THE WAR FOR AMERICA

1775-1783

THE WAR FOR AMERICA

AMERICA

1775-1783

PIERS MACKESY

HARVARD UNIVERSITY PRESS

CAMBRIDGE MASSACHUSETTS

1965

FOR MY GRANDMOTHER

NORAH C. E. COOK

CONTENTS

PART TWO: THE WORLD WAR
1778

PART THREE: THE BOURBON ALLIANCE
1778–9

ILLUSTRATIONS

MAPS

THE SERVANTS OF KRONOS

The Muses attend the births of gods and nations: Clio to record and Calliope to adorn the great event. They tell how the infant Zeus was snatched from the jaws of his father Kronos; and inevitably it is the infant who is sung, while old Kronos fades back into the mists of antiquity, the half-forgotten symbol of an outdated and regrettable past.

So it happened with the American Revolution. The triumph of the rebels was of overwhelming importance for the future of the world, and the struggle was recorded in terms of American battles on American soil. The red coats of old Kronos's hirelings are visible; but the mind that moved them, the Kronos of Whitehall and St James's, was thrust aside to be forgotten or turned into a background buffoon.

This treatment accentuated a characteristic feature of British historiography: the distortion of diplomacy and warfare by the elimination of strategy. Strategy falls between two kinds of history. For the political historian it is a marginal activity of government which occasionally erupts to disturb the course of diplomacy, debate and electioneering. For the military historian it is a background to operations in the field and on the seas; and the decisions of governments are too often seen through the eyes of distant and half-informed commanders. Sir John Fortescue, the historian of the British army, was a devoted operational historian; and the thirteen volumes of his history, magnificent in their energy, style and range of narrative, form a splendid monument to the vanishing regiments which made the British empire. Yet his devotion to the army narrowed and warped his judgment. In the sphere where strategy merged with policy, he was incapable of justice. For him the appalling problems of the government which waged the war for America were reduced to 'the folly and ignorance of Germain'.

Though strategy has emerged to take its rightful place in the history of the twentieth century, the direction of war before 1914 is a little known area of British history. In no war has less attempt been made to strike the balance between strategy and operations than in the War of American Independence. There is now much interest in Lord North's administration; yet though the war covered seven of its twelve years of life, the task of assessing its efforts to direct the war in the context of eighteenth-century warfare remains to be done. The neglect is largely due to the consequences of the war, which concentrated the interest and emotions of historians on the struggles of the new state and its embryo armies beyond the Atlantic. Yet the injustice which has been done in the past to Lord North and his colleagues has two other causes: that the war was lost, and that George III and his Ministers were blackguarded by domestic enemies.

The men who conduct a war are more intemperately and uncharitably criticised than those who run an administrative machine in peacetime. Statesmen and commanders are equally victims; for in war the results are swift, harsh and measurable, and censure readily precedes understanding. The vilification of the Ministry was perpetuated because the most accessible and digested source of information was the Parliamentary Debates. There one may read the half-informed and largely disingenuous criticisms of the Opposition, and the misleading and partial replies of the Ministers. The failure to blockade Brest will demonstrate the effect. The Ministry's enemies maintained that if it had been done the enemy would have been unable to seize the initiative: his overseas expeditions and his concentrations in home waters would have been prevented, and England would have maintained her maritime ascendancy. Yet Lord Howe, whose slow mind required time to choose its political stance, flatly declared in the House of Commons that Ushant was no station for a fleet. Though naval historians are aware how great a margin of superiority was necessary to maintain a close blockade, it is rarely asked whether the country had the necessary means, and whether the policy which had succeeded in the Seven Years War and was to succeed again in the struggles with revolutionary France could have been applied in the different circumstances of the American War.

The *Parliamentary History*, supplemented by the *Annual Register* and memoirs like Horace Walpole's, dominated the entire history of the reign for generations: they are riddled with lies, special pleading and gossip. Though the political history is being re-written from better sources, the major decisions of the war have not been re-assessed. Yet better sources are freely available, and some of the most important have been in print for many years. It is not necessary to accept opinions as facts, or to mistake uninformed hindsight for wisdom.

The American War was Britain's only clear defeat in the long contest with France which began with the Revolution of 1688 and ended at Waterloo. Unique characteristics explain the uniqueness of the failure. England was maintaining nearly 60,000 soldiers beyond the Atlantic, most of them in a hostile country: a feat never paralleled in the past, and in relative terms never attempted again by any power until the twentieth century. The territory was vast, and the people were in arms. Even so the resistance of the Americans might have been worn down and a settlement (though probably a temporary one) achieved. But for the first time England faced what she had always dreaded and averted: a coalition of maritime enemies undistracted by war in Europe.

In simple terms of power the consequences are clear, and after a struggle of several years a momentary tilt of the naval balance brought the disaster at Yorktown which broke the country's will to fight on. The same factor made the strategic choices which faced the North Ministry infinitely more complicated than those which faced the two Pitts. With a general command of the sea it was possible to take as much or as little of the war as one desired: to feed the war fronts in Europe as much as one judged necessary, and to take the initiative in colonial warfare. In other words it was possible to a considerable degree to treat the theatres of war in isolation, and to neutralise one theatre in order to act in another. But for Lord North's government, whose enemies had free access to ocean communications, all problems of war were interrelated. An additional effort in North America might expose in the West Indies, a strong fleet in the Channel endanger India.

The Ministry which faced these problems was not a strong one. Its parliamentary majority was insecure, it was troubled by internal stresses, it lacked leadership, and it waged war without gusto. But weak leadership was not unique in English warfare. The Elder Pitt had been a brilliant exception – perhaps the only exception in two centuries. And he had everything in his favour: a European war which engaged the resources of the enemy, friendly colonies in America, Spanish intervention delayed till the French navy and empire had been broken. The country and Parliament were united behind the war, and Pitt's junction with the Newcastle system gave the government an unbreakable majority. One often hears how the North government alienated its generals and admirals; yet only one, Keppel, was court-martialled, and he through unhappy circumstances. The reason for the government's forbearance was timidity and fear of outcries. In the Seven Years War two successive commanders were recalled from America with no outcry; the general at Gibraltar was court-martialled, and a 'revision' of his sentence was discussed when he was acquitted; Sackville was broken, and Byng was shot. What would have been the fate of Burgoyne under the régime of Pitt and Newcastle? How long would Clinton have held his command?

There was much administrative inefficiency in the American War. But North was using the machinery he had inherited; and the more one lifts the curtain of adulation from the Ministry of the Elder Pitt, the less does the scene appear to match the script, and the more one uncovers the characteristic inefficiences of the age. One finds the same delays in despatching expeditions; vital reinforcements held up by contrary winds; time lost by naval commanders in securing prizes. There are the same shortages of shipping, the same departmental friction over transports, the same slow and piece-meal embarcations. Pitt and his friends planned distant offensives in the same manner as Germain, with no allowance for wastage from sickness and the same optimistic reliance on precise timing.

If one looks forward the same scene is revealed. In the American War much was made of the Ministers' summer habit of haymaking in the country; yet as the Helder expedition prepared to embark in the summer of 1799 the Younger Pitt was to write that in a few days he and many of his Cabinet would be out of London. His faults as a war minister were shrouded by the necessity of his leadership, to which almost all subscribed. The Ministry of All the Talents of 1806–7 were less fortunate: their failures were scrutinised under the microscope; and even their successes were harvested by their opponents, for the swift and secret Copenhagen expedition of 1807 sailed in transports which they had assembled. If one contemplates the arrangements for the Mediterranean in the autumn of the same year, one may wonder how far Castlereagh and Canning excelled Germain and Sandwich in overcoming the difficulties of slow communication and uncertain weather.

The first purpose of this book is to examine the making and execution of strategy in one of England's great eighteenth-century wars, and to create a detailed model of the machine at work; the second, to judge a war Ministry in the light of circumstances rather than results. This is how one at least of the Ministers wished to be judged. Defending the Admiralty after Yorktown against charges of operational mismanagement, Lord Sandwich wrote: 'These charges are not so easily answered, because there is no demonstrative evidence that the orders given have been right; the event certainly does not decide that question; but those who mean to find fault, wait the event, and then adopt whichever side of the question best suits their purpose.'[1] To understand the war, one must view it with sympathy for the Ministers in their difficulties, and not with the arrogant assumption that because they were defeated they were incompetent, and that all their actions proceeded from folly.

This, then, is not a history of the War of Independence, but a study of British strategy and leadership in a world war, the last in which the enemy were the Bourbons. I hope that American readers will not be disconcerted by the Whitehall perspective: that they will forgive my disregard of the great moral truths of the struggle, and bear with the habitual designation of the Patriots as rebels. The term is used with deliberation. It was the contemporary British usage, and any other would alter the perspective. 'Patriots' is the language of opposition, not of those who fought the rebellion. 'American' in many contexts is misleading. And rebels are conceded to be Revolutionaries only when they have succeeded, whereas the struggle was waged by men who believed that the rebellion could still be defeated.

A work which covers such well explored campaigns owes debts to many predecessors; particularly, among recent writings, to the scholarship of Professors J. R. Alden, G. S. Graham and W. B. Willcox; and to Douglas Southall Freeman's monumental life of Washington. Dr Howard C. Rice of Princeton University cleared up a number of topographical problems. Mr J. D. Spinney gave me valuable information about Lord Rodney, though he will dispute some of my views on the Admiral; and Father J. S. Benedict Cullen about Father Hussey. Mr M. W. Williams generously lent me his manuscript on the naval administration of Lord Sandwich and transcripts of unpublished letters in the Sandwich papers. The Marquess of Bath allowed me to see the papers of Lord Weymouth, later first Marquess; and the Earl of Mansfield had the great kindness to send me copies of some papers left by Lord Stormont, though there are hopes that more may one day come to light. Through the kindness of the Hon. R. P. de Grey I was able to see some papers of the 2nd Lord Walsingham, in the possession of Lord Walsingham at Merton. I have the Librarian of Duke University to thank for permission to quote from three manuscript letters in the Library; and Dr Howard H. Peckham and William S. Ewing of the William Clements Library for their help and courtesy. The research was begun, and a study made of the collections at the William Clements Library, when I held a Commonwealth Fund Fellowship of the Harkness Foundation; and the manuscript was completed during a visit to the Institute for Advanced Study at Princeton.

Pembroke College, Oxford.
September 1962.

[1] G 3510.

The Cabinet 1775–83

	LORD NORTH'S (to March 1782) Lord North	LORD ROCKINGHAM'S (to July 1782) Marquess of Rockingham	LORD SHELBURNE'S (to Feb. 1783) Earl of Shelburne
First Lord of the Treasury			
Secretaries of State	1. Northern Department: (a) Earl of Suffolk (b) Viscount Stormont (from Oct. 1779) 2. Southern Department: (a) Earl of Rochford (b) Viscount Weymouth (from Nov. 1775) (c) Earl of Hillsborough (from Nov. 1779) 3. For the American Colonies: (a) Earl of Dartmouth (b) Lord George Germain (from Nov. 1775) (c) Welbore Ellis (from Feb. 1782)	1. Foreign Affairs: Charles James Fox 2. Home and Colonial Affairs: Earl of Shelburne	Foreign Affairs: Earl of Grantham Home and Colonial Affairs: Thomas Townshend
First Lord of the Admiralty	Earl of Sandwich	Viscount Keppel	(a) Viscount Keppel (b) Viscount Howe (from Feb. 1783)

Commander-in-Chief	General Conway	General Conway
Lord President of the Council	Lord Camden	Lord Camden
	Lord Amherst (from March 1778)	
	(a) Earl Gower	
	(b) Earl Bathurst (from Nov. 1779)	
Lord Privy Seal	Duke of Grafton	Duke of Grafton
	(a) Duke of Grafton	
	(b) Earl of Dartmouth (from Nov. 1775)	
Lord Chancellor	Lord Thurlow	Lord Thurlow
	(a) Earl Bathurst	
	(b) Lord Thurlow (from June 1778)	
Chancellor of the Duchy of Lancaster	Lord Ashburton	Lord Ashburton
Chancellor of the Exchequer	Lord John Cavendish	William Pitt
Master-General of the Ordnance	Duke of Richmond	Duke of Richmond
Lord Steward of the Household		Duke of Rutland (from Feb. 1783)

xix

Abbreviations used in footnotes

Add. MSS.   Additional Manuscripts in the British Museum.

Adm.   Admiralty Papers in the Public Record Office in London.

CL   William Clements Library, Ann Arbor, Michigan (followed by name of
            collection).

CO   Colonial Office Papers in the Public Record Office.

Eg   Egerton MSS in the British Museum.

G   Correspondence of George III (ed. Fortescue).

Knox   MSS. of Captain H.V. Knox (Historical MSS. Commission).

Sackville   Stopford-Sackville Papers (Historical MSS. Commission).

SP   State Papers in the Public Record Office.

WO   War Office Papers in the Public Record Office.

A GOVERNMENT AT WAR

1. *And Great Bellona Smiles*

The Peace of Paris in 1763 had left England alone in splendid but perilous eminence. She had crushed her enemies, but lost her friends. Her former ally Austria, turning from Flemish interests and obsessed by the rise of Prussia, had looked to France since the *renversement des alliances* of 1756. Prussia, the ally of the Seven Years War, was alienated, for Frederick the Great chose to regard the peace as a desertion. Holland had gradually retreated from the role of a Great Power. Spain was a defeated enemy. France, once the arbiter of Europe, stood humiliated before the nations. She had been stripped of her colonies. Her resources were exhausted, her prestige was demolished. While her former client states, Poland and Turkey, were plundered, she stood a helpless spectator. At foreign courts English ambassadors claimed the precedence of victors.

But within a few years a shadow was dimming the glory of England's triumph, and giving hope to the defeated. It had been foretold that the ejection of the French from Canada would bring to a head the discords of England and her American colonies. In 1765 the Duc de Choiseul traced out the course by which France would rise from her defeats. The colonies would cast themselves loose from British tutelage; and if France was to find her revenge she must seize that moment. She must turn her back on the battlefields of Europe, and fight in alliance with Spain for the supremacy of the seas. A year later he thought the time was approaching. But rebellion had not yet ripened in America, and France was weak. The years still slipped away.

Yet the stage was being prepared. Stamp Act, Customs disputes, mob violence and military retaliation were building up a pressure of animosity which was soon to burst the shell of the old British Empire. By 1774 civil government was near its end. The courts could no longer administer justice, and the people of New England were arming and training for war. Parliament closed the port of Boston, and General Gage returned to America to combine the offices of Governor of Massachusetts and Commander-in-Chief of the troops in North America. Before the end of the year he was warning the government at home that only a great army could end the troubles, and that a bloody crisis was at hand.

Little had been done to meet the storm. A few regiments were ordered to Boston early in 1775 to reinforce the garrison, and with them sailed three active Major-Generals to inject some vigour into Gage's irresolute command. But Gage himself had been writing for many months that nothing short of an absolute reconquest of New England could end the mischief, and it would need 20,000 men. The Cabinet was reluctant to face the truth. Aware of England's diplomatic isolation, it hesitated to disperse its exiguous forces beyond the Atlantic; and, committed as the Ministers were to a policy of financial retrenchment, they were reluctant to face the expense of placing the army on a war establishment. Violence in the Boston area seemed to have been the work of a rabble without leadership or spirit, and they clung to the hope that a small force used quickly would open the way to a political solution. Gage was encouraged to try to disarm the provincials and protect British cargoes arriving in American ports, even if it forced the Americans to take up arms prematurely.[1] But of reinforcements only a dribble had been sent: now three guardships and 600 marines; next a regiment of cavalry and three of foot. An addition to regimental establishments was authorised early in 1775; but in May the Admiralty asked Parliament for fewer seamen and less money than in the previous estimates. When Gage struck his blow at the rebel armaments, as he had been ordered, the British government was still unprepared for a serious struggle.

On 29 May a rumour of war ran through Whitehall and St James's. There had been fighting between armed Americans and a detachment of troops which was marching to seize the magazines at Concord. The rebels seemed to have been bolder than might have been expected; but the report came from an American source, and might be exaggerated. 'Be that however what it may', wrote an official in the American Department, 'the die is cast, and more mischief will follow.'[2] A decade of dispute had ended in bloodshed.

The despatch from Gage arrived a fortnight later, and confirmed the seriousness of the affair. As he had long since warned the Ministry, the King's enemies were not a Boston rabble, but the farmers and freeholders of the country,[3] and they had turned out in strength. Another couple of weeks went by before further news confirmed the scale of the insurrection. The forts of Crown Point and Ticonderoga on the boundary between New England and Canada had been surprised and captured with all their cannon and stores.

For the moment little could be done to strengthen Gage. Four more frigates were ordered to America to isolate New England, and the Black Watch stood by to embark in Scotland. No further reinforcements could

---

[1] Gage Corr., II, 174–5, 179–83.   [2] Knox, 118.   [3] Gage Corr., I, 374.

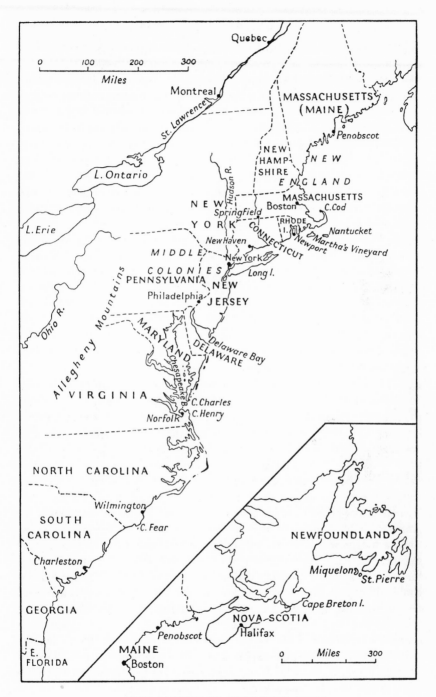

THE AMERICAN COLONIES, 1775

reach Boston from home during the present campaigning season; but seven battalions of infantry and a cavalry regiment were on their way there, and the Ministers hoped to hear that Gage had broken out of the city and re-opened his access to the countryside.[1] The answer to their hopes was Bunker Hill.

Towards the end of June Gage had received his reinforcements, and re-solved to dislodge the rebels from the heights of Brede's Hill and Bunker Hill which commanded the town and upper harbour. The attack was launched without reserves or any preparation for the wounded, in full confidence that it would achieve its object without trouble. The works were stormed and the Americans forced to retreat; but in successive frontal assaults and bitter fighting the British regiments were shattered. The soldiers' gal-lantry had cost them forty per cent of their strength. The news of this Pyrrhic victory cast its shadow across Whitehall on 25 July, and it was clear beyond doubt that New England was organised and determined. The Ministry had a foreign war on its hands.

2. A War of the Ancien Régime

The struggle which opened at Lexington was the last great war of the *ancien régime*. In the American War there first appeared the fearful spectacle of a nation in arms; and the *odium theologicum* which had been banished from war-fare for a century returned to distress the nations. As a civil war in America the struggle was often characterised by atrocious cruelty between rebels and loyalists; and even between the rebels and the British the conventions of warfare sometimes threatened to break down. But the European participants kept hatred within bounds and observed the rules. Indeed Englishmen in France fared better than in the Seven Years War, when Gibbon's dry phrase recorded how the seizure of French shipping before the declaration had 'rendered that polite nation somewhat peevish and difficult'. In the war for America civilised amenities were better preserved. In the summer of York-town a tourist at Chepstow saw miles of iron waterpipes on the quay for shipment to Paris. French artists were given passports to collect drawings for a book of travels; and on the other side of the Channel George Selwyn could still export the Paris gossip and another Member of Parliament find refuge from his creditors. The Master-General of the Irish Ordnance spent the autumn of 1778 in Provence for the sake of his health. Englishmen were banned from French ports; but an influential woman was able to arrange matters for Henry Ellis, the explorer and colonial governor, and he passed the first winter of the French war very agreeably in Marseilles society. So

[1] Sandwich, I, 62; Gage Corr., II, 200-2.

agreeably, that he had to retire to Spa and take the waters in the spring of 1779. There the French and English were mixing freely; and if his own government had not inconveniently stopped the Dover–Calais packet after being at war with France for a year, he might have imagined that the whole world was at peace. Even the absurdities were preserved. At New York Lord Carlisle used an insulting phrase about France, and was rewarded with a challenge sent through the lines by Lafayette.[1]

The amenities were preserved because France and England were not divided by fanaticism. They were fighting over quantitative issues of wealth and power. The stakes were high, and the danger grave. Yet the challenge was limited. The belligerents looked to a future when they would live together and the balance of power once more be called into play. They knew, moreover, that social stability transcended frontiers. A decade later the doctrines of the French Revolution brought a new intensity to warfare, and since that time almost every major conflict has led to revolution on the losing side. But in 1778 England faced no threat to her social or political structure, but only to her power and wealth. Wraxall's Memoirs struck the note: 'No fears of subversion, extinction, and subjugation to foreign violence, or to revolutionary arts, interrupted the general tranquillity of society.'

Limited objects called forth limited efforts. There are bounds to the sacrifices which people will make for material and measurable ends, and neither the wealth nor the man-power of the warring nations could be fully deployed. Governments might totter into bankruptcy, but they were bankrupt while their countries' wealth lay untapped. Armies might be raised at a price, but there was no conscript population to provide a cheap reservoir of replacements. Nor did the princes and oligarchies of Europe wish it otherwise. A whole nation could not be called to arms without at least the illusion of political partnership; and the ruling classes of the eighteenth century had no intention of paying the price of total war.

With no threat to their domination, the ruling classes of England had no challenge to throw off the sloth of old ways. England was not forced to re-examine her political life, to remould her institutions and administration, or to overhaul her war machine. The war of 1793 was to have a very different effect. The revolutionary challenge was to unite the propertied classes, and lead to the overhaul of much antiquated machinery and habits. But the war for America left the country politically divided. Patronage raged without check. In every sphere of government the old ways which had served in the past continued. It was not that the country lacked vigour. The year of the

[1] Torrington Diaries, 41; G 3321; I. R. Christie, *The End of North's Ministry*, 302; Carlisle, 374, 422; Lothian, 339; Knox, 158.

American Declaration of Independence saw the first publication of three masterpieces. Adam Smith's *The Wealth of Nations* pointed the way towards a new concept of imperial and commercial relations. Bentham's *Fragment on Government* was a first devastating assault on the English constitution and the assumptions on which it rested inert. And a friend of Lord North's, soon to accept a minor place in his administration, had been at work on the greatest of historical apologias for a rational liberty: the first volume of *The Decline and Fall of the Roman Empire* burst on the world in February 1776, as England gathered her forces for the counterstroke in America. David Hume lived to congratulate Gibbon on his masterpiece, and died in Edinburgh three days after Howe's landing on Long Island.

The tragedy of administrative apathy was revealed in horror wherever soldiers and seamen were collected. The troops of Revolutionary France were to be allowed to die because they could be replaced; the fighting men of England in the last war of the old Europe were killed by neglect. Of scurvy in the navy we shall have more to say; but a microcosm of the system and its effects on the army can be found in Jamaica. There the waste of life was more than a tragedy: it threatened the island's safety. The Governor was convinced by experience that the fever could be controlled by building barracks and hospitals and providing skilled doctors. He declared that the loss of life bordered on murder: 'seven out of ten of the soldiers who perish in this country might be saved, if due attention was paid to them when sick'. But the Jamaican Assembly would not bear the cost; and the government at home would not take over the expense which it was the Jamaicans' interest and duty to bear.[1]

Nor was cruel neglect excused by financial stringency.[2] Though country gentlemen disliked heavy taxation, they had no means whatever of controlling expenditure in detail; and in spite of Pitt and Shelburne matters continued much the same throughout the Napoleonic Wars. The Estimates and Extra Estimates voted by Parliament bore no relation to requirements. The real 'extraordinary' expenditure required by changing circumstances was not authorised by Parliament at all: it was met simply by running up departmental debts, and at the time of Yorktown the interest-bearing Navy Debt was above £11 millions. The spending of the money was unchecked. The Treasury did not control departmental spending; and Parliament, unable to limit expenditure in advance, was equally impotent to audit it

---

[1] CO 137/75, ff. 200–1; CO 137/76, f. 144; CO 137/78, ff. 58, 135. The years are 1779–80, the Governor the otherwise deplorable Dalling.

[2] Naval finances are examined in R. G. Usher's unpublished thesis, *Civil Administration of the British Navy during the American Revolution*, pp. 20–30; the subject in general in J. E. D. Binney, *British Public Finance and Administration, 1774–92*.

afterwards. Auditing meant merely the checking of arithmetic. There was no check on excessive spending, or on the delivery of what had been paid for. Nor did the Admiralty attempt to use parliamentary grants for the purposes for which they had been voted; and Lord Mulgrave, a Lord of the Admiralty, said this had been the practice since the reign of James II.

Such as it was, the auditing was yet twenty years in arrears. The Paymaster-General treated the balance in his hands as his own until his accounts were finally passed; and Henry Fox was still enjoying an income of £25,000 at his death in 1774 from his unaudited balances, though he had resigned in 1765: four years later his executors paid in £200,000. Lord North's Paymaster, Richard Rigby, handled his funds so freely that he was threatened with impeachment. It seems a miracle that the machine continued to revolve. But as a Napoleonic general was to observe,[1] the corruption of English life in itself imposed certain bounds; 'and generally speaking the thefts are not so scandalous as they would be elsewhere under the aegis of so convenient a legislation'.

3. 'John will wallow in preferment'

Long after the years of his great victories, Lord Chatham recalled that there had been no party politics at that time, and that conversations between Ministers had been the most agreeable he could remember in his long experience. His son was to enjoy a similar immunity from faction when he fought the French Revolution. It was not so in the time of North.

The rancour of George III had driven into opposition the ablest men in politics: the aristocratic Rockingham group, who numbered one in seven of the House of Commons and commanded in Burke, Sheridan and Fox a peerless team of orators; and Chatham's odd and brilliant political heir Lord Shelburne, with about ten votes in the House. The committed Opposition in 1780 numbered about a hundred in a House of five hundred and fifty-eight members.[2] Against them Lord North ranged a typical eighteenth-century coalition, bound together by the desire for office: more stable than many, because it had the King's confidence and a leader who was a brilliant manager of the House of Commons; yet the more bitterly assailed because its monopoly of power seemed so impregnable. Lord North himself had one of the largest followings in the House, held together by their leader's position at the Treasury. Lord Gower and Weymouth led the old Bedford group with about a dozen followers held together by family and electoral interest. Lord Sandwich, once a member of the Bedfords, was by now the leader of his own

---

[1] Foy, *Peninsular War*, I, 189.

[2] The composition of the parties in 1780 is analysed by I. R. Christie, in his *The End of North's Ministry*, esp. pp. 198 ff., 218 ff.

faction, based on the patronage which he controlled at the Admiralty and East India House. The survivors of the old Grenville group were led by Lord Suffolk. With a scattering of other leaders controlling a vote or two, and the steady support of the court and administration votes, Lord North could count on about 220 members in the House of Commons.

The Ministry's majority of committed supporters did not guarantee a majority in a division. An absolute majority of the House required another sixty votes; so that like all eighteenth-century governments it depended on the goodwill of a body of independents. Conversely, the Opposition could succeed only by persuading enough independents that the Ministers were leading them to disaster. Unlike many Oppositions of the century, the Rockinghams had a programme to offer, which they developed during the course of the war: to end the American War, and to break the power of the King's political patronage. But neither object commanded much support outside the group. The attack on patronage could too easily be interpreted as a desperate expedient of self-interested men who had once been happy to use the same royal influence for their own purposes. Still less was the American War an effective issue, till its failure alienated the country. The Rockinghams were divided from the Shelburne group on the question of peace terms, for the heirs of Chatham were not willing to surrender the sovereignty of America; and from the country at large, or from the country gentlemen who represented it, by their attacks on the policy of coercion. The spectacle of politicians avid for office crowing at the nation's disasters disgusted the ordinary backbencher. 'The parricide joy of some at the losses of their country makes me mad', wrote a member after Yorktown, though he was by no means an admirer of the Ministry. Nor, in spite of their intellectual brilliance, did Charles Fox and his friends command confidence. 'Such farceurs as are in opposition, or such a desperate rantipole vagabond as our Charles' were not likely to proselytise. The country had a long road to travel before the House would vote Fox 'from a Pharo table to the head of the Exchequer'. Year after year Lord North held his own in his lonely forensic battle against a battery of great orators. Through seven disastrous years of war he rode out the storms, because there was no alternative Ministry to continue the struggle. Mediocre the Ministers might be, unfortunate they certainly were; but their 'principles respecting America were agreeable to the people, and those of Opposition offensive to them'.[1]

Nevertheless the Ministers' majority was often precarious. And in 1775, as the crisis in America approached, they continued to give priority to the political game at home, and treated the American problem as an embarrassment to be shed at the lowest cost. From this stemmed their reluctance to

[1] *Life and Letters of Sir Gilbert Elliot*, I, 74, 77; Carlisle, 553, 584.

strengthen the armed forces and increase expenditure. Even when the war was fairly launched, the government continued in its political chains; chains which the Elder Pitt in his great Ministry had shaken off. Perhaps the most pernicious of the pressures exerted by political weakness was on the appointment of generals and admirals.

Who were the wartime commanders? Most of the generals had been born in the seventeen-twenties, had grown up in the era of Walpole and the Pelhams, and were around their fiftieth year when the war began; rather younger than the admirals who were nearer sixty. Almost all were men of social rank and connection. The generals were sons of peers, cousins and neighbours of dukes, school friends of earls. The admirals' backgrounds were more varied, for the sons of peers and baronets were mixed with the sons of simple naval officers, and occasionally with lucky men like Arbuthnot, of obscurer pedigree. Nevertheless the nobility predominated in the higher ranks of both services. Lord Howe was an Irish peer, by the death of his elder brother at Ticonderoga. Keppel, Barrington and Byron were sons of peers, Digby a grandson, Pye and Rodney related to the nobility. Drake, Hotham and Ross were sons of baronets (the latter also a peer's grandson); Hyde Parker was the heir to a baronetcy.

Social ties clashed with military heirarchy. The aristocratic structure of the services affected their discipline. Military subordination among officers may be strictest in an egalitarian society where no superiority but rank is acknowledged. The violent quarrels between generals, admirals and governors which characterised the war might have taken a more inhibited form in a society where social and military rank did not compete. Their chief cause, of course, was the spoils system which still ruled supreme in every walk of life. Mere rank was not enough. As courtiers sought places and the clergy rich livings, so a seaman hoped for a station or a ship to command, with a share of prize money and the control of promotions; a soldier for the colonelcy of a regiment, the sinecure governship of a fortress, or the perquisites of a command. Hard work and ability might help, but favour counted most; and a seat in the House of Commons was an instrument for obtaining it. Lord Hardwicke had long ago deplored the number of men of quality in the army as an obstacle to efficiency and a cloak for failure; and the Elder Pitt had unsuccessfully promoted a bill to exclude junior officers of the two services from the House. The twenty-three generals in the House in 1780, who included Howe, Clinton, Burgoyne, Cornwallis and Vaughan, shared between them twenty-one colonelcies, nine governorships, and six or seven staff appointments. Any failure which the Ministry dared to notice was likely to send the perpetrator into opposition.[1]

[1] Namier, *Structure of Politics* . . ., 73; Whitworth, *Ligonier*, 194; Christie, 178-9.

The system was as harmful to military efficiency as to the peace of the Ministry. The hunt for profitable places might have placed the army at the mercy of politics had it not been for the royal family. Like his father, George III took his military prerogative seriously. He at least, as Captain-General, was sufficiently above the crowd of petitioners to defy their importunity. Where military and political considerations did not conflict, he was ready to manipulate the army for the sake of the government's majority: for he regarded military sinecures as a fair prey. But invariably he placed military interests above political calculations, and sheltered the army from the worst effects of the spoils system. He resisted the raising of new regiments to confer rank on the Ministers' friends; and when votes in the House were at issue his hand was light on the reins. Even the King's aides-de-camp could not be relied on to vote with the government. Of the seven Generals in the House of Commons who voted with the Opposition in 1780, only Burgoyne had no regiment, having lost it when he quarrelled with the Ministry after Saratoga.[1]

In peacetime and in the absence of a Commander-in-Chief, the direct patronage of the army rested in the hands of the Secretary at War, Lord Barrington; but when Amherst was made Commander-in-Chief on the outbreak of the French war, Barrington relinquished the patronage to him. When Jenkinson, a Treasury man of business, succeeded Barrington, he introduced a vigorous political supervision; but his powers were circumscribed. He could canvas voters, and grant them leave at election-time; but in Amherst he found a drag on political action. 'Incapable of doing a favour to his nearest connections', Amherst obstinately opposed political promotions. Jenkinson could only refer applicants to him; and he in turn found shelter in the formula of 'putting names before his Majesty'.[2]

The system for naval appointments was more invidious. Naval patronage was not controlled by the sovereign or the professional head of the service, but by the First Lord of the Admiralty, who was usually a leading politician. During the American War faction and indiscipline were rife in the fleets; and Lord Sandwich, much hated by those whose claims to employment he passed over, has been branded as the source of the trouble. His fortune was rumoured to be below his station, which exposed him to damaging insinuations; and as the leader of a political faction he had strong inducements to misuse his control of appointments. His power rested on the seventeen votes

[1] Pares, *George III and the Politicians*, 19; Christie, 178–9.

[2] Add. MSS. 38306, ff. 136, 138, 149; Olive Anderson, 'Army and Parliamentary Management in the American War' (*J. Soc. Army Hist. Research*, 1956, pp. 146–9). Amherst's reference of applicants to the King's will is habitual throughout his correspondence (WO 34/226–41). For his opposition in later life to political promotions, see Clode, *Military Forces of the Crown*, II, 94.

which he controlled in the House of Commons, a private empire of patronage which made him formidable to his colleagues and a wayward and independent force in the Cabinet.[1]

With friends to be fed and a majority to be kept up, the temptations were strong. Ministers faced a barrage of fawning flattery alternating with outraged denunciation. 'My Lord', wrote a naval Commander-in-Chief to Lord George Germain, 'the very idea in having thought my conduct worthy of your notice and approbation transports me almost to a frenzy.'[2] The importunities to which Sandwich was exposed are astonishing. His patronage papers are full of them: of Collier's complaint on being sent to sea just before a parliamentary election; Captain Cornwallis's untimely remonstrance and hasty apology; Gambier's growing brood of infants and flattery of Sandwich's mistress; Samuel Graves's innumerable nephews. One is led to ask whether a professional First Lord like Anson would have tolerated such insolence; and, indeed, whether it was Sandwich's resistance to private importunity rather than his compliance with it which caused the feeling against him. Royal patronage might have saved him much unpleasantness, though it would have reduced his influence.

Against the ravening hordes of suitors it was not easy to hold out. Yet on the whole Sandwich withstood the pressure well. His appointment books reveal how few appointments were available to satisfy the torrent of applications, and how seldom influence prevailed. Even Middleton's complaints of political appointments in the dockyards do not stand up to scrutiny. The real source of trouble in the navy did not lie in Sandwich's general handling of appointments.[3]

Some of the trouble lay in the characters of naval officers. As the urbane Rodney observed, sea officers were a censorious lot. Living together in seaport towns, they knew little of the world: hence their violence in party, their partiality to those who had sailed with them, their gross injustice to others.[4] Combined with a spleen strained by heavy eating and drinking in the confinement of a ship, it was a formidable recipe to nourish faction. These footballs of fortune[5] were ill-equipped to do justice even to the most scrupulous of civil administrators.

[1] Christie, 203–6; Sutherland, *East India Company in Eighteenth-Century Politics*, 271, 277–9; Wraxall Memoirs, II, 507; Sandwich, III, 179–81.

[2] CL, Germain, 13 Sept. 1780, Arbuthnot to Germain.

[3] Mr M. J. Williams has analysed the Appointment Books and produced remarkable figures in defence of the disinterestedness of Sandwich's practice (pp. 233, 266–7, 273–4). For Middleton, see *ibid.*, 281–2.

[4] Mundy, *Life of Rodney*, II, 358.

[5] Admiral Lord Shuldham: 'I have been made the football of fortune my whole life' (William Transcripts, 28? Aug. 1777).

But the real trouble was political. During Lord North's Ministry politics reached heights of bitterness unequalled since at least the later years of Walpole or perhaps the reign of Queen Anne. A comparison with Anson's navy in the Seven Years War is scarcely valid. Still less so is comparison with the next war, when the ruling class closed its ranks against a terrifying social threat. For in the American War the political world was still torn apart by the events of the early 'sixties. The fall of Newcastle had broken the united Whig front, and driven into opposition men who would have been bought in by the Pelhams, but with whom George III stubbornly refused to come to terms till they stormed the closet after Yorktown. A fair comparison is with the War of the Spanish Succession, when the country's political passions had been mirrored in the careers of Marlborough, Peterborough, Argyll and St John. The appointments which caused most of Sandwich's difficulties were not the commands of ships, but the Commands-in-Chief to which well-placed political admirals laid claim. Above all, the trouble was rooted in the Channel fleet, rising out of the disappointments of the first campaign and the breach with a politician-admiral, Augustus Keppel. Sandwich may have handled the affair unwisely, but he was not the original source of the mischief.

4. The Blueprint of the War Machine

Just as the North Ministry inherited political troubles, so it inherited and used the machinery which had operated with varying efficiency through many emergencies. At the heart of the machine was the Cabinet, which planned; and the Secretaries of State, who executed. The Cabinet made or approved the policy. The Secretaries of State carried its resolutions to the King, and transmitted them into executive channels. An official thus explained their roles:

Cabinet. To consider and determine what expeditions are to take place, and at what periods; what troops are likely to be sent abroad, *when, where,* how, and the number. What services are to have preference.

Secretary of State. To issue timely orders, to the Treasury, Admiralty, Ordnance and Commander-in-Chief of the Army on these heads, so that every necessary preparation can be made, and no delay nor disappointment happen when the services take place.[1]

Lord North's Cabinet consisted of the eight or nine chief Ministers. The large Outer Cabinet of the first half of the century had withered like the Privy Council before it to a purely formal body; and deliberations of state

[1] CL, Shelburne, Vol. 151, No. 38 (Sir Charles Middleton to Shelburne).

were now confined to the responsible holders of major offices. The First Lord of the Treasury presided. With him at the table sat the three Secretaries of State; the Lord Chancellor, Lord President of the Council, and Lord Privy Seal; the First Lord of the Admiralty; and from 1778 the Commander-in-Chief. The average attendance was six or eight; a better number for efficient discussion than the ten or eleven hungry mouths of the second Rockingham Ministry which succeeded North's. In moments of crisis business was done by hastily convening the four or five members whose departments were directly concerned with the war. There were weekly Cabinet dinners, and when the cloth had been removed those who could stay awake discussed the nation's business. Meetings to discuss specific problems as they arose were called by the Ministers concerned at their own offices or private residences. Decisions were embodied in a minute or draft despatch and forwarded for the King's approval.

At times the Cabinet was still absurdly said to be unknown to the Constitution. It is true that Ministers were not bound to lay the business of their departments before it; but they preferred to do so, for its collective decisions already sheltered them from personal responsibility, and major decisions were rarely taken without its approval. Though attempts had been made by individuals early in the reign to repudiate their share of responsibility for a Cabinet decision, or to lay dissenting minutes before the King, unanimity was the rule in matters of national policy. In the heated political atmosphere of the American War, the shelter of a Cabinet minute was particularly attractive; and North, Sandwich and Germain all claimed the protection of collective Cabinet responsibility and insisted on Cabinet authority for inflammatory measures. 'Every expedition', Lord Sandwich declared to the House of Lords, 'in regard to its destination, object, force and number of ships, is planned by the Cabinet, and is the result of the collective wisdom of all his Majesty's confidential ministers. The First Lord of the Admiralty is only the executive servant of these measures.'[1]

This tendency became most marked when the Ministry was crumbling after Yorktown. Neither Germain nor Sandwich would then order controversial measures without the authority of a Cabinet minute. 'I conclude you have the minute of a Cabinet to justify my proceedings,' Germain wrote to his Under-Secretary in January 1782, 'for in the precarious situation in which I stand, I can take no measures of consequence upon myself.'[2]

Beneath the Cabinet, and controlled through the machinery of the Secretaries of State, were the executive Departments. Four had major

[1] Pares, *George III and the Politicians*, 160; Sandwich, II, 255, 259; Costin and Watson, *Law and Working of the Constitution*, I, 238–9.

[2] Knox, *Extra-Official State Papers*, I, Appendix p. 7. See also below, p. 452.

responsibility for war administration: the Treasury, Board of Ordnance, Admiralty, and what for simplicity may be called the Army. Between them they dealt with supply and transport, man-power and movements. The planning of operations lay largely outside their control.

The army was controlled by a system in need of great reforms. The engineers and the admirable Royal Artillery were administered by the Board of Ordnance. The rest of the army was ruled by a system which provided neither a regular military leader nor a responsible Minister in the Cabinet, for the army lay within the sphere of the royal prerogative. The King was Captain-General, and might or might not appoint a professional Commander-in-Chief. To assist him there was a Secretary at War, a professional politician of the second rank who invariably sat in the House of Commons but rarely in the Cabinet. His position was ambiguous and ill-defined. Constitutionally he was the servant of the Commander-in-Chief and a mere agent of the royal pleasure, who could disclaim responsibility in Parliament; in reality a powerful official who in the absence of a professional Commander-in-Chief might annexe the whole field of military administration and patronage.[1]

But administration and finance were all that the Secretary at War could supervise. For the training and discipline of the army at home there was no fixed provision. The Hanoverian Kings were soldiers who took pride in the personal exercise of their military prerogative; and like his predecessor, George III preferred to control the army without an intermediary. From 1770 until 1778 there was no Commander-in-Chief. When France entered the war, the King was forced to appoint Lord Amherst Commander-in-Chief with a seat in the Cabinet; and Amherst was succeeded by General Conway on the fall of the Ministry. But as soon as the King escaped from the shackles of Charles Fox, he resumed his personal control.

There was thus no effective machinery for inspecting the army; and hence no uniformity of drill or doctrine. The small peacetime army was scattered across the country in regimental detachments. 'A British army', Castlereagh was to say of this period, '. . . had no more uniformity of movements, of discipline, and appearance in its various regiments than one composed of the troops of different sovereign states.'[2] Here as elsewhere the French Revolution was to be a turning point. From 1793 there was always a Commander-in-Chief; and in the following year was created the office of Secretary of State for War with a seat in the Cabinet.

The operational control of the army was exercised directly by the Cabinet and Secretaries of State. Neither the Secretary at War nor the Commander in-Chief were responsible for strategy or for the strength of the army. This

[1] Clode, *Military Forces of the Crown*, II, 253–60, 698–705.   [2] Clode, II, 359.

has often led to confusion, for the Secretary at War sometimes complained of being left in the dark. But both Lord Barrington, the Secretary at War in 1775, and his successor Charles Jenkinson, were explicit about the bounds of their responsibility. 'Augmenting the forces is purely a matter of state', wrote Barrington, 'and the functions of the War Office do not begin till both the measure and the manner of executing it, have been settled in the Cabinet.' Jenkinson did not go so far. He had to introduce the Army Estimates in the House of Commons, and felt that he should be consulted about the method of achieving the strength which the Cabinet had fixed. But about strategy he was as clear as Barrington: he 'was no minister, and could not be supposed to have a competent knowledge of the destination of the army, and how the war was to be carried on'. If he was told the destination of troops, it was for his private information as a matter of administrative convenience. There is no substance in the claim which has been made for him,[1] that he 'furnished what co-ordination there was' between the departments of the war machine.[2]

Lord Amherst's departmental responsibilities as Commander-in-Chief were equally circumscribed. He was the chief military administrator of the army, and commander of the home forces. Though he had his share as a member of the Cabinet in discussions of policy and strategy, his executive duties were confined to administration. The Cabinet's strategic decisions were executed through the Secretaries of State; and operational instructions went directly to the commanders in the theatres of war.

Very different was the navy's position. In matters of patronage it may have been more vulnerable than the army, since it did not enjoy the same royal protection; but in administration and strategy the Admiralty was united and formidable. Instead of a dubious official on the fringes of the Ministry, and a Commander-in-Chief appointed intermittently at the King's pleasure, the navy was ruled by the Lords Commissioners of the Admiralty; a body in which professional knowledge was balanced with political power to produce a voice of commanding authority. The First Lord was no minor figure, like the Secretary at War, on the boundary between politics and public service, but a magnate with a seat in the Cabinet.

It had to be so. For this department, on whose efficiency England's security rested, controlled one of the most complex machines on earth: several hundred warships, most of them carrying enough cannon to equip an army; as many men as the entire British army; a vast network of dockyards, victualling yards and storehouses throughout the globe; a great purchasing

---

[1] *Journal of Modern History*, XXVI, 123.

[2] Lothian, 324; *Journal of Soc. for Army Hist. Research*, 1959, p. 167; Add. MSS. 38213, f. 243 (11 April 1780, Amherst to Jenkinson); below, pp. 369–70.

organisation; a great recruiting system. Only foresight, authority and professional skill could manage the navy.

The Board itself exercised direct control of operations, and of manning, promotions and discipline. Shipbuilding, supply and transport were delegated to the subordinate Navy Board over which the Comptroller presided. The Navy Board built and fitted out ships; purchased shipbuilding materials; managed the dockyards throughout the world; and transported troops. It had greater autonomy than the subordinate boards of other departments, and the Comptroller claimed a status second only to that of the First Lord of the Admiralty.[1]

Unlike the army, the navy retained a high degree of control of its own operations. Though the destinations of squadrons and reinforcements were determined in the Cabinet, they were determined with the First Lord's advice and assent. It was most unusual for the Cabinet even to discuss a naval question in his absence, and when they did so they deferred their decision till his return. Rare, too, were direct instructions to admirals from the Secretaries of State. It was very occasionally done for speed and secrecy[2]; but normally the Secretary of State's letter was addressed to the Board of Admiralty, who made out their own operational instruction from it. We shall find that the Admiralty's institutional solidarity and professional character made it the department least susceptible to Cabinet control.[3]

The contrasting characters of the two service organisations were reflected in the organisation of supply and transport. In most respects the navy was autonomous in these matters; the army was not. Three separate departments supplied the armed forces, and four transported them. The navy's provisions were procured by its own Victualling Board; the army's by the Treasury. Shipbuilding materials were purchased by the Navy Board; and though other stores and equipment for both army and navy came from the Board of Ordnance, the army having no political head in the Cabinet could indent only through a Secretary of State.[4] Sea transport, which kept open the Atlantic supply-lines, was yet more diversely organised. The navy's victualling ships were hired by the Victualling Board; army victuallers by the Treasury till 1779, and thereafter by the Navy Board; troopships by the Navy Board. Artillery, engineers and ordnance stores were shipped by the

---

[1] 'The Comptroller is next in consequence tho' not in rank in the sea line to the First Lord of the Admiralty' (Sir Charles Middleton, in CL, Shelburne, Vol. 151, No. 40).

[2] Commodore Johnstone's expedition to the Cape in 1781 is an instance (see Harlow, 111). As soon as Shelburne became Secretary of State in 1782 he assumed the correspondence with the naval Commander-in-Chief in America (see below, p. 475).

[3] See below, p. 19.

[4] Thomson, The Secretaries of State, 75–7.

Board of Ordnance in ordnance transports. The problems raised by this multiplication of authorities will become apparent[1]; for the moment it is enough that operational planning was linked to this complex system of logistics.

5. The Machine in Motion

The nexus of the system was the office of Secretary of State. It was the Secretaries who translated planning into preparation. 'However well your Lordship as conductor of the war may plan', Sir Charles Middleton was to tell Lord Shelburne, 'it will avail but little if preparation or execution do not go hand in hand.' Legally each of the Secretaries could sign any act of state; but in practice they divided the world between them. The Northern and Southern Departments conducted the diplomatic correspondence respectively of northern and southern Europe, while a third Secretaryship had recently been created to deal with the West Indies and North America.[2] Military and naval plans were divided on the same geographical principle. Operations in the American sphere belonged to the Colonial or American Secretary; and Gibraltar and the Cape of Good Hope, for example, fell to the Secretary of State for the Southern Department. The Secretaries of State alone signified the King's pleasure to' the departments which had to implement a Cabinet decision. Even when the head of a department was in the Cabinet, he normally required a letter from a Secretary of State to authorise any important undertaking. 'All warlike preparations, every military operation, and every naval equipment must be directed by a Secretary of State before they can be undertaken.'[3] So wrote the Under-Secretary of the American Department.

The Secretaries of State were therefore much more than departmental Ministers. It was they who powered the war machine. They provided at once a Cabinet Secretariat and executive supervision. By their hands the complex of supply and transport, military movement and naval preparation was drawn together and given life. Only their directing hands could break into the departmental pyramids and keep measures moving down the channels of administration. If an integrated expedition was successfully assembled with its proper equipment, provisions and transport, and at the place and time which the Cabinet had decreed, this was the achievement of the responsible Secretary of State.

Thus the efficiency of the whole system could turn on the efficiency of the Secretaries; and it was from the Southern Department that the Elder Pitt had directed the Seven Years War. 'It is said our constitution is not well

---

[1] See especially Chapter III below. [2] For the Third Secretary see below, p. 47.
[3] Thomson, 75.

calculated for war', Sir Charles Middleton once wrote to Shelburne. 'I know of no reason why, but because men cannot be found to attend to business.'[1] For in 1775 the Ministry contained no statesman of Pitt's calibre. At the Southern Department Lord Rochford retired in the autumn to make way for the indolent and easily frightened Weymouth, a Bedford Whig who resigned with his friends in 1779 and was succeeded in turn by the plodding inefficient Hillsborough. At the Northern Department was the bibulous Lord Suffolk, who knew no French though he shared the conduct of foreign policy. He was disliked by the Bedford faction in the Ministry, and proved a wretched leader in the House of Lords. He died in 1779 after a long decrepitude, and was succeeded by a professional diplomatist, Lord Stormont.

These men shared the control of military affairs at home. The Mediterranean, South Atlantic and Indian Ocean belonged to the Southern Department, and were to become important theatres as the war expanded. But the most important theatre of war lay in the north-west Atlantic, and was controlled by the American Department. The American Secretary at the outbreak of the rebellion was the pious Lord Dartmouth, a relation by marriage and a close friend of Lord North. Hating and dreading the struggle, he was unlikely to pursue it with resolution. Nor was he to remain long at the helm. Before 1775 was out a more resolute leader was sought; and the Ministry turned to Lord George Germain.

Each executive Department presented a separate problem of control. The Treasury, efficient in itself, was hampered at every turn by the difficulty of obtaining the co-operation of the army commanders in America. It was charged with procuring and delivering the army's provisions. But indents from America were late and sketchy, and tonnage needed for shipping the supply was detained in American ports without authority. The supervision of a Minister above the two authorities was needed to reduce the friction. The Board of Ordnance was a different problem: its trouble was its own gross inefficiency. It moved with agonising slowness. Clothing, entrenching tools, or chapel hassocks – whatever the need, months and even years went by before an indent was satisfied. Warships were detained for weeks and months after they were ready for sea because their armament had not been delivered; and when the guns at last arrived they might lack their complete equipment. 'Mortifying beyond imagination', wrote Sandwich of one such delay; and Sir Charles Middleton declared that the only remedy was the creation of a new office of sea-ordnance controlled by the Navy Board. The Master-General of the Ordnance was Lord Townshend; and even by the standards of the day he seems to have spent an unconscionable time at his home in Norfolk. He was not in the Cabinet, and appears to have been

[1] Barham, II, 67.

critical of the Ministry and to have treated his office, like Richmond later,[1] as a purely military one on which he depended for the salary. The Lieutenant-General of the Ordnance was Lord Amherst; a conscientious though unimaginative administrator, but from 1778 too deep in the duties of Commander-in-Chief to supervise the Ordnance effectively. In this sphere of the war effort, supervision might have been effectively flavoured with a dash of Chatham's terror.[2]

The Admiralty, by contrast, was wayward and independent. By tradition it distrusted Cabinet direction, and guarded its independence jealously. There was a well-developed technique of obstruction to defeat a Cabinet which interfered directly in fleet operations and attempted to override the Board. Sometimes it was possible to use the First Lord against the Cabinet: a pliant one like Lord Spencer in the Younger Pitt's war Ministry was dominated by the naval members of the Board. A different technique, used in the War of the Austrian Succession, was to feign ignorance and withhold co-operation. By withholding data or misrepresenting the dockyard situation the Admiralty could make planning impossible.[3]

Yet it was the Cabinet's business to control the war: to see the situation as a whole, and to strike the balance of risk and advantage. Systematic evasion of political control could lead to disaster. And in the Seven Years War Pitt had effectively asserted his control, ruling through a professional First Lord with close and ruthless personal supervision which reached down to the subordinate boards. Perhaps a seaman at the head of the Board was the best answer to the problem of control; for though a professional scrutiny of Cabinet instructions may have been necessary, a political filter in the shape of an amateur First Lord was not. When Lord Barham became First Lord in the Trafalgar era, it was arranged[4] that he should not attend Cabinet meetings except on naval questions.

A political filter was precisely what Lord Sandwich imposed on his colleagues in the American War. His power as a party manager was skilfully combined with his special knowledge of the highly technical naval situation to extend his influence from naval patronage to strategy. 'I must always desire to be understood that I do not speak with precision as to the time of the readiness of any ship', he wrote in the autumn of 1779. This was reasonable in itself, for bad weather, the diversion of workmen to tasks with a

[1] See below, p. 509.

[2] E. E. Curtis, *Organisation of the British Army in the American Revolution*; Sackville, II, 195; Sandwich, II, 143; CL, Shelburne, Vol. 151, No. 15; WO 34/137, f. 49; Hutchinson Diary, I, 553; Leeds Political Memoranda, 44.

[3] Richmond, *The Navy in the War of 1739–48*, I, 82, 195–7, 223, 235–6; II, 70, 85 87–8; III, 16–7.

[4] English Historical Documents, XI, 17.

higher priority, and a hundred other unpredicted obstacles might delay a ship's fitting out. But it could be made a convenient smoke-screen. 'I never could understand the real state of the fleet', Germain once wrote to North. Towards the end of the war he declared that if the First Lord approved of a Cabinet proposal there were always ships to carry it out; but if he disliked it none could be found. To the Prime Minister Sandwich was even more cavalier. He treated his information and suggestions with such contempt that North was reduced to passing intelligence through a subordinate to disguise its origin.[1]

A voice from a different walk of life shows the disjointed nature of the system. In May 1776, the colonial governor and merchant Thomas Hutchinson visited the American Department. He found the two Under-Secretaries searching the letter-book to discover by what ship certain orders had been sent. As a merchant he had never written an important letter without tracking the ship from the moment she sailed; but in government the system was to send letters from the office of the Secretary of State to the Admiralty, who forwarded them at their convenience. The appointed ship might be delayed at home for weeks without the Secretary of State being informed. 'This', said Hutchinson, 'shows the want of one great director to keep every part of the operations of government constantly in his head.'[2]

6. 'One Great Director'

'One great director': the phrase was everywhere. The conduct of a great war called for strong leadership in the Cabinet, and energetic supervision of the executive departments; for strength to weigh the risks and courage for great decisions. It called for a dominating leader who rejoiced in war. Lord North knew it as well as any. The war, he told the King at a critical moment, 'can hardly be well conducted unless there is a person in the Cabinet capable of leading, of discerning between opinions, of deciding quickly and confidently, and of connecting all the operations of government, that this nation may act uniformly and with force'. But North knew equally well that he was not the man.[3]

Neither appearance, nor character, nor interests equipped Lord North to dominate a war administration. His figure was clumsy and his movements awkward. A large tongue thickened his articulation. Two prominent myopic eyes rolled about in his face to no purpose, and with his wide mouth, thick lips and inflated cheeks 'gave him the air of a blind trumpeter'. His skills

---

[1] G 2776; Knox, 180; CL, Germain, 11 Jan. 1779 to North; ibid., 31 Oct. 1781, from Knox; Abergavenny, 25; Sandwich, III, 244–5.

[2] Quoted by Anderson, p. 87.   [3] G 2446.

were those of peace. He was a man of culture and personal charm; of patience for dull understandings, wit which never wounded, humour which never ridiculed. He was proud of being a good manager of the House of Commons, and few surpassed him in the political arts: the manoeuvre by which he jobbed his half-brother into the bishopric of Winchester ranks high in the tactical annals of patronage. Almost single-handed he defended his Ministry in Parliament year after year against the bitter invective and dialectical brilliance of a ferocious opposition. His knowledge of the House, his accessibility, his even temper and his aptitude for raising a laugh baffled and infuriated his rivals. But of war this civilised man knew nothing: 'Upon military matters I speak ignorantly, and therefore without effect.'[1] He did not enjoy war; nor was he even confident of victory. As misfortunes accumulated he grew increasingly despondent and weary of responsibility. But the hypochondria which always deepened as Budget day approached puzzled his friends. He talked of wanting to retire; but they could not tell if this was more than a temporary symptom of ill-health, and the King could not bring him to a forthright declaration whether he really meant to go. It has been suggested that duty prevented him from telling the King clearly that he disagreed with his American policy, and gratitude to the monarch who had paid his debts prevented him from deserting the ship. But even today one cannot be sure that he was kept unwillingly: his love of the political game was so mingled with his neurosis.[2]

There was nothing in the constitution to tie the leadership of a war government to the Treasury. It was not long since the Secretaries of State had vied with the head of the Treasury for primacy in the Cabinet; and only fourteen years earlier Pitt had run a great war from the Southern Department. But now things had changed. It was partly that the weakness of the Ministry increased the importance of the Treasury's patronage; partly that no politician in office now commanded Pitt's weight with the country; and partly an increasing conviction that finance was decisive. In the next war, when the primacy of finance was becoming doubtful, Dundas and the Younger Pitt were to reiterate the doctrine: all modern wars are a contention of the purse, and the war minister should be the Minister of Finance.[3] Thus the leadership of the war government was thrown upon a man who carried the full burdens of political and financial management. North's position

---

[1] Ritcheson, *British Politics and the American Revolution*, 198. The great British war ministers have been men who throve on war. Lord Hillsborough once remarked that the North ministry was too backward in firing guns for victories and in those marks of triumph which the Elder Pitt had used on all occasions (WO 34/131, ff. 64, 66).

[2] Pares, 172; G 2854, 2856, 2872.

[3] English Historical Documents, XI, Nos 62, 64.

may be contrasted with Newcastle's in the Seven Years War. Newcastle had been a miserable war leader, terrified of responsibility and ludicrously ignorant of geography. But from 1757, when he withdrew to the Treasury and Pitt took control of the war, Newcastle became the indispensible political manager of the team. North had to be his own party manager in a time of violent contention, bearing a burden of detail which distracted his wits. And in one respect his civil burden was heavier than Newcastle's; for being in the House of Commons he followed custom and combined the Treasurer-ship with the Chancellorship of the Exchequer, carrying on his own back the undivided weight of the finances. He accepted these burdens from in-clination, both as a party leader and as a sound financier. History has con-firmed his financial abilities; but sound financiers make the worst war ministers. North, with his 'parsimony of public treasure',[1] his ignorance of war, and his opposition to re-armament, was of the lineage of Walpole and the Younger Pitt; of Gladstone and Neville Chamberlain.

Distracted and gloomy, the Prime Minister gradually withdrew deeper into the sheltering recesses of his departmental routine. He became inaccess-ible to his colleagues, and only a few junior officials were able to approach him. With these he conducted his business in holes and corners, always ready to take flight at the hint of a difficulty. The Ministry had never worked as a single co-ordinated machine; and more and more it became a govern-ment of separate departments. For this situation the King's supposed desire to rule in person has been blamed; but the truth is that it was a recent historical accident which North perpetuated. In 1766 Chatham had formed a miscellaneous Administration of clever young men with no bond of union but himself. When he fell ill the Duke of Grafton at the Treasury refused to act as effective Prime Minister in his place, and the Ministry was reduced to a collection of independent departments without a head. This was the system which North inherited: 'I found it so, and had not the vigour and resolution to put an end to it.' Perhaps the saddest spectacle of the war is the Prime Minister, with the clearest self-knowledge, helpless to correct his faults or to resign.[2]

In a moment of depression North seems to have implied that the true director of affairs was the King.[3] This view would have suited the book of

---

[1] Knox, 156. In 1779 William Eden reproached North for devoting two-thirds of his time to contractors' jobs, Custom House scruples, and memorials of individuals about pounds, shillings and pence (Butterfield, 61). A year later the King wished that North could be persuaded to appoint a Secretary to the Chancellor of the Exchequer to see that letters were answered promptly (Add. MSS. 37835, f. 164).

[2] Butterfield, *George III, Lord North and the People*, 21–2; Russell, *Memorials of Fox*, II, 38.

[3] G 2845.

Charles Fox; but it was not so. North himself was quite specific about it to Fox: 'the appearance of power is all that a King in this country can have. Though the Government in my time was a government by departments, the whole was done by the Ministers, except in a few instances.'[1] Though still in constitutional theory the head of the executive, and though still generally conceded to have the right to choose Ministers whose views he approved, George III did not direct the war. He received Ministers individually, and commented on their views; but beyond insisting in general terms on the subjugation of America he made no attempt to steer strategy. Military administration he rightly regarded as lying within his prerogative; and in this sphere he was active, resisting the worst abuses of patronage and retaining a say in the appointment of commanders. But these were matters of administration rather than policy. About the strategic movement of troops he was always punctiliously consulted by Amherst before orders were issued; but though he was capable of rejecting Cabinet advice to send a regiment to Jamaica, it went there just the same.[2]

The King neither could nor would provide the missing leadership. His contribution to the war was a moral one. He could try to see that the Ministers held together and did their duty. He would put heart into the hesitant, stir up the idle, and check the treacherous. He never wavered from the chosen object of the war. His own firm spirit helped to hold the Ministry together and encouraged resolute measures; in the darkest crises he never lacked confidence or courage. 'If others will not be active, I must drive', he remarked of an occasion when he summoned the Cabinet to his presence. His aim was not to direct policy, but to infuse his own energy into those who ought. He knew the importance of pushing slothful administrators, and gained his servants' respect. 'I have always observed', wrote a junior Minister, 'that the Admiralty can be expeditious when the King is inquisitive or anxious about their preparations.' 'The more the Ministers know of their Master', Germain wrote in his retirement, 'the more will they incline to merit his good opinion.'[3]

With regard to North's leadership, the King knew what was lacking. 'I fear', he wrote contemptuously in 1779, 'his irresolution is only to be equalled by a certain vanity of wanting to ape the Prime Minister without any of the requisite qualities.' Yet it was his own deliberate choice which kept the wretched North in harness. He preferred administration paralysis to the political difficulty of replacing him. He never hoped the

---

[1] Russell, *Memorials of Fox*, II, 38. Lord Hillsborough 'thought the King would never thwart his Minister, and would rather, when dissatisfied, change him'. (Hutchinson Diaries, II, 187).

[2] Knox, 155; CO 5/254, ff. 125–6.

[3] Sandwich, III, 26; Knox, 130; Sackville, I, 141.

impossible: he never expected to turn North into an effective leader. But he believed that, while confining himself to financial matters, North could be persuaded to fill vacant offices with the best men, and keep in touch with what was going on; could be steered into methodical habits; and above all could be persuaded to remain in office. The King described his ambition for North in a letter to John Robinson in November 1778: 'he must cast off his indecision and bear up, or no plan can succeed; he must be more exact in answering letters or let others do it for him; and he must let measures be thoroughly canvassed before undertaken, and when adopted must not quit them'. It was a modest pattern for the head of a government at war.[1]

[1] Add. MSS. 37834, ff. 39, 133; Knox, 155, 157; Pares, 151.

PART ONE

THE CITADELS OF
REBELLION

1775–7

CHAPTER I

LORD DARTMOUTH'S WAR

1. *The Watching Enemy*

The task which the unfortunate Ministers faced was enough to daunt the most stout-hearted. They had not sought it. But with the attack on Bunker Hill they had crossed the Rubicon. Nothing had been prepared, everything had to be done. In America there was not a single requisite for waging a war except gunpowder. The one gleam of light was that the rebels had shown their hand, and Parliament would now vote supplies which might have been questioned a few weeks earlier. Only the King was cheerful and energetic. 'We must persist and not be dismayed', he replied to a jeremiad from North.[1]

The most threatening aspect of the situation in the long run was not in America but in Europe. If the struggle should be prolonged, it was not likely to remain a private colonial quarrel. Paris, like London, had watched the news from Boston. In the Foreign Ministry of the young Louis XVI there were men who waited for the day that would right the balance and restore France to her greatness. At their head stood the Comte de Vergennes, a statesman without the brilliance of Choiseul, but endowed with a patience which groped its way through the tangled politics of the nations towards it goal. One of his subordinates later described the aims which inspired them. For her honour France had to seize this opportunity to rise from her degradation. 'If she neglected it, if fear overcame duty, she would add debasement to humiliation, and become an object of contempt to her own century and to all future peoples.'[2]

In seeking independence for England's colonies, Vergennes challenged tradition. The Americans would expect the opening of French colonial trade to their shipping and the final renunciation of Canada. Yet most French officials believed the price should be paid. Vergennes' way was clear; and in surveying his country's alliances he followed the path mapped by Choiseul. In Europe, the Austrian alliance should be maintained, but only as a tranquillising agency: Austrian aggressions were not to be supported. The corner-stone of French foreign policy must be the Family Compact with Spain. On the Continent the Compact would help to restrain Austria: on the seas France and Spain together could outnumber the British navy.[3]

From the beginning of the war, Vergennes believed that the reconquest of

[1] G 1682–3.   [2] Doniol, I, 2 ff.   [3] Doniol, I, Chap. 2 and p. 241.

America was impossible. He was convinced that Britain had lost her chance; that her slow and deliberate building up of strength would now enable the Americans to organise and prepare; and that all her wealth and resources would not enable her to succeed. 'It will be vain for the English to multiply their forces there', he wrote in July 1775; 'no longer can they bring that vast continent back to dependence by force of arms'.[1]

Yet there were reasons for treading carefully. In the first place Spain was an uncertain factor. Though she coveted Minorca and Gibraltar, and was embroiled in a dispute with Portugal which brought her into collision with England, her interests were less clear-cut than those of France. Her colonies were more extensive and vulnerable; and even if they survived a war with England, the rise of an independent America might create a new threat to their security and loyalty. The internal politics of Madrid brought further confusion. The Prime Minister, Grimaldi, was a foreigner, and anxious not to affront Spanish opinion by too Francophile a policy. This anxiety was accentuated in the summer of 1775 when the King admitted his heir-apparent to a more active share in his deliberations; for round the Prince of the Asturias were grouped Grimaldi's most active opponents. When the rebellion broke out in America, Spain seemed more anxious to secure her own possessions than to embarrass England's.

Further reasons for caution lay in the English political scene. In the long run defeat in America might tempt England to seek compensation in the West Indies. More immediately, the surprise attack in 1755 was remembered. A preventive attack on France did not seem beyond the bounds of possibility. The North government was pacific; but under public pressure it might turn belligerent. A couple of days after the news of Bunker Hill, Lord Rochford unmistakably showed his claws to the French ambassador. And behind the North Ministry stood the shadow of Chatham. If North fell from power, the King might be forced to recall the architect of victory; and that restless and ambitious spirit might reconcile the Americans and turn the united forces of England and her colonies against the West Indies. Already England had ten thousand troops beyond the Atlantic with warships and transports, and at home a powerful fleet in good condition and ready to be manned. The pick of French seamen were exposed in the Newfoundland fisheries, and her commerce and colonies were unprotected. There was much reason for care.[2]

Lord Rochford's threat, however, was used to good purpose in Madrid. The two Courts drew closer together, and Spain urged France to keep sixty sail of the line in good condition, which with Spain's fifty would balance the British fleet. The two governments were thus closely linked against the

[1] Doniol, I, 89, 171-2.   [2] Doniol, I, 41-3, 61-2, 68-71, 81, 116; II, 90-1, 223.

supposed danger, even to the point of concerting war plans, when on 23 August the British Ministry issued the Proclamation of Rebellion. All intercourse with the rebel colonies was forbidden, and the seizure of rebel shipping at last began. This was the real declaration of war. It marked the British government's recognition that unless it strengthened its hand by the use of force it would negotiate in vain.[1]

The Proclamation gave confidence to Vergennes. Hitherto he had feared that reconciliation was imminent. But now the door was closed. England's forces would be contained by the vain effort of reconquest, and the immediate danger of an attack on French and Spanish colonies receded. England could be left to destroy her forces and exhaust her finances. In a burst of optimism Vergennes and Guines, his ambassador in London, wrote as though revolution in England was imminent. They pictured the country engulfing itself in civil war, George III as another Charles I, with scaffolds for the Ministers and exile for the royal family. It was not, alas, the British Ministers who were to tread the scaffold.

For France the critical moment would come when England gave up the struggle in America and withdrew her forces; and the degree of danger would depend on how far those forces might remain intact. Vergennes' business was to see that they did not; and he began to feel his way cautiously towards active help for the rebels. Early in September an agent sailed for America to transmit information; and in the same month Beaumarchais, the begetter of Figaro, returned from the colonies to urge the necessity of acting now as the future allies of America. For if England subdued her colonies she would turn on France. France must support the colonies to ensure her own survival.[2]

2. The Rebels

The population of the American colonies was estimated by Congress as nearly 3 million. The American Department made it something under $2\frac{1}{2}$ million, of whom 600,000 were negroes. If one supposed that a quarter of the white population could bear arms, there were about 450,000 fighting men in the American colonies, from whom loyalists, pacifist sects and seamen had to be deducted. Nine years earlier Benjamin Franklin had calculated ironically in a London newspaper that America had a quarter of a million fighting men; but since one Englishman was as good as five Americans, an army of 50,000 could quell the colonies in three or four years at a cost of 10 or 12 million pounds a year.[3]

[1] Doniol, I, 43, 51–6, 123–7.   [2] Doniol, I, 90, 149, 171–4, 204.

[3] Knox, 288; CL, Germain, Vol. 17, p. 24; Theodore Thayer, *Pennsylvania Politics and the Growth of Democracy*, 125, n. 54. The population of the British Isles was about 11 million; but no comparison can, of course, be drawn from the figures.

Superficially, of course, the argument was fallacious, for America was geographically and politically divided, and her economy would not allow her to mobilise more than a fraction of her fighting men for regular service. Nevertheless a very high proportion of her men would turn out with the militia to defend their own districts; and if the Americans were fighting for principles a very high proportion of their strength could intermittently be brought to bear.

The total was formidable. But whether it consisted of reliable fighting men was another question. With the possible exception of Lord Amherst, those among the government's friends who knew the Americans best rated them lowest. Wolfe at Quebec had called the American Rangers 'the worst soldiers in the universe'. His successor, General Murray, was now Governor of Minorca, and as late as 1777 he guessed that Washington's only reliable men were recent immigrants: 'the native American is a very effeminate thing, very unfit for and very impatient of war'. Admiral Rodney had met them when he was Governor of Newfoundland, and despised them. Some of the reports on Lexington and Concord had tended to confirm these estimates. Though astonishing numbers had turned out, it was suggested by friendly Americans that if the rebels had shown skill and courage the tired British detachment could not have retired twenty miles without ammunition.[1]

Bunker Hill produced a different impression. Fighting on ground which was ideal for their tactics, among small enclosures and narrow lanes, the Americans had defended their position inch by inch. Their steadiness was far beyond what could have been expected. They showed, wrote Gage, 'a conduct and spirit against us, they never showed against the French, and everybody has judged them from their former appearance and behaviour'. His subordinates all agreed. The American defence had been well planned and obstinately maintained, and their retreat had been covered with skill and courage.[2]

In face of such evidence, British Ministers have been accused of obstinate blindness to the quality of the rebels. But the first American successes were followed by a long succession of tactical defeats. Indeed, they probably never succeeded in equalling either the British regulars or the British-trained loyalist regiments. The Americans could handle firearms, but at first they had little training or discipline. They could not manoeuvre in the field, and were only happy skirmishing in the woods or digging in on a strong position. 'We must learn to use other weapons than the pick and spade', said John Adams. 'Our armies must be disciplined and learn to fight.'[3]

[1] Reilly, *The Rest to Fortune*, 223; Sackville, I, 371; CL, Wedderburn, II, Nos 49, 51 (No. 49 is misinterpreted in a manuscript note as referring to British troops).
[2] Rutland, III, 2; Dartmouth, 381; Gage Corr., II, 686; G 1670.
[3] Freeman, *Washington*, IV, 141–2.

For British statesmen it was extraordinarily difficult to assess the enemy correctly. A revolutionary struggle which involved an armed insurgent population was unique in the memory of the age. And the hostility of a great part of the population and the passion of the loyalists made accurate and objective intelligence scarce. How, for example, was Germain to assess the views of Dr Berkenhout, who went through the lines in 1778? If his report was to be believed, the Continental army consisted chiefly of transported Irishmen; and if Washington could ever be defeated and resolutely pursued, his troops would disperse. 'They are not, as they have been represented, a respectable body of yeomanry, fighting *pro aris et focis*; but a contemptible body of vagrants, deserters and thieves.'[1]

The idea that Washington's Continentals were mainly Irishmen and other recent immigrants was widely held. We have seen that General Murray believed it: so did Clinton and his staff at New York; and few of the Provincial troops in British service were native 'Americans'.[2] This much was certain: that Washington had the greatest difficulty in keeping an army together. For the rest, Englishmen at home had no yardstick to measure such statements. American society was unlike any other in the world; and its peculiar strength had the appearance of weakness to the aristocratic statesmen of Westminster. Lord Carlisle, comparing the revolts of America and the Netherlands, argued that America was in its infancy and lacked the strength and vigour of age and 'a proper division of different ranks of men'. When he saw New York for himself in 1778 he noticed that in spite of the wretchedness and poverty among the victims of the war, he was never asked for charity. Yet in face even of the refractory obstinacy of rebel prisoners, well-informed and sensible Englishmen returned again and again to this error. Admiral Rodney supposed that Washington could be bought with honours. In 1778 a particularly acute memorandum on the conduct of the war which circulated in Cabinet circles urged the distribution of titles and honours 'to hasten the natural progress of an aristocracy on that Continent in order to correct the levelling spirit of the people'.[3]

The loyalists, of course, nourished the idea that the enemy were a mob led by demagogues; the contrast between the rebels' talk of rights and liberties and their actual oppression of the loyal minority made it hard for the victims to credit them with honesty of purpose. But the British themselves had reason for their low opinion of American troops. In the Seven Years War the colonials had lost confidence in their ability to face the French

[1] CL, Germain, 24 Aug. 1778.
[2] Mackenzie, 81; Willcox, *American Rebellion*, 110. See also Hastings, III, 186; Howe's *Narrative*, 43.
[3] Carlisle, 447; Sackville, II, 194; WO 34/110, ff. 144–52.

regulars and the disciplined Canadian militia. In part their weakness is explained by the failure of the separate colonial legislatures to combine and contribute adequately, a failure which the British government could now reasonably hope to see repeated. But it was also a product of the American way of life: of the individualism and passion for freedom which made them suspicious of standing armies and impatient of discipline; of the absence of dependence and poverty on which the recruiting sergeant could feed; and of the lack of that social subordination which was the root of eighteenth-century discipline. Of all this the Americans themselves were aware. Petitioning for British troops in 1755, the Massachusetts Assembly had explained:

our people are not calculated to be confined in garrisons or kept in any particular service; they soon grow troublesome and uneasy by reflecting on their folly in bringing themselves into a state of subjection when they might have continued free and independent.[1]

Throughout the rebellion the difficulty of getting Americans to serve outside their own militia areas continued. Even Congress was reluctant to see a standing army. 'Long enlistment is a state of slavery', a member declared. Thus the Continental army was hampered by short enlistments, and was continually dissolving and being reformed. In some respects the British estimation of American strength in the field was not wide of the mark. Their real miscalculation lay elsewhere.

3. Conscience and Policy

This miscalculation was the strength and vitality of the loyalists and the effectiveness of the rebel militia. And the loyalists were essential because none of the great maxims of strategy applied in America. The weighing of ends and means, the magnitude of the object against the cost of achieving it, provided little guidance. For both sides the political objects of the struggle were absolute. For the Americans, before the first British counterstroke was even launched, the object was defined as absolute independence. For Britain the object was the overthrow of the revolutionary government. Yet this British object was, paradoxically, not an unlimited one of simple conquest. Her ultimate desire was the political one of restoring union and harmony between the colonies and the mother-country. Force was adopted with reluctance, and throughout the struggle the attempt to seek a solution by

---

[1] L. H. Gipson, *The British Empire before the American Revolution*, VII, 71. See also Vol. II, Chap. I, and Vol. VII, Chap. IX. Since the above was written, fresh light has been shed on the misleading lessons of the Seven Years War by Mr. John W. Shy in 'A New Look at Colonial Militia' (*William and Mary Quarterly* 1963, pp. 183–5).

political means was never abandoned, though at times it was temporarily shelved while the army attempted to crack the shell of American obstinacy.

Thus a war of unlimited destruction was ruled out. There were limits to what conscience and policy would allow. Clinton would not countenance the murder of the enemy Commander-in-Chief.[1] Nor could the country be ravaged as Marlborough had ravaged Bavaria. The systematic burning of towns was an expedient sometimes considered but never adopted. Occasionally a coastal town was burned, but always with some sense of shame and usually with a military purpose such as the destruction of stores or privateers. When General Tryon burned New Haven and Fairfield in 1779, he thought it necessary to make the following apologia to his chief.

I should be very sorry if the destruction of these two villages would be thought less reconcilable with humanity than with the love of my country, my duty to my King, and the law of arms, to which America has been led to make the awful appeal.

The usurpers have professedly placed their hopes of severing the Empire, in avoiding decisive actions, upon the waste of the British treasures, and the escape of their own property during the protraction of the war.

Their power is supported by the general dread of their tyranny, and the arts practised to inspire a credulous multitude with a presumptuous confidence in our forbearance.[2]

The British army's attitude to the struggle was ambivalent. They were professionals doing a duty, but they could not easily forget that they were fighting against men of their own race. 'Here pity interposes', wrote General Phillips, 'and we cannot forget that when we strike we wound a brother.' Even the King, whose heart was hardened against the rebels, never forgot that they were his subjects. Thus his reaction to Howe's successes at New York in 1776: 'Notes of triumph would not have been proper when the successes are against subjects not a foreign foe.' And in 1777 on a foreigner's proposal to raise a force on a peculiar system: '. . . very diverting, a Corps raised on the avowed plan of plunder seems to be curious, when intended to serve against the Colonies'.[3]

It was not easy to determine the limits of such a policy, and the difficulty can be seen in the diary of a humane and intelligent staff officer. When the rebels in Fort Washington rejected Howe's summons, was he right to restrain the troops from carrying the inner fort by assault? The Hessians, irritated by their losses, would have inflicted dreadful carnage in the crowded enclosure; and without overstepping the laws of war a lesson could have been inflicted which might have made it impossible for Congress ever to

[1] Mackenzie, 585.
[2] CO 5/98, f. 122.
[3] Royal Institution, I, 254; Add. MSS. 37833, ff. 99, 139.

raise another army. On the whole Major Mackenzie thought that Howe was right 'to treat our enemies as if they might one day become our friends'. Yet it was hard to stomach the sight of uniformed rebel officers walking the streets of New York on parole, disgusting the loyalists and inviting sabotage. In the last stages of the struggle, when he considered the possibility of pursuing Washington on his march from New York to Yorktown, Mackenzie was to suggest that on moving into the Jerseys Clinton should issue a proclamation that men taken in arms without uniforms should not be treated as soldiers; for he believed that a severe example on the first party of militia would clear the line of march. That this had never been done is a remarkable illustration of the moderate temper with which the rebellion was fought.[1]

It is true that as the war dragged on the army's dislike of the rebels increased. The conventions of civilised warfare were not invariably observed by either side. The British refused to exchange naval prisoners till 1780, and the Americans to honour the Convention of Saratoga. Both these departures from the norm were the result of Britain's extended ocean communications, which made the army's existence dependent on clearing the sea lanes and its losses on land all but irreplaceable: disadvantages which the British could not easily accept nor the colonists forbear to exploit. The refusal to exchange was also due in part to the equivocal position of the colonists. Were they rebels and traitors, or a nation with belligerent rights and status? They were anxious to assert that they were full belligerents; the British to maintain that they were not. The British were therefore reluctant to enter into a regular cartel for the exchange of prisoners, and left it to the commander on the spot to effect it at his discretion 'without the King's dignity and honour being committed'. The Americans, determined to assert their independence to the letter, conducted their necessary correspondence with the British commanders in tones of prickly rudeness. 'The Congress of the United States of America make no answer to insolent letters', was the reply to Clinton's demand for the fulfillment of the Saratoga Convention; words which Germain justly characterised as a 'very indecent answer'. The delay in granting Cornwallis his exchange after Yorktown provoked this comment from the honourable Carleton: 'Instead of that humane attention to the rights of individuals which prevails in Europe, they seem to practice in this country a studied incivility.'[2]

---

[1] Mackenzie, 110–12, 639. There was some suggestion in 1776 that the British did not give much quarter on Long Island; but this was a period of initial confusion, to which the rebels contributed by fighting with the desperation of men whose leaders had warned them to expect no mercy. (See Lowell, *The Hessians*, 68.)

[2] CL, Germain, 1 Feb. 1776 to Howe; CO 5/96, Germain's of 2 Dec. 1778; Cornwallis Corr., 141.

But studied incivility was very far from a war of indiscriminate ravaging and reprisal. The ordinary means of forcing an enemy to submit to one's will was to strike at his military or political centre of gravity. But where did it exist? It was far from clear that the destruction of the Continental army would prove decisive, though it would be a help. Nor was this easy to effect. The opportunity was lost in 1776 and perhaps again in the winter of Valley Forge. But Washington had no intention of risking a defeat, and had a great depth of country into which he could retire where the difficulties of regular movement and supply impeded pursuit. Nor was there a political centre whose capture would break the American will to resist. There was no equivalent of London, Paris or Vienna. Cities meant little, and the rudimentary political institutions of the United States were not anchored to places. Boston, New York, and the first seat of Congress at Philadelphia were all occupied by the British without visible effect on the rebels' determination. The fragmented political and economic structure of the colonies was a protection to them as well as a handicap.

Without the possibility of a single decisive blow, the cost of resistance might yet have been raised to a pitch where the majority of the population would have preferred submission. How this might have been achieved was sketched by General Murray. He, indeed, in spite of his contempt for the American fighting man, agreed with Lord Barrington in reprobating the idea of military conquest. He foretold that in prolonged military operations numbers would favour the rebels. They could replace their own losses, the British army could not; and a series of Pyrrhic victories might end in a fatal reverse which would destroy the moral idea of its superiority. British troops should not be exposed in offensive battles. Instead, they should be used at New York as an anvil on which to hammer the New England rebels. New England, the heart of the trouble, must be severed from the Middle Colonies, ruined by the annihilation of her trade and fisheries, and harried by Canadian and Indian raiders till she turned to the British army for protection.[1]

This prescient analysis had two flaws. The first was the restraint imposed on British policy by the aim of reconciliation. The second was the hardening of American resistance. American opinion often faltered under the pressure of war and commercial blockade: 'We can't drive the British Army away, and the length of their purse will ruin us', was reported to be the common talk at the end of 1779.[2] But they were led by a hard core of revolutionaries with everything to lose by submission; and in the last resort independence meant more to the Americans than reconquest to England. The Younger Pitt once boasted that he could predict to the day the financial collapse of

[1] CL, Germain, 27 Aug. 1775, Murray to Germain encl.
[2] Carlisle, 433.

Revolutionary France. 'But who', Wilberforce is said to have replied, 'was Attila's Chancellor of the Exchequer?'

Ultimately the recovery of America required the re-occupation of the colonies, after the Continental army had been either smashed or contained. And permanent success would depend on the loyalists. Loyalist administrations and loyalist militias alone could consolidate the gains.

'I may safely assert', wrote General Howe to a constituent early in 1775, 'that the insurgents are very few, in comparison with the whole of the people.'[1] On this assumption the British war effort went forward. How many loyalists were there? They have been estimated at the highest as half the population: perhaps one-third is nearer the mark. But it is clear that the British assumption was nearer the truth than was once supposed. The Tories were weakest where the colonists were of the purest English stock. In New England they may have been scarcely a tenth of the population; in the South a quarter or a third; but in the Middle Colonies including New York perhaps nearly a half.[2]

Most revolutions are made by highly organised minorities, and Germain was right in believing that the dedicated nucleus of the rebellion was small. He was not blinded by the *Schwärmerei* which beset the French. Franklin might masquerade at Versailles as a noble savage, but the British knew the political Americans better: a wealthy sophisticated society with a high standard of living, and as aggressive as the British themselves in the pursuit of commercial gain. Germain's error, if he made one, was the assumption that the mass of the population was actively friendly and could be organised in the face of terrorist reprisals: an assumption occasionally justified in more recent British history but often disastrously misleading. The American loyalists were indeed numerous. But they were not evenly distributed, and they lacked organisation, unity of interests, and a common standard round which they could rally. Where they were weak they were intimidated by the organised violence of the Sons of Liberty: in the north by mobs and committees, in the south by terrorist posses invading their plantations. As the war progressed, intimidation was increased, systematised and blessed by the law. Even in districts where they had an overwhelming superiority the loyalists were quickly overrun and broken up by neighbouring rebel militias. The rebels had the initial advantage of prior organisation and intact leadership.

---

[1] Anderson, *Command of the Howe Brothers*, 49. See also *ibid.*, pp. 10 *et seq*, for a striking discussion of the courses open to the British government.

[2] This is the distribution suggested by William H. Nelson, *The American Tory*, 92. R. R. Palmer (*Age of the Democratic Revolution*, 188) hazards a guess that the refugees by the end of the war may have numbered 24 per thousand, compared with about 5 *émigrés* per thousand in the French Revolution.

If the British were to use the loyalists, they would need faith in their strength, and a consistent policy of rescuing and protecting them from oppression to restore their shaken confidence. These may have been foundations of sand; but there were no others on which to build[1].

4. *The Decision to Fight*

With or without French intervention, the coming struggle would be one of peculiar difficulty. It would be waged three thousand miles beyond the ocean, by methods in which political and military calculations would be awkwardly entwined. If France stood behind the rebels, the possibility of disaster was real. Was America worth the risk and effort?

There were many who believed that their own prosperity or the nation's depended on the political control of the colonies. Mercantile protectionists feared the development of American manufactures and the repudiation of their London debts; country gentlemen irrationally feared a higher land tax if the fiscal resources of America were lost. Post-war experience was to prove the falsity of the economic arguments; and already they were being challenged. Even at the outbreak of the rebellion a few sceptics like Dean Tucker and Adam Smith were arguing that England would gain by discarding her colonies. By 1778 Charles Jenkinson was beginning to argue this very thesis at the Treasury Board. For the rebel embargo on British goods had revealed to the observant how much the Americans really depended on British imports. The prohibition was defied. Through neutral channels the Americans continued to buy British goods on a large scale. Nova Scotia was importing ten times what the colony could consume; and almost certainly the surplus was being smuggled along the coast to New England. Whatever the effect of American independence might be, it was unlikely to mean the loss of the American market.[2]

Yet the decision to hold America was more than a commercial calculation: it was an imperial dream of power. American independence, wrote the British ambassador in Paris a year or two later, 'would be of signal advantage to France, and the deepest and most disgraceful wound that Great Britain could possibly receive'. For George III and most of his subjects concessions far short of independence would strike at the roots of the Constitution and at Britain's standing among the Powers. And this belief was more than a constitutional superstition, or a confusion of prestige with power. Statesmen

[1] For a clear analysis of the coercion and subjection of the loyalists in the first year of the rebellion, see Nelson, 93–115.

[2] See below, p. 158, for Jenkinson's memorandum; Harlow, 198–222; Williams Transcripts, 6 Dec. 1777, Commodore Collier to Sandwich (from Halifax).

feared, and even Adam Smith admitted, that the end of the Navigation System would be the end of Britain's naval strength. We should find ourselves like the Dutch, wrote Lord Sheffield in his decisive study in 1783, 'rich perhaps as individuals, but weak as a state'; 'opulent merchants for a time, if riches are our only object'. If a sophisticated mind like Sheffield's could plead for salvaging the system when the American War was lost, it is small wonder that ordinary ones clung to the entirety from the beginning. The King's derision of 'weighing such events in the scale of a tradesman behind his counter' was a simple person's expression of the same belief. 'A small state may certainly subsist', he declared in 1780, 'but a great one mouldering cannot get into an inferior situation but must be annihilated.'[1]

Thus from the outset, and until inevitable defeat stared the country in the face, the American War was popular. 'The executive power', wrote Edward Gibbon, 'was driven by the national clamour into the most vigorous and coercive measures.'[2] And when Parliament assembled in October after the plunge was taken, the Ministry was backed by overwhelming majorities in both Houses, and a four shilling land tax was accepted without a murmur.

Nevertheless the difficulties were very apparent. Even if Europe stood aside from the struggle, there were some who shared Vergennes' belief that the task was impossible. Within the Ministry the first news of bloodshed had revealed weakness and division. Lord Suffolk and Wedderburn, survivors of the old Grenville group, favoured large military reinforcements and headlong coercion, though they recognised that England always entered her wars unprepared, and predicted initial reverses. Lord Gower, the leader of the Bedford group, contemplated another campaign without dismay. But at the vital American Department the pious Dartmouth dreaded the coming struggle; and his friend and family connection at the head of the Ministry, Lord North himself, led the faint-hearted. Like Suffolk, North expected initial reverses; but he showed no conviction that matters would improve. As always, the chief source of purpose and confidence was the King: 'When once these rebels have felt a smart blow, they will submit; and no situation can ever change my fixed resolution, either to bring the colonies to a due obedience to the legislature of the mother country, or to cast them off.'[3]

But how to proceed? The two senior administrators of the army declared that military reconquest was hopeless: 'as wild an idea', said the Adjutant-General before the news of Bunker Hill, 'as ever controverted common sense'. And Lord Barrington, the Secretary at War, declared that the Americans 'may be reduced by the fleet, but never can be by the army'.

---

[1] SP 78/306, 26 Feb. 1778; Harlow, 221–2; G 2649, 3155.
[2] *Autobiography*, 324
[3] Abergavenny, 9; Doniol, I, 153; Sandwich, I, 63; Dartmouth, II, 407.

Perhaps no one imagined a British army rolling triumphantly from end to end of America. But the rebels must be taught the superiority of trained British troops, and the economic consequences of their defiance. Then from the general distress a political harvest might be reaped. To achieve this, naval pressure alone was not enough. Lord Howe, the future naval commander, was clear that troops were needed; and even Lord North, much though he still hoped that the struggle might be averted, was sure that a large land force would be needed to make the naval pressure effective. At the very least, troops were needed to sever the colonies from each other and secure bases and supplies for the fleet. And to ease their task, one hard blow was needed to smash the rebel army.[1]

On these grounds the decision was taken to send a major force to America. An army of 20,000 men would strike in the following spring. No major effort could be mounted earlier[2]; and the immediate tasks were to prevent further losses during the autumn and winter, and to prepare the force. To these ends the winter's efforts would be directed.

Lord Barrington's gloom was caused by the shortage of troops rather than the operational difficulties they would meet. Barrington was an old woman[3]; but for once the facts supported him. The separate Irish establishment of 13,500 infantry was down to about 7,000. The British establishment was small, and already heavily committed to colonial garrisons. On paper it had 29,000 infantry of all ranks; but of these more than 10,000 were already in America and Canada or on their way there; and another 7,700 in Gibraltar, Minorca, the West Indies and minor garrisons overseas. In England and Scotland there were only 10,975 infantry of all ranks on paper, of whom 1,500 were invalids fit for light duties. Thus England and Scotland had only 9,500 infantry to defend the country and reinforce America. Nor were all these fit to take the field, for some of the regiments were mere cadres.

But the King, the head of the army, was determined. In the face of the difficulties raised by his Secretary at War, he set vigorously about the task of finding more troops. The most shattered of the Bunker Hill regiments were summoned home to recruit, and five regiments of the Irish establishment placed under orders to relieve them. Five regiments of the royal Hanoverian army were taken on the British estimates, to serve at Gibraltar and Minorca and release British battalions from the Mediterranean. At

[1] Fortescue, *History of the British Army*, III, 167; Shute Barrington, *Political Life of Viscount Barrington*, 148–51; Sackville, II, 6; Abergavenny, 9; Feiling, *The Second Tory Party*, 129.

[2] G 1683, 1794.

[3] For Barrington's pessimism in the previous war see Rex Whitworth, *Lord Ligonier*, 269–70, 273.

home an augmentation of regimental establishments was decreed; but the difficulty was to find the recruits to complete it, for the War Office could not be sure of raising more than four or five thousand men by the following spring. Lord North, impressed by Barrington's warning, suggested the raising of new regiments by individual officers with the bribe of quick promotion. But the King was not yet ready for this expedient. It would open the way to abuses, and the new regiments would not be ready for service inside a year, whereas the existing cadres could take the field in three months if they were completed. What the King needed was a swift deployment; and the readiest source of fresh troops was not new regiments, but foreign armies. In the last war foreign troops had formed a very high proportion of the army, and a search for these was begun. Catherine the Great held out hopes of 20,000 Russians; and the Northern Department opened negotiations with the German states.

5. Damming the Flood

In the meantime the American theatre had to be made secure for the winter. The first step was to reorganise the command. There had been some talk of sending Lord Amherst out to replace Gage, but this had been frustrated by the King's opposition to disgracing Gage, and probably a refusal on the part of Amherst. Instead, three Major-Generals had been sent out to Gage's assistance. But after Bunker Hill the Cabinet resolved that Gage must go, and he was recalled for 'consultations'.[1] In the ordinary course of events he would have been succeeded by General Carleton, the Governor of Quebec. But instead the opportunity was taken to split the American command. The overland communications between Quebec and Boston were now severed by the rebellion; and the sharper pace of war would not admit the transmission of orders, stores and men by sea round Cape Breton and up the St Lawrence, which was ice-bound for several months of the year. Carleton was therefore given an independent command at Quebec, where he would be fully employed, it was imagined, in raising and organising Canadian forces. General Howe at Boston was appointed Commander-in-Chief in the Atlantic colonies from Nova Scotia to West Florida. The new system reverted to that of 1759, when Wolfe had commanded in the St Lawrence and Amherst on the Hudson. It was intended that Carleton should assume the command of the whole if the two armies joined forces.

Neither Howe nor Carleton could take much comfort from the prospect of the coming winter. Quebec had been stripped of troops to reinforce Boston, and was now exposed to invasion by the fall of Ticonderoga. On

[1] Knox, 257; Dartmouth, I, 370; G 1556, 1592, 1630, 1685, 1794; Gage Corr., II, 203.

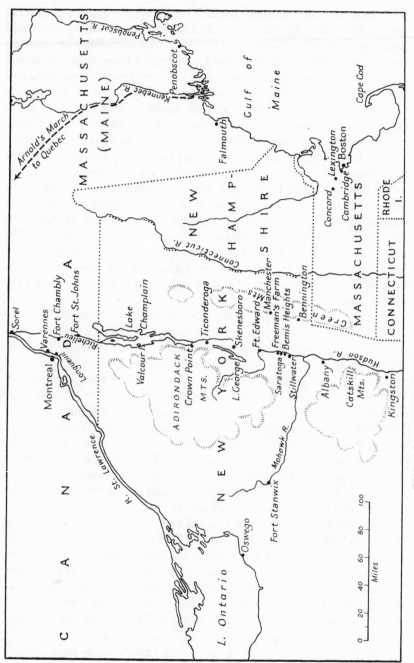

THE NORTHERN SPHERE OF OPERATIONS, 1775–7

the Atlantic seaboard the whole British force, except the garrison of Halifax, was blockaded in a city which it barely had the strength to hold. Nor could Boston be regarded as a useful base for the coming offensive. The besieging Americans were strongly entrenched, and behind them stood the armed population of New England in a broken country of woods, enclosures and ravines which was ideal for irregular fighting. Gage, Howe and Burgoyne were united in thinking that an advance would be fatal. Burgoyne urged Gage to abandon Boston before the winter and shift his base to New York, to avoid delay in opening the campaign in the spring. Gage heartily agreed. To attack the rebels at Boston was taking the bull by the horns. 'I wish this place was burned', he wrote privately; 'the only use is its harbour, which may be said to be material; but in all other respects it's the worst place either to act offensively from, or defensively.' Even subsistence was difficult. The rebels were withholding supplies of every kind. There was no fresh meat; no flour except a little from Canada; no straw for bedding. The coast was policed by Nantucket whalers to prevent the fishermen from supplying the garrison. Indeed, three weeks after the news of the first fighting reached England, the Treasury had placed its contracts to feed the army from home.[1]

All this helped to turn the Ministers' thoughts to New York. More loyalists were expected there; and its position at the mouth of the Hudson gave it the appearance of a strategic key to the northern colonies. The great river thrust like a highway into the heart of the rebel country, into the back of New England and towards Canada. Already ideas were beginning to form of a converging movement from Montreal and New York to unite the two armies on the backs of the New Englanders. The importance of New York had been recognised on Gage's recall by giving latitude to Howe to recover it with part of his force. But the accumulating weight of intelligence and authoritative opinion soon produced a more positive instruction. At the beginning of September orders were sent for the withdrawal of the whole force from Boston before the winter, and its removal to New York or some other port where the fleet could lie in safety.[2]

By this decision the Cabinet relieved itself of anxiety for Howe. But Halifax and Quebec were also weak. Halifax, though not immediately threatened, was of such importance as the base of the North American squadron that it was thought necessary to reinforce it; and on 17 September a letter from Gage warned the Ministry that Carleton had found the Canadians slow to organise for defence, and had asked for 4,000 reinforcements. On 25 September the five Irish battalions intended for Boston were therefore

---

[1] G 1663, 1668, 1693; Gage Corr., I, 403, 409; II, 679, 686-7, 690.
[2] Sackville, I, 3, 135; Gage Corr., II, 206; G 1794; Howe's Orderly Book, 300.

diverted; one to Halifax and four to Quebec. When these orders reached Cork, two of the battalions for Quebec had already sailed to join Howe, and by now the year was too far advanced for the remainder to get up the St Lawrence; but the senior officer had orders to disembark if he could not enter the river, and march overland to Quebec. If all now went smoothly, the city should be safe for the winter.[1]

6. A Winter Offensive

By the end of September the American theatre of operations had apparently been battened down for the winter. Quebec and Halifax would be made secure, and the Boston garrison shifted south to New York, a safer post and a springboard for the coming offensive. Thus, with no fear of untoward developments, preparations to strike at the heart of the rebellion could be put in hand. It was to be a winter of twilight war.

But within a few weeks the Cabinet learnt that the winter need not be wasted. Since early September reports had been arriving from the southern colonies of the strength of the loyalists. Governor Martin of North Carolina had been driven out of his province; but from his refuge in a warship he reported that he had received addresses signed by thousands of loyalists in the back settlements. He was sure that with a supply of arms and a nucleus of regular troops he could raise a loyalist force to subdue the Carolinas and overawe Virginia. This view accorded with the belief in England that the south was too much dependent on seaborne trade to hold out for long. The problem of supporting the loyalists was studied in the American Department; and after consultations with General Amherst, Lord Dartmouth ordered the Board of Ordnance to send out 10,000 stand of arms, and recommended Howe to send at least a battalion from Boston.[2]

Such were the modest origins of the Charleston expedition. Soon other evidence poured in to support Martin's advice. The Governors of South Carolina and Virginia were confident that with a small force of troops they could restore order; and a variety of other intelligence supported them. People of property in the south complained that the loyalists were being neglected. It is true that the information came from interested parties; but disinterested intelligence was unobtainable. In the American Department the Under-Secretary, William Knox, was a property-owner in Georgia and Agent for the colony; and throughout the war he was to argue for the

[1] Gage Corr. I, 413, II, 206; Howe's Orderly Book, 301; SP 42/49, Nos. 41-2; Dartmouth, I, 387.
[2] CL, Germain, précis in Vol. I, Suppl.; Dartmouth, I, 390; Gage Corr., II, 196; Sackville, I, 136; G 1712, 1714.

preservation of the south even at the cost of throwing off and annihilating the northern colonies. There is no evidence that his influence was decisive with Lord Dartmouth; but his presence in the Department may well have influenced the decision to intervene.[1]

By the middle of October the Cabinet was persuaded. Some of the troops under orders for America were ready; and rather than keep them in idleness through the winter till the northern Atlantic passage was fit for transports, an immediate blow was to be delivered against the southern periphery of the rebellion. Five regiments on the Irish establishment which had been promised to Howe were chosen. It was thought that they could sail before Christmas if the orders were given at once, and achieve their purpose in time to rejoin Howe at New York early in his campaign. Thus the expedition was not intended to dilute the concentrated blow in the north, but to use the interval before the main effort could be deployed.[2]

Approval was not unanimous. The Adjutant-General feared the risk of dispersion; and the Secretary at War, Lord Barrington remonstrated strongly when he arrived at the War Office on the following Monday. Learning that five regiments were to be sent abroad, he guessed their destination from common report, and wrote at once to Dartmouth. 'Allow me, my dear Lord,' he begged him, 'to remind you of the necessity there is in all military matters, not to stir without full consultations of able military men.'[3] It has often been remarked as curious that the Secretary at War should have been kept in ignorance of the plan; but Barrington had no grounds for complaint. He was an administrator, not a strategist. He had certainly been kept in the dark about operational plans in the Seven Years War; and in November 1780 the same secrecy was observed about the proposed River Plate expedition, to the annoyance of his successor.[4]

The rendezvous of the expedition was off Cape Fear on the coast of North Carolina, where Governor Martin promised a large force of highland immigrants. A cruiser sailed at once to find pilots and alert the Governor. If the regiments were to sail from Cork at the beginning of December speedy organisation was needed. The Navy Board's transports were ready to leave the Thames by 9 November, and the enterprise seemed fairly launched. Clinton was to come down from New York to command the troops, with whom Cornwallis sailed from England; and Sir Peter Parker

---

[1] CL, Germain, loc. cit.; CL, Knox, Vol. 9, Nos. 21–2 (précis in Knox, 289); Knox, 122, 258–60, 276. Nelson, 110–13, provides facts which support the British assessment of the Southern loyalists.

[2] G 1724, 1727.

[3] Fortescue, II, 173–4; Barrington, 151–2.

[4] Whitworth, Ligonier, 215; Harlow, Founding of the Second British Empire, 111.

commanded the naval task force with his flag in the *Bristol*, 50, and half a dozen frigates under command to operate in the shallow approaches to Charleston.[1]

Two more regiments were added to the force. Their provenance was ominous. For these were the two battalions which had been despatched to Quebec in October. By this time they should have been approaching the St Lawrence, and their story provides a foretaste of much that was to follow. A few day out in the Atlantic the transports had been struck by a gale and driven back to Milford Haven, where ten days were lost in repairing damage. By then it was too late to make the St Lawrence before the spring, and the troops were diverted to the Carolinas. It was typical of the improvisations with small bodies of men which characterise the outset of a British war. Thus the safety of Quebec and the future of British Canada lay in a couple of weak battalions in the St Lawrence basin, two companies of the Royal Irish in the far posts of the Illinois, and a levy of highland immigrants just forming at Sorel. General Howe, aware of Carleton's nakedness, wanted to send him a regiment of Marines from Boston, but the attempt was vetoed by the Admiral.[2]

[1] SP 42/49, Nos. 46, 54, 56; Adm. 2/1333, 30 Oct.; CL, Germain, *loc. cit.*
[2] SP 42/49, No. 49; G 1734; Howe's Orderly Book, 307.

CHAPTER II

THE COMING OF GERMAIN

1. *The Third Secretary*

On 15 September William Eden, Under-Secretary of the Northern Department, wrote to Lord George Germain expressing a guarded hope that the government was beginnning to see the danger of half-measures. More had been done in the past three weeks, he said, than in the preceding three years; but much was still needed 'to make up a real systematical and efficient exertion'.[1]

The recipient of this letter was soon to be called on to provide the needed effort. Many people in the summer of 1775 had begun to think of Lord George as the man to 'repair Lord North's indolence and inactivity'. General Burgoyne, quick to spot a star in the ascendant, told him he was 'the man who my best judgment tells me is the most capable of any in England to redeem America by his counsels'.[2] Germain's attitude to America had endeared him to the King and Lord Suffolk. Since the start of the troubles he had held that they could have been checked by timely firmness. He shared the King's conviction that the government had played into the hands of the seditious few by coupling the pusillanimous repeal of the Stamp Act with the imposition of other duties which were at once more irritating and less easy to collect. With impatience he had watched the Ministry's slow reaction to the fight at Lexington, convinced that a prompt mobilisation of loyalists and Canadians would be better than a ponderous build-up of regular troops. Bunker Hill gave the situation a different turn. 'One decisive blow on land is absolutely necessary', he wrote to his friend General Irwin, 'After that the whole will depend upon the diligence and activity of the officers of the navy.'[3]

In November a ministerial crisis gave the Ministry a chance to resolve the problem of effective leadership. For some time past the Duke of Grafton, the Lord Privy Seal, had been showing his discontent with the government's American policy. Cynics speculated on whether he could face the financial loss of resigning; but on 9 November the King cut the question short by dismissing him. At the same time Lord Rochford retired from the Southern

[1] CL, Germain.
[2] Marlow, *Sackville of Drayton*, 161; CL, Germain, 20 Aug. 1775.
[3] Sackville, I, 135–6.

Secretaryship and was replaced by the Bedford Whig Lord Weymouth. Grafton's place was filled by Dartmouth, who was transferred from the American Department after feeble struggles and changes of mind. He remained ostensibly in the Cabinet, but disappeared to the country whenever he could and played no further part in directing the war.

The vital department was now cleared of its incubus, and Germain stepped into the breach. His authority was to be wider than his predecessor's. Hillsborough and Dartmouth had never been regarded in the full sense as Secretaries of State, and their powers had been confined to colonial matters. But this created a difficulty. For if the office was not a Secretaryship of State, it must be a new office; and Germain, who sat in the House of Commons, would have lost his seat on accepting it. The solution was to give him parity with the other Secretaries. Suffolk and Weymouth resisted this dilution of their authority, but gave way to the King. Weymouth and Germain were sworn in together, and Germain thus became 'one of His Majesty's Principal Secretaries of State'.[1]

Thus there came to power the statesman who more than any other became identified with the direction of the war and its prolongation. This strange man is perhaps the most traduced of all English statesmen. The common verdict of history is summed up in an astonishing phrase of F. V. Greene[2]: 'probably the most incompetent official that ever held an important post at a critical moment'. For judgments such as this there is no basis but ignorance of the facts, unfamiliarity with eighteenth-century government, and credulous gorging on the malice of Lord Shelburne and the *Parliamentary History*.

He was born a proud Sackville, a younger but favourite son of the first Duke of Dorset, and in later life heir-presumptive to his nephew the third Duke: reared at Knole, schooled at Westminister, a graduate of Trinity College, Dublin, during his father's first period as Lord-Lieutenant of Ireland. Like the Duke of Wellington, he served his political apprenticeship in the exacting *manège* of Irish politics, and became Irish Secretary at the age of thirty-five. But before everything he was a soldier. Hit by a musket ball at Fontenoy at the head of his regiment, which had 139 casualties in the battle, he was carried into one of the French King's tents to have his wound dressed. After the 'Forty-five rebellion, the Duke of Cumberland wrote that he was 'exceedingly sorry to lose Lord George as he has not only shown his courage

---

[1] Thomson, *Secretaries of State*, 60; Knox, 256–7. See also A. H. Basye, *The Lords Commissioners of Trade and Plantations*, for the history of the Third Secretaryship. On Suffolk's behalf William Eden made a further attempt after Germain's appointment to have his status reduced, but without success (see Valentine, 105–6).

[2] Quoted by Christopher Ward, *The War of the Revolution*, 878.

but a disposition to his trade which I do not always find in those of higher rank'. The Seven Years War brought him the Lieutenant-Generalcy of the Ordnance, and he served as second in command of the St Malo expedition of 1758. Officers who served under him are said to have affirmed 'that in his behaviour as a man, and in his deportment as a commander, dignity was most happily tempered with ease, and the strictness of military discipline with mildness and affability; that he was a most instructive and engaging companion, a most faithful and zealous friend, and a most humane protector of his dependents'. His relations with Wolfe confirm the picture. He was Colonel of the regiment which Wolfe commanded, and took great pains to push him on. It is possible that he suggested his name for the Quebec expedition; and Wolfe's correspondence with him during the Seven Years War was full, friendly and without disguise. Sackville was evidently a man whom he trusted. [1]

When Pitt offered him the command of the St Cas expedition, Sackville is said to have replied that he was tired of buccaneering: a blunt unconciliating reply to the author of the policy of breaking windows with guineas. He went to Germany instead, as commander of the British contingent serving under Prince Ferdinand of Brunswick. Then came disaster. At the battle of Minden he lost time in obeying orders from Ferdinand to attack with the cavalry of the right wing; was scathingly rebuked in General Orders; and on returning to England was dismissed from the army.

The mystery of that day has never been cleared. Sackville's conscience was clear. He dined at Ferdinand's table on the evening of the battle; forced his government to try him on a capital charge; and appeared in the House of Commons on the day the sentence was published. Personal resentments were at work, possibly in the battle and certainly in the subsequent treatment of Sackville. He had criticised Ferdinand's mishandling of British subsidies; and he asserted to Ligonier that Ferdinand had been trying to pick a quarrel since Sackville had criticised his abandonment of Münster without a fight, exposing the British lines of communication. There was vindictiveness, both personal and political, in the conduct of the Ministry. Sackville's second in command and successor, Lord Granby, with whom he had been on hostile terms before the battle, had been pushed up by the Ministry before the war to secure the Rutland interest. The Sackvilles themselves had fallen from grace at Court, and he was known to be connected with the young Court at Leicester House, which ensured the King's dislike and prevented him from obtaining a ministerial office. While George II ardently supported the German war and his kinsman Ferdinand, the Princess Dowager of Wales

[1] Almon, . . . *Anecdotes*, II, 119. For Germain's relations with Wolfe, see Robin Reilly, *The Rest to Fortune*.

opposed the one and hated the other. Sackville is said to have been given the German command against the King's wishes, and to have left the country without kissing hands: it is certain that he was not granted his predeccessor's power of promotion.

When Sackville returned to England demanding a court-martial, he was certain to encounter royal prejudice: the loyalty of his friends remained to be proved. He was not left long in doubt. Pitt, so friendly before Minden, changed his tone sharply. That smooth operator, his old friend Lord Ligonier, whose nephew had brought one of Ferdinand's messages during the battle, refused him a court-martial and told him to go seek it in Germany. This was strange, for it was not a Ministry which ordinarily flinched at courts-martial. When Minorca was lost, it had shot the Admiral and dismissed the General. The commander of the Rochefort expedition had been tried, and on his acquittal Ligonier had talked of 'revising' the sentence. Sackville insisted on his right to a trial; was told that as a civilian he could not be tried; after delays succeeded in having his case referred to the Judges of the High Court; and in spite of lobbying by Lord Mansfield obtained a ruling that he could be court-martialled. Only confidence in the strength of his case could have led him to court this risk. For the public was clamouring for his blood as it had clamoured for Byng's; and the King sent him a message that, whatever the sentence of the court, it would be carried out.

When the court assembled in March 1760, it could find no motive for Sackville's alleged behaviour. He was not charged with cowardice, though one witness suggested it; but he was found guilty of disobedience. Seven of the fifteen members of the Court voted for death, but a two-thirds majority was needed, and Sackville was declared unfit to serve His Majesty in any military capacity. The aged King ensured that every humiliation attended the sentence. He struck him off the Privy Council; and at Ligonier's suggestion the sentence was read out to every regiment, with a rider composed by Ligonier himself. 'So finishes', wrote Ligonier's secretary, 'the career of a man, who was within ten minutes of being the first man in his profession in the Kingdom whenever it had pleased God to take Lord Ligonier from the world.'[1]

The King's malice extended even to the prosecutors. Lord Albemarle had raised the question whether some other sentence than death was open to the court. George II struck his mother's name from the list of those invited to evening parties, and decreed that she should be ignored in the Drawing Room. Six months later the petty tyrant was dead. Soon Pitt was dismissed, Ligonier was humiliated, and the days of the Newcastle Whigs were numbered. Sackville's friend Bute came to power. For a while expediency delayed his rehabilitation; but in due course he was restored to the Privy

[1] For Ligonier's part in the proceedings, see Whitworth.

Council, and held minor office in the first Rockingham administration. A duel with Governor Johnstone satisfied the witnesses of his courage. In 1770 he changed his name to Germain to inherit a fortune and the great house at Drayton in Northamptonshire under the will of Lady Betty Germain.

2. *A Man with a Past*

When Germain was called to high responsibility in 1775 he was sixty years of age. Who can describe his character with confidence? Even his appearance is a subject of difference. Wraxall tells us that he was tall, muscular and active, and capable of sustaining much physical and mental fatigue; Shelburne that he was 'of a large make, though rather womanly'. Shelburne's sketch of his character says that the officers of the Twentieth Regiment which he commanded used to find him listening outside their tents in Scotland to hear what they said of him. Must we believe this of the young Colonel who, on a rare visit to his regiment in Scotland, formed a lasting friendship with the commanding officer Major Wolfe? Of whom Wolfe feared on his relinquishing the Colonelcy that 'none will be found that can in any manner make amends for the loss of him'? Was he, as Shelburne tells us, a vindictive intriguer and a master of the art of influence, who pushed his way to the top by cunning imposition? Or a clear direct speaker who scorned all disguise? An incompetent coward and designing catamite? Or a brave and wronged officer, and a Christian gentleman with the manners and benevolence of Sir Roger de Coverley? Shelburne's sketch bears the unmistakable marks of relentless malice. Though he left in writing for posterity the statement that Germain was corrupt in spite of an ample fortune, he confessed in opposing Germain's admission to the House of Lords that he had no complaint to make of his personal conduct in office. The intemperance of Shelburne's detraction destroys its credit. I prefer the testimony of Lord George's friends.[1]

Romney's portrait shows a clever, strong, commanding face. He had once been called 'the gayest man in Ireland', but melancholy shadowed his features. A reserved and lonely figure, he rarely dined from home during the war except at the weekly Cabinet dinners, though he dropped in at White's occasionally in the evening. There his outward equanimity hid

---

[1] Fitzmaurice, *Shelburne*, I, 75, 248–50; II, 86; Reilly, *The Rest to Fortune*, 76. In assessing Shelburne's reliability, the common opinion of him must be borne in mind. 'His falsehood,' wrote Walpole, 'was so constant and notorious, that it was rather his profession than his instrument.' 'His oratory,' said Wedderburn, 'resembled more a cunning woman's than an able man's address.' Neither Pitt nor Ligonier escaped abuse in his secret pages.

every trace of the strain of his responsibilities. Yet clearly there were tensions beneath the surface; and his unpopularity in some quarters was inflamed by the belief that he was a homosexual. This was fair game to Granby's old friends who flung it about with relish.[1] But Germain's association with the young American loyalist Benjamin Thompson (later Count Rumford), whom he took into his household about 1778 and made Under-Secretary of his department in 1780, caused comment among people of a friendlier disposition.[2]

But whatever the truth of all this, he had a greater internal enemy in his bearing of proud reserve. His habitual politeness framed a haughtiness, says an admirer, 'which depressed and darkened all that was agreeable and engaging in him; it . . . naturally, and very fairly, hurt the reasonable self-love of his acquaintance and friends. His integrity commanded esteem, his abilities praise; but to attract the heart was not one of those abilities . . .'[3] Perhaps his outward melancholy went deeper than the Minden reverse. Both his brothers were a prey to melancholia[4]; and Shelburne asserts that difficulties threw Lord George from arrogant presumption to abject despair. Depression would be a convenient explanation of Minden; yet Cumberland denies it, and Wraxall's portrait constantly emphasises his equanimity. And his subordinates in office discovered that his exterior was deceptive. Though he was impatient of delays and frustrations, his Under-Secretaries liked him, and found him a hospitable and unassuming friend. In his contracted circle he was an agreeable talker and a patient listener. His family life was happy, with a sensible wife and lively affectionate daughters. His easy communicative letters to his sons suggest sympathy and mutual confidence.

His impatience belonged to a facet of his character which is common among successful war leaders, indeed essential in them. The view of Germain as a pathetic creature trying desperately to redeem a tarnished reputation is far from the truth. A high-spirited and courageous youth, a successful

[1] Lord Herbert (ed.), *Henry, Elizabeth and George*, pp. 290, 372, 405; and his *The Pembroke Papers*, 179, 195. Lord Pembroke, whose own preference ran rather to his friends' wives, had been A.D.C. to Lord Granby.

[2] For this association, see Sackville, I, 340; II, 250–6; Hutchinson Diaries, II, 184, 289, 337, 339, 344, 404. Valentine, pp. 472–4, examines the question. Benjamin Thompson later earned an inflated reputation as a scientist, and has been coupled with Benjamin Franklin as one of the greatest Americans. What emerges from his biographies, however, is good looks, charm and a striking taste in dress, attibutes which he exploited without scruple for his own advancement. Beginning with a marriage to a rich older woman, he progressed through Governor Wentworth of New Hampshire to the Secretary of State for the American Department, and at last to the Elector of Bavaria, who satisfied his passion for decorations and titles.

[3] Stockdale, I, 436.

[4] Valentine, 466–70.

career as regimental commander and military administrator, the arrogant public manner: these denoted a sanguine temperament, too much wedded perhaps to its own preconceptions,[1] but in Richard Cumberland's words 'incapable of despondency'.[2] He brought into office a considerable reputation as an administrator. This Shelburne attributes to his 'talents for imposition' and 'a naturally clear understanding, which prevented his taking up any argument . . . of which he was not a complete master'. These attributes, says Shelburne, combined with his fortune, connections and inclination for intrigue to make him so formidable, that 'I do not conceive that anything but the checks which stopped his military career, could have prevented his being Prime Minister'. The reader must judge the truth from the record. Germain was certainly tough, difficult to work with as an equal, and possibly not over-scrupulous. But so are many ambitious and successful men, including other war Ministers of his day and ours. For the moment it is enough to say that he won the respect of the most formidable of his colleagues, Lord Chancellor Thurlow; and that Horace Walpole, who nourished a fancied slight, acknowledged 'his great abilities'. A subordinate in his office, who saw him at work and held him in affection, had an estimate of his powers equal to Shelburne's, though on different grounds. 'He had', wrote Richard Cumberland, 'all the requisites of a great minister, unless popularity and good luck are to be numbered amongst them.'[3]

As a political asset Germain's value to the Ministry was less clear. In the House of Commons he had long ago proved his skill when he succeeded the politically ineffective Ligonier as Lieutenant-General of the Ordnance, and North welcomed the support of a Secretary of State who was not in the House of Lords. His Irish apprenticeship had made him a clear and ready speaker. Walpole refers to his attack on the expedition against the Caribs in 1773 as 'one of his most pointed speeches, full of pith, matter, irony, and satire'; and the back-bencher Wraxall was to recall that no one better understood the management of the House and the art of prolonging or shortening a debate to suit its temper.[4] Yet his early handling of the Irish had shown more of the sanguine confidence of a future war minister than of sensitiveness to a proud people.[5] And since those days misfortune had sapped his position. His enemies fastened on his combination of personal

[1] Cf. Wortley, 146; Hutchinson Diaries, II, 25.

[2] Here, again, Shelburne's description conflicts with the bulk of the evidence: see Fitzmaurice, I, 75, and compare below, p. 472, on Shelburne's own administrative character.

[3] Fitzmaurice, I, 239, 250; Walpole, *Last Journals*, II, 136; Cumberland, *Character*, 12.

[4] James Harris, M.P., often referred to Germain's able speeches in letters to his son, the Minister at St. Petersburg. See also Valentine, 98.

[5] Valentine, 23–9.

reserve and readiness in debate to insinuate that he was cunning; and his court-martial was a gift to unscrupulous opponents. Their use of it disgraced the Opposition. 'The Ghost of Minden' was for ever being wheeled in. They began at once. Wilkes said that he might conquer America, but it would not be in Germany, a sally which Lord George found funny enough to retail in the Cabinet; Luttrell that the only safety of the army was flight, in which Germain was fit to lead them. Germain had 'either to turn absolute knight-errant, or else put up quietly with constant affronts'.[1] He brought to these trials reserves of contemptuous dignity. Yet the equanimity described by Wraxall did not preclude a sharp and hasty temper. Sometimes he gave way to the goading of Charles Fox and his friends, and once threw the House into an uproar by challenging an opponent on the spot. He could be irritated into revealing what the easy-tempered North had managed to conceal. Fox claimed that he knew how to exploit his 'unwary frankness'; and Jenkinson in 1778 described his conduct on the question of investigating General Howe's campaigns as indiscreet beyond description.

In these circumstances, and without a personal following in the House, Germain's contribution to the Ministry's strength could only be his achievements in office. His enmities were widely spread. The Graftons had long disliked him, and the Duke's brother had been a hostile witness at his trial. He cannot have loved the Rutland family connection, for Lord Granby had been his rival and Lord Robert Manners had sat on his court-martial. Lord Albemarle, the head of the Keppels, whose family included a prominent general and Admiral serving in the American War, had been a chief examiner at the trial. The Duke of Richmond, a violent and wrong-headed politician of the Rockingham connection, had served on Ferdinand's staff at Minden, and twenty-two years later in the House of Lords malevolently exaggerated the time lost by Germain's delay; and Shelburne had been with Granby in the battle. It was a time of unrestrained parliamentary language, and political enmities need not be taken too seriously: Fox found no difficulty in alternating ferocious denunciation of Lord North with intimate gossip with the victim. Perhaps more serious for Germain was hostility within the Ministry. Lord Amherst, who joined the Cabinet as Commander-in-Chief in 1778, had been a friend since childhood. But Lord Bathurst disliked him, and Lord Barrington, the Secretary at War, had arranged his court-martial.

These coolnesses may not have mattered much: his relations with the First Lord of the Admiralty undoubtedly did. Sandwich was the man with whom a close understanding was most essential for the efficient conduct of the war. In wartime a harmonious inner circle of Ministers was needed to

[1] Walpole, *Last Journals*, II, 26–7; Carlisle, 311.

reach decisions quickly and steer business through the Cabinet. It was all the more necessary when the presiding Minister in the Cabinet was as evasive and undecided as North. Friction between Germain and Sandwich began early. It started with Germain's criticism of naval weakness in America, and was kept alive by disputes over naval appointments and letters of marque. The two men had little in common. Sandwich was a political jobber, gamester, and man of fashion, Germain politically solitary with the stately manners of an old-fashioned country gentleman. To spur the sluggish Admiralty on was a duty in the Secretary of State; and Germain made no effort to conceal his low regard for the navy, its operations and its Admirals. Their lack of mutual confidence must have brought many matters unprepared before the Cabinet.

A constitutional historian has described Germain's position as very similar to Pitt's in the Seven Years War.[1] As Secretaries of State, both controlled the main operations of a war; and just as the Elder Pitt had used his office to dominate the Admiralty and quicken the Ordnance, so Germain could try to make the wheels of administration revolve with the faster tempo of war. He had faults of temper, but so had Pitt. If he lacked the touch of genius which in Pitt was allied with madness, he was a more orderly administrator. But one asset of Pitt's he lacked: the weight of transcendent political authority. He had not, like Pitt, been summoned by the nation; he did not hold the Ministry's fate in his hands; he could make no claim to share the political supremacy with the First Lord of the Treasury. And, for all his talents, he lacked the magic gift of Pitt: the power to frighten and inspire.[2]

3. The First Weeks in Office

Lord George Germain's country seat was Drayton in Northamptonshire. His London retreat was his favourite house, Stoneland Lodge[3] near Tunbridge Wells, convenient for his London friends and close to the Sackville family seat at Knole and to his friend Amherst's home at Montreal. For his working days he took Lord Waldegrave's house in Pall Mall, in the heart of official London. Across the way in St James's Square lived Admiral

[1] Thomson, *The Secretaries of State*, 86.

[2] No biography of Germain based on archival research existed till the recent publication of Alan Valentine's *Lord George Germain*, where much information and many leads on sources may be found, though on many points Mr Valentine's judgments are contrary to my own. A highly sympathetic sketch is Louis Marlow's *Sackville of Drayton*. Wraxall and Cumberland show Germain through the eyes of friends; and there is interesting material in C. J. Phillips, *History of the Sackville Family*, George Coventry's study of Junius, and in the *Memoirs* of Percival Stockdale.

[3] Now Buckhurst: he rented it from his nephew the Duke of Dorset.

Palliser of the Board of Admiralty. A few steps beyond, Lord Suffolk lived in Duke Street, and the Secretaries' offices were nearby in Cleveland Row. Germain's own office was across the Park in Whitehall, conveniently near Downing Street and the Admiralty.

The impression Germain made in his Department was immediate. From the beginning he showed the qualities which had brought him to the top of the army. He was punctual and precise, quick and impatient of delays.

There was at once an end [the Under-Secretary Richard Cumberland recalled] to all circumlocutory reports and inefficient forms, that had only impeded business, and substituted ambiguity for precision: there was ... no trash in his mind; he studied no choice phrases, no superfluous words, nor ever suffered the clearness of his conceptions to be clouded by the obscurity of his expressions, for these were the simplest and most unequivocal that could be made use of for explaining his opinion, or dictating his instructions. In the meanwhile he was so momentarily punctual to his time, so religiously observant of his engagements, that we, who served under him in office, felt the sweets of the exchange we had so lately made in the person of our chief.[1]

The decision to use a large army in America had already been taken when Germain became responsible for the war. But he had wholeheartedly approved the measure. After the first rebel successes a sharp lesson was needed. Germain never deluded himself that America could be conquered by force from without; but he believed that England was dealing with a seditious minority, whose power must be broken in order to crack the unity of Congress and enable the people, under pressure of commercial blockade, to turn to the loyalists for a lead. But the blow must be delivered swiftly. 'As there is not common sense in protracting a war of this sort', he had written in September,[2] 'I should be for exerting the utmost force of this Kingdom to finish the rebellion in one campaign.' Events were to prove the wisdom of this. Not only did the prolonging of the struggle tempt the European powers to intervene, but the accumulated bitterness of protracted war was to divide the Americans from England as no merely constitutional struggle could do, and make for ever unattainable the political settlement for which England embarked on the struggle.

In a war so distant it would have been improper for the Secretary of State to dictate the course of operations or the disposition of the troops in the fighting theatres. The Elder Pitt had tried to do it; and from lack of confidence in the energy of Loudon and Abercromby he had dictated the strength and composition of every body of troops down to companies. But his intervention was as unpractical as it was unusual, and with increasing experience and greater confidence in his generals he came to allow a larger

[1] Richard Cumberland, *Memoirs*, 289.
[2] Sackville, I, 135-7

degree of operational autonomy to the theatre commanders. Germain in 1776 made no attempt to repeat Chatham's early experiment. 'The distance from the seat of Government necessarily leaves much to the discretion and resources of the General', he had said recently.[1] His proper sphere as Secretary of State was the appointment of commanders, the allocation of resources between theatres, and the organisation of movement and supply at home: in a word, grand strategy. The commanders he inherited: in Howe he had confidence, in Carleton less. He did not dictate their operations in detail. Not till Howe and Carleton had failed and Clinton had shown his feebleness did he begin to press detailed proposals on the general. His misfortune was to be that, a member of a weak and embarrassed government, he was unable to replace his commanders as he might wish.

The strategic situation when Germain took over his Department seemed to be well in hand. It was hoped that Howe's force was already transferred from Boston to the more useful base at New York, ready for the spring offensive; and that Canada was safe for the winter in spite of the failure to get the reinforcements through. The only operation immediately on foot was the small expedition of seven battalions for Charleston, for which preparation had begun. The path seemed clear for the orderly preparation of the spring offensives in the Atlantic colonies and Canada; and through the rest of November and most of December Germain pressed on with their organisation. But in the closing days of the year news arrived from both Howe and Carleton which shed a very different light on the prospects.

From Boston came General Burgoyne, eager for Parliament and society bearing the latest news from Howe. The withdrawal to New York had been frustrated. The victuallers from England had gone astray in the autumn storms, and Howe found himself without the necessary shipping to lift his whole force at one time. To move it in two échelons was most hazardous, in view of the extent of the lines to be held and the uncertain winter weather which might delay the rescue of the second division.[2] Thus the army remained immured in Boston through a dismal winter. The infantry battalions defending the long perimeter were on the low peacetime establishment and had been further reduced by wastage and casualties. At the beginning of the winter their average strength had been only 400 of all ranks, and sickness had been increasing. While Howe remained in Boston it would be difficult for him to keep a reserve in hand to meet an emergency; and when the spring came he would lose part of the campaigning season in taking New York.

Still worse was the news from Canada. Two days before Christmas a

[1] Marlowe, 175
[2] Howe's Orderly Book, 302-7; T. S. Anderson, *Command of the Howe Brothers*, 86.

frigate hastened in from the St Lawrence with despatches reporting that the Americans had burst into Canada from two quarters, and Quebec itself was in danger. Many months earlier, the loss of Ticonderoga and Crown Point had revealed a threat to Canada. But Germain's predecessors had delayed reinforcements until they miscarried in the autumn gales south-west of Ireland. Now General Montgomery had swept forward from Ticonderoga, and Carleton had sacrificed most of his regulars in defending the approaches to Montreal. Then behind him a second enemy had burst from the wilderness of Maine. Arnold's force debouched on the St Lawrence opposite Quebec. The city's fortifications were in disrepair, there were few troops, and the shortage of stores and provisions was desperate.

Germain did not despair. He suspected that Carleton had painted the situation blacker than was necessary. But there was no time to lose. The provisions in Quebec could not last beyond the middle of May, just after the ice broke up in the St Lawrence, but long before the main spring convoys reached the river; and Carleton had suggested a small emergency relief. There was nothing for it but to trust an emergency supply to the wintry ocean. Germain hastened to the Admiralty. No one was there except Palliser. The First Lord and every other member of the Board was in the country for Christmas; and according to the gossip Lord North was also on the point of slipping away to his villa at Bushey when Germain laid him by the heels and forced him to attend to the problem. Palliser was summoned at once to plan an emergency shipment to Quebec with Germain and the Prime Minister. The last news before a curtain of silence fell on the besieged city was growing worse. But if Quebec could hold out till the ice broke up, relief would come. A fifty-gun ship and three cruisers were ordered to stand by; three victuallers were loaded; and a regiment of foot embarked in Navy Board transports. The force sailed from the Nore on 22 February, with orders to push singly and with all speed for the St Lawrence; and the little expedition was scattered forth upon the Atlantic.[1]

4. The Strategy of Reconquest

Scarcely had the relief been set in motion when Palliser learnt with alarm that shipping was needed for a second wave of 10,000 troops for Canada. This was on 3 January, and their purpose was indicated to Howe as the relief

[1] Sandwich, I, 85; CL, Germain, Suppl., I (24 Jan. to Admiralty); Adm. 2/372, 15 Jan.; CO 5/254, pp. 4, 6, 9; CO 5/93, p. 335; Walpole, *Last Journals*, I, 531. Walpole's story that Palliser had to inform Germain that the St Lawrence was frozen need not be credited. Even if Germain had incredibly been ignorant of this, the appeals from Quebec made it clear.

or recovery of Quebec. Palliser's surprise might suggest that the reinforcement was a response to the rebel invasion.[1]

Yet much more was ultimately intended. There had been talk in the previous summer of building up a striking force in Canada and retaking the lost frontier forts; and Carleton had asked for an army of ten or twelve thousand men to invade New England. In September he had been warned to expect the bulk of the 20,000 Russians whom it was hoped that Catherine the Great would provide; and soon after the news of the attack on Quebec Palliser had been warned that boats would be needed for the frontier lakes, on which he innocently observed: 'I don't foresee when we shall be in possession of the Lakes.'[2]

It is therefore clear that the plan to advance from Canada had old roots; and every plan which had been canvassed advocated it. New England was rightly assumed to be the core of the rebellion; and though a policy of attacking the softer areas was to be adopted later in the war, it seemed natural at the outset to break the heart of the movement by striking at New England. She must be isolated at the least, and squeezed by economic pressures; at the best, invaded and crushed. Seize control of the Hudson crossings and cut New England off from the Middle Colonies; dominate Upper New York and enlist the help of the numerous loyalists in the area; open the communications between New York and Canada so that the reservoirs of Indian and Canadian help could be tapped in support of the regular striking force.

The importance of the Hudson valley had been grasped by the rebel Congress from the outset, and in November 1775 they had sent a committee to report on the fortifications which guarded its northern and southern entrances. The committee found that at the Canadian end the fort at Crown Point would be too expensive to repair, and recommended that work should be concentrated at Ticonderoga; while in the Highlands which blocked the approach from New York they urged the obstruction of the channel and the strengthening of the existing fortifications.[3] On the British side the same basic proposal for a joint operation from New York and Canada had come from Gage, Burgoyne and finally Howe, with the possible variants of simultaneously holding Boston or of seizing Rhode Island to pin down the militias of Connecticut and Massachusetts. The incursion from Canada had also, as we have seen, been urged by General Murray, who had commanded there in the previous war, and by Carleton, who was there at the moment. Carleton had always been sure that the Hudson link was vital; and eight years earlier

---

[1] Sandwich, I, 94; CO 5/254, f. 2; CL, Germain, 5 Jan. to Howe, and Suppl., I, 15 Jan. to Admiralty.

[2] Gage, II, 202; CO 42/34; Sandwich, I, 87–8.

[3] Harvard, Sparks MSS., 52/11.

he had urged the creation of strongholds at New York and Quebec, linked by restoring the fortifications of Crown Point, Ticonderoga and Fort George. He did not doubt that Canada would provide a great reservoir of loyal helpers, sharing and indeed promoting the extravagant expectations of Canadian assistance which pervaded every quarter.[1] The views of Burgoyne, who was to be so intimately connected with the execution of the plan, ran thus:

I have always thought Hudson's River the most proper part of the whole continent for opening vigorous operations. Because the course of the river, so beneficial for conveying all the bulky necessaries of an army, is precisely the route that an army ought to take for the great purposes of cutting the communications between the Southern and Northern Provinces, giving confidence to the Indians, and securing a junction with the Canadian forces. These purposes effected, and a fleet upon the coast, it is to me morally certain that the forces of New England must be reduced so early in the campaign to give you battle upon your own terms, or perish before the end of it for want of necessary supplies.

For Burgoyne, then, the New Englanders in 1775 were an enemy entrenched in an unassailable position, who must be compelled to sally forth or be starved into surrender.[2]

This was the plan which led two years later to Saratoga: but it should not be judged in the light of the errors of Howe and Burgoyne. It was framed before the armies of the Revolution took shape, and was executed when they seemed continually on the point of dissolution. The harassing of the western frontier was expected to dry up the rebel armies' flow of supplies. On the authority of men like Governor Tryon of New York and Colonel Skene of Skenesborough, it was believed that numerous loyalists in the Champlain and Hudson areas awaited the moment to throw off the oppression of the rebel committees.[3] Refugees are often deceptive advisers; but Tryon dwelt in no fool's paradise, and in the previous August he had advised Dartmouth to withdraw the claim to tax America, in order to rally the Crown's supporters, who were between Scylla and Charybdis.[4] Again, though a past war is often a deceptive guide to a present one, the Seven Years War seemed to show that the advance from Canada would be possible and effective. A handful of French troops backed by militia and Indians had kept the frontiers of New York in flames, and contained a considerable force of regulars and provincials to protect the settlements. In 1758

[1] General Murray had advocated using 12,000 Canadians against New England in his letter of 1 July to Barrington.

[2] G 1662, 1670; Gage, II, 413, 418; Howe's Orderly Book, 302, 304; Thynne Papers, American Affairs, Nos. 21–2 (a copy of Burgoyne's answers to queries from Gage, supplied to Lord Rochford); Burt; Carleton.

[3] As late as June 1777 Carleton gave credit to this belief (CO 42/36, f. 172).

[4] Add. MSS. 38650A, ff. 1–2.

15,000 men had marched from Albany on the Hudson by Lake George to attack Ticonderoga. The fortifications of Ticonderoga had administered a bloody repulse; but in the following year Amherst had taken Ticonderoga and Crown Point and invaded Canada by Lake Champlain and the Mohawk. Nor had the Americans, in the course of these operations, shown the military virtues they were soon to display.[1]

Howe's own proposals were received on 14 November, and approved by Germain on 5 January in a letter which announced the major reinforcements for Canada. Assuming that he would have the promised 20,000 men, Howe proposed to use his main force at New York. He would isolate New England from the Middle Colonies, strike up the Hudson, and open communications with Canada. Having secured these with proper posts, his own army and Carleton's might invade the back of Massachusetts by separate routes. A further despatch brought by Burgoyne on 27 December advocated the evacuation of Boston and the seizure of Rhode Island.[2]

While Quebec was still in danger, Germain was cautious of committing his hopes for Canada to paper. 'Major-General Burgoyne', he wrote to Carleton on 17 February, 'will be so fully instructed in every point in regard to the important services that are to be carried on', that he wrote nothing on the subject himself. But a flotilla for the Lakes was being proposed; and the prospect that it would be used in the coming campaign brightened in the second half of February when news came from enemy sources that an assault on Quebec had been defeated. Thus, when Burgoyne left London at the end of March bearing the orders for Canada, Germain felt justified in indicating the full scope of his hopes. Carleton was ordered to endeavour to pass the Lakes as early as possible, and in his progress 'contribute to the success of the army under General Howe'. But Germain had no intention of dictating Carleton's operational plans. 'These operations must be left to your judgment and discretion, as it would be highly improper, at such a distance, to give any positive orders, especially as so much confidence is placed in your knowledge and military experience'. To Howe he wrote at the same time in a similar strain. If the rebels had given up hope of conquering Canada, 'there is good ground to hope, that the army will be able to advance into the other colonies, by the passage of the Lakes': that was to say, 'as far as I can judge of what is likely to be the general plan of operations in North America'.[3]

[1] The Ministerial viewpoint on the prospects offered by the advance from Canada is précised in CO 5/253, ff. 21–30.

[2] Howe's Orderly Book, 302, 304, CO 42/35, f. 3; G 1826; Howe's of 23 Jan.

[3] CO 42/35, f. 7; CO 5/93, p. 72.

CHAPTER III

THE GREAT CONCENTRATION

1. *The Timetable*

'Our disgraces have been great and repeated in America', wrote Sandwich when the news of the invasion of Canada reached him, 'but I am clear in the opinion I allways [sic] had, that they are entirely owing to our having begun too late, and having suffered ourselves to be amused by what were called conciliatory measures; fleets and armies, admirals and generals, can do very little without ships, troops, and orders . . .'[1]

It was Germain's task to make up for lost time: to supply the orders and the men. Howe had asked for six or seven thousand recruits and 4,000 foreign troops, in addition to the seven regiments which were coming out by way of Charleston. Germain promised better. Not only would he find 10,000 men for Canada: Howe should have 4,400 British reinforcements and 10,000 Germans, a total of more than 14,000. And even this figure was to be improved.[2]

The reinforcements had not been easy to find. The Tsarina had dashed the summer's hope of Russian troops. At home the Ministry had been at its wits' end to find recruits. The East India Company had refused to suspend its own recruiting – a measure of the weakness of executive government in the eighteenth century – and would certainly siphon off a thousand recruits. As for completed regiments, the Charleston expedition left only four battalions fit for immediate service in England and Scotland apart from the Foot Guards; and the old croker Lord Barrington declared that there were not enough troops at home even to keep public order against 'the very levelling spirit among the people'. In Scotland, where four or five battalions were needed, there would not be 600 infantry to maintain order and collect the revenue. There was a large force in Ireland; but the executive in Dublin Castle refused to take German mercenaries or the Scots-Dutch brigade in exchange for their own regiments, on which the Protestant ascendancy depended. Their contribution was reduced, but at the expense of the force in England.

Foreign troops were the only answer to the shortage. As soon as the Russian refusal was known, the Cabinet had resolved to close with the offers

---

[1] Duke University MSS., XVIII: 30 Dec. 1775, Sandwich to unidentified correspondent.

[2] CL, Germain, 5 Jan. to Howe (précis in Howe's Orderly Book, 308).

from Hesse-Cassel and Brunswick, and hire Germans. The German regiments were originally intended to relieve British troops in Ireland; and when the Irish executive protested, to be used in garrison in America to release all Howe's troops for the field. Only gradually did the King and his Ministers accept the necessity of using Germans for general service. In January 1776 treaties were signed for 18,000 German troops. These were tough and disciplined regulars officered by veterans trained in the school of Frederick the Great and Ferdinand of Brunswick. By accepting them England solved her man-power problem for the moment. Without them the attempt to subdue America would have unthinkable.[1]

Thus the troops were secured. But the greater task was to deploy and maintain them on battlefields 3,000 miles beyond the ocean. This colossal task was shouldered by Germain. In high spirits he set to work to sweep away the legacy of Dartmouth's timidity, confident that one bold stroke would settle the American question and irradiate his reputation.[2] And if organisation alone could have conquered, he would have succeeded. To the American Department flowed in reports of the Germans' progress towards their ports of embarkation; intimations from the War Office of British troops ready to embark, from the Ordnance of artillery loaded and storeships ready to sail, from the Admiralty and Navy Board of transports mustering and escorts preparing for sea. Five major embarkations had to be arranged for the spring: the Guards at Spithead, the Highlanders in the Clyde, Irish infantry for Canada at Cork, Germans in the Elbe and Weser. Innumerable other embarkations and convoys were required: for recruits, for tents and camp equipment, for artillery and ordnance stores, for provisions. From Germain's office went forth the ceaseless stream of instructions which were to marshal troops, stores and landing craft in the approaches to New York and the St Lawrence. He had to see that the Admiralty hired and equipped the transports for men, baggage and horses, and assembled them at widely scattered loading points; that it found the escorts for large convoys and single storeships; that it duly forwarded sailing orders and intructions for the disposal of troops at their destination. Embarkation orders went out to bat-

[1] G 1708, 1710, 1725, 1727, 1760, 1769, 1771, 1774, 1776-7; Sackville, I, 243; Barrington, 153-7; CO 5/254, f. 15. The original treaties with the German princes took into the service 12,500 men from Hesse Cassel, 4,000 from Brunswick, 900 from Hesse Hanau and 750 from Waldeck. Offers from Bavaria and Würtemberg were refused because of the poor quality of the men and their equipment. In 1777 1,285 men were accepted from Ansbach-Bayreuth, and in 1778 1,160 from Anhalt-Zerbst. Small augmentations and drafts of recruits brought the numbers of Germans sent to America and Canada in the course of the war to 29,166.

[2] Carlisle, 306; Hastings, III, 166, 168.

talion commanders. More than a hundred landing craft were eventually to be sent to Howe: by the end of 1775 the first thirty had gone, and forty more were being got ready, with ten yawls and ten cutters. There were batteaux to be prefabricated for the Canadian Lakes, and shipwrights to be engaged and sent out to assemble them. Three hundred heavy waggons were to be built and shipped by the Ordnance; camp equipment for twenty-nine battalions to be ordered and shipped. All this had to be superintended on top of the routine work of the Department: disposal of prisoners, prevention of smuggling to the rebel colonies from St Eustatius, arrangements to watch for suspected vessels, and all the endless necessary trivia of war administration.

The most difficult of Germain's problems was shipping. Indeed, in combination with the winter's reverses in America the shipping bottleneck was to kill the hopes of decisive victory in the openning campaign. In the first weeks of Germain's administration the Charleston expedition provided him with a microcosm of the problem. The force was intended to sail on 1 December, and the Navy Board transports were ready at the beginning of the month. So were the warships, except the *Bristol*, 50, which was delayed in dock for four or five days. But the Ordnance Department was behind its schedule. Not till the middle of December were its storeships and bomb-tenders ready to leave the Thames. Then the wind intervened. Blowing steadily from the east, it held the ordnance ships fast in the river; and not till the 29th, four weeks after the appointed sailing day, was Sir Peter Parker able to collect his convoy at Spithead. He sailed for Cork to pick up the Irish regiments, but in the face of storms and adverse winds he did not make the port till 5 January. At Cork another five weeks slipped past before the whole expedition was collected and ready to sail. On 12 February it put to sea; but a few days out it was scattered by a violent south-wester. The shipping dispersed and ran before the gale for different ports, and several transports arrived disabled and distressed.[1]

It was now the middle of February. Perhaps the enterprise should have been abandoned and the troops sent straight on to join Howe, who feared (though this was not known) that the southern expedition might delay his own operations. But an operation once launched is not easy to dismantle. Clinton was on his way from Boston to command the force, the loyalists were ready and perhaps already committed, and the task force was assembled in its interlocking intricacy. It would have been hard to throw the opportunity away and perhaps cost England her friends in the southern colonies. For these reasons the expedition sailed again in spite of its delays. But a couple of weeks after the transports finally cleared the Irish coast, a despatch from Howe revealed his disapproval of the southern expedition. He regretted

[1] CL, Germain, I, Suppl. précis.

that the southern colonies had not been left in a state of false security while he crushed the rebellion in the north, and feared that it would delay his reinforcements. He also reported that private letters arriving in the same packet as the Secretary of State's despatch had made the force's destination public knowledge in Boston, and he had little doubt that the news had reached the enemy.[1] In this he was mistaken; but the breach of security and his general uneasiness about the expedition threw a different light on its retarded timetable. Germain therefore sent Clinton latitude to abandon the whole project if nothing of real advantage could be gained, and to join Howe at once. A months later news from General Cornwallis, who was with the convoy, gave good reasons for satisfaction that Clinton had this discretion. For the transports had been delayed and scattered once more, and were now unlikely to reach their rendezvous till the end of April. Strategic movements in the Atlantic in midwinter were not calculable.[2]

All this time the preparations for shipping the main forces were under way. There were eight British regiments and 5,000 Brunswickers for Canada; and for Howe 12,000 Hessians, 3,500 Highlanders and 1,000 volunteers from the Guards.

By the end of December the negotiations with the Admiralty for transports had made considerable headway. Admiral Palliser, holding the fort in Sandwich's absence, agreed to have 20,000 tons of shipping ready in the river by February to fetch the first contingent of Germans, and 3,200 tons in the Clyde by April for the Highlanders. But he saw these requirements with alarm in view of the supply-needs of the army already in America.

It seems [he wrote to his chief] the demands from the small army now in America are so great as to be thought impossible to furnish. The waggons and draft cattle is prodigious. If this is the case, what will it be when we have another army there above 20,000 men, if they can't make good their quarters, and command carriages and cattle, and subsist and defend themselves without the aid and defence of the fleet, who whilst so employed can perform no other service? I think some people begin to be astonished and staggered at the unexpected difficulties we are in.[3]

Palliser's dismay can therefore be understood when he learnt in the New Year of the 10,000 troops for Canada, and of the need for additional seamen to complete the transports and bring the warships to war establishment. He could see that the reinforcement for Howe might prove decisive if it arrived in time, and promised that the Admiralty would break every record to get

---

[1] CO 5/93, p. 33; EHR 1951, p. 552. (Eric Robson, *Expedition to the Southern Colonies*.)
[2] CL, Germain, Suppl. I, Précis; CO 5/93, p. 379.
[3] CL Germain, Supp. I, 26 Dec.; Sandwich, I, 88. 'Cattle', of course, means horses.

it there. But as for the Canada force, he declared flatly that if it had to fight its way up the St Lawrence, the seamen to man the transports could not be found. The Admiralty had already been required to provide at short notice more transports than the highest number collected in the course of several years in the Seven Years War. Sandwich carried the matter to the King; but he received a characteristic reply: 'You call it unprecedented: the expression in ordinary times ought undoubtedly to be attended to; but when such acts of vigour are shown by the rebellious Americans, we must show that the English lion when roused has not only his wonted strength, but has added the swiftness of the racehorse.'[1]

Sandwich protested that 'unprecedented' was not used in complaint[2]; and in spite of misgivings the Admiralty set to work to find the shipping. In this way was launched a logistical effort on the oceans which had no parallel till 1944; an effort of whose duration the British government had no conception when it was undertaken. For the truth was that no one foresaw how the army would continue to depend on supplies from home. The distress of the Boston garrison was treated as a temporary difficulty which would end as soon as an adequate foraging area was seized.[3] This was never to happen; and the British army in America rested on lines of communication which were strained to the uttermost. Already the shipping shortage was restraining the despatch of troops, and North predicted that even if more men could be hired on the continent, the transport situation would prevent their deployment in America that year.[4] There was truth in William Patterson's lament three years later: 'at the distance of above a thousand leagues they will ever outnumber us'.

2. *Shipping the Supplies*

It was clear from the beginning that virtually all the weapons, ammunition and stores would have to cross the Atlantic.[5] Nor could Canada and the West Indies even provision their garrisons. The temperate Atlantic colonies could at least be expected to feed an army; but even this hope was disappointed. For the British forces were to remain for the most part confined to narrow bridgeheads. Some provisions could be obtained locally at a price: some rice, and some flour if it could be milled and baked. Fresh meat had to be supplied by raiding the rebel coasts, for in spite of the Treasury's efforts it proved impracticable to ship live cattle from England.

[1] Sandwich, I, 94, 97, 102; G 1809; CO 5/253, f. 114.
[2] G 1824.
[3] Add. MSS. 38208, f. 180; Add. MSS. 38209, f. 163.
[4] Add. MSS. 34413, f. 5.
[5] A shipment of camp equipment is listed in Appendix I.

Fodder in general was bulky to ship, and hay out of the question, so that extended cantonments for foraging became a dangerous but necessary feature of military operations. Everything else crossed the Atlantic: oats for the horses; salted beef and pork, butter, oatmeal, pease and flour for the men. Every year a third of a ton of food was needed for each man in America, besides the weight of the casks in which it was packed. Without reckoning packaging, 29,000 tons of provisions were shipped to the army all over the world in 1782.

At every stage of the long journey from the farms of the British Isles to the distant theatres of war the provisioning system contended with obstacles and delays. Even to forecast the need was difficult, for returns were unreliable and commanders indented late and inaccurately. At home contractors delivered late to the depots, bad provisions were rejected by the Commissaries, damaged barrels and casks had to be repaired before reshipping. There were delays in assembling convoys and appointing escorts; delays from the weather, which might blow the North American victuallers as far as the West Indies; delays through the retention of transports at their destination to provide storage or for amphibious operations. The wastage was immense. Bad quality, packing and loading; theft, storage and climate; changes of destination imposed by the requirements of strategy: all contributed to the immense loss of treasury provisions.[1]

Added to troop movements, naval victualling, and the storing of foreign dockyards, the shipping of army provisions and equipment imposed a crushing burden on the country's shipping resources. By July 1776 the Navy Board alone controlled 127,000 tons of transports, though it was not yet responsible for the army's provisions, and by 1782 the army's needs absorbed 120,000 tons of shipping. The army transports were mostly small ships of between 250 and 400 tons burthen, and three or four troopships were needed to move a battalion.[2] Germain's initial demand for transports in January 1776 had driven the Navy Board to scour the ports of Holland and North Germany, but the shortage continued; and when the Treasury was called on to send out the army's provisions at the end of the month all the available shipping had been pre-empted by the Navy Board. This shipping responsibility was new to the Treasury. As late as October 1775 the freighting of provisions to America had been left to the contracting suppliers, on the supposition that it was a temporary measure. But it became clear that victualling from Europe would be necessary for some time to come, and the

[1] E. E. Curtis, Chap. IV; Usher, 289–90, 297–305; G 2700; Royal Institution, I, 37, 46, 48, 54, 102; II, 20, 257, 262, 367; CL, Germain, 6 and 13 Oct. 1780; CL, Clinton, 28 Aug. 1779 from Germain; Sandwich, I, 84.
[2] Williams, 68 n.; Usher, 292, 325–6, 335–6.

contractors were unwilling to arm ships or expose their cargoes to rebel privateers. The Treasury asked the Admiralty to undertake the shipping, but received the blunt reply that the transport of army provisions was not its business. The Treasury was thus saddled with the duty of hiring its own victuallers.[1] Depots were opened where a Commissary could take delivery of the provisions. The first and most important was at Cork, a capacious anchorage well placed for the Irish trade in beef and butter; but the expense of deliveries from English contractors later caused other depots to be opened in the Thames and Solent. Here the provisions were inspected and shipped, before the victualling transports sailed on their long voyage to the western depots which stretched from Montreal to St Lucia.[2]

The Admiralty's refusal to help meant that four departments were competing for the available resources. They competed for crews. The seafarers of America had been lost; and only 50,000 merchant seamen were estimated to sail from British ports, a very small reservoir from which to man a navy whose strength rose to more than twice that figure in the course of the war. The transport services naturally went to the wall, and the navy pressed transport crews whenever they dared. In the course of 1776 the Navigation Laws were modified to enable shipowners to man with foreigners up to two-thirds of their complements. But still the shortage was felt, and seamens' wages soared in response to it.

The competition for shipping became acute again at the end of April 1776, when an urgent call for horse-transports brought the departments into collision. At the navy's request the Treasury restrained its agents from paying the full Navy Board price for transports, and till midsummer no victuallers could be hired. By this sacrifice twenty-one horse-transports were collected. Every precaution was ordered by the American Department for the horses' health, and some Dutch ships which were too close between decks to give them air were ordered to have their decks scuttled. Nevertheless, of 950 horses which embarked more than 400 never reached New York.[3]

It was largely to eliminate this competition that the Navy Board at length accepted its natural responsibilities in 1779, and under the departmental imperialist Sir Charles Middleton took over the army victuallers. The Navy Board was technically more competent to administer a transport fleet. The Treasury had hired without inspection or supervision through a firm of agents, at a higher rate than their rivals; but the Navy Board had the resources to survey the ships, insist on a fair price, and supervise the Masters

---

[1] Add. MSS. 38343, f. 1: an important Treasury memorandum of 1 Jan. 1778 to which further reference is made below.

[2] Usher, 285–90; Royal Institution, I, 34.

[3] Treasury memo. *loc. cit.*; CO 5/254, f, 37; CO 5/93, p. 499.

through its Agents when the transports were abroad. In the last stages of the war, when Middleton had the ear of Shelburne, he was to advocate the rationalisation of the whole transport service by the transfer of Ordnance and Victualling Board shipping to his own department.[1]

Yet whatever the administrative and financial advantages of a unified service, the army was better served by the Treasury than by the Navy Board. When the Navy Board took over the victuallers, it insisted that they should sail unarmed and in convoy, which delayed their departure till the victualling fleets were assembled about three times a year. On this Germain blamed the victualling shortage at New York in 1780. He preferred the Treasury system of arming the victuallers and despatching them singly as they were loaded. This policy the Treasury had adopted in February 1776 on a warning from General Howe of the risk to unarmed ships in convoy through separation in fogs and gales.[2] The ships were to be armed, and the guns manned by recruits on their way to America. The difficulties of a new enterprise had to be overcome. The Ordnance could produce no suitable guns, and very few of the ships had a tier of ports for cannon. Everything had to be made, and the materials collected from the various iron-works, before the victuallers could be brought into service. But the result repaid the trouble. When the embargo on Treasury hiring was lifted again in June 1776 enough ships were eventually found; and from that time, as the Treasury claimed eighteen months later, the victualling service 'has never stood still an hour for want of shipping, or of armament'.

The original plan had been that the ships which carried the first quarter's provisions should return to carry the third quarter's, and the second likewise the fourth. This intention was unhinged by delays at home and in America, so that the ships did not return in time to execute it. But the arming of the transports served its purpose. The small oat-ships, armed with only a few swivels, were convoyed by the large transports. In 1776 only six Treasury victuallers were taken. Five of these had no troops on board and, with only the ordinary transport complement of seven men per hundred tons, could make little resistance; but the sixth, with thirteen soldiers, fought till six of them were killed and the captain lay unconscious, when she was boarded. In the following year not a single Treasury ship was taken, with the possible exception of an oat-ship. The vicuallers' freedom from convoy made the army's provisions certain and regular at least till France entered the war; and

[1] Curtis, 121, 129; CL, Shelburne, Vol. 153, No. 11; Barham, II, 169. For the jobbery and abuses which governed the hiring of transports, see Porritt, *Unreformed House of Commons*, I, 217-18.

[2] Later supported by Lord Howe: 'the protection of convoy . . . is not to be relied on in this precarious navigation' (Adm. 1/487, f. 25).

from the latter part of 1776 the Ordnance armed its storeships on the same principle. The Treasury calculated that by the end of 1777 its method had saved the navy the escorts for twenty-nine separate convoys. The department was rightly proud of its achievement.[1]

3. A Bid for Decision

Excusing the Admiralty for the delays to the Charleston expedition, Lord Sandwich bluntly told the King that 'I fear your Majesty will never have a sea expedition that will be in readiness so near the given time as this has been'.[2]

The punctual arrival of reinforcements was vital to the coming operations in America. Howe and Carleton had a long way to march from New York and Lake Champlain before they joined hands on the Hudson, and once the New England winter descended on the armies again no movement would be possible. The failure to withdraw from Boston and the loss of all Canada as far as the city of Quebec meant that the first part of the campaigning season would be lost in merely taking possession of the starting points; so it became the more important that operations should begin the moment the weather allowed troops to take the field.

Germain had counted on getting the reinforcements away in the course of March. But the shortage of shipping, and a month of severe frosts and snow in January which held up work in the dockyards, made this impossible.[3] February saw the departure of the Charleston expedition and the first relief for Quebec. But it was not till April that the main convoys for Canada, which had priority over Howe's force, were ready to depart. On 7 and 8 April the eight British regiments and the first contingent of 2,000 Brunswickers sailed from Cork and Portsmouth. Howe's reinforcement did not begin to leave till the 29th, when 3,500 Highlanders sailed from the Clyde; and about the same time the 8,200 Hessians of the first contingent reached Spithead under General Heister. Here they embarked in fresh transports for the longer part of the voyage, their water was laid in and their hospital ship fitted up. The Guards, who had been waiting for them, now embarked; and early in May the whole force of 9,300 men sailed under the protection of Commodore Hotham, with nine navy victuallers in company.[4] There still remained the balance of the Germans: 4,000 Hessians for Howe and 3,000

[1] Treasury memo., *loc. cit.*
[2] G 1809 (11 Jan.).
[3] Howe's Orderly Book, 310; CO 5/253, f. 17; CO 5/93, f. 69; Walpole, *Last Journals*, II, 8.
[4] CO 5/93, pp. 409, 422, 424.

Brunswickers for Canada. But shipping was the difficulty. The Brunswickers eventually sailed from England late in June. At the end of March the transport shortage had made it impossible to guess when the second division of Hessians would embark, but by the second half of May 10,000 tons of transports reached the Weser and they arrived at Portsmouth a month later.[1] On 7 July they were married to their escorts and despatched to the westward.

That the reinforcements were late was no fault of Germain's. Their despatch with the necessary supplies was an impressive achievement, as General Howe was the first to acknowledge. 'I cannot take leave of your Lordship', he concluded a letter on 8 June, 'without expressing my utter amazement at the decisive and masterly strokes for carrying such extensive plans into immediate execution as has been effected since your Lordship has assumed the conduct of this war.' An American authority on the warfare of the twentieth century has endorsed the praise. 'The bureaucratic achievement', Walter Millis has written, ' . . . is surely entitled to the respect of modern staff officers and logisticians.'[2]

The despatch of these forces was a calculated risk, for by the end of 1775 the foreign mails were reporting that France and Spain had begun to arm. To send across the Atlantic all the good infantry in the country and most of the navy's frigates was an invitation to our enemies in Europe; and at the Admiralty Palliser for one was haunted by the fear of a sudden emergency at home. Yet it was also becoming clear that France and Spain intended to supply the rebels, while the Dutch islands in the West Indies were ready to furnish the gunpowder which the colonies could not provide for themselves. The rebellion had to be broken if possible before it could organise and arm its forces with foreign help; and at the same time a rapid success might avert the danger in Europe. Considering the distance of the theatre of war, England was making an effort without parallel. 'It is the plan of a campaign which they do not want to repeat', wrote the French chargé d'affaires, 'and not of a systematic war calculated on the means, the interests and the relations of the two countries.' The political aim behind the effort may have been mistaken; but in the military means there was more calculation than Frenchmen realised. A 'systematic' war was the last thing England desired or could afford: she preferred a bold decisive stroke to crack the shell of the rebellion.[3]

In selecting the military means the political object of the war had not been forgotten. But Germain intended to treat from strength. As Burgoyne had

---

[1] CO 5/93, f. 69; G 1870.
[2] CO 5/93, p. 212; Walter Millis, *Armies and Men*, 18.
[3] Sandwich, I, 76, 90; G 1806, 1857; Doniol, I, 448.

written to him in August 1775, if the extremist view continued to prevail in the colonies, 'America . . . must be subdued or relinquished'. With this view Germain agreed; and he believed that it could be done without making concessions. He was not an advocate of barbarity: the destruction of Falmouth by Admiral Graves gave him no pleasure, and he remarked that Graves had shown no grounds for his action.[1] But he believed that if the objects of the war were to be assured, the Ministry must stand firm on them from the start.

This became clear when the machinery of pacification was discussed in the Cabinet. Since the early autumn Lord North had been thinking of sending peace commissioners to America to investigate on the spot and negotiate directly with the separate colonies. This was common sense; and as the military preparations reached their climax a Commission to make peace was placed in the hands of the new Commanders-in-Chief on the Atlantic seaboard, Admiral Lord Howe and his brother the General. North had once hoped for a negotiated settlement without a war; and now that fighting had begun he hoped that the strength of the British effort would weaken American determination and at the same time reassure the more bellicose of his colleagues. But the terms of the Commission were vital.

When the Commissioners' instructions were discussed, only Dartmouth resisted the prevailing view in the Cabinet that the colonies must be forced to acknowledge the supremacy of Parliament. North, however, while agreeing that this acknowledgment must be written into the final settlement, did not want to make it a preliminary condition of negotiation. Germain knew the Prime Minister too well: if the demand was postponed, he suspected that North would end by letting it be shelved altogether. Rallying the support of Suffolk and his friends, he insisted that no colony should be restored to the King's peace till it had acknowledged the supremacy of Parliament.

'The truth was', wrote William Knox, the Under-Secretary of the American Department, 'Lord George having now collected a vast force, and having a fair prospect of subduing the Colonies, he wished to subdue them before he treated at all.' His stand produced a deadlock, with Dartmouth and North talking of resignation; but through the mediation of Lord Mansfield a compromise was reached.[2] The paradox is that in the context of the decision to coerce, Germain was probably right; for by now no terms which the British government or Parliament could have swallowed were acceptable to the Americans. Though few American patriots had wanted to cast themselves off from Britain when the rebellion broke out, the British actions which

[1] CL, Germain, 5 Jan. 1776 to Howe.
[2] Sackville, II, 10; Knox, 258–60; Ritcheson, 201–6.

followed Bunker Hill had produced a rapid change of feeling; and the news that foreign mercenaries were to be used seemed to make the breach irreparable. If the British intended to treat the struggle as a foreign war, as foreigners they should themselves be treated. A steady current of opinion flowed towards Independence. The colonies would no longer listen to terms which England could accept, nor would piecemeal offers to the separate colonies be considered by a united and undefeated America. The relative strength of the contenders would have to be changed by battle to make a solution possible.

CHAPTER IV

THE ARRESTED OFFENSIVE

1. *These Noble Heroes*

The task in America cried out for men of stature. For when the Ministry at home had allocated the reinforcements and expressed its general hopes for the campaign, it could exercise no further control. News from America ran with the prevailing wind and at the most favourable might take a month. But a westerly passage from England with the Cabinet's instructions very rarely took less than two months from office to office, and many despatches from home took three or four months to reach their destination. Weather and enemy cruisers took their toll; but by far the greatest cause of delay was the shortage of despatch ships. Forty Post Office packet-boats were lost during the war.[1] The generals were periodically accused of hoarding packet-boats in America, which they denied; but whatever the real cause, no regular and frequent service could be maintained. If the Admiralty was asked to help, it was quite capable of sitting on the despatches for weeks before it found a conveyance. The slowest recorded transmission was probably that of the accumulated despatches which were sent out by the September packet of 1781. The packet was taken, and for some reason the duplicate copies sent out in a warship went astray. The triplicates reached New York on 11 April 1782, six or seven months after they were written.[2]

The responsibility for bringing strategy to the battlefield therefore lay entirely on the commanders in the theatre. Between January and March of each year Germain allocated the reinforcements and approved the plans.

---

[1] Ellis, *Post Office in the Eighteenth Century*, 96.

[2] A rough check of letters sent by Germain to Clinton on sixty-three days between May 1778 and Feb. 1781 yields the following passage times:

less than two months	6	days' letters
2 months	12	,, ,,
2–3 months	28	,, ,,
3–4 ,,	11	,, ,,
4–5 ,,	4	,, ,,
5–7 ,,	2	,, ,,

(counting all the despatches sent by the packet of Sep. 1781 as one).

Thereafter he could do nothing to influence the course of events. His summer despatches were little more than a running commentary of applause and disapproval. Conscious of their isolation from the source of political direction, both Howe and Burgoyne had suggested in the previous summer the appointment of a viceroy with full powers to co-ordinate operations. 'There is no possibility', Burgoyne had written, 'of carrying on a war so complicated as this will be, at the distance we are from the fountain head, without these full powers being at hand.'[1] Such an office would have been as foreign to the constitution as was the Congress of the colonies, and might, in acknowledging the unity of the rebellion, have implied the right of the colonies to negotiate in unison. By appointing two brothers as General and Admiral, and vesting them jointly with the power of negotiation, the Ministry may with reason have hoped to provide both sufficient authority and sufficient unity in the theatre. The inclusion of Canada in a unified military command was out of the qestion as long as overland communications were closed.

The history of the Howes' appointment was rather curious. The General, William, had had the imprudence to tell his parliamentary constituents at Nottingham that he condemned the government's American policy and would not accept a command there. But he had been looking for employment; and the offer, very lucrative and made perhaps in a manner which was difficult to refuse, was evidently more than he could bear to turn down.[2] His elder brother Admiral Lord Howe, was in an equally ambiguous position. He was favourably disposed to the Americans; but he wanted employment, and was bought by the Ministry for political reasons. He had served on the Board of Admiralty under Sandwich and Egmont in the 'sixties, but had recently quarrelled with Sandwich over a sinecure. Lord North had promised him the reversion of the Lieutenant-Generalcy of Marines on the death of Sir Charles Saunders; and when it went instead to Sandwich's friend Sir Hugh Palliser, Howe was, like Admiral Keppel, violently offended. If Horace Walpole can be trusted, the Ministry hastened to buy off his resentment with the American command.[3] It was a high price, for Howe made his own terms. Sandwich's friend Shuldham had just reached America to replace Graves, and to save the Admiralty's face North suggested carving out a separate command for him in the St Lawrence. But Howe would not hear of it, and Shuldham's supersession had to be softened by the unusual dis-

---

[1] Sackville, II, 9; G 1693.

[2] Anderson, *Command of the Howe Brothers*, 47–9. For Burgoyne's account of the manner of his own appointment at the same time, see Fonblanque, *Burgoyne*, 120.

[3] But Germain's friend Sir John Irwin recorded that the appointment was due to pressure from Germain (Hastings, III, 169).

tinction of a peerage. Over the terms of the Peace Commission Lord Howe also made difficulties, in opposition to the tough line advocated by Germain. But though he went through the motions of preparing to resign, the politicians guessed that in the last resort he would not refuse the command. This was not the way Chatham would have appointed; but a weak Ministry could not take a strong line with politicians in uniform.[1]

The Howe brothers were courageous and popular leaders: tall, dark inarticulate men of proved tactical skill. William Howe had done well on two continents in the Seven Years War. He had led the forlorn hope which scaled the Heights of Abraham, and was a master of light infantry tactics. Both the brothers were regarded as moderate, level-headed men for a delicate task, and tolerably well-disposed to the Ministry. It was said that Lord Howe had not spoken to Germain since the St Malo expedition of 1758; but the brothers launched their American careers on friendly terms with the American Secretary and possibly under his patronage. Before Germain entered the Cabinet, Lord Howe had written acknowledging his 'particular goodness to my brother on his late appointment'. Germain was warmly congratulated by General William when he took office, and again on his preparations for the campaign; and Germain was equally warm in his approval of the General's operations.[2] Though the Howes certainly felt some sympathy for the Americans, they accepted the need to check America's drift from the colonial system. Lord Howe wrote to his old acquaintance Benjamin Franklin of 'the necessity of preventing the trade from passing into foreign channels'. He regarded Barrington's fear of military operations as pusillanimous; and the only anxiety to which the brothers confessed before the opening of the campaign was that the effort might be too small.[3]

Yet their taciturnity made them difficult to measure. In the House of Commons the General was no master of argument; and Lord Howe's dark ambiguous speeches were scarcely comprehensible.[4] They had no profound knowledge of the American political scene. Their attitude to the struggle was somewhat ambivalent; and their known professional abilities were those of tacticians. For the Admiral this was almost enough. He had only to control the rebels' trade, protect British shipping, and support the army. The technical difficulties were considerable; the strategic choices few. The General's task was more complex. He was to command the greatest army

[1] Anderson, 52–4; Sandwich, II, 201; G 1816, 1818, 1836.
[2] CL, Germain, 22 July 1775, Lord Howe to Germain, and *passim*; Sackville, II, 11, 30. cf. Wykeham-Martin, 315. For their earlier bad relations, see Valentine, 39, 46: Walpole appears to be the only evidence.
[3] Add. MSS. 34413, f. 56; CL, Germain, 29 July 1775.
[4] Anderson, 7, 43; Wraxall, II, 288.

ever sent across the oceans, in a situation of deep political and military confusion. Colonel Stuart feared he would be imprudent[1], but the guess was wide of the mark. For as Clausewitz was to observe, the boldest subordinate rarely makes a resolute chief. The highest levels of command press harder on the intellect; and with time to ponder, doubt and confusion creep in. In putting forward his plans of campaign in the autumn of 1775 Howe had written that it was 'of greater compass than he feels himself equal to direct'. Would he rise to the challenge; or had he already reached the ceiling of his ability when he was entrusted with supreme command?

Of Howe, at the outset, Germain and his colleagues seem to have felt no doubts. With Carleton in Canada it was different. The recall of Gage had made Carleton the senior General in America; and at first he had been intended to command all the forces on the continent if his own troops should form a junction with the army on the Atlantic seaboard. But for reasons buried in their past[2] Germain distrusted him. 'I take the General to be one of those men who see affairs in the most unfavourable light', he wrote to Sandwich on learning of the American invasion of Canada; 'and yet he has the reputation of a resolute and persevering officer.'[3]

Carleton was ruled out as supreme commander when the Howe brothers were appointed sole Peace Commissioners; and Germain did not intend him to command the advance from Canada in person. Clinton would have been sent from Boston to act as his field commander, with instructions to place himself under Howe's orders when the two armies joined; but Clinton had already been ordered south to command the Charleston expedition, so instead John Burgoyne was sent out with the reinforcements as second-in-command in Canada.[4] When he arrived, however, he found operations already begun under Carleton's direct control; and in the absence of an order from home to relinquish them to his subordinate, the Governor continued to command his army in person.

As a Governor Carleton had many admirable qualities. His financial integrity, humanity and conscientiousness were beyond dispute; and his breadth of vision had created the Quebec Act which made it possible to fit the French-speaking Catholic Canadians into the structure of the empire. Yet a temper which could bear no criticism led him to arbitrary removals of councillors and judges who spoke out against his views; and his largeness

[1] Wortley, 73.
[2] Horace Walpole conjectured from Carleton's friendship with the Duke of Richmond that Germain knew he was unfavourable to him on the Minden question.
[3] Sandwich, I, 86.
[4] CL, Germain, 1 Feb. 1776 to Howe.

of vision was accompanied by a flawed judgment. In administering the Quebec Act he had committed two important errors: he failed to realise that the seigneurial régime in Canada was an empty shell, since seigneurs competing for tenants were in no position to exact tenurial obligations; and contrary to the British government's intentions he withheld from the English-speaking minority the protection of English law in civil suits. The result was that he greatly over-estimated the loyalty of the population and the help which the army could expect from the machinery of the feudal régime. In this fool's paradise he had sent two of his four regiments to Boston in response to Gage's appeal in 1774, and had allowed the government to believe that Canada would defend itself and provide a well-served military base against the Revolution. These dreams were shattered by the events of 1775–6.

As a commander in the field Carleton's abilities have also been rated high; but the evidence is slender, for by 1777 he was displaced from the control of operations, and coming home in 1778 he returned to America only to superintend the final evacuation. His military reputation therefore rests on his defence of Quebec in the first winter of the war – which was no very severe test once the first shock had been met – and on the subsequent advance to the frontier; and on the latter the evidence is not as unequivocal as his admirers claim.

The appointments of Howe and Carleton were confirmed in the spring by the revocation of Gage's commission as Commander-in-Chief, though he was left the now sinecure Governorship of Massachusetts. Howe and Carleton were promoted to the local rank of General, and Clinton, Burgoyne, Cornwallis and Percy became local Lieutenant-Generals. Germain let it be known that the King would employ no General senior to them in the rebellious colonies, thus granting to the officers who had come forward promptly at the outset a vested interest in the expanding theatre. They had a great opportunity; but not everyone believed that they would rise to it. A captious but able Colonel at Boston had complained during the winter that the army had the most ordinary men to command it: 'I hope to God they will send us some Generals worthy the command of a British army', he wrote.[1]

Their tactical instrument, at any rate, was superb. British infantry in battle were among the best in the world, and the artillery among the most efficient. In open country or a well-planned assault they were invariably successful. Their trust was not in marksmanship, but in the close-order volley and the bayonet charge. 'It will be our glory and preservation to storm where possible', ran Burgoyne's orders to his troops. Howe's first campaign was to

[1] Sandwich, I, 119; CL, Germain, 1 Feb. 1776 to Howe; Gage, II, 207; Wortley, 74.

prove the virtues of the army and its tactics. The Americans hated the bayonet, which they resented just as the British resented the sniping of officers by rebel sharp-shooters; and they respected the close order drill of the German plains enough to learn it from European instructors.

Yet in many ways the British army was not suited to American service at the beginning of the war. It marched slowly and with too much baggage. A battalion embarking for foreign service was allowed sixty women and eighty tons of baggage: a General and his staff might take as much for themselves. A German officer writing of the Seven Years War censured the officers' love of comfort; yet in America it was the German troops who showed themselves least ready to relinquish their baggage and indulgences, as both Howe and Burgoyne were to complain in their separate theatres. All, whether British or German, were professional eighteenth-century troops performing one more duty. Campaigning for years in a harsh and distant country, they could not be expected to forego their comforts as the short-service American armies and the inflamed militiamen would do. Nor could their commanders afford to let them freeze or starve: they were not expendable. A British army needed warm clothing, tents, and cooking equipment.

The tactics, too, so effective in open country and against regular entrenchments, were not good enough in forests and enclosures. The lesson of Braddock and the Indian Wars might never have been learnt, for all that was remembered of light infantry tactics by Gage's troops when the war began. After Braddock's defeat in 1755 light infantry had been trained to protect the main body from ambush and sniping. But as Germain recognised at once,[1] the losses on the retreat from Concord had the same cause as Braddock's disaster: against an enemy who refused to stand and face them, the troops kept together and volleyed. If the Boston garrison had kept up its light infantry training, the embattled farmers would have been brushed off with ease.[2] But the art of open-order fighting had to be relearnt, and Howe was the man to brace the army's discipline and teach them. One of his first steps was to group the regimental light companies into separate battalions, as Wolfe and Amherst had done. As the war progressed, the infantry as a whole learnt to hold their own in extended order in the woods. In most tactical situations their discipline and experience told against the individual initiative, marksmanship and speed of the Americans. Their slowness lost them some opportunities. But the two great defeats of the war at Saratoga and Yorktown were strategic rather than tactical. The soldiers so curiously crimped and scraped together bore their burden nobly.

[1] Sackville, II, 2.
[2] So Fuller argues in his British Light Infantry in the Eighteenth Century, 125.

2. The Winter at Quebec and Boston

It was to Quebec that the Minister looked anxiously for the first news of the year. The February report of a rebel repulse was true; but it was an anxious and critical winter for Canada. When Montgomery's Americans advanced 2,000 strong from Ticonderoga in September 1775, Carleton had only 800 seasoned troops to oppose them; and in spite of the support of the seigneurs and the Catholic heirarchy, the Canadians had been slow to come forward to his help. Carleton concentrated most of his little force in front of Montreal, and threw the bulk of the men into Fort St John's in the path of the enemy. Major Preston defended his wooden ramparts with gallantry; and without trained men or cannon Montgomery was baffled. Probing forward with a small detachment in the rear of the fort, he attempted a *coup de main* against Montreal and was repulsed. But Fort Chambly surrendered to the rebels, giving them the equipment to press the siege of St John's. On 2 November it surrendered after a resistance of fifty-five days, and Montreal was abandoned.

A two-months' delay had been imposed on the rebels, and winter was closing in on them. But in the approaches to Montreal Carleton had sacrificed most of his seasoned troops. Quebec was almost defenceless when, a few days after the surrender of St John's, a second and totally unexpected American force burst from the wilderness of Maine on to the banks of the St Lawrence opposite the city. Only the river stood between the survivors of Benedict Arnold's heroic march and the helpless capital. But while they prepared to cross, the news of their coming travelled up the river to Sorel. There Colonel Allan Maclean was forming a regiment of highland immigrants. He moved at once by forced marches, and entered the city with nearly 400 levies as Arnold was scaling the Heights of Abraham. Maclean's decisive march made him the saviour of British Canada.

Besides these recruits there were about 100 British regulars in the city; and with seamen, marines and armed inhabitants, Maclean and the Lieutenant-Governor collected a motley garrison of 1,300 men. When Carleton arrived in disguise from Montreal, he found enough men to hold Arnold in check. Even when Montgomery appeared early in December, the 1,600 Americans were baffled. A siege by regular approaches was impossible, for their light cannon were overwhelmed by the artillery on the ramparts. Starvation might have reduced the garrison in due time, but the American enlistments were about to expire, and Montgomery was driven to the desperate expedient of a *coup de main*. In the snow and darkness of 30 December the Americans stormed and were repulsed. Arnold was seriously wounded, and among the dead was Montgomery.

This was the only attempt to storm Quebec. But reinforcements enabled the wounded Arnold to maintain a blockade, though his force was drained by smallpox, expiring enlistments and desertion. The garrison's provisions shrank; but winter was dissolving, and the vanguard of Germain's relief was on the way. On 6 May, three days short of sixteen years since the *Lowestoft* had raised the French siege in 1760, the *Isis* and *Surprise* burst through the ice. Canada had been snatched from the ruin of the American Empire, and the bridgehead saved for the army which was coming.

At Boston General Howe had endured a winter as trying as Carleton's. Since Bunker Hill he had been closely beset by Washington, who had arrived to assume the command of the rebels. The enemy had great difficulties of their own. They were short of powder, and their troops were continually melting away like Montgomery's at Quebec. But they were strongly entrenched, and backed by the armed population. Howe, deprived of intelligence, saw little to be gained by a sortie and perhaps everything to lose; for he had less than 9,000 men of all arms to hold the long circuit of the city whose fortifications an officer had judged to need two years' work and a garrison of 20,000 men.[1] Supplies were very short, and the ships expected from England did not appear. In the New Year an officer sailed for the West Indies in search of the missing victuallers, and found twenty-six vessels which had been blown off their course to Boston lying at Antigua in various states of damage and loss. By March there was less than three weeks' supply of meat in Boston. Yet though Howe was anxious to evacuate the town and be early in the field at New York, only the arrival of transports from Europe would make an orderly embarcation possible.

The impasse was broken by the enemy. With characteristic energy the artillery captured in Ticonderoga had been dragged across the snow-bound hills of New England; and on the night of 4 March Washington occupied Dorchester Heights and threw up batteries to command the harbour. The ingenuity which entrenched the frost-hardened peninsula in a single night deserved success. Howe had either to retake the heights or lose Boston. An assault planned for the night of the 5th was frustrated by a heavy storm; and the Americans pushed their lines forward till they flanked the British lines on Boston Neck. Howe had to leave while he could. Into seventy-eight ships of an average burthen of 250 tons were crammed troops, loyal inhabitants, stores and horses. Much had to be sacrificed: a hundred pieces of ordnance, a hundred irreplacable trucks and waggons, eighty horses, and large quantities of barrack stores and forage. On 17 March, St Patrick's Day, the British army left Boston for ever.[2]

[1] Wortley, 70.
[2] The happy coincidence with the feast of the Irish saint preserves Evacuation Day among the numerous public holidays of Massachusetts.

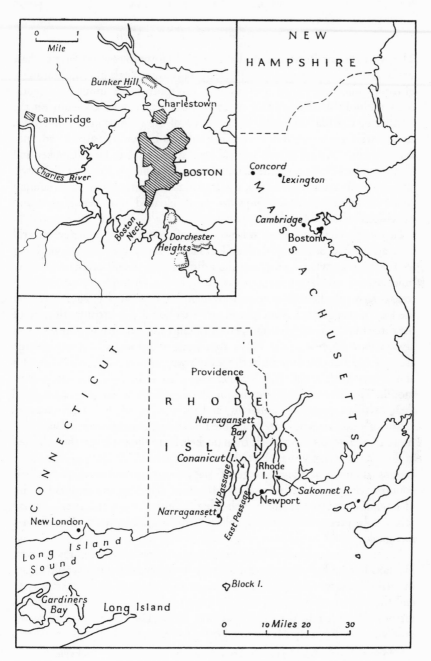

BOSTON AND RHODE ISLAND

3. The Concentration off New York

The evacuation of Boston might have enabled Howe to establish his new base without trouble by forestalling Washington at New York. But the confusion of troops and stores in the overcrowded transports made immediate operations unthinkable. The spring of 1776 should have seen Carleton on the frontier of Canada, thundering at the gates of New England; while Howe, after a winter comfortably entrenched on Manhattan, prepared to advance and meet him. Instead, Carleton had been swept back as far as Quebec and prevented from collecting the material needed for his advance; while Howe, after a winter chained in Boston, was steering for Halifax. No tactical landing could be attempted till the ships had been reloaded at a friendly port and provisions collected for the campaign.[1]

Howe was clear that there was no hope of conciliating the Americans till their armies had been roughly handled. He foresaw some difficulty in doing so; for with the whole country at their disposal they could easily retire a few miles back from the navigable rivers, and Howe with his shortage of land transport would be unable to follow them.[2] This difficulty, aggravated by the loss of waggons at Boston, was never to be fully overcome. In spite of the three hundred waggons shipped from England that spring, transport was always short. A few of the heavy four-horse waggons which supplied the army in the field were built in the army's waggon yard at New York. But about two-thirds of the army's vehicles were hired in America by the day or month. The shortage was a fertile source of corruption. Commissaries hired their own waggons to themselves; and the officers of the Quartermaster-Gerneral's department were computed at the end of the war to have put more than £400,000 into their own pockets from the contracts they allotted in the course of five years. Nevertheless it was the vulnerability of communications as much as the shortage of waggons in an extensive and hostile country which hampered the army's freedom of movement. It was the risk of having convoys attacked which Charles Stuart two years later said had 'absolutely prevented us this whole war from going fifteen miles from a navigable river'.[3]

In spite of the difficulty which he foresaw, Howe was in a hurry to leave Halifax. For he hoped that elation at the recovery of Boston would tempt the Americans to offer the battle which he believed was the shortest way to end the war; and the health and discipline of his troops made him sure of victory. He still hoped to join Carleton in the Hudson valley before the year was out. By early May he had collected enough additional tonnage to

[1] Howe's Orderly Book, 319; Anderson, 105.   [2] Sackville, II, 30.
[3] Curtis, 136, 144-5; Clode, I, 136; Wortley, 113.

embark his force in tactical order. But he still lacked provisions. Only one of the numerous Treasury victuallers which had sailed between August and November had yet arrived; and on 7 May there was less than a fortnight's meat. June came in before the army could move; but at length it sailed 9,000 strong on 11 June for New York.[1]

The entrance to New York harbour is guarded by a narrow passage between Staten Island and the western end of Long Island. Howe's first object was to open the passage for shipping by securing these points. On 29 June the convoy reached Sandy Hook in the outer approaches to New York, and four days later the troops landed on Staten Island and secured their first objective. But here the operation halted, for Howe had changed his mind about hastening on the battle, and resolved to wait for reinforcements before he tackled Long Island, where the Americans had had time to fortify the heights of Brooklyn. For seven weeks the troops idly watched the summer gliding away. Not till 22 August did the assault begin.

Even before he left Halifax the General had begun to hesitate. He had written to Germain that in his early operations he would bear the coming reinforcements in mind, and risk no difficult attacks without them. As it happened, a letter was then on its way from the Secretary of State which expressed a similar line of thought: it applauded his expressed intention to make an early attack on New York, but hoped that 'as such large reinforcements are going to you, I wish they may arrive before the time of carrying it into execution'. This was not an instruction to wait but a hope of timely help; and since it only reached Howe when he had been twenty-four days on Staten Island, it can have had no influence on his decision, though it may have encouraged him to stick to it.[2]

From Howe's caution some of his contemporaries deduced that he had never shaken off the effect of his losses at Bunker Hill. But this is a highly speculative subject. The whole demoralising experience of the months in Boston continued to oppress the army's command. Sir William Howe's first introduction to the loyalists as a frightened handful of New England refugees must have prejudiced him permanently, and made him disinclined to encourage them in areas where they were thicker on the ground; and the winter shortages in Boston may have had a lasting influence on his conduct of operations.[3] Yet whatever the particular experiences which may have influenced him, the core of his thinking concerned the conservation of his force. Even when enough troops reached him he still waited for the camp

[1] CO 5/93, pp. 135, 153; Sackville, II, 32; Royal Institution, I, 46.
[2] Sackville, II, 33-4; CO 5/93, f. 119.
[3] These influences are suggested respectively by Nelson (p. 139) and by Anderson (pp. 71, 97).

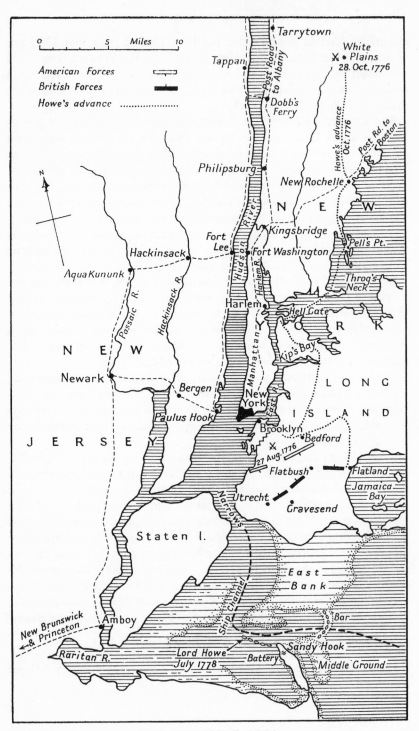

THE NEW YORK AREA

equipment. To take the field without camp kettles would have risked the health of his men; and these, as he explained, were the irreplacable 'stock on which the national forces in America must in future be grafted'.[1] This thought had been in many minds since the rebellion broke out: in Lord Percy's this summer when he wrote that 'our army is so small that we cannot even afford a victory'; in the Adjutant-General's when he had feared that the army would be 'destroyed by damned driblets' if no settled plan of operations was fixed; and far off in Minorca in General Murray's when he rejoiced that Howe had not risked a general engagement. 'The fate of battles at the best are precarious. When Burgoyne gets over the Lakes, and Sir John Johnstone [sic] penetrates with his Indians, Sir William Howe's detachments co-operating with them, must open the eyes of the deluded, unshackle the constrained, and accomplish your most sanguine wishes without much bloodshed.' For as he had written to Lord Barrington in the summer of 1775, the Americans' plan ought to be to lose a battle every week, till the British army was reduced to nothing: 'it may be discovered that our troops are not invincible, they certainly are not immortal'.[2] Howe's situation, far from home in command of his country's only army, was a characteristic British one. Wellington in the Peninsula was to operate under the constant restraint of knowing that his army was England's last, and that one serious defeat would be the end of his campaigns.

If all had gone as Germain had planned, Howe's reinforcements should have reached him much earlier. But the transport shortage, aggravated by the winter frosts and the stringent priority of saving Canada, had delayed the embarkations. The first to sail had been the Highlanders at the end of April: late, yet in another sense too soon, for a few days later, when it was too late to change their destination, news arrived of the evacuation of Boston eight weeks earlier. Through some neglect by the navy, no warships were left off Boston to meet them, and several transports fell a prey to rebel cruisers. The remainder were dropping in early in July; and on the 12th Lord Howe arrived in the *Eagle* to command the fleet, after a voyage of two months by way of Halifax. Hotham's convoy with the Guards and Hessians sailed from England late enough to be diverted from Boston. The Admiralty had intended to send them to Halifax, but on Germain's suggestion the Commodore had been given latitude to seek the army where he was most likely to find it.[3]

One further contingent remains to be accounted for: the regiments

[1] CO 5/93, p. 228.

[2] Anderson, 90; Sackville, I, 371; CL, Germain, enclosure in Murray's to Germain of 27 Aug. 1776.

[3] Adm. 2/1333, f. 39; G 1859; Adm. 1/310, Hotham's of 5 May 1776.

borrowed from Howe's reinforcements to recover South Carolina. By now they should have completed their mission and joined the main army; but as he had feared, they were still absent from his order of battle. Retarded by its many misfortunes, the expedition had not reached Cape Fear till 2 May. Clinton had been waiting there for eight weeks to assume command; and in that time the situation in the southern colonies had changed rapidly for the worse. The loyalists of North Carolina had risen in February, when the British troops should have been at hand to support them, only to be defeated and scattered, and their leaders imprisoned. In South Carolina, where the back country was even more hostile to the Revolution, the loyalists had been defeated in November, through lack of leadership, by an inferior force of rebel militia; and Clinton at first saw little point in taking Charleston, a difficult operation in itself, since the loyalist strength was in the interior and his amphibious force could not move far from its transports. Georgia was ruled out by the approach of the hot weather. In these circumstances Clinton's first instinct was to call off the operation and move northwards to look for an opening in the Chesapeake till he was needed by Howe.

The despatch which was on its way from Germain gave him the latitude to do this very thing. Unfortunately Clinton had second thoughts before its arrival. Learning that Howe did not expect him in time for the opening of the northern operations, and hoping to achieve some sort of diversion in the south, Clinton changed his mind and decided to attack Sullivan's Island in the approaches to Charleston, where the rebel fortifications were still unfinished. It was planned as a probing attack, with no follow-through unless rapid success seemed certain, so he was not deflected from his purpose by the arrival of Germain's permission to abandon the whole enterprise.[1] On 28 June the squadron engaged the batteries of Fort Moultrie, and the troops landed. But the tidal shoals where they disembarked proved to be unfordable; and after ten hours of costly and ineffective bombardment the fleet retired, with 200 casualties and the loss of a frigate. Three more weeks were wasted with no clear purpose before the expedition sailed to join Howe at the end of July. Germain's chagrin at the affair can be understood.[2]

On 1 August Clinton arrived at Staten Island from Charleston; and on the 12th Hotham brought in the Guards and Hessians. Howe had an army of 25,000 men, 'for its numbers one of the finest that ever was seen'.[3] More

---

[1] CO 5/93, pp. 459, 463, 473.

[2] CL, Germain, 22 Aug., Germain to Burgoyne. Lord Huntingdon told Hutchinson that Clinton had been constantly sea-sick for two months before the attack on Charleston. If this was true, it is not the only occasion on which sea-sickness has caused a British operation to miscarry (Hutchinson, Diaries, II, 177).

[3] Rutland, III, 6.

important to Howe was the arrival of the camp equipment. At last he was satisfied and ready to act. But most of the summer had been wasted, and he no longer expected the campaign to be decisive. He hoped for no more than the capture of Rhode Island and New York, and even Rhode Island would have to wait. The enemy had had time to concentrate their army at New York, and against it Howe would deploy his whole strength.[1]

4. The Clearing of New York

During the long pause at Staten Island, the Howes had made their first overture as Peace Commissioners. They published their powers in a Proclamation which promised pardon and a fair consideration of measures to re-establish lawful government. It was sent to Washington with a covering letter; but since it was addressed to him as a private person and not an American General he refused to receive it. The bearer retaliated by refusing him a copy; and Washington 'expressed some concern at the idea of all communication being at an end, as he was fully convinced how much we had already suffered for want of that free intercourse subsisting among all civilised nations though at war'. The sentiment marks the reluctance even of the rebels to fight without restraints. But whatever Washington's views about protocol, the overture was vain. Ten days earlier the Congress at Philadelphia had approved the Declaration of Independence; and now only victory in battle could pave the way to negotiation.[2]

On 22 August Howe made his landing unopposed on Long Island. The landing craft from England put down 6,000 men on the beaches in the first wave. Commodore Hotham organised the naval side, and his experience was later to be valuable against the French. It was a smooth operation which spoke well for the commanders, troops and equipment.

Washington's plan was to hold the fortified heights of Brooklyn. He took up a covering position to the eastward and prepared for his first battle in the field. His army had good material; but it was raw, unformed and badly officered. At Bunker Hill and Boston it had learnt to rely too much on entrenching. 'The practice we have hitherto been in, of ditching round our enemies, will not always do', John Adams foretold.[3] Washington himself was misled by past success. At Bunker Hill the British had underrated the rebels and tried to teach them the sharp lesson of a frontal attack, and he assumed that they would not try to manoeuvre now. But while General Putnam walked up and down repeating his Bunker Hill injunction not to

---

[1] Sackville, II, 38; CO 5/93, p. 228.
[2] Royal Institution, I, 50; Anderson, 153–5.
[3] Freeman, IV, 141–2.

fire 'until you see the whites of their eyes', the Americans were surprised by a swift and undetected turning movement which sent them flying from their positions.

Howe had begun the game like a skilled tactician. He had inflicted 2,000 casualties at the cost of 300, and driven the Americans back against the East River. He had only to storm the Brooklyn lines to win his decisive victory. The troops were on the point of storming the main redoubt, and Howe thought it would certainly have fallen. But he 'would not risk the loss that might have been sustained in the assault'. His victorious soldiers were stopped in full cry, and set down to attack by siegecraft a ditch three miles long and three or four feet deep, which General Robertson said would not have stopped a foxhunter.[1] It is a puzzling episode, never satisfactorily explained. Stedman and others have suggested that Howe was reluctant to shed American blood; but all the evidence shows that it was British lives he cared for. On the other hand he was soon to prove his willingness to storm entrenchments at Fort Washington. His later statement at the parliamentary enquiry suggests that he thought there was a second shorter set of lines in the rear of the one he faced, to cover the enemy's embarkation and rob the British of their reward for storming. The lines were evidently difficult to reconnoitre, and without full knowledge of the situation one must be cautious of criticising his decision, though many later episodes repeated the pattern. But whatever the truth, the decision was a misfortune. Ground was broken, and regular approaches begun. But while the north wind still barred the East River to British warships, Washington snatched his army away by a swift and silent evacuation.[2]

Thus victory eluded Howe; and on 2 September he reiterated that a second campaign would be needed to kill the rebellion. Yet there was still reason to hope for victory by the end of the year. The enemy had been outmanoeuvred and thrown into confusion; British and Hessian morale was high; and the reception on Long Island was encouraging. This was the real key to success: 'I never had an idea of subduing the Americans', General Robertson was to say; 'I meant to assist the good Americans to subdue the bad.' And the attitude of Long Island promised success. 'The inhabitants received us with the greatest joy', wrote a field officer, 'seeing well the difference between anarchy and a mild regular government.' There was a general belief that the raw rebel army would break up in adversity, and General Lord Percy drew a conclusion: 'Everything seems to be over with them, and I flatter

[1] Hutchinson Diary, II, 260. cf. Mackenzie (89), who wrote two months later that though many thought Howe had missed an opportunity at Brooklyn, his cautious conduct in not risking a check in the first battle was generally approved.

[2] Anderson, 134-40; Howe's *Narrative*, 5, 64.

myself now that this campaign will put a total end to the war.'[1] Perhaps this hope had been the explanation of Howe's conduct before the Brooklyn lines. With the rebel army apparently in his grasp, and the civil population on his side, what need to shed vain blood in an unprepared assault?

While the next assault was prepared, a second and more hopeful attempt was made to negotiate. General Sullivan had been taken on Long Island, and was used as an intermediary. He went to Philadelphia, carrying the impression that the Commissioners had wider powers than Congress believed; and an embassy from Congress, which included Lord Howe's old friend Franklin, met the Commissioners on Staten Island on 11 September. But the meeting confirmed their first impression, that the Howes could not discuss independence or allow Congress to treat on behalf of the colonies; and they replied that America would consider nothing less. Even now military success had not ripened the situation as Germain had hoped.[2]

In the meantime seventeen golden days sped by. From 29 August, when Washington evacuated Brooklyn, till 15 September, the army made no move. Howe always insisted that the time had been spent in necessary preparations; and indeed he was mounting the most difficult of all operations, an opposed landing. He had to cross the wide East River and land a force on the Manhattan shore. The landing craft had first to move round the end of Long Island and up the East River under the enemy's batteries. To stem the strong current a north-flowing tide was needed; to pass the batteries a full night's darkness. The first boats made the passage on 3 September; but conditions were not right again till the 12th or 13th.[3] On the morning of the 15th eighty British guns began to roar; and about one o'clock the first wave of assault craft burst through the drifting smoke and disgorged their infantry on the Manhattan shore above New York.

The defence had been deceived. Only a thin line of musketmen behind a breastwork guarded the beach at Kip's Bay, and their supports would not come up under the warships' fire. They broke and ran in disgraceful panic, with Washington raging vainly to check them. Clinton commanded the first wave; and if he could have thrust two miles across Manhattan to the Hudson, several thousand Americans in New York would have been cut off. But he had no artillery, his orders were to hold a bridgehead for the second wave, and he stood fast on high ground to cover the landing place. Later he felt that a chance had perhaps been missed, though Lord Rawdon thought otherwise. More curious, however, is a staff officer's journal which records that the

[1] Wortley, 82; Hastings, III, 183; Wykeham-Martin, 315; Anderson, 145–6
[2] Anderson, 155–60.
[3] This was Anderson's contention. But Mr Ira Gruber of Duke University informs me that he believes the boats were moving in the intervening period.

escape route was still left open by the dispositions for the night, when Howe rejected his advice to post troops across the road by the Hudson. But Howe he wrote, was 'slow, and not inclined to attend to whatever may be considered as advice, and seemed more intent upon looking out for comfortable quarters for himself . . . '[1]

The landing had been a brilliant success. But before the assault Clinton had shown the misgivings which haunted the British command. He foretold strong resistance and a possible reverse, and later maintained that only the American blunder about the British plan had enabled him to succeed. 'My advice has ever been to avoid even the possibility of a check', he had written that morning. 'We live by victory.'[2] The British superiority was moral, not numerical. Hitherto the Americans had fled before them; raw men, whose military spirit, far from being broken, had not yet been created. In normal warfare risks are justified to exploit success. But the Americans had the resilience of innocence. Reverses quickly intimidated them; but the slightest run of success might transform them into an army. This was indicated the day after the landing. Washington had drawn away to the north and occupied a strong position on Harlem Heights. Two light infantry battalions supported by the Black Watch pressed impetuously forward into a disadvantageous action in front of the advanced posts, and were quickly withdrawn by Clinton on instruction from Howe. To the British it was an outpost skirmish; but the Americans had seen the redcoats' backs, and thought they had won a major success.

Howe entered New York unopposed, and took possession of sixty-seven guns and much abandoned equipment. Then there was another lengthy pause of four weeks. To the north Washington's flanks rested firmly on the Hudson and the Harlem Creek. Howe spent his time in consolidating a base at New York, necessary if his assumption was correct that there would be another campaign. A line of redoubts was formed across Manhattan, and a post at Paulus Hook on the Jersey shore to make the harbour safe. This achieved, the army was free to manoeuvre. The reception at New York had been disappointing, and Howe regarded further progress that year as doubtful. He intended, however, to make a push. His aim was to threaten Washington's communications with Connecticut by an amphibious movement, and manoeuvre him out of his Harlem position. But the tactical requirements of the army and navy diverged, and there was much discussion before a plan was agreed. At last it was settled that a landing should be made on an isthmus called Throg's Neck in the East River behind the American lines. The boats, skilfully

[1] Anderson, 169–79; Hastings, III, 184; Mackenzie, 49–50.
[2] Willcox (ed.), *American Rebellion*, 46, n. 12. See a similar sentiment in Hastings, III, 186.

manoeuvred by the navy, moved through Hell's Gate in a dense fog and the landing was made. But failing to surprise the Americans and seize the exit from the Neck, the troops were re-embarked and landed again a mile to the north- ward, on which they thrust six miles inland to New Rochelle. There had never been much doubt that Washington could slip away, but the aim of the opera- tion was achieved. The rebels were forced out of their entrenchments, and once more the armies were in the open field.

Washington, however, had learnt his lesson on Long Island. He had had enough of pitched battles for the moment: 'We should on all occasions avoid a general action, or put (sic) anything to the risk, unless compelled by a necessity into which we ought never to be drawn'.[1] This resolution, flexibly interpreted, became the foundation of his strategy. It did nevertheless present him with a difficult choice. He could slip away into the mountains higher up the Hudson, and be safe for a considerable time from pursuit. But he wished also to prevent a penetration of the lower Hudson, in order to protect his lateral communications between Connecticut and New Jersey. He had blocked the river at the northern end of Manhattan with a line of sunken hulks, commanded by the fire of Fort Lee on the Jersey shore and Fort Washington on Manhattan. He had left garrisons to hold them when he retreated, and took up a position at White Plains to remain in supporting distance. His flanks were secured by a river and a marsh, and his numbers were about equal to Howe's. Howe promptly seized a height which dominated the American right flank. But instead of pressing his success at once, he began to construct batteries which would sweep the American position, and prepared for a general assault on 31 October. Rain postponed the attack for twenty-four hours, and during the night Washington was able to evacuate his position and slip away to a stronger one in his rear. Without accurate maps, Howe had to feel his way into the country to the north. He was convinced that Washington did not intend to stand and fight, and that there was no point in continuing to push him northwards. On the night of 4 November he decamped and fell back south- west to the Hudson. And on the 16th he stormed Fort Washington.

When the British army marched away from his front, Washington had divided his force to meet the various dangers which its movement suggested. He left 7,000 men under Lee in his present area; sent 5,000 into New Jersey to guard against a thrust at Philadelphia; and posted 4,000 up the Hudson at Peekskill to guard the entrance to the Highlands. This dispersion meant weakness everywhere; yet 3,000 men still lay locked up in Fort Washington, at the gates of New York. Between these four packets of troops lay the British army. Washington considered abandoning Fort Washington. Its usefulness was in doubt, for British frigates had forced the barrier of hulks

[1] Freeman, IV, 217.

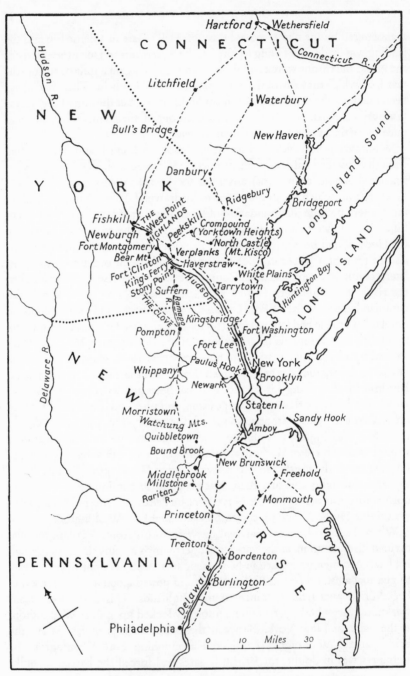

THE LOWER HUDSON VALLEY AND NEW JERSEY

which it protected, and passed up the Hudson. But he was overpersuaded by the advice of Greene, the preference of Congress, and the confidence of the garrison's commander. He believed until it was too late that the garrison could be withdrawn across the river at any time. Howe's preparations were thorough and unhurried. No memory of Bunker Hill deterred him. No misdirected leniency deflected the blow. British and Hessians stormed through the outworks, and the inner fort surrendered. For 440 casualties Howe had taken a fortress which the Americans believed impregnable. Three thousand prisoners fell into his hands. There and in Fort Lee, which the enemy precipitately abandoned, he took 146 cannon, 12,000 shot and shell, 2,800 muskets, 400,000 rounds of ball; tents, entrenching tools, and a mass of other equipment. The material and moral loss to the rebels was immense.

From Fort Lee a corps under Cornwallis drove forward into New Jersey. Washington summoned Lee from White Plains to his help; but the response was slow, and to save his army he could do nothing but fall back. Cornwallis raced forward to the Raritan, where his half-starved troops found the bridges broken. Here he stopped as he had been ordered, seeing no prospect of catching Washington. But Howe joined him at New Brunswick on 6 December and resumed the advance. At Princeton he was only an hour behind Washington; but here he halted for seventeen hours, and reached the Delaware just as the last American boat grounded on the further bank. The pursuit was over. Washington had swept up every boat, and Pennsylvania remained inviolate behind the river.

In the meantime another corps under Clinton had taken Rhode Island, which was occupied without opposition at the beginning of December. The harbour there was wanted by the Admiral, for the ice-bound rivers of New York offered no shelter to his larger ships in the winter. Rhode Island had a deep and defensible harbour for the fleet; and with the anchorage at Gardiner's Bay on the eastern end of Long Island it could close the seaward end of Long Island Sound and bottle up all the shipping of Connecticut.

5. The Arrested Offensive

So ended Howe's advance, far beyond New York, yet on the Delaware instead of the Upper Hudson. The direction of Washington's retreat caused some comment, for he had been expected to take refuge in New England. If his army survived the winter, its position to the south-west might cramp the British plan to crush New England when the campaign was resumed. But in any case a British junction on the Hudson was still far off. For while Howe had turned away to the southward, the northern army of Carleton had closed its operations without unlocking the northern gates of the rebel colonies.

Carleton had proved a cool and resolute commander in adversity; but he had still to prove his vigour in exploiting advantage. When the relieving ships reached Quebec at the beginning of May, the garrison already outnumbered the diseased and starving rabble which beleaguered it. Carleton sallied forth from the walls when the relief appeared, and the Americans abandoned their stores and fled. He did not press them far, for he knew that the main reinforcement under Burgoyne was on the way. At Sorel the Americans were met by a strong reinforcement; and with the quick recovery of the offensive spirit they so often showed after extreme adversity, they rallied and counter-attacked. Blundering forward through forest and swamp against, as they supposed, 800 regulars and Canadians, they ran into the main body of Burgoyne's force. Repulsed, pursued, and cut off by river-borne forces, they lost a general and four hundred men. The demoralisation of the American army in Canada was complete. Starving, ravaged by smallpox, their reinforcements cut to pieces, they fled for the frontier.

Carleton now had the 10,000 men for which he had asked; and the arrival of the second Brunswick contingent in the middle of September was to bring his force to nearly 13,000. He had wanted the troops in order to drive into New England, and there were high expectations at home of what he might achieve.

The British fleet was at Sorel within an hour of the last rebel's departure up the Richelieu. The wind was favourable, and had Carleton pressed on up the St Lawrence to Longueuil, opposite Montreal, it was suggested that he might have marched across the neck of land to the Richelieu and cut off the enemy. There would then have been nothing to oppose him on the Lakes. But instead he halted at Sorel to organise a body to advance up the Richelieu, and before the rest of his force reached Longueuil the wind in the St Lawrence changed and checked them. The moment was lost, and Arnold and the survivors of the American army escaped to fight again.[1]

It was now necessary to fight for the Lakes. Long weeks had to be spent in dragging past the Richelieu rapids the prefabricated sections of gunboats from England, and heavier ships which had been dismantled for the portage.

Carleton had sent home a naval lieutenant at the time of the American invasion, to ask Germain for the means of crossing Lake Champlain. He wanted boats, materials and artificers. But all he received were the fourteen gunboats, capable of carrying one gun apiece, and ten 'flat-bottomed boats', the landing craft of the period, Artificers were sent, but few and late. There

[1] A. L. Burt suggests that even though Carleton had lost the wind for Longueuil, he could have marched across the peninsula from Varennes to cut off the Americans. He believes that Carleton deliberately refrained from pressing the enemy to avoid pushing the 'deluded people of the colonies' over the brink into irreconcilable war.

can be little question that Germain had done what he could. The pressure on the dockyards and skilled labour during the winter must have made it almost impossible to conjure up a lake fleet and ship it to Canada. And Howe had the first claim on amphibious equipment, just as Carleton had had priority of reinforcements. The Atlantic army had no useful foothold in America, and the large fleet of landing craft which Howe was sent was essential if he was to force a landing at New York. But in consequence Carleton's difficulties were severe. The resources of Canada had been won back; but it had been impossible to make any preparations while he was besieged in Quebec, and now the country had been swept of much that was useful by the rebels. He had not a boat for the Lakes, except the few from England and twenty-five longboats borrowed from the transports. There were no materials or workmen ready to build more. Amid the confusion of an exhausted province he had to assemble axemen and fell the timber for his shipyards.[1]

Delay was inevitable. Yet there were those who felt that Carleton settled down too stoically to build his fleet, and without regard to the urgency of the situation or the enemy's difficulties. So desperate were the Americans that at the beginning of July a conference at Ticonderoga almost resolved to abandon the frontier and withdraw to Albany. Only Arnold prevented it. There were two sloops and two schooners on Lake Champlain; and he argued that if they disputed Carleton's passage the British would lose the rest of the year in building a fleet. He was given command of the flotilla; and under immense difficulties he began to build an auxiliary fleet to support it.

Carleton did nothing to reconnoitre or harass the enemy's preparations. The troops lay in cantonments, the Indians were sent home till the spring, and during the whole period of ship-building the only military operation was an ambush by four soldiers and six Indians. Not even a reconnaissance party seems to have been sent to see what the rebels were doing. A staff officer painted a curious picture of Carleton at this time, and although, for reasons which will appear, he was violently hostile to the General, it may have some semblance of truth.[2] Absorbed within himself, saying little and giving answers to few, Carleton followed a plan which none could grasp; handling every detail himself; spreading confusion and embarrassment.

A dozen gunboats and 560 flat-bottomed boats were built on the Lake, and 120 more flat-bottomed boats in other parts of Canada. But something more

[1] Carleton described his difficulties to Germain in CO 42/36, ff. 99–103.

[2] Sackville, II, 45–6. For the writer, Colonel Christie, see below, p. 105. Carleton's reserve is confirmed by another officer (Valentine, 184).

formidable than this was needed to blast aside the fleet which Arnold was gathering. By the end of August when Carleton returned from re-establishing civil government at Quebec, he had assembled a capital fleet of two schooners of twelve and fourteen guns, which had been taken apart and carried past the Richelieu rapids; a huge radeau with sixteen heavy guns; and a six-gun 'gondola' captured from the rebels: altogether forty-eight guns, with another twenty-four in the gunboats.[1] The fleet was manned by 700 officers and men from the warships and transports at Quebec. But still Carleton was not satisfied. A square-rigged three-master called the *Inflexible* mounting eighteen guns was knocked down and brought up from the St Lawrence. In twenty-eight days from the relaying of her keel she was ready. It was a remarkable feat, but the time lost was fatal.

Early in October the fleet put out on the Lake and felt its way cautiously southwards. On the 11th it met the enemy, lying in wait behind Valcour Island. Arnold had three eight-gun schooners, a ten-gun sloop, three galleys and a number of gondolas. Carleton's fleet could discharge almost twice the weight of metal, and the result of the battle was certain. Without bringing his radeau and gondola into action, Carleton won a crushing victory. Arnold abandoned Crown Point and the way to Ticonderoga was open.

But now the weather broke. Ticonderoga lay in the army's path, formidable in appearance with its fortifications strengthened by Kosciousko; and the cruel northern winter was coming on. Yet the fort was held by defeated men, so demoralised that a British party drove off 150 head of cattle under their eyes. General Phillips and other officers thought it was worth while to push forward and try to frighten the enemy out of the fort. But there was 'neither reconnoitring post nor scout sent forward, but as the whim of a drunken Indian prevails'. Instead, even Crown Point was abandoned. Its barracks had been burnt and its defences were crumbling; and deciding that it was too late in the year to fortify it or provide winter shelter for a garrison, Carleton withdrew his advanced force to the bottom of the Lake. The army dispersed into winter quarters in Canada. So much had Arnold's show of a fleet accomplished. 'If we could have begun our last expedition four weeks earlier', the Brunswick General Riedesel was to write in 1777, 'I am satisfied that everything would have ended this year.' Four weeks was exactly the time it had taken to build the *Inflexible*.[2]

[1] CO 42/35, f. 176; James, *The British Navy in Adversity*, 429.
[2] Ward, *The War of the Revolution*, 385, 393, 473; Riedesel, Memoirs, I, 79–83; Hutchinson Diaries, II, 117; Fonblanque, *Burgoyne*, 218 (quoting General Phillips) Jane Clark has used letters from Burgoyne in CL, Clinton (Canadian Historical Review, 1929). The most unfavourable interpretation of Carleton's conduct of the campaign is to be found in a ministerial précis in CO 5/253, ff. 21–30.

6. Gains and Losses: The Failure of the Blockade

When Carleton closed his operations, he had done no more than press the enemy back to the point from which they had launched their offensive, and the northern advance to the Hudson had still to begin. At that time Howe's southern army was still flailing the enemy; and by the middle of December resounding successes had been won. Washington's army had been hustled, shaken, thinned by casualties and desertions, and at last driven back almost to the doors of Congress. During the pursuit across New Jersey the Howes issued a fresh proclamation promising pardon for submission within sixty days. The effect was striking. All New Jersey appeared to submit or intend to, and many important Pennsylvanians came in. The Middle Colonies seemed on the point of collapse; and the next effort promised success against New England. At New York and Rhode Island firm bases were held for thrusts against the heart of the rebellion. Only Washington's position to the southward was unexpected; but his soldiers' time would expire at the New Year, and his army was not likely to remain much longer in being.

The position which the British had acquired at New York was to dominate the strategy of the American campaigns to their end. To the British army it was of course a heavy defensive liability, for though Manhattan island was defensible against assault if the Harlem heights were fortified and the surrounding waters commanded by the navy, the town and harbour could soon be made unusable and local supplies cut off unless a larger area was controlled. Long Island, Staten Island, and Paulus Hook on the Jersey shore had therefore to be held. The safety and mutual support of all these posts depended on commanding the intervening waters, and the freezing of the river or the appearance of a hostile fleet could place them in peril.

Nevertheless the possession of New York was a great strategic asset. Militarily it was the only vital city in the rebel colonies, for it dominated the communications. The bight of sea at whose apex it stands channelled the direct roads between New England and the Middle Colonies into a coastal defile. Its possession gave the British army an interior position, and pushed Washington's lateral communications back to the Hudson crossing at King's Ferry between Stony Point and Verplanck's Point, some thirty miles north of the British lines. Thus a body of American troops marching from Princeton towards lower Connecticut had to make a long detour behind the Watchung Mountains to Pompton, proceeding thence by the Ramapo Valley to Suffern and Haverstraw. The Stony Point crossing was guarded by two forts, but if these were taken and the crossing severed, the American communications would be pushed back behind the Highlands to the crossing near Fishkill. To reach the Fishkill crossing at Newburgh meant leaving the

Stony Point road at Pompton or Suffern and marching by a road constructed during the war through the deep upper valley of the Ramapo called 'the Clove' to pass to the west and rear of the Highlands.[1]

As the war developed, Washington's normal posts astride the Hudson from which his army watched New York were at White Plains on the east side of the river, and on the west some strong position such as Morristown or Middlebrook in northern New Jersey. But since the British could sail up the Lower Hudson at any time, his main depots were collected at Fishkill behind the barrier of the Highlands. The importance of the Highlands, already appreciated by the rebels, was driven home to them by the events of 1776, and in May 1777 Nathanael Greene and three brigadiers made a further examination of the fortifications and reported that if the river at Fort Montgomery could be obstructed by a boom and covered by row-galleys and batteries, it would be impossible for shipping to penetrate. They were confident that the British would not attempt to operate by land owing to the difficulty of the passes.[2] The forts and batteries guarding the Highlands became the key to the rebel's position, as New York was to that of the British. They were sited first at Fort Montgomery near the present Bear Mountain bridge, and later further up the river at West Point, where a sharp bend in the river covered the chain-boom. The validity of the British plan to penetrate the Hudson valley is confirmed by the concern of the Americans from the outset, and their rage after several years of war when Arnold attempted to betray the West Point position.

The most serious failure of the year had been at sea. Much depended on denying munitions from Europe to the rebels. But hitherto the navy's achievement had been disappointing. Though the fleet exercised unchallenged command of American waters, cargoes continued to run the blockade from the Bay of Biscay and the neutral ports of the West Indies. Thus the rebel armies were equipped with the arms and munitions they could not

[1] In detail, the three chief routes between New Jersey and Connecticut were:
  (i) The main peacetime road, roughly the present U.S. Route I: Trenton – Princeton – New York – Kingsbridge – New Rochelle – New Haven, where the road to Providence diverged from that to Hartford – Springfield – Boston
  (ii) The upper road by the Stony Point crossing: Princeton – Millstone (then called Somerset Court House) – Whippany – Pompton – Ramapo Valley to Suffern – Stony Point – Verplanck's Point – Northcastle (the present Mt Kisco) – Ridgebury – Waterbury – Farmington – Hartford. This (in reverse) was Rochambeau's route from Rhode Island to Yorktown in 1781.
  (iii) The Fishkill crossing: Princeton . . . Pompton – The Clove – Newburgh – Fishkill crossing – Fishkill – Bulls Bridge – Litchfield – Farmington – Hartford.
[2] Harvard, Sparks MSS. 52, Vol. III.

produce in sufficient quantities at home; and American shipping continued to export the goods to pay for them. Nine-tenths of the powder available to the rebels up to the end of 1777 was imported by sea.[1] If these supplies had been stopped, the rebellion would have withered away.

Was it negligence or design which caused the failure? When England next fought America she imposed a complete blockade, and in 1813 American shipping scarcely moved. The contrast is no mystery: it was partly a matter of sufficient ships, partly of the demands of General Howe's army. In 1813 England had a vast fleet in commission, with a full complement of cruisers swelled by twenty years of war and eight of unchallenged supremacy. She had only to redeploy a part of this force on the American coast to bring American trade to an end. The foreign terminals of that trade were already closed: France was under rigorous blockade, Spain had been wrested from the Bonapartes, the West Indian islands were throttled or in British hands. In December 1813 the Caribbean stations had thirty-eight warships; and on the American station were a dozen ships of the line and fifty-six cruisers.[2]

Contrast the situation in 1776. The navy had been on a peace establishment with a low proportion of cruisers. The ports of Europe and the West Indies were open to the rebels, and there were only ten British warships in the Caribbean. In July 1775 when only New England was in armed rebellion, Palliser calculated that fifty warships were needed on the American station: at that moment there were only thirty-three, and the rebellion was spreading fast. With these Admiral Graves had to secure the army's movements and supply-lines against a swarm of privateers; to support military operations; and to search for local provisions for the troops. There was little to spare for commerce-destruction. Nor, however, did Graves satisfy the army. He failed it at Bunker Hill; he showed little energy in finding supplies; he did not squeeze the rebels as he might. Sandwich warned him against quarrelling with General Gage, and of the complaints coming in of his lackadaisical delicacy towards the rebels. At last in September 1775 the First Lord yielded to pressure at home and recalled him.[3]

Graves resented his disgrace. He refused the command at Plymouth in 1777, and signed the memorial against the trial of Admiral Keppel. Though he had shown little energy, there was some substance in his complaint of lack of ships. 'Judge', he exhorted Sandwich two years later,[4] 'if the small leaky half-manned squadron under my command did not as effectively

[1] A calculation by O. W. Stephenson in *Amer. Hist. Rev.*, XXX.
[2] Adm. 8/100; Adm. 1/505, ff. 320-2.
[3] Sandwich, I, 60, 64-7, 73-4; II, 233; Abergavenny, 11.
[4] Williams Transcripts, 22 Sept. 1777, Graves to Sandwich.

serve their country and protect the trade as the numerous and well-appointed squadrons have done since I left America.'

Here was a charge against Shuldham and Howe. By May 1776 there were fifty-nine substantial warships on the station, besides eight small brigs and schooners. Yet not only did the Americans continue to sail: half a battalion of Highlanders fell to them off Boston because no cruisers were there to meet them. Yet Shuldham's apparent strength was deceptive. Of his fifty-nine ships, fifteen were on Atlantic convoy-duty or under orders for home, and eight with the Charleston expedition; while of the remaining thirty-six stationed between Quebec and Florida, two were in the St Lawrence and others with the army at Halifax. After Lord Howe's arrival the needs of the army expanded. The flotilla on the Canadian lakes had to be manned. The great army in the Atlantic called endlessly for help as it shifted from Boston to Halifax, from Halifax to New York; as it crept from island to island at the mouth of the Hudson; as it spread its tentacles to New Jersey and Rhode Island. On the eve of the landing on Long Island, twenty-three ships were concentrated off New York to support the army. Ten more were in the St Lawrence, and three were coming up from South Carolina with Sir Peter Parker. This made a total of thirty-six warships engaged in supporting the army; and others were needed to take home the empty supply ships. Only nine ships remained to blockade the innumerable ports between Halifax and the eastern end of Long Island, compared with twenty-nine in 1814. To the southward, watching the Delaware, the Chesapeake, and the Carolinas, were six cruisers of fourteen guns and upwards, and two eight-gun brigs; and four more were protecting East Florida and Bermuda. This compares with sixty-eight ships between Rhode Island and New Orleans in 1814. And this slender chain of cruisers had many difficulties. Off New England summer fogs and winter storms interrupted the watch, and the numerous exits from Boston were difficult to seal. To the southward there were no bases, and the cruisers had to quit their stations and return to New York for water, requiring a regular succession of wasteful reliefs. In spite of these handicaps, an incomplete return of prizes taken between March and December shows 140 American vessels taken and twenty-six British recovered. These figures were substantial, but they were not decisive.[1]

The burden of supporting the army was reduced in the winter, when New York had been taken and land operations were over. In March 1777 there were twenty-six ships on the coasts of New England and Nova Scotia.[2] 'Prizes are now brought in on every side', a letter to William Eden reported

[1] Adm. 1/487, ff. 24, 55, 86–7, 104, 211, 254, 325, 338, 382, 401. The problem of blockading Boston was never satisfactorily solved in the war of 1812.

[2] Compared with fifteen in April 1814 (Adm. 1/506, f. 44).

in the New Year; 'for since the island Manhattan was all cleared and our troops began to act in Jersey all the men of war were sent out: the long stay of the ships in this harbour gave great openings to growlers, who would not consider the good effects resulting from the good agreement and co-operation of the two services.'[1] The growlers must certainly have included naval officers. For there was a feeling in the service that Lord Howe's co-operation with his brother showed a devotion altogether excessive, and educated the army to expect too much. Admiral Gambier was to complain in the winter of 1778-9 that the Generals demanded protection and help for every trifling movement; and in 1781 Thomas Graves lamented that it had never been possible to wean the army of this habit contracted in the time of Lord Howe.[2]

Perhaps it was really impossible to combine major land operations with successful blockade. And yet a certain doubt persists. For there were many at home who attributed the failure of the blockade to lukewarm officers. Germain was among them, exasperated at the loss of the Highlanders off Boston, the prolonged neglect of Dartmouth's orders to blockade the Delaware, and the removal of the two cruisers which were eventually sent there.[3] Lord Howe seemed so reluctant to distress the rebels, so lenient towards their trade. There was a story in circulation that he had been asked for letters of marque against the small rebel craft plying between the Carolinas and the French West Indies, and replied with heat: 'Good God! Will you never have done with teazing me? will you leave no room for reconciliation?' It might, as he claimed, be wisdom to let the Americans use their fishing boats, for fear of driving the fishermen into the privateers for a living. Yet his instructions when he sent Commodore Hotham to blockade the southern colonies in December 1776 suggest a deliberate leniency with a political motive. His captains were 'to . . . cultivate all amicable correspondence . . . and to grant them every other indulgence which the necessary restrictions on their trade will admit, in order to conciliate their friendly dispositions and detach them from the prejudices they have imbibed'. *Necessary restrictions on their trade*: it is not the strict meaning of the words which makes one pause, but the whole tone of the instruction. Its ambivalence may have been political wisdom; but it was unlikely to indoctrinate the captains with the idea of relentlessly suppressing the rebels' means of continuing the struggle. 'Lord Howe', Germain was to write ironically in June

[1] Add. MSS. 34413, f. 152.

[2] Williams Transcripts; Sandwich, IV, 177. To the cynical the navy's motive for preferring commerce-destruction to military operations was not far to seek, and it was suggested that they preferred to let a few rebel ships through the net 'to encourage others to risk their property on the ocean' (Verulam, 129).

[3] CL, Germain, 22 Aug. 1776 to Howe; CO 5/254, f. 44.

1777, 'is the most disinterested man I know, in permitting the trade of Charleston to be carry'd on without interruption, when he might avail himself of so many rich prizes.'[1]

The balance between conciliation and coercion was not easy to strike. In this and every respect a limited war was being waged: limited by the nature of its object, by sentiments of race and language, and by the size of the forces which Britain could raise and deploy. The factor which above all had caused the first campaign to fall short was the length of the Atlantic communications and the transport problem to which it gave rise. Delays in fitting out followed by bad weather at sea had caused the design against the Carolinas to misfire so completely; the shipping shortage had postponed the evacuation of Boston and then caused it to take place in the most disadvantageous manner; the miscarriage of supplies had delayed Howe at Halifax. It was the shipping shortage which had retarded Howe's reinforcements from Europe, further delaying his offensive. It was very probably the pressure on the dockyards which had prevented Carleton from being supplied early and adequately with the means of commanding Lake Champlain. Perhaps the influence of the ocean was never again to appear in so visible a form during the course of the war. But always the cold wastes of the Atlantic were to exert their invisible stranglehold on the British operations.

[1] Sackville, II, 68; Anderson, 133-4, 313; G 2072; Knox, 131. In 1779 Germain felt that Commodore Collier had done more to destroy rebel shipping with his small force than his predecessors with their great fleets (CL, Germain, 27 Sept. 1779 to Clinton).

CHAPTER V

THE PLANNING OF SARATOGA

1. *A Need for Victory*

As the New Year dawned on 1777 Germain could look back with pride on his first year in office. Large armies had been conjured from nothing, wafted across the Atlantic, and maintained there. Canada had been cleared of the enemy. New York had been secured. The last despatches to arrive in 1776 told of Cornwallis's victorious advance across New Jersey, and of Clinton's departure to take Rhode Island, which Germain regarded[1] as vital for the future in war and peace. Nevertheless the campaign had not been decisive. The swift and overwhelming blow which Germain had designed had all but crushed the rebellion; but still a further effort was needed.

To deploy so much of England's resources beyond the ocean had been a bold but calculated risk. Against the danger of a French attack had been weighed the advantage of overcoming the American rebellion before Europe could intervene. The more cautious policy of insuring at home might well in the long run prove the less safe. But time was vital. And in the course of 1776 France had made it clear how much would turn on a speedy solution in America.

The magnitude of the British effort had encouraged rather than checked the hopes of the French. In the Cabinet only Turgot opposed preparations for war. To him it was internal reform which mattered; and ten years later many had cause to regret that he had lost the debate. He believed that the whole colonial system was doomed by the American example, and that the colonies of France herself were no longer worth a war to defend. For him the real danger was that England would collect the profits of the new economic system which would replace the restrictive colonial one; and the cost of armaments might make internal reform for ever impossible and prevent France from collecting the fruits of peace.[2] His views were parallelled by the most far-sighted opinion in England; but they were shrugged off as a narrow focussing on internal affairs. The great game of foreign policy carried the day. Whether America were freed or subjected, said Vergennes, the prospect for France was equally dangerous, and she must arm. The Ministers of Marine

---

[1] Sackville, II, 43.

[2] Turgot, Œuvres, V: 'Réflexions . . . suite de la querelle entre la Grande-Bretagne et ses colonies.'

and War supported him; and Sartine, the Minister of War, looked forward openly to an offensive war.

Vergennes' reasoning was strengthened by the English parliamentary debates of March 1776. Member after member exhorted the Ministry to beware of France and not to strip the British Isles of their defences. The chargé d'affairs in London painted the picture of a government slothful yet imprudent; pacific, yet, in its weakness, at the mercy of the actions of bellicose generals and admirals. The French Ministry resolved to give immediate assistance to the rebels, and to begin arming the navy. Unofficial relations were established with the Americans. Silas Deane arrived in Paris, armed with congressional warnings to avoid the pleasures of the great city. Money was advanced for munitions, and technical advice made available. From Nantes the first trickle of supplies began to cross the Atlantic, and young officers of noble family – Lafayette, Noailles, Ségur – embarked as volunteers in the cause of liberty. In the naval bases the replenishing of storehouses and refitting of ships went forward. Twelve sail of the line were to be kept ready for manning in Brest; and since the port would probably be blockaded in the event of war, a squadron of eight was commissioned in the Mediterranean, to intervene wherever it might be needed. Thus, two years before the breach with England the strategic stroke of April 1778 was planned.

Much of this was known in England. From the Paris Embassy, the British Minister in Brussels, and a continental intelligence centre in Amsterdam, a stream of accurate information arrived to be digested by William Eden's bureau. And there was a more remarkable source. For William Bancroft, the secretary and confidant of the American Commissioners in Paris, was a British spy.[1]

During the summer of 1776 Vergennes was feeling his way towards war; wary of the dangers, fending off his bellicose rival Choiseul, yet sure that France faced a great opportunity. In August he presented the case for war to a Cabinet committee and passed it on to Madrid. Yet all depended on what was happening in America. 'From the indications of the present campaign', wrote the Spanish Prime Minister, 'we shall discover how far one can count on American resistance if the war continues.' About the same time Lord George Germain warned the Spanish Ambassador that though the Declaration of Independence might encourage other powers to make treaties with the United States, he expected news which would change their tone.[2]

[1] There is much material about intelligence in the Auckland Papers (British Museum). See also *Amer. Hist. Rev.*, XXIX (S. F. Bemis, 'British Secret Service and the Franco-American Alliance'). For Bancroft, who was a double-spy, see *William and Mary Quarterly*, 1959 (Julian P. Boyd, 'Silas Deane: Death by a kindly teacher of treason').
[2] Doniol, I, 579, 586.

Lord North, depressed by Howe's delay to wait for reinforcements, did not share Germain's optimism, an attitude which deprived his opposition to naval rearmament of its most solid justification. But the news from Long Island came as Germain had promised. The Brooklyn victory created a general contempt for the Americans; and Germain was right when he wrote to Howe on the news of the battle that great success in his operations would be the country's best security against France and Spain. Vergennes drew back. Now he talked of the financial need for peace, and argued with a strange ignorance of maritime possibilities that a safe winter base at New York made the British less dangerous than if they had been seeking an asylum on the seas. 'Rien ne presse plus en effet', he declared. Thus England's victory in America held her enemies in check.[1]

2. Germain and the Generals

The despatches which told of Cornwallis's swift advance into New Jersey arrived on 30 December, and were followed by the expected news that Rhode Island had fallen. Germain could feel that Howe had finished his campaign honourably and gloriously. He did not share the view that he had been too cautious. For though the Americans had not stood against the King's troops in the open, their skill at entrenching called for uncommon ability to keep the casualties low, and Howe had 'infinite merit in that particular'. Germain's only reservation about the campaign concerned the offer of pardon, which seemed to him to offer indemnity for rebellion and oblivion for loyalty. 'A sentimental manner of making war', he called it in private. But in the military sphere he had given Howe a free hand in the last campaign, and saw no cause to interfere with his plans for the next.[2]

Very different were his feelings towards Carleton. The mutual antipathy at which Walpole hints had been increased by an incident at the beginning of the year. When the reinforcement for Canada was mounted early in 1776, Germain had named his friend Colonel Christie as Quartermaster-General of the force. But before the force was sent, Carleton had asked that his own brother should be appointed; and Horace Walpole described the choice of Christie as a signal affront to the Governor. He called him obscure and a Scot (two decisive disqualifications in Walpole's eyes); yet Christie was a competent officer who later rose to be a Major-General, and the choice had Amherst's approval. At the time of the appointment it was still possible that Quebec had fallen; and Germain argued that the experience of Christie, who knew Canada intimately, would be needed by the force sent for its recapture.

[1] Doniol, I, 610–20, 680–8; Add. MSS. 37833, f. 32; Sackville, II, 42.
[2] Knox, 128; Add. MSS. 34413, f. 2.

On Christie's arrival he found that Carleton had already appointed his brother, an appointment which Germain confirmed in due course. In the meantime Christie, who had incurred Carleton's hostility in the past by signing a petition against the Quebec Act, had been packed off up country and subjected to such ill-treatment that he had to be recalled, and returned to England with no favourable account of Carleton's management of supply and transport. Carleton was certainly intemperate in his quarrels. In 1777 he broke with his Chief Engineer, who appealed to Germain for leave to come home, alleging that the service was being mangled and his suggestions dismissed as impertinences.[1]

Perhaps with the treatment of Christie in mind, Germain opposed the award of a red ribband to Carleton. And in June, after congratulating him on the defence of Quebec, he lamented that he had said nothing in his despatches of the enemy's force, the attitude of the Canadians, or his own intentions, which made it impossible to send him any instructions. Carleton replied with asperity that he could have only one great object, the expulsion of the rebels, which was done long before he could profit by any instructions with which Germain might think it necessary to favour him; and in retaliation he complained that he had not been sent the boats and materials he had demanded for the next phase of his operations, the crossing of the lakes.[2] Neither the manner nor the content of this letter was warranted. 'Expelling the rebels' was not a sufficient object to assume in a commander who had asked for his reinforcement with the intention of invading the rebel colonies; nor a clarification of the Canadians' attitude unreasonable to ask of a Governor who was indirectly known to have reversed his earlier assessment; nor information about the enemy superfluous when he intended to advance on a line which would carry him into the rear of the rebels facing Sir William Howe.

It will be remembered that since Carleton was not a member of the Peace Commission, Germain had not intended him to command the troops which would cross the frontier[3]; and in August 1776 he ordered him to return to Quebec and leave the pursuit to Burgoyne. He softened the blow by stressing the importance of Carleton's civil task of restoring peace and order after the rebel invasion; an argument supported by the Law Officers' opinion that he ought not, as Governor, to advance beyond the borders of his province. By the same ship Germain wrote privately to Burgoyne, referring in un-

[1] CL, Germain, 23 Aug. 1776, to Burgoyne; 11 Sept. 1777, from Gordon; Add. MSS. 38210, f. 8; Sackville, II, 45; Walpole, *Last Journals*, II, 21, 61; Burt, *Canadian Hist. Rev.*, 1930.
[2] CO 42/35, ff. 40, 171-2.
[3] Above, p. 76.

friendly terms to Carleton's treatment of Christie and his hesitation about using Indians.[1]

The officer carrying these letters failed to get up the St Lawrence before it froze, and Carleton continued to lead the frontier operations. At the beginning of December Burgoyne arrived to spend the winter in England, bringing amongst other letters Carleton's insolent reply to Germain's remonstrance. It naturally increased Germain's hostility, and he began to agitate for the Governor's recall. This the King refused, for there was no mistaking the American Secretary's rancour. He warned Lord North to expect an attack on Carleton at the next Cabinet dinner, and advised him to play for time till all the Cabinet were in London. Nevertheless both the King and the Prime Minister shared some of Germain's dissatisfaction. The information available suggested that only Carleton's slowness had prevented the frontier of New England from being burst open. Instead, Lake Champlain would have to be crossed a second time, and Ticonderoga still stood intact in the invaders' path. There was a general clamour at the withdrawal from Lake Champlain, and one M.P. commented that it was not conceivable that Carleton should be relied on to conduct the operations of the next campaign. Even North wondered at the delay in embarking on the Lake; and on learning that Carleton had closed his campaign by abandoning Crown Point, the King agreed that he had not been sufficiently warm and active, and that a more enterprising officer should lead the thrust to the Hudson.[2]

The obvious choice was Burgoyne. Not only was he at hand; he knew Canada, and claimed to have opposed the evacuation of Crown Point. Burgoyne had had a curious career, His father was a baronet's son who had died a debtor in the rules of the King's Bench. As a young officer Burgoyne had eloped with a school friend's sister, the daughter of the Earl of Derby. Finding that two could not make ends meet where one had failed, he sold his commission in 1747 and retired for seven years to the continent till Lord Derby forgave him. In 1756 at the age of thirty-four he was re-gazetted in the army as a junior captain, an almost unprecedented favour probably engineered by the Derby influence; and after seeing service in the raids on Cherbourg and St Malo he was favoured again with a commission to raise the Sixteenth Light Dragoons. When war broke out with Spain his regiment was sent to serve with the army defending Portugal against the French and Spaniards. Burgoyne, now acting as brigadier, distinguished himself by a daring regimental exploit, the raid on Valencia d'Alcantara, where he surprised and destroyed a Spanish regiment. His only other notable experience was the direction of a raid on Vilha Velha which was executed by Washington's

[1] Sackville, II, 39; G 1930; CL, Germain, 22 Aug. 1776 to Carleton; Fonblanque, 227.
[2] Hastings, III, 189; G 1930, 1936 1938.

future second in command, Colonel Lee. In temperament, experience and interest Burgoyne was a light cavalryman.

The war over, he returned to England. He had not done badly for himself. On the strength of two or three coastal raids and some skirmishing in Spain, he had risen in six years from junior captain to brigadier, with the command of a regiment to line his pockets. He and his regiment were favourites of the King, whose intervention may have saved the Sixteenth from being disbanded at the peace. Their Colonel continued to flourish. The lucrative governorship of Fort William fell to him in 1768, a sinecure rarely held by an officer below the rank of general. With this and the fortune which his wife inherited about the same time, he could give rein to his expensive tastes. Acting and playwriting kept him amused, and politics and the society of Charles Fox employed his money. In 1769 he barely escaped imprisonment for inciting his supporters to violence in a contested election.

Burgoyne had many of the qualities of a good regimental commander and leader of men. But merit alone was not enough to explain his success. He had pushed the claims of family connection so ruthlessly as to shock even a hardened Secretary at War.[1] About his intrinsic worth the diarists on both sides of politics were for once agreed. 'A vain, very ambitious man', wrote Horace Walpole, 'with a half-understanding which was worse than none.' Wraxall gave credit to Junius's portrait of him at the gaming table, waiting with sober attention to engage some drunken young nobleman at picquet. But he had no lack of energy, which he employed in pushing his own claims to high employment. On his appointment to America in 1775 he exerted pressure in many quarters to shake off the seniority of Sir William Howe and obtain an independent command at New York; and failing, filled the idle months at Boston with letters of enormous length to all the Ministers he knew. In a very long letter complaining of his position to Lord Rochford, he gave this estimate of General Gage, his Commander-in-Chief: 'capable of figuring upon ordinary and given lines of conduct; but his mind has not resources for great, and sudden and hardy exertions, which spring self-suggested in extraordinary characters, and generally overbear all opposition'. The denigration of Gage was careful and moderate, the contrasted character a fantasy-projection of himself.[2]

This was the officer who arrived on the eve of the planning period for the campaign of 1777, armed with a letter from Carleton referring the Minister to him for advice. He landed at Portsmouth on the afternoon of 9 December,

---

[1] Fonblanque, 47–8. In America he evidently did not consider it necessary to expand his social charm on General Riedesel's German wife (see, e.g. Mme Riedesel's Memoirs, 199).

[2] Anderson, 45; Wraxall, II, 293; Fonblanque, 125 *et seq.*, 148–9.

and was in Germain's office at noon on the following day. After Saratoga he strenuously denied the report that he had tried to undermine and supplant his Commander-in-Chief, and was always afterwards careful to praise Carleton in the House of Commons. It is probably true that he put on a show of loyalty for his friends at large. But he informed Germain that he had opposed the withdrawal from Crown Point; and a précis among the papers of the American Department shows that what he told Germain of the summer's operations was not all to Carleton's advantage. He gave Germain detailed observations on Carleton's requirements for the next campaign, in a tone which conveys the feeling that he was supplanting his chief. And in his own suggestions for the campaign there is a reference to Carleton which his biographer omits. He wrote that in the matter of supply everything depended on the 'peremptory powers, warm zeal, and consonant opinion of the governor; and though the former are not to be doubted, a failure in the latter indicated . . . by the plausible obstruction that will not fail to be suggested by others, will be sufficient to crush such exertions as an officer of sanguine temperament, entrusted with the future conduct of the campaign, and whose personal interest and fame therefore consequentially depended upon a timely outset, would be led to make'. Here is the same technique of tempered criticism and suggestive contrast which he had used against Gage. 'Under these considerations', he continued, 'it is presumed that the General Officer employed to proceed with the army will be held out of the reach of any possible blame till he is clear of the province of Canada, and furnished with the proper supplies.'[1]

3. Howe's Plans of Campaign

Thus it happened that by the end of 1776 General Howe enjoyed the Ministry's confidence; but Carleton did not. Howe's proposals for the next campaign arrived on 30 December in a despatch written a month earlier which brought news of the swift pursuit across East Jersey.[2] He expected the enemy to stand on the Raritan or perhaps not till the Delaware, and to try to cover Philadelphia, and he expected to close his operations for the winter in possession of East Jersey, which he needed as a foraging area. He had learnt of Carleton's withdrawal from Lake Champlain; but he assumed that though the northern army was unlikely to reach Albany till the following September, its advance from Canada would be renewed in the spring, and

[1] Fonblanque, 226; Parl Hist., XIX, 1187; CO 5/253, ff. 26–9; CL, Germain, 28 Feb. 1777, Burgoyne to Germain, and his observations on Carleton's requirements placed at the end of the 1777 papers; G 1936.
[2] Howe's of 30 Nov. (Sackville, II, 49–50).

that both armies would continue their concerted offensive against New England.

Howe therefore proposed to switch the main weight of his own army back to the northward. He would leave 8,000 men to cover New Jersey and check Washington, and 7,000 to hold New York and Rhode Island. Two offensives, each 10,000 strong, would be mounted against New England and Upper New York: one on the Hudson towards Albany and the Canadian army, the other from Rhode Island toward Boston. If these operations were successful, he would reduce Pennsylvania and Virginia in the following autumn and South Carolina and Georgia in the winter. By this design he hoped to finish the war in one more campaign.

This plan called for 35,000 men. By the last returns Howe had some 27,000 effectives, and the Cabinet might reasonably infer that 7,000 reinforcements would give him the strength he needed. But his proposals ended with a highly ambiguous and very disturbing paragraph: 'South Carolina and Georgia must be the objects for the winter, but to complete this plan, not less than ten ships of the line will be absolutely requisite, and a reinforcement of troops to the amount of 15,000 rank and file.' This reinforcement, he continued, would give him 35,000 'effective men' which he would need to face the 50,000 which Congress had voted for the next campaign.

What could be made of this? The 35,000 he demanded were, in fact, the force postulated in detail in his plan of campaign; but 15,000 effective reinforcements would give him many more than this, and the figure was coupled with the southern colonies in a manner which suggested that it was what he would ultimately need to re-occupy the whole of the rebellious provinces. The impression that the requirement was an ultimate and not an immediate one was strengthened by his suggestion that the troops might be had from Russia or Hanover, which he could not suppose could be done in a hurry.

The precise meaning was important; for though 7,000 reinforcements might be collected for him, there was no hope whatever of finding 15,000. Not many Germans could be got; and those sure recruiting grounds, the Highlands of Scotland, were said to have been exhausted in the previous winter. England was producing a mere trickle of recruits, and the few formed regiments left at home could not be spared in face of the uncertain intentions of France. The only means of finding more troops would have been to raise new regiments, for which men were easier to find; but the expense would be heavy, the regiments could not be ready for the field till 1778, and the King was as reluctant to raise troops as to commission ships for a campaign which might never be fought. Germain talked of new Highland regiments, but the King and Lord North nipped the plan in the bud.[1]

[1] G 1938; Add. MSS. 37883, ff. 165–70.

To later eyes it appears that in spite of his phrase 'effective men' Howe was not reckoning in effectives, a term which included sick, prisoners of war, and detachments, but from a base figure of his 20,000 men who were present and fit for duty. But the inducement to interpret the phrase literally was strong. Moreover Germain was rightly incredulous of Congress's ability to raise anything approaching 50,000 men; and could they have done so, he was confident that they would not stand up to Howe's splendid troops. He read Howe's despatch to the Cabinet on 10 January, and it was agreed that 4,000 additional Germans should be taken into British pay, making a total reinforcement including recruits of 7,800, which it was understood from the latest returns would give Howe 35,000 effectives. Germain therefore wrote to Howe on 14 January that he hoped these reinforcements would meet his requirements. Not all of them would reach him at the outset of the campaign; but, Germain argued to Eden (though here perhaps he was stretching the point), the mention of Russians and Hanoverians suggested that his need was not pressing. In the event the Northern Department was to be disappointed of its full quota of additional Germans, and only 1,285 were obtained; but by giving Howe priority over Canada, about 6,100 reinforcements were sent to New York in the course of the summer, of which the bulk arrived in May and the balance of 1,700 recruits in September.[1]

Comment on the details of Howe's operational plan was deferred till the end of the campaign was known. Howe's next despatch was written on 20 December, but it limped in to Whitehall two months later on 23 February. Events had moved rapidly in New Jersey, and instead of halting on the Raritan he had pushed forward across the whole state to the Pennsylvania boundary on the Delaware. He was now within easy distance of the seat of Congress at Philadelphia, and the rebellion seemed to be on the brink of complete disintegration. Here rather than in New England he was now sure of finding the main army of the rebels. The inhabitants of New Jersey and Pennsylvania were flocking in to collect their pardons. The apparent change in American sentiment persuaded Howe that the fall of Philadelphia would be decisive, and that one short stroke would end the rebellion in the Middle Colonies. He therefore proposed a change of plan to seize the opportunity. Instead of waiting for reinforcements to mount his offensive against New England, he would exploit his success to the southward, and strike with 10,000 men at Philadelphia. This would mean cutting his other commitments to the bone. The Rhode Island offensive towards Boston would have to wait for fresh

[1] The above reading of Howe's despatch and the reinforcement figures differs from those in most authorities. For the despatch and its interpretation see Sackville, II, 49–50, 56–7; CO 5/253, f. 256; Thynne Papers, Cabinet Minute of 10 Jan. (précis in Dartmouth II, 432); Add. MSS. 34413, f. 2 (31 Jan. Germain to Eden). For the reinforcements, see p. 118 below.

troops from England; New York would lose a thousand men of its intended garrison; and instead of 10,000 men to surge towards Albany and the Canadian army, there would be a defensive corps of 3,000 on the Lower Hudson to cover New Jersey and 'facilitate in some degree the approach of the army in Canada'.[1]

With this despatch Howe broke from the design which had ruled British strategy since Bunker Hill. Instead of a concerted thrust into the back of New England by the full weight of both the Canadian and Atlantic armies, he intended Carleton's force to make its dilatory way against the disintegrating enemy, while his own army overran the Middle Colonies and the political capital of the rebels, and thus put an end to the rebellion. This was still Howe's intention when the plans for Canada were worked out in London. But the Ministers were aware that there had been some change of fortune since it was drawn up; for simultaneously with its arrival came the official news of a sharp reverse in New Jersey.

To cover the loyalist areas which he had overrun, and enable the army to drive across the Delaware as soon as it froze, Howe held a very wide cantonment area, protected by a chain of posts extending from the Hudson as far as the Delaware, and anchored at its southern extremity on two Hessian posts at Trenton, on the high road to Philadelphia, and at Bordentown. He knew that the line was too extended, but trusted to the submission of the country beyond the southern end of his line, and the strength of his advanced positions.[2] In Trenton Colonel Rahl had 1,300 men. He was close to the Delaware, the enemy had boats, and he had been ordered to entrench. But he had neglected to build redoubts, and his immediate superior General Grant had failed to visit the post. Early on Christmas morning Rahl was surprised and killed by Washington. His brigade laid down its arms. The neighbouring Hessians at Bordenton abandoned their heavy baggage and beat a hasty retreat, and Washington raided deep into the British winter quarters. The rebels recovered their nerve. Many who had taken King George's pardon now took the precaution of submitting to Congress. The loyalist units forming in New Jersey dispersed to protect their homes. And though Howe drove the Americans from Trenton he did not stay, but fell back and abandoned all his gains in New Jersey except a shallow bridgehead at Brunswick and Amboy. This was the first of many evacuations which were to shatter loyalist confidence.

4. The Plan for Canada

On New Year's Day Burgoyne had written to tell Germain that he was going for a cure to Bath. He told him that he had informed the King of his departure, and 'as the arrangements for the next campaign might possibly

---

[1] Sackville, II, 52-3.   [2] Cornwallis Corr., I, 25.

come under his royal contemplation before my return, I humbly laid myself at his Majesty's feet for such active employment as he might think me worthy of'. He ended by soliciting Germain's 'patronage in this pursuit'. It is clear what he had in mind. But Clinton was also in England that winter, irritably trying to clear himself of blame for the Charleston failure, and had a certain claim to the field command in Canada, though he did not press it. As late as 24 February, the day after the receipt of Howe's change of plan, the King wrote to tell Lord North that Germain was about to propose Clinton for the Canadian appointment, and Burgoyne to join Howe; an arrangement of which he thoroughly approved. Yet on the following day the Cabinet agreed to employ Burgoyne again in Canada. On that day Germain told William Eden that he despaired of success in Canada if Carleton was not removed; and since he was to stay, Burgoyne may have seemed to possess just the boldness and vigour needed to counterbalance the faults which the Secretary of State saw in Carleton. Clinton was a very different character from Burgoyne; and whatever his weaknesses he would not have let himself be trapped in the Saratoga net.[1]

The choice of Burgoyne was the worst ministerial error of the campaign: perhaps the only avoidable one. But whoever was chosen, it might have been better if Carleton had been removed from Canada as Germain desired. It could have been done, though at the cost of some scandal, for in the previous war Pitt had successively supplanted Loudon and Abercromby in that very theatre, though Carleton's civil Governorship might have complicated his removal. The result of the King's refusal to replace him was a strange dual command, with Burgoyne dependent on Carleton for his base and transport, yet marching independently to place himself under the orders of another General, while Carleton disowned all responsibility for events beyond the frontier of Canada.

On 28 February Burgoyne sent Germain a long memorandum on the coming campaign from his house in Mayfair. He assumed, as everyone did, and as he had suggested in the winter of 1775-6, that the Canadian army ought to advance southwards in the general direction of General Howe's command.[2] The only alternative would have been to switch the striking force by sea to operate on the Atlantic seaboard. Burgoyne considered this,

[1] CO 42/36, f. 1; G 1964; Sandwich, I, 285; Willcox, *American Rebellion*, 65, n. 14; Add. MSS. 34413, f. 267. (25 Feb., Germain to Eden). In the letter of 24 February the King also wrote that Germain 'wants Cramahe to be recalled, but I have thrown cold water on that.' Cramahe was Lieutenant-Governor of Quebec. Though Fortescue transcribed the sentence accurately, the name is misread in Donne's edition as '(Carleton ?)' and many historians have followed this reading. Miss E. Price Hill, Registrar of the Royal Archives, has kindly checked the original for me.

[2] CL, Germain, and CO 42/36, f. 23; Fonblanque, 208-10, for his earlier plan.

and suggested that the commander should have latitude to do so. He afterwards made much of the omission of this latitude from his instructions. But
his memorandum pointed out that this course would be wasteful of troops,
since it would tie up a larger garrison in Canada. Nor did he think it
would be effective: 'I do not conceive any expedition from the sea can be so
formidable to the enemy, or so effectual to close the war, as an invasion from
Canada by Ticonderoga, this last measure [i.e. the movement by sea] ought
not to be thought of, but upon positive conviction of necessity.'

Carleton had suggested that the main thrust should come from Oswego
on Lake Ontario, striking down the Mohawk towards the Hudson.[1] It was
the route which Amherst had travelled in reverse in 1760, and was generally
regarded as the easier way.[2] But Burgoyne preferred to advance by Lake
Champlain, with only a very light demonstration on the Mohawk. He
argued rightly that the enemy were unlikely to fight for the Lake again, and
he expected Ticonderoga to fall in the early summer. From there the line
of advance would depend on the object. If he was to assist Howe, either
by joining him or by acting on the Hudson to enable him to use his whole
force to the southward, then it would be necessary to break through the
difficult country from Ticonderoga to the Hudson. The enemy would
probably block the road by land and fight for Lake George with a flotilla.
But, Burgoyne continued, if the force now at Rhode Island could remain
there a second course might be considered. Instead of making for the
Hudson, the army might turn eastwards from Ticonderoga, and strike
straight into the heart of New England to the Connecticut River. The march
of sixty miles through the Green Mountains would be very difficult for
artillery and stores; perhaps more difficult than the route to the Hudson. But
on reaching the Connecticut valley he would fortify a position and post
Indians to protect his communications. 'Should the junction between the
Canadian and Rhode Island armies be effected upon the Connecticut, it is
not too sanguine an expectation that all the New England provinces will be
reduced by their operations.'

These proposals show that Burgoyne recognised from the beginning that
Howe's main force might turn southwards into Pennsylvania instead of
striking up the Hudson to meet him. They suggest, indeed, that he knew of
Howe's revised plan to do exactly this which had arrived four days earlier
and was under consideration. One ambiguous sentence in Burgoyne's plan
might suggest that he depended on Howe's initial co-operation. It runs:

These ideas are formed upon the supposition that it be the sole purpose of the Canadian army to effect a junction with General Howe, or after co-operating so far as to

[1] Sackville, II, 222.
[2] E.g. by Clinton (Willcox, *American Rebellion*, 70, n. 25).

get possession of Albany and open the communication to New York, to remain upon the Hudson's River, and thereby enable that general to act with his whole force to the southward.

This might be taken to mean that even if Howe intended to operate in Pennsylvania, he must first clear the lower Hudson and help Burgoyne to establish himself at Albany. But it does not mean that Howe had to employ his whole force on the Hudson, or meet him at Albany: and both then and later Howe intended to favour Burgoyne's advance in some degree with a detachment. Nor did the prospect of operating without Howe's support alarm Burgoyne. He believed till his campaign was far advanced that with or without Howe's help he could subdue New England.

For these operations Burgoyne said that 8,000 regular rank and file would be needed, with 1,000 Indians or more, and 2,000 Canadians including hatchet men and other workmen; and he had already written in his observations on Carleton's paper that 3,000 troops should be left in Canada, for reasons which included the control of the *corvées* on which the supply of the army would depend. His own suggestions were shown by the King to a military authority, who doubted whether, allowing for sickness, more than 7,000 effectives could be provided for the advance. Burgoyne had also named in astonishing detail the units he wanted for his own advance, those for the Mohawk, and those which should be left in Canada. Such detailed requisitions scarcely flattered Carleton, but the King's military adviser agreed that they were proper, and that it was important that the exact numbers to be left should be laid down by the Ministry.[1]

In broad outline Burgoyne's suggestions were accepted; and to make sure that he had his way they were drawn up as an instruction for Carleton.[2] Burgoyne was to 'force his way to Albany', seconded by a diversion on the Mohawk, and place himself under Howe's command. But till Howe's orders were received, he was to act as his judgment and the situation required, never losing sight of the junction with Howe as the main object. It was not suggested that the advance to Albany would be seconded by Howe himself. The two alternatives Burgoyne had suggested were omitted: the Connecticut River plan because Howe had already cancelled the striking force which he had intended to base on Rhode Island; and the movement of the army by sea because, as Burgoyne had pointed out, it would be wasteful of troops. The merits of the Connecticut plan will be examined in due course. But if Burgoyne had had permission to join Howe by sea, he would not have done

---

[1] Burgoyne's memorandum, *loc. cit.*; G 1996–7. Fonblanque omits the requisition of units from his version of Burgoyne's memorandum. The King's notes and comments on G 1996–7 are in Fonblanque, 486–7.

[2] Sackville, II, 60–3.

so, for though he had fewer men than he had asked for, we shall see that he set forth from Ticonderoga without a doubt of success.

In every other respect Burgoyne had his way. The military business of the American Department was then in the hands of Mr D'Oyly, one of the Under-Secretaries, who had been Deputy Secretary at War and was a close friend of General Howe. He and Burgoyne drafted Carleton's instructions together; and, according to Knox, Burgoyne went in to the King and got his consent to his having the command and everything as he wished.[1] Even his suggested distribution of the units in Canada was exactly incorporated in the instructions for Carleton. The Commander-in-Chief in Canada, who had once been intended to take Howe under his command if the two armies joined on the Upper Hudson,[2] found himself deprived of all latitude in the disposal of his army: even the brigading of Burgoyne's force was prescribed. Coupled with an offensive reference to the abandonment of Crown Point, it was enough to wring from the quick tempered Carleton a demand for recall; and perhaps it was intended to. But there had been no dictation to the commander of the advance. To the last detail, the organisation and the plan were Burgoyne's.

It remained only to inform Howe of the plan for Canada. It contained nothing which he had not expected; but the resurgence of the Americans after Trenton threw open to debate the wisdom of his abandoning Burgoyne to his own devices. Germain had instantly divined on the news of Trenton that it was not the loss of men which mattered, but the effect on French and American opinion.[3] Howe, too, had been concerned at the probable effect, and feared that instead of the present winter seeing the end of the rebellion, another whole season's campaigning would be necessary. Nevertheless he was still convinced that the rebels were at the end of their tether, and were buoyed up only by hopes of help from France. If that door were shut, he wrote a week after Trenton, he believed it would put an end to the rebellion when British reinforcements arrived in the spring; 'such is the present eagerness of the inhabitants . . . for peace and pardon'. This seems to have remained the general impression in America. 'The back of the snake is broken', declared a letter from New York on 3 January. Even when the full effects of Trenton had been unrolled in an irritating skirmishing war, the impression survived. The critical and pessimistic Colonel Stuart was confident that the struggle would soon be over. 'In spite of all our blunders, fortune declares in our favour . . . there is a strong appearance of its being at an end before the autumn'.[4]

[1] Knox, 277.   [2] Howe's Orderly Book, 300.   [3] Add. MSS. 34413, f. 267.
[4] Sackville, II, 53–5; Add. MSS. 34413, ff. 152–5; Wortley, 109.

When, therefore, a letter written by Howe in the middle of January demanded 20,000 reinforcements, it was puzzling to know what to make of it. Howe said nothing concrete about his difficulties increasing, but merely wrote that it would now once more be necessary to defeat Washington in battle, and enlarged his original demand, pointing out that without such a reinforcement his operations against both Philadelphia and New England would be cramped. The implication was that the stroke against Philadelphia would now be neither as swift nor as immediately decisive as Howe had hoped in the triumphant week before Trenton. General Clinton was in London, and he later claimed that he had suggested the propriety of ordering Howe to co-operate with Burgoyne by using his whole force on the Hudson. But Clinton's fear for Burgoyne rose solely from the possibility that Washington would leave Howe undisturbed to take Philadelphia, and turn his own force against Burgoyne. This in fact was never to happen; and it was in any case reasonable to assume that Howe would take the necessary measures to prevent it. When Germain replied to Howe's despatches on 3 March, a few days after the receipt of Burgoyne's proposals for Canada, he made no comment on the demand for 20,000 men, but warned him that he might be disappointed of fresh German units, and that his reinforcement might therefore be reduced to 5,500. As to Howe's proposal to switch his main effort to the southward, Germain called his reasons 'solid and decisive', and gave it his approval.[1]

Thus, while Burgoyne's proposals for Canada were being translated into instructions for Carleton, Germain gave his approval to Howe's invasion of Pennsylvania. The plan for Canada was launched in the full understanding that though Howe's army would eventually co-operate with Burgoyne's on the Hudson, it could not support his advance to Albany in strength. Carleton's instructions were signed on 26 March, in time for Burgoyne to take them to Quebec; and a copy was sent to Howe which he acknowledged before his departure for Philadelphia. But a legend was launched by Shelburne that through the idleness of Germain and the carelessness of his office, Howe was never informed of Burgoyne's intentions. Knox, however, left a note which explains the truth. When Howe's friend D'Oyly had drafted the despatch for Carleton, Germain came down to the office to sign it on his way to Stoneland. Knox pointed out that there was no

---

[1] CO 5/94, f. 100; Willcox, *American Rebellion*, 60–1; Sackville, II, 58. The figure 5,500 is reached by deducting the Germans of whom the Ministry had been disappointed from the original total. Germain warned Howe that his forces (i.e. fresh regiments) might be only 2,500 strong (2,100 Germans and 400 Highlanders). The phrase has misled some historians into the belief that only 2,500 *reinforcements* were promised; but Germain's figure specifically excluded recruits.

letter to Howe. Germain started, and D'Oyly stared, but said he would write a few lines in a moment. 'So', said the impatient Germain, 'my poor horses must stand in the street all the time, and I shan't be to my time anywhere.' D'Oyly then said that Germain should go on, and he would write to Howe himself enclosing a copy of Carleton's instructions; 'and with this', Knox recalled, 'his Lordship was satisfied, as it enabled him to keep his time, for he could never bear delay or disappointment'. D'Oyly sat down and wrote to Howe; but he kept no copy for the file, and if Howe had not acknowledged it, it would have been impossible for the American Department to prove that he had ever seen Burgoyne's instructions.[1]

5. Supplies and Reinforcements

The operations were now in the hands of the generals. It remained for Germain only to see that they received the men and supplies which they needed. In the course of the summer Howe received a thirty per cent reinforcement of 6,100 men. Carleton had asked for 4,000 reinforcements in addition to recruits, and these Germain at first hoped to give him. But after Trenton, on the failure of the Northern Department to obtain troops from Würtemberg to replace Howe's lost Hessians, Germain was unable to allocate anything approaching 4,000 men to Canada. Only 1,600 recruits and reinforcements were despatched to Quebec.[2]

In the matter of supplies, Germain had determined that the late deliveries of 1776 should not be repeated. 'The Admiralty may want a little enforcing', the commentator on Burgoyne's plan had shrewdly predicted; and the first half of the year was a continual struggle against Admiralty delays. By 11 January Germain had prevailed so successfully over the War Office and Board of Ordnance that the camp equipment for Howe was ready for shipping in the Thames, and the first contingent of recruits was assembled at Chatham. But the Navy Board had still to be overcome. The Secretary at War discovered that the transports for the equipment were quite unfit to defend themselves against attack. Their safety would thus depend wholly on keeping in convoy; and without naval officers or seamen to control the masters it was improbable that they would do so in this stormy season. Germain must have sighed for the powerful armed victuallers run by the Treasury. He ordered the Admiralty peremptorily to take measures for the transports' safety, and arranged for parties of recruits to sail with them for their defence. Soon afterwards a storeship hired by the Navy Board for the Quebec run was found to be inadequately defended, and

[1] Knox, 277.
[2] Sackville, II, 222; G 1938; Add. MSS. 34413, ff. 202, 267; CO 5/253, ff. 256–7.

was ordered to sail in convoy with extra seamen and a large detachment of troops.

Pressed by the Secretary of State, the Admiralty got the equipment and recruits for Howe away in the middle of March, followed by a German contingent from Dort in the middle of April. But there were the usual maddening delays. Howe's clothing issue for 1776 had been intercepted by the rebels, and it was vital that the new supply should reach him safe and soon. The Admiralty was ordered to load the clothing in a warship capable of protecting herself, to be ready to sail by 10 March. 'Very extraordinary delays' ensued, for which Germain conveyed the royal dissatisfaction to the Admiralty. Finally at the end of April he learnt that even then not all the clothing was on board. Twenty tons of stowage space had been occupied by a huge machine for carrying landing craft. He ordered the Admiralty to enquire why the captain had embarked it.

Such was the detailed supervision which made the war machine revolve. There was more trouble over the clothing for Canada. Again the Secretary at War objected to the weakness of the transport, and the Navy Board professed itself unable to find a better. Germain himself found a ship with a respectable armament, ordered fifty soldiers to sail with her, and required the Admiralty to supply a naval officer to fight the ship if she were attacked. The Board objected, and was sharply overruled. Germain's tone to the Admiralty was peremptory, but necessary. It was certainly not sharper than the Elder Pitt's; nor did he bypass the Board of Admiralty to deal directly with the Navy Board as Pitt had done. But Pitt had been dealing with a professional First Lord. Sandwich the politician had the means to show his resentment.[1]

From these experiences Germain learnt that if he waited the outcome of the present campaign to judge the requirements for the next, the difficulties of organising shipments would never be overcome in time for the start of operations in the field. He therefore resolved to make every preparation for the campaign of 1778 so early that the troops could take the field without delay. As early as August 1777 he issued his instructions to the Admiralty to have transports capable of beating off rebel cruisers ready in December to load camp equipment, stores and tents for America, and to assemble them at Spithead under convoy and ready to sail by 1 February.[2]

The provisioning system, in contrast to the Navy Board shipping, was now on a reliable footing. These supplies at least were free of the treacly complacency of naval administration. Though the contractors' deliveries of bad flour continued to distress the commanders and the Ministry, the exertions

[1] Précis of American Department's measures to supply the forces, CO 5/254, ff. 58-83.
[2] *Ibid.* ff. 88-9.

by which the Treasury had collected and armed a fleet of powerful victuallers were bearing fruit. In June 1777 Howe sent the Treasury his warmest thanks for providing him with every necessity.[1] When provisions ran short again at New York in the following year, the fault lay not in London but in America.[2]

[1] Abergavenny, 16.   [2] See below, pp. 222–4

CHAPTER VI

PHILADELPHIA AND SARATOGA

1. *Howe and Burgoyne*

When Howe withdrew from New Jersey into a shallow bridgehead after Trenton, he did not relinquish his intention to make Philadelphia his first objective. But the survival of Washington's force after its flight across the Delaware removed the immediate prospect that the rebellion in the Middle Colonies would collapse. The Continental army had lived to fight again. Though it virtually disbanded itself when enlistments expired at the end of the year, the cadre survived on which to build afresh. Not that the American prospects were good: so far from it that when the captive Lee invited peace delegates from Congress to visit him in prison in February, Washington and opinion in the army was in favour of complying, and it was Congress which rejected the opening. Nevertheless Howe knew that he still needed the victory which he had missed on Long Island. Only the destruction of the enemy's army in battle would end the war.

This was the reasoning behind his huge demand for reinforcements in the middle of January.[1] But an enemy who moved fast and did not intend to fight was not easy to bring to action. Howe complained of the slowness of his Germans, who were 'much attached to their baggage, which they have in amazing quantities in the field'. At the end of January he reinforced Cornwallis with troops from Rhode Island so that he could move as soon as the weather improved. Washington had taken up a strong flank position to the north-west at Morristown, from which he harassed the British bridge-head at Brunswick and Amboy. There he could maintain his communications with the Hudson and New England, and threaten the British rear if they marched on Philadelphia. His new army was still in the making, and in March he had only 3,000 men of whom two-thirds were militia. 'If Howe does not take advantage of our weak state', he wrote on 12 April, 'he is very unfit for his trust.' Howe's intelligence, however, gave the enemy at least 8,000 men. The Morristown position was strong and difficult to approach; and he had decided that the cost in men of several weeks' winter campaigning in the open would be too severe for an army which could not replace them that year. By the beginning of April he had learnt that his demand for reinforcements would not be met. In the light of hardening

[1] CO 5/94, f. 100 (Howe's of 20 Jan. – see above, p. 117).

enemy resistance he decided that if he could not get an advantageous battle with Washington, he must modify his plans.[1]

Philadelphia remained his goal. But Washington's presence on his flank ruled out a direct advance across New Jersey. To bridge and cross the Delaware, with ninety miles of exposed communications in his rear, was not in Howe's view a feasible operation until Washington was defeated. On 2 April he put his new plan into a despatch for Germain. Instead of thrusting overland to Philadelphia, he would invade Pennsylvania by sea. With a bridge-head in the Chesapeake, his communications with New York would be secured by his brother's fleet.

The cost would be heavy. To find the necessary force, Howe warned Germain that he would probably have to abandon New Jersey. The evacuation in the presence of the enemy would probably delay the opening of the offensive; and from this, and the weakness of his force, he now saw no hope of ending the war in the present campaign.[2]

This despatch reached the American Department on 8 May.[3] Howe's pessimism was disappointing, but Germain did not share it. Daily intelligence of the rebels' difficulty in raising troops reassured him; and accounts from all quarters supported Howe's belief that a loyalist defence force could be raised in Pennsylvania so that the army could maintain the offensive. In only a minor degree did Howe's new plan affect the operations of Burgoyne. He had dropped the active force of 3,000 men on the Hudson, which had been intended to cover New Jersey and favour in some degree Burgoyne's advance; but he intended a force of 3,000 Provincials to act on the Hudson or in Connecticut. Howe enclosed a copy of a letter which he was sending by frigate to Canada, warning Carleton that he would be unable to support the advance from Canada at the beginning of the campaign, but hoped to provide a force to break through the fortified Highlands when Burgoyne reached Albany. He told Carleton that he regarded the advance on Albany as of the utmost importance to his own operations, and that an officer on his way to Canada for exchange would give him his reasons, which were too delicate to commit to paper. The numerous loyalists in the area, he said, were an assurance that the more rebellious parts of New York would be easily reduced. Thus, though Howe had not received his copy of Burgoyne's instructions when he wrote the despatch, he had no doubt what they would be. He saw no difficulty in the thrust from Canada, and regarded it as vital to his own plans; and his intention to aid Burgoyne, not in his initial advance to Albany, but in maintaining himself there, was in harmony with the general plan of the Ministry.

---

[1] CO 5/94, ff. 100, 121; Fortescue, III, 211; Anderson, 236–7.
[2] Sackville, II, 65–6.   [3] Not 18th as in Sackville.

Trusting therefore to Howe's assertion of the importance of Philadelphia, Germain agreed to his change of plan: he only added the hope that Howe would really complete his operation in time to co-operate with the Canadian army. Indeed the plan had reached London so late that Germain had no choice but to agree; and his answer, though promptly given, did not reach Howe till the middle of August, when the dilatory expedition was already in the Chesapeake. The responsibility was Howe's alone; and Howe had no reason to fear that the plan would hurt Burgoyne. On 16 July, before he sailed for the south, he received a letter from Burgoyne himself, written before Ticonderoga in high spirits and only lamenting that he had no latitude to reduce New England on his own. Howe foresaw only one danger to the northern army: that Washington would leave Philadelphia to its fate and turn against Burgoyne. To guard against this he resolved to make his own approach to Philadelphia by way of the Delaware instead of the Chesapeake, in order to be in closer supporting distance of the Hudson. If Washington marched north to attack Burgoyne, Howe thought Burgoyne was strong enough to check him; while if he merely attempted to retard Burgoyne's advance on Albany he ran the risk of being caught between two British forces.

But if Washington stayed to defend Philadelphia, Howe could see none but administrative obstacles to Burgoyne's advance. Scarcely anyone, least of all Burgoyne, seems to have realised the real nature of the danger, which lay in the difficult country and the New England militia. Only that able and difficult officer Charles Stuart, the future conqueror of Minorca, saw what might happen. He could scarcely believe, when the army embarked, that it was not a feint; for if Howe's army went south instead of north, Burgoyne would have to fight his way unaided against the most powerful, inveterate and populous of the colonies. 'I tremble for the consequences', he wrote.[1]

In England the slow unrolling of Howe's campaign was also watched with an eye to its effect on Burgoyne. But Howe was no letter-writer; and when he did write he said little to reveal his intentions or explain the long delay in embarking. In the middle of August Burgoyne was known to be on the move and about to invest Ticonderoga. Howe had sallied out to look at Washington, and it was known by a private ship that he had then embarked; but whether for Philadelphia or the Upper Hudson was a mystery. The summer was already far gone, and fears began to be aired that he would leave Washington free to turn on Burgoyne. Robinson tried to reason himself and others into believing that Howe would go northwards; but though North, Germain and the Adjutant-General agreed with his logic, they still feared that the army had gone to Philadelphia. On 22 August there was still

[1] Sackville, II, 66–7, 73; CO 5/94, ff. 269, 286; Fonblanque, 233; Wortley, 113.

no news of his intentions, 'for which and for something effectual to be done we grow very impatient'. That very day, however, despatches arrived, including his letter of 16 July with his cheerful news of Burgoyne. Even then he had not sailed, and gave no reason for his delay. But Germain had at least the assurance that he was acting on the fullest information, and did not doubt that he would take the best measures to meet the situation. Robinson was more sceptical. Howe had written that he 'trusted' Burgoyne would be able to give a good account of the Americans on the Hudson even if they were aided by Washington; which Robinson thought was trusting a good deal. 'In this case *we here trust*, and we hope Howe had provided so, that Sir Henry Clinton may be able to move from New York to aid Burgoyne . . .'[1]

2. Delays in the South

The Ministers at home had good reason for their bewilderment. For by September even Howe expected Burgoyne to reach Albany. Yet it was not till the last days of August that he made his landing in Pennsylvania and opened the campaign. The southern army would not be ready to open the lower Hudson and co-operate with the Canadian force before the winter. How had Sir William wasted the whole summer before he struck his blow?

Though he had written in his despatch of 2 April that he meant to avoid offensive operations in the Jerseys unless a very good opening appeared, Howe resolved in the end to offer one final challenge to Washington before he embarked, in order either to bring on a battle or at least to secure his embarkation, about which he felt some anxiety. It was not till the end of May that he took the field, a delay later attributed by Cornwallis and General Grey to the necessity of waiting for green forage on the ground.[2] On 8 May he received Germain's approval of his second plan, the march on Philadelphia. On the 24th drafts from England began to arrive, which raised the strength of his whole command to 27,000 men; and about the same time Washington moved south with 8,000 men to be nearer the British road to Philadelphia, and took up a new position near Bound Brook. Here he was only eight miles from Howe's post at New Brunswick, and seemed to offer a good chance of forcing him to battle.

Washington's new position was judged too strong to attack. But Howe hoped to lure him into the plain; and marching from New Brunswick, he thrust forward to cut off an enemy detachment under Sullivan at Princeton. But Sullivan was hastily and successfully withdrawn without a fight; nor was

[1] Add. MSS. 38209, ff. 152-3, 155; Knox, 136; Sackville, I, 138-9.
[2] Anderson, 240-7.

Washington impressed by the threat to Philadelphia, for he knew that Howe had left his heavy baggage and bridging train at Amboy. 'The idea of offering them battle is ridiculous', wrote Colonel Stuart, 'they have too much caution to risk everything on one action . . . If we wish to conquer them we must attack him [Washington], or if his posts are too strong, by a *ruse de guerre* place ourselves in that situation he may expect to attack us to advantage.' [1]

Washington had been tempted in vain; and he was thought too strong to be attacked. It only remained to try a ruse. On the night of 19 June Howe suddenly decamped, and fell back rapidly on Amboy with all the appearance of a disorderly retreat. Washington moved forward from his hill position, ready to hinder the British embarkation; and on the night of the 26th Howe dashed forward to cut his line of withdrawal. Washington escaped precipitately to the mountains before the trap closed, though one of his divisions was roughly handled, and at last Howe was satisfied that he would not fight in New Jersey. He had lost a month in the experiment, but secured a peaceful embarkation. It now remained to be seen whether a seaborne threat to Philadelphia would give him the decisive battle.

The hottest months of the year had now arrived, and a seasonal southwest wind blew unfavourably. Nearly 14,000 rank and file embarked in their hot and crowded transports between 9 and 11 July; but Howe still waited for news of Burgoyne. On the 16th came the cheerful letter written before Ticonderoga, and Howe, informed and reassured, at last commited his own force to the sea.

Yet, dismissing the risk to Burgoyne, as Howe had reason to do, what merit had his own plan? Since Trenton had renewed his conviction that the Continental army must be destroyed before the rebellion would break, the plan made sense only on the assumption that Washington would fight for Philadelphia. But would he? As Colonel Stuart observed, the name of 'capital', so impressive to Europeans who did not know America, had almost no significance in the decentralised federation of colonies. Moreover, the rebels had had time to remove the military stores whose loss might have proved decisive at the time of Trenton. Yet for the sake of a doubtful profit, Howe was abandoning posts in New Jersey which had cost him nearly 2,000 men, and deserting the inhabitants who had served him. It is said that every general in his army except Grant and Cornwallis disliked the plan. Only two satisfactory choices were open to Howe: to accept the risks and losses of attacking Washington in New Jersey; or to leave a covering force there as he had originally planned, and strike northwards to open the lower Hudson. Howe's own course promised few risks, but fewer gains. [2]

[1] Wortley, 113.   [2] Wortley, 113; Anderson, 263; Clinton, 61 *et seq.*

On 23 July a favourable wind at last carried the army to sea. But at the mouth of the Delaware it was met by a frigate long stationed in the estuary; and so emphatic was her captain about the hazards of navigation and the strength of the enemy defences that on Lord Howe's advice the fleet changed its course and steered for the Chesapeake. A year later Sir William was to tell Lord Carlisle that he had switched to the Chesapeake on learning that the enemy's main magazine was not in Philadelphia but in northern Virginia. But he made no mention of this at the time; and the whole record is so bedevilled by subsequent polemic that when the source is a man as inarticulate and unclear as Howe, one must doubt the story.[1] In any event, the wisdom of the decision is in doubt. Evidence suggests that the fleet could have gone up the Delaware without difficulty as far as Newcastle, only a dozen miles across the peninsula from the eventual landing place in the Chesapeake.

The voyage from the Delaware capes to the head of the Chesapeake took twenty-five days. Not till 25 August did the army land. During the voyage Howe received Germain's letter of 18 May, approving his plan and echoing his hope that he could co-operate with Burgoyne before the end of the campaign. But this was no longer possible; and he replied on the 30th that it was too late. And in spite of reports of a reverse to the northern army at Bennington, he trusted that Burgoyne would not be prevented from pursuing the advantages he had gained.[2]

3. The Campaign of Philadelphia

The army which landed at Head of Elk on 25 August had been embarked for forty-seven days, and was as far from Philadelphia as it had been when it went on board the transports. Its long voyage had meant many days of anxious speculation for Washington. When the embarkation began he knew, which Howe did not, that Burgoyne had taken Ticonderoga without a shot and was pushing for the Hudson; and he assumed that Howe was embarking to pierce the Highlands and join him. Moving towards the Hudson, he sent two divisions across it to Peekskill to guard the Highland passes. When the British put out to sea, he recalled his detachments and countermarched to the Delaware, only to fear that he had been misled by a deep feint when the fleet showed itself off the Delaware and vanished again. After days of indeterminate movements and faulty guesses came the news that the British were high up the Chesapeake. Washington marched, not north against Burgoyne, but south to oppose Howe, who was to have

---

[1] Carlisle, 254. Cf. the evidence given at the enquiry, that the Delaware was impracticable (Howe's *Narrative*, 71 ff.).

[2] Sackville, II, 74; CO 5/94, ff. 313-4.

his battle; and only a handful of riflemen from the main army reached General Gates in the north. The danger to the force advancing from Canada was a different one, which no British planner had foreseen. 'Now', wrote Washington, 'let all New England turn out and crush Burgoyne.'

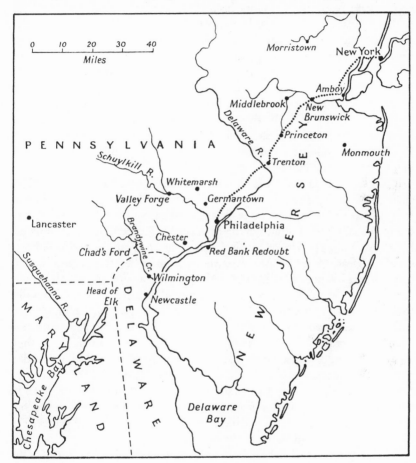

HOWE'S PHILADELPHIA CAMPAIGN, 1777

In Pennsylvania the odds were less favourable to Howe than in 1776. The two armies were about equal in numbers. But the Americans now had European instructors, and French arms and cannon. Nor were their backs to a great river, as they had been on Long Island: there was infinite room for retreat. Howe, for his part, would have to exploit a victory with speed and energy to reap its benefits. But by choosing an amphibious strategy he had imposed on his army the defective mobility on shore of an amphibious force. He had two regiments of cavalry in America; but he had brought only Burgoyne's Sixteenth Light Dragoons to Pennsylvania, leaving the other regiment in readiness to follow him. Thus the only cavalry at hand to exploit success were three squadrons shared between the divisions of his army. Nor were they fit for a hard day's work. The heat of the voyage, the rough seas, confinement and shortage of provisions had made the men suffer. But for the horses it had been catastrophic. They had embarked with three weeks' forage for a voyage of seven. Many dead and dying horses had gone overboard, and the rest were mere carrion. A Quaker youth saw Howe himself on the day of the battle of Brandywine 'mounted on a large English horse, much reduced in flesh'. If the Commander-in-Chief could not keep his charger in condition, the troop horses of the Sixteenth must have been in a wretched state indeed.[1]

If it is true that Howe's first object in the Chesapeake had been the maga-zines in Virginia, it was changed on secret intelligence that Washington intended to risk a battle. The plan was now to push for Philadelphia and tempt Washington to fight. On the Brandywine Creek Washington formed his army, and gave Howe his first chance since White Plains to inflict a decisive defeat. Howe's tactics were the ones he had used so successfully on Long Island. While Knyphausen with 5,000 men and plenty of cannon demonstrated above the ford on the main road to Philadelphia, Cornwallis took a wide sweep round the American right flank and made an unopposed and unobserved crossing of the Brandywine. The Americans had neither re-connoitred nor patrolled the country properly. Struck in front and flank, they were driven into a general retreat. Washington however had responded correctly to the crisis by sending a reserve under Greene to hold the road open for his routed right wing. Cornwallis's men had marched eighteen miles in the heat of the day, and were unable to break Greene's fresh division and join hands with Knyphausen before dark. Howe halted his troops and allowed the enemy to retire unmolested into the night.

The ground was said to have been unfavourable for his cavalry. But as the Americans fell back, the road to the rear became a scene of hopeless confusion. For twelve miles they streamed along in the darkness, intact companies mingling with dispersed and beaten fugitives. Only at the Chester Creek did Lafayette post a guard on a bridge to stop the mob, and Greene and Washington arrived to restore order. A cavalry force properly proportioned to Howe's army and fit for duty might have prevented the enemy from rallying. Two or three regiments of boldly led dragoons sabreing the

[1] Curtis, 126; Ward, 332, 348.

stragglers and penetrating the flanks of the retreating column might have spread such confusion as to give a different turn to the campaign.

So ended a battle which was nearly decisive. Howe's problem was now to cross the Schuylkill and enter Philadelphia. There followed a period of manoeuvring in which the Americans showed a resilience in defeat which was astonishing in an army of amateurs, and a power of marching which put the British and Hessians to shame. But at length, by a series of perplexing movements which alarmed Washington for his right flank and supplies, Howe drew him away to the west. Then, by a swift march to his right he threw his army across the river. Washington was twenty miles in the wrong direction, and the road to Philadelphia was clear. On 26 September Cornwallis entered the city with four battalions. Eight days earlier the Congress had fled to Lancaster.

The success at the Brandywine was spent, and a period of consolidation followed. The immediate task was to clear the lower Delaware and open communications with the sea. Three battalions crossed the river to clear the forts commanding the channel, and 3,000 men were sent back to bring up supplies from the beachhead on the Chesapeake. To cover these operations Howe encamped with the remainder of his force, fewer than 9,000 men, on the western side of Philadelphia at Germantown. Washington, having summoned reinforcements from the Hudson, had at least 8,000 Continentals and 3,000 militia. He had just lost the largest city in America; but neither the moral nor the physical effects were what they would have been nine months earlier. Almost all the stores had been removed; and his army now had a steadiness on which the purely symbolical loss of the 'capital' had no effect. And there was news to lighten the load on their spirits. On 28 September, the army celebrated with gunfire and rum the first exaggerated reports of Gates's victory over Burgoyne in the first battle of Freeman's Farm. Washington could now 'count on the total ruin of Burgoyne'. He prepared to take the offensive himself, and moved forward to within twelve miles of the British camp. At the beginning of October he had accurate intelligence of Howe's detachments and the position at Germantown; and with the unanimous support of his generals he resolved to attack it.

A long night march, a complicated plan and a morning fog would have stretched an experienced staff and veteran troops. The attack was pressed with courage, but it was confused, ill-concerted, and easily unhinged. After initial success the Americans were repulsed with nearly 1,100 casualties, against Howe's loss of just over 500. Physically it was a reverse; but the Americans carried off the illusion that the British had been on the point of a general retreat, the persuasion that Howe's casualties were larger than their own, and the moral sensations of victory. For Howe the battle could not be wholly gratifying. He had not expected so determined a riposte so soon after the Brandywine. Though the attack was expected, his camp was not entrenched, which he later explained as a deliberate omission 'to create always an impression of superiority'. But Colonel Stuart may have been nearer the truth with a phrase he had used a month earlier[1]: 'our usual carelessness prevails'.

Philadelphia was now secure. It remained to open the Delaware. This proved a long and costly operation, comparable in importance and trouble with the clearing of the Scheldt in 1944. The army was immobilised for many weeks. A Hessian assault on one of the American forts was beaten off on 22 October with the loss of the commander and nearly 400 officers and men. On the same day one of Lord Howe's few ships of the line grounded in range of enemy batteries and became a total loss. Not till batteries had been laboriously brought to bear by land and water in the middle of November was the river cleared and the shipping able to move up to Philadelphia.

General Howe, in the meantime, had concentrated his force in Philadelphia. Across the peninsula above the town he drew a line of fourteen redoubts connected by a strong stockade, anchored on its flanks to the Schuylkill and the Delaware. Here he was safe from further American insults till the Delaware operations were finished. Then, on the night of 4 December he sallied to attack Washington's camp at Whitemarsh. But the ground was strong, and after attempting to feel his way round the American flank he desisted and withdrew to his comfortable winter quarters in Philadelphia. As yet he had no certain news of the fate of Burgoyne; but rumour was bleak.[2]

4. The Advance from Canada

Burgoyne had reached Quebec in the first days of May to encounter difficulties which he had not anticipated when he laid his plans before the Minister. He had expected 2,000 Canadians and at least 1,000 Indians. But these could not be found. Only 500 Indians came forward; no great loss, for except as scouts they proved worse than useless, and their savagery made effective propaganda to rally the enemy's militia. But the Canadians were a different matter. On them Burgoyne had counted to clear his path through the forest. But only about 650 Canadians and loyalists served with the army.

Transport and supplies proved harder to organise than he had imagined. To make good the deficiency of armed men, Burgoyne suggested a *corvée*

[1] Wortley, 115; Howe's *Narrative*, 108.
[2] The above account of Howe's operations is based largely on Fortescue, Anderson, Ward, and Freeman.

of 1,000 men and 800 horses. But Carleton had long since given warning (or so he claimed) that little help could be expected from the Canadians after the long disuse of their tenurial obligations: they had been governed, he said, with too loose a rein for many years.[1] As he expected, the response was reluctant. Drivers could not be obtained for the provision carts; and wet weather and bad roads delayed the movement to the frontier. And Burgoyne intended to take a powerful train of artillery to the Hudson. Twenty-four pounders and twelve-pounders meant water-carriage; and there was further delay in making boats for the cannon.[2]

It was on 20 June, six weeks after Burgoyne's arrival in Canada, that the army assembled on Lake Champlain, soon after the departure of St Leger's diversionary force to the Mohawk. As had been expected in England, there were only 7,000 regulars, of whom 3,000 were Germans. But they were good troops, and well led. In General Phillips and the brigadiers, Burgoyne had brave and proficient subordinates. The Brunswickers were led by Major-General Riedesel, aged about thirty-eight and recently promoted from the rank of Colonel to lead the contingent: an excellent officer who spoke English and had made English friends when his regiment was stationed near London in 1756. Above all, Burgoyne had the confidence of his men.

The start had been slow. But Burgoyne set forth with all the optimism of favourable auguries and a sanguine temperament. And his cheerfulness was soon increased. For on reaching Ticonderoga he found that the American garrison, 3,000 strong, had failed to occupy a hill commanding the fort. He promptly erected a battery on it, and the enemy abandoned the works and fled. It was a heavy blow for the rebels. But Washington had taken Burgoyne's measure, and sent words of reassurance to General Schuyler on the Hudson: ' . . . the confidence derived from success may hurry him into measures which will in their consequences be favourable to us'. Burgoyne's own deduction from his success may have had its influence on his later decisions. It was that the enemy 'have no men of military science'.[3]

It was now the first week of July; and the army had at last reached the point which some believed that Carleton could have gained in the preceding autumn. Here, if he had had the latitude for which he had asked, Burgoyne might have turned aside from the path to the Hudson and marched eastwards to the Connecticut valley in the heart of New England. Much was later made by Burgoyne and his apologists of his lack of choice in the matter; and it is true that at Ticonderoga he voiced regrets that he had no such latitude. Since it was afterwards implied that this course would have given

---

[1] CO 42/35, f. 175; CO 42/36, ff. 211, 326-7, 329. But cf. p. 59 above.
[2] Sackville, II, 112.
[3] Fonblanque, 247, 253.

the campaign a happier ending, the nature of his regret at the time must be made clear. On his arrival in Canada he had written to Howe regretting that he had no latitude to make a *diversion* towards the Connecticut; but on 11 July, as he committed his force to its southward advance towards the Hudson, he wrote in more precise and ambitious terms to Germain: 'As things have turned out, were I at liberty to march in force immediately by my left instead of my right, I should have little doubt of subduing, before winter, the Provinces where the rebellion originated. If my late letters reached General Howe I still hope this plan may be adopted from Albany . . .' Burgoyne was not concerned for his army's safety: he believed that with his own resources, and without the help of troops from New York or Rhode Island, he could end the rebellion.[1]

Subsequent events made it clear that he was wrong. New England was not to be subdued by six or seven thousand regular troops. Nor is there any reason to think that a march into New England would have been safer than an advance on Albany. Burgoyne's communications would have been exposed to the force on the Hudson instead of to the New Hampshire militia; and the distances were as great, the country as difficult, the population as inveterate.

From Ticonderoga there were two routes to the Hudson. The one generally regarded as the easier was by Lake George, from which there was a practicable waggon road to the Hudson where it became navigable at Fort Edward. This route was eventually cleared and used for the army's supplies. But the retreating garrison of Ticonderoga had been pursued up the narrow southern arm of Lake Champlain to Skenesborough, from which there was a long forest trail to Fort Edward. Having started on this line Burgoyne held to it. The decision was much criticised; but he reasoned that the enemy would probably have blocked the road from Fort George as effectively as they blocked the road he took, and that by using the Skenesborough route he forced the Americans to abandon Fort George without a fight. These reasons may have been valid. He did however employ a third argument, that a withdrawal from Skenesborough to start again on the Lake George route would be discouraging. This contention was curiously similar to Howe's reason for not entrenching at Germantown; and it is odd that two commanders whose troops' morale was high should both have accepted unnecessary disadvantages for fear of damaging the spirit of their men.[2]

---

[1] Fonblanque, 233–4, 256. His letter of 11 July to Germain (CO 42/36, f. 361) seems to show that he was in fact perfectly ready to turn his whole force towards the Connecticut in spite of his orders; but finding the enemy preparing to strengthen themselves on the Hudson, he would 'employ their terrors that way, and after arriving at Albany it may not be too late to renew the alarm towards Connecticut.'

[2] Fonblanque, 264, 267.

Right or wrong, the advance from Skenesborough proved very difficult. The winding trail had been blocked systematically by felling trees, destroying bridges and damming and diverting streams. Innumerable trees were cleared, forty bridges and causeways were built. In this way twenty miles swallowed twenty days. At last, on 30 July, the army emerged at Fort Edward. Schuyler withdrew his force to Stillwater, thirty miles above Albany, and before Burgoyne stretched the wide valley of the navigable Hudson.

If the army could have advanced at once, Burgoyne could have driven the Americans before him and reached Albany with scarcely a pause. Though the long toil from Lake Champlain had given the enemy time to collect about 4,500 men, of whom three-fifths were Continentals, their morale was very low and desertions were numerous. But Burgoyne could not move forward till he had collected thirty days' supplies at Fort Edward; and he could not bring up enough to form his magazine. Time was needed to open the Lake George route; no Canadian porters had materialised; and the Canadian contractors had furnished only a third of the horses they had promised. And on this ill-found transport service he threw the burden of bringing up his artillery and batteaux. Twenty light six-pounders with 124 rounds per gun could have moved with eighty horses, and marched as fast as the army. But against an ill-equipped enemy and in a situation where mobility was everything, Burgoyne elected to bring a train of fifty-two cannon. 'The artillery, after the light troops, is the important arm in the American War', he had written in England; and he maintained afterwards that numerous and heavy guns were essential against an enemy who could throw up wooden forts and abbatis in a matter of hours, as well as to defend the camp he intended to entrench at Albany. As a result of this precaution he was never to reach his destination. 'All his wants', wrote an eyewitness, 'were owing to his having too great an abundance.' [1]

Burgoyne, however, was far from despair. 'Nothing', he wrote to Germain on the day he reached Fort Edward, 'has happened . . . to change my sentiments of the campaign.' The determination with which the rebels had driven off the cattle and population 'seems to me an act of desperation and folly. The only purpose it can answer is to retard me for a time, which it certainly does; it cannot finally impede me.' A week later, he wrote to Howe that he hoped to move to Saratoga in a few days, though even if the enemy did not fight he could not get to Albany before 22 August. [2] Unable to bring up his supplies from the rear, he intended to seize them from the enemy in front. Riedesel had suggested a raid to the left into the Connecticut valley,

[1] CO 42/36, f. 7; CL, Germain, 'Remarks' at end of 1778 volume.
[2] CO 42/36, f. 386; CO 5/94, f. 352.

to collect pack-horses which would free the army from its dependence on Canadian carts and increase its mobility. Vital time had elapsed since the suggestion was made, but Burgoyne now resolved to adopt it.[1] Then, hearing of an enemy magazine thirty miles south-east of Fort Edward at Bennington, and on the near side of the Green Moutains, he radically altered the plan and made this the object of the foray. The commander he chose was a brave German dragoon called Colonel Baum, who qualified for marching through a country of mixed friends and foes by speaking no English. His force was remarkable. He had fifty picked British marksmen and 100 German grenadiers and light infantry; 300 Tories, Canadians and Indians; to preserve secrecy, a German band; to speed the column, 170 dismounted German dragoons in search of horses, marching in their huge top boots and spurs and trailing their sabres. They were reinforced on the march by fifty Brunswick Jäger and ninety local Tories who brought Baum's force to 800 men.

Burgoyne had been assured by Colonel Skene that the country was full of loyalists. He knew that the remains of a militia regiment scattered at Ticonderoga had assembled north of Bennington at Manchester, but thought it highly probable that they would retreat. If they did not, he left it to Baum's discretion whether to fight them, with the warning that his force was too valuable 'to let any considerable loss be hazarded'. What Burgoyne could not know was that a remarkable cross-grained fighter called John Stark had just reached Bennington with 1,500 New Hampshire militia whom he had raised in a single week. At Bennington Stark found 500 militia-men from Massachussets and Vermont; and on 16 August he fell on Baum's 800 men from all sides. Baum thought that the shirt-sleeved farmers approaching his rear were loyalists coming to join him. His Indians fled at the first discharge; the Tories were rushed and scattered. For two hours the regulars fought off their attackers till their ammunition ran out. Then, leading his dragoons in a desperate sabre charge, Baum fell mortally wounded and the fight was over.

Back on the Hudson Burgoyne had received a call from Baum for reinforcements; and 600 Germans under Colonel von Breymann were slowly approaching the battlefield as the fighting died down. Stark's men had scattered to loot, and for a time the Americans' position was dangerous. But the arrival of a small reinforcement enabled them to check Breymann's attack till he too had exhausted his ammunition, when he fell back into the night with the loss of both his guns and two-thirds of his men. The two combats at Bennington had cost Burgoyne 900 men, and half of them were regulars.

[1] Riedesel, I, 247–61.

5. The Fatal Decision

The losses at Bennington were the more serious because Burgoyne had found himself unexpectedly forced to garrison Ticonderoga. He had asked Carleton to find a garrison; but Carleton, still wearing the mask of civility, had stood by the letter of his instructions. He had no authority outside the borders of Canada; the force to remain in Canada had been prescribed; and he refused to help.[1] Burgoyne's insistence on having his own way had recoiled on him, and the force for the Hudson offensive was reduced by a further 900 men. His resources were rapidly shrinking; and he knew that he could expect no immediate help from Howe, for he had received Howe's letter of 17 July, with the news of his embarkation for Pennsylvania.[2] On the Mohawk, St Leger's miscellaneous detachment had been held at Fort Stanwix and then scattered with the loss of guns and baggage by the mere approach of a force under Arnold.

The prospect was rapidly changing. A diminishing force, vulnerable communications and a strained supply system had reduced his thrusting power. From New York he had little to hope, on the Mohawk nothing. But more serious than his own changing strength was the increasing power of the enemy. On his front, the long pause at Fort Edward had enabled the Americans to collect their strength. Arnold returned from the Mohawk, and 300 picked riflemen under Daniel Morgan arrived from Washington. By the middle of September Schuyler's successor, Gates, had six or seven thousand men in the Hudson valley. The position on the flank was worse. Bennington had revealed that the country towards the Connecticut was no loyalist stronghold but a hive of determined rebels.

Burgoyne was alive to the dangers. The moment he advanced, the New England militia on his left would close on his communications; and if he failed to reach Albany and open a supply route from New York he could not maintain himself on the Upper Hudson. All the premises of his plan had collapsed. His supply system had failed him. The General whom he had elbowed out had denied him help. The loyalists of Vermont and the Upper Hudson were a negligible force. He had a superior enemy strongly posted in front, and a swarming militia on his flank. To advance was folly.

The choice which faced Burgoyne at Fort Edward was not a pleasant one. To halt where he was or withdraw to Ticonderoga would be an admission that his plan had failed, and public opinion might not understand his difficulties.

[1] Fonblanque, 261, 276.
[2] Burgoyne later argued in the House that this letter indicated an intention to co-operate with him, and that it thus cancelled Howe's earlier warning to Carleton: but Howe only promised to pursue Washington if he turned against Burgoyne.

What, as he later asked the House of Commons, would the govern-ment, the army and the country have said of him?[1] To a man of Burgoyne's vanity and ambition, the humiliation would have been unbearable. To escape the dilemma, he seized on a twisted reading of his instructions. 'Had I a latitude in my orders', he wrote to Germain after Bennington, 'I should think it my duty to wait in this position . . . till some event happened to assist my movement forward; but my orders being positive to "force a junction with Sir William Howe" I apprehend I am not at liberty to remain inactive.' This was his first complaint that the positive nature of his orders compelled him to advance; and the words which he misquoted were 'to force his way to Albany'.[2]

'It is notorious', wrote Macaulay, 'that the great men who founded and preserved our Indian Empire treated all particular orders which they received from home as mere waste paper. Had not these man had the sense and spirit so to treat such orders we should not now have had an Indian Empire.'[3] Burgoyne, two or three months distant from England in the wilds of America, was asserting that though his own circumstances and Howe's had changed utterly he was bound by the letter of his orders. After the final disaster he refined his theory still further. His advance, he argued had been part of a closely interlocking plan. The Ministry had chosen to risk his force 'to assist the great general arrangement of the campaign'. It was not his business to halt from motives of prudence. To do so would leave Gates at liberty to turn against Howe; 'and I reasoned thus: the expedition which I commanded was at first evidently intended to be *hazarded*; circumstances might require it should be *devoted*'.[4]

Not a syllable in Germain's instructions could justify this interpretation. But Burgoyne plunged forward to his fate. By 13 September he had collected thirty days' provisions; and on that day and the next his regiments crossed the Hudson on a bridge of rafts, and put the river between themselves and their base. And so Burgoyne advanced to meet the very difficulties he had foreseen, and to surrender his army to the enemy.

6. The Last Scenes on the Hudson

Scarcely had Burgoyne crossed the Hudson when the enemy fell upon his communications. General Lincoln had been sent across the Hudson from

---

[1] *Parl. Hist.* XIX, 1189.
[2] Fonblanque, 274-6. See above, p. 115.
[3] Quot. Richmond, *Navy in India*, 110.
[4] Sandwich, I, 307; Fonblanque, 291-2. If anyone urged that Burgoyne's advance was vital to Howe's operations, it was Howe himself in his letter of 5 April to Carleton.

Stillwater to collect the militia of Vermont; and 1,500 of these were detached to raid the British rear. On 18 September they captured the British shipping at the head of Lake George, and the three companies of infantry guarding it; and even Ticonderoga was threatened for a time. But of this Burgoyne knew nothing as he closed with the main American force on his front. On the 19th he assaulted Gates's position on Bemis Heights. He was ignorant of the ground and the enemy dispositions, for his Indians and scouts had been driven within his lines by American irregulars. Groping forward to out-flank Gates's position, he was checked and counter-attacked by Arnold. His failure cost him 600 men. The loss of officers to American marksmen was very severe; and three weak British battalions which bore the brunt of the action lost 350 men out of 800. Two days later Burgoyne was ready for a second attempt; but that morning he at last heard news from the south. A message arrived from Clinton that he intended to make a push against the forts in the Highlands about the 22nd. Hoping that the pressure would force Gates to divide his force, Burgoyne called off his attack, and entrenched his position to await events.

Sir Henry Clinton had been left with a force to guard New York while Howe was operating in Pennsylvania. There seems to be an ancient law of warfare that a general shall measure his own strength by the numbers fit for duty, and his subordinates' by their total strength on paper. It was obeyed by Howe. To Germain he calculated his strength by the numbers present and fit; but in his subsequent narrative he called Clinton's strength 8,500, reckoning it by total effectives of all arms. Clinton's real strength in infantry fit and present was 6,900, of whom 3,000 were newly raised Provincials. With this force he could do no more than defend his own position as long as Washington was in striking distance; for he had a perimeter of 100 miles with extensive works on three separate islands and the Jersey shore. As for an offensive up the Hudson, it would remain out of the question, for Washington had detached Putnam with 4,000 men to guard the passes of the Highlands, and if Clinton had been able to spare every man of his garrison he could not have opened that strong and fortified country. Nor did Howe suppose that he could; for he left him with no instructions to help Burgoyne.[1]

It was with some surprise that Clinton received a letter from Howe dated 30 July, reminding him of the usefulness of any diversion in favour of Burgoyne's approach. Far from being able to take the offensive, he was being assailed at several points by the enemy. The pressure on New York was eased when Washington crossed the Delaware to follow Howe; but Clinton's force was still too small to crack open the Highlands. Nor did he fear for Burgoyne; for he had his letter of 6 August, written at Fort Edward

[1] Willcox, *American Rebellion*, 63, 83.

before the reverse at Bennington, which indicated that he expected to reach Albany about the 23rd, and made no mention of expecting assistance from New York. Early in September, however, recruits were due from England. On the 11th Clinton learnt of the defeat at Bennington. He read it as a successful feint to open the road to Albany[1]; and it was now that he sent his promise to make a push at the Highlands. The undertaking on which Burgoyne built so much was to be a demonstration with 2,000 men when the reinforcements arrived from Europe. Clinton had not designed a rescue operation, but a feint to assist success.

The expected fleet from England arrived on the 24th with 1,700 recruits. About the same time Clinton learnt that Washington had drawn off a very large detachment from Putnam's force guarding the Highlands. He was now in a better position to threaten the Highlands; and on the 29th an answer arrived from Burgoyne, that an attack or even a demonstration would be of great help. The messenger said that Burgoyne's provisions were low and his communications with Canada severed, and that he intended to form a junction with the southern army. Clinton therefore hastened to strike his blow; and with the first suitable tide, on 3 October, he moved up the North River with 3,000 men.

Surprise was complete. On the morning of the 5th the expedition appeared off Verplancks, whose garrison was not in strength and fled in confusion. Clinton was preparing to land when an officer arrived from Burgoyne with news which gave a new and unexpected turn to the situation. The position of the northern army was desperate. Losses had reduced it to 5,000 men; the enemy had double that number strongly posted on its front, and another considerable body hanging on its rear; while its provisions would not last beyond the 20th. Burgoyne said he had no doubt he could force his way to Albany; yet being uncertain of supplies when he got there, he wished to know before he tried it whether Clinton could open communications and supply him from New York. He demanded Clinton's most explicit orders either to attack the enemy on his front or to retreat to Canada; 'hinting at the same time', as Clinton was to recall, 'that he would not have relinquished his communication ... had he not expected a co-operating army at Albany'.[2]

Clinton was alarmed for Burgoyne, and resolved to do his utmost to relieve the pressure on him. He was also angered by his message. Burgoyne had an independent command, and was now trying to climb out of his scrape by asking orders of an officer who was separated from him by 100 miles of unknown enemy country. Nor was it possible that Burgoyne believed Clinton could force a passage to Albany with the force he had

---

[1] Willcox, *American Rebellion*, 70 n. 26
[2] *Ibid.* 73.

promised to use. He sent off the messenger with a stiff letter in the third person:

Not having received any instructions from the Commander-in-Chief relating to the northern army, and ignorant of even his intentions concerning its operations (except his wishes it may get to Albany), Sir Henry Clinton cannot presume to send orders to General Burgoyne. But he thinks it impossible General Burgoyne could really suppose Sir Henry Clinton had any idea of penetrating to Albany with the small force he mentioned to him in his letter of the 11th September. What Sir Henry Clinton offered in that letter he has now undertaken. He cannot by any means promise himself success, but hopes the move may be serviceable to General Burgoyne, as his letter of the 21st intimates that even the menace of an attack will be of use.[1]

Clinton's opponent, General Putnam, had indeed been weakened by detachments to north and south, the most recent a reinforcement for Washington after the Brandywine battle; and he had now been reduced to 1,200 Continentals and 300 incompletely armed militia. The demonstration at Verplancks had induced him to withdraw his force at Peekskill four miles inland and to summon part of the garrisons of the river forts. At daybreak on the following morning Clinton flung his force across to the west bank of the Hudson. Leaving his cannon, he marched his infantry twelve miles by a path through the hills, surprised the two main forts commanding the river, and stormed them with the bayonet. Sixty-seven cannon and many stores fell into his hands; and the American flotilla guarding the Hudson boom was caught by foul winds and destroyed. On the 8th he scribbled a short note to Burgoyne: 'Nous y voila,[2] and nothing now between us but Gates. I sincerely hope this little success may facilitate your operations . . . I heartily wish you success.' But it never reached Burgoyne, for the messenger was intercepted and hanged.

Clinton had intended to halt where he was, and keep the Highlands open by dismantling Fort Montgomery and strengthening and holding Fort Clinton, with a force lower down the river which could either succour the fort or fall back on New York as might be needed.[3] But at that moment a letter arrived from the commander at Rhode Island, offering to spare a thousand men from his garrison. Clinton leapt at the offer, and having returned momentarily to New York he ordered three more regiments to the Highlands, and boats to be loaded with six months'

[1] Ibid., 74, n. 35, 378–80.
[2] Sic in CL, Germain.
[3] These forts were near the site of the modern Bear Mountain bridge. The West Point fortifications were developed later, when Forts Clinton and Montgomery were abandoned. The main fort at West Point was also named Clinton, ensuring future confusion. The military topography of the Highlands is lucidly described in Nickerson.

provisions for running up the river to Burgoyne. He then pushed General Vaughan up the Hudson towards Albany with 2,000 men in transports, to feel his way to Burgoyne and do his utmost to assist him. Vaughan reached Kingston[1] on the 15th, destroyed it to secure his communications, and felt his way further up the river. But he was still forty-five miles from Albany when the pilots refused to take the transports any further. The Americans had taken post on both banks, and he was unable to communicate with Burgoyne. But all accounts agreed that his position was desperate.

For eighteen long days Burgoyne had waited in his position below Bemis Heights. Sickness and a steady trickle of desertions were daily reducing his force, while reinforcements were pouring in to Gates. Lincoln's militiamen arrived from Vermont, and other armed men were appearing in their hundreds, enraged by carefully propagated stories of Indian atrocities. On 5 October Riedesel and Brigadier Fraser urged Burgoyne to retreat while there was still a chance; but in the teeth of their advice he hung on for two more days, and on the 7th launched a final attack to turn the American left. Gates now had 11,000 men. The result was disaster: another 600 men and ten guns lost; Fraser and Breymann dead; and the loss of a vital redoubt which made the British position untenable.

Burgoyne, in Clausewitz's memorable phrase on Waterloo, had thrown his last farthing. On the following day he fell back to Saratoga, abandoning 500 sick and wounded. His exhausted men dropped to the ground as they came into camp without cutting wood or making fires, and slept in the heavy rain. On the 9th the enemy were entrenching the heights on the far bank of the river to prevent a crossing. Short of a great American blunder, only one chance remained. Riedesel proposed to abandon guns and baggage and retire by forced marches to cross the Hudson above Fort Edward. At first Burgoyne refused; but on the 12th he yielded, and agreed to march in the darkness of the coming night. Rations for six days were distributed, and all was ready when Burgoyne cancelled the march. He had learnt from his scouts that no movement was possible without instant discovery; and on a height north of Fort Edward 2,000 New Hampshire militiamen were already posted to prevent his withdrawal. By the next day the unpredictable Stark had joined the enemy with his militia and the camp was closely beset on every side.

Nothing now was left except to wait in hopes of Clinton. But even time was short. The encircled army was under ceaseless fire. By day and by night the roar of cannon and the crack of rifle bullets continued, and the militia-

[1] Actually to Esopus, which Ward identifies with the modern Kingston. The present Esopus in 8 miles south of Kingston.

men swarmed round the lines. The ground was covered with the corpses of shot or starved horses. For the wounded there was no shelter from the bombardment even while the surgeons dressed their injuries. And for the unwounded there was neither safety nor rest. They stood to their arms by day and night. With only 3,500 men fit for duty, the fight could not continue long. On the 13th Burgoyne summoned his generals, field officers and captains commanding units, and all agreed that he should seek a capitulation. The next morning negotiations were opened. There was a brief moment when Burgoyne hoped that Vaughan's push for Kingston meant relief; but his officers advised him that it was now too late to withdraw from the negotiations. Gates for his part was eager to hasten the surrender. The capitulation became a convention and the beaten army was granted the honours of war and a return to England on condition of serving no more in America.

On 17 October the army from Canada marched out. They had fought a splendid fight; and it is sad that Burgoyne, who had retained their confidence to the last, should have blamed their courage among the reasons which he published to the world for his failure. If the whole army, he wrote to Howe, had been in spirit for a hardy enterprise, he could have cut his way through to Ticonderoga. But his Germans would rather be prisoners than endure hard blows. 'In short, my army would not fight and could not subsist.' Yet it was the German General who had begged him to try the retreat while there was still a slender chance.[1]

7. Conclusion

In round figures the British loss at Saratoga was not large. But it would be difficult to replace, and more serious still was the proof of what the perceptive had long suspected: that the American country with its armed population might be beyond the power of Britain to reconquer with any force which she could raise and sustain in America. The grand design of 1775 lay in ruins. For two seasons the British counter-offensive had hammered the Americans; and its failure marked the end of the private conflict between England and her rebel colonists. Saratoga was the sign for which France had waited; and the Great Powers began to enter the arena.

There was blame to apportion. The Opposition wanted a scapegoat in the Cabinet, the generals to defend themselves at the Ministry's expense. They joined forces in a general assault on Germain. But the generals'

[1] Royal Institution, I, 140. There is some suggestion in the German memoirs that Burgoyne had lost the confidence of General Phillips and other senior officers: he had never had Riedesel's (see Riedesel Memoirs, I, 238; Lowell, *Hessians*, 136–7; Eelking, 135; Madame Riedesel, 174, 176. The Brunswickers resented the imputation in Burgoyne's despatch, and Riedesel wrote a long defence of their conduct to the Duke of Brunswick.

needs diverged. Burgoyne wished to show that Germain had interfered too much; Howe that he had not intervened enough. 'The noble Secretary for the American Department', Howe was to declare to the House of Commons,[1] 'had not used him well; had often left him without instructions, to shift for himself at the opening of a campaign, without sending information how to act.' Burgoyne on the contrary complained that he had been tied by rigid dictated instructions which left no latitude.

Burgoyne's complaint seems to be supported by a letter which Carleton sent after his surrender. It has often been used against Germain.[2] 'This unfortunate event', it runs,

... will in future prevent Ministers from pretending to direct operations of war in a country at three thousand miles distance, of which they have so little knowledge as not to be able to distinguish between good, bad, or interested advices, or to give positive orders upon matters which, from their nature, are ever on the change.

What was in Carleton's mind? Resentment, certainly. His conduct of the campaign of 1776 had been criticised, and he had been deprived of the command of his own field force and the prospect of taking Howe under his command. But it has been shown, and Carleton well knew, that the chief source of interested advice was Burgoyne himself. The positive order to which Carleton most objected concerned the disposition of troops, and was dictated by Burgoyne. It had precedents in the time of Chatham[3]; had military approval; and was forced on Germain by his failure to remove Carleton, which obliged him to cast Burgoyne's requirements in the form of an order. The plan itself was Burgoyne's. The deletion of his two suggested alternatives had no effect on the outcome of the campaign; and the prescribed object of pushing through to Albany was not one which any commander at that distance in time and space should have treated as absolute. It was Burgoyne's use of this defence which convinced at least one contemporary that he was in the wrong: 'Men of lively imagination', wrote Henry Ellis from Berlin, 'are not fit for real business military or political, they make apt comparisons, ingenious metaphors and very probably fine speeches or florid despatches, but they are neither statemen nor soldiers'.[4]

The weakness of Burgoyne's defence is clear. To Howe's, Germain gave this reply, which might have served for them both[5]:

If the Hon. General had not immediate instructions when he called for them, it was because many things depended upon unforeseen circumstances; and as it was im-

---

[1] *Parl. Hist.*, XIX, 1395.
[2] E.g. James, 61; Fortescue, III, 244.
[3] See Whitworth, *Ligonier*, 241, 278, 286, 297–8.
[4] Add. MSS. 34415, ff. 3–7.   [5] *Parl. Hist.*, XIX, 1397.

possible to send letters every day beyond the Atlantic, the General must necessarily, in many respects, be left to his own discretion.

Germain knew Howe's plan just as he knew Burgoyne's, and he let him follow it. There was no need to provide him with a detailed recapitulation of his own proposals; for unlike Burgoyne he had no hostile superior between himself and the Minister. It has been argued that Germain should have intervened to veto his first change of plan, and prevent him from turning south to Pennsylvania. But it must be remembered that from the beginning Howe had framed all his own plans on the assumption that the advance from Canada would be resumed. It was no part of the general plan that he should support Burgoyne's initial advance to Albany. On both sides of the Atlantic it was assumed that the rebellion was on its last legs. The only danger to Burgoyne which was foreseen was that Washington might leave Pennsylvania undefended and turn on him with his whole force; a danger which became likely only when Howe abandoned the Jerseys and put out to sea. It seemed right to accept Howe's judgment of the decisive importance of Philadelphia, and to let him strike in that direction before joining Burgoyne, who in the meantime would have established himself on the Upper Hudson.

It remains, however, to ask whether the failure of the strategy which had been pursued though two campaigns proved it to have been unsound. Given that the rebellion had to be crushed quickly, and by an offensive on land, was the plan to dominate the Hudson valley a realistic and useful one? It was easy to say in retrospect that the distance between New York and Montreal was 300 miles, and that no chain of posts could be made secure enough to protect the communications over this distance: but till Burgoyne was defeated no one fully grasped the danger from the New England militia.[1] The advantage of controlling the Hudson line would have been great. It would have reduced the handicap of operating on exterior lines, for instead of the slow communications by sea which were shut entirely in the winter, there would have been a direct land route between the two bases. The unified command which had ceased in 1775 could then have been restored, and the two armies could have acted as one.

For the enemy, British control of the Hudson would have been disastrous. Permanent control of the whole length of the river was unnecessary, for if the British held the Highlands they could use the waterway beyond at any time, and cut the last link in Washington's lateral communications. His supplies and reinforcements would have been strangled with decisive effect: so at

[1] Least of all Burgoyne, though he had warned against underrating them in the first winter of the war (Fonblanque, 209).

any rate Benedict Arnold was to assert when he deserted the rebel cause.[1]

The irony of the campaign is that the keys rested for a moment in British hands. To check Howe in the south and Burgoyne in the north, the Americans had fatally weakened the nexus between the two fronts. By one of those bold tactical strokes which contrasted so oddly with his strategic timidity, Clinton had seized the forts of the Highlands which six days earlier or six hours later would have resisted the whole army of Howe. In spite of Burgoyne's disaster and the coming intervention of France, it is conceivable that the future pattern of the war would have been altered if the gateway could have been kept. But the day after Burgoyne's surrender, Clinton received an order from Howe to send five battalions and the remaining cavalry regiment immediately to garrison Philadelphia. Though Howe knew of Burgoyne's peril he gave Clinton no latitude, beyond a few days' delay if he should be engaged in operations on the Hudson. This order was followed shortly by instructions to dismantle and evacuate Fort Clinton, and forbidding the loan of troops from Rhode Island. Clinton therefore had no choice but to abandon the Highlands to ensure the safety of New York. Years later in his retirement he was to write that he had hoped Howe would strain every nerve to keep open the door of the Hudson: ' . . . had this been done, it would most probably have finished the war'.[2]

[1] Fortescue, III, 338: 'The supplies of meat for Washington's army are on the east side of the river, and the supplies of bread on the west; were the Highlands in our possession, Washington would be obliged to fight or disband his army for want of provisions.'

[2] Willcox, *American Rebellion*, 80-1; CO 5/94, f. 335.

PART TWO

THE WORLD WAR
1778

CHAPTER VII

THE MORROW OF SARATOGA

1. *Resignation of the Commanders-in-Chief*

The defeat at Saratoga is the clearest turning point of the war. It marked the beginning of a general war waged throughout the world; and it was the beginning of North's real parliamentary troubles. In the House of Commons and the Lords a hurricane broke over the heads of the Ministers. For a time the country gentlemen held firm, and Lord North maintained his large majority. But as the session dragged on and war with France drew near, these supporters began to fall away, and at the beginning of March an Opposition motion on the Budget was defeated by only six votes in a House of 288. Much of the political trouble turned on the treatment of the generals.

Saratoga was marked by the resignation of all the Commanders-in-Chief in America, and was the beginning of what was soon to become a characteristic misfortune of the war: bitter feuding between the Ministers and their naval and military commanders. By the end of 1777 both Carleton and Sir William Howe had resigned; and their example was to be followed by Lord Howe in the course of the coming year.

Carleton's resignation was not a consequence of the disaster, but of his feud with Germain. When he learnt that he was to hand over the bulk of his army to Burgoyne, he had treated it as a mark of disapprobation for his withdrawal from Lake Champlain, and replied to the Secretary of State in language of intemperate violence, reflecting with savage irony on Germain's military knowledge and personal integrity. 'An officer entrusted with the supreme command ought, upon the spot, to see what was most expedient to be done, better than a great General at three thousand miles distance . . . A little reflection on the nature of this climate will, I hope, convince your Lordship . . . a little military reasoning might prove . . . ' He accused Germain of having intended from the start to remove him at the first opportunity, and in the meantime to make his situation intolerable by every kind of slight, censure and disregard. 'Constitutionally I am not inclined to think it possible, that, from private enmity . . . a Secretary of State should avail himself of the trust, confidence and power of his office, to insult the authority of the King his Master, in a distant province'.

Carleton was moving from insolence to hysteria, but his letter measures the length to which the feud was carried, and the insinuations to which Germain's past misfortune could expose him. As Major Carleton wrote with satisfaction to Lord Shelburne, the Governor's 'correspondence with *Cain* will not dispose the latter to continue him in his government'. In all his correspondence with Germain it was Carleton who took the offensive. 'His nature had an ugly twist', says a Canadian historian who has done much to revise the unqualified admiration of Carleton which reigned half a century ago. Intolerance of criticism, a treacherous temper, and a ruthless determination to cut his way out of the difficulties it raised, did much to undermine his better qualities. How can one explain the passionate excesses of 1778? The same scholar suggests chagrin that his high promises of Canadian support had not been fulfilled, an uneasy conscience at the result of his lenient pursuit of the rebels in 1776, and the frustration of his hope that he might retrieve his errors by a successful campaign.[1]

Germain replied strongly, as Carleton's letters warranted, but with more restraint and a better aim. He remonstrated against the 'very extraordinary manner' in which Carleton had expressed himself, and reminded the General of what was constitutionally true, that he was the executive agent of measures which had been carefully canvassed by the government and approved by the King. 'It would ill become my situation to enter into an ill-humoured altercation with you.' He declared that he would never be so mean as to let personal resentment interfere with his duty, and that the imputation of personal dislike was without the least foundation. 'I trust you did not so lightly give credit to intelligence when you were to decide upon measures relating to the public service'.[2]

This reply crossed Carleton's formal resignation, which he sharpened with the parting hope that after his removal 'at least . . . the dignity of the Crown may not appear beneath your Lordship's concern'. General Haldimand, the commander in East Florida, was named as his successor. Like Prevost in Georgia, he was a Swiss who had never learnt to speak English well; but though he could not pretend to Carleton's qualifications for civil government, he was a thoroughly professional soldier of whom the German officers in Canada formed a high opinion.[3] Haldimand could not get up the St Lawrence till the summer of 1778; and Carleton made use of the delay to

[1] A. L. Burt, *Guy Carleton* . . . , summarises briefly the lifetime's reflections of a scholar on the subject. For fuller accounts see his articles, *inter alia*, on the case of Chief Justice Livius and Carleton's quarrel with Germain, in *Canadian Hist. Rev.*, 1924 and 1930.

[2] This correspondence is in CO 42/36, ff. 94-9, 136-7, 140, 165-71, 291; and Sackville, II, 133.

[3] Walpole's statement (*Last Journals*, II, 135) that Carleton had been a witness for the prosecution in Germain's trial, and Haldimand a witness for the defence, maintains his usual standard of accuracy. Both officers had been in America or Canada at the time.

dismiss Chief Justice Livius who had been appointed by Germain, an arbitrary gesture probably prompted by the Chief Justice's defence of the legal rights of the English-speaking minority.[1] When the Anhalt-Zerbst Regiment reached Quebec in May 1778 he refused to let it land as he had had no official notice of its coming, and the troops remained in their transports for three months while their Quartermaster went back to England for the necessary papers.

Carleton's conduct was a strange mixture of pettiness and magnanimity. On his return to England his personal feud with Germain continued to burn. He refused to justify his dismissal of Chief Justice Livius before the Privy Council, and the Chief Justice was reinstated. Germain for his part felt the General's insolence so deeply that he refused to sign a letter put before him by Knox which said that Carleton's information would be helpful to his successor. When the King rewarded the General's services with the Governorship of Charlemont, Germain threatened to resign; while Carleton for his part neither applied for the salary nor appointed anyone to look after the lands of the Governorship. Yet he did not intend to inflate his quarrel with Germain into a great public issue. In the Parliament enquiry of 1779 he refused to become the tool of the Opposition, like the Howes and Burgoyne. 'He answered like a gallant and wise man', wrote an M.P., 'scorning to make his court to a faction, either by abusing Lord George Germain or exculpating Burgoyne.'[2]

Carleton was an able man, but he did not make it easy to use him. He 'dislikes Lord Amherst so much', the King told Lord North in 1779, 'that it is not very easy to employ him'. Nor could he work again with the American Secretary after the letters he had written: letters, said Germain four years later, of which 'the style and manner . . . were improper to have passed between one gentleman and another'. Carleton was not re-employed in the army as long as Germain remained in the Ministry, but in 1780 Lord North gave him an important civil employment as head of his new Commission of Accounts.[3]

The trouble with General Howe ran a different course. Throughout 1776 his relations with Germain had been excellent. But in the course of 1777 they deteriorated; and after his resignation Howe complained in the House of Commons that Germain had not given him his co-operation or confidence, nor accepted his recommendations for promotion. Germain's reply, as clear-headed as Howe was confused, turned the House against the General.[4]

---

[1] See A. L. Burt's articles in *Canadian Hist. Rev.*, 1924 and 1930.
[2] G 2202; WO 34/138, f. 82; Malmesbury Letters, I, 410.
[3] G 2754; CL, Germain, 16 Dec. 1781.
[4] Germain's reply is in Parl. Deb., XIX, 1395 ff. Walpole reports the impression it made.

In the matter of favours only three of Howe's recommendations had been held up; one for three days till a promotion of Colonels took place, and two for solid reasons which Germain explained to the House. The withholding of co-operation alleged by Howe can have referred only to Germain's inability at the beginning of 1777 to reinforce him to the full extent of his unreasonable hopes, and like several commanders in the course of the war he treated the failure to fulfil his demands for reinforcements as a personal slight. The complaint of lack of confidence must be based on two criticisms which Germain had made in the course of 1777: his infrequent letters, and his failure to distress the rebel coasts. The Ministry had endured long periods without news in 1776; and when Howe's A.D.C. returned to him at the opening of his second campaign with Germain's remarks on his plans, he carried a verbal request for more frequent and explicit despatches. The message had no effect. The silences were long, the hints of his intentions vague. 'It is surprising that the General should be so fond of concealing his operations', Germain wrote to the King. News of the army had to be gleaned from Admiralty despatches. Not a line did Howe pen from 17 July, before he sailed from New York, till 30 August five days after his landing in the Chesapeake; nor did he write again till 10 October. His evacuation of New Jersey and his embarkation were known from private letters from America and reports from France. Germain may be forgiven for writing that he awaited Howe's despatches with impatience.[1]

This was a small complaint. On the conduct of operations Germain voiced a more serious dissatisfaction. He had always been anxious to distress the rebels in every possible way. But the Howes seemed to let American shipping come and go as it pleased; and the American Secretary's dislike of their liberality with pardons seemed to be vindicated by the defections after Trenton. If the two brothers, the King wrote to Robinson,

will act with a little less lenity (which I really think cruelty, as it keeps up the contest) the next campaign will bring the Americans in a temper to accept of such terms as may enable the mother country to keep them in order; for we must never come into such as may patch for a year or two, and then bring on new broils; the regaining their affection is an idle idea, it must be the convincing them that it is their interest to submit, and then they will dread further broils.

It is now that Sandwich, probably prompted by the King, remonstrated with Admiral Howe at the one-sided lenity of letting the inhabitants use their fishing boats. Germain, in accepting Sir William's plan to switch his main effort towards Philadelphia, suggested diversions against the New England coast to impede their recruiting and secure the British trade.[2]

[1] Knox, 130; G 2010; CO 5/94, f. 242.
[2] Sackville, II, 58; CO 5/94, f. 106; Sandwich, I, 288; Add. MSS. 37833, f. 137.

Coastal raiding was of real military importance. In April 1777 a raid on Danbury in Connecticut destroyed a large quantity of stores, including 1,700 tents which Washington could only replace from abroad. One effect of the raid was to make the Connecticut authorities reluctant to send militia to Peekskill and relieve the Continentals guarding the Highlands: a hesitation which gave Clinton his chance at Forts Clinton and Montgomery. Washington believed that Connecticut was indefensible to the depth of a full day's march from the coast, and argued that the only provident course was to move all valuable large stores further north.[1] But Howe in 1777 believed he could spare no troops for coastal raiding. This Germain perhaps unwisely lamented. He accepted that Howe on the spot was the best judge; but rebel privateers were very active that summer, and public opinion at home would have welcomed counter-measures against the enemy's coast. People were looking for bold and enterprising measures; and he told Howe that he would have liked to see him win the applause of the ignorant as well as of better judges.[2]

These were the slender grounds which Howe offered for his resignation. But there is a more probable explanation than these. His resignation accompanied the first rumours of Burgoyne's disaster. Anderson, in his sympathetic study of the Howe brothers, came to believe that some time after Trenton Sir William began to realise the vastness and complexity of his task, and his own inadequacy to surmount it. This was reflected in both his private and public life: in public by a desire above all else not to make mistakes, and in private by recourse to the bottle. An American brigadier remarked that he was 'certainly too indolent and too ignorant for the command of such an army'; and General Lee, his prisoner and a former British officer, described him as 'totally confounded and stupefied by the immensity of the task imposed upon him. He shut his eyes, fought his battles, drank his bottle, had his little whore . . .' Anderson calls this a caricature. But several field officers lend credit to the view that Howe's limitations were becoming apparent to others, and that the hand which disciplined the army was growing lax. Colonel Stuart complained of the habitual carelessness and neglect in the field, and the relaxed discipline which allowed the campaign in Pennsylvania to open with every kind of irregularity. Allen Maclean, the saviour of Quebec, saw the same deficiency of leadership in the war of posts after Trenton, and declared that the successes hitherto gained had been due solely to the bravery and impetuosity of the troops. Sir William he called 'a very honest man, and I believe a very disinterested one. Brave he certainly is, and would make a very good executive officer under another's command,

[1] Freeman, IV, 410–11.
[2] Sackville, II, 68; CL, Germain, 4 Aug. to Howe.

but he is by no means equal to a Commander-in-Chief' Major Wemyss, wrote thus in retrospect:

he succeeded General Gage with the good opinion of the army; but it was soon discovered, that however fit to command a corps of grenadiers [he] was altogether unequal to the duties of a Commander-in-Chief. . . . His manners were sullen and ungracious, with a dislike to business, and a propensity to pleasure. His staff officers were in general below mediocrity, with some of whom, and a few field officers, he passed too much of his time in private conviviality.

On the quality of his staff Maclean agreed: 'none but very silly fellows about him – a great parcel of old women'.[1]

By the spring of 1778 Howe seems to have lost the confidence of his best officers. He was given a convivial farewell, as befitted a convivial man. But dissatisfied field officers were not his only critics. The loyalists naturally criticised him bitterly for despising their help and missing his opportunities. The Hessians too, who liked his easy ways and hospitality, criticised his professional conduct. From White Plains to Germantown they saw a long procession of missed opportunities, costly delays, omissions of planning, and carelessness in details. On any single occasion Howe's apologists can find plausible explanations of his conduct. But the weight of the indictment lies in the cumulative impression of his actions, and in failures which run through the whole scale of events from the great decisions to the details.[2]

2. A Distracted Leader

The first storm, however, was raised by Burgoyne. When Parliament learnt the news of Saratoga on 3 December, Germain was bitterly assailed by Fox and Richmond. When he expressed a hope that Burgoyne would not be condemned unheard, Fox flared in the General's defence, charging Germain with the whole responsibility for the disaster and hoping that he would be brought to a second trial. Germain had wished to defer an enquiry into the campaign till Burgoyne came home to defend himself; but Burgoyne's letters were so clearly intended to incriminate him that under Fox's attack he felt justified in proceeding at once to a military enquiry on the limited question whether the orders to push for Albany had been absolute. The Adjutant-General supported a limited enquiry on this crucial point, but the King felt that not only Germain's conduct was in question, and that the enquiry ought to be a general one into the whole failure of the expedition.

[1] CL, Germain, Dr Berkenhout's journal, 1778; Anderson, 320, 331, 337, 342; Wortley, 101–2, 104–5, 115–6; Harvard, Sparks MSS. XXII, p. 214 (character sketch by Major Wemyss).

[2] Nelson, 135–8; Eelking, 26–7, 50, 52, 105, 112–13, 116–20.

With this doubt in the air, the Cabinet divided evenly on whether the partial investigation should be ordered, and for the moment Germain allowed it to drop.[1]

The case of Sir William Howe did not develop into a parliamentary battle till later; but his resignation produced an immediate conflict in the Cabinet. Permission to quit his command was deferred till the end of the campaign ; but at the beginning of February the Cabinet, torn between the danger of employing an unwilling commander under a hostile Minister and the difficulty of replacing him, reluctantly agreed that he should be ordered to hand over to Clinton and come home. Germain read the letter to the Cabinet before it was sent; but Lord Bathurst had left the meeting, and ten days later he suddenly resigned because the letter had been coldly phrased.

Bathurst seems to have been moved by personal hostility to the American Secretary. But as a matter of political calculation North and the King both hoped for several weeks that Germain would resign in order to make way for a reconstruction of the Ministry and a new peace policy. And for a time he talked of doing so. In January he received a severe personal blow by the sudden death of his wife from measles. It could have struck him at no more vulnerable moment, and only the support and encouragement of Suffolk persuaded him to remain in office. Bathurst was induced by the King to withdraw his resignation, for fear that it would be the last straw which would make North give up; and Germain was persuaded to send off a conciliatory letter to Howe.[2]

North had been begging for release from the moment when the Saratoga disaster was known. In the face of French preparations he had long since lost whatever faith he had had in total victory. Weeks before the Saratoga news he had characterised the struggle as 'this damned war'. 'I am very melancholy notwithstanding our victory', he had remarked on the news of Brandywine: 'my idea of American affairs is, that, if our success is as great as the most sanguine politician wishes or believes, the best use we can make of it is to get out of the dispute as soon as possible'.[3] He felt, however, that the Ministry in its present form could not honourably abandon its American policy, and his thoughts turned to Chatham: the man to rally the country

[1] Suffolk, Sandwich and North supported Germain, while Bathurst, Dartmouth and the two 'Bedfords' opposed him. How far hostility to Germain himself can be read into this division is a matter of doubt, since we do not know the course of the discussion or the objectors' reasons. Ritcheson (241–2) is perhaps more positive than the evidence warrants. See G 2108, 2122, 2124, 2126–7, 2161. The draft (probably by Eden) on which the Cabinet divided is Add. MSS. 34414, f. 497 (see also ff. 461, 501).

[2] CO 5/94, f. 376; Sackville, I, 73, 139; II, 90–3; G 2152, 2154, 2156, 2161, 2194, 2195; Bathurst, 17–8.

[3] Add. MSS. 34414, ff. 309–10.

in its hour of defeat, to reconcile America without conceding independence, to marshal the nation's resources against the danger from France. The times indeed required a Chatham, confident, ruthless and domineering. Lord North knew it well. 'Whoever comes to the assistance of government', he told the King, 'must be the director and dictator of the leading measures of government . . . Lord North's diffidence of himself is grounded upon seven years' experience, and will for ever render it fatal to His Majesty to continue him at the Treasury.'[1]

The appeal was vain. The King was willing to admit Chatham to the existing Ministry; but he feared that if he formed one of his own it would be to shackle the Crown. Deaf to Lord North's entreaties, he clung to his present servants. They would survive in office because the Opposition was too deeply divided on the question of American independence to unite in the House of Commons. In April Chatham's death removed the possibility of his accession, and the Ministry struggled feebly on into the great war which lay ahead. And at the head of affairs was a man who 'had become the mere sum of the forces acting upon him'[2]: Lord North remained at the Treasury, the distracted leader of a divided Cabinet.

3. A Strategic Re-appraisal

The lack of a leader was apparent on the day after the news of Saratoga. It was clear that even if France did not enter the war, the assault on the citadels of rebellion had failed, and some new plan was needed. 'I can think and speak of nothing but America', Germain told Eden. For the time being the catastrophe had destroyed his confidence in the policy of military reconquest, and he fell back on the idea of a naval war. Troops should be used only to hold the navy's bases and raid the coastline, under commanders with full powers to treat for peace. But North was too distracted by the political clamour to initiate a re-appraisal. It was a situation often repeated in the years to come; and the means used on this occasion to force the problem on the Prime Minister's attention were to become standard techniques as North's will increasingly broke down. The approaches were two: from below through underlings, and from above through the King.

Germain was working for a meeting with North and Suffolk. But instead of approaching the Prime Minister directly, he sent his ideas to Suffolk's Under-Secretary, Eden, whose influence with North was then in the ascendant. Eden put down on paper some of the questions it was essential to decide, in the hope that North would focus his mind on them. Should we

[1] G 2239.   [2] Ritcheson, 251.

reduce our effort in America to a maritime war? If so, we must decide
what bases to keep, how to hold them, and what ships to employ. Should
the Howes be recalled, and the naval command split into three separate
blockading stations? Above all, what were the political implications of such
a war? It would end the quest for a decisive victory and a dictated peace.
The struggle would become one of attrition in which weariness might draw
both sides towards a compromise. The ground must be prepared for a new
negotiation; and Eden suggested a clean sweep of existing Acts of Parliament
and a new Commission to investigate colonial grievances and devise a
settlement. Such a descent from the proud expectations of 1775 might
discredit the Ministry, and particularly the American Secretary. In the first
black days after Saratoga, when Germain had confessed that he began to
despair of victory if the rebels continued united, he had declared in the House
his opposition to a federal union, and said that if the colonies could not be
brought back to a state of constitutional obedience, he would prefer to break
all political connection with them. With this in mind, Eden suggested
privately to North that the way might be cleared by the removal of the
unbending Secretary to the House of Lords.[1]

The King was pressing independently for a radical review of strategy.
Like Germain he believed that the army would have to be reduced to the
defensive, and he urged North to consult Amherst and others who knew
America. Under this pressure North assembled the Cabinet, and matters
began to move. Sandwich was asked by the Cabinet to produce the naval
view, while the King sought a military opinion from Amherst, who was
interviewed first by North, Suffolk and Sandwich, and then by the whole
Cabinet. Sandwich and Amherst were found to be in complete agreement:
military reconquest must give place to maritime pressure. Sandwich, indeed,
in the light of French intentions, challenged the fundamental assumption
that America was the vital theatre; a doubt which was to permeate his thought
from this time on. But if the colonies were still to be the main point of effort,
he agreed with Germain that we should rely on naval pressure. Hitherto the
blockade had failed because Howe's ninety ships had been absorbed in
supporting the army's offensives, enabling the enemy to import and survive.
A new directive should now be sent to Lord Howe to concentrate his
resources against the rebels' ports, including (Sandwich added on Germain's
suggestion) support for coastal attacks by the army.

Amherst regarded conquest as impossible without a reinforcement of thirty
or forty thousand men; but even a sea-war would need additional troops.
England would need 33,000 men in America and Canada to secure the navy's
bases, and 12,000 more if Philadelphia was retained. Thus, surveying the ruins

[1] Add. MSS. 34414, ff. 394–8; Parl. Hist., XIX, 530.

of past strategy, the King, the American Secretary, the First Lord of the Admiralty, and the Ministry's most trusted General were united in disavowing the attempt to reconquer America on land. When the attempt was resumed in 1779 it would take a very different form.[1]

If the blockade was to be made effective more naval bases were needed, for the Halifax yard was too remote to service squadrons blockading the whole length of the American coastline. The professional members of the Board of Admiralty were questioned by the Cabinet; and their advice was to separate the blockading fleet into several squadron stations with their own yards. It was agreed that a Navy Commissioner should be sent to New York to create a proper dockyard for that station; but about bases for the southern squadrons the Board had little information, for though Lord Howe had long since been ordered to report on suitable harbours he had not complied. But for the central station Mulgrave and Palliser suggested Hampton Roads or Norfolk in the Chesapeake. In this proposal lay one of the germs of Yorktown.[2]

The new strategy was one of dispersed security. Instead of reinforcing the main army to maintain the offensive, a reinforcement was hurried off to defend Canada, and another to strengthen Halifax, whose loss would be irreparable. Only three or four thousand men could be spared for the main theatre.

On 8 March, five days before the rupture with France threw these plans into the melting pot, Germain signed the orders to Clinton.[3] The diversion of troops to Canada and Halifax as a result of Burgoyne's surrender left only seven regiments and some recruits immediately available to strengthen Clinton. Therefore if he could not bring Washington to a decisive battle at the outset of the campaign, he was to cease offensive operations inland and assail the coasts of New England. He should hold Philadelphia if he could spare the force; but if he needed its garrison for his coastal attacks, he was authorised to withdraw it.

The orders continued with a glance to the future. In the following autumn (by which time it was hoped that new regiments raised by bounty subscriptions would enable further reinforcements to be sent), an attempt should be made to recover Georgia and South Carolina. If all the colonies south of

[1] G 2092, 2094, 2131, 2170, 2172; Sandwich, I, 312, 327 ff., 355-9; Sackville, II, 94-9; Willcox, *JMH*, 1947.

[2] Willcox's suggestion that the plan to extend the bases southwards was opposed in Admiralty circles is based on the correspondence with Shelburne of Robert Gregson, a malcontent Navy Board clerk. But it should be borne in mind that Palliser and Mulgrave, professional members of the Board of Admiralty, were advocates of the extension.   [3] Sackville, II, 94-9 (fuller version CO 5/95).

the Susquehanna could be recovered, the northern ones might be left to their own distress, and the operations confined to a blockade. These suggestions were so pregnant with triumph and disaster that their origins deserve a closer examination.

It will be remembered that Howe's original plan for 1777 had foreseen a winter conquest of the southern colonies from Virginia to Georgia.[1] The prospect had made a strong appeal to Germain, and with the southerner Knox at his back he felt sure that Georgia at least could be recovered with ease.[2] His hopes were sustained in the late summer of 1777 by a memorial from the southern Governors and Lieutenant-Governors in England, based on information from returning officials and refugees, which set forth the practicability and importance of recovering the southern colonies that winter. On 3 September, before the shadow of the coming disaster at Saratoga fell across the future, he communicated the Governors' memorial to General Howe, with a reminder that the conquest of the south in the course of the winter formed part of his eventual plans. If Howe would carry any part of his army to the south this winter, he told Knox privately, 'I should have little doubt of their success.'[3]

Before Howe took up his reluctant pen to reply, the disappointments of his Pennsylvania campaign and the disaster to Burgoyne had unrolled. His answer in January 1777 damned the plan out of hand. No force could be spared for the south; he intended to concentrate against the main army of the enemy; and past experience had proved that nothing more could be expected from the mass of the population than an equivocal neutrality, so that the army could not rely on the loyalists to hold its gains.[4] This letter has been used to deride the whole southern concept. Yet it specifically referred to 'this winter', and though Howe was unable to forecast a date when the plan could be attempted, he did not condemn it for ever. Moreover, the letter was questionable in its sentiments and irrelevant to the new conditions which were emerging. In the first place, as a recent writer on the loyalists has said, Howe had never shaken off his early experience of their weakness in New England and disorganisation in the Middle Colonies. Indeed Howe was himself to own, when it pleased him to regret the evacuation of Philadelphia, that his firm possession of the city had encouraged the numerous loyalists of the Middle Colonies to arm and assist him.[5]

Two circumstances had altered the outlook since Howe had written. One

[1] Above, p. 110.
[2] CL, Germain, 2 April 1777 to Mr Stuart.
[3] CO 5/95, f. 299; CL, Knox, 13 Sept. 1777.
[4] CO 5/95, f. 64.   [5] Nelson, 139; Howe's *Narrative*, 32.

was that the army was now to disengage in the northern interior if it could not bring Washington to an early and decisive battle; the other, a revulsion in England against the northern colonies and a feeling that they were not worth the effort of recovering. This had long since been argued by Knox, and it may have been now that he wrote two memoranda which assailed the past strategy of the war. He asserted that in attacking the rebels where they were strongest, England had begun at the wrong end. Instead of pressing south from Pennsylvania against Virginia, the army should begin its assault by taking Georgia, when South and North Carolina would fall in succession; and Virginia, with the navy on the coast, the Indians on their backs, and the main army on their north, would then be seriously pressed.[1]

Here lies the germ of the future campaigns in the south. A supporting argument, equally persuasive and perhaps more influential, was being pressed on the Cabinet by that authority on commercial questions, Charles Jenkinson of the Treasury. At some time after Saratoga he discussed the American situation with North or Germain, and urged that if England was to contract her operations in America the wisest course would be to give up New England altogether and make the barrier of the Empire on the Hudson. He amplified these views on paper. His military argument was that there were no important militia forces south of Pennsylvania; and that the main militia forces of the rebellion belonged to New England, which could neither afford distant operations nor intervene to the southward if the British army fortified and held a blocking line on the Hudson. But Jenkinson's commercial arguments were more unusual: revolutionary indeed from the pen of a Minister. He reasoned that England had no need to control New England's trade. Of all the produce of the rebel colonies only the tobacco of the south was worth monopolising by restrictive trade laws; and of England's exports to America only linen and some silks would suffer if every Act of Trade were repealed. New England would always buy British woollen goods, hardware and India goods because we sold them cheapest: indeed, if the swollen import figures of Canada and Nova Scotia meant anything, the New Englanders were buying them by stealth at that very moment. Most of their other British imports were for re-export to the Spanish Main, and were finding their way there through other channels. New England's own exported products mostly went to foreign markets; and the enumerated articles, potash and naval stores, could be got elsewhere except for the great masts of New Hampshire. New England, in a word, could be cast out of the Empire without damage to Britain's wealth or security. 'If I should happen to be right, how much mistaken and deluded have been the people of this country for more than a century past. I bow

[1] CL, Knox, Vol. 9, Nos. 21–2.

with reverence to the Act of Navigation, but I pay very little respect to the Acts of Trade.'[1]

The view that the British effort should be concentrated against the south was a plausible one after Saratoga. The southern colonies were in many ways the soft underbelly of the rebellion. It was not only that there were loyalists in the back country. Though the population was expanding rapidly, it was sparser than in the north, and lived in fear of a huge slave population which was suspected of Tory sympathies. There were three-quarters of a million whites spread from Maryland to Georgia, and nearly half as many negroes. These southern colonies, with their thin populations, their slave problem, and their dependence on exporting their crops, might well prove easier to subdue and more profitable to hold than the populous and stubborn New England.[2]

The political aspect of the new plan was tackled as Eden had suggested. Even the King recognised that the political objects of the war had to be lowered: a sea war could do no more than force the Americans to 'come into what Britain may decently consent to'; a vague formula, but humble compared with the proud aims of 1775. Before the Christmas recess North had promised the House that he would introduce new peace proposals; and in the New Year he closeted himself with Eden and the law officers to draft the bills. For some weeks their contents remained a mystery even to the Cabinet; but early in February they were passed by a silent and gloomy House. England was to renounce the right to tax America except for the regulation of trade; and new Commissioners were appointed with full powers to treat for any terms short of independence.[3]

On the new Commission was Eden himself. Eager to be dissociated from the foundering Ministry, he had prepared a rewarding post at a safe distance. The nominal leader of the mission was his young friend the Earl of Carlisle, needy son-in-law of Lord Gower, trailing a seedy crew of gamblers and place-hunters in his wake: 'very fit', said Horace Walpole, 'to make a treaty that will not be made'.

4. The Breach with France

Walpole's comment reached the heart of the matter. For the centre of gravity was no longer in Philadelphia, but in Paris. If France entered the war, the Americans were unlikely to consider any terms short of independence. This was well recognised; and as soon as the news of Burgoyne's

[1] Add. MSS. 38210, ff. 187–91.
[2] For the southern population, see Alden, *The South* . . . , 7–10.
[3] For the origins of the Carlisle Mission, see Ritcheson, 258ff.

capitulation reached London, North and Eden had sent off an unofficial emissary of American birth to talk with Franklin and his fellow Commissioners in Paris. But so secret was the mission, and so devious the course North was steering through the ministerial shoals, that Germain knew nothing of it, and independently allowed an emissary of his own to contact Franklin.

Lord North's instrument was the intelligence agent Paul Wentworth. His purpose, like that of Germain's agent William Pulteney, was to head the Americans off from a French alliance. But the effect of his mission was the opposite. The astute Franklin played him off against the French. When Wentworth reached Paris Louis XVI had already authorised treaty negotiations with the American Commissioners; and his arrival merely frightened Vergennes into speeding up the discussions. Without even waiting to refer to Madrid, he promised recognition of America's independence and a treaty of alliance. It was a critical decision for France, for about that time war broke out between Austria and Prussia, and presented her with a choice between Europe and the oceans. On 6 February 1778 treaties of Commerce and Alliance were signed with the Americans. Louis XVI resigned his opportunity to exploit the troubles of Germany, and France went forward into a maritime and colonial struggle: to triumph, bankruptcy and revolution.

When the bills for the new Peace Commission were passed by the House of Commons, the news of the French treaties was already speeding across the Atlantic to close the doors on compromise. Of this the Cabinet was well informed. By the end of January the Ambassador in Paris had convinced the Ministry that France's pacific declaration was a mask for treachery.[1] And from Bancroft, Secretary to the American Commissioners and British spy, Eden's office received every detail of the treaties' contents.

At the beginning of March a French squadron in Quiberon Bay was known to be preparing to escort an American convoy into the Atlantic. No ink was wasted on remonstrance, for the French had weighed the consequences, and no British arguments were likely to deflect them.[2] Instead, orders went out on 10 March to naval Commanders-in-Chief to seize all vessels trading with the rebels, regardless of whether they were escorted by a foreign Power. A clash at sea now seemed inevitable; but the rupture of relations came more formally. On 13 March the French Ambassador informed Lord Weymouth of his government's Treaty of Commerce with the United States. Nothing was said of the Treaty of Alliance, but the commercial treaty in itself meant recognition of America's independence. The same night Lord Stormont was recalled from Paris.

[1] SP 78/306, Stormont's of 25 Jan. and Weymouth's of 30 Jan.
[2] SP 78/306, 6 March, Weymouth to Stormont.

This was not war. Many weeks were to pass before fighting began. Every shot would reverberate through the close network of European alliances; and while England still hoped that the Carlisle Mission might persuade Congress not to ratify the treaties, France was anxious not to forego her defensive alliances by appearing the aggressor. The French Foreign Office drew up a remarkable study which showed that there were almost no grounds on which France could with prudence justify a declaration of war. Anglo-American ideas of the rights of man were not generally received in the political society of Europe; and it would not be wise to appeal to these, putting in the mouth of a French king assertions of natural liberty, popular sovereignty, and inalienable rights straight out of Rousseau's *Social Contract*. Nor could France set herself up as an arbitrator between England and her colonies, after evading her duty as a guarantor of the Peace of Westphalia and allowing the annexation of Bavaria. Nor was it wise for one colonial power to lecture another on constitutional principles. The author's recommendation was to avoid all discussion of the American treaties, which were indefensible, and to concentrate on France's own grievances against England. These were slight, but noise and hyperbole could be used to swamp England's weightier complaints. The only reply to protests against the treaties must be the cannon. Restrained by these considerations, France like England waited with matches lighted for the smoke of the first shot to break from a warship's battery.[1]

[1] Harvard, Sparks MSS., LXXV (18 March, Favier to Vergennes).

CHAPTER VIII

THE NAVAL MOBILISATION

1. Sandwich and the Admiralty

This was the moment of truth for Lord Sandwich. For seven years he had been at the head of the navy; and now his work was to face the test of major operations. In no earlier war had France and England committed their fates so completely to the seas. France had chosen to forego her opportunities on the continent, and England had no bridgehead or allies in Europe to enable her to harass the enemy by land. Both powers could use their military forces only to the extent which sea power allowed. Everything depended on the control of maritime communications.

Something has already been said about Lord Sandwich's place in the political scene, and his share of responsibility for the divisions in the navy.[1] He was an unpopular figure in many quarters. The rakes had not forgiven 'Jemmy Twitcher's' prosecution of his friend Wilkes; and the respectable abhorred the looseness of his life. Yet there was much to be said for this tall, shambling, vigorous man. If his London house was embellished by Martha Ray the actress and her two bastards, his life had been clouded by the madness of his wife. He had great social charm, and the atmosphere of his home was relaxed, pleasant and musical. When the French war approached he was in his sixtieth year, with a long and varied experience behind him: Fellow of the Royal Society, soldier, plenipotentiary at the Peace of Aix-la-Chapelle. He had served on the Board of Admiralty in the War of the Austrian Succession, and then as First Lord till 1751; and had returned to the Cabinet for two years in 1763 as First Lord and then Secretary of State.

A very hostile account of his career[2] admits that Sandwich was esteemed and loved by his subordinates at the Admiralty; and Philip Stephens, who served as Secretary to the Admiralty for thirty years and remained in office when Sandwich retired, took much trouble to draw up the case for his defence. A legend persists that he was a slothful Minister; but contemporaries as well as his own voluminous correspondence bear witness to his industry. His enemy Lord Howe owned in 1779 that 'to give him his due, he is seldom backward . . . in answering letters'.[3]

[1] Introduction, pp. 7–8, 10–12.   [2] Sir Charles Laughton in *DNB*.
[3] Huntington Library, HO 11 (29 June 1779, Howe to Capt. Curtis). See also Wraxall Memoirs, II, 180; Butler, *Reminiscences*, 71.

The most persistent critic of Sandwich's office habits was Sir Charles Middleton, who succeeded Sir Maurice Suckling as Comptroller in 1778. This great administrator was commanding a fifty-gun ship on the stocks when Suckling's death in July 1778 called him from a seaman's life to the administrative career which was to bring him to the head of the Admiralty in the year of Trafalgar. His predecessor Suckling had served the country well by bringing his nephew Horatio Nelson into the navy. But his three years at the Navy Board had been marred by failing health; and according to Middleton he had been unable to get business through the Board in the face of some contentious and domineering colleagues. Middleton was a more formidable chairman. Thorough, capable of sustained effort, and patient in the pursuit of long-term objectives, he applied himself to the task of improving the navy's administration. His first task was to end the contention at the Navy Board. By bringing everything to the vote at once, he silenced the endless debate which clogged its business. He threw himself whole-heartedly into the work of his office; labours which increased continuously as the war went on. 'The Comptroller', wrote an Official of the Navy Board, 'is the most indefatigable and able of any in my time. The load of business he gets through at the Board, at the Treasury, at the Admiralty and his own house, is astonishing, and what I am confident no other man will be able to execute.'[1]

But his own labours alone could not make administration flow. If we are to believe him, there existed above his own Board a greater clog to efficiency in the Admiralty itself. There action was held up because letters lay un-answered. Ships ready in harbour awaited the Admiralty's orders for stores and victuals, or for the appointment of boatswains and carpenters to receive them. Middleton contended that there were two causes: lack of supervision by the First Lord, and lack of professional knowledge on the Board. Too much was left to the Secretary, who could not take decisions or remove difficulties without time-wasting reference to the Board. The management of 400 warships required unremitting application, and Middleton begged the First Lord to read the correspondence from the Navy Board himself, and take the necessary action. This, rather than the juggling of appointments, would save the Ministry: 'measures are more likely to support your Lordship's administration than men'.[2]

The portrait of Middleton which emerges from his letters shows a gentle-man of independent fortune who had occupied himself with farming before the approach of war brought him back to active service. He said that he had no interest in the emoluments of his office; his interest was in its duties.

[1] Barham, II, 209; CL, Shelburne, Vol. 151, No 87.
[2] Sandwich, III, 181; IV, 385; Barham, II, 41.

In Middleton and Sandwich the coming age confronted the *ancien régime*. One was the head of a great Whig family; the other the son of a Scots Customs collector, with two generations of Aberdeen professors behind him. Sandwich was a political jobber, for whom public service was to a considerable extent a matter of pushing one's friends and interests; Middleton a professional seaman and public servant, and a censorious advocate of administrative reform and of professionalism and integrity in government. The new Comptroller was a friend of Lord Shelburne, and a forerunner of the administrators who were soon to convert the archaic racket called government into the efficient instrument which transformed Victorian England. His principles, so different from the First Lord's, are concentrated in a single phrase: 'right measures will always make their own way, if supported with integrity and disinterestedness'.[1]

Yet there is another side to the picture. Middleton seems to have created his own legend by persistent self-advertisement. 'My turn to business and application' was the constant theme of his letters to Sandwich and later to Shelburne. 'The truth is . . . I suffer no object to divert my attention from the public business, and therefore I am seldom wrong in my information concerning it.' He was exceedingly ambitious and by no means as free from connections as he liked to imply. Before he became Comptroller he was not above promising the First Lord his vote and influence in East India Company affairs. He was related to those Scottish political manipulators, the Dundases; and before discussing his appointment to the Navy Board with Sandwich he told him he wished to talk the matter over with 'some confidential friends (who by their intimate connection with my family are particularly interested in any change of my destination)'. He repeatedly solicited Sandwich to find an appointment for his brother. Nor was his long connection with Shelburne a wholly disinterested, though it was a devious one. 'The only return I expect', he wrote of his private reports on naval reform when Shelburne was Prime Minister, 'is to be kept out of sight in all the particulars . . . I may furnish your Lordship with on public subjects.' He had backed a winner who might soon become a loser.[2]

Middleton's desire for a new office of Sea Ordnance[3] may have been in the best interest of the navy; but it also bears the stamp of his engrossing ambition. His heavy load of work was caused in part by over-centralisation. He wished the office of Comptroller to carry a seat on the Board of Admiralty; and he wanted a professional seaman (and who better qualified

---

[1] CL Shelburne, Vol. 151, No. 54
[2] Williams Transcripts, 23 March 1776 and 8 March 1778, Middleton to Sandwich; Williams, Thesis, 277; Sandwich, IV, 371; CL, Shelburne, Vol. 151, No. 41.
[3] Above, p. 18.

than himself?) in the Cabinet. He got his seaman in the Cabinet in the end: it was Keppel. A short experience of Keppel as First Lord persuaded him that the head of the Admiralty should be a politician, with a statesman's power to support his subordinates and a landsman's humility in naval matters.[1]

The Navy Board had long been extending its authority. Captain Lord Mulgrave, whose junior rank attracted Middleton's criticism of his seat on the Board of Admiralty, was deeply suspicious of the Navy Board's tricks and of its greedy over-centralisation of dockyard administration. Rodney attributed the Admiralty's frequent ignorance of the real state of the fleet to the lack of regular statements from the Navy Board, and advocated tighter supervision: 'The Navy Board . . . has ever been ambitious of rendering themselves an independent Board. They have never carried their point, and I hope never will'.[2]

It is in this context that Middleton's criticisms of Sandwich must be judged. There was certainly some substance in his views, and they were echoed by Germain. Yet Middleton was at least as critical of Sandwich's successors: he disliked his masters, whoever they might be. Sandwich was the prisoner of an over-centralised and inflexible machine; and if he kept short office hours, he must be judged by the standards of the age: in indicting Sandwich, Middleton was indicting the business methods of a class and a generation. To Middleton himself the frantic overwork of a modern war-administrator was unknown. In 1779, at the height of the naval danger, he complained that he could only devote one day a week to private business, and needed five whole days to get through his duties. By 1782 he claimed that he could only keep abreast of his work by keeping office hours six days a week from ten till five, and longer when Parliament was sitting. Yet having private business in the country a few days later, he informed the Prime Minister that he would be out of London from Friday evening until Monday morning for the next month. And this was no great nobleman, but a man of business with his way to make.[3]

2. The Peacetime Fleet

The work of Sandwich must be judged by two separate standards which are often confused: the upkeep of the navy through the years of peace, and its mobilisation for war. The first meant the preservation, repair and building

---

[1] Below, pp. 484–6.

[2] Usher, 71–3; Lewis, *Navy of Britain*, 372; Sandwich, IV, 380–1; Mundy, *Rodney*, II, 356–7.

[3] Sandwich, III, 181; CL, Shelburne, Vol. 151, Nos. 31, 41. The weight of trivial detail which over-centralisation threw on Sandwich is described by Williams, 19–20.

of ships of the line, most of them to lie 'in ordinary' without crews, rigging or stores; and the provision of a proper reserve of materials. The second meant preparing the ships to receive men, and then their commissioning, manning, and final preparation for sea.

This was the only war of the eighteenth century in which England failed to win ascendancy at sea. Lord Sandwich was chosen as the Opposition's scapegoat for the navy's weakness. For weakness, not indiscipline, was the cause of failure. From Spain's intervention in 1779 England was fighting against odds which to doubters often seemed hopeless. The situation was extraordinary. Though England had fought the Bourbon powers together in the last two wars, and was to fight them again in the next, this was the only occasion on which she faced them simultaneously with their fleets and finances intact. In 1779 she faced their full combined strength, and eighteen months later they were joined by Holland. In this war England needed a navy of more than two-power standard. She did not achieve it.

By the autumn of 1779, within a year and a half of mobilisation, the navy had a battle fleet in commission which could compare with the highest strength achieved in the Seven Years War: about 100 ships of fifty guns and upwards, compared with about 118 including ten prizes at the end of 1759. Of the fleet of 1759, fifty were Fourth Rates; in 1779 there were only twenty; and the more powerful ships of 1779 carried a total complement of nearly the same number of seamen as the more numerous ships of 1759.[1] Judged therefore by the standard of past achievement, the navy of 1779 was adequate; but judged by present need it was not. It is very difficult to discover the whole truth, for the parties to the controversy drew up conflicting lists of ships and stores to suit their case. Nor do the bare figures tell the whole story. Was a ship listed as in commission really a fighting unit, manned and in good repair? Were new ships built to satisfy the Surveyor's vanity at the expense of repairing old ones? Were stores accumulated when they should

[1] Sandwich, III, 316, checked against list supplied to Shelburne in CL, Shelburne, Vol. 142. In the Fourth Rate the ships of sixty guns were classed as ships of the line, while the fifties were not. Middleton maintained that the distinction between fifties and the line was ridiculous; and for simplicity the whole Fourth Rate is included in the line in the figures above. The exclusion of the fifties from the line is rather more favourable to Sandwich. In approximate figures the more detailed breakdown is:

	1759		1779	
	Numbers	Tonnage	Numbers	Tonnage
1st to 3rd rates	68 }	137,000	82 }	140,000
Sixty-gun ships	29 }		6 }	
Fifty-gun ships	21	21,500	14	15,000
Totals	118	158,500	102	155,000

have been used for repairs? Comparison is impossible, for there is no serious study of preceding administrations of a later date than the reign of William III; and for evidence one is confined to the assertions of Sandwich's parliamentary enemies.

The Opposition alleged that Sandwich had inherited eighty-six serviceable ships of the line from Lord Hawke, and had allowed this powerful force to waste away. An analysis by Philip Stephens, who had been Secretary to the Admiralty since 1763, reached a different conclusion. Hawke's ships were the hulks of the fleet which had won the Seven Years War. The navy of 1763 had been the largest in English history, but in the worst condition. Many ships had been kept in service at great risk, and another year of war would have seen the fleet begin to dwindle. Of the new ships, many had been built with green timbers during the emergency and decayed rapidly after the peace. Hawke had repaired twenty ships of the line, and left fifteen new ones on the stocks. But he had not kept ahead of the rising flood of decay, and Stephens declared that most of the ships on the serviceable list in 1771 had been kept there for political reasons by the very men who now assailed Lord Sandwich. Sandwich's inheritance was a paper-fleet.[1]

From the moment when he came into office Sandwich had foreseen that the next war would see France and Spain in alliance, and that this time England might not be allowed to beat them separately. The state of the fleet was desperate, and he was convinced that if the Falkland Islands crisis had led to war we should have lost India and perhaps Gibraltar before enough ships were ready to provide detachments from home. With his Comptroller, Palliser, he began the uphill task of restoring the fleet. Two years later Palliser could praise 'the noble foundation your Lordship has laid for building a real serviceable fleet'.[2] Economy dictated the removal of the useless ships, and by 1778 half of Hawke's fleet had vanished from the serviceable list. The fleet which remained was regularly inspected and repaired. Financial stringency had prevented all from being done that Sandwich had wished; but of the forty-three of Hawke's ships which remained in service, twenty-six had undergone considerable repairs, though seventeen were still serving without repair.[3]

Two bottlenecks had threatened the navy's recovery at the outset: a shortage of timber, and a shortage of slipways and skilled labour for building. The whole stores situation was disastrous, for a fire in the Portsmouth yard in 1770 had destroyed all the stores and furniture of twenty-five ships of the line, including their masts, yards, sail, cable and cordage. But the

[1] Sandwich, IV 303 ff.
[2] Williams Transcripts, 23 June 1773.
[3] Ritcheson, 173 ff.; Sandwich, II, 183; IV, 303–8; Williams, 447.

most intractable need was timber for building: the yards were empty and the Navy Board despaired of getting more. Sandwich bent his energies to the problem. 'I was one of the few that did not despair', he claimed: 'I set my hand and heart to the work.' One cause of the shortage was excessive building by the East India Company to obtain the builders' votes in parliamentary elections: against warm opposition a bill was passed to force the Company to reduce its fleet. But the main reason for the timber shortage was said to be the exhaustion of the English woodlands. This Sandwich investigated; and he found that the scarcity was artificially created by the timber merchants to keep the price up. He set to work to break the combination. A subsidy was introduced for the carriage of distant timber which could not be brought out of the woodlands at the ordinary price; and a large contract was placed for foreign timber. But the second expedient was to exact an unforeseen penalty. The Stettin oak which was floated down the Oder to break the English monopoly had only a quarter of the life of English oak; and foreign oak was just beginning to reveal its defects when the American Revolution surged in.[1]

By 1777 the three years' reserve of timber which Sandwich had ordered to be maintained had been accumulated. The opposition alleged that timber was laid down which should have been used for repairing and building; but Sandwich could point out that a large stock in his new seasoning sheds allowed ships to be built of thoroughly seasoned timber. Every other store except masts was plentiful. There was more hemp in store in the spring of 1779 than had ever been known at that season, and great quantities were under contract for delivery. There was two years' supply of pitch, three of tar, four of iron. Middleton could assert in 1779 that the Channel yards were prepared for accidental and current services, and that the naval arsenals had never been so fully supplied with stores. By 1781 a vast additional reserve of hemp had been laid down as a precaution against the hostility of the Baltic powers, and seven times as much was in store as in 1759. The quantities shipped to stations abroad were unparalleled. Seven thousand tons of stores had already been shipped to seven destinations, and another 1,800 tons were ready or in course of shipment. If overseas yards were short of stores, this was caused by the accidents of war and the shortage of shipping rather than by any failure to procure.[2]

It has been alleged, however, that if the stores in general were satisfactory,

---

[1] Sandwich, II, 259; *Ibid.* IV, 28, 281 ff., 303–8; Lewis, *The Navy of Britain*, 105–6. Mr Williams throws doubt on the existence of the timber ring, and suggests that the cause of Sandwich's success was a more enterprising Navy Board headed by Palliser. He amply vindicates Sandwich's claim to have stockpiled timber.

[2] CL, Shelburne, Vol. 142, No. 10; Sandwich, II, 263; IV, 281 ff.

there was one vital exception: the 'great masts' of over 27-inches diameter
for the lower masts of ships of the line.[1] Since the days of Cromwell England
had relied for her great masts on the pine forests of New Hampshire, a
safer source than the Baltic. When this supply was cut off in 1775, Sandwich
had a three years' reserve in hand; but nothing was done either to find a
new source of supply or to revive the art of making composite masts from
smaller trees. The charge is that at the moment when France entered the
war the stock of great masts was exhausted; and that the shortage imposed
crippling difficulties on fleet operations. But a close and recent investigation
has shown that there was no alarm about the stock of great masts till 1780,
when the apparent scarcity of great masts in Europe threatened the fleet's
consumption. The scarcity of 1778 was not of mast-poles but of 'made-
masts', the composite masts which were stronger than pole-masts and
which, in spite of assertions to the contrary, supplied all lower masts of
capital ships. Experience had never shown a reserve of made-masts to be
necessary; but at the battle of Ushant in July, 1778, Keppel's fleet suffered
unprecedented damage aloft from the new French technique of firing into the
masts and rigging. Though some masts were borrowed from ships lying in
ordinary, the fleet could only be refitted quickly by wholesale 'fishing' of
old masts; and many of these fished masts were sprung in the gales of the
autumn. The deficiency was cured in due course by building up a reserve of
made-masts; and its cause was not neglected to stockpile, but a tactical surprise.

It had become clear during the Seven Years War that the royal dockyards
were unable to build and maintain the expanding navy. Storehouses, docks
and slipways were all inadequate. A long-term plan to expand the western
yards had been drawn up in 1764; but when the Sandwich administration
investigated the situation in 1771, the work everywhere was behind its
schedule. It was now pushed on as fast as funds allowed. But even in the years
of peace the docks in the royal yards had been too few; with the result, if
an embittered Navy Board clerk is to be believed, that repairs were often
disastrously delayed for the sake of new building. The only solution was to
contract with merchant builders. Till 1778 about a third of all new building
was done outside the royal yards: thereafter the proportion in the private
yards gradually drew ahead. Every available slipway was brought into use.
Ships of the line were built at three places where none had been in the
previous war; and at the end of 1781 thirty-seven ships of the line were
building. 'Every slip in England', wrote Middleton about this time, 'where
a line of battle ship can be built with safety and advantage is at this moment

[1] The theme is in Albion, *Forests and Sea Power*, 276–90; the critique in Williams,
esp. pp. 317–9, 326–7, 451, 456–7.

occupied by the Navy Board and new ships contracted for as fast as they become vacant.'[1]

In the royal yards shipwrights were as short as slipways. Three companies of shipwrights, each of fifteen men and six boys, could build a seventy-four in a year. These craftsmen, often illiterate, built by eye and tradition, and imposed their variations on Admiralty designs. Such traditional skills could not be learnt in haste; nor could artificers be recruited from other yards. The law allowed no compulsion except for seamen; and to raise wages merely sent up wages in the merchant yards in competition. Unable to increase the shipwrights' numbers, the Admiralty tried to raise their productivity. Task work, which cut costs and time, was introduced to the royal yards. The system shortened working hours and raised wages; but there were immediate strikes in all the yards except Deptford. The Channel yards could not be coerced, for the loss of a month's work in Portsmouth and Plymouth might have been fatal; nor was the system easy to apply to their main wartime work of refitting. In the eastern yards, where most of the building was done, task work was gradually established, and without powers of compulsion the government could do no more. 'There is a line', said Sandwich, 'beyond which the exertions of every country cannot go'; and in England before the French Revolution the line was sharply drawn by concern for individual liberty and low taxation.[2]

3. The State of Readiness

Low taxation and balanced budgets meant stable Ministries; and from the beginning of Sandwich's administration, he had been in conflict with the Treasury. His revenue threatened by the near-bankruptcy of the East India Company, Lord North looked to cuts in naval expenditure to balance his budgets and reduce the National Debt. This meant not only curbing expenditure on the maintenance of the fleet in reserve, but cutting to the bone the force in immediate readiness. North knew very well that England had been caught unprepared at the beginning of the past two wars; but 'great peace establishments will . . . prove our ruin', and [in 1772], 'I do not recollect to have seen a more pacific appearance of affairs than there is at this moment.' He wanted to reduce the squadrons abroad and put four guardships out of commission. The squadrons abroad were reduced as he wished, but to

---

[1] Williams, 341–92; Usher, 387–8, 395–400; Sandwich, IV, 281 ff.; CL, Shelburne, Vol. 151, No. 37; Add. MSS. 38344, ff. 310, 312. Between 1778 and 1781 there were 151 dockyard refits of ships of the line, and 36 dockyard repairs (Add. MSS. 38344. ff. 320–3).

[2] G 3510; Sandwich, IV, 308 ff.; Add. MSS. 38344, f. 306.

Sandwich the twenty guardships at home, ready for sea and manned by skeleton crews, were the foundation of British security. He called Lord Rochford to his support, and his resolute stand maintained the guardships at twenty.[1]

These twenty guardships were enough until the middle of 1776, when it became clear that France and Spain were arming. By then the real strength of the home fleet had been undermined by the war in America. Every frigate in good repair was abroad, and all the fifty-gun ships; so were 15,000 seamen, leaving only 8,000 at home to protect the trade and man a battle fleet. These facts Sandwich put repeatedly to the Cabinet. If no countermeasures were taken, France and Spain would soon have as many ships ready in Europe as Britain had, and before much longer would have double the British force.

But the King and Prime Minister were reluctant to accept his reasoning. George III counted on a rapid victory in America to dispel the crisis, and was unwilling to embark on further naval expenditure which might never be needed. He and Lord North were all too ready to be soothed by Vergennes' assurances. Sandwich was not. Whatever the intentions of the present French Ministry, France was preparing for a war. Rearmament would indeed be costly and might be dangerous; but he remembered the Falkland Islands crisis, and knew that the greatest danger was to be weak. He wanted more guardships commissioned, and more ships brought forward from ordinary and prepared to receive men. In June 1776 he persuaded the Cabinet to commission three more guardships, augment the Marines, and make secret arrangements for a press. But it took another month and further alarming intelligence to get Cabinet sanction for a dozen more ships to prepare to receive men, though this committed the country neither to heavy expenditure nor to increasing the fleet actually in commission.[2]

That autumn the Spanish dispute with Portugal reached a crisis; and the news of French preparations were so alarming that Sandwich was able to obtain much more extensive measures. The twenty-three guardships were manned to full crews by a general press; other ships were commissioned to replace them in immediate reserve; and more were prepared to receive men. Admiral Keppel was nominated as Commander of the Channel fleet in the event of war. These precautions brought thirty-six ships of the line into commission at home by the end of 1776, and would have been satisfactory if the gain could have been held. But almost at once it began to be dissipated by a call from America.

At the end of the summer Lord Howe had asked for a large reinforcement of two-deckers for the next campaign, evidently to increase his manpower

[1] Sandwich, I, 19–30.
[2] G 1894–6, 1905; Sandwich, I, 213, 215–16; Ritcheson, 209.

for assisting the army. Sandwich hoped that fifty-gun ships and frigates with their shallower draught would be at least as useful on the American coast as ships of the line. He explained the danger of dissipating the battle fleet in Europe; but Howe felt that the possibility of French intervention merely strengthened his case for more ships of force on the station, and asked for six more ships of the line to bring his squadron to eight. Sandwich was anxious not to deny him; and in February 1777 the Cabinet resolved to send him five ships of the line from home, and make up the number he required by putting a fifty-gun ship in the St Lawrence at his disposal. But the same meeting decided not to replace them at home by commissioning others. Sandwich would not be put off. By letter and conversation he continued to press for their replacement, using Robinson as his channel to urge on North the necessity of keeping pace with the Bourbons. In March he confronted Robinson with fresh intelligence of preparations in France, and begged for a decision.[1]

North had been laid low by a cough and could not be seen; but his attitude as revealed by Robinson was a very curious one. At that moment he regarded the international situation as so threatening that he was enquiring about plans to resist an invasion. Yet though he insisted that Howe must have all that he asked to mollify him for his brother's lack of military reinforcements, he still hedged about the fleet at home. If French armament continued, his objection to keeping pace would cease; but the French preparations must first be proved, and since there was a Cabinet minute on the subject, the Cabinet ought to decide. All this emerged when the King grew curious. For though King George was anxious not to alarm the French by military precautions, he regarded naval readiness as a different matter. If the Prime Minister agreed on replacing the ships going out from home, the King intended to encourage the other Ministers to support him in the Cabinet. The royal intervention may have been decisive; for the decision to commission replacements was duly taken.[2]

Thus Sandwich won the battle to keep the home fleet at thirty-six. But as the summer of 1777 drew on, a different anxiety developed. American privateers had multiplied at an alarming rate, and with French connivance were swarming in the British seas. From every quarter came cries for convoy and protection. The few cruisers left in home ports were hopelessly over-stretched, and the battle fleet had to do their work. The ships of the line were scattered on cruising stations and with Mediterranean and South Atlantic convoys. On the American coast the privateers and rebel cruisers were

---

[1] Sandwich, I, 160, 163, 170, 285; Sackville, II, 50, 52; Add. MSS. 37883, f. 163.
[2] Add. MSS. 37883, ff. 161–70; G 1974; Thynne Papers, American Affairs 1777–8, No. 6 (Cabinet Minute of 15 March 1777).

becoming very bold. The frigate *Fox* fell a temporary prize to the 32-gun *Hancock*; and the Admiralty feared that if the rebels cruised in small squadrons they could overmatch our single cruising frigates. Palliser argued that Howe should be ordered to pursue American squadrons with his own two-deckers. 'For if we are to disperse our home guard after every squadron of privateers in distant parts, whilst the fleets of Spain and France are armed, we certainly shall not be safe at home.' Nevertheless a ship of the line was detached from the home fleet in August to sustain the frigates on the Newfoundland station against the Boston cruisers. 'The sea is now overspread with privateers on every part', Sandwich told Lord Howe, 'and the demands for convoys and cruisers so great that we know not how to supply them.'[1]

Meanwhile French actions continued to belie their soothing professions. In June Captain Jervis fell in with a small squadron whose Admiral said frankly that he was cruising to protect American shipping. In French ports privateers were being armed for American captains, and merchantmen laden with clothing and munitions for the rebel armies. From Dunkirk to Bordeaux the French were sheltering and equipping the King's enemies. So outrageous were their breaches of neutrality that in the summer of 1777 Germain thought that immediate war was inevitable. Yet North, in spite of his earlier enquiry about plans to resist invasion, had 'no idea of taking any public steps that would cause any alarm whatever'. To tread so warily, yet knowing that French supplies alone might be sustaining the rebellion, seems at first sight a strange policy. Yet as Suffolk reminded Sandwich, it was of immense importance to preserve the peace for that year, while the campaign which might still be decisive unrolled in America. For England had staked on the army: that effort must not be jeopardised by fighting France for the sake of a sea blockade.[2]

At the beginning of August Sandwich tackled the Prime Minister again. The presence of Spanish and probably of French ships of the line in the Antilles had prompted the Prime Minister to suggest yet another detachment from the home fleet. Admirable, said Sandwich; but they must be replaced by commissioning more. 'I lay it down as a maxim that England ought for her own security to have a superior force in readiness at home to anything that France and Spain united have in readiness on their side.' Later in the month it was learnt that the French were preparing troops and frigates for the West Indies. North caught the alarm. Postponing a visit to Somerset, he hastened to London to summon a Cabinet. Such bewildering fluctuations and inconsistencies in the conduct of France momentarily convinced him that England should no longer depend on her professions, and must be ready

---

[1] Sandwich, I, 181, 223, 224, 229, 233–4, 294.
[2] Sackville, II, 73; Sandwich, I, 221–3, 226; Abergavenny, 18; G 1975.

for war by October. The balance of forces at the moment appeared thus: the French and Spaniards were believed to have forty sail of the line in commission in Europe, with another four about to be commissioned in Toulon. Against their forty-four, of which twenty-three were French, the Royal Navy had only thirty-six, and of these twenty were dispersed on cruising stations or distant convoy duty, and one had just been ordered to Antigua. In immediate reserve England had six ships ready to receive men, while the Bourbons were believed to have many more in the same state which they could man much faster. Seven thousand five hundred seamen would be needed to complete the ships in commission and man the six which were ready to receive men. The frigate situation was catastrophic. There were only ten at home not under orders for America; and of these six were paying off or docking, and the remainder cruising for privateers. There was not a single frigate to send to sea with the fleet.

Abroad the disbalance was worse. England had eight ships of the line overseas, six of them in America and two in the West Indies. Against these there were thought to be twenty Spaniards and one French ship of the line. Sandwich had already given warning that the opening of a war would find England on the defensive, and the initiative in the hands of the enemy. If the Brest fleet went to New York, it 'might give such a blow to the English fleet that it would be difficult ever to recover. The loss of America would in such an event be far the inferior consideration.' On the first suspicion that the French were about to strike, America and the West Indies must be reinforced. But how should we then stand at home? The country drained of troops, the coasts swarming with privateers, and the French at liberty to invade the British Isles or take the offensive overseas as they might choose. 'In this situation', Sandwich demanded, 'are we safe at home, and can we in any emergency venture to detach, without more ships being immediately commissioned?' It was a prescient forecast of the situation in March 1778.[1]

By now Sandwich was preaching to the half converted. North remained bewildered by the contrast between protestations of friendship reported by the Paris embassy and the intelligence collected in William Eden's bureau. The British Ambassador pointed out the difference between promise and performance; yet in September 1777 North was 'more sanguine than I have been for some time past in my expectations of the continuance of peace'. Still he thought war was not inevitable, and that we must tread delicately; still he selected from Stormont's letters to present French conduct to Parliament in its most favourable light.[2] Nevertheless it was clear that amid these

[1] G 2049; Sandwich, I, 205-6, 231, 235-8, 241-5; Abergavenny, 17.
[2] Add. MSS. 34414, ff. 195-6, 335-6.

contrarities, the navy's strength must gradually be increased. By November forty-two sail of the line were in commission at home, thirty-five of them completely manned for sea. In the space of a year Sandwich's importunity had converted twenty guardships into twice that number of seagoing ships of the line.

4. Mobilisation

When Parliament reassembled late in November 1777, the debate on the address in the House of Lords opened with a furious attack by Chatham on the defenceless state of the country. To this Lord Sandwich replied that the navy had fifty-four ships of the line in service or fit for service at home; and of these thirty-five were completely manned and seven more ready in all other respects. This force, he declared, was superior to anything which France and Spain together could muster in Europe. 'Our navy is more than a match for that of the whole House of Bourbon.'[1]

At that moment the statement may have been the strict and literal truth. But Sandwich added a flourish for which he was not to be forgiven: 'I should, my lords, be extremely sorry, as presiding at the Admiralty-board, if I permitted at any time the French and Spanish navy united, to be superior to the navy of this country; I should indeed be wanting in the discharge of my duty.' There spoke the politician; but the views of the administrator appeared a few days later in his Cabinet memorandum on the effects of Saratoga. France and Spain had at least as many ships in commission in Europe as Britain's forty-two, and many more ready to receive men. Abroad, the Spaniards could collect a formidable fleet in the West Indies without detaching a single ship from Europe; and the French would certainly send a squadron overseas the moment they determined on war. Britain was vulnerable to hostile fleets in the West Indies and America; and to amphibious attack in India and the Mediterranean. The moment war began she must be ready to send large reinforcements to all these theatres: and the forty-two ships of the line in commission could not supply these detachments. England must arm. 'What shall we have to answer for if we are taken unprepared, and reduced to the necessity of either leaving our distant possessions undefended or seeing France and Spain in the Channel with a superior fleet?'[2]

The worst danger was not realised in 1778: Spain did not enter the war with France. Yet in spite of Sandwich's boast in the House of Lords the navy was found inadequate in the first weeks of crisis. A week before the breach with France, the French and Spaniards together were believed to have sixty-five

---

[1] *Parl. Hist.*, XIX, 376–8.   [2] Sandwich, I, 333–5.

ships of the line in commission in Europe, thirty-three of them French. Sandwich stated the British fleet at home as fifty, of which only forty-one were ready. So much for his assertion that England could outmatch the combined House of Bourbon. Against France the force seemed adequate; but the story is in every book of how Keppel went down to Portsmouth to take command of a Channel fleet of twenty ships and found only six in a true state of readiness. What had become of the powerful forces at home of which Sandwich had boasted in November? And what had been done in the three intervening months to increase their strength?

The truth was that since December the navy had continued to expand rapidly; and the real state of the fleet was very much better than Keppel's first report suggests. Of the forty-two which had been ready in November, two had since dropped out; but a great number of ships were in course of being prepared for sea. By October 1778 sixty-two ships were in full service throughout the world, and another eight lacked only men. Seventy ships in the first months of a war was no mean achievement: it far outstripped what the French could do, and speaks well of the ships and stores in reserve. If naval considerations had prevailed, these ships would have been ready in the first weeks of the emergency. 'It is not your Lordship's fault', Palliser told Sandwich, 'that our fleet is not in more forwardness: it was no reasoning of ours that we should not equip long ago for fear of alarming France, whilst they were exerting themselves to the utmost in equipping theirs, and thus they have got the start of us.'[1]

The real trouble, then, was the late mobilisation. Many ships were still being rigged and stored; but the chief difficulty was seamen. France, with her register of seamen, could man a fleet rapidly: England, with her clumsy apparatus of pressing by an Order in Council, could scarcely find the men at all. Manning had always been a bottleneck; but the American rebellion had made it all but insoluble. America's seamen had gone, and the vast transport service which supplied the army had engulfed the British.

The method of raising seamen had been established for a century: first, a royal proclamation; then an embargo on the sailing of merchant shipping while the fleet was being manned; and simultaneously the issue of press warrants to the captains of ships being manned and to the impress service which recruited for the navy as a whole. Throughout the war the manning difficulty continued. Landsmen had to be conscripted in a proportion variously estimated at from a quarter to nearly half of the ships' complements. The wastage was colossal. In the course of the war 171,000 seamen were raised. Only 1,240 were killed in action; but 18,500 died of disease and 42,000 deserted. The impress service of 1780 was nearly three times as large as in 1760, but

[1] Sandwich, II, 111, 183, 349–52.

its need far outran the reservoir of trained seamen. Of all the branches of naval administration, it was recruiting which bore with deadliest effect on strategy.[1]

The manning shortage made the sickness rate calamitous. Every year thousands retired to the hospitals or were lost to the service for ever by death. The navy's medical record from 1778 was a bad one; and the most sickly command was the Channel fleet, which received a large proportion of the new entry. The effect on fleet operations was crippling. Admiral Keppel reckoned that no large fleet should stay at sea for more than six or seven weeks; and old Hawke, who had kept a fleet at sea for months in the Seven Years War, surprisingly supported him. 'Six weeks is long enough in all conscience', he wrote in 1780 to Geary. 'I wish the Admiralty would see what was done in former times.'[2]

How far must the Admiralty be blamed for the sickness? The figures make it clear that in this war, and in the succeeding one against the French Revolution, the sick rate followed the navy's rate of expansion. The worst year, 1780, was the year of the greatest increase of seamen; and the sudden influxes of verminous recruits from 1778 onwards evidently swamped the machinery. Scurvy remained proportionately steady; but the fever-rate soared. Towards the end of the war, however, the figures improved as the machine got into its stride; and the influence of the great naval physician James Lind helped to reduce the spread of typhus and typhoid. It was Lind who observed the dissemination of typhus from ship to ship, and from his hospital at Haslar to the surrounding countryside. Of the agents of that transmission, the flea and the louse, he never had the smallest suspicion; but observation taught him that infection could cling to clothing, tents and furniture. He ordered the scouring of cots and quarters, and the airing of bedding on the decks of ships; and he recommended that doctors and nurses should change their clothes on leaving the hospital. At his suggestion Receiving Ships were established in 1781, where recruits were examined, issued with new clothes, and quarantined. His influence may have had much to do with the remarkable dropping off of the hospital rate in the last two years of the war.[3]

Yet the greatest killer raged unchecked. Scurvy is a deficiency disease, and the therapeutic value of lemon juice had been known since the reign of James I. Thirty years before the American War, Lind had proved the superiority of lemon juice as an anti-scorbutic, and had described a method

[1] Usher, 155–74, 221 ff; Lloyd and Coulter, *Medicine and the Navy*, III, 137; Williams, 490–501.
[2] Lloyd and Coulter, 126.
[3] *Ibid.*, 137, and tables on pp. 371–2; Roddis, *James Lind*, 68, 134, 152–5.

of concentrating and preserving it. In 1775 Captain Cook had returned from his second navigation of the world without losing a man from scurvy, proving how careful victualling could eliminate the disease. Yet throughout the war the application of the lessons was left largely to private enterprise. A general sailing for India in 1781 complains that the East India Company had provided only a small quantity of lemons for his troops, and demands a large supply of anti-scorbutics.[1] Individual captains and ships' surgeons see that their crews are adequately supplied with fresh fruit and vegetables. Yet the Admiralty continued to experiment with half-measures and useless nostrums. Sauerkraut did some good, extract of malt little and elixir of vitriol none. Rodney's physician, Sir Gilbert Blane, sent the Admiralty a memorial in 1781 in which he urged them to supply the seamen with lemons; but fourteen years later when he became a Commissioner for the Sick and Wounded he found that nothing had been done. In that year, 1795, he persuaded the First Lord to order a regular issue of lemon juice. The effect was miraculous. Within five years scurvy was almost unknown. Fleets could stay at sea indefinitely, and the long blockades which broke the naval power of Napoleon became possible. In 1807 one man in twenty was sent to the hospitals: in 1779 it had been one in three.

It is a striking example of the gap between the scientific recognition of a technique and its administrative adoption. The same administrative apathy which was killing off the garrison of Jamaica may have contributed to the delay[2]; yet Blane himself has other explanations which do something to excuse the Admiralty, gripped as it was by circumstance. Blane himself was an eminent physician; but ships' surgeons had a low social status and could not easily make their opinions audible. Again, scurvy was rare on land, so eminent doctors did not have to give their minds to it. And finally, the cure seemed too simple to be true.[3]

The forty-two ships in commission in November 1777 had been short of 3,000 seamen and nearly as many marines; and many smaller vessels had been crying out for men. But the measures needed to complete the complements – bounties, embargo, and impressment – were acts of state, controversial, portentous and risky. The government had hesitated to injure the hopes of peace by taking these steps, and the wretched seamen already raised were turned over from ship to ship without ever setting foot on shore. And thus it came about that when Keppel went down to Portsmouth in March 1778 he found the Port Admiral's pool of seamen stripped to man

[1] WO 34/138, f. 202.
[2] See above, p. 6.
[3] Lloyd and Coulter, III, 130–6, 319 ff.

the armed ships and cruisers at sea with convoys. If we could raise eight or nine thousand men, he said in April, the whole situation would change. Every little batch was counted greedily. A lieutenant put in to Plymouth with 150: 'That 150 here would give us another 74-gun ship', wrote Palliser from Portsmouth. A Scots captain sent his tender to Scotland, and it returned with 200 men for his ship. Lord Longford sent to his own countryside in Ireland. And still the delayed mobilisation exercised its galling influence.[1]

[1] G 2312; Sandwich, I, 76–81.

CHAPTER IX

WAR PLANS AND PREPARATIONS

1. *Lord Amherst*

Lord Barrington, faithful servant of the Crown, had for a long time past wanted to retire. When France entered the war he went straight to Court and had a curious interview with his sovereign. He told him frankly that the Ministry was inadequate, but if he would not change his Ministers he must change his military advisers. There was not one general, he said, on whom the King, the nation or the army could rely if the British Isles were invaded. He then made the extraordinary suggestion that Prince Ferdinand of Brunswick, the victor of Minden, should be invited from Germany to be Commander-in-Chief.[1]

This gross insult to Germain came more naturally from the lips of Chatham, who is said to have been on the point of making it when he was struck down by his fatal fit in the House of Lords.[2] But there were others who shared Barrington's opinion of the generals. 'I do not know whether they will frighten the enemy', North is reported to have said, 'but I am sure they frighten me whenever I think of them.' The flabby borrowed joke reflected on the head of the government as much as on the generals. But it was clear at least that the peacetime system of direct royal control of the army was no longer enough, and a Commander-in-Chief was needed. General Harvey, Adjutant-General and the King's chief military adviser, had just died. The Duke of Gloucester came up from the New Forest, where he had been convalescing from asthma, to offer his services. This was embarrassing, for the Cabinet had already resolved that the King must release the command of the army from the hands of his family. The obvious choice was Lord Amherst. To protect the pride of Gloucester the title of Commander-in-Chief was withheld; but on 19 March Amherst was effectively appointed to the command of the army with a seat in the Cabinet.

The choice was widely welcomed. In America he had shown administrative capacity and unusual care for his mens' health and welfare, and had earned a reputation for temperance and honesty. 'A valuable man . . . a choice no one disapproves of', an M.P. reported. In Minorca General Murray was delighted: 'I love and esteem the man, and I think him the fittest person

[1] Shute Barrington, *Life of Barrington*, 186–7.
[2] Walpole, *Last Journals*, II, 254.

for the great task he has to perform of any of our Generals.' His actual performance in office did not sustain his reputation. Walpole's opinion that his mind had gone to seed, and that he revealed himself as self-interested and obstinate, is too harsh. But Lord Gower grumbled at his choice of men, and even the King was to own that he was not perfect.[1]

Amherst's correspondence in the years which followed give an impression of good sense, integrity, and friendly relations with the generals serving under him. His resistance to political pressure on the army has been mentioned[2]; and he made determined efforts to compel officers whose regiments were in America to join them. This meant resisting Lord North's suggestions for employing them at home[3]; but North could forgive a capable and honest administrator, 'the most attentive to public economy', he told him,[4] 'of any military commander that I ever knew'. His common sense and tact in dealing with the oddities of the militia show that he was neither inflexible nor a martinet.[5]

Amherst's responsibilities as a strategic planner consorted oddly with his other duties. The chief administrator and inspector of the army was not out of harmony with the Chief of Staff, which is what he, like Ligonier, really was, in spite of his seat in the Cabinet. But he was also Commander-in-Chief of the home forces in England and Wales; and we shall see that his interests as a theatre commander could conflict with his role as a maker of national strategy. And as a Minister he was something of a disappointment to his colleagues. Unlike his predecessor and patron Ligonier he was not at his ease among politicians, and became as monosyllabic as his successor in the First World War, Sir William Robertson. He would give his opinion in his taciturn way; but his reasons were hard to extract.[6]

2. The Redeployment

Amherst had often been consulted about the strategy of the war; and before his new appointment was announced he was already embroiled in the problems of redeployment against France. For France with its great military and naval forces would open new theatres of war in the West Indies, the Indian Ocean and European waters. The Cabinet was now squarely faced with the question which Sandwich had asked after Saratoga: ought the American war still to be treated as the main effort?

---

[1] Namier, . . . *American Revolution*, 306–7; Malmesbury Letters, I, 384; Sackville, I, 372; Walpole, *Last Journals*, II, 315–16; G 2828, 3099.
[2] Above, p. 10.   [3] E.g. WO 34/231, pp. 254–6.
[4] WO 34/127 (31 Oct. 1780).   [5] E.g. Long, *Lord Jeffrey Amherst*, 248–9.
[6] Wraxall Memoirs, II, 194.

Lord North remained detached from the coming crisis. Ten days before the breach with France he left it to Sandwich to arrange a Cabinet meeting to take the necessary naval measures. 'I am at present engaged from morning till night with the House of Commons and the loan, but will attend any meeting where my presence is required.'[1] There could be no better illustration of North's preoccupation with finance and politics: a Newcastle without a Chatham. In the great crisis of the war the initiative devolved among the American and Southern Secretaries, the Admiralty, and the King.

The first and most frightened voice which had been raised against the effort in America had been Lord Chancellor Bathurst's. On the news of Saratoga, he had foretold the loss not only of America but of the West Indies as well; and in tones of deepest defeatism concluded that the only safe course was to stop reinforcing America, concentrate our forces for the defence of the British Isles and the Mediterranean, and seek peace on any terms.[2] With the evasiveness of a legal careerist, he shied away from saying so in a forthright manner to the Cabinet; but when the French war became inevitable others had similar thoughts.

The other declared pessimist in the Cabinet was Sandwich. He was not irrationally frightened like Bathurst. But in his Cabinet memorandum after Saratoga he had pointed out how vulnerable we were in every overseas theatre with France's capital fleet uncommitted in her home ports. To meet the threat we needed a powerful strategic reserve at home. At the Cabinet meeting which followed the French Ambassador's declaration, he produced a new paper which contemplated a suspension of operations in America. If this was resolved on, he suggested either recalling Lord Howe with the army and most of his capital ships, leaving a force at Halifax; or ordering him to detach Commodore Hotham with a squadron of fifty-gun ships and frigates to secure the West Indies.[3]

The West Indies: there lay a capital danger. The French were thought to have 9,000 troops in their islands. while the British garrisons scattered throughout the Leeward Islands and Jamaica had only 1,800 effectives of all ranks, and many of them were sick. But if a combined force from America could seize the island of St Lucia, in the Windward Islands, we would gain a fine harbour dominating the main French base at Martinique. Sandwich had before him a detailed proposal from another member of the Board, Lord Mulgrave, to do exactly this. Speed and secrecy would be the essence of this opening blow. Mulgrave suggested that from St Lucia the expedition might go on to St Nicolas Mole in Haiti, a new French establishment which they were developing into the Gibraltar of the West Indies. With our port at

---

[1] Sandwich, I, 347.   [2] Bathurst, 16.   [3] Sandwich, I, 333, 359.

Pensacola in West Florida, Mulgrave said that St Lucia and St Nicolas Mole would make us masters of the Caribbean from the Bahamas to the Spanish Main, and give us the control of both the outlets from the Caribbean. He thought this might be accomplished in time for the ships to return to Europe or America before the hurricane season in August.[1]

These proposals were after the King's heart. He had seen the approaching war, not as a matter for dread, but as an opportunity to be grasped. England could compensate herself for the loss of America by completing Chatham's work in the Caribbean, and driving the French from their remaining possessions in the West Indies.[2] This view would have caused no surprise in France, where it had been feared from the beginning of the rebellion that England might seek compensation at the expense of the French Empire.

But why this obsession with the West Indies? Sandwich had predicted that the war aims of France would be to overturn the peace of 1763 and regain her empire and her markets; and that for the sake of the American alliance she would forget her claim to Canada, and look for her reward in the sub-tropics – in India, West Africa and the Caribbean. And he was right. The French navy was to neglect America for the West Indies. There most of the naval fighting took place; and there in 1782 the greatest British victory of the war was won by Rodney. With the fate of North America in the balance, the maritime Powers of Europe threw their strength and hopes into a chain of small, fever-ridden islands in the Caribbean. 'The war', wrote one of Shelburne's correspondents in the year of Rodney's victory,[3] ' has and ever must be determined in the West Indies.'

A powerful and noisy pressure group represented the West India interest in London. In 1775 the Society of West India Merchants and the Agents for the Planters had joined forces to represent the West India interest as a whole; and they were to exercise some influence over the government's strategy. But their clamour was not the main reason for the Ministry's interest in the islands.[4] The real issue was concerned with national policy. In the long run England might or might not recover America; but whatever the course of the war in the Caribbean, the Antilles could not sustain an independent existence and would remain colonies of one Power or another. The wealth they produced from sugar and its by-products was still vast. It is said that the West Indies accounted for a third of the overseas trade of France. Much of the

---

[1] Sandwich, I, 357–60; CL, North's return-books of the army.
[2] G 2182, 2251.
[3] CL, Shelburne, Vol. 72, p. 377.
[4] The West India interest in Parliament before the war is analysed in Namier's *England in the Age of the American Revolution*, 271–9. In the 'sixties they numbered some twenty votes in the House of Commons.

British trade passed through Bristol; but into London alone the British islands sent nearly 300 ships in an average year, with a 100,000 hogsheads of sugar and 11,000 puncheons of rum. The West India imports in 1776 had been valued at £4¼ millions, compared with the East India Company's £1½ millions. And for a mercantilist the sub-tropical products of the West Indies fitted much better into the British economy than the products of American farms and fisheries, which were not needed and were generally excluded from the home market. The planters' produce was needed, and favoured the balance of trade by saving England from the need to buy from foreign rivals. As a market for English manufactures the planters were also more satisfactory than the Americans: with their sugar profits they could at least pay their debts. The sensible Sir Charles Middleton believed passionately in the islands' importance. 'The sugar islands', he wrote,[1] 'are the best and surest markets for our staple commodities, and the most productive of all our colonies. They are the easiest source of our revenues.'

There was thus a general belief that the British economy and finances depended on the West Indies. And conversely it could be argued that nothing but their West India commerce had enabled the French to equip the fleet which successfully confronted Keppel in the course of 1778; and that the conquest of the French islands would ruin the enemy's finances. And by conquering them all it was argued that England would obtain an economic grip on the American colonies. 'Let therefore the dance of rebellion go round', wrote a West India correspondent to Germain on the eve of the French war,[2] 'while we appropriate the islands and emancipate the continent [i.e. the Spanish Main]. The full possession of the West India islands will soon repay the expenses of the war, and this with a proper guard on the Mediterranean would soon bring America to our beck.' A note among the Germain papers at the end of 1778 urges the same view. 'Having them in possession, instead of cringing to an American Congress for peace, we shall prescribe the terms, and bid America be only what we please.'[3]

For England, the islands held the lure of compensation for her losses in America, finance to pay for the war, a favourable balance of trade, an economic lever to coerce America. For the chance of conquering the French West Indies and 'avenging the faithless and insolent conduct of France', the King had said he was willing even to come to terms with America. As early as the end of January he had been contemplating a complete withdrawal from the rebel colonies, retaining only Canada, Nova Scotia and Florida. More than this, he had suggested that if Spain was not very explicit about

---

[1] Barham, II, 70.
[2] CL Germain, 2 March 1778 from (?) the Rev. James Ramsey.
[3] CL, Germain, 5 Dec. 1778, 'Thoughts on the Caribbean Station'.

her intentions we should seize New Orleans from her. On the day when France declared her intentions, he insisted that all thought of reinforcing Clinton so that he could resume the offensive was dead. England must form front against the French, and gather a force from America for the West Indies. In America two or three thousand of the remaining troops could be set apart to attack the rebel ports: the rest should be distributed in fixed garrisons to hold New York and Rhode Island in the colonies, and Nova Scotia and the Floridas at the extremities. Philadelphia must be abandoned.[1]

It was on the following day that a Cabinet meeting at Weymouth's house received the views of Sandwich. It was agreed that the Howes should detach most of their ships of the line and 4,000 troops to defend the Leeward Islands. The question of evacuating America was not decided. But Amherst was consulted by the King on the 17th, and opposed the total abandonment to which Sandwich[2] had inclined. He feared that to concentrate the fleet at Halifax as Sandwich wished would open the American coast and invite the rebels to collect a fleet of their own and attack the West Indies; and his advice was to abandon only Philadelphia, to hold New York as the fleet rendezvous, and to use the warships to destroy all vessels in American harbours. If the Peace Commissioners found on their arrival that the Americans were determined to join the French, New York and Rhode Island should be evacuated and the troops used for a West Indian offensive.[3]

On the next day another Cabinet meeting at Weymouth's heard Amherst's views and amplified their plans. Lord Howe was to send a squadron of four sail of the line, three fifties and four frigates to the Leeward Islands; and (to satisfy Sandwich and Admiral Keppel), to send home twenty frigates and sloops to make good the desperate shortage of cruisers in British waters. Five thousand troops from Philadelphia should attack St Lucia; and 3,000 more should be sent to reinforce the Floridas. The gutted remnant of the army in Pennsylvania should withdraw to New York, and thence make yet another detachment to strengthen Halifax. The Peace Commissioners should be sent to New York at once; and if they found no prospect of success, or that the army and fleet were in danger, Clinton should prepare to evacuate the city.[4]

The orders were signed on 21 March. Extraordinary steps were taken to prevent a leakage, which might bring out an intercepting force from Brest. A rumour was floated in London that the army in America was coming

---

[1] G 2182, 2190, 2204, 2243, 2251. No. 2243 must have been written about 13 March rather than on the 23rd as printed.

[2] G 2227; Sandwich, I, 359.

[3] G 2229. This is the King's account of Amherst's views; but Amherst may perhaps have thought New York should be evacuated only if the Commissioners found it to be in danger, as the consequent orders directed.

[4] Sandwich, I, 363–5; G 2227, 2229.

home. In the American Department only the Under-Secretary who wrote out the orders was in the secret. At the Admiralty the most secret part of Howe's instructions was handled by the First Lord in person, so that even the Board should not see them. And the Peace Commissioners sailed for America in ignorance that Philadelphia was to be abandoned.[1]

These orders reduced the forces in America to the defence of Britain's undisputed possessions on the flanks of the rebellion, with only two posts in the rebel colonies themselves, at New York and Rhode Island. Canada and Newfoundland would be reinforced from home; but for Nova Scotia and the Floridas, which lay within Clinton's command, he would have to provide part of the reinforcements from his own depleted force. And no replacements would be sent: no new regiments except the three already promised for Nova Scotia; and no recruits, for they were needed to fill the battalions at home. Clinton would therefore have to draft his weakest regiments and send their cadres home. His marine battalions were called home to man the fleet; and one of his cavalry regiments, unlikely to be needed for the defensive warfare to which he was reduced, was to be dismounted and shipped back to England. No more would be heard of the development of a naval base at New York. Its evacuation was not mentioned in his instructions, as its possession was important to the Peace Commissioners' negotiations, and it was hoped that he could keep up the alarm on the American coasts and reduce the attacks on British trade which had been the curse of 1777.[2]

Scarcely had these orders been signed when despatches were opened which gave a distressing account of the state of Lord Howe's fleet, and raised doubts of his ability to provide the full force intended for St Lucia. So anxious was the King for the secret expedition to proceed that he would have been willing to spare two or three ships of the line from the exiguous home fleet; but the Admiralty sent Howe a supplementary order drafted by Amherst, to explain why he should make every effort to provide at least part of the force named in his orders. 'The object of the war being now changed, and the contest in America being a secondary consideration, our principal object must be distressing France and defending . . . His Majesty's possessions.'[3]

3. The Peace Commission

The St Lucia expedition had been considered with care, and was far from being the senseless diversion of effort which it has sometimes been called.

[1] CL, Germain, 31 July 1778 to Eden; 21 March to Sandwich; Sandwich, I, 369.

[2] CL, Germain, Amherst's minutes of March 1778, and 21 March, Germain to Clinton; Sandwich, I, 363-70; II, 29; G 2229.

[3] Sandwich, I, 365, 370; Adm. 2/1334; despatch to Howe of 22 March.

The Peace Commissioners were to argue that it blasted the hopes of a settlement with America, and asserted that one more determined effort in the colonies would have brought peace on the terms which they were empowered to offer. It is just possible that they were right, though the refrain that the rebellion was on its last legs was already depressingly familiar. But the Commissioners saw only a part of the game. The fact was that France had a striking force poised in her home ports, and the West Indies were almost defenceless. Another effort in America would have staked the probable loss of the West Indies against the lesser probability of detaching the rebel colonies from the French alliance, on terms which at the best would have left them in a state of near-independence. It might be argued that though the West Indies needed reinforcements for their defence, this was very different from the offensive planned against the French islands. But the truth is that an offensive was the islands' best and cheapest defence. Dispersed garrisons in the Caribbean were wasteful of men, led to weakness everywhere, and required the permanent attendance of a superior fleet. Preventive attacks on the French bases were a cheaper policy in the long run. Though the French were to disrupt the plan, the plan itself made sense.

In reorientating strategy to face the French, constructive parts had been played by Sandwich, Germain and the King.[1] Through the unanimity which shrouds the Cabinet minutes, only one unhappy voice is heard in feeble protest: it is the Prime Minister's. When the orders had been signed and despatched, he wrote to the King predicting disaster. The country was not equal to a war with France, Spain and America. Borrowing would dry up and England would be ruined by the expense. 'Great Britain will undo herself while she thinks of punishing France.'[2]

North had never really thought that Congress would listen to any terms which his colleagues could swallow.[3] And with France standing by the side of America it was still less probable. But there were signs of a change of heart in England. It would be worth great concessions if our hands could be freed for the fight with France: a price which in the last resort might mean even independence for America. Even the King was coming round: 'so desirable to end the war with that country, to be enabled with redoubled ardour to avenge the faithless and insolent conduct of France . . .'. His sticking point was no longer independence, but the fate of Canada, Nova Scotia and Florida, the possessions still uncontaminated by rebellion. These

---

[1] Germain consulted Amherst, drew up the orders, and later defended the plan to Clinton. A letter to him of 24 March (CL, Germain, from John Drummond) suggests that he had personally been investigating the possibilities in the West Indies.

[2] G 2246–7.

[3] G 2164.

we must retain: 'for it is by them that we are to keep a certain awe over the abandoned colonies'.[1]

When the King had shifted so far, the atmosphere had changed indeed. The Commissioners' instructions had not been settled when Noailles presented the French declaration; and the draft from the American Department was referred by North for revision to the Attorney-General and Solicitor-General, who had helped to draft the preparatory Acts. Wedderburn was pressing for larger powers for the Commissioners, on behalf of his ally Eden. Knox of the American Department held forth on his favourite theme, that the northern colonies were dangerous commercial rivals who should be cast off and annihilated; to which the formidable Thurlow replied that if the northern colonies where we still had a foothold were not worth keeping, the southern ones where we had not were not worth invading. After some sulking and bickering Wedderburn had his way; and the Commissioners were empowered to offer terms so generous that the conservative Knox thought the Americans would enjoy all the advantages of being British subjects without any of the burdens. Great Britain, he lamented would be depopulated and reduced.[2]

A note among Lord Weymouth's papers suggests that the Cabinet regarded these terms as a surrender of Britain's war aims, but an inevitable one in the light of French intervention. 'The basis of the whole', it runs, 'is that in the present state of things . . . the object, although just and well founded in the principles of our Constitution, is not valuable enough, to countervail the expense which must attend even the successful enforcement of it.'[3] The Commissioners' instructions were indeed a dramatic surrender of British claims. The Acts authorising the Commission had already renounced Grenville's touchstone of parliamentary supremacy, the right to tax for revenue. The Commissioners were empowered to treat with Congress 'as if it were a legal body'. Then the catalogue of concessions: no standing army in the colonies in time of peace without the assemblies' consent; the colonies to maintain their own military forces; their charters secured; offices reserved for Americans; judges' tenure secured; Congress to continue in being if the Americans insisted, provided it did not infringe the sovereignty of Parliament. And of this sovereignty what was left? A power to regulate the trade of the empire, and to tax non-British imports to the colonies, thus maintaining the protected American market for British manufactures; the Americans to maintain no ships of war; provincial officers to hold the

[1] G 2251.

[2] Carlisle, 377; Knox, 277-8.

[3] Thynne Papers, American Affairs 1777-8, No. 1 (probably in Lord Weymouth's writing).

Kings's commission; no independent coinage (but help from the home government to secure the debts of Congress and sink its vast issues of depreciating paper currency); American debts to British merchants to be honoured; loyalists restored to their estates. But this was not the whole tale of concession. Additional and secret instructions provided for the probability that the Americans would insist on the recognition of independence before they would treat. This was not to be refused. The Commissioners were to refer it to London for instructions, and arrange an armistice while they awaited the reply.[1]

The Commissioners embarked on 16 April; and so well had the secret of the new strategy been kept for a whole month that they were still ignorant of the coming evacuation of Philadelphia. At the last moment their destination was changed from Philadelphia to New York; and when Carlisle asked the reason Germain replied briefly but truthfully that 'perhaps the city may not be in your hands on your arrival'. When Carlisle learnt the truth on reaching America, he asserted in his rage and wounded vanity that if he had known it he would have refused to sail, rather (he improbably asserted) than receive the public wages for a useless task. From this it was a short step to the imputation of motives: soon he was saying that he had been deceived to ensure his departure.[2]

Lord North declared that he thought Eden knew of the orders; Germain that he had had no idea of the Commissioners' ignorance, and that since he had not been a party to their appointment and instructions he had never thought information from himself to be necessary. In this the American Secretary may not have been entirely candid. But he added a better reason: that he had not been at liberty to reveal the secret. Full knowledge of the plans were virtually confined to the Cabinet; and who was Carlisle that he should be excepted? An ambassador on an important mission, to whom the information was relevant; but also a smart penurious young man who had been appointed to please his father-in-law or provide a front for Eden. He was surrounded by fashionable gossips from his old school. Anthony Storer was going out with him, and that connoisseur of executions, the *larmoyant* George Selwyn, hung about his coat-tails. Perhaps the country's secrets were safest out of the Commissioners' keeping till they had crossed the Atlantic.

---

[1] The Commissioners' instructions are admirably presented in Ritcheson, 268–71. But contrary to his statement Carlisle's father-in-law, Gower, did in fact attend the vital Cabinet meeting which ordered the evacuation.

[2] Carlisle, 335–45, 378–80.

CHAPTER X

THE COMMAND OF THE SEAS

1. *The French Initiative*

The new war plans of March 1778 assumed that England would retain the initiative in the western Atlantic, and could shift her forces between the American colonies and the West Indies without interference. But in the coming struggle the initiative lay with the enemy. For the French navy was uncommitted, whereas England had already locked up a large naval force, especially of frigates, in America. The French were in a more forward state of readiness than the British home fleet; and the day after the decision was taken to attack St Lucia, a letter from Lord Stormont gave warning that Admiral d'Estaing had left to take command of the Toulon fleet. The British Isles were weakly garrisoned and vulnerable to invasion. And France could choose the moment to sally out of her harbours and strike. Only a great margin of initial superiority at sea could have enabled England to throttle the French initiative; and she did not have it.

The French navy was faced with two broad strategic alternatives. It could concentrate in the English Channel and force a decisive battle to open the way to invasion. Or it might contain the British main fleet in home waters and strike in an overseas theatre. Invasion made little appeal to Vergennes. A victory so decisive might bring other states into the war to redress the balance of power. 'Even if I could destroy England, I would abstain from doing so, as from the wildest folly.' He was fighting for limited objects, and they could be attained with less risk of international repercussions by striking at England's economic strength through her trade and colonies than by invading her homeland.[1]

Vergennes therefore preferred the plan of the Ministry of Marine, which considered that the French navy lacked the decisive superiority to win a battle of annihilation with the rigid linear tactics of the day. Nor had the French much confidence in their ability to match the British fleet in equal combat. In spite of the efforts to reform the French service since the last war, they felt that the Royal Navy was trained in the tradition of victory and at least partly seasoned by three years of war service. They would enjoy 'l'avantage que donne la science et l'expérience'.

The French plan was therefore to rivet the attention of the British home fleet in the Channel, and detach a force to seize the local command of an

[1] A. Temple Patterson, *The Other Armada*, 37–9.

THE EUROPEAN THEATRE

overseas theatre with decisive effect. For this purpose they had an immense asset in their Mediterranean base. Brest could menace the Channel, but it could also be closely watched by the British Channel fleet based on Portsmouth and Plymouth. It was much less easy for the British to control the distant exit from the Mediterranean, though they held bases at Minorca and Gibraltar from which it might be done. The French preparations were complete. The fleet which they had begun to assemble two years earlier in Toulon had a dozen sail of the line in readiness. In February the command of this force was given to the Comte d'Estaing, with orders to cross the Atlantic and strike as opportunity served. At the same time eighteen sail of the line, the forerunners of a larger Channel fleet, were ordered to lie ready in the Brest roads to threaten the English Channel; and a large camp of exercise was to be formed in Normandy to simulate invasion.

These preparations could not be concealed from the British government. Intelligence from inside France was regular and accurate: so accurate that a note by Sandwich towards the end of the war asserts that even in wartime it proved a more reliable source than the cruisers which hastily looked into Brest.[1] When France made her declaration, the Cabinet knew of the squadron arming in Brest, and of d'Estaing's departure to command at least ten of the line at Toulon. But his destination remained a secret. All sources agreed that he would not stay in the Mediterranean, but beyond that there was no certainty. Bancroft had written that he would strike in America, but there was no corroboration from the Paris embassy. Was it safe to act on Bancroft's word? Or would d'Estaing join the Brest fleet in the mouth of the Channel? Or the Spaniards at Cadiz, whose intentions were distrusted? Or was it India? Stormont's reports from Paris did not penetrate its purpose.[2]

The existence of this striking force explains Lord Sandwich's anxiety to strengthen the West Indies. He had long foreseen that a rupture with France would find England's overseas possessions in danger. But it was not an easy decision. England had never had such a surplus of naval force that she could be strong everywhere in face of an uncommitted enemy. The central pillar of the system evolved in the eighteenth century was the Western Squadron or Channel fleet. It had two functions: to blockade Brest, and thus simultaneously secure the Channel and prevent the enemy from despatching an expedition overseas; and to act as a strategic reserve, which could detach flying squadrons in pursuit of enemy expeditions or task forces to support British overseas offensives. From the Channel, said Lord Sandwich, 'all our exterior efforts are derived'.[3]

[1] Sandwich, IV, 329.
[2] SP 78/306, Stormont's of 3, 12, 15 and 16 March 1778; Patterson 97–8.
[3] Sandwich, I, 333–5.

The system has sometimes been represented as a straight alternative to an evil system of dispersion. But this is too simple. In the first place local squadrons were needed on foreign stations, to protect the trade and garrisons in quieter periods and meet the first impact of an emergency till relief arrived from home. Secondly, the blockade of Brest was a more complex operation than is sometimes allowed. Its usual form in the eighteenth century was an open blockade, with the fleet lying in an anchorage on the coast of England and cruisers off the enemy port. This left the Atlantic wide open to the French, and the only method which offered a good chance of intercepting enemy expeditions was a close blockade off Brest by the battle fleet itself. But a close blockade was so taxing that it was never adopted as the regular method till after the conquest of scurvy at the end of the century, and in 1778 the only precedent for it was Hawke's blockade of 1759. The parliamentary opposition argued when it suited their purpose that Sandwich should have kept the fleet off Brest and thus throttled the enemy's overseas efforts at the source; but in attacking the Ministry's orders of 1778 to Keppel, Lord Howe revealed a contrary opinion, which his experience in the next war was to confirm. He told the House of Commons that 'stationing a large fleet off the coast of France, was a very improper and hazardous measure'. The ships were exposed to great damage, the crews became sickly, and any southerly wind put the fleet in peril from the difficulty of weathering Ushant. 'A station off Brest', he concluded, 'was a dangerous station, and should never be taken but upon great emergencies.'[1]

Keppel was never as explicit as this; but on one aspect of the policy of keeping the seas he was very positive. This aspect was winter cruising. The Ministry was blamed, both then and subsequently, for not attempting to intercept de Grasse when he left Brest in March 1780.[2] For such a winter interception there was a precedent in Hawke's autumn cruise of 1759. But even Hawke had acted against his better judgment under pressure from Anson, and Keppel condemned the system utterly while he commanded the Channel fleet. 'The French can have no better wish than to know you keep your large fleet collected at sea in the winter: their fleet in port quiet, recruiting and waiting the moment of the storm's separating and demolishing your fleet, while theirs remains perfect to go upon some settled service when the English fleet is in port from disaster and sickness.'[3] Middleton, who was responsible for the fleet's repairs and upkeep, was equally opposed to keeping it at sea in the winter.

But the decisive objection to a close blockade was the lack of a margin of superiority to allow for refits. In the Napoleonic Wars a superiority of one

[1] *Parl. Hist.*, XX, 202–3. [2] Richmond, *Navy in India*, 137–9. [3] Sandwich, II, 166.

third over the enemy was considered necessary, and in the American War the British fleet was never strong enough to impose a sustained blockade. In the absence of effective close blockade, readiness to detach was vital. France was a great military power which did not fear attack, and her navy was free to take the offensive where it pleased. Only a swift riposte could check it. But the British home fleet's flexibility was constricted by fear of invasion. It was an old bugbear, which the First Lord of the Admiralty always feared more than his colleagues in the Cabinet: Anson more than Pitt, Sandwich more than Germain, Spencer more than Dundas and Grenville. There was a constant temptation to forget the Channel fleet's role in global strategy: to over-insure in home waters and detach late and reluctantly. The Admiralty was too apt to treat the home fleet as a static shield rather than a strategic reserve. By the end of the war Sir Charles Middleton was convinced that too many ships had been kept in the Channel: that other objects had been sacrificed to the maintenance of a Channel squadron which was too weak to block the enemy's ports and command the Channel, yet stronger than was necessary to hamper an invasion.[1]

In March 1778 the local squadrons scarcely existed. Only the American station had a respectable squadron of five sail of the line backed by five fifties. As Sandwich had pointed out, it was necessary to reinforce all the overseas theatres at once. At home were forty sail of the line more or less ready, with another thirteen in commission which would soon be ready if men came in fast. Sandwich intended Keppel to have a Channel squadron of twenty powerful ships, to be augmented from time to time as other ships became ready and the enemy's strength required. This left twenty ships for other services; and from these the Admiralty intended to form its overseas squadrons including one for the Mediterranean.[2] Of these the Mediterranean squadron was incomparably the most important. It was much more than a local squadron charged with the safety of Gibraltar, Minorca and the Levant trade; for it confronted one of the enemy's main European bases, and was in fact an extension of the home fleet which jealously watched Brest. In 1757 the Mediterranean had been watched so successfully that the French had been unable even to prepare a squadron in Toulon which they had intended for the relief of Louisburg in the following spring. On the French declaration Sandwich persuaded the Cabinet to order the immediate formation of a Mediterranean squadron to follow this precedent.[3] But within a short time he began to lose his nerve.

[1] Barham, II, 37–40, 54.
[2] The sources of these figures are at first sight confusing. Compare: G 2218; Sandwich, I, 350–1; II, 5 n., 19–21, 183, 269,274, 369; CL, Shelburne, Vol. 142, No. 39.
[3] Sandwich, I, 359–61.

The force in immediate readiness at home was less than appeared on paper. Fourteen ships had been cruising since early February in the Bay of Biscay, doing the work of the frigates which were absent in America, and did not come in till 2 April, when they required extensive refitting and provisioning. Four others needed docking, and all were still short of men. But the question whether England could afford to detach to the Mediterranean was not debated on grounds of readiness. Sandwich began to doubt the sufficiency of twenty ships in the Channel, although thirteen more would soon be ready. In this he was almost certainly influenced by Keppel, the Commander-in-Chief in the Channel. Keppel approved in principle of a Mediterranean squadron to stop d'Estaing, but he was becoming insistent that twenty were not enough for the Channel, and that we should make no detachments till we were certain that the enemy had committed their forces.[1] On 4 April Sandwich gave his written opinion to the Cabinet that it would be unsafe to leave England and Ireland without a very much larger force than Keppel's twenty sail of the line. Two days later he reiterated to the Cabinet, and later the same day to the King, that it would be impossible at that moment to form a separate squadron to meet the Toulon fleet without sacrificing every other service. The only possibility was to send the Channel fleet itself, which was too great a risk in the face of the Brest fleet and the possible intervention of the Spaniards.[2]

Sandwich's theme was that we must be secure at home before we detached. His argument of numbers was a weak one: the Brest fleet was no more ready than the British, and it was not conceivable that they could mount a serious invasion before Keppel was strengthened by the ships which were nearly ready. If there was weakness at home it lay rather in the shortage of frigates to defend the trade and intercept landing craft or raiders like Paul Jones. Lord North suspected that the French were not so ready as Sandwich supposed, and intelligence in the middle of April supported him. But he was in no state to dispute the issue with effect. He was standing up badly to the pressure of political tension, and was so harried and confused that he fled from London to collect his scattered wits in the country. He did no more than lament feebly to the King that no squadron had been sent out to intercept the Toulon fleet. Germain pressed for a reinforcement, and the King persuaded Sandwich to see if Keppel could be induced by the promise of additional ships to detach a force to Gibraltar.[3]

But the First Lord had allowed Keppel to dominate him; and Keppel was dominated by the fear of invasion. Though ships were coming forward

[1] Sandwich, II, 19–21; G 2263, 2312.
[2] Sandwich, II, 22–3; G 2275.
[3] G 2301, 2304, 2309.

rapidly in March and April, he remained adamant. The fleet must be kept together, he replied to Sandwich on 16 April, with a squadron ready to follow the enemy if they detached abroad.[1] It is true that the army at home was very weak. Many points were vulnerable to a raid; and the French would not need to pass a very large force across the Channel to mount a full invasion. Yet even Lord North doubted the reality of the danger. There were reports of troop concentrations in Normandy, but none whatever of landing craft. Keppel, however, swallowed the French demonstration. He was certain that an invasion was coming, and haunted by fear that Spain would join the enemy as soon as her galleons were home. He lamented the lack of frigates to intercept the enemy transports. 'I am not brave enough to go to my bed with the confidence of the country's being in security', he wrote.[2]

Keppel and Sandwich might have recalled that at the opening of the previous war the priority given to the fitting out of the Channel fleet had delayed Byng's departure for the Mediterranean and lost Minorca. Exactly twenty years later another First Lord was to face a similar problem and give the same answer as Sandwich. In 1798 Lord Spencer was asked to find a force to intercept the expedition being prepared by Napoleon in Toulon. With the advice of his naval colleagues on the Board he answered that the ships could not be spared with safety from the Channel. But the Younger Pitt and his Secretaries of State were a tougher team than North's; and in view of the political and strategic issues at stake they induced the First Lord to accept the risk in the Channel, which his advisers had greatly magnified. The consequence was the annihilation of the Toulon fleet by Nelson at the Nile. Perhaps the parallel is not entirely fair: for in 1778 Sandwich faced an efficient, undefeated and well prepared enemy, while in 1798 the French navy had suffered from revolution, defeat and lack of sea training. Yet in both cases the army at home was depleted, the fleet was short of men, and Ireland was restless. In April 1778 a dozen ships of the line might have been spared for Gibraltar.

2. The British Riposte

Keppel's reply to Sandwich on 16 April killed the last opportunity to send a fleet to the Straits. No squadron was sent; and on the 20th the *Proserpine* frigate sailed with orders for the Admiral at Gibraltar to station her with one of his own frigates on either side of the Straits to watch for d'Estaing and determine his course. Another cruiser was sent to reconnoitre Brest.

[1] Sandwich, II, 31.   [2] Sandwich, II, 53–4, 64–5, 82–3.

At this moment a preliminary warning should have been sent to Lord Howe. He was still under orders to detach most of his force to the West Indies; and though he had been warned in March that a squadron was out from Brest, the Admiralty had informed him on 2 April that it had put back to port. He was thus allowed to presume that there was no further danger. Nor should there have been; for at the time when his orders for the West Indies were drafted, the Cabinet had resolved with the First Lord's advice to send a force to the Mediterranean. It was not till far into April that the hope of a Mediterranean squadron was finally lost; and it was at this point that Howe should have been warned that the Toulon fleet would not be intercepted. This was admitted by the American Department within its own office walls. Under the existing orders the army in America would be at sea and Lord Howe's little squadron divided when d'Estaing reached the Delaware. Only a lucky decision by Clinton was to avert the danger.[1]

On 27 April, six weeks after the French declaration of alliance with the United States, came the first positive intelligence of the Toulon fleet. The sources were an agent in Paris, and the bankers of Amsterdam, whose news was relayed by the British Minister at The Hague. D'Estaing had sailed on the 11th with eleven sail of the line, a fifty-gun ship, and several frigates. His nine months' provisions made a destination outside Europe virtually certain; and the personnel embarked confirmed the Paris rumours that it was the Delaware or Boston.[2] To Germain the news portended the ruin of all his work: the loss of command in American waters, and the fall of Philadelphia, Halifax or Quebec. He had done all he could to have a fleet sent to Gibraltar. Now it was too late, and to avoid a small risk we had exposed ourselves to a great disaster. He entreated North to act on the intelligence and send part of the home fleet to America. That this was the enemy's destination no one doubted. Yet still Sandwich hesitated, unwilling to stake everything on a probability and maintaining that we could not detach from home with safety. He had fixed a Cabinet for the 29th to discuss the news. By that day Germain was desperate at the inaction, and he made a formal protest in writing to the King and Cabinet. At least twelve sail of the line should be sent to America immediately. He presumed that the ships which would remain in the Channel would be enough for home defence; but in any case he insisted that in war risks must be run, and it was better to fail in a vigorous effort than tamely submit to the loss of our distant fleets, armies and possessions.[3]

[1] CL, Germain, précis at end of 1778.
[2] SP 78/306, copy of Yorke's of 24 April.
[3] G 2316; Sandwich, II, 35–6, 38; CL, Germain, 29 April, Germain to King and Cabinet.

Germain's protest was decisive. The Cabinet resolved the same day to send thirteen ships of the line to America, and he had the satisfaction of sending the order to the Admiralty. On his suggestion, the squadron was to make for Halifax, and proceed to the West Indies if there was no sign of the enemy in American waters. Should there be no intelligence of the enemy in either theatre, the commander was to bring his squadron home to the Channel.[1]

It remained to send a belated warning to Howe. Germain's paper had demanded a frigate to warn the commanders in America. But Sandwich sent word that the relieving squadron would have only a single frigate to meet the numerous cruisers believed to be with d'Estaing, and none could be spared for despatches. He asked the American Secretary to arrange a special packet boat, and the despatches were sent down to Falmouth by express on 4 May. But only one packet on the American run was available, for none of the last five sent out had returned. The West India packet was taken off its run and ordered to Philadelphia, and the American packet was sent off with duplicates to New York. The American packet was taken on passage by the enemy; but the West India packet joined Howe off the Delaware on 29 June with the news that she had been chased by a French battle squadron.[2]

The relieving squadron called for a senior Admiral. Lord Howe was probably coming home; and no one wanted Gambier, who had sailed with a convoy in March, to command so large a force. Vice-Admiral Byron, who was under orders to take the command in India, was summoned to the Admiralty. He dashed up from Pirbright as soon as he could get horses, to learn that he was to be switched to America. Much of his baggage had been sent ahead to India, and the rest was in London. He hired a waggon which trundled his things towards his ship at Plymouth, but if his squadron sailed as soon as the Cabinet expected, there was a good chance that he would put to sea with a purser's kit. Byron was the second son of Lord Byron and nephew of the Lord President, Gower. Now in his middle fifties, his experience was of exploration rather than fleets; and the nickname of 'Foul-weather Jack' ominously suggested the shape of his luck.[3]

Whatever the merits of Sandwich's reluctance to despatch the squadron, the ships should have been ready to sail at a moment's notice when the decision

[1] G 2320; CL, Germain, 29 April to Admiralty.

[2] Sackville, II, 110; CL, Clinton, Secretary of State Out, 4 May, Germain to Clinton; CL, Germain, 29 April to King and Cabinet, and précis at end of 1778; Royal Institution, I, 260. Germain attributed the shortage of packet boats to their unnecessary detention at New York. The precariousness of the communications were underlined later in the summer, when the August packet from New York was taken by a privateer and the bearer of the despatches was killed.

[3] Sandwich, II, 43.

was taken. And Sandwich evidently imagined that they were. He went down to Portsmouth on 1 May to accelerate their departure, followed the next day by the King. But Byron would sail with his baggage. For the ships, with one exception, were still stored and provisioned for Channel service, and according to Keppel two of the ships which were to remain in the Channel were stripped of their running rigging to fit out those for America. While the Channel ships had to embark a further four months' provisions, the gun-decks of Byron's flagship at Plymouth were crammed with provisions for a voyage to India, and these had to be returned to the Victualling Office.[1]

Everything possible was now done to hasten the squadron to sea. Eight hours should have been enough to complete the provisions. But rough weather prevented the victuallers from lying alongside the ships at Spithead. Finding that some of the ships could not fix their sailing date, the King resolved to stay and chivvy the Port Admiral. He remained for a week, taking notes on the state of the shipping, inspecting the fleet, and walking about in the rain among the dockyard puddles. In his absence the House of Commons stormed at the squadron's unreadiness, and the loss of an east wind to carry it out of the Channel. One member demanded the heads of North and Sandwich; a call for retribution curiously seasoned with a letter assuring North that no personal attack had been intended.[2]

Even now, however, the battle to despatch the squadron was to be resumed. The Lords of the Admiralty at Portsmouth – Sandwich, who was visiting, and Palliser and Mulgrave who were serving in the Channel fleet – were anxious that Byron's squadron should not winter abroad, as its absence would be very dangerous and prevent any further detachment from home. Germain laid the First Lord's letter before the Cabinet, and once more persuaded them to turn it down: an intervention which was to save the West Indies in the coming winter. But when the preparation of the squadron had been hastening forward for a week, advices from Paris and a letter from the Admiral at Gibraltar brought reports that the Toulon fleet had gone to Cadiz, and a list of the Spanish fleet. Keppel once more fell a prey to doubt, and drew Sandwich in his wake. Though every day strengthened the evidence that d'Estaing was bound for America, they felt that in view of the combined strength of the Brest fleet and the Spaniards it would be wrong to detach Byron without absolute certainty that when d'Estaing left Cadiz he would cross the Atlantic. The French design to hold the British navy in the Channel was bearing fruit. The latest reports from France were that the Brest fleet of twenty-five of the line was nearly ready, and that a French victory over Keppel would be followed by an invasion. Of all this North

---

[1] G 2318, 2327–8
[2] G 2328, 2330, 2324–5.

remained sceptical; and on receiving a letter of 7 May from Sandwich at Portsmouth urging further delay, he took the lead for once.

North replied to Sandwich that the *Proserpine* would probably return from Gibraltar with positive news before Byron could sail, and warned him not to retard the squadron for a moment without an order from a Secretary of State. He then collected the opinions of all the members of the Cabinet who were in London. From Weymouth, Germain, Gower and Dartmouth he obtained the same answer: unless Sandwich received positive information before the squadron's departure that the Toulon fleet had not gone to America, Byron should sail as soon as possible. Though North did not regard invasion as impracticable, and thought it possible that the French and Spaniards would try it, he did not believe they could do so for some time. The danger in America was more probable and immediate. The episode reveals North in a moment of unusual decisiveness and activity. It is interesting that the King was far away at Portsmouth. Perhaps the royal presence sapped rather than vitalised the Prime Minister.[1]

3. Byron sails for America

On the evening of 17 May the wind dropped at Spithead, and under a clear moon the ships began to complete their stores. The King went out from Portsmouth to hurry the work, and returned to London on the following evening satisfied that the fleet would weigh with the first fair wind. For now the fatal south-west wind which blew across the Channel ports in the spring had interposed. The fleet, ready at last, was held up by the weather. The Admirals of the Channel fleet were happy to see the Cabinet's intentions thus frustrated; for Palliser agreed with Keppel in his reluctance to see Byron away till d'Estaing's destination was known beyond human doubt. The natural instinct of a fleet commander was to over-insure, and to see the danger in his own command writ larger than that in a distant theatre. And Sandwich had been excessively influenced by these partial views.[2]

The squadron was still waiting for the wind on the 13th when news of d'Estaing burst like a thunderclap on the Ministers. He had been sighted off Algiers on 28 April. The *Proserpine's* long absence was explained. Far from having entered Cadiz or set its course for America, the Toulon squadron had not even left the Mediterranean a fortnight after it had sailed. The chances were now very good that the frigate would pick up the enemy and discover their course. With the King's approval Sandwich anticipated the Cabinet's decision

[1] Sackville, II, 110; Sandwich, II, 41–2, 48, 49–54; G 2326, 2329.
[2] G 2330, 2333; Sandwich, II, 55–8.

which was given the next day, and sent an express dashing off to Portsmouth to stop the fleet from sailing.[1]

There followed three torturing weeks of uncertainty. Contradictory reports flowed in, rumours flew about, and plans were canvassed for every contingency. The Toulon fleet was to destroy Howe and enter the St Lawrence – had put back to Toulon – would join the Brest fleet off Finisterre – was steering for Brest. In the meantime the ships at Spithead dropped down the Channel to join their Admiral at Plymouth; and the squadron's destination was changed from Halifax to New York. This alteration had been suggested to the King and Sandwich by Commodore Hood on the ground that it was easier to get north from New York than south from Halifax. It was adopted by North with a timid reference to 'the opinion of the best seamen', as he thought it increasingly probable that d'Estaing would go direct to New York. This was accepted by the Cabinet on the 16th. The loss of Halifax would have been a crippling blow; but the Cabinet took into consideration the three regiments believed to be on their passage to reinforce the garrison. In this they were misled. The transports for the Halifax force had been ordered in February for 2 April, but had not reached the Clyde till May. The troops were on board on 12 May; but without consulting or informing Germain the Admiralty had postponed the sailing to wait for Byron's departure.[2]

At last on 2 June the *Proserpine* sped into Falmouth after nearly seven weeks' absence. In company with the *Enterprise*, which reached Plymouth on the 3rd, she had sighted the Toulon fleet in the Straits on 16 May, and followed it for a short distance south-west into the Atlantic. From its regular course and great press of sail her captain supposed it was bound for the West Indies; but when his report reached the Queen's House on the following morning, the King reasoned that the enemy's course was more probably intended to catch a good wind for America. 'The Cabinet cannot meet too soon, nor Byron be ordered to sail', said his note to Sandwich at half-past nine.[3]

The Cabinet faced a harassing decision when it met later in the morning: a wrong one would bring great losses. But they had before them a mass of digested intelligence which had not been available to the *Proserpine's* captain. The King's guess was supported by the accounts of persons and material on board the enemy, which all suggested that d'Estaing was bound for America and was steering an indirect course to catch the trade wind for the Delaware.

---

[1] Sandwich, II, 57–8, 375; Wortley, 124–5.

[2] Sandwich, II, 56, 62, 74–5, 370, 374–5; G 2332, 2346; CL, Germain, 17 May to Admiralty; *ibid*, précis at end of 1778 correspondence.

[3] James, 92–3; Sandwich, II, 8, 89.

The Ministers resolved that Byron should sail at once for America. At three o'clock on the morning of 7 June he was roused by sailing orders from the Admiralty. The wind was blowing into Plymouth Sound at the time; but two days later he was at sea, and his squadron was dropping down the Channel for New York.[1]

4. Keppel and the Channel Fleet

The Ministry had staked its forces, and could do no more. Byron's despatch was the last action by which it could influence the summer's campaign beyond the Atlantic. The Government's attention was now claimed by the Channel fleet, which was ordered to sea at the same time as Byron.

Admiral Augustus Keppel had been chosen as war-commander of the Channel fleet when the guardships were manned in the autumn of 1776. By birth and connection he was a Rockingham Whig, and his brother the Bishop of Exeter had recently died thanking God that he had never given a vote for shedding American blood. The Keppels were a close-knit clan. The eldest brother, Lord Albemarle, after sitting on Germain's court martial, had commanded at the capture of Havana in 1761, with his brother General William Keppel serving in his force and Augustus as second in command of the fleet.[2] Both Albemarle and his brother Augustus had been in office in Rockingham's administration, Augustus at the Board of Admiralty for fifteen months in the period of the navy's rapid decay. He was a close friend not only of Rockingham, but of Richmond and Fox, to both of whom he was related.

Keppel's conduct since the beginning of the American rebellion had matched his connections. He refused to serve against the Americans, actively opposed the war, and at the end of 1775 quarrelled violently with Sandwich over the disposal of a sinecure. This was the Lieutenant-Generalcy of the Marines, which went to Palliser though both Howe and Keppel had wanted it. Palliser was Keppel's junior; but Generals of Marines were not appointed by seniority. Palliser was a member of the Board of Admiralty, and as Comptroller had been Sandwich's closest colleague in the reconstruction of the fleet. Sandwich followed precedent, and would have been a fool to hand over the plum to his political enemy. But this dispute must be remembered when Palliser appears as Keppel's second in command in the Channel fleet.

'When men do not draw with men in power, they should not be entrusted with the command of the King's ships.'[3] Keppel's political friends assiduously

[1] Sandwich, II, 91, 371, 375.

[2] There is some reason to suspect that the Keppels did not emerge with completely clean hands from the administrative duties of the expedition.

[3] Barham, I, 89 (Captain W. Young in Dec. 1780).

planted in his mind the idea that he had been chosen as the future scapegoat for the navy's weakness. By nature he was open to this kind of suggestion. He was a small man with a broken nose; popular with his seamen, and physically courageous. But more than physical courage was needed for his coming task. What of his moral powers? He had been a member of Byng's court-martial, and though he had made some effort to obtain Parliament's intervention after the sentence, he had been 'too frightened to lift up his voice' when he was questioned by Mansfield and Hardwicke at the bar of the House of Lords.[1] The memoirist Wraxall took a view of him which his letters do not contradict: 'in self possession, judgment, superior maritime skill, and presence of mind; in all those endowments of a great commander which ensure victory, I have always regarded him as deficient.'[2] His health was bad. He suffered constant pain from an old injury to his back, and at times it prevented him from walking.

This was the man who had been chosen to command the main fleet of England: a comparatively junior vice-admiral, of good reputation but questionable firmness of character, and a personal and political enemy of the First Lord. Only a few weeks before the breach with France he had complained to Sandwich of delay in promoting him, which he attributed to his political opinions.[3] Since Saratoga he had taken a most dispirited view of the country's prospects. 'Full of alarm and uneasiness', he had predicted the loss of India and the West Indies if France entered the war. When the time for action came, he saw the King; and in accepting the command of the Channel fleet he asked that he should take under his orders only ships which he had inspected and agreed to be properly manned. His motive was fear that he might have to 'answer for operations proportionate to my apparent, not my real strength'. Since Sandwich's treatment of Keppel has been indicated, it is as well to be clear about Keppel's attitude to Sandwich from the outset of his command.[4]

The weeks which followed were loud with Keppel's lamentations. On taking command he was promised twenty sail of the line alleged to be ready in home ports, but only six of them were really ready for sea when he came to inspect the list. The remainder, of course, were either refitting after their winter cruise or fitting out for the first time as a result of the delayed mobilisation, and the work was slowed by the shortage of hands. To Rockingham, whom he invited to visit him at Portsmouth, Keppel expressed

[1] Nothing in the American War equals the baseness of these lawyers in procuring Byng's execution.
[2] Wraxall Memoirs, I, 386.
[3] Williams Transcripts, 27 Jan. 1778.
[4] Keppel, II, 13–15; Sandwich, II, 17.

'much anxiety'. 'The good opinion the country in general expressed towards me, gives them expectations, I fear, much beyond my poor abilities to perform.' Yet war was still four months off, and under Sandwich's eye the fleet was rapidly being brought forward from ordinary. As Keppel was making his first conditions and complaints, additional workmen were being taken on in the yards, extra time was being worked, and all hands were turned to fitting ships for sea. The ships on the stocks were ordered to be hastened on, as they had been in the previous war, without waiting for their timbers to season. From the dockyards of southern England ships were dropping down towards the fleet anchorage. Army recruits held back from America were lent to man them till the Marines returned from Nova Scotia. The line of battle, Captain Jervis wrote on 15 April, was 'the most formidable, for its numbers, I ever saw'.[1]

Keppel's first sailing orders were to put to sea with twenty-nine sail of the line and escort a convoy past Ushant with reinforcements for Gibraltar. But they were suspended on the news that the Toulon fleet was at sea, and his fleet was gutted to make up Byron's squadron. Eleven of his ships were taken, and the tacks and sheets in two others were unrove and made over to Byron. As a result of this set-back, when Keppel sailed in June he had only twenty sail of the line; but other ships joined him steadily as they completed their crews. When fighting began in the middle of July he had thirty, and by the end of September thirty-three, while twenty-five others had gone abroad since the spring. It was no mean achievement on the part of Sandwich; and Keppel's fleet was amply sufficient to hold the Channel against the French.

Keppel's fear of invasion was one which always afflicted seamen more than soldiers or statesmen. But in this case perhaps it also reflected the wishful thinking of the opposition. Their desire to bring home the army in America was voiced in Parliament on 1 April on a motion by the Duke of Richmond[2];

[1] Keppel, II, 19; CO 5/254, f. 108; Sandwich, I, 363; II, 93; *Amer. Neptune*, 1947, p. 95.

[2] *Distribution of the British army, November 1778*

	Cavalry Regiments	Infantry Battalions
England	16	23
Scotland	1	3
Ireland	11	11
America	2	45
Mediterranean	—	7
West Indies	—	6
East Indies	—	1
Africa	—	1
TOTAL	30	97

(WO 34/111, f. 32).

(*Continued opposite*)

and Rockingham was at Portsmouth to prime Keppel. 'God send the fleet and army safe home from America', Keppel wrote to Sandwich on May 30th. 'I have long wished to see it, every hour of its absence now is critical. I must here finish upon this or I shall be led to my political ideas upon this subject, which I do not mean and will therefore confine myself to my profession, where the King called me to act in.'[1]

But in his profession he was equally beset by fears. From the first he seems to have swallowed the opposition line that the Ministry intended to use him as he had allowed Newcastle to use Byng. Lord Weymouth had remarked that he seemed more inclined to do his duty at sea than to give advice; and he was pressing that his instructions should be explicit on every point. Should he give battle with twenty or thirty sail of the line, he asked in April, if d'Estaing joined the Brest fleet and brought the enemy's strength to nearly forty? Sandwich replied that if the enemy's superiority was not very marked, he should fight; but if the Brest and Toulon fleets united, he should return to collect the reinforcements which would assemble at St Helen's as they were manned. It was a fair and obvious answer. But early in May, with his best ships gone to Byron and few of the remainder collected, Keppel was asking what to do if the French came up the Channel; and a couple of weeks later he asked for a Cabinet ruling on whether to risk a battle. 'I am not the person that will offer an opinion upon a matter of such

Forces in England, June 1778

Encamped:

9 regiments of cavalry	2,919
11 battalions of infantry	7,810
39 corps of militia	19,503
	30,232

To guard coasts:

2 regiments of cavalry	570

Cantonments:

1 regiment of dragoons (Scotland)	285
2 battalions and 5 companies (England)	2,086
28 corps of militia	10,516
	13,457

Serving in the fleet:

1 battalion of infantry	710

TOTAL:	44,399

(Thynne Papers)

[1] Sandwich, II, 83.

THE ENGLISH CHANNEL

Harwich
Colchester
ESSEX
Gunfleet
The Nore
Tilbury
London
Sheerness
Gravesend
Chatham
Thames
KENT
Dover
The Downs
Strait of Dover
S. Foreland
Calais
Boulogne
Rye
Beachy Head
SUSSEX
Chichester
Portsmouth
Gosport
Spithead
Solent
St Helens
Isle of Wight
The Needles
Salisbury
Bath
Bristol
Bristol Channel
DEVON
Torbay
Start Point
Plymouth
Eddystone
CORNWALL
Falmouth
Lizard
Land's End
Scilly Is.
ENGLISH CHANNEL
le Havre
NORMANDY
Cherbourg
Channel Isles
Jersey
St. Malo
BRITTANY
Brest
Ushant

Proposed invasion routes 1779

nice importance. I hope I shall do my duty becoming an officer in every situation; and I might perhaps not be sorry, if I considered myself *only*, to give battle to the French fleet when I might not dare as a councillor to my King to advise it.'[1]

5. The Campaign in the Channel

On 13 June, a few days after Byron's departure, the Channel fleet of twenty ships of the line weighed anchor for its first cruise, with orders to see the Gibraltar reinforcement safe past Brest. Keppel's orders were to seize any French frigates which tried to shadow him, and give battle if the Brest fleet came out. Before he sailed he expressed his satisfaction with these very explicit instructions.[2]

The fleet worked its way down the Channel, and west of the Lizard two French frigates were sighted. If they had followed the usual custom and come alongside the Admiral, he could have done nothing but get their promise not to follow the fleet, and wish them *bon voyage*; and a monotonous proceeding it would have been, for eleven French frigates were reported in the chops of the Channel, and the performance would have been repeated every day. But, instead, one of the Frenchmen answered the Admiral's summons by pouring a broadside into a sixty-four, and after a two-hour fight was forced to strike. The first shots had been fired.

In the captured frigate was a list of the Brest fleet. It showed twenty-seven sail of the line ready for sea, and five more preparing. Keppel turned home for reinforcements, and on the 27th he anchored off the Isle of Wight. After the campaign he was to plead that he came in because he dared not risk a battle knowing that there were no naval stores to repair his damage. But he did not say so at the time, and hitherto his complaints had been about manning and not stores.

There was general dismay at the fleet's return. Keppel's withdrawal might expose the Gibraltar convoy to capture, and the homeward-bound East Indiamen and large West India convoys due in the Channel were at the mercy of any raiding force the French might send out. The King was 'much hurt' at his reappearance, and hoped the Cabinet would order him back to his cruising station at once. Germain, too, remembered with impatience how Hawke had kept the seas. 'I long to hear of Mr Keppel's return to Brest', he told Knox, 'and if ever I am concerned in drawing instructions for Naval operations I will strike St Helen's out of my Dictionary.' Keppel's return when the French were still in harbour showed an unnecessary haste.

---

[1] *Ibid.*, II, 17 ff., 24ff., 54, 69, 77, 79.
[2] Sandwich, II, 88, 93 n.

He had said that five of the Brest ships had already sailed, which reduced their force in harbour to twenty-two, and he now had as many himself. But he took refuge in his orders. 'To have fought with such inferiority, and to have been totally routed, would have merited censure; it would have been justly said that I had proper orders to return to St Helen's, and that an additional force was collecting in case of such an event.'[1]

The Admiralty did what it could to hasten Keppel to sea. He was ordered to return off Brest as soon as four more ships were ready, a number later reduced to three. Sandwich went down to Portsmouth again, but Keppel treated his suggestions for getting men with obstructive contempt, and declared that he must be equal to the French, 'ship for ship in the line', before he would sail. He complained that his return to port had not received approval. Sandwich's irritation shows through one of his replies, but generally he answered with patience and good temper. Palliser, who was doing all he could to smooth the way, assured the First Lord that Keppel was perfectly satisfied with his treatment, and that his disposition was 'of the fairest and most honourable kind'. But the tone of Keppel's own letters to Sandwich does not support this. An anonymous letter to Sandwich hit near the mark: 'If His Majesty *will* employ Opposition admirals of great political connexions and family, he will undo his ministry, the nation, and himself.'[2]

The shortage of men was increased by sickness in the ships which had cruised in the winter. But the Leeward Island convoy passed safely up the Channel, bringing a welcome supply of seamen for the press. On 9 July Keppel sailed again with twenty-four of the line for the rendezvous off the Lizard, to await the Jamaica convoy and collect his reinforcements as they came out to him. Five more ships followed him within a couple of days.

The safety of the convoys was not the only reason for wishing to keep the fleet at sea. There was intelligence from Paris that Spain would enter the war when Congress ratified the French treaties; and if this was true the French must be fought and beaten before the Spaniards could join them. There was thus a conflict between the need for time to complete the British mobilisation and the need for a rapid decision. Even Lord North hoped the French would try their strength with Keppel quickly. So did the King, who never doubted the outcome of a battle.[3]

But such firmness of spirit in the Prime Minister was becoming rarer. At the beginning of June the King was so exasperated by North's vacillation and talk of retirement that he wrote him a lecture on his duty, and hoped

---

[1] Sandwich, II, 98, 100; Knox, 144.
[2] Adm. 2/1335, 26 June and 3 July, Admiralty to Keppel; Sandwich, II, 101–10.
[3] Sandwich, II, 115–17; G 2391.

that 'the summer's repose will enable you to rouse your mind with vigour to take the lead again in the House of Commons, and not let every absurd idea be adopted as has too often recently appeared'. About this time the King began his confidential relationship with North's friend and Under-Secretary John Robinson, whom he enlisted for the work of keeping North at the treadmill. Robinson assured him that North had made a resolution to concentrate his mind on public affairs and to start a vigorous drive on the backlog of work.[1]

On 17 July a dilemma faced the Ministry which measured North's painful indecision. A fugitive arrived with news that a declaration of war had been read on the quay at Dunkirk, and an intercepted letter reported that orders had been given for the destruction of British shipping. A formal declaration in reply would require a Cabinet meeting, and the Ministers had scattered to their summer retreats. Should orders be given to attack French shipping without a declaration? To the King the issue was clear: the French had cast off the mask, and open warfare should begin. Lord Weymouth, the responsible Secretary of State, agreed. So did North, who went off to dine with Sandwich and talk about encouraging privateers.

But by the morning North had developed scruples. He now insisted that on the question of reprisals the Cabinet's views must be sought. But he was not sure how to discover them: the only suggestion he could make was that he should write off to those members of the Cabinet who were in reach, and either ask their opinion or arrange a Cabinet meeting. This was too much. 'You have already this morning settled with Lord Sandwich', wrote his irritated sovereign. '... There can be no reason to delay issuing the orders till a Cabinet is summoned; what is so clear ought never to be delayed for that formality.' This decided the matter, and on the following day Keppel was ordered to attack French shipping.[2]

The clash was now approaching. The militia spent those late July days in camp, grumbling at their confinement and wondering if the French fleet was at sea. An invasion alert went out from Amherst's headquarters to the district commanders, and secret plans were made to drive and burn the countryside in front of the enemy. Amherst's dispositions followed Ligonier's classic pattern. The seaports were garrisoned, and the coast patrolled by a forward screen of dragoons. But the main counter-attack forces were held together in reserve, in camps astride the Thames in Essex and in Kent (where Keppel's brother commanded), to cover the capital against a landing in any quarter. The two groups were linked by causeways across the Thames

[1] G 2369; Add. MSS. 37883, ff. 225-8.
[2] SP 78/306, 17 July; G 2393, 3108 (wrongly dated 1780); Sandwich, II, 123-6, 373; Dartmouth, II, 467.

between Tilbury and Gravesend, protected on the seaward side by obstructions, so that either force could cross the river rapidly in three columns if the enemy landed.[1]

Meanwhile the fleets of France and England converged. Admiral d'Orvilliers had put out from Brest on 10 July with thirty sail of the line and two of fifty guns; but three of them were of weak scantling and unfit for the line of battle, so that his real strength in the line was twenty-nine including a fifty. His orders were to cruise for a month, but not to seek out and attack the British fleet. On the afternoon of 23 July, sixty-six miles west of Ushant, he sighted Keppel. During the night he worked to windward, and manoeuvred with the weather gage for three days without closing for action. But on the 27th the wind changed and enabled Keppel to pounce on the French rear. D'Orvilliers turned to meet him.

Two of the French ships had parted company in the night, and d'Orvilliers had only twenty-seven ships in his line of battle against Keppel's thirty, and 1,950 guns against 2,280.[2] He did not want a close action, and the fleets passed each other firing on opposite courses. Keppel was unable to collect his damaged ships and renew the action in daylight; and during the night the French crept off, covered by deceptive lights. The French had suffered greater casualties, 736 against 408; but their guns, firing langrage high into the British rigging, had so shattered the British masts and sails that Keppel was virtually immobilised. Both sides claimed a victory which neither had won, though Keppel was left in possession of the watery battlefield. The action proved that the enemy lacked the strength and the will to win the command of the Channel and invade England that summer. The Ministry had produced a fleet which could hold the French in check.

Keppel took his battered ships into Plymouth, where a survey showed the damage to be severe. The dockyard toiled to restore the fleet to service; but the shortage of great masts forced Keppel to patch his damaged ones and make do. Sandwich offered to come down in person, and was soundly snubbed – 'If you are so obliging as to delegate a little authority to us here, I think your Lordship's coming will only give you unnecessary trouble.' He stamped on Sandwich's suggestion that his foulest ships should be docked and cleaned, and the crews sent to man the new ships waiting at Portsmouth; and Sandwich acquiesced, though convinced that it would have increased the fleet more rapidly. Keppel wrote that he was fretting himself into illness; and after many complaints of bad health he withdrew to Mount Edgecumbe for a few days' rest. From there he wrote that he was such an invalid that rest

[1] Ducane MSS. 239–40; WO 34/226, p. 325 and *passim*; WO 34/227, pp. 3, 58.

[2] Lists in James, 432–3, and Chevalier, 87, with slight discrepancies. D'Orvilliers had another 174 guns in his three ships which were not fit for the line.

would be essential when the winter came on; and once again he lamented the American War as a fatal drain on our seamen.[1]

On 23 August the fleet put to sea again, to seek the French in the mouth of the Channel. The King hoped for another battle: 'Some decisive blow is necessary to rouse the nation from a lethargy which may prove fatal, if unanimity and vigour is shown Britain is capable to cope with her enemies.'[2] But d'Orvilliers was cruising in the Bay of Biscay, and Keppel's few frigates failed to find him. Convoys came safely in from Jamaica, the Baltic and the Mediterranean; but Keppel's health had not recovered, and after several weeks at sea without finding the enemy his spirits were falling. The lack of intelligence he found 'very trying to an anxious mind' – a phrase often echoed in the letters of Nelson and Collingwood a generation later, for Keppel was a victim of the uncertainty which always preyed on admirals searching the empty waters. Sickness was increasing in his ships, and provisions were running low, but he stayed at sea, himself a prey to crippling spasms. October came in with dirty blowing weather and large seas. The patched masts were showing the strain, 1,000 seamen were sick, and Keppel was anxious to bring his fleet right up to Spithead for the winter refit. To this the Cabinet agreed, and at the end of the month the fleet worked in to Spithead.[3]

The campaign had not been unsatisfactory, for decisive blows were seldom struck in the first year of war. The navy's mobilisation had been accomplished without misfortune, and no convoys had been lost. Only men and masts still cast their shadow. At the beginning of October eight more ships of the line were ready for sea, but for want of 2,500 seamen lay captive in their harbours.[4]

[1] Sandwich, II, 136, 139, 147, 150.
[2] Add. MSS. 37834, f.5.
[3] Sandwich, II, 154, 159, 173ff.; G 2414, 2418.
[4] Sandwich, II, 177.

CHAPTER XI

CRISIS IN AMERICA

1. *Sir Henry Clinton*

Much more caution is necessary in conducting this than any former war',
wrote Palliser after the Battle of Ushant. North and his colleagues were men
walking a tightrope with a heavy burden, the American rebellion. They
could not have turned back if they had wanted to; for the country's shipping
resources were unequal to the evacuation of the army in America, and the
operation would have had to be spread dangerously over two years. They
were forced to move on with resources so slender that a single mistake might
bring them tumbling to disaster. They had kept the command of the Channel
in dispute, but had no surplus of vessels to protect the coastal shipping against
Paul Jones and his fellow raiders, or to form the flying squadron at Kinsale
which was needed to protect the convoys in the Western Approaches. Nor
could a squadron be spared to hold the Mediterranean against the enemy
ships which remained in Toulon.

The precarious balance must have been constantly in their minds that
summer as they waited for news from America. Byron's arrival might save
the situation there; but if he had gone astray the plight of Clinton's great
army would be alarming indeed. For their peace of mind it was lucky that
the Ministers' eyes could not follow Foul-weather Jack into the Atlantic.
For only three days out his squadron was scattered by a violent gale, and
bad weather pursued it across the ocean. The first ship did not reach New
York till 30 July, nor a second till the middle of August. Six more came in
at the end of August, nearly three months after they had sailed, with crews
exhausted and rigging in disarray. Byron himself arrived at the end of
September from Halifax. Others had fetched Newfoundland in a shattered
state, and one sixty-four which had been driven south as far as Portugal and
been remasted at Lisbon appeared in October. Only one ship from England
reached Lord Howe before the crisis was weathered.[1]

General Howe and the main force in America had spent the winter comfortably in Philadelphia, while Washington watched him in discomfort
twenty-six miles away at Valley Forge. The Americans suffered in their hut-
ments through the harsh winter. Supplies of every kind were short, many
deserted, and Washington's strength once more ebbed away. But his lines

[1] Compare James, 108–11; Sandwich, II, 286; Albion, 297–8.

were reported to be strong; and Howe, who had declined to attack his entrenchments at Whitemarsh in December, saw no point in exposing his force to a winter offensive in which an initial success could not be exploited. April arrived, and still Howe stayed in his winter quarters, believing that Washington had strengthened his camp and waiting for green forage to grow before he would take the field. The order of 8 March to detach a force against the New England harbours arrived and was dismissed as impracticable – he could spare only two thousand men, the operation would need twice as many, and the coastline was difficult to navigate. Even in Pennsylvania he saw no hope of ending the rebellion with his present force.[1]

In any event Sir William had no intention of staying in America to try it. On 8 May Sir Henry Clinton arrived from New York to succeed him in the supreme command. He was to hold it for four years, and his name was for ever to be linked with the downfall of the American empire. He was, wrote Major Wemyss who served under him, 'an honourable and respectable officer of the German school; having served under Prince Ferdinand of Prussia and the Duke of Brunswick. Vain, open to flattery; and from a great aversion to all business not military, too often misled by aides de camp and favourites'. The vitriolic Colonel Charles Stuart had called him 'fool enough to command an army when he is incapable of commanding a troop of horse'. But this is unfair. He was a very capable general in the field; and Wemyss laid his finger on Clinton's real weaknesses. His interests were narrow, and he was crippled by self-distrust. In a station where political and administrative questions crowded in on the commander, he lived retired with a staff of whom Stuart said that the Adjutant-General Lord Rawdon was the only man of integrity. Thus he insulated his mind from the realities of American opinion and the doings of loyalists, refugees and commissaries. He was a difficult colleague, for he was jealous, hot tempered, and quick to take dislikes and to notice slights. At the beginning of 1778 he had been bespattering Howe with abuse; and his command was marked by endless quarrels with the admirals on the station.[2]

This touchiness was the outward sign of a deep self-distrust. On paper a bold memorialist with a powerful and persuasive style, he was timid in action. Shortly before he relieved Howe he was protesting that the command should not fall on his shoulders. 'Naturally of an unsteady disposition', he was easily cast down by minor reverses. His appointment to command England's largest army was due to circumstance rather than deliberate choice. He had gone to America in 1775 with Howe and Burgoyne, one of a trio

[1] CO 5/95, ff. 86, 116; Sackville, II, 107–8; Anderson, 299–300.
[2] Harvard, Sparks MSS., XXII, 214; Wortley, 83, 154; Carlisle, 432. Clinton spoke German and was liked by his German troops.

enjoying a reputation as high as any in the army. Howe and Burgoyne had had their chance and failed, and he was next in line of succession. For two years he had held a dormant commission as Commander-in-Chief in case of accident to Howe. Nevertheless he seems to have succeeded Howe by default rather than the active preference of the government. Amherst had once again refused the command; and as late as the middle of February the government seems to have intended to send out a general from home.[1] It would have been easier to prevent Clinton's appointment than to supersede him when he was installed.[2]

2. The Evacuation of Philadelphia

Clinton had only been in Philadelphia for a day when the *Porcupine* sloop arrived from England with the Cabinet orders of 21 March. They changed the whole character of his task. France was now an enemy in fact if not yet in name. Clinton learnt that he was to expect no reinforcements and no recruits, and would loose 8,000 men to Florida and the West Indies. His first act as Commander-in-Chief would be to abandon Philadelphia and remove the gutted remnant of his field army to New York. There was no glory in this.

The army in the rebel colonies had a strength at that moment of nearly 27,000 rank and file fit for duty: 8,400 at New York, 3,500 at Rhode Island, and 14,700 with the main force in Philadelphia. The detachments for the West Indies and Florida would leave about 8,000 rank and file fit for duty to withdraw from Philadelphia.[3] But Clinton resolved to postpone the departure of the expeditions to the southwards till his own movement to New York was complete. His reason was the impossibility of providing simultaneous naval protection for both movements. The last news from Europe was that a squadron under la Motte-Picquet was at sea, while Lord Howe had only five ships of the line and three fifties, of which he would have to detach all but two sixty-fours with the St Lucia expedition. It seemed wiser to keep the squadron together till the evacuation of Philadelphia was complete.

This decision gave Clinton the extra troops which enabled him to take a second resolution. He lacked the shipping to take off the whole army with its horses, if 3,000 loyalists who could not be left to the rebels' mercy were

[1] So G 2194 seems to imply.

[2] Willcox, *JMH*, 1947, p. 109; Wortley, 150; G 2194. In conjunction with Frederick B. Wyatt, Willcox has made an experimental study of Clinton's psychology in the *William and Mary Quarterly*, 1959.

[3] CO 5/95, ff. 222 *et seq.* (returns for March). Figures include Germans and Provincials. Total *effective* strength was 33,756 (Philadelphia 19,530, New York 10,456, Rhode Island 3,770).

to be embarked. The army could have cut the throats of its 5,000 horses, but the loss and humiliation were too much to bear. Instead Clinton resolved to march his army overland to New York, freeing the shipping for stores and refugees.[1]

On 18 June, when the embarkation was complete and the transports had left the quays, Clinton set out on his march. It was not a simple movement. He had 90 miles of rebel country and obstructed roads to cover, and might have to fight on the way; and since he was casting loose from his base he took with him what he confessed was an 'enormous' provision train stretching over nearly twelve miles of road. To protect it he marched in two divisions. Knyphausen's escorted the train, and Cornwallis's acted as an offensive rearguard to pin the enemy if they attempted to work their way up the flanks of the column towards the supply train.

The long, vulnerable column gave Washington an opportunity which he could not ignore. With a force rather greater than Clinton's he marched from Valley Forge in pursuit, while the Jersey militia turned out to harass the British flanks. Washington had many veterans, and his army had been drilled for three months by Steuben: it was the most refined instrument he had yet commanded. The American force converged with the British at Monmouth Court-house, and General Lee advanced to strike at Cornwallis's rearguard. Clinton was there in person. In suffocating heat he took the offensive, drove the enemy back for two or three miles, and disengaged without interruption in the cool of the night.[2] The army made good its retreat, and crossed unmolested to Manhattan to rejoin Lord Howe and his convoy. Thus the evacuation of Philadelphia was accomplished. By skill on land and good fortune at sea the army returned without loss to New York, drawing in its horns in America to strike at the French in the West Indies.

Yet it had been a narrow thing. If Clinton had adhered to his orders and sent off the St Lucia expedition from the Delaware, he would have taken much longer to embark his forces and stores, and the greatest part of the army in America would have been at sea in 400 sail of transports when d'Estaing swooped on the American coast. Off the Delaware Howe learnt for the first time from Germain's packet-boat that an enemy fleet was approaching. There was much indignation at the neglect to send early warning; indignation which was increased in July when a fleet of victuallers from Cork entered the Delaware in ignorance of the evacuation.

The hazarding of the victuallers concerned the Treasury. They had sailed

[1] CO 5/96, f. 20; Carlisle, 380; Willcox, *JMH*, 1947, p. 120.
[2] CO 5/96, f. 27. Numerous Hessians are said to have deserted on the march. The actual number of Hessian desertions in the six months to 24 June 1778 was only 219 NCOs and men.

from Cork at the end of May, two months after the order to abandon Philadelphia was sent to Clinton; entered the Delaware to find the enemy in possession; and by mere luck escaped to New York with their vital cargoes. The blunder seems grotesque. But its cause was not ministerial negligence, but friction in the badly oiled eighteenth-century machinery of war.

When the decision was taken to abandon Philadelphia, Lord North was under the impression that the arrears of the 1777 provisions were on the point of sailing, and would reach Clinton before the withdrawal. This was confirmed by the Commissary at Cork; and it was not till the very end of May that a further letter from Cork informed the Treasury that six more victuallers were on the point of sailing. This reached Robinson at midnight on 4 June, and he wrote at once to divert them to New York, but the ships had already gone. The error was due to a misunderstanding. The Commissary had spoken the strict truth when he said that the New York supplies were about to sail: he referred to the supplies furnished by the 'New York' contractors. But the Treasury had instructed him that the supplies from the 'Canada' contractors should also be sent to Clinton; and it was these, believed by the Treasury to have sailed in March, which formed the later shipment.[1]

The incident is a salutary reminder that in this war both sides were operating in an eighteenth-century time-scale and with eighteenth-century standards of efficiency. The worst consequences of misunderstandings were seldom reaped, because the enemy worked at the same pace and were subject to the same chances. Neptune was no partisan, and the hazards of the ocean afflicted French as well as British. If d'Estaing, sailing on the favourable southern track from Gibraltar, had made his landfall on the American coast ten days earlier, he might have destroyed Lord Howe and his convoy. But his passage took twelve weeks from Toulon; and when he sighted the Delaware capes, Howe was safe in New York. In this war time was vital, but it could not be calculated.

3. The Crisis Weathered

With Clinton's return to New York the contraction in America was complete. But before the next phase of the Cabinet's plan could be mounted, and the battle shift to the West Indies, Lord Howe had to face d'Estaing. His appearance on the American coast might sever the strategic communications and throttle the southward shift of forces.

Lord Howe had thrown out a chain of frigates to the southward to watch for the enemy. On 7 July they brought news of a French squadron at anchor in the Delaware; and a few days later a sloop came in which had sighted

[1] WO 34/113, f. 172; Thynne Papers, American Affairs, 1777–9, No. 23.

twelve French ships of the line steering for New York on the previous evening.

The French line of battle mounted 850 guns against Howe's 534, and d'Estaing had six frigates against his three. Perhaps the danger has been exaggerated; but it was serious. The loss of Howe's fleet and seamen would have been a difficult blow to repair, and Clinton's army would have been in peril; caught, says one writer, like rats in a trap. Cut off they would certainly have been; but they could look after themselves. In the New York area, Clinton had perhaps 24,000 men fit for duty, divided between Manhattan, Staten Island, Long Island and Paulus Hook. Manhattan itself had 14,000, and Washington, who had forborne to press the detachment marching from Philadelphia, would certainly have found it impossible to assault the same troops in their redoubts and entrenchments. The real danger lay in the shortage of provisions. The six Cork victuallers which escaped in the Delaware did not arrive till the crisis was past; and even with their cargoes the army's reserves were low, for reasons which will appear.[1] Had Howe lost the command of the sea it is possible that Clinton would have been starved into surrender during the autumn. Possible, but no more. For the French squadron based on Boston or perhaps Rhode Island might have found it hard to maintain an efficient blockad of the approaches to New York when the gales began to blow; and great efforts would have been made to succour the garrison.

Howe met the superior forces of the enemy by anchoring his squadron in a defensive line. It was a method later discredited by Brueys' use of it at Aboukir; but properly employed it was used several times with success by outnumbered British fleets in the course of the American War. As the British had reason to know, the shallow bar at Sandy Hook was very hazardous for ships of the line, and several ships struck on it in the course of the war. D'Estaing would not find it easy to feel his way into the harbour under fire. An advanced squadron would harry the enemy as they sounded their way across the bar; and behind it Howe placed a line of ships to cover the main channel with their broadsides, with springs on their cables so that they could swing as the enemy came up the harbour. The seaward flank of the line was covered by a battery and a brigade of infantry on the Hook.

For eleven days the two fleets watched each other across the bar, while d'Estaing waited for wind and tide to carry him into the harbour. On 22 July the French fleet weighed with a spring tide and a following wind. But d'Estaing's pilots reported that there was not enough water at the bar for the ships of deep draught; and he allowed himself to be deterred and made sail to the southward. For this he has received much blame, and probably with

[1] Below, pp. 222–4.

little justice. The pilots' advice was checked by soundings, and was found correct. Even if the French fleet had penetrated the harbour, Howe was confident that he could beat them: 'We should succeed at no time if we fail on such as occasion.'[1]

New York was saved, but the danger shifted now to Rhode Island. General Pigot's garrison had been threatened for several months by Sullivan; but while d'Estaing awaited the spring tide off Sandy Hook, Clinton had anticipated events by slipping a reinforcement of five battalions through Long Island Sound to Newport. On 27 July Howe became convinced that Rhode Island was d'Estaing's next target. 'Where is Byron?' Clinton exclaimed, surveying the exiguous squadron. But help was beginning to arrive. The principle had come into operation by which the navy, scattered to exercise the command of the sea, would concentrate on a point of crisis. A sixty-four and a fifty joined from Halifax, another fifty from the West Indies; and on 30 July a seventy-four, the solitary forerunner of Byron's fleet, came in with its tale of misfortune. No one could guess when the rest of Byron's ships would appear; but already the balance of force was beginning to be redressed. There were now thirteen weak ships of the line, if the five of fifty guns could be so classed; and Howe felt better able to face the sickly fleet of d'Estaing. Foul winds detained him till 6 August, when he weighed for Rhode Island.

Sullivan, with the support of two French ships of the line, had pressed in on the British garrison, and Pigot, in expectation of an enemy landing, had burnt the four frigates in the harbour and withdrawn into the lines outside Newport. On 8 August the French fleet entered the passage to Newport, and French and American troops began to land. At that moment the British fleet appeared. 'The surprise was complete', d'Estaing reported, 'and the day very exactly calculated with reference to our projects.' He attributed the precision of Howe's timing to spies, as people will when they are surprised; but he was wrong. Howe's action was the consequence of a sensible deduction from his cruiser-reports; his timing dictated by the wind. He had 772 guns in his line of battle against d'Estaing's 850[2]; but he was on the open sea, while the enemy was involved in the support of a military operation.

As Howe discovered when he communicated with General Pigot, there was very little he could do to help the garrison. But d'Estaing allowed himself to be diverted. Disliking the prospect of being blocked up between channels commanded by the enemy, he profited by a rare north wind and put to sea. Howe bore away to the south, hoping for a change of wind to give him the weather gage. For two days he manoeuvred for an advantage

---

[1] Quot. Willcox, *JMH* 1947, p. 111.

[2] Ward gives Howe 914 guns by including his frigates and flotilla.

to offset his weakness, but the cleaner French ships outsailed him; and on the night of the 11th a full gale scattered both the fleets. The weather moderated on the 13th, and as the Admirals collected their squadrons several indecisive single-ship actions were fought. On the 17th Howe reached Sandy Hook, to find that three of his ships had severe damage.

Sullivan had been pressing his siege at Newport, confident that the French troops would return to help him. The fleet returned indeed, but d'Estaing had learnt that the first of Byron's ships were arriving. He refused further help and sailed for Boston to refit his damaged ships while he still had time, for his orders if a superior British fleet appeared were to retire to Boston to revictual, and from there to sail for the West Indies. Howe followed him, leaving Sullivan a clear retreat from the island; and when Clinton appeared from New York with 3,000 troops in transports to cut him off, the last of the Americans had just crossed to the mainland. When Howe reached Boston the French had had two days to fortify their anchorage, and were beyond his reach.

This was the end of operations in the northern theatre. Howe returned to New York to learn of his promotion to be Vice-Admiral of the Red, an occasion which he used to complain of his omission from the last promotion, when he had been left second on the list. 'I cannot cease to lament the public testimonies of their Lordships' disesteem.' He had long since made gestures of resigning, and is said to have had motives of disappointed avarice; but his real reason for quitting at this critical moment seems to have been his desire to support his brother. He knew that his action would cause criticism; but with the enemy still on the coast, and Byron on the way to relieve him, he handed over his command to the unpopular and incompetent Gambier, and sailed for England.[1]

4. Failure of a Mission

It was under the shadow of these critical operations that the Peace Commissioners shot their bolt. They had made their approach to Congress, offering a union of Great Britain and America under a common sovereign, acting together in peace and war 'on a basis of equal freedom and mutual

---

[1] Adm. 1/488, f. 343; Walpole, Last Journals, II, 121. He explains his unwillingness to let his brother down by remaining in a letter to an unidentified correspondent which was catalogued in Messrs Sotheby's sale of 6 Oct. 1958 (Item 44).

Gambier had probably been sent to America to make room for Samuel Hood as Commissioner at Portsmouth. He bitterly regretted the move when he found himself relegated by Howe to be Port Admiral at New York; an inadequate reward for quitting 'an honourable lucrative safe post, a loved and amiable wife big with child of a fifth produce of our conjugal happiness'.

safety'. Short of independence, there was nothing more to offer. But Congress's answer was an assertion of that independence. They would negotiate for peace when England had recognised the United States or withdrawn her forces.

In different circumstances the British offer would have been attractive and generous. Americans had been offered the liberty 'to dispose of their property and to govern themselves without any reference to Great Britain, beyond what is necessary to preserve that union of force in which our mutual safety and advantage consist'.[1] Carlisle had small hope of success. But he believed that his terms offered real advantages to the Americans: a continued connection with Britain, which he thought essential to them; help in restoring their currency; free commerce; political stability, so rarely the reward of revolution; and at a safe distance the cohesive force of the monarchy to hold the states together. Like most Englishmen he believed that for England total separation would mean the loss of the West Indies, and probably of Canada and Nova Scotia; and that in time of war a hostile America could inflict deep injuries on England's major trade routes. Time proved his fears unnecessary; but they were not groundless or irrational.[2]

In retrospect it is easy to say that in withholding independence at this moment Britain was blind and foolish; and that by cementing the American alliance with France she ensured her own downfall in a ruinous double war. But there is another side to the question. The Commissioners had indeed latitude to entertain a demand for independence. But now that America had bound herself to the French alliance, and French forces were actually on the coast, to concede independence as a preliminary would throw away one of the few negotiating cards that England held. The Americans would be free to assert that they could not treat separately from the French, and to fight on for Canada with French assistance. Four years later the British government did recognise American independence without a treaty, but they obtained an equivalent: a separate negotiation with the United States.

Carlisle spent the rest of summer hanging about New York with his fellow-Etonians, abusing his patrons in England and complaining of the heat and the monotonous scarlet uniforms. His disappointment at the loss of Philadelphia had warped his judgment; and he and Eden worked themselves up to such a pitch that they implored the government to cancel the St Lucia expedition so that Clinton could resume the offensive. If they had had their way, d'Estaing's arrival would have caught the army scattered in weak detachments from Philadelphia to Newport, with Howe's handful of ships attempting to cover every part. In the autumn, on the eve of their departure,

<hr>

[1] Ritcheson, 278.
[2] Carlisle, 353ff.

they were agitating for a systematic war of destructive raiding. But as Colonel Stuart observed, America was almost invulnerable to a war of destruction. Boston and Philadelphia were the only important towns in the rebels' hands (for Charleston had been almost destroyed by fire); and to destroy either of them the whole army would have to be used, in the type of large-scale operation hitherto so unsuccessful. Our barbarities, said Stuart, had already planted an 'irrecoverable' hatred, and it would be rash to incur the American's enmity for ever. 'I doubt whether they have, on this point, either power or understanding to advise; I fancy private resentment has drove them to adopt quite contrary opinions from those they came here with, not from a greater or more extensive knowledge of the country, but from a deep sense of the insults they have received.'[1]

But in the malcontent Clinton, the Commissioners found a ready sympathiser. Since the moment when he assumed the command he had been distressing the Ministry with his complaints of personal neglect and inadequate forces. Instead of the usual calculation of total effectives he chose to reckon his force by the rank and file fit for duty. Eden fed his chagrin at the order to detach to the West Indies, and urged him to ignore it. And in the middle of September, when news of the relief of Rhode Island had eased the anxiety at home, a letter arrived from Clinton which threw the Ministry into fresh consternation. Written when Rhode Island was still in danger, it forecast his future prospects in tones of deepest gloom. When he detached to the West Indies and Florida, and complied with the demands for help which he expected from Canada, he would probably be forced to abandon New York and withdraw to Halifax.[2]

Clinton had made his calculation by assuming that Haldimand would call for a third of his remaining force. The depth of his pessimism is plumbed in a letter written the same day to his cousin the Duke of Newcastle. 'By the present arrangement I wish one half [of the army] may not be underground by Christmas, and the rest reduced to an ignominious flight to avoid still further disgrace.' His prophesy was received at home with utter dismay. Though the King was still prepared in the last resort to abandon New York in order to beat the French, even the timid North could not see that the moment for the sacrifice had come. If Clinton withdrew to Halifax, every hope in America would be blasted, and the army destroyed by a Nova Scotian winter under canvas. Germain tried to strengthen the General's nerves by painting a more cheerful picture. The large force collected by Washington was no more than might have been expected for a special

---

[1] Wortley, 132-3.
[2] Royal Institution MSS., I, 435; Knox, 150; Sackville, II, 116-7; Willcox, *JMH*, 1947, pp. 112-13, 118.

effort; and the disgraceful failure of his co-operation with d'Estaing might cause a revulsion of public opinion. 'In no light do I see anything but good in prospect.' Canada seemed safe enough; but if Clinton was forced to send help to Haldimand, Germain begged him to evacuate the dependent post of Rhode Island and keep New York.[1]

Mercifully Clinton recovered his balance. It dawned on him that Canada was in no danger and had probably received its reinforcements from Europe. Halifax, too, had been strengthened from home. He resolved to send off the expeditions to the West Indies and Florida as soon as convoy could be provided. He was now willing to hold New York with the balance of his force, which he called 13,000. This figure was derived from the lowest basis of assessment, and even then he underestimated, for when the expeditions had embarked he still had nearer 14,000 rank and file fit for duty in the New York area. On the usual basis of calculation he had 17,452 effectives.[2]

The departure of the expeditions left a melancholy body of officers at New York.[3] Their depression was not in itself very alarming: it was the natural result of a dull and circumscribed defensive, and spirits would rise again with the prospect of action. Its sinister aspect was that the croakers were led by the Commander-in-Chief. Clinton filled his despatches with laments, and hinted at his wish to quit a post which he had not sought. He did not wish to remain there, 'a mournful witness of the debility of an army at whose head, had I been unshackled by instructions, I might have indulged expectations of rendering serious service to my country'. 'Do not let anything be expected of me, shackled as I am.'[4] These 'shackling instructions' were part of a general redeployment of the country's forces to meet the danger from the Bourbons. Not for a moment did Clinton admit that other theatres had claims on the nation's resources, or that his own renown should not be the Ministry's chief concern.

5. A Provisioning Crisis

D'Estaing's threat to New York brought home the need for a proper reserve of provisions, not only to give the army a degree of strategic flexibility but to enable it to survive if its lifelines were cut. The threat passed, but the

[1] Willcox, *JMH*, 1947, p. 113; G 2405; Knox, 150-1; CL, Clinton, 25 Sept. Germain to Clinton.

[2] CO 5/96, ff. 110, 211. His complaint of the shortfall of numbers was an old one. Cf. Wolfe at Quebec: ' . . . the army 9,000 men; in England it is called 12,000' (Reilly, 223).

[3] Wortley, 139.

[4] CO 5/96, f. 161-2; CO 5/97, f. 28.

autumn of 1778 saw a crisis developing in the army's provisioning system. In spite of the Cork victuallers' escape from the Delaware, the stock of provisions dwindled as the year drew to its close. By the middle of December Clinton had only a fortnight's flour in hand. Another victualling fleet sailed from Ireland in October, but the first ships did not reach New York till January. By that time the troops were living on indifferent oaten bread to which British soldiers had not been accustomed for a generation.[1]

The British Government had not expected, when it resolved to coerce America in 1775, that the initial supply burden would continue. But as the years passed and no conquests in depth were consolidated, the commissariat continued to draw the greater part of its needs from home. At such a distance the Treasury could not question the commanders' estimates of their needs. 'We are in their hands', wrote Robinson, 'and must submit.' After the initial difficulties, the department had maintained a transport fleet adequate to the needs, and at the beginning of 1778 there were enough ships at Cork to complete the 1777 supply.[2]

The difficulty was not primarily shipping, but indenting. From the beginning the Treasury had been starved of accurate information of the army's needs. General Gage had kept the department in the dark, so that 'we are obliged I may say to grope for it',[3] Commissary Weir was sent out to introduce an orderly system of indenting, but confusion continued. The shortage of 1778 burst on the Treasury without warning. Weir's returns had not revealed whether the refugees from Philadelphia had increased the army's consumption, as Whitehall had intelligently expected; nor could the officials make out whether his returns included the Rhode Island garrison, and whether the army was eating 46,000 rations a day, or 10,000 more. What did suddenly become clear was that without the Treasury's knowledge the army had consumed in seven months an additional $3\frac{1}{2}$ million pounds of bread and flour, and nearly 2 million pounds of meat.[4]

The fault, as the King said, lay in America. Nor could it be quickly remedied. When the July returns first revealed the coming shortage, arrangements were made at once to ship additional supplies. But so many transports had been detained in New York that none were available to take out the

[1] CO 5/95, f. 114; CO 5/97, ff. 28, 66, 76. Ligonier had persuaded the Treasury to sanction wheaten bread in 1743.

[2] Add. MSS. 38209, f. 163 (5 Sept., Robinson to Jenkinson); Add. MSS. 38343, f. 1 (memo. on transport service). On 1 January 1778 the Treasury had 72 victuallers and storeships in service (23,080 tons), besides 43 small oat ships (6,972 tons) which were under orders to be discharged. The total cost of shipping engaged in the two years to 30 Sept. 1777 was £438,460 (Add. MSS. 38375, f. 47; Add. MSS. 38343, f. 9).

[3] Add. MSS. 38208, f. 180 (19 Sept. 1775, Robinson to Jenkinson).

[4] Usher, 297–8; Add. MSS. 37834, f. 1.

emergency supply; and before it could be sent, the Treasury had to hire an entire cargo fleet of twenty-two sail.[1]

The inefficiencies of paleotechnic man astound his descendants. Yet 3,000 miles of ocean were only bridged by the irregular Post Office packets or the chance of a warship's sailing; and the headquarters at New York were insulated from the parent body's supervision. Through the channels of indenting, purchasing, collecting and shipping, supply followed lamely in the wake of demand.[2]

[1] CO 5/96, ff. 129-30. The transport state at New York in Oct. 1778 was:

Preparing for St Lucia expedition	.	.	32 ships of	9,357 tons
Unfit, should return home	.	.	42 ,, ,,	11,423 tons
Fit to remain in North America	.	.	72 ,, ,,	20,335 tons

(Adm. 1/488, ff. 477-81).

[2] Two difficulties of a different kind confronted the Treasury in the winter of 1778-9. In October the garrison of Senegal was known to have provisions only till Christmas. A ship with urgent provisions was ready to sail; but the underwriters refused to insure her at any price unless she had separate convoy, as the West India convoy with which she was to sail would only touch at Madeira, not at Teneriffe. This ship was still awaiting Admiralty convoy at the end of January (CO 5/254, ff. 120-1, 125).

A second difficulty was caused by the effect of delayed troop movements on victualling arrangements. When the St Lucia expedition was ordered in March, 1778, three victuallers were sent out to Barbados to meet it. The expedition did not arrive till the following December, by which time the provisions were not surprisingly rotten (Add. MSS. 37834, f. 106).

CHAPTER XII

THE SOUTHERN OFFENSIVES

1. *The West Indian Theatre*

It had been an anxious summer in England. The French were in the mouth of the Channel, and homebound convoys at hazard in the Atlantic. But, above all, Ministers were oppressed by the uncertainty which hung over the American theatre when d'Estaing vanished to the westward. In the second half of July they learnt that Clinton was about to evacuate Philadelphia; and for a long-drawn month Lord North waited for the despatch which would tell him of the army's safety or annihilation. On 22 August came the news that the fleet and army had reached New York.

Germain was triumphant: 'The evacuating Philadelphia will *now* possibly be approved by the Commissioners.'[1] There was still danger to be weathered. Lord Townshend rose from the muddy depths of the Ordnance Department to remind his colleagues that they had lost the command of American waters, and might yet lose the fleet and 30,000 irreplacable veteran troops.[2] But good news continued. Howe was reinforced, and Rhode Island relieved; and by the middle of September the Cabinet knew that the worst was over. The dangerous period of mobilisation and redeployment had passed, and the offensive for which Philadelphia had been sacrificed could begin. As operations closed in the Channel and the northern colonies, the campaigning season opened in Georgia and the Caribbean.

The British West Indies consisted of two widely separated naval and military commands, based on Jamaica and the Lesser Antilles. Jamaica, with 16,000 white inhabitants, was by far the richest of the British islands, producing two-fifths of the sugar and nine-tenths of the rum. But it was isolated 1,000 miles to leeward of the other British possessions, which lay in the chain of islands enclosing the eastern end of the Caribbean. They are known to the geographer as the Lesser Antilles. To the strategist they had various names, but were most commonly known collectively by the name of the naval command as the Leeward Islands, from the northern group of British islands where lay the naval rendezvous and fitting port at Antigua. Far to the south lay St Vincent, Grenada and Tobago, more properly known as the Windward Islands; and 100 miles to the east of them was

[1] G 2411.   [2] Knox, 149.

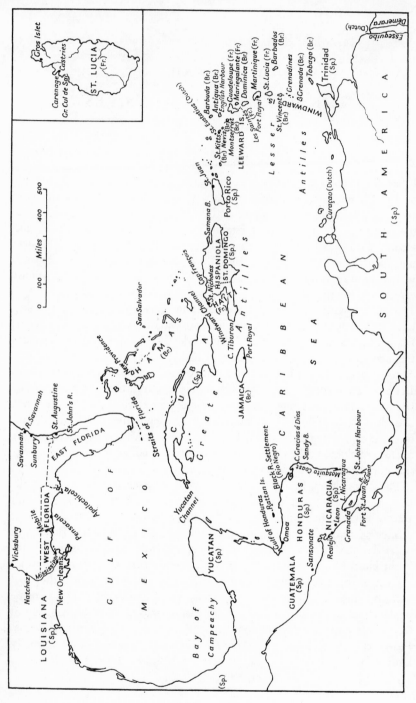

THE CARIBBEAN AND CENTRAL AMERICA

Barbados. The whole of this group of British islands, with 42,000 white inhabitants, stretched for 500 miles from north to south; and interposed between the Leeward and Windward Islands was a closely knit group of French possessions enclosing the solitary British island of Dominica.[1]

These scattered possessions, intersected by the enemy, posed a formidable defence problem; and the troops at hand in the autumn of 1778 were quite inadequate for their safety. The whole military force in the Caribbean had sunk to fewer than 1,600 effectives of all ranks, and so sickly that only 1,060 rank and file were fit for duty. Of these Jamaica had 440, and the whole of the scattered Leeward Islands little more than 600. These diminutive forces were useless for defence unless they were kept together. But the planters called continually for troops, partly to relieve the militia of nightly guard duties, and in the southern islands to protect them from the indigenous Caribs. The result was that Dominica had a garrison of sixty men fit for duty, Grenada 100 and the far off Tobago thirty.[2]

This dispersion meant that scarcely any one island could resist the lightest attack. The white population was large, and every island had its militia; but the paradox of West Indian strategy was that those who appeared to have most to lose were the least inclined to defend it. The poor whites and free negroes might wish to offer a vigorous defence; but faint-heartedness was rooted in their natural leaders, the planters and overseers. The educated class of whites was shrinking, as more and more of the planters hastened home to spend their money, leaving their estates to bear an increasing load of debt under the supervision of neighbours or overseers. Those who remained to vote in the island Assemblies were chiefly interested in low taxation. Fortifications and batteries were allowed to decay, and the army's requests for help to strengthen the defences were ignored.

Islands with adequate garrisons were reluctant to spare help to a threatened neighbour, while in the weaker islands where immediate relief was unlikely, the propertied class had more to lose than to gain by fighting. Resistance meant withdrawing into fortifications or holding out in the hills and forests, leaving their estates to the enemy's mercy. And the plantations were heavily capitalised and very vulnerable. Houses, mills and workshops would burn like torches. If the sugar canes were destroyed, they would take years to return to production. And above all the slaves could be carried off. These were the heaviest capital item, and the real cause of the planters' financial dependence on the merchants at home. Why should they ruin themselves by a vain resistance, when capitulation to a polite French officer would safeguard their property and food supplies? Their only fear was that British

[1] The estimates of population are for 1773, in Namier, . . . American Revolution, 274.
[2] WO 34/111, f. 215.

forces might set the French the evil example of seizing property. British admirals might sigh, like Hood, at 'labouring to protect men who wished not to be protected.'[1] They sighed in vain.

In these circumstances the islands' safety depended on the fleet. Nor were they vulnerable only to military action. The West Indies depended on imported provisions, and could quickly be reduced to starvation if they were cut off from the beef and butter of Cork. So little did their own food production meet their needs that the decline of the free negro population in the course of the eighteenth century may have been caused by starvation. The slaves, being chattels, fared better; but for all classes the safe arrival of the provision ships was vital. They, however, were preyed on by the privateers who swarmed in the islands, and interception was easy. Without reliable chronometers to determine longitude, ships approaching from Europe sailed down the latitude of their destination till they sighted it; and privateers had only to place themselves in certain latitudes to intercept the merchantmen as they came down the wind to their landfalls. Since many ships refused to wait for convoy, only numerous fast cruisers could protect them.[2]

The task of protecting the trade was further complicated by the pattern of trade routes, which were determined by the prevailing trade winds from the east. Outward convoys for the whole West Indies sailed together and made their landfall at Barbados, where the Leeward Island ships scattered to their several destinations, while the Jamaica trade continued in convoy across the Caribbean. But the homeward voyage required separate convoys. The Leeward Island ships assembled at St Kitts and made their way northwards to the latitude of Bermuda to pick up a west wind. But the Jamaica ships could not beat back across the Caribbean. Instead of rejoining the Leeward Islands convoy they used the Gulf Stream; and passing through the Windward Passage or the Straits of Florida steered northwards till they felt the wind.[3]

The Navy's problem was how to protect simultaneously the Leeward Islands and Jamaica and their separate trades. For routine patrols and convoys it was enough to maintain a squadron of cruisers supported by a few heavier ships on each station, basing them at English Harbour in Antigua, and Port Royal in Jamaica. The real difficulty appeared with an enemy battle fleet. Then a major fleet was required. But to divide it between the Leeward

---

[1] Sandwich, IV, 243.

[2] For West Indian society and the problem of local defence, see Pares, *War and Trade in the West Indies*, esp. pp. 227, 230-4, 248, 260, 288 *et seq.*; and his *West India Fortune*, esp. 16-20, 24-5, 30, 45, 47, 92, 107-9, 126, 350; Sackville, II, 290-2; Fortescue, III, 6, 42, 262-5.

[3] James, 85.

Islands and Jamaica would be fatal. The navy would be strong on neither station, and ships committed to Jamaica could not beat back against the east wind to the relief of the Leeward Islands. The main fleet was therefore held together at Antigua, ready if need be to run down to leeward and succour Jamaica. There was some risk that Jamaica might be surprised and captured before help arrived, for it was not easy to send intelligence of an attack up wind to the Leeward Islands. The Jamaica interest asserted that their defence rested entirely on the local squadron, and demanded that it should be strong. But in practice the danger from the French was slight. They were as reluctant as the British to surrender the windward position, and the two fleets fought out their campaigns among the Lesser Antilles. The real threat to Jamaica would come from a Spanish squadron based within striking distance at Cuba; for Spain had no possessions to defend in the windward sphere.

In the short run the islands could be defended by a complete command of the sea. But naval power was expensive to maintain and uncertain in operation; and few of the islands' garrisons were capable of holding out if relief was delayed. In the long run the best guarantee of safety was the destruction of the enemy's means of attack by the conquest of his bases.

The planters, though unwilling to exert themselves in their own defence, still felt some of their old reluctance to see the danger ended by the conquest of the French sugar islands, which might threaten their monopoly of the British market. But a more serious obstacle to an offensive strategy was disease. The climate was fatal to unseasoned European troops.[1] Howe and Clinton were convinced that the force ordered to the West Indies from America would be destroyed. Its commander, General Grant, predicted that only half his troops would be fit for service after a short stay in the West Indies; and St Lucia, his destination, was reputed to be the most unhealthy of the Leeward Islands. The sickness was deadliest in offensive operations, and a protracted spell in the siege trenches could soon reduce a force to helplessness. Nevertheless offence was the best defence. Dispersed garrisons, faint-hearted planters, vulnerable plantations and shortage of provisions all worked against passive security.

2. St Lucia

Admiral Barrington had sailed from England in May to take up the command in the Leeward Islands. He had two ships of the line on the station, the French none; and a sixty-four was also sent out to strengthen Sir Peter

---

[1] Not least the voyage from England. The average loss was 11 per cent; the highest, 25 per cent. See table in Appendix I.

Parker's force of cruisers on the Jamaica station. But such was the French superiority of land forces in the Leeward Islands that Barrington was unable to use his command of the sea to attack the French islands. His orders were to assemble his squadron at Barbados, where it was hoped that the expedition from America would join him before the hurricane season in August. He would then be in a position to take the offensive. Howe was to inform him if the expedition was postponed.[1]

At Barbados Barrington lay throughout the summer, expecting the expedition at any moment and little guessing that Clinton had postponed it. For Lord Howe had not sent a frigate as he should have done, to tell him of the delay. Thus immobilised at Barbados, Barrington could do nothing; and the Governor of Martinique profited by his absence to seize the initiative. On 7 September he landed a force of 2,000 men on Dominica, which surrendered after a brief resistance.

On the news of this misfortune Barrington at last felt free to depart from his instructions, and sailed to protect the defenceless naval yard at Antigua. There he found a storeship with a guarded letter from Lord Howe, who had taken no other steps to warn him that the troops from America were delayed. Barrington's position was now uneasy. The capture of Dominica had grouped the French islands into a solid bloc which cut the British islands in two, and deprived him of a fine anchorage for watching the French. If he remained in the north at Antigua, the southern islands with their scattered companies of troops would be exposed to another sudden blow. Fortunately the enemy did not follow up their success at Dominica, and when the hurricane season ended in October Barrington put to sea and cruised off Martinique, the French base and the only station where he could cover all the islands.

The squadron was replenishing at Barbados in November when a frigate arrived with the news that the expedition from America was on its way at last; and on 10 December the convoy entered Carlisle Bay escorted by Commodore Hotham. The offensive could begin. Its object, St Lucia, was the nearest neighbour to Martinique. Less heavily fortified than the French base, it had nevertheless good anchorages, and would provide an admirable position from which the fleet could watch Fort Royal. From the Gros Islet anchorage shipping movements off Fort Royal could be clearly seen; and though lee currents made a closer blockade difficult, the watching squadron would have a fair chance of intercepting French reinforcements as they made their landfall.

General Grant had been chosen to command the troops by Clinton; but he was also personally known to Germain. He was a man of independent

[1] Sandwich, II, 333.

fortune, and a *bon viveur*. The only estimates of him come from comparatively junior officers, but they are not flattering. Colonel Stuart detested him; and Major Wemyss painted a highly coloured portrait of a cunning, ignorant officer solely devoted to pushing his own interests: 'insensible of the ties of blood, incapable of friendship or a generous action. He was a gamester, a glutton, and an epicure. In short, it may be truly said that he lived only for himself.'[1] But his period of command in the Leeward Islands suggests an officer with some of Clinton's own qualities and defects: competence in the field, and incapacity to look beyond his own sphere of endeavour.

The General lost no time on his arrival, but at once concerted a plan with Barrington; and three days later the expedition anchored off St Lucia. Hotham, who had organised the efficient landing on Long Island in 1776, put the troops ashore with the smoothness of experience, and the three brigades quickly overran the key points of the island. They were a force of high quality. Germans and Provincials were excluded from the West Indies by their terms of service; and Grant's ten regiments were all British and good.

The first success had been easy; but there was peril in the offing. Though the British commanders did not know it, the French had also turned south-wards for the winter. At Boston d'Estaing had rejected American demands for further assistance, and refused either to dislodge the British from the coasts of the colonies or to attack Quebec and Halifax. France, like England, had fixed her eyes on the Caribbean, and had no wish to help American expansion into Canada. On the day when Grant's force sailed from New York, d'Estaing had left Boston; and for five weeks the two fleets had sailed on parallel courses. Three British transports fell into the hands of the French, betraying Grant's movement; but though their course suggested Barbados as the British rendezvous, d'Estaing made for Antigua in the hope of intercepting them there, and when they failed to appear he continued on his way to Martinique. There on 13 December an American privateer informed him that Barrington was at sea.

On the morning of the 14th the British troops on St Lucia had scarcely taken up their positions when a frigate was seen coming in under a cloud of sail and flying the signal 'enemy in sight'. Barrington had only seven ships fit to lie in the line of battle, including three of fifty guns; and d'Estaing was coming up with twelve of the line and a superiority of 700 guns.

Twenty-four hours earlier the British expedition would have been caught on the open sea. But now Grant and Barrington were able to meet the danger as Howe and Clinton had met it at New York. Barrington anchored his line in the mouth of the Grand Cul de Sac, with the transports inside it; and a

[1] Wortley, 135; Harvard, Sparks MSS., XXII, 216.

couple of miles to the north the entrance to the Carenage was commanded by
the guns of Brigadier Medows's brigade. Beaten off at both points by the
seaward defences, d'Estaing resolved to take them from the rear. He had
9,000 troops commanded by the Marquis de Bouillé, and these were landed
five miles north of the British position. On 16 December 5,000 French
infantry advanced against Medows's three battalions entrenched on a
peninsula north of Castries. Three times they assaulted, and three times
they were beaten off with heavy losses. From this Bunker Hill of the
Caribbean the enemy retired with casualties of thirty per cent; and finding
that Barrington had strengthened the fleet's position in the Grand Cul de Sac,
d'Estaing gave up as he had given up at New York and Rhode Island, and
sailed for Martinique. Grant was left in possession of St Lucia, a window
overlooking the French base which was to be of decisive importance in the
coming years.

D'Estaing had missed a great but fleeting opportunity. With a naval and
military superiority he had accomplished nothing; and he had allowed
inferior British forces to make good their foothold on his doorstep. Soon
the moment passed. Byron was coming to the rescue, and on 6 January he
arrived from America with eight sail of the line. For the moment superiority
in the West Indies had passed to the British.

3. The Conquest of Georgia

On the day when d'Estaing withdrew baffled from St Lucia, the other expedition from New York began its operations. Clinton's detachment to the
Floridas had two objects: a defensive one based on the Cabinet orders of
21 March, and an offensive one based on the earlier orders of 8 March.

East and West Florida were composed of the former Spanish colonies
east of the Mississippi, which had been ceded to Britain in 1763 with the
exception of the 'island' of New Orleans. From these acquisitions the
British had formed two colonies with a boundary on the Apalachicola
River; so that East Florida consisted roughly of the modern state of Florida
with its capital on the Atlantic coast at St Augustine, and West Florida of a
coastal strip of modern Alabama with its capital at Pensacola. The northern
boundary of West Florida had subsequently been extended up the Mississippi as far as the modern Vicksburg, to take in some settlements in the
Natchez districts.[1]

In the autumn of 1778 the entire garrison of the two colonies consisted
of the Sixteenth Foot and a few companies of the Sixtieth, numbering
about 1,400 effectives. They were menaced from the north by the rebels,

[1] Harlow, 304.

and from the south by the Spanish bases in the Caribbean. Pensacola was uncomfortably close to Cuba and New Orleans in the event of war with Spain, and on the northern boundary the rebels had been raiding down the Mississippi and disposing of their loot at New Orleans with the connivance of the Spanish authorities. But though the Governor had reports of batteaux assembling on the Ohio for a regular invasion, his troops were so few that their commander kept them together for the defence of the capital at Pensacola. The back settlements had no protection till June, when a company was sent up the Mississippi and defeated a party of rebels at Natchez. The reinforcement from New York, 1,000 Germans and Provincials under Brigadier Campbell, was vital for the colony's safety.

East Florida, too, was menaced by French and Spanish bases in the Caribbean; and it was this which had prompted the Cabinet to order reinforcements from Clinton on the outbreak of war with France. For though the King had considered the possibility of evacuating the Thirteen Colonies in order to fight the French, the Floridas were not 'American' colonies but, like Canada and Nova Scotia, prizes of recent victory. The British were determined to hold them.

But by the autumn of 1778 Britain was no longer playing a purely defensive game in the south. It will be remembered that the superseded orders of 8 March had suggested a winter offensive against the southern colonies; and in August Germain reminded Clinton of these orders, and instructed him to adopt them as far as circumstances allowed. He argued that Georgia and South Carolina would provide not only the replenishing station which the navy needed at the southern end of its blockade line, but provisions and timber for the West Indies to replace the North American supplies cut off by the rebellion. Indeed he seems to have regarded the recovery of the two colonies as essential to enable war to be sustained against France; a view which the officer who conquered Georgia was to argue[1] long afterwards when they were abandoned again under another Ministry. In the course of August the American Department pursued its enquiries; and James Simpson, the royal Attorney-General of South Carolina, propounded the advantages of Charleston as the starting point.[2]

In America the warmest advocate of an attack on Georgia was the Governor of the neighbouring province of East Florida. His boundaries were harassed by Georgian rebels, who were beating up the settlements on the St John's River and gathering in menacing numbers along the border. Governor Tonyn believed that the mischief could be stopped by invading

[1] Below, pp. 475–6.
[2] CL, Clinton, 5 Aug., from Germain; CL, Germain, 1 Sept., J. A. Simpson to Richard Cumberland.

and overrunning Georgia with a force of regulars and loyalists, and had repeatedly put this to Clinton. But he had been opposed by his military commander, Prevost, and the ill-feeling which had long existed between Governor and General ran still higher. Clinton now cut short the argument; for on 10 October he received Germain's August letter urging the importance of Georgia, and responded by ordering the reinforcement already destined for East Florida to act offensively towards Savannah. Characteristically he covered himself with a prediction that as soon as Washington knew he had been reduced to the defensive at New York, the Americans could send a force to the south which might recover all that the British gained.[1]

The force for East Florida and Georgia consisted of nearly 3,000 rank and file fit for duty.[2] Like the Pensacola force it consisted largely of Germans and Provincials, since the St Lucia expedition had taken British regiments; but the commander, Lieutenant-Colonel Archibald Campbell, had his own two-battalion regiment, the Seventy-first Highlanders. On 29 December he landed near Savannah. Guided by a negro he groped his way through the swamps, and surprised and routed a rebel force. Soon the whole of Georgia was cleared; and this vigorous highlander could claim to be 'the first officer . . . to take a stripe and star from the rebel flag of Congress'.[3]

[1] CO 3/96, f. 174.
[2] There are discrepancies in the returns.
[3] Carlisle, 413.

PART THREE

THE BOURBON ALLIANCE
1779

CHAPTER XIII

THE CRACKS IN THE FOUNDATIONS

1. *The Keppel Affair*

The conquest of St Lucia brought to a close the phase whose foundations the Cabinet had laid in March 1778 on the breach with France. Considering how long England's war preparations had been delayed, the balance was not unfavourable. She had more than held her own in home waters. In North America Pennsylvania had been evacuated without loss, the strategic flanks in Florida, Nova Scotia and Quebec had been strengthened, and Georgia had been recovered. In the West Indies the loss of Dominica had been balanced by the conquest of the strategically more valuable St Lucia. Above all, the year had provided a vital breathing space. If the Spanish navy had intervened, disaster might have followed in the Channel or the Caribbean. But Spain held back, as she had done in 1756. By the autumn of 1778 the mobilisation was well advanced, and the navy was in sight of re-establishing its ascendancy over France.

To the Ministers and the country the account did not appear so favourable as the autumn closed in. The loss of Dominica was a shaking revelation of the military weakness in the Leeward Islands; and the forces from New York had not yet sailed to redress the balance. Not till February 1779 were the fall of St Lucia and the conquest of Georgia known. Long before then Spanish intentions had begun to cast their shadow over the future. And for the Ministry there were more immediate embarrassments at home.

For the past year the defection of the commanders in America had been a mounting embarrassment. Carleton had confined his feud with Germain to a personal level, and the Howes had held their hand for the moment. The first political explosion was detonated by Burgoyne, who came home on parole and left his army at the mercy of a Convention which his indiscretions had given Congress a specious cause to repudiate. He landed at Portsmouth in May, 1778, while Byron's squadron lay at Spithead waiting for news of the Toulon fleet. He was unlikely to be retained in the Ministerial interest, in view of his contention that his disaster was caused by the inflexibility of his orders, and his friend Fox apparently settled the matter by hiring a carriage and hurrying down to meet him on the road from Portsmouth. In the Seven Years War Burgoyne might well have been court-martialled and disgraced. But he was popular and well connected, and with passions running high in the House over the escape of d'Estaing, and the country gentlemen out of humour with the Irish Trade Bills, the political scene did not invite the government to handle him roughly. His welcome, however, was not calculated to conciliate him. In self-defence Germain had produced the papers which showed how far the Saratoga plan was Burgoyne's own.[1] On the General's arrival at his office he gave him friendly reception, but informed him that as an officer whose conduct was under enquiry, he was excluded from Court. A Board of General Officers was assembled at once, but reported that the enquiry must be deferred, since Burgoyne was a prisoner on parole and might be recalled at any time by Congress. Within a few days Burgoyne was assailing Germain's role in his disaster, and the Ministry's supineness in the face of France.

The occasion was seized by the Opposition to provoke Germain. Temple Luttrell compared Burgoyne's conduct favourably with that of the American Secretary, who he said had been promoted for disobedience and cowardice. Two years earlier Germain had sat quiet under a similar shower of Luttrell insults; but now he started up in a rage, and denounced him as an assassin of the most wretched character and malice. 'Old as I am', he continued, 'and young as is the hon. member, I will meet that fighting gentleman and be revenged.' There was an immediate uproar and two hours of confusion. Germain retracted, but Luttrell had to be ordered into custody before the two men would satisfy the House with an apology.[2]

Against Burgoyne retaliation was prompt but ineffective. A letter from the Secretary at War ordered him back to rejoin his troops in America as a prisoner of war as soon as his health was re-established. He did not go, and for a year and a half no steps were taken to force him although his health was good. In October 1779 the Secretary at War wrote to reproach him with disobedience and neglect of duty; on which Burgoyne replied that it was useless for him to surrender himself, that he demanded a court-martial, and wished to resign all his military appointments except the rank which entitled him to trial. Amherst had always been reluctant to rouse passions by treating him harshly; and even now he hesitated to accept his resignation. The letter was referred to the King, who was revolted by 'so Attorney-like an epistle' and insisted that it should be noticed. Burgoyne was deprived of his regiment and his governorship of Fort William, leaving him only his pay and the hope of future favours from the Opposition.[3]

---

[1] See above, p. 152.   [2] Parl. Hist., XIX, 1199; Walpole, Last Journals, II, 34, 180.
[3] On the behaviour and treatment of Burgoyne, see Sandwich, II, 45; Wraxall Memoirs, II, 293–4; Knox, 277; Long, Amherst, 248–52; Add. MSS. 38210, ff. 62–8; Add. MSS. 38212, ff. 144–7, 155, 175; Add. MSS. 38383, draft speech by Jenkinson; G 2794–5; Hutchinson Diaries, II, 210; and Parl. Hist., passim.. Valentine devotes a chapter to the subject.

Burgoyne was a light-weight and his case was weak. More extensive was the trouble brewing in the navy as a result of the summer's operations. When the Channel fleet returned to port at the end of October, Admiral Palliser found an attack in an Opposition newspaper on his conduct at the battle of Ushant. The bare facts are that when Keppel had tried to reform his line and renew the battle, Palliser had not conformed with the order to wear his ships. He commanded the most damaged division; and his own flagship had been reduced to confusion by an explosion and was visibly in no condition to manoeuvre. From accounts of the battle one very able officer who had not been present formed the impression that the masts and rigging of the British fleet had been so damaged that it lay at the enemy's mercy after the first exchange of fire[1]; and Palliser always maintained that Keppel's intention of re-engaging that day was mere pretence.

Keppel and Palliser had been friends since they had returned from America together in 1756, though there had been jealousy on Keppel's part when Palliser was appointed Lieutenant-General of Marines. It was Palliser who had brought Keppel the invitation to command the Channel fleet, who had promoted his reconciliation with Sandwich, and who had smoothed the relations between the two men in the early weeks of the campaign.[2] But Palliser took strong exception to the newspaper article, which he attributed to friends of his Commander-in-Chief. He wrote at once to Keppel demanding his signature to a contradiction and a statement that he had not intended to re-engage till the following day. Keppel made no answer. Palliser called on him in person, and after an angry altercation he published his own version of the battle in the ministerialist *Morning Post*. The quarrel shifted to Parliament; and on 11 December Palliser suddenly produced charges against his Commander-in-Chief and demanded that he should be brought to trial. The same day the Admiralty informed Keppel that he would be court-martialled.[3]

The very haste of the Board had an indecent air, though Sandwich pleaded the need to act while witnesses were still in England. The Opposition maintained that the First Lord could have stopped the whole affair by rejecting the charges, though the Crown lawyers and the members of the Board argued with conviction that it was not open to the Admiralty to reject a charge by a high-ranking officer. Yet there were peculiarities in the case. Keppel, a political opponent of the Ministry, had had two members of the Board of Admiralty in his fleet; Palliser had continued to serve under

---

[1] ''Tis plain to me that our fleet after that action, for all the first part of the afternoon, was at the mercy of the French' (Kempenfelt). (Barham, I, 291).

[2] Sandwich, II, 88, 110.

[3] A balanced account of the affair is J. H. Broomfield's in *Mariner's Mirror*, 1961.

him for five months before he charged him; and the circumstances suggested malice. Palliser denied on his honour that he had had collusion from the Board; but in the circumstances it was important that there should be no suggestion of a plot against Keppel.

Palliser's reply to the anonymous newspaper attack and his charges against Keppel were a calamitous error of judgment. Yet there is another side to the case. For Palliser had believed from the first that Keppel intended to fix the blame on him for the failure to renew the attack: so much so that when the fleet put to sea again he left a paper in his bureau for the First Lord in case he should be killed and his memory aspersed.[1] Though Keppel had commended Palliser's conduct in his official despatch, he had sent his flag captain to tell Sandwich that he had private matters to communicate; and his young protégé Lieutenant Berkeley whispered it about that Palliser had disobeyed Keppel's order to come up with the French again.[2] Palliser believed that in private conversation Keppel had contradicted his public despatch; and Keppel's refusal to contradict the press attack confirmed his suspicion that a plot for his ruin had been formed on the day of battle. Ill-health may have nourished his suspicions; for like Keppel himself he had been in pain throughout the operations, and came in to Spithead ill and exhausted.

On the first day of the new session of Parliament Lord Bristol had demanded an enquiry and declared that in view of Palliser's newspaper attack Keppel would never serve with him again. A few days later a Commons debate on the Navy Estimates brought the two admirals into personal collision. Pressed by Temple Luttrell, Keppel confessed that Palliser had shown 'no want of what was most essential in a British seaman – courage'; and proceeded to say that he would never sail with him again unless the newspaper article was explained. Palliser complained that Keppel gave the appearance of withholding something; and Keppel rose again to say that the signal for coming into his flagship's wake had flown for five hours unobeyed. Luttrell attempted to move for an address for the trial of Palliser, and renewed the motion a week later on the day when Keppel had been charged.[3]

Palliser now stood under the shadow of an oblique accusation. For some days he waited for Keppel to prefer a charge against him; but Keppel seemed intent on ruining his reputation without a trial. And in a campaign of slander the Commander-in-Chief enjoyed overwhelming advantages.

[1] Sandwich, II, 198, 218.
[2] Walpole, Last Journals, II, 309; G 2460. Berkeley, who became an Admiral and seventeenth Baron Berkeley, was an Opposition politician. He was a lieutenant in the Victory in the battle, and Keppel afterwards promoted him to command a fireship.
[3] Parl. Hist., XIX, 1300, 1380-6.

LORD GEORGE GERMAIN
Engraving of 1780 after Romney

GIBRALTAR—A STRATEGIC MAGNET
View of the grand attack of 1782, from the Spanish lines

Palliser was the son of an obscure Yorkshire army officer. By merit alone he had risen to flag rank and a baronetcy; and he lacked the advantages of education, deportment and polish.[1] His hard-won reputation was now threatened by the noble house of Albemarle and its extensive connections. Keppel had started on the ladder with every advantage, and quick promotion had come to him as of right. He was three years younger than Palliser, but had got his flag thirteen years earlier; nor was he ashamed to press this advantage, for it was on rank that he had grounded his objection to Palliser's Lieutenant-Generalcy of Marines. Behind him stood the menacing ranks of the aristocracy. With reason Palliser might think that his only defence was to strike back and bring the matter into the open.

Sandwich had shared Palliser's suspicions of the Opposition faction in the Channel fleet.[2] Hitherto he had stood fast against an enquiry, recalling the mischief done by the Mathews-Lestock affair in 1744; and in the House of Lords he had described the conduct of both admirals as gallant and able.[3] He had had no intention of making Keppel an unofficial scapegoat; but a formal charge was a different matter. The delayed charge, and the charging of a senior by a junior, were justified by precedents: in the Austrian War Admiral Knowles's captains had accused him more than a year after his battle off Cuba, when they discovered that he had censured them in public and private letters. Yet twelve admirals now petitioned the King that the charge was destructive of discipline: 'It will not be easy for men attentive to their honour to serve your Majesty, particularly in situations of principal command.' This protest was organised by two Opposition admirals, Lord Bristol and the Duke of Bolton. The aged and infirm Lord Hawke was induced to head the list; and among those who signed Samuel Graves had refused at first and afterwards apologised to Sandwich. Some may have recalled how Hawke had twenty years earlier been superseded in the command of the Channel fleet for 'a high breach of discipline'; and how the Duke of Bolton had accused his senior officer Admiral Griffin. But the petitioners' aim was not to further justice: it was to create prejudice.[4]

The trial opened at Portsmouth in January 1779, in circumstances which the Opposition exploited to the utmost. Because of Keppel's poor health Parliament had passed a bill enabling it to be held on shore, which allowed the Rockingham party to fill the courtroom with a claque headed by the great leaders. The Ministry was to pay not only for Sandwich's error in allowing the trial, but for their predecessors' wicked execution of Byng;

---

[1] Wraxall, I, 385; Sandwich, I, xvi.   [2] G 2403, 2460.
[3] Parl. Hist., XIX, 1298, 1302.
[4] Sandwich, II, 213; Pack, Anson, 216–17; Walpole, Last Journals, II, 324; Williams Transcripts, 22 June 1780, Palliser's observations.

for the charges against Keppel were capital, and while the navy rallied against the sacrifice of a second scapegoat, the politicians whipped up sentiment for a man ostensibly on trial for his life.

It was a highly charged courtroom over which Admiral Pye presided. The passions beneath the smooth surface of eighteenth century life welled up. Tears were shed, witnesses were hissed, the Deity was invoked. The court made no pretence of fairness, and Admiral Montagu's bias was so glaring that Walpole thought Palliser should have refused to proceed before such partial judges.[1] Palliser was hampered at every turn in conducting his case. His flag-captain giving evidence was threatened by Keppel, and Palliser censured for asking the court to protect him. Witnesses were required to give their opinion of the charges as though they were judges; and after repeated refusals to hear Palliser, the court in acquitting Keppel passed a sort of judgment on the accuser by describing the charges as 'malicious and ill-founded'.

Violent demonstrations followed the verdict. The London mob forced householders to illuminate for Keppel's 'victory': a victory which the Opposition was forced to claim, though it had been won by Sandwich's fleet. Even Ministers put candles in their windows to save their glass. Palliser's house in Pall Mall was gutted. In the early morning Fox and Burgoyne's Stanley relations left their bottle at Almack's and led the mob to smash Germain's windows, and thence to the Admiralty, where the gates were unhinged and the windows broken. Society joined the celebrations of the mob with illuminations, processions and balls. And while Lord North's carpets were strewn with broken glass, Thurlow and Amherst celebrated the acquittal.

Palliser's career was finished. The Opposition shed crocodile tears at the prospect of his conviction and execution, but Keppel still wisely refused to charge him. The King wanted to dismiss him at once to forestall a parliamentary petition, and found some support in the Cabinet though North pointed out that it might prejudice his defence if he were brought to trial. But Sandwich stood loyally by his old friend, and forced a compromise. He went down with Robinson to meet Palliser as he returned from his place of refuge when the disorders had ended, and persuaded him to resign. On 21 February Palliser resigned his Lieutenant-Generalcy of Marines, his governorship of Scarborough, and his seat in Parliament. Fox had demanded that he should be deprived of his rank, adding that like Germain he could still have a court-martial.[2]

[1] Walpole, *Last Journals*, II, 343; Hutchinson Diaries, II, 243. Montagu was surprised when he was immediately removed from the Newfoundland command. In spite of his applications he was never re-employed.

[2] G 2539, 2540, 2542, 2547–50; Walpole, *Last Journals*, II, 350.

Palliser insisted on a trial to clear his name. With no specific charges, it took the form of an enquiry without a prosecutor. He stood under the prejudice of Keppel's acquittal and of the votes of both Houses of Parliament, and his judges under threats and the fear of unpopularity. Nevertheless his conduct in the battle was found to have been exemplary and meritorious, the Court merely observing that he should have informed Keppel by the frigate which brought the order to rejoin the Flag that he was disabled; a fact which Palliser had regarded as too apparent to be worth reporting. After this acquittal he asked for reinstatement. From this Sandwich shrank for the moment; and for a time Palliser lived in reduced circumstances near Knaresborough. But in 1780 Sandwich manoeuvred him into the Governorship of Greenwich Hospital, and gave him one of his seats in the House of Commons 'to curb Keppel'. In spite of attacks in Parliament Palliser survived in his post to an honourable old age.

2. Generals and Admirals

Keppel was not slow in opening his counter-offensive. In a long letter to the King he set forth his ill-treatment and implored the King not to send him to sea again under the present Ministers. His motive was thought to be to force the King to dismiss him. The Admiralty asked him whether he intended to serve, received an offensive answer, and replied in the same manner by ordering him to strike his flag. Several of his captains thereupon resigned; and Admiral Harland, who had commanded a division in the battle, struck his flag, 'convinced that it cannot be for the public service nor my own safety to serve with or to command men high in rank who differ so much in opinion with me on the great points of naval discipline'. Palliser could take comfort from the fact that the Keppelite captains had all been in Keppel's own division on the day of the battle.[1] Nevertheless the Channel fleet was now deprived of all its commanders of divisions, and the navy was split from top to bottom. Even the 'common sailors' were involved. The *Victory* and *Formidable*, flagships of Keppel and Palliser, were docked separately for fear that their crews would fight it out with fatal results.

Nor was the mischief confined to the navy. Three days before Keppel was charged, his brother had resigned his military command. The camps had just broken up for the winter, and the General's ostensible reason was that he had been unsupported and uninformed during the summer. But the tone and volume of Amherst's correspondence suggests that this was no more

---

[1] Captain Ross was suspected of being a Keppelite though he had been in Harland's division. But Leveson-Gower and Lindsay, who resigned, and Walsingham, Jervis and Macbride, who took Keppel's side, had all served in his division.

than a malicious pretext. General Keppel was soon taking his part in the debates on his brother's trial.

The Ministry had now had its fill of enquiries; but scarcely had the naval trials reached their noisy conclusion when a new devil was raised by the hasty temper of Germain. When the Howe brothers returned from America in 1778, efforts had been made to conciliate them. After the Keppel trial, the King hoped to bring Lord Howe to the Admiralty in place of Sandwich, and looked round for a suitable governorship for Sir William. The General had promised the King that he would not follow Burgoyne into opposition, but reserved the right to defend himself against Germain and the pamphlets which the American Secretary was, with small reason, suspected of having inspired. In the autumn of 1778 the Howes moved for papers in the House, but the Ministry had no intention of making scapegoats of them, and even Germain showed no great desire to defend himself at their expense. One opponent of the enquiry used an argument which had been used against Palliser, that they should take no notice of scribblers. But under an attack by Burgoyne, Germain allowed himself to be pushed into specific disapproval of the landing in the Chesapeake. After this it was impossible to refuse the Howes an opportunity to defend themselves. A muddy enquiry dragged through May and June of 1779 till the adjournment of Parliament brought it to an inconclusive halt.[1]

Graves, Carleton, Burgoyne, the Howes, Keppel: the list was already long. Would Clinton's name be added? His complaints had reached a climax in the autumn of 1778, and just when the Keppel affair was brewing an officer arrived from New York with his application to resign. His request was supported at home by his cousin the Duke of Newcastle. The real cause of his discontent was still the beggaring of his striking force to reinforce Florida and the West Indies. Following on his endless complaints of neglect, his letter must have tested the not inexhaustible patience of Germain; and a commander who showed so grudging a spirit and so little willingness to see his task in perspective ought to have been removed at once. But the Ministry had lost the services of too many commanders; and its political weakness made it clumsy in handling the recalcitrants and frightened of alienating those who remained. Germain could not afford to lose another general; and he refused Clinton's application to resign with assurances of his confidence and a promise to do all in his power to reinforce him. He explained that the disposition and employment of the troops had always

[1] Anderson, 322–4; Valentine, 351–2; G 2387, 2470, 2485, 2506, 2540; Sandwich, II, 325; Add. MSS. 38210, ff. 62–8. The chief pamphlet attack on Howe was written by Mauduit, a man of good reputation whose nervous fear of the consequences does not suggest powerful backing (see Hutchinson Diaries, II, 203–4).

been left to Clinton's own judgment: the sole exception had been the order to evacuate Philadelphia and detach to Florida and St Lucia. This, said Germain, had been done with regret, not least because of the chagrin it would cause Clinton; 'but the intelligence we had received of the intentions of France . . . would not allow of an alternative, and I am persuaded you will now join in opinion that those measures were unavoidable'.[1]

This apology for the government's major strategy was a remarkable concession to the sulks of a theatre commander. The King had already had to apply an emollient K.B. to 'heal his mind' after the Charleston failure, and a couple of Colonelcies were now thrown in to sweeten his temper.[2] If anything short of unlimited acquiescence in his demand for troops could have satisfied the egoism of Clinton, German's reply should have done so. Henceforth the American Secretary was obliged to handle the Commander-in-Chief in America with velvet gloves. Not least of the misfortunes which sprang from the alienation of the Howes and Keppels was that the North government was saddled with Clinton for the rest of its existence.

3. The Disintegration of North

Throughout these troubles North had remained his amusing and baffling self in the House of Commons; but behind the scenes his political leadership had disintegrated. The successful strategic defensive in 1778 had lent him no confidence, for it was already clear in the autumn that the breathing space which had been gained was the prelude to greater dangers. Once again he implored the King to release him. 'In critical times', he reiterated, 'it is necessary that there should be one directing Minister, who should plan the whole operations of government, and controul all the other departments of administration so far as to make them co-operate zealously and actively with his designs even tho' the contrary of their own.' The attributes of a great war leader have seldom been better drawn. But the letter continued: 'Lord North . . . is certainly not capable of being such a minister as he has described.'[3]

In the Ministry as it existed, even his patient Under-Secretary Robinson acknowledged that North was the insurmountable barrier to energy. As 1779 went by, paralysis continued to creep over his will, and his incapacity for taking or adhering to decisions was becoming worse. The exasperated King lamented the frequent changes of mind which stopped all business.

---

[1] CL, Clinton, 3 Dec. 1778.
[2] Walpole, *Last Journals*, II, 108; Add. MSS. 37833, f. 155; CO 5/96, f. 194; CO 5/97, f. 191.
[3] G 2446.

In Cabinet his weak chairmanship held up decision, and more and more he did his work in holes and corners with a few junior confidants – 'the flimsy way of doing business' of which Hillsborough complained.[1]

The effect on strategy of North's weakness can be exaggerated. Particular items of war business seldom depended on his initiative, for departmental Ministers followed the established practice of taking the lead in Cabinet on their own affairs. Though urgent general questions like Ireland and India might be delayed or evaded, specific decisions on strategy were rarely if ever held up by North's remissness. Yet a stronger man might have reconciled the conflicting views of Sandwich and Germain, and forced the executive departments out of their leisurely pace.

What drove North's friends to despair was his political leadership. His majority in the Commons was becoming less stable, and a motion of censure on the weakness of Keppel's fleet was defeated in March 1779 by only thirty-four votes, a slender margin in the unreformed House of Commons where weakness bred desertion. To hold the Ministry together through such trials it was vital to wield patronage firmly and fill the vacant offices promptly and well. This was what North was failing above all to do.

At this critical period of the war, one of the Secretaryships of State fell out of play. Lord Suffolk had had a fit in June 1778, but was forced to linger on in the Northern Department, 'dead to the state long before he was dead to nature'. He died in March 1779, but still no successor was appointed. After being tenanted for nine months by a moribund man, this key office lay vacant through the fateful summer of 1779, and its duties were discharged by the inattentive Secretary for the Southern Department. 'The whole of the laborious and arduous correspondence of this Empire, rested solely upon the activity and energy of Lord Weymouth', said the ironical Burke. Weymouth's neglect of business was thought by Robinson to be due to a settled intention to desert the Ministry.[2]

Suffolk's place was vacant because North was incapable of contending with his colleagues' rivalries. Before the death of Suffolk he had toyed with the idea of pushing Sandwich upstairs into the Secretaryship, as his presence at the Admiralty was embarrassing after the Keppel affair; but Lord Howe, who was designed as his successor, posed terms which were repugnant to the King, and at the Admiralty Sandwich remained.[3] When Suffolk was truly dead and North could no longer pretend that the Secretaryship was filled, he hoped to bring in his friend Lord Hillsborough. But here as elsewhere the hatreds generated in the 'sixties were at work. Hillsborough was disliked

---

[1] G 2741, 2775; Add. MSS. 37834, f. 133; Sandwich, III, 164; Abergavenny, 28.
[2] Butterfield, *George III, Lord North and the People*, 34–5.
[3] On Germain's position in this negotiation, see Valentine, 390–2.

by the Bedford group, who had driven him from the Ministry in 1772 and now made known their objection to his appointment.[1]

The Bedfords had an axe of their own to grind. Lord Gower's son-in-law Carlisle had returned from America and needed a new job. It was not clear that provision for Carlisle would keep the Bedfords in the Ministry; but it was quite certain that if he were not given a salary and if Hillsborough were brought in, they would go. The King would not hear of Carlisle as Secretary of State; but there was always the Board of Trade. It had been annexed to the American Department for the past ten years; but by separating it and doubling the salary North could give Carlisle £2,000 a year for very little work. A happy conception; but the difficulty lay in Germain, who said that the separation of the Board from his own department would degrade him. This deadlock continued throughout the summer.

More demoralising to North than the open designs of the Bedfords were the intrigues of his own lesser confidants. William Eden returned like Carlisle from America in need of a place; but lacking Carlisle's connections he had to work more deviously. He opened his campaign in January 1779 by stirring up that ambitious Scots lawyer, his cousin Wedderburn. What they wanted was a matter for speculation. Knox thought Eden was after the Legation at The Hague. Robinson believed that they were ultimately seeking the highest offices of state. At the least they hoped to prevent the appointment of Hillsborough, and to obtain a Secretary of State who would give them the influence which Suffolk had done. Eden managed to extort a pension of £600 settled on his wife; but Wedderburn's demand was more difficult to satisfy. He wanted the Chief Justiceship of the Common Pleas with a peerage, so that he would be irremovable if the Ministry foundered. But the Chief Justiceship was not vacant; and to force the incumbent to retire and give Wedderburn a peerage would create more jealousies and enmities than it would buy off.

Eden's tactics were devious but simple: they were to harry and frighten North. It was easily done. He opened the campaign by holding conversations with Shelburne's party, which he followed up with talk of the Ministry's failures and possible resignations, 'knowing well how that operates to carry any Job he wants'.[2] Intrigues were more than North's nervous system could bear, and before long he had become quite incapacitated for decisions. Incapable of saying no, he had already ensnared himself in careless promises to other junior Ministers.

Behind North in his own department stood two sturdy inelegant figures, the Secretary John 'Ratcatcher' Robinson, and Charles Jenkinson, a junior

[1] Thomson, *Secretaries of State*, 58; Knox, 264.
[2] Knox, 261; Add. MSS. 38210, ff. 22–5, 293–7.

Lord of the Treasury who had succeeded Lord Barrington as Secretary at War in the autumn of 1778. These two men figured as *eminences grises* and unseen agents of the Crown in the lurid imagination of Burke: in reality they were useful hard-working props of the faltering system. Robinson was North's expert in the management of the House of Commons, and ranked in the Treasury as 'one of the most active and essential functionaries of the executive government'.[1] Over the past two years he had, through the agency of Jenkinson, developed a confidential relationship with the King, who was becoming increasingly distressed by his Prime Minister's irresolution. In North's equable and conciliating assistant he recognised an ideal go-between to fathom the Prime Minister's intentions and keep him on course. No one who exercised the patronage of the Treasury could be universally popular; and 'low Secretary' and 'low Attorney' were frequent sneers among the place-hunters of Lord Carlisle's set.[2] But he had a moralising vein which appealed to the King: 'by severe sumptuary laws', he replied to a royal letter in the war crisis of 1778, 'a reformation of manners should be endeavoured to be brought about, and oeconomy, temperance and industry introduced'.[3] Through him the King tried to fight the forces of confusion in the government; but North could not be brought to make a firm stand. Robinson found it impossible to make his chief discuss political appointments calmly, and was forced to put his ideas on paper in the hope that North might read them at leisure.[4]

[1] Wraxall *Memoirs*, II, 225–6.
[2] Carlisle, 540, 542.
[3] Add. MSS. 37833, f. 239.
[4] Add. MSS. 37834, f. 76.

CHAPTER XIV

THE STRATEGY OF
1779

1. *The Autumn Deployment*

The return of the Channel fleet from its summer operations always marked the start of a new period of naval planning, and was followed by a winter deployment. Reinforcements were found for the campaigning seasons in the Indian Ocean and the Caribbean, and the remainder of the fleet was brought in for its winter refit. When Keppel returned, the situation had improved so much since the spring that a small squadron could now be spared for the Mediterranean, to check the French squadron which remained in Toulon and keep the trade routes open. Enemy squadrons were preparing in Brest for overseas service; and five British ships of the line were therefore intended to reinforce the Leeward Islands, and three to strengthen the Indian squadron whose reinforcement had been postponed in the spring for the sake of America. The ships for India could even create an opportunity for a small operation in West Africa, a battalion attack on the French slave settlement of Goree.

But towards the middle of October the prospect was darkened by an intervention from Madrid. The Spaniards came forward with an offer of mediation whose hostile tone suggested that they would soon align themselves with the enemy. Spain was the third naval power in the world, and her intervention would utterly change the prospect for which Britain was laying her plans. The King stood firm against a compromise; for with Spain and France armed to the teeth he argued that only from the test of war could stability emerge. And if the Spaniards could be kept quiet through the winter, he thought the navy might be strong enough to face both the Bourbon Powers.[1] But Sandwich, though equally convinced that Spain would enter the war unless she were bought off at a high price, could not treat the danger so boldly. Better than anyone he knew the facts about the country's naval strength; and he feared that if Spain entered the war that autumn England would pay for her late start in the armaments race. Jamaica and Minorca might be lost at once; and though Gibraltar could stand a long siege it would also fall in the end if the fleet could not relieve it. So near were the Spaniards to achieving their objects.

We must temporise, said Sandwich. Two months could be gained by asking for explanations: time to reinforce Minorca, to send a squadron to

[1] G 2434, 2464.

Jamaica, and to strengthen the Channel fleet. The proposed Mediterranean squadron must be dropped. France and Spain together had about eighty ships of the line in commission at home; and Sandwich calculated that by the end of the year England could have only fifty-four in the Channel, including five old receiving ships which could be used in home waters. But the deployment of this force depended absolutely on getting the seamen; and troops should be called from their winter quarters to bolt them from their lurking holes. The army at home must be strengthened by every possible means; and Sandwich suggested asking Russia for a squadron for the Channel: 'for everything is now at stake'.[1]

Though Sandwich talked of a fleet for Jamaica, he knew that it was easier to propose than to provide.[2] For he still held that the proper strategy was to concentrate in the Channel. But at the end of October he was shaken by news of the loss of Dominica. By then the ships and troops from America should have been in the islands, but by the latest report no sailing date had been fixed for the expedition. It was rightly suspected that d'Estaing's French squadron would winter in the West Indies instead of coming home, and further losses in the Leeward Islands seemed inevitable.[3]

The West India merchants were baying for blood. The loss of Dominica had disclosed to a shocked public the weakness of the West Indian garrisons; and the Committee's representatives visited Sandwich and Germain to remonstrate. They were sent away with a promise of reinforcements but a refusal to specify the force; and they were back again in the evening with a renewed demand for a strong and adequate reinforcement. The weak Ministry would have found it hard to withstand this pressure if they had wanted to. On the same day three ships of the line were added to the force for the Leeward Islands; and a strongly worded order was sent to New York for the immediate despatch of Grant's convoy to Barbados. Byron's arrival in America was not yet known, and Gambier received the blame for the delay which, said Sandwich, 'subjects you . . . to the blame and clamour that will be the consequence of the loss of our islands'. He censured the commanders' preoccupation with their own problems and indifference to the general situation. 'For believe me', he warned Gambier, 'this is an object which all sorts of people here have set their hearts on, and upon which they are much in earnest.' His relief was immense when news arrived that Grant's force had sailed. 'You cannot conceive the sudden alteration that was occasioned among us.'[4]

---

[1] Sandwich, II, 179–82.   [2] Sandwich, I, 419.
[3] Knox, 151, 153; CL, Germain, 4 and 13 Nov. to Clinton.
[4] CO 5/254, ff. 121–3; Sandwich, II, 328, 341; CL, Germain letterbook, 4 and 13 Nov. to Clinton.

If there had been any serious question of reinforcing Jamaica, the danger in the Leeward Islands ruled it out. A regiment was embarked to strengthen the garrison; but rather than add to Sir Peter Parker's squadron, Sandwich relied on the reinforcement of the Leeward Islands to protect Jamaica.[1] Eight ships of the line sailed in December to join Barrington.

The West India merchants were not the only pressure group whose anxiety pressed on strategy that autumn. In December there was intelligence of a squadron under de Ternay preparing to leave Brest for India. Its real strength was five ships of the line, but six or eight were reported. The East India Company appealed for reinforcements; and three ships of the line were added to the force preparing to go out under Admiral Hughes, making six in all. A regiment of foot would sail with them.[2]

2. A Fresh Start in America

Thus the French initiative was dispersing Sandwich's strategic reserve in home waters. But his preference for a concentration in home waters and a holding strategy abroad had never been shared by Germain. If Sandwich had had his way, Byron's squadron in America would have been ordered home for the winter instead of pursuing d'Estaing to the West Indies, and disaster in the Leeward Islands might have followed. Germain had himself had doubts about the future of the American theatre when the Spanish threat began to take shape in October, and recognised that with the army and navy at full stretch against the Bourbons England might have come to the end of her offensive capacity against the rebellious colonies. At the end of 1778 only 3,000 recruits were allotted to Clinton as reinforcements for the next campaign; and Germain expected little more than coastal raiding in the theatre.[3] But in the New Year the danger from Spain seemed to have receded; and in spite of Sandwich's doubts about the naval situation, Germain believed that more troops could be found for Clinton and that the reduction of the colonies could be resumed.

While the Opposition was crowding the court-room at Portsmouth in January for the Keppel trial, a series of consultations was held in London from which a new plan for America emerged. There was fresh evidence to consider. The renegade Congressman Joseph Galloway had recently arrived in England, and through Robinson had conveyed some lengthy reports to the King, who referred them to Amherst. The Peace Commissioners had also returned, and at North's suggestion Germain summoned Eden and Johnstone to meet such Ministers as were in London. Germain was

---

[1] Sandwich, I, 406.   [2] Richmond, *Navy in India*, 87–93.
[3] CL, Germain, 4 Nov. to Clinton; CO 5/96, f. 193; Knox, 153.

determined to enlist North's support. Convinced that the Cabinet at that time would automatically reject any suggestions of his own, he prepared the ground for a full Cabinet discussion by priming North with a long paper explaining the views he had formed as a result of his talks with the Commissioners. 'If he adopts them', he told Knox, 'they may be of use; if they come only from me, I know their fate.'[1]

In the first two campaigns of the war, the aim had been to break the rebellion by crushing its army and overrunning its political centres. The result had been that while the American army had survived, the British had failed to consolidate their territorial gains. The army's motion, as Admiral Samuel Graves observed, was like 'the passage of a ship through the sea whose track is soon lost'.[2] The military master-plan having failed, it was necessary to attempt a more systematic consolidation: to break away from the search for an enemy centre of gravity, to recognise the atomised political and social structure of the colonies, and to subordinate the military to the political aspect of the problem. The germ of the idea is contained in a memorandum on the southern colonies in the Germain papers of 1778.[3] 'The great point to be wished for, is that the inhabitants of some considerable colony were so far reclaimed to their duty, that the revival of the British constitution, and the free operation of the laws, might without prejudice be permitted amongst them.' The advantages of British sovereignty would then become apparent; 'and a little political management, would with ease bring about what will never be effected by mere force'.

If this reasoning was sound, the piecemeal reduction of separate colonies might achieve what the search for a single point of effort had failed to do. If the regular army could not destroy Washington, its role must be to drive him out and fend him off, while internal order in the recovered colonies was established by a loyalist militia. Secure from within and without, the colony could then send representatives to an assembly, and political reintegration with the Empire could proceed. The role of the militias had been sketched by Germain a year earlier in his instructions of 8 March 1778 for an attack on the southern colonies. Though farmers and men of means could not be expected to serve as soldiers for an indefinite period and far from their homes, the British might use them as the rebels did, by embodying them under their own officers to co-operate with the regular troops in their own district, or defend a post in their absence. 'Such appear to be the methods taken by the rebels for strengthening their own army.'[4]

---

[1] Knox, 155: the paper referred to is CL, Germain, 11 Jan. 1779, cited below. There appear to have been Cabinet meetings on the 12th and 16th.

[2] Williams Transcripts, 6 Aug. 1778 to Sandwich.

[3] CL, Germain, II, Suppl.   [4] Sackville, II, 98.

The new system depended on a large and active body of loyalists. The refugee officials from the southern colonies had unanimously assured Germain that it existed; and for the Middle Colonies Galloway had made himself the spokesman. He had long been in touch with Lord Dartmouth, to whom he had written on the capture of Philadelphia to report that the rebellion in the Middle colonies had collapsed. When Philadelphia was evacuated, he made his way to England, where he arrived about the beginning of December 1778, asserting that the Middle Colonies were tired of the war, and that if the army had not abandoned Philadelphia all Pennsylvania and New Jersey would have returned to their allegiance. In the memoranda which were passing through the hands of the King he declared that if the British army would drive Washington away, the loyalists could disarm the rebel minority by their own efforts.[1]

Galloway was persuasive. Lord North, who had never been an optimist, was satisfied by him that a vigorous campaign at that moment had every hope of success. Yet the opinions of exiles are notoriously unreliable, and in matters of this kind, where opinions must predominate over facts, the Ministry could only act on what seemed to be the most trustworthy or the most agreeable advice. Colonel Stuart was later to assert that the plan had been foisted on the Ministry by a set of sycophantic refugees; and it is true that General Howe had denied that the liberated loyalists could even protect themselves, let alone disarm the rebels in the first instance.[2] Yet Howe in his own fashion was perhaps no more dispassionate than Galloway and the southern officials; and to all appearances Germain and the Ministry were not building solely on the quicksands of refugee opinion: they had, or thought they had, better authority. General Robertson was home from New York for the winter, and the Peace Commissioners were at hand. They unanimously endorsed the optimistic view of American opinion.

Yet was this enough? Reading another loyalist, we slide back into the nightmare world of the refugees: a world of insubstantial fears, jealousies and plots. Thomas Jones was to write in his history of the rebellion that the evidence on which Germain relied was a tangled scheme for self-advancement concocted between Eden, General Robertson, and the loyalist William Smith: that Smith, a renegade rebel like Galloway, remained a fellow-traveller of the rebellion, and was the moving spirit of the conspiracy. Where is there firm ground among these quicksands? Perhaps a voice may be allowed to speak from the other side of the fence which divided the combatants, to show at the least that if the British government was deceived by appearances it was not alone. Two months after these discussions the

[1] Dartmouth, II, 449; Hutchinson Diaries, II, 226; G 2467, 2492–3.
[2] Wortley, 152; above p. 157.

French Minister with the rebels, writing in the heart of Galloway's Penn-sylvania, opposed the idea of a long-term truce between the Americans and the mother-country on the ground that the people were naturally favourable to England, and could never be roused a second time to resume the struggle.[1]

General Robertson, at any rate, firmly endorsed Galloway's assertion that most Americans opposed the rebellion; 'and it is on this foundation we should build our hopes'. Carlisle and Eden came home convinced that the lower country round New York was ready to be reclaimed. In conference with Germain they recommended the seizure of the Highlands between the Hudson and Connecticut Rivers, to cover the fertile lower country of Connecticut. The people would then be free to send representatives to an assembly in New York, and civil government could be restored.[2]

Translating this plan into military terms, Galloway had urged a main effort in the Middle Colonies from New Jersey to northern Virginia. At the other extreme Amherst, while he thought opportunities might occur to attack Georgia from East Florida and New Hampshire from Nova Scotia, still favoured the systematic coastal raiding which he had advocated after Saratoga.[3] But Germain's instructions to Clinton followed Robertson and the Peace Commissioners. Carlisle and Eden had recommended the New York area as the starting point of political re-absorption; and their suggested occupation of the Connecticut Highlands would have the further military advantage of cutting New England off from supplies and succour. General Robertson took a similar line. The army should not wander from place to place, nor call people to arms who could not be sustained, nor scatter troops in battalion packets to defend them. The people who might arm and protect themselves, and could be reached faster with the help of water carriage by the British army than by the enemy's, should be put under civil government and their trade encouraged. He thought the government of New York might soon be able to support itself; and that this example, combined with negotiations and military pressure, would bring in the other colonies. Like Carlisle and Eden, he saw the Highlands as the vital country. Their occupa-tion would cut off New England, almost starve the rebel army, open communications with the Indians, and enable the loyalists to defend them-selves. He advocated raiding on the New England coast to call home the local forces and weaken once more the defences of the Highlands.[4]

Robertson added the rider that a plan for the campaign could be formed

---

[1] Thomas Jones, *History of New York*, I, 160–1; Harvard, Sparks MSS., 78, Gérard's of 8 and 10 March 1779.

[2] G 2494; CL, Germain, 11 Jan. 1779 to North; CO 5/97, 23 Jan. to Clinton.

[3] G 2492, 2494.   [4] CL, Germain, 11 Jan. to North; G 2494.

only by the Commander-in-Chief in America, from circumstances which could not be known in England; and that he should therefore be vested with every power to form and execute his own plans. Yet Clinton was not of a stature to frame a large design and adhere to it. Ministerial guidance was needed. Remembering his susceptibilities, and the charges of ministerial dictation which had been levelled after Saratoga, Germain presented the instructions as suggestions, whose execution was left to Clinton's absolute discretion. Yet perhaps the orders which were signed on 23 January contained too much military detail, and insufficient broad direction on the political concept which underlay it.[1]

Germain's orders assumed an army of 29,000 men at New York and Rhode Island. The last return showed Clinton to be 7,000 short of this target; and the numbers would be made up by transferring 1,000 men from Halifax, no longer threatened by d'Estaing, and adding three regiments to the reinforcements from England, making the total from Europe 6,600. Clinton would then have enough troops to provide garrisons 9,000 strong for New York and Rhode Island, a main field force of 12,000, and coastal raiding forces of 8,000. Germain hoped, too, that Clinton could increase his Provincial forces. In the past year their strength had more than doubled, to over 7,000, as a result of the enlarged recruiting area while the army was at Philadelphia. Germain believed that by restoring to Provincial officers the status granted by Amherst during the Seven Years War, and offering permanent rank and a right to half pay to efficient units, their numbers could rapidly be increased.

For the main army the most effective course would be to bring Washington to decisive action at the start of the campaign. But if this proved impossible, the Continental army should be driven into the Highlands, leaving the lower country at liberty to return to their allegiance as the Commissioners said that they desired. The majority of counties could then send members to the Assembly, and the Constitution could be restored to New York. To prevent the reinforcement of Washington by the militia, two amphibious forces each of 4,000 men should raid the coasts of New England and the Chesapeake, while parties of Indians and troops harassed the back areas from Canada. If Washington was forced to concentrate for the defence of the Highlands, the raiding force in the Chesapeake might be strengthened with new levies of Provincial troops so that they could liberate and organise the loyalists of New Jersey or the Delaware peninsula. And thus the reoccupation might be extended into the Middle Colonies.[2]

---

[1] G 2671; CO 5/97, ff. 12–16 (23 Jan. Germain to Clinton, which should be read in conjunction with Germain's of 11 Jan. to North in CL, Germain).

[2] Anderson, 314; CL, Germain, 11 Jan. to North; Royal Institution, I, 427; CL, Clinton, 25 June, 1779, from Germain.

One apparent disharmony between the military and political aims lurks in these plans. A civilian commentator had pointed out in the previous autumn that destructive coastal raiding was likely to implant an irremovable hatred in the victims.[1] Yet there were arguments in the other direction. One was the menace of the rebel militias. Experience had shown that only a small nucleus of Continentals was needed to turn them into a formidable menace to their loyalist neighbours and at times to the army. The Danbury raid in the previous spring and General Grey's autumn raid on New Bedford had shown what might be achieved by raiding; and Germain accepted the proposition that in addition to the damage it could do to privateering and the rebel economy, the raiding policy offered the best means of pinning down the militias and securing the peace of areas which returned to their allegiance.[2]

Taken as a whole, the arrangements for 1779 were moderate and sensible. Clinton was to argue that the dispersion of force they entailed robbed him of the hope of beating Washington. Yet he had orders to attempt this if he thought it could be done; and how often had military victory eluded the commanders in America? If Washington could not be assaulted in his mountain strongholds, there was little point in pitting the maximum force against him. What the army in the field had always lacked was not mass but speed and flexibility. The raiding forces might prove a powerful asset on the rebel coasts. And if the attempt to recover America was reasonable at all, Germain's proposals, a nice balance of military and political considerations, had a better chance of success than a military policy of concentrated blows against the small and elusive Continental army.

3. The Erosion of the Plan

Such were the plans: it remains to consider the machinery for their execution. Germain was aware that the constructive political part of his proposals required something more than the machinery at the disposal of the Commanders-in-Chief. The most urgent problem was in Georgia, which Colonel Campbell was expected to attack. To profit by its occupation civil government would have to be established; for as William Smith was to write, 'if all America becomes a garrison, she is not worth your attention'. A number of southern officials were despatched at once from their refuge in England to assist the soldiers in restoring civil government; among them James Simpson the Attorney-General of South Carolina, whom Germain had already con-

---

[1] A commentary in WO 34/110, ff. 141-52.
[2] CL, Germain, 4 Nov. to Clinton; Knox, 153.

'RODNEY INVESTED—OR ADMIRAL PIG ON A CRUIZE'

Caricature by Gillray of Rodney's supersession. Pigot sets forth in a ship of cards, his sail the Knave of Hearts. Pigot was said to owe £17,000 to Fox's faro bank, and Fox in the distance explains that he has given Pigot the appointment to enable him to pay off the debt.

GENERAL ELIOTT ON THE KING'S BASTION AT GIBRALTAR

From a drawing by his Aide de Camp

sulted about the recovery of the south, and whom we shall meet again in this connection. On the news of Campbell's complete success, Sir James Wright returned to enjoy three more years as Governor, and the Peace Commissioners signed a proclamation to be published on his arrival, restoring the colony to the King's peace. Georgia was to be the only province where the Carlisle Mission's procedure for restoring civil rule was used.[1]

In the summer of 1779 a more general measure of political control was framed. A critic of the policy of coastal destruction had recently advocated a Council of State for America, to be composed of the two Commanders-in-Chief and a number of civilians.[2] It should administer all civil matters lying within the royal prerogative, with power to restore the provincial governments and prepare for a general Congress or Parliament for all America. Whether or not Germain saw the proposal, he adopted a measure on similar lines. A new Commission was drawn up in the summer on news of good progress in South Carolina. Carlisle and his friends were superseded, and Clinton was now to be sole Commissioner, with a council of civil and military members to advise him. The new Council had power to offer pardons; to restore districts to the King's peace; and to investigate American opinion on taxation and all proper subjects of negotiation.[3] Alas for this admirable and overdue arrangement: the chief obstacle to its usefulness was the Commissioner himself. Clinton became a consistent opponent of civil government.

At the remote outset of the rebellion in 1775, Sir William Howe and Burgoyne had suggested the appointment of a Viceroy to co-ordinate policy and strategy in America.[4] After Saratoga there was renewed interest in the idea. 'That a Lord Lieutenant be sent over to America', runs one proposal, 'vested with the powers . . . to superintend and direct the military operations, and to establish civil Government as soon as the Colonies shall be reduced.' Opposed to the idea was the characteristic English obsession with tyranny and usurpation, the cry which had been raised against Marlborough and prevented an adequate military establishment in time of peace. The objections were answered; but nothing was

---

[1] Carlisle, 414, 418; CL, Germain, 19 Jan. to Lt-Col. Campbell; CO 5/97, ff. 144, 183; CL, Clinton, April 1779, No. 34.

[2] WO 34/110, ff. 141–52. The author was probably William Pulteney: see CO 5/174, No. 15

[3] CL, Germain, Clinton's Commission of 22 July 1779. The military members of Clinton's Council were to be Cornwallis and Robertson; the civilians Governors Franklin of New Jersey and Martin of North Carolina, Chief Justice Fred. Smith and Attorney-General John Tabor Kempe of New York, Andrew Elliot (Superintendent of the Port of New York), and William Smith.

[4] Above, p. 74.

done, and both military and political control remained in the hands of the commanders.[1]

For a different reason the naval and military commands themselves required a degree of higher supervision which could not be supplied from home. The effect on the Hudson valley plan of separating the American and Canadian commands was already apparent. And the intervention of France brought a third theatre of operations into the struggle in the Western Atlantic. For the North American and West Indian theatre were indissolubly linked by geography and climate. This central truth was grasped by Germain. He did not intend the transfer of troops from America to the Leeward Islands to be a fixed and permanent arrangement; for he dreamed of the Western Atlantic as a single vast theatre of war. Between Quebec and the Antilles 50,000 soldiers were deployed. When ice gripped the harbours of North America, and frozen ground and rivers kept the troops in their cantonments, the Caribbean stirred from its long siesta; and when the summer spread green forage across the northern colonies, operations in the West Indies were stopped by heat, disease and hurricanes. Germain visualised a succession of offensives by troops and squadrons switching their blows between north and south as the seasons changed, using the command of the sea to achieve a superiority on each front in turn.

In practice this alternation produced its difficulties. The campaigning seasons overlapped, ships were transferred late and without refits, troops expected in America were detained to protect the islands against enemy fleets. Yet it had been done in the last war, when the Cuba expedition of 1762 had been concentrated in part from England and in part from North America, to which part of the force returned at the end of the campaign. And it was to be done again with resounding success in 1781: but not by the British.

Both Clinton and the Peace Commissioners had grasped how the theatres interlocked. Clinton's aide-de-camp was in England that winter, with instructions to press for the return of General Grant's force in the West Indies for a summer campaign against Charleston; and the Commissioners recommended that the North American squadron should no longer be confined to its station, but should act in intimate connection with the Leeward Islands fleet.[2] Much would depend on the reciprocal goodwill of the commanders. Clinton suggested a single generalissimo to control both

---

[1] One such proposal is an undated plan, later than 1777, in the British Museum, Eg. 2135, f. 14. There is a long refutation of the danger of usurpation among Lord Stormont's papers at Scone. Germain raised the question again after Yorktown (see below, p. 462).

[2] Willcox, *American Rebellion*, 119–20; CL, Germain, 11 Jan. to North.

theatres; 'indeed an *admiralissimo* would be equally necessary'.[1] Rodney was to suggest the same arrangement to overcome the selfishness of rival admirals. Whether the structure would have worked is another matter. Unified command in the west was tried by the navy for a year in the War of 1812, with three station commanders at Halifax, Jamaica and the Leeward Islands under the general direction of Admiral Warren, but the experiment was dropped in 1813. Both an American Viceroyalty and a Supreme Command in the Western Atlantic would have been easier to decree than to fill. Either would have required a public servant of great stature. Rodney may have felt that this was his mission: but it was Rodney himself who sent an incomplete squadron to America in 1781 as the crisis mounted at Yorktown.

When the plans for 1779 were drawn up in January, there was no immediate prospect of returning Grant's troops to Clinton, for the news that Byron had allowed d'Estaing to sail from Boston to the West Indies without pursuing him roused much anxiety for the fate of Grant's expedition.[2] But in March it was learnt that Byron had joined Hotham in the Leeward Islands and restored the British ascendancy. The islands were safe, and it became possible to think of restoring the borrowed battalions to Clinton. This was the more fortunate in that the hope of 6,600 reinforcements for Clinton from Europe was doomed to disappointment. Of the 3,000 promised British recruits, only 1,300 were to materialise.

With the fall of St Lucia Germain regarded the winter operations as complete. The defence of the islands till the next campaigning season was the responsibility of the fleet assisted by garrisons; and the balance of Grant's force could be returned to America for the summer, giving Clinton two or three thousand seasoned troops of the highest quality to compensate for the deficiency from England. But Sandwich was reluctant. Characteristically he wanted the troops to stay in a defensive posture where they were: perhaps he already felt some foreboding about the naval balance in the islands. Germain insisted on putting the question to the Cabinet without loss of time, and on 1 April orders for the transfer were sent to Grant. If there was no prospect of taking the offensive again before the hurricane season, he was to distribute garrisons where they were needed, remembering that the British fleet was always intended to be superior to the French, and to embark the remainder for America. On the same day Clinton was informed of the coming accession from Grant, and the news was broken that the recruits from home were short of the promised strength. He was asked to return

1 Willcox, *American Rebellion*, 120 n.
2 Sackville, I, 139.

Grant's men at the end of the summer for a renewed offensive in the islands; and the admirals on both stations were ordered to consider their two squadrons as one. For the moment Byron's fleet was not to be replaced at full strength in America; a small task force of four ships of the line was ordered out under Arbuthnot, but the security of American waters would depend on mutual support with the West Indian fleet. The government declared that it intended any future offensive in the West Indies to be mounted from America, and the troops to be brought back there when the campaigning season was over.[1]

Thus by one means or another Clinton's reinforcements seemed secure. And once again Germain had every reason to hope that those from England would make an early passage. He had warned the Admiralty of his shipping requirements as early as 11 December, long before the operational plan was drawn up: transports for 3,000 recruits and 1,500 tons of camp equipment and stores were to complete their loading by 20 February. When three regiments were added in January, the Admiralty was at once ordered to send transports to the Forth to collect them.[2] But, as usual, hopes of an early sailing date were cruelly disappointed. In spite of fine weather and favourable winds Germain discovered at the end of February that the transports he had ordered to the Forth five weeks earlier were still in the Thames. It was not till early April that they returned with the troops. Germain watched the wind with relief as it set fair for them to enter the Downs. But already he knew that they would arrive late in America.[3]

Admiral Arbuthnot, who was to succeed Byron in the American command, was ordered to take his convoy to sea at once, without waiting for the German recruits. Germain's spirits rose. 'We have charming weather', he wrote cheerfully from Stoneland, 'but we farmers are never contented; the wheat wants rain, and we shall all be undone.' But not only the farmers were at the mercy of the weather. The wind turned up Channel, and Arbuthnot was still detained in Portsmouth at the end of April.

At last the convoy put to sea. But as it turned down Channel, a privateer swept in from Jersey with news of a French attack. The Channel fleet was not ready for sea; and Arbuthnot, dropping his merchantmen in Torbay, rushed to the rescue with his warships and troops. Before he arrived, a frigate force had driven off the enemy, and he turned back to his proper mission.[4]

This chapter of accidents had brought round the campaigning season in

[1] G 2589; CL, Knox, 27 March from Germain; CO 318/5, 1 April, Germain to Grant; Sackville, II, 152; Adm. 2/1336, f. 21.
[2] CO 5/254, ff. 123, 125.
[3] CO 5/254, ff. 127–8; Sandwich, III, 121; CL, Knox, 4 April from Germain.
[4] Sackville, II, 127–8.

the Channel; and the enemy were by now in a position to dispute the convoy's passage. A squadron of five sail of the line under la Motte-Picquet was ready in Brest, and Lord North pointed out that heavy insurance costs could be saved if an additional escort could be found to see the convoy clear of the Channel. On 11 May the Cabinet ordered Arbuthnot to remain in Torbay till ten sail of the Channel fleet were ready to accompany him. Not till the 24th was he off the Start with his 215 sail and an escort from the Channel fleet under Admiral Darby; and when Darby turned back on 4 June he left him struggling forward with a foul wind and an inattentive convoy. Not till 25 August did the reinforcements reach New York.[1]

The retarding of Clinton's reinforcements is one more instance of the fatal dependence of military on naval planning. The St Lucia expedition had been planned in separate compartments; and so were the general plans for America for 1779. In forming his plans for America, the only naval factor for which Germain could provide was a task force for the local support of the army. He had to assume that the general command of the western Atlantic would be assured; for as he complained to North,[2] he could never understand the real state of the fleet. To such uncertainty Sandwich's autarchy and the lack of a supreme director had brought the country's planning.

The unity of the North American and Caribbean theatres depended absolutely on commanding the sea communications; and this in turn depended on an accurate assessment by the Admiralty of the enemy's intentions. In January 1779 Byron's arrival from America ended the temporary superiority of d'Estaing; but in the next few months miscalculations in London were to forfeit the command of the Caribbean and destroy Germain's hopes that troops could be switched from the Leeward Islands to Clinton.

The eight ships of the line which had sailed for the West Indies in December joined Byron in February, and more than balanced four ships with which de Grasse reached Martinique a week later. But in April two more ships joined the enemy; and at the end of June la Motte-Picquet arrived with his five ships from Brest, finally turning the balance in favour of the enemy. Two separate errors or misfortunes had allowed this to happen. The first was the despatch to India with Hughes of three additional ships in the belief that the French were about to reinforce the Indian Ocean. Too late it was discovered that the French force had been cancelled. A frigate was sent to Goree to recall three of Hughes's ships; but the whole squadron had rounded

---

[1] CO 5/97, f. 216; Sandwich, III, 130–1; Adm. 2/107, 11 May to Arbuthnot. The insurance money saved was £12,000.
[2] CL, Germain, 11 Jan. to North.

the Cape of Good Hope and been swallowed by the Indian command.[1]

The second misfortune was the failure to deal with la Motte's five ships which were bound for the West Indies. After a false start in April he was allowed to get clear away at the end of May. At almost the same time Arbuthnot sailed with a very similar force of four ships of the line for America; and if these had been diverted to the West Indies they could have preserved the balance in the Leeward Islands. But though Germain thought la Motte's destination was the Caribbean, there was intelligence that he was going to North America. Even if Arbuthnot's great convoy could have sailed without his protection, the American command could scarcely have been left destitute of ships of the line: the French carried no such drag on their strategic freedom as the British did in their great army under Clinton. There was one other way of defeating the enemy's purpose: by intercepting la Motte when he sailed, a course which Keppel strongly maintained should have been adopted. But the Channel ships which were ready at the end of May were detached to see Arbuthnot out of the Soundings; and had they been sent off Brest instead, the enemy could have sent out their main fleet to protect la Motte and his convoy. The implications of la Motte-Picquet's departure were not fully grasped at home. On 2 June Germain wrote to General Grant[2] lamenting that de Grasse's squadron had got safely into Fort Royal; but he added that Byron's force was still superior, and hoped Grant could send off his troops to North America as he had been ordered.

4. In the Teeth of Spain

The New York convoy was gone, and on 16 June the Channel fleet put to sea to seek the French; but on that very day the Spanish Ambassador waited on the Secretary of State with a declaration. He set forth a series of trumped-up grievances, complained that the mediation of Spain had been rejected, and concluded that she was now forced to use every means to procure the justice she had solicited in vain. The language was veiled, but the meaning clear. In April France and Spain had signed an offensive alliance against England, the Convention of Aranjuez. The two Powers were to fight together till Spain had recovered Gibraltar. To France the alliance promised Newfoundland, the recovery of Senegal and Dominica, re-establishment in India, and a share of the Honduras logging. The declaration had been carefully timed to follow the departure of the Brest fleet for its rendezvous with the Spaniards.

The British reply was pacific, but all recognised the Spanish note for what

[1] G 2586; Adm. 2/1336, f. 15; Richmond, *Navy in India*, 18–93.
[2] CO 318/5 [CO 318/5].

it was: a declaration of war. On the following day Lord John Cavendish moved a resolution in the House of Commons that all the forces of the country should be collected against the Bourbons. It was defeated by two to one; yet it was a very real issue. Shelburne and Richmond described the crisis as the most awful the country had ever experienced, and comparable with the Armada. Should not England abandon the war in America in order to face the threat to her other possessions?

Only a few days earlier the King had heard Lord North lament that the objects of the war were not worth the cost. He would have none of it. 'This', he replied, 'is only weighing such events in the scale of a tradesman behind his counter.' Once again he restated the beliefs which underlay the attempt to recover America. America's independence would be followed by that of the West Indies; and then England would be a poor island indeed. His response to Cavendish's motion was the same. America and the sugar islands could not be treated as separate issues. To abandon the first was to lose the others. 'Therefore we must stretch every nerve to defend ourselves, and must run some risks, for if we play only a cautious game ruin will inevitably ensue.'[1]

The King was determined to play for the whole stakes, believing that the only alternative was ruin. He was sustained by the stubborn strength which he had drawn all through his life from the faith that God was with him; and in this dreadful summer of 1779 the Providence which guarded the country's destiny was often in his thoughts and on his lips. 'I wish Lord North could see it in the same light for the ease of his mind', he told the Prime Minister.[2] He was sure of the justice of his cause, the approval of the Almighty, and the superiority of British fleets. To the navy he confided his youngest son. The child who was to become William IV was nearly fourteen, the latest age at which naval officers said a boy could enter the navy with success; and he went to sea with Admiral Digby in the Channel fleet. The reports of the Prince's conduct seemed to the royal father to compare well with that of some of his Ministers. 'If all my servants in their different departments will be as zealous, I shall yet guide the country out of its present difficulties. . . .'[3]

The harrying of North by Eden and Wedderburn was now at its height. The King was profoundly disturbed by the sight of the Prime Minister running in circles like a hunted hare instead of confronting 'the most serious crisis this nation ever knew'. If North would not give the lead and unite his Cabinet against the danger, King George must do what he could himself.

[1] G 2649, 2662.
[2] G 2719.
[3] Sandwich, III, 20; G 2639.

'It is an hour that requires every exertion', he told Lord Weymouth, in asking for a division list on Cavendish's motion; 'despair should never be harboured but by those who cannot dare to examine that inward Monitor who cannot disguise the truth'.[1] For a few days after the Spanish declaration he waited for signs of a new spirit, but in vain; and on 21 June the sovereign stepped into the arena and summoned the Cabinet to his presence. The Spanish challenge had cast his thoughts back two centuries to another war crisis: 'It was the vigour of mind shown by Queen Elizabeth and her subjects, added to the assistance of Divine Providence, that saved this island when attacked by the Spaniards.'[2] As he waited for his Ministers in the library of the Queen's House his mind may have dwelt on Queen Elizabeth. But his own discourse was very different from her Tilbury declamation. He was a gentleman talking in his library. For the first time in his reign he asked the Ministers to sit down, and addressed them in a plain conversational way about the crisis and its background. He began by reflecting on the past. He blamed himself for only two acts in his life: for changing his Ministry in 1765 and for consenting to the repeal of the Stamp Act. He assured them that he had never thought of injuring the Constitution or abridging liberties; nor had he ever opposed any man's admission to office on grounds of prejudice if he approved his principles. If his Ministers thought they needed strength, he was willing to bring in new blood.

King George then turned to the conduct of the war. He thanked Sandwich for the respectable condition of the navy, and the Treasury for the abundant supplies which reached America. As for the commanders there, he had sent the generals who were considered the best in the army; and when Howe, Burgoyne and Clinton were appointed, everyone had approved. He appealed now for unity. Conscious of the rectitude of his conduct and intentions, he had confidence in the favour and protection of the Almighty. His duty to God and his people was to preserve his dominions entire, and he would part with his life rather than allow them to be dismembered. Therefore, said the King, he expected firmness and support from his Ministers.[3]

This plain stout-hearted declaration was heard with respect; and the King was hopeful that it would change the atmosphere. 'If others will not be active I must drive'; and a day or two later he wrote to North that he would soon infuse some of his own spirit into his servants. But of North this was too evidently untrue. After the meeting he went down to the House to be assailed for corruption and treachery. He had just lost a favourite child, his fourth son aged two. On referring to his 'pretty numerous family'

[1] Thynne Papers, XXXVIII, No. 54.
[2] Sandwich, III, 20.
[3] The substance of the speech was collected from Germain by Knox (pp. 260-1, 267).

he was overcome by tears. But the same day Eden, unabashed by sorrow, renewed his pressure; and the wretched North was 'quite unhinged' by a stormy interview with Wedderburn over a bill to double the militia. Robinson feared that the trouble over the Militia Bill would destroy the Ministry, 'if His Majesty from his firmness and good sense cannot save it.'[1]

Here lay the one hope. If it was the King's obstinacy which kept the unhappy North at the helm, the King was also his one firm buttress. In the summer of 1779 George III stepped forward to save his tottering servant. 'His weak mind only wants *support*, which your Majesty may give it', wrote Jenkinson.[2] It was the King who by appealing to the practice of William III had combatted the fear that a chance defeat in the House of Commons would bring the Ministry down; who had urged the coercion of recalcitrant members; and who now tried to speed the prorogation and end the quest for majorities in a dwindling House.[3] It was he too who checked Wedderburn. He at least could not be frightened by hints and threats; and he insisted that in the last resort North could manage without Wedderburn in the Commons. To the Attorney-General himself he made it plain that his true interest was to stand by the Ministry. There lay the prospect of emoluments and promotion: if he joined the Opposition, he consigned his future to men with whom the King was determined never to treat as a party. Wedderburn saw where his interest lay, and was quieted.[4]

Yet all these efforts could do no more than check the rout. They could not rally North for a firm stand. Like Robinson, the King was baffled. 'His conduct is inexplicable', he wrote in July; 'yet I will do all I can to push him on; but find by experience on paper I can sometimes succeed, but conversation never does anything with him.'[5]

On the day after his address to the Cabinet, the King declared that he would accept no help from the Opposition without a written undertaking to withdraw no forces from America. This was his final answer to Cavendish's motion. To pull out of the rebel colonies would throw away the hope that one more push would win them back, leaving England free to turn against the Bourbons without sacrificing the main object of the war. He believed that the end of the rebellion was only postponed by the tonic of the Spanish intervention; and his view had the same grounds as the operational plans for the

[1] Add. MSS. 38211, ff. 173–4.
[2] G 2637.
[3] G 2536, 2572, 2677; Sandwich, III, 25–6.
[4] Add. MSS. 37834, ff. 77, 83, 90, 101, 103; G 2637, 2695–9. Wedderburn's ruthless ambition must be balanced against the debt which we owe him for enabling Gibbon to scribble in greater comfort as a Lord of Trade.
[5] Butterfield, 60.

year: the belief that most Americans were loyal. It was shared by Germain. On the day of the King's declaration a despatch arrived from America showing that Clinton intended to take the field early in pursuit of the Ministry's plans; and letters by the same packet from South Carolina indicated growing dissatisfaction with the rebel cause. Germain hoped that the recovery of Georgia might have opened the way to an unopposed re-occupation of South Carolina; and on the King's initiative a firm assurance was sent to Clinton that no troops would be withdrawn from America.[1]

For three years England had kept far more men in America than had beaten the French out of Canada, and she maintained them without the resources of the American colonies. The decision to persevere committed the country to three more years of exhausting effort in America; and its immediate effect was that no fresh resources could be deployed against the Spaniards in the Caribbean. Germain, however, was determined that the forces already in the West Indies should do everything in their power to wrest the initiative from the enemy. As soon as the Spanish declaration was received, he ordered General Campbell in West Florida to seize New Orleans, which was thought to be weakly garrisoned, and thus to secure the navigation of the Mississippi. For speed and secrecy the orders were sent direct to Pensacola, with an apology to Clinton for bypassing him. Sir Peter Parker at Jamaica was ordered to co-operate when he could spare a naval force in the hurricane season, and Haldimand in Canada was directed to assist by harrying the Spanish posts in the Illinois country. On the Central American isthmus too the Spaniards might be harried. It was suggested to the Governor of Jamaica that freebooters and Mosquito Indians might be armed to harass Nicaragua and pave the way for a regular attack.[2]

These ideas did not prove easy to realise. Yet it was right that the home government should suggest them; for however petty and irrelevant to the main objects of the war they may seem, it could not be wrong to bring every pressure to bear on the military and moral resources of the enemy. We shall find that they were the germ of a more significant effort.

[1] G 2674, 2686; Sackville, II, 130–1; CL, Germain, 25 June to Clinton; CL, Clinton, 5 May from Germain; Sandwich, III, 28.

[2] CL, Germain, 17 June to Dalling and Haldimand; 25 June, to Campbell; June, to Clinton; Knox, 158; Sandwich, III, 123.

CHAPTER XV

THE WESTERN ATLANTIC:
THE DESIGN MISCARRIES

1. *The Rebel Colonies*

Germain's highest hopes for America now rested on the southern colonies. He ordered Clinton to leave Campbell's force intact in Georgia, so that it could pursue its career of conquest into South Carolina. Campbell was a vigorous and able officer, and in his fortieth year he still had the flexibility of youth. He had urged from the first that a Governor should be sent out to restore legal government in Georgia, and his period of independent command was popular and successful. But it did not last for long. General Prevost marched from East Florida to join him, and his coming brought a different atmosphere. His advance across Georgia was more like a plundering expedition than the prelude to a permanent occupation. A Swiss like Haldimand, he showed no grasp of the British veneration for property; and he despised the officials on whom the pacification of Georgia depended. Much of the good which Campbell had achieved was undone. Houses were destroyed, property illegally requisitioned, slaves and private effects appropriated by the General. Arrivals from South Carolina were harshly received, as were all who had in any way submitted to the rebels. Prevost was no more and no less than a well-meaning and not very able soldier of fortune, bent on lining his pockets and promoting his family. But he was not the man to undo the work of rebellion.[1]

With the arrival of the reinforcements from East Florida a fierce little war flared up on the borders of South Carolina, with hard-fought actions and hangings of captured loyalists. At the end of April Prevost thrust boldly into South Carolina to counter an incursion into Georgia by General Lincoln; and finding resistance light he pushed on towards Charleston, in whose neighbourhood he left a detachment under Colonel Maitland when he withdrew. These were attacked by General Moultrie with a superior force at Stono Ferry; but by the efforts of the gallant Seventy-first he was repulsed with loss. Yet the cost to the Highlanders was severe. As Colonel Stuart said, it proved the superior valour of British troops; but the loss of so many gallant

---

[1] CL, Germain, memorandum at end of 1779 papers; Harvard, Sparks MSS., 22, p. 216 (Major Wemyss's character of Prevost); Royal Institution, II, 59, 88.

men detracted from the advantage, 'and I am afraid proves what I have said, that that Army in the end will be overpower'd and beat'.[1] But the fulfilment of this prophesy was still far off.

The hot weather brought operations in the south to a close, and the pick of the British force was quartered for the summer at Beaufort on Port Royal Island, where their presence gave security to Georgia by threatening Charleston. The offensive was now taken up in the northern sphere by Clinton.

The opening of the year had found the British forces in their winter quarters round New York, while Washington's army lay hutted and cantoned astride the Hudson with their centre secured by the fortress of West Point in the Highlands. The severe winter was taking its toll of the rebels, but Clinton found it hard to obtain intelligence 'divested of the too sanguine reports of the zealous friends of his Majesty's Government'. Nevertheless the evident condition of the rebels created the same atmosphere of optimism as had conditioned the Ministry at home. Chief Justice Smith wrote to Carlisle in February that if proper attention were paid to restoring civil government, 'no person informed of the divided, exhausted and debilitated condition of the revolted Colonies, will believe it possible to maintain the Rebellion . . .' He continued throughout the early summer to assert that the common people were oppressed and sickened by a hoard of officials and profiteers who constituted the core of the revolt. Nothing, he said, was needed to restore the King's government but the absence of the Continental Army till the loyalists had been armed for their own defence. This accords precisely with the views on which Germain had based his plans for the year. Nor was it merely the opinion of a 'sycophantic refugee'; for Sir George Collier, the senior naval officer when Gambier departed in the spring, expressed 'some confidence that rebellion is thrown on its back, and that this campaign will be the *last* of this unnatural civil war'.[2]

But Clinton continued to bathe in self-pity over the reduction of his force. His sense of grievance was not assuaged by the latitude which Germain was careful to give him in his orders. On the contrary: while he seized on the orders respecting the rank of Provincial officers as a harsh example of the American Secretary's dictation of detail, he complained that the latitude left to him over strategy was designed to throw the responsibility for a failure on his shoulders. 'For God's sake', he exclaimed, '. . . if you wish that I should do anything leave me to myself, and let me adapt my efforts to the hourly change of circumstance. If not tie me down and take the risk of my

[1] Wortley, 158.
[2] CO 5/97, ff. 71, 75; Carlisle, 418, 424, 429, 430; Sackville, II, 128–9; Sandwich, III, 133.

want of success.'[1] Clinton was demanding what no commander in that war or the previous one had enjoyed: complete control over policy and strategy in America. The Ministry should feed him with troops from Britain and the West Indies, place Canada under his requisition, and leave him to play the game as he fancied. American strategy involved the resources of other theatres, and policial decisions such as a soldier should not be asked to take without a directive. Germain however shrugged his shoulders at this new outburst, and despaired of managing him. He pointed out that the instructions about Provincial rank merely confirmed the advice of a Board of General Officers convened by Clinton himself, and were drawn up in consultation with officers from Clinton's own headquarters. 'I could not conceive that anticipating your wishes could have proved the occasion of offence.' Clinton, however, had some grounds for his fear that the new seniority of Provincial officers would give offence to British regulars; and he blamed two of his officers whom he had sent over to Germain for the misunderstanding.[2]

It must not be supposed that Clinton differed from the Secretary of State about the prospect of reducing the colonies. But he placed less faith in re-establishing loyalist administrations and more on making the rebels' condition intolerable. If his later account states his view with accuracy, he believed that a field force of 30,000 British troops on the Hudson and the Connecticut, with expeditions at proper seasons to the Chesapeake and the Carolinas, would drive the rebel Congress to such straits that the people would soon force them to accept the British terms.[3] He had no such force at the outset of the campaign; but with the promise of 6,600 reinforcements and the hope of more from the West Indies, he could look forward to an active force of at least 20,000 men in the course of the summer.

The Secretary of State's orders of 23 January did not reach New York till 24 April; and already Clinton and Commodore Collier had devised a series of coastal raids on the lines suggested by Germain in the autumn. They were to begin in Virginia, and switch to New England in the hot weather. This course was chosen in preference to exploiting the success in the south, where the summer heat and the near presence of d'Estaing's fleet in the West Indies were likely to make operations precarious. Two thousand troops under General Mathew sailed for the Chesapeake, with the objects of preventing reinforcements from marching to join Washington, destroying shipping, and seizing the magazines accumulated against the return of the

---

[1] CO 5/97, ff. 160, 302, 330–1. The letter quoted is printed in full in Willcox, *American Rebellion*, 407, and illustrates in a striking manner Clinton's relations with his government.

[2] G 2671; CL, Clinton, 25 June from Germain; Willcox, *American Rebellion*, 128, 404–10.

[3] Willcox, *American Rebellion*, 119.

French fleet. Portsmouth was seized, and a fortnight's operations resulted in the destruction of immense quantities of military stores and tobacco intended for export, and of about 150 vessels of different sizes. Collier found enough support among the inhabitants to judge it feasible to retain Portsmouth, 'the finest yard on this continent' and a much needed southern base for the fleet. Mathew, however, returned to New York in obedience to his orders, which warned him to give no encouragement to the population to endanger themselves by active support.

During Mathew's absence Clinton had been planning a movement which would place him in a position to exploit the arrival of his reinforcements. On 1 May there were 14,500 rank and file present and fit for duty at New York; and he resolved to strike up the Hudson to the forts covering the crossing at King's Ferry. Their possession would sever the shortest lateral road open to the enemy, and force them to use a detour of at least sixty miles with two crossings of the mountains. Washington might then be induced to risk a battle; and at the least the threat to the Highlands should prevent him from detaching to seize the initiative in other parts. As soon as Mathew's force returned from Virginia the advance began. The attack was made with the good fortune and skill which characterised most of Clinton's minor operations, and by 1 June the two forts of Stony Point and Verplancks were in his hands.

Washington was forced by the British movement to take the field before he was ready, drawing his troops in to West Point from both sides of the river. The early start promised well, and Clinton paused to wait for the reinforcements which were due at any moment, keeping his troops together within twenty-four hours' march of Stony Point in the hope that Washington would try to recover the forts. But no reinforcements appeared.

In the meantime Washington's concentration was believed to have weakened the Connecticut coast. Collier had been anxious to continue the coastal raids by striking at New London, 'that thorn in our sides,' and Clinton ordered General Tryon to take an expedition up Long Island Sound. Losing hope of striking directly at Washington, Clinton moved his army across to the East River to support Tryon, hoping to induce Washington to cross the Hudson and give him an opening. Washington did not; but on the night of 15 July Stony Point was stormed by General Wayne.

The loss of Stony Point threw Clinton into a depression far beyond what it warranted. The fort was recaptured at once, and Wayne's exploit cost the British no more than the several hundred men of the garrison. But when Colonel Stuart returned from England soon afterwards, the Commander-in-Chief told him with tears in his eyes that he was an altered man. He had lost all confidence in himself. 'Let me advise you never to take command of an army', he said. 'I know I am hated, nay detested by this army. . . . The Minister has used me so ill I can no longer bear with this life.'[1]

His state of mind percolated to the public of New York that autumn, and a new arrival in November may have reported the common opinion when he wrote home: 'no abilities to plan, nor firmness to execute, the most trivial military operation . . . an ignorant, capricious, irresolute commander'. Clinton was much better than that, but his temperament was his undoing. 'I indulge a hope', wrote a loyalist who had endured the spectacle of Howe's missed opportunities, 'that I shall yet have a chance of seeing a General that's neither a Rebel nor a Histerical Fool.'[2]

A demand arrived from Haldimand for 2,000 men to strengthen Canada, with which Clinton complied; and Commodore Collier sailed soon after to repel an attack on a new post on the Penobscot River in Maine. Clinton, aware that the naval balance in the western Atlantic was turning in the enemy's favour, began to draw the army into a tighter perimeter round New York. There was a fresh pinprick in the middle of August when 'Light Horse Harry' Lee surprised and almost captured Paulus Hook. Clinton was 'tremendously depressed'. The next day he sent off a renewed demand to be recalled. He wrote that his spirits were worn out by adversity, and he had abandoned every hope of an effort in the north. In this mood he received Admiral Arbuthnot and the reinforcements.[3]

The long-expected convoy brought only 3,800 rank and file, for the German and Irish recruits were to follow, and did not arrive till 21 September, the Germans about 1,000 of all ranks. Arbuthnot's troops were very sickly after their long confinement in the transports, and brought a fever which swept through the army and put 6,000 men into hospital. Though the 2,000 men detached to Canada failed to get through to Quebec before the winter and returned to Clinton, their absence and the sickness killed the northern operations, of which Clinton had already despaired. He prepared instead to open an autumn campaign in the south.

Germain had written at the end of March to urge once more the importance of reducing Charleston in the autumn. About the time of Arbuthnot's arrival at New York, James Simpson the Attorney-General of South Carolina appeared from the south. He had been sent from England to Georgia in the spring with orders to cultivate a correspondence with the back

[1] Wortley, 151, 186-7.
[2] Verulam, 127; Nelson, 143. There is a suggestion in Hutchinson Diaries, II, 296, of a revulsion against Clinton in England.
[3] CO 5/98, ff. 201-2, 287.

country of South Carolina. He had long since urged Charleston's superiority over Savannah as a base to protect the trade of the West Indies, and he now presented himself to Clinton with an optimistic account of opinion in South Carolina. He was confident that a strong British force would be supported by many of the people, and that the province could be subdued with little difficulty. Thereafter he believed that with proper management royal government would strike firm and permanent roots.[1]

These were the hopes on which Clinton was now to build. He had intended to attack South Carolina in the past summer if Grant's troops had arrived from the West Indies, and had had little doubt that he could seize Charleston without them, though he might not be able to hold it.[2] General Cornwallis and 3,000 troops prepared to embark for the south, and Arbuthnot planned a naval diversion in the Potomac.

2. The Loss of Command at Sea

The chapter of accidents which delayed Arbuthnot's convoy has already been explained. Not so the absence of Grant's troops which he had been ordered to return to Clinton. He had indeed promised these on receiving Germain's letter, and Clinton had built considerable hopes on these good regiments.

On reading the order to detach towards the end of May, Grant resolved to send six regiments back to America. Two others were serving as marines in the fleet, and he planned to keep the remaining three together on St Lucia. His prediction that half his force would be out of action soon after it reached the West Indies had proved too gloomy. He had arrived in the healthy winter season, and careful administration kept the sick rate in the spring down to little more than the average rate in America. But it was still high. Of the 4,945 rank and file fit for duty when the force arrived in December, 1,400 were sick or dead by 1 April; and by the middle of May the total had risen to over 1,800.

The intended distribution of troops assumed a continuous protection of the British islands by the fleet; and since Byron's arrival in the Leeward Islands he had been keeping watch on the enemy in Martinique from his new anchorage at St Lucia. But though he knew that la Motte was on his way with reinforcements from Brest, and cruised for a few days in the hope of intercepting him, he left his station at the beginning of June and sailed northwards to protect the homeward-bound convoy which was gathering

---

[1] Sackville, II, 137; CO 5/97, f. 144; and above, pp. 233 and 256–7.
[2] Willcox, *American Rebellion*, 120 n.

at St Kitts. His absence in the northern islands was used by the French. Four hundred troops were sent southwards past St Lucia and attacked St Vincent, whose derisory garrison capitulated at once.

In the meantime la Motte-Picquet had got safely into Fort Royal, with a desperately needed provision fleet and a reinforcement which turned the scales against Byron. The British fleet was now slightly inferior in capital ships, and in frigates very weak indeed, for Vaudreuil and la Motte between them had brought eight from Europe. D'Estaing had the superiority he needed for another blow. On 2 July he attacked Grenada; and on the following day Lord Macartney's 159 regulars and 300 militia capitulated. The richest British sugar island in the Lesser Antilles had gone the way of Dominica and St Vincent.

Byron had returned to St Lucia on 1 July to learn that the enemy were steering for Grenada. A frigate was sent to look into Fort Royal; but the enemy's cruiser screen kept her at a distance, and her captain wrongly reported that thirteen ships of the line were still in the harbour. Byron concluded that only a weak detachment had gone to Grenada, and in the hope of falling on it he made sail with twenty-one of the line and a convoy of troops. When he sighted the island he could see d'Estaing's ships straggling out of harbour, and came down widely spread in a General Chase to attack them before they could form their line. Before he knew that he was in the presence of a superior force he was closely engaged. The British fleet was lucky not to lose its damaged ships in the battle, and had d'Estaing ordered his frigates to chase the unguarded convoy, the whole of the military force would have been taken.

Byron now knew that he had lost the command of West Indian waters. It was out of the question to escort troops to America; and the troops themselves were now needed to defend the islands. The regiments which had been told off for America were thrown into garrison; and once again sea-power and land forces were proved to be inseparable. For want of ships in the West Indies, the six battalions were denied to Clinton.

The loss of St Vincent was known in England at the beginning of August, and caused much concern. Grant had been ordered to distribute his troops through the islands where garrisons were required; but in the light of Germain's assurance of superiority at sea he had reasoned that small garrisons would make his command weak everywhere, and that a disposable force kept together at the fleet base was the islands' best security. This reasoning Germain acknowledged to be sound in general; but it could not apply to islands which were liable to surprise or could not be immediately succoured by the navy, and St Vincent had been snapped up by a contemptibly small enemy force. For the order to disperse, Germain has been savaged by

Sir John Fortescue,[1] who attributes to it General Vaughan's difficulty in re-concentrating the force in the following year before he could resume the offensive. Yet Germain's order had been conditional on Grant being unable to take the offensive; and though Grant had not acted on the order, he did so without a reminder and in spite of his own previous reasoning as soon as the naval superiority was lost. The regiments which had been intended for America were not kept together on St Lucia, but stationed on St Kitts and Antigua; and it was these which Vaughan had to reassemble when he was able to go over to the offensive. It was Grant, in other words, who dispersed his force; and he did so because the command of the sea had been lost and there was no dependence on relief by a mobile reserve. He held only the most important islands, and held them in some strength; and there was no other means of securing them against an enemy who controlled the water.[2]

3. Disintegration of the Western Theatre

The hurricane season was now approaching; and in August d'Estaing left the Leeward Islands for Haiti. From the British fleet first Barrington and then Byron went home, leaving the enemy in a central position from which they might move northwards to the American coast or westwards against Jamaica. D'Estaing was said to be impressing Jamaican pilots, but he had used this artifice before.

In the western Caribbean towards which d'Estaing was pointing, the intervention of Spain had opened a series of petty operations and great alarms. In West Florida General Campbell found it beyond his power to attack New Orleans as Germain had suggested. His British regiment was worn out and only fit to be drafted; and the Germans and Provincials whom he had brought from New York at the end of 1778 were too few to defend Pensacola and simultaneously protect the settlements on the Mississippi. His only warship was an armed sloop, and a large Spanish schooner in the mouth

[1] ' . . . the folly and ignorance of Germain . . . this deplorable Secretary of State' (Fortescue, III, 275).

[2] Fortescue, III, 274-5, 341; CO 318/5, Germain's of 1 April and 6 Aug., and Grant's of 6 Jan., 25 May, 8 and 17 July, 10 Oct. Grant's distribution of troops was:

St Kitts	.	.	.	3 battalions
St Lucia	.	.	.	3 battalions
Antigua	.	.	.	1 battalion (equivalent)

Total strength: rank and file

fit	.	.	.	1,775
sick	.	.	.	495
effectives	.	.	.	2,521

(CO 5/318, f. 19).

of the Mississippi effectively cut his command in two. Colonel Dickson's force on the Mississippi was isolated, and in October it was forced to surrender to the Spaniards.

Though West Florida was nominally Clinton's responsibility, it was too distant for effective communication. The naval responsibility however lay with Sir Peter Parker on the Jamaica station, and it was to Jamaica that Campbell looked for support. But Parker and the Governor, Colonel Dalling, were involved in operations in another quarter. In obedience to Germain's suggestions contact was made with the Mosquito Indians. A small naval force was cruising in the Gulf of Honduras, with Captain-Commandant Dalrymple and a dozen of his soldiers on board, when it was learnt that two galleons were sheltering under the fort of S Fernando de Omoa. English settlers were collected from the Bay of Honduras to swell the party, and in October Omoa was stormed and a rich treasure taken. Dalrymple appropriated for his dozen soldiers the credit which properly belonged to the seamen and marines. It was the opening of a curious and unhappy enterprise on the Isthmus.[1]

In Jamaica itself Parker and Dalling existed in a continual state of fear. Cries for help were flying to and fro across the Gulf of Mexico. When General Prevost marched into Georgia from East Florida, he left only a few hundred troops to hold St Augustine. The officer whom he left in command feared the Spaniards at Havana and the French at Haiti, and appealed to West Florida and Jamaica for men and powder. But d'Estaing's central position equally threatened Jamaica, and Sir Peter Parker and Dalling dashed off their own cry for help to New York.

Clinton received this appeal on 15 September, at the moment when he was preparing to switch his own effort to the Carolinas. On receipt of Parker's letter, with its news that d'Estaing's fleet and transports were at Haiti, the southern expedition was instantly dropped, and Cornwallis was embarked with 4,000 men to save Jamaica.[2] On the 24th the transports were over the bar and standing out to sea when a privateer came in with the news that d'Estaing no longer threatened Jamaica: he was already on the coast of Georgia.

Thus for the second time Clinton's army was pinned down by the arrival of a French fleet. Mutual support between America and the Caribbean became impossible. Grant had been unable to send his regiments to Clinton; and now Clinton, ignorant of d'Estaing's intentions, was unable to send help to Dalling or even shift his forces within his own command. From Quebec

[1] James, *Journal*, 71–8
[2] Governor Dalling very characteristically protested on learning that Cornwallis would come to supersede him after he had borne unspecified distress, fatigue and difficulties in his quiet Jamaican backwater.

to Tobago 55,000 British troops now lay in isolated pockets where before they had been linked by the navy. Haldimand's thin forces in the St Lawrence basin, the scattered garrisons in the Leeward Islands, Dalling's troops in Jamaica and the garrisons of the Floridas were strong only so long as secure intercommunication made them one army. In Clinton's command only the main force at New York was strong in itself. Rhode Island, Halifax and Savannah lay vulnerable to an attacker who commanded the intervening water.

Everything came to a halt. Cornwallis returned with his transports to the shelter of New York, while Arbuthnot prepared to repeat Howe's defence of Sandy Hook, and quarrelled with Clinton about whether to reinforce Halifax. Though he had only been at New York for a month, there had already been friction between the two commanders; and on this occasion the old admiral told Colonel Stuart with tears in his eyes that he was tired to death of Clinton, and abused him for his folly and want of candour. Stuart returned to Clinton, who abused Arbuthnot in the grossest terms for his deceit and artifice. Later, however, they met and agreed to send no ships of the line to Halifax. 'This indecision seems to be the rule of those from whose conduct the American conquest is expected', wrote Stuart.[1]

The most serious consequence of d'Estaing's intervention was the abandonment of Rhode Island. Realising that they were incapable to supporting the garrison if it were attacked by a French fleet, Clinton and Arbuthnot agreed at the end of October to withdraw it. This decision is often represented as a disastrous error. Rodney called it 'the most fatal measure that could possibly have been taken', and described Rhode Island as the only all-weather harbour in America. His motive was probably to discredit Arbuthnot with Germain; and it is a fact that the British had never used Newport as a fleet base during three years of occupation. It had proved a less satisfactory winter anchorage than had been hoped when it was taken; and Howe's ships had driven there owing to the badness of the anchoring ground and the roughness of the sea. For cruisers there was a good anchorage at Gardiner's Island on the north-east end of Long Island; and it was arguable that if the force which held Rhode Island could be spared for garrison duties, it could be better employed in holding an anchorage in the Chesapeake.

Germain had already heard the arguments for evacuating Rhode Island when he learnt that it had been done, and he gave it his approval: 'Indeed if in consequence of your withdrawing the troops from thence the southern colonies are recovered this winter, the wisdom of the measure will be fully manifested and the authors universally applauded.' The strongest argument for retaining Rhode Island was the negative one of denying it to the enemy.

[1] Wortley, 161.

As Lord Howe wrote, 'd'Estaing will be found a more troublesome neigh-bour, than in our time, if he makes his headquarters at Rhode Island'; and in 1780–1 a French fleet and army did indeed find there the secure base from which they contributed to the victory at Yorktown. But Arbuthnot and Clinton had immediate realities to face. Its possession tied up 5,000 troops and half a dozen warships at a time when all quarters were crying out for help. And if d'Estaing came north it could not be relieved: Howe had barely been able to save it in 1778, and Arbuthnot with only five ships of the line could certainly not save it from d'Estaing's twenty. Five thousand troops might make a new Saratoga for a possession whose value was small to Britain and uncertain to the enemy; troops which were needed for the coming expedition to South Carolina. It is true that the evacuation eventually assisted the enemy, but in war it is impossible to insure against every risk.[1]

D'Estaing had first proposed a return to America in the previous spring, suggesting a joint expedition with Washington against Halifax or New-foundland. Washington had been discouraging. He could not spare the troops for these divergent objects; and he doubted whether New York could be attacked, though the French might burn the British transports and attack Staten Island. D'Estaing remained in the West Indies throughout the summer; but in August he received an appeal for help from the Governor of South Carolina. Prevost was threatening Charleston; and the Governor's appeal was supported by French representatives on the spot. They painted a frightening picture of confusion: shortage of regular troops, a feeble un-disciplined militia, and quarrelling leaders. But they believed that if the French fleet could appear in September, the British army and flotilla could be destroyed by a single stroke.

D'Estaing could see the difficulties; but his original orders had demanded a *coup d'éclat* to demonstrate the value of French support, and he was in-fluenced by his failure at Rhode Island in 1778. He warned the American Governor that his absence from the West Indies would have to be brief, and that success would depend on the speed and promptitude of the American troops. '*M. Rutledge m'a demandé de venir frapper un coup, c'est tout ce que je peux.*' On 1 September he swooped on the coast of Georgia with twenty ships of the line and 5,000 troops.

Surprise was complete. The fifty-gun ship *Experiment* fell into his hands with pay for the troops in Georgia; so did a frigate and two storeships. But

---

[1] CL, Germain, 10 Oct. 1779, William Pulteney to Germain; CL, Clinton, 4 Dec. from Germain; Huntington Library, HO 15 (13 Dec., Lord Howe to Captain Curtis). For some contemporary estimates of Rhode Island as a base, see Pulteney's letter cited above; Mundy, *Rodney*, I, 428–32; and for alternative bases, Sandwich, IV, 174, 180, 196, 197.

here his luck ended. Maitland's troops at Beaufort slipped through his fingers, and made their way south by creeks and inlets to rejoin Prevost in Savannah. D'Estaing was on their heels, and on 16 September he summoned the town to surrender. But Prevost had two great assets: an able Engineer officer, and the brave Seventy-first Highlanders. When the enemy's batteries opened on 3 October his little force was ready. For six days cannon and mortars pounded the town, and as time went by d'Estaing grew increasingly uneasy. The season was late, his anchorage bad, his seamen and guns on shore. At last he persuaded General Lincoln to cut short the siege by attempting to storm. Before daybreak on the 9th the French and Americans assaulted. A redoubt was penetrated; but a determined counter-attack by two companies of the Sixtieth and a party of Marines drove the enemy back with heavy loss. D'Estaing was wounded in the fight; and he gave up as he had given up at New York, Rhode Island and St Lucia. Troops, stores, and guns were re-embarked, and before the end of October the French had quit the coast of America for the second time.

While Clinton and Arbuthnot awaited the outcome of d'Estaing's operations, they had pressed on with their preparations for the expedition which they had planned against South Carolina. The news of the enemy's repulse at Savannah reached them on 18 November, and they waited only to be sure that the French fleet had left the coast. Before the end of the year Clinton sailed with his expeditionary force for Georgia. Large-scale operations in the northern colonies were over, and the great adventure in the south had begun.

The American operations of 1779 have been called 'the disjointed offensive'. The name is misleading. It was not a single offensive, but a series of spasmodic local efforts by forces crippled by external circumstances. Nor was it the realisation of Germain's conception.

For it was not the lack of a plan which disjointed the operations, but the maritime failure to secure the early passage of Arbuthnot's convoy of reinforcements and the command of the western Atlantic. The retention of a large fleet in the Channel to meet the French and Spaniards, and the last-minute failure to reinforce the West Indies, gave France the game in the west: it was only good fortune that averted the worst consequences in the Leeward Islands and Georgia. Britain's American strategy was strangled. Only at New York was there a disposable force to retain the initiative; but Clinton was distracted by cries for help from Jamaica, Halifax and Quebec. He was obliged to abandon Rhode Island, and his expedition to the southern colonies was delayed for three months. Whatever the condition of the rebel colonies, whatever the grounds for believing that capitulation was near, a shadow hung over the British path of conquest: the shadow of the French fleet.

CHAPTER XVI

THE DEFENCE OF ENGLAND

1. *The Invasion Plan*

Hitherto Spain had remained neutral because she had settled her quarrel with England's ally Portugal, and because in the way of her ambitions there stood rebellious America, a fatal example to her own colonies. Nor were her own resources such that she could lightly engage them. Nevertheless she longed to wipe out her past defeats. On her own coasts there were Gibraltar and Minorca to be regained, and beyond the seas Jamaica and Florida. In Honduras there were British settlements to dislodge; and she hoped for a share in the Newfoundland fisheries. The Foreign Minister, Floridablanca, was determined on war. But he was playing a devious game in the political thickets of Madrid, and before he could commit his country he had been forced to concede to King Charles III his wish to mediate.

Vergennes disliked the delay, but was forced to defer to the temper of the Spanish Court. A further consideration held the allies apart: the strategy of the coming alliance. Vergennes remained hostile to the idea of invading England; but the Spaniards could not contemplate a long struggle to undermine the British economy, and hoped for a short decisive war. One carefully planned blow against the English homeland would achieve their end. For this they held out; and when the indecisive battle of Ushant had convinced Vergennes of his need of the Spanish fleet, Floridablanca was able during the course of the winter to shepherd him gradually into accepting the Spanish strategy. By the beginning of March Vergennes was converted to invasion.[1]

Many plans for invading England had been examined in the past eighty years. The Comte de Broglie's of 1765, for a landing in Sussex and a march on London, offered the most decisive results. But Vergennes still feared that the other Powers would take fright at so resounding a victory. He preferred a more limited success. England's public wealth was believed to be an unstable credit structure founded on public confidence; and an attack on Portsmouth would not only blast her naval power but cause a panic which would wreck her credit system. The plan which Vergennes proposed was to concentrate fifty French and Spanish ships of the line off Corunna by the middle of May, and establish command of the English Channel. Twenty thousand troops would cross from Normandy to seize first the Isle of Wight,

[1] Patterson, *The Other Armada*, 39–47.

and then a beachhead at Gosport from which to shell and burn the Portsmouth dockyard. Subsidiary operations might be launched against Bristol and Liverpool, and afterwards against the victualling depot at Cork; and if the Isle of Wight attack miscarried, Plymouth might be made the main object. In the couple of months which followed the French proposal, the plan was extended under Spanish pressure to include the capture and occupation of Portsmouth itself; and the military force was raised to 30,000 men.[1]

In this plan the time factor was vital. The Spaniards insisted that their ships must return at the end of August, before the weather made navigation hazardous in the Channel; and in any case a longer cruise would strain the victualling arrangements and tell on the health of the crews. This deadline gave the allies four months from the beginning of May to concentrate the fleets on the Spanish coast, train them in combined manoeuvres, win the command of the Channel, and accomplish the invasion. Until late in April Vergennes believed that the Brest fleet would be ready to sail on 1 May and could join the Spaniards in the middle of the month; but when d'Orvilliers arrived in Paris on 21 April he revealed to the Minister's disgust that he could not sail before the end of May. The sailing date was put back to early June, and the Brest fleet put to sea five weeks behind its schedule. But Vergennes little suspected how much further the Spaniards would fall behind their promises.

D'Orvilliers reached the rendezvous near Corunna on 10 June, where he was joined before long by two ships from Toulon which completed the French component to thirty of the line. The Spaniards had originally been intended to contribute twenty, and to send another twenty to blockade Gibraltar or pursue Arbuthnot's convoy; but to ensure an overwhelming superiority in the Channel they agreed to transfer sixteen ships to the main force, making it a vast armada of sixty-six sail of the line. But where were the Spaniards? After making every conceivable excuse and betraying his repugnance to the French, the Admiral of the eight Ferrol ships at last came out and joined d'Orvilliers on 2 July. But though Vergennes had begged the Spaniards to lose no time by waiting for news that the Brest fleet had sailed, the Cadiz fleet had not sailed till 23 June; and meeting the north winds which blow on the coast of Portugal at that season, it did not reach the rendezvous till 23 July.

The French had now been waiting for six weeks. They had been hurried to sea without their full four months' supply of water and provisions, and many ships were without surgeons or adequate medical supplies. The fleet had now consumed half its victuals, and fevers and smallpox had begun to ravage the crews. Time was running low. But though the French signal codes had

[1] Patterson, 5, 7, 46–7, 149.

been sent to Spain, they had not been properly issued to Cordoba's fleet. A week slipped away in translating signal books and agreeing on orders; and d'Orvilliers foresaw that the unwieldy mass of ships would be too numerous and inexperienced to manoeuvre well. On 30 July the Combined Fleet sailed for the Channel with only a month in hand; but the wind off Ushant turned contrary, and ten more days were lost in doubling the cape. At last on 15 August the Lizard was sighted; and on the following day the armada was seen from Plymouth.[1]

2. The British Fleet

So England was faced, for the first and only time in the war, with what Keppel had wrongly feared in 1778: an invasion across the Channel. Thirty-one thousand men were concentrated at St Malo and le Havre to seize the Portsmouth area; and the Bourbon fleets were in the Channel to protect their crossing. At that moment the British Channel Fleet was far to the westward and ignorant of the enemy's presence.

To trace the policies which laid the Channel open to the enemy, one must turn back to the opening of the Channel fleet's operations at the beginning of June. It was maintained by Keppel that if Hardy had been sent south in pursuit of the French he could have fought and beaten them before the Spaniards reached the rendezvous. But this supposed that the Cabinet were certain of the enemy's intention, which they were not; and that they could guess what delays would retard the Bourbon concentration. Hardy did in fact sail with orders, issued a couple of weeks before the Spanish declaration, to prevent the enemy's junction. An additional instruction, so secret that he was to issue no copies and inform only flag officers, authorised him to intercept any Spanish ships of the line which were clearly bound for a French port.[2]

Thus at the outset of the second campaign the Admiralty felt strong enough to re-institute the blockade of Brest; and if Hardy could have been off Ushant in time he might have put an end to the enemy's plan. But when his orders were issued the fleet was still unready. Darby's squadron had been sent out to protect Arbuthnot and the New York convoy; and at the beginning of June twelve ships left at Spithead lacked 1,400 men. On 4 June, a week before Darby's return and long before the other ships had completed their crews, d'Orvilliers sailed from Brest.

The news that the enemy were out reached the Cabinet on 11 June. Sandwich sent off a messenger the same evening to urge Hardy to sail. But Darby had only returned on the 10th and needed a few days to complete

[1] Patterson, 59–61, 160–9.
[2] Adm. 2/1336, ff. 23, 25

his provisions. There was much criticism of the delay; and Keppel implied that the interception of the French fleet should have had priority over the despatch of a convoy. But even when Darby returned, the rest of the fleet was still short of men; and it seems clear that Hardy could in no circumstances have been off Ushant on 4 June to stop d'Orvilliers.[1] One other point may be made in defence of the Admiralty. The French had hustled out before they were ready, and paid a heavy price for being first at sea; the British fleet sailed with healthy crews and adequate provisions.

Hardy put to sea on 16 June with thirty sail of the line, leaving another half dozen nearly ready to follow him. He cruised off Ushant for several days before he learnt for certain that the enemy were indeed away and had been sighted by a neutral off Finisterre. His orders were to follow the French only if it would not expose the British Isles, and otherwise to fall back and wait off the Lizard. There was no sense in crossing the Bay after an enemy who in all probability had long since joined the Spaniards and left the rendezvous; and Hardy returned off the Lizard for news and orders.

The position of Commander-in-Chief of the Home Fleet has often been an uncomfortable one. His was the only command whose operations were subject to daily interference from London. Hardy was spared the wireless communications with which the First Lord plagued Sir Charles Forbes in 1940; but his slow movements and long spells in port exposed him to letters and visits from Sandwich. Like Keppel he was anxious for the protection of specific orders; but this was not the form of Sandwich's directions as the Bourbon fleets approached.

Sandwich's attitude to Hardy must have been influenced by the manner of his appointment. The Keppel affair had deprived the Channel fleet of its Commander-in-Chief and both its commanders of divisions. In Ross, Darby, Digby and Thomas Graves the Admiralty found satisfactory substitutes for Palliser and Harland; but a Commander-in-Chief was less easy to find. Many good officers felt that Keppel had been wronged, and would not take his place. Howe was not even approached, and Mann pleaded poor health. On scanning the list of admirals the King's eye fell on Sir Charles Hardy, Admiral of the White and Governor of Greenwich Hospital, who had offered his services. Hardy was sixty-four, in poor health, and had not been to sea for twenty years. His recommendations were an amiable temper and great seniority, which the government hoped might place him above faction; but to introduce some competence he was compelled to take a seaman of the first order as his Flag Captain. Richard Kempenfelt was an officer whose ability had somehow failed to bring him to the top of his profession.

[1] Keppel, II, 334; Patterson, 105.

He was only two years younger than Hardy, and diffident of the burden which he was to shoulder for the next two years. But his merits were widely known. Middleton had wanted him for the Navy Board: 'Captain Kempenfelt is not merely a sea officer, but a man of deep knowledge in most professions.'[1]

There was much to be said for the choice of Hardy, for a conciliator was needed at that moment. The navy's unity had been torn to shreds by the court-martials, yet Sandwich could not surrender to the opposition and restore the command to Keppel, whom he now feared and distrusted. And Lord Mulgrave reported from the fleet that Hardy was diligent and much liked. But Kempenfelt saw him at closer quarters and was appalled. He found the Commander-in-Chief to be a bad administrator, inaccessible to advice, and no leader. He took no forethought, and did not know the important from the trivial. 'There is a fund of good nature in the man, but not one grain of the Commander-in-Chief. . . . My God, what have you great people done by such an appointment.'[2]

Sandwich had been driven to appoint a Commander-in-Chief in whose ability it was difficult to have confidence. His own nerve had been shaken by the Keppel affair; and in April he suffered a personal sorrow which undermined him further. Martha Ray, the actress, was shot dead at Drury Lane. Germain had lost his wife on the heels of Saratoga: Sandwich now lost his mistress. He had taken her from a milliner's shop sixteen years earlier, when his mad wife had long since left him. She lived in his house, sang at his parties, and bore him two sons. Even the puritan King pitied his loss. 'I am sorry Lord Sandwich has met with any severe blow of a private nature', he wrote to him; ' . . . the world scarcely contains a man so void of feeling as not to compassionate your situation.' Sandwich, 'robbed of all comfort in the world', found himself for a short time unequal to his burdens. A week after the murder, Lord Bristol was due to introduce a motion against him in the House of Lords; and Sandwich had to beg him for the sake of their former friendship to postpone the debate. Bristol, whose days were numbered, used a touch of the gout as a convenient excuse to comply.[3] This generous action shed the only ray of warmth in the weeks which followed the courts-martial.

The effect of these successive blows was betrayed by Sandwich's increasing eagerness to shelter from responsibility behind the Cabinet and the fleet commanders. When Spain entered the war, his colleagues had the greatest difficulty in persuading him to press from exemptions without waiting

[1] G 2209; Sandwich, III, 3, 43.

[2] Sandwich, III 17; Barham, I, 293, 323.

[3] Sandwich, II, 249, 256–8; CL, Lacaita-Shelburne, I (12 April 1779).

for an Act of Parliament, though the fleet at that moment was still under-manned. Even Lord North intervened against delay, and promised the Cabinet's support in obtaining a bill of indemnity.[1] With Hardy Sandwich's loss of nerve led him to the calculated substitution of personal conversations and private letters for official instructions.

3. Suspense in the Channel

The intervention of Spain and the escape of the Brest fleet made Hardy's orders obsolete, and brought a new sharpness of anxiety to the Admiralty's deliberations. He had scarcely sailed, in ignorance of the Spanish declaration on that very day, when intelligence reached the Admiralty from the Consul at Cadiz that the Spanish fleet was ready for sea. Coupled with the Spanish Ambassador's note, the news suggested an overwhelming concentration against Hardy; and on 19 June instructions were drafted that if he found himself too weak to risk a battle he should come up the Channel for orders.

At this the King protested. It was the eve of his address to the Cabinet; and the magnitude of the danger and his ministers' disunity were propelling him into an unusually persistent course of advising on the operations of war. He was convinced of the British fleet's superior quality and morale, and lamented that the draft left so little latitude to Hardy. With such orders, he told Lord Weymouth, and in Hardy's situation, he would instantly return to Torbay. 'I know the zeal and excellence of the fleet under his command; if its spirit is damped it may prevent its acting with that vigour the occasion requires, over caution is the greatest evil we can fall into.' He suggested adding a few words trusting that Hardy would not execute the instructions further than his own judgment made him think absolutely necessary, and desired Lord Weymouth to show his letter to the Cabinet. The instructions went out unaltered, but on 3 July an amendment was sent which followed closely the words the King had suggested.[2]

One may ask, as the fleet clears the Devon coast, how England could hope to hold off the great fleets which were gathering against her. Thirty or forty ships of the line could scarcely face sixty-six in battle; and it may seem that nothing but the enemy's mistakes could save the country. The enemy suffered indeed from sickness, shortages and inexperience, and his weaknesses were guessed. But there were more positive grounds for hope. For d'Orvilliers and Cordoba had been charged with one of the most difficult operations of war. To cover an invasion it was not enough to possess the general command of the sea. They would have to exercise continuous local command of

---

[1] G 2666, 2672–3; Sandwich, III, 26, 28–9.
[2] Thynne Papers, XXXVIII, No. 55; Adm. 2/1336, ff. 30, 34.

the invasion line over the whole period of the landings. If Hardy refused to fight, the unwieldly armada would have to protect the transports in every wind against both the fast two-deckers of Hardy's fleet and the frigates which were charged with their interception.

An active fleet in being might well make the passage too perilous to attempt. And Hardy had one revolutionary asset. By July he had seven swift coppered two-deckers in his fleet. In the late summer of the previous year Keppel had reported fourteen of his ships as foul beyond all hope of over-hauling an enemy, though some of them had been off the ground for less than a year, and another thirteen foul after only six or nine months out of dock. But when Hardy faced the Bourbon fleets in 1779 the experiments of the past nine years were bearing fruit.

In 1770 the hulls of one or two frigates had been experimentally sheathed with copper plates to prevent the growth of barnacles and the boring of the sea-worm. Success came with Middleton's introduction of a preservative to prevent the copper from corroding the iron bolts which held the frames of ships of the line; and just when the intervention of Spain put the British fleet at a hopeless numerical disadvantage, it became possible to increase its real efficiency. 'Twenty-five sail of the line, coppered, will be sufficient to hazard and tease this great, unwieldly, combined armada, so as to prevent their effecting anything.'[1] So Kempenfelt was to write from the Channel in September. England's technological victory was to have immense import-ance in the years to come.

The choice in the weeks which followed was between a position to the westward in the open sea, and one inside the Channel; and to some extent this was also a choice between risking everything on a battle and frustrating the enemy with an active fleet in being. The King was for fighting. Only the Ferrol squadron was known to have joined the French, making an estimated thirty-nine ships of the line against the thirty-two which Hardy had collected by the middle of July; and the King regarded these as fair odds which were unlikely to improve. Middleton, it is true, did not share his optimism, for though seamanship and courage might be on the British side, the letters he was receiving from Kempenfelt made him doubt whether they would enjoy the same pre-eminence in manoeuvring a line of battle. Yet as Pye and Mulgrave pointed out, the larger the fleet the more difficult its manoeuvres, and the enemy had the handicaps of divided nationality, unfamiliarity, and the low standard of manoeuvre of the Spaniards. Mulgrave considered the British fleet to be equal to anything; and Captain Walsingham, whose lean-ings were towards the Keppel faction, shared his confidence.

There was nevertheless much to be said for avoiding battle. The King

[1] Barham, I, 297.

with his taste for Providence might have remembered the *flavit deus* of the Armada medallion: 'God blew with his winds and they were scattered.' The position of the British ports on a lee shore, so hampering when spring convoys were imprisoned by the wind, could be the country's saving when an enemy was master of the Channel. The British could safely keep the seas, knowing that they could find shelter from a south-wester and a retreat for ships damaged in battle. For the French and Spaniards it was otherwise. In a westerly gale they would have no resource but to run up the Channel as the Armada had run two centuries earlier; and a southerly wind might drive them on to the English coast.

Yet till the enemy's plans were known it was not possible to retire inside the Channel and yield the western position. Not only were convoys due from the Caribbean and India: Ireland was vulnerable, and could not be covered by a fleet inside the Channel. Its defences were weaker even than England's, and its internal peace a hundred times more precarious. There were fewer than 10,000 regular troops, and the regiments grew weaker daily, as recruits were outnumbered by deserters whom the civil power refused to apprehend. Nor was their commander, Sir John Irwin, highly regarded. But the King, with the Howe enquiry still on its last legs, refused to remove him and disgrace an amiable man. He suggested instead the device already used in the Channel fleet, of putting in a good subordinate to manage him.[1]

Irish discontent was aggravated by economic troubles. Linen exports to America had been blocked by the war, and the price of black cattle had tumbled when the sale of provisions to the French was banned. Money flowed out to pay the troops abroad and support the absentee landlords who fled from the country's poverty. These troubles made the oppressive trade laws intolerable; and Protestant resentment at their economic fetters rivalled the Catholics' hatred of their religious oppressors. The French and Spaniards were well aware of these troubles. Their agents were in the country, and they had discussed an attack.[2]

For these reasons it was right that Hardy should remain to the westward. At the beginning of July he ran in to Torbay before a westerly gale, learning for the first time that the country was at war with Spain, and was promptly ordered to resume his station west of the Lizard as soon as the weather allowed. Whether he should give battle there was still an open question. 'I sigh for an action', wrote the King, while Middleton urged the postponement of the battle at least till six more ships which were nearly ready could join the fleet. Sandwich fell in with the King's suggestion by writing a personal letter begging Hardy to get to the westward and meet the enemy before they had time to collect their strength. But he emphasised that these were

[1] G 2685, 2687.   [2] See Patterson, 72 ff.

his private views, and not instructions: the Commander-in-Chief must interpret his orders for himself.[1]

Hardy sailed again on 14 July; but by now the enemy's intentions were beginning to take shape. Intelligence from the Norman and Breton coasts showed that the enemy was assembling his invasion shipping inside the Channel at Le Havre and St Malo; and a few days after the fleet's departure reports reached Wentworth's intelligence bureau from Holland and Paris which revealed the Cadiz fleet's intention to join d'Orvilliers, and the strength of the Combined Fleet of the enemy as sixty-six of the line.[2] If this was believed, everything pointed to an overwhelming concentration in the Channel and an invasion of the south coast of England.

The invasion craft were the immediate care of frigate squadrons which the Admiralty had stationed on the flanks of the invasion coast in the Downs and the Channel Islands. Supported by fifty-gun ships, they had been active for some time, and as soon as the enemy transports' assembly points were known, the Jersey squadron had sailed to scour the French coast. At that point Amherst had pressed the Prime Minister to attack the huddled transports, now more vulnerable in their harbours than they might ever be again. His plan to bombard le Havre was examined and turned down by Admiral Mann. But Rodney, who had bombarded the port in 1759, believed that it could be done; and for the next two months his friend Germain pressed for the attempt to be made.[3]

Meanwhile Hardy had chosen a position thirty to sixty miles west-south-west of the Scillies, which he considered the best station to protect the trade and meet the enemy if they tried to come up Channel. Its danger was that they might slip past unseen into the mouth of the Channel, a risk which had to be balanced against the increasingly unlikely threat to Ireland. In the light of the latest intelligence there was something to be said for a position inside the Channel off Start Point, relying on the light forces to prevent the transports in St. Malo from slipping away towards Ireland.

At the end of July there was a last opportunity to consider the fleet's position, for Hardy was blown up Channel again by a gale. The chance was rejected. On the 28th an official letter from the Admiralty regretted that he had been driven so far to the eastward, exposing the East and West India convoys and uncovering Ireland. There was some anxiety that he might come into port, and the Admiralty promised him reinforcements and supplies at sea. The same day Sandwich wrote again privately that his coming into port would arouse 'very extraordinary sensations in this country'. At

[1] Sandwich, III, 40–1, 43.
[2] Sandwich, III, 47; G 2702, 2716; SP 78/306, intelligence of 9 July.
[3] WO 34/230, p. 407; Knox, 162; Sandwich, III, 31, 55.

the same time he was fearful of blame for any misfortune which might result from keeping the fleet to the westward. He emphasised that these were only his private opinions, and that Hardy must act in the light of his own experience. 'Your enemies and mine are watching to take every advantage against us . . .'[1]

On the following day Sandwich was to find better cover in a Cabinet instruction, a form of protection to which he increasingly resorted. The King had already canvassed North, Weymouth and Amherst; and on the morning of the meeting he wrote to the First Lord strongly urging the modification of Hardy's old orders to come into port if he were outnumbered. Most of the reinforcements had now joined the fleet, and there was not enough prospect of additional ships to justify Hardy in delaying the battle, while retreat might damage the fleet's morale. He did not mean that Hardy should be ordered to risk a battle at all events, but that he should be authorised to watch the enemy and exploit an opening. He dreaded the disgrace and political confusion of a retreat into harbour. The Cabinet meeting went as he hoped, and a more positive order went out to Hardy. In view of the threat to England, Ireland and the convoys he was to go to the westward as far as he judged necessary to frustrate the enemy; nor was he to quit his station while his provisions held out unless he were driven off it.[2]

The Leeward Island convoy was spoken on 30 July, and passed safely up the Channel. Germain, watching the naval operations with sardonic detachment, hoped that by then Hardy had resumed his station; 'but I think we have more reason to trust in Providence than in our Admirals'.[3] Hardy was slowly working his way to the westward to resume his station. In spite of the growing indications that the invasion would be inside the Channel, the King at least still feared for Ireland; and his uneasiness was fed by a letter from the Bishop of Derry in Paris and an intercepted Swedish despatch. He was aware that independence would be a powerful bait for the Irish.[4]

Whether Hardy should fight remained an open question. The King still doubted if the whole Spanish fleet was fit to come north to the Channel, and preferred the alternative (and not ill-conceived) theory that it was bound for Gibraltar. Even if he were wrong he still wished for a battle. 'I may appear strange, but I undoubtedly wish for the action and feel a confidence in the success that never attended any other event.'[5] Yet Hardy's orders by no

---

[1] Adm. 2/1333, f. 64; Sandwich, II, 49, 55.
[2] G 2722–3; Adm. 2/1336, f. 46.
[3] Knox, 160.
[4] G 2726, 2728.
[5] G 2717–9; Sandwich, III, 49.

means made clear what he was intended to do. He regarded himself as confined to a defensive station, and his Secretary was writing to urge that he should have positive orders to seek the enemy. Mulgrave wrote from the fleet that he regarded the present position as the best one to cover both Kingdoms and the convoys; but if the fleet was intended to seek the enemy Hardy should have explicit orders from the highest quarters, since nothing less would justify him in leaving the country exposed. These views had not reached London when the Cabinet agreed that if Hardy had any reason to think the enemy intended to avoid an engagement by returning to Brest, he should be free to leave his station and prevent their retreat by battle. This order was sent on 14 August, without delaying to refer the decision to the King. Sandwich excused his haste, 'being unwilling to lose any time, and knowing that your Majesty would not withhold your sanction from any measure that is likely to add to the probability of bringing the fleets to action'.[1]

The Ministry was still acting on the presumption that the odds would be fifty ships of the line against thirty-nine. Mulgrave had supposed that as soon as the Indiamen were safe home Hardy's mission would be to guard the Channel, since all the enemy's preparations seemed to be against England. But on this point no instructions were sent. And soon none were needed. For as the *Marlborough* made her way down Channel on the 15th to join Hardy, she sighted sixty-three enemy ships in the chops of the Channel. Her First Lieutenant was put on board a sloop which ran in to Plymouth; and twenty hours later he was hammering on Sandwich's door at Blackheath.[2]

The First Lord sent off a messenger at once to the Admiralty with orders to summon North, Weymouth and Amherst to London; and expresses dashed off with warnings to the Admirals at Portsmouth and the Downs. By then the enemy fleets were far inside Hardy's position, riding unchallenged off Plymouth Sound.[3]

4. The Plymouth Panic

The worst had happened. For the first time in ninety years an enemy fleet was in possession of the Channel, and the safety of the Kingdom apparently

[1] Sandwich, III, 56–8; G 2741.

[2] Patterson, 181.

[3] G 2742, 2747. The Opposition made much of the Ministers' absence at their country houses for the summer. But they were conforming to custom – a custom which had surprised the French Embassy before the war (Doniol, I, 216, 583 n.). Shelburne's Cabinet continued the practice (see below, p. 482); and in 1799 Pitt's colleagues marked the imminent departure of the hastily gathered expedition to Holland by scattering to their country retreats.

rested on the army. Since Saratoga new regiments and a general augmentation of establishments had brought the home forces up to a more respectable strength. There were about 21,000 regular cavalry and infantry of all ranks in England, backed by 30,000 militia. Amherst had begun to encamp his regulars in May; and on the Spanish declaration tents were ordered to enable the militia regiments which were not on coast duty to take the field.

In making his dispositions Amherst faced the inevitable dilemma of a commander preparing to meet an invasion: the choice between dispersing his force to hold the beaches and keeping them together for a counter-stroke. His solution was concentration and his dispositions much as they had been in 1778. A screen of dragoons patrolled the coast of Kent and Sussex, while the striking force lay back round London: the infantry of the line and militia astride the Thames in Kent and Essex, with the cavalry of the northern force at Colchester; the Household Cavalry and Foot Guards in the capital from which they could move out on either side of the river. This left very little to defend the coast. A battalion thrown forward to Rye and a cavalry regiment at Chichester would impose some delay where landings were most likely; and the naval bases of Portsmouth, Plymouth and Chatham had garrisons and encampments to meet the first onslaught. But beyond Plymouth the coast was almost naked, and Cornwall had only a single regiment of militia.[1]

These arrangements were bound to cause alarm; and it was not confined to country gentlemen whose local beaches were undefended, but extended to the highest quarters. Lord North harried the Commander-in-Chief to strengthen Plymouth and Portsmouth, and even to shift the whole weight of his force to cover London against a landing in Sussex. When the enemy appeared off the coast Sandwich wanted Torbay to be fortified; and later, when Hardy came up the Channel and left the south-west uncovered, North agitated for troops to be moved to the west. But some militia regiments had already gone down to the west, and unlike Hardy in the Channel the Commander-in-Chief of the Army was free to post his forces as he pleased. Throughout the summer he steadfastly refused to weaken his *masse de manoeuvre*. Till the enemy committed his forces, the most critical areas were Kent, Sussex and East Anglia, and the place for the counter-offensive reserve was in the London area. His patrolling dragoons would report a landing immediately, and the army would have to use its mobility to intercept the enemy as he pushed for the capital. To deal with the first impact of a landing at Portsmouth or further west the cavalry south of the Thames were posted at Salisbury; and in August a gentleman was organising a loan of horses to move the infantry rapidly from their camps round London at a

[1] WO 34/112, and CL, Lord North's return books.

moment's notice. Amherst's reply to Sandwich's demand for troops at Torbay sums up the situation with bluntness and force:

Your Lordship must know as well as I do that the number of bays and length of the coast will not admit of defences being made to prevent an enemy from landing, and if they were, your Lordship likewise knows the number of troops will not afford a sufficiency for guarding those defences, besides there are other bays nearer the capital, as likely for an enemy to land in, and it is necessary to consider the whole.[1]

Amherst was confident that if invasion came the people would fly to their country's defence. The Lords-Lieutenant and magistrates were ordered to make arrangements for 'driving the country' in the path of the enemy, and for collecting all able-bodied men at the sound of church bells to dig entrenchments. The Duke of Richmond, who was Lord-Lieutenant of the vital county of Sussex, gave a characteristic display of wrong-headed scruples about these measures; but his attitude did not reflect the tone of the country as a whole. Patriotism was as evident as in other crises. Volunteer companies sprang up everywhere. At Plymouth the gentry greeted the enemy by raising a force to march the prisoners of war inland, and the Cornish gentry sent miners to work on the fortifications. From the behaviour of all classes on the arrival of the Combined Fleets, Amherst felt hopeful[2] that the national resources could beat off any attack.

A different picture has usually been painted, of a panic-stricken population and defenceless ports. It was said by the Opposition, and has been repeated, that the enemy rode within twelve hours of Plymouth for a fortnight, while the batteries guarding the harbour were incapable of resistance for lack of ammunition, gunners and equipment. The source of most of these tales was the garrison commander. While the Governor of Portsmouth put the best face on his difficulties and prepared to do his utmost, the Governor of Plymouth, Lord Waldegrave, was sulking in London because he had been passed over for Commander-in-Chief. Thus the organisation of the defence was left in the hands of three unco-ordinated authorities, the Port Admiral Lord Shuldham, the dockyard commissioner Ourry, and the garrison commander Sir David Lindsay.[3]

Lindsay had revealed himself to Amherst as 'diffident from the beginning',

---

[1] WO 34/115, f. 116; WO 34/118, f. 61; WO 34/231, pp. 190, 254–6; WO 34/232, p. 448.

[2] WO 34/231, pp. 254–6. Hutchinson lamented the general apathy, but he was in London, where he was unlikely to receive a faithful picture.

[3] For the troubles at Plymouth see Patterson, Chaps. VIII, X; J. C. Long, *Amherst*, 264–8; Sandwich, III, 64–83; G 2752–3; WO 34/116, ff. 218 *et seq*; Malmesbury Letters, I, 422, 427, 429.

and would probably have been removed before the crisis but for his connection with Lord Mansfield. He had pestered the Commander-in-Chief for written instructions on the defence of the dockyards, and had talked of disowning responsibility unless the fortifications were strengthened and reinforcements sent. On 10 August he had gone so far as to refuse to give any orders for the defence of the harbour without Amherst's express approval. And still he was not replaced.

When the enemy appeared, there was consternation among the townspeople of Plymouth. The thud of gunfire as a ship of the line ran by mistake into the enemy fleet, followed by the sight of the enemy standing in towards the Sound, was enough to send the shopkeepers and their families scurrying inland. The town with its 4,800 troops and weak fortifications was certainly vulnerable to an attack on the landward side, if the enemy could land a force at Torbay which was strong enough to make the long march and force the many deep defiles on the road; but it was not vulnerable to a *coup de main* by a fleet. Ships could not come within bombarding range of the dockyard till the batteries in the Sound had been silenced by landing parties; and this Amherst had made arrangements to prevent. He had been down at the beginning of July to give the directions which Lindsay demanded, and had ordered the only possible landing places to be blocked with trees and defended by concealed infantry and masked cannon. With three battalions to hold the western shore of the Sound, there was little likelihood that the enemy could land a force capable of seizing the batteries.

So at least thought Sandwich and Middleton; and at Plymouth Admiral Shuldham agreed. But Commissioner Ourry and General Lindsay saw it in a different light. When the enemy stood in towards the Sound, they were convinced that the dockyard would be in Bourbon hands in a matter of hours, and Ourry talked of setting fire to it before the enemy did. He suspended all work in the yards, banded his artificers into companies as the Admiralty had suggested to Shuldham, and demanded the rank of Colonel.[1] A floating boom was built across the harbour with the agreement of Lindsay and Shuldham.

In London, where heads were cooler, these activities caused much dismay. Sandwich was horrified at the thought that Ourry might burn the dockyard; and he shared Middleton's fear that if the Commissioner's military activities continued indefinitely work would cease in the yards. Hard though the Navy Board was pressed, a Commissioner was spared for Plymouth to restrain Ourry's enthusiasm. When he arrived the enemy had gone, and he ordered some labourers back to the yards. On 26 August Shuldham con-

[1] On 15 July the Admiralty had ordered Shuldham in consequence of a letter from Amherst, to train the artificers in military exercises and co-operate in the defence of the dockyard (Adm. 2/107).

ferred with Lindsay, and withdrew the 200 seamen he had lent to man the batteries. At this Lindsay exploded. Though Shuldham promised to restore the gunners if the enemy returned, the General wrote a violent protest at the withdrawal of seamen and artificers. He declared that if they were not restored he would wash his hands of the defence of the place beyond what concerned the troops, and asked to be placed under another general.

It was now plain that Lindsay must go. Amherst and the King did what should have been done before, and obtained Mansfield's approval for Lindsay's exchange with the commander of the north-western district at Whitehaven. But Lindsay refused the exchange, denied that he had intended to resign, and threw up his appointments. To justify his stand he declared that he could not have fired a single gun without the co-operation of the Commissioner and Admiral. He complained of his shortage of troops; but troops were short everywhere, and always had been when England was engaged in serious fighting abroad. His successors were confident that they could put up a stout defence; and the Chief Engineer declared that the batteries were admirably sited, equipped and manned. But Lindsay spread reports that ammunition had been short, though the Ordnance officers at Plymouth denied it; and in the following year he primed the Duke of Richmond for his attack on the state of the Plymouth defences. Had the government had the confidence to break with Lindsay in time at the risk of offending Mansfield, it is unlikely that he would have remained long enough in his command to do such mischief.

5. The End of the Affair

But though the danger at Plymouth was exaggerated and the Ministry knew it, it cannot be said that they were at ease. The King's spirits soared at the prospect of a naval battle: 'Decision is the joy of my life.' But the Cabinet had been completely surprised. The Ministers were outside London; and the fleet was outside the Channel. Hardy had learnt of the enemy's presence on 17 August; but an easterly wind was driving him before it, and by the 25th he was 100 miles beyond the Scillies.

'God grant that you may send me good news in the course of tomorrow', Germain wrote to Knox on the 17th. The disgraced Palliser wrote to Sandwich pointing out the danger that with the easterly wind and Hardy so far to the west the enemy army might make its crossing. He begged the First Lord to take the advice of reliable sea officers, and send frigates off the invasion ports to intercept the transports. This was taken in hand, and on the 23rd Captain Brisbane sailed from the Downs with a squadron of copper-bottomed frigates to scour the invasion coast from Boulogne to

Cherbourg, where he joined Sir Hyde Parker and the force from the Channel Islands.[1]

'No news of Sir Charles Hardy', the embittered Navy Board clerk Robert Gregson wrote to Shelburne. 'I am afraid our fate is sealed . . . delivered up by a set of the most abandoned villains that ever disgraced a nation.' 'Nothing but croaking', Shelburne wrote in the margin.[2] And indeed if the Ministers and the frightened people of Plymouth could have seen what was passing in d'Orvilliers' cabin in the *Bretagne* their minds would have been eased. For the tide was on the turn, and the great armada which seemed to dominate the English coast had reached the limit of its effort. Provisions were low, the sick in the French ships equalled the healthy, and so many dead were going overboard that Devon gave up eating fish. Becalmed off Plymouth, and supposing the British fleet to be in harbour up the Channel, d'Orvilliers was impatient to push on to the Isle of Wight and bring it to action while his own ships were still capable of fighting. But a frigate arrived with orders which put a different light on his task. On 1 August the Spanish Ambassador in Paris had despaired of executing the original plan after the long delays in concentrating the fleets, and persuaded Vergennes to revert to an alternative which had been discussed when d'Orvilliers' instructions were drawn up. Instead of seizing Portsmouth, d'Orvilliers was to land the army at Falmouth when he had cleared the Channel of the enemy, and Marshal Vaux would then overrun and hold Cornwall as a bridgehead through the winter. To enable the fleet to keep the sea through the autumn it would be revictualled by a convoy from Brest.[3]

D'Orvilliers read the new orders with distaste. Instead of a safe anchorage at Spithead, he faced months of cruising on a hostile lee shore, with water and provisions gone, and no real possibility of revictualling at sea whatever the Ministry might hope. Only one chance to salvage the campaign remained: to bring the British fleet to battle and release the French from the prospect of conducting a winter blockade of Plymouth and Portsmouth. The remaining provisions were divided between the ships, extending the fleet's cruising time till the middle of September.

The wind which had driven Hardy beyond the Scillies was neutral; and on 17th August, as the alarm on shore rose to its *crescendo*, the Combined Fleets weighed and ran before it. By the 20th they were fifty miles south-south-west of the Lizard; and here d'Orvilliers wrote to the Minister suggesting the abandonment of the campaign till the following year. But five days later, on 25 August, a passing vessel revealed that Hardy was not up the Channel

[1] CL, Knox, 17 Aug.; Sandwich, III, 63–4, 73; Adm. 2/107, to Sir Hyde Parker.
[2] CL, Shelburne, Vol. 146, No. 145.
[3] Patterson, 150, 205–6.

but in the open sea to the westward. Here lay the last chance of success. A Council of War was summoned in the flagship, and agreed that in view of disease and shortage of supplies the fleets should not re-enter the Channel but seek battle with Hardy: in any event the cruise should end on 8 September and the fleets return to port.

It was on the day after this conference that the wind veered to the south and Hardy began to work his way back towards the Channel. On the 29th he was off the Scillies in thick weather when one of his ships sighted the enemy. They were seen again on the 30th, and on the 31st they sighted Hardy for the first time and gave chase. But by then the British had worked far to the eastward, and the sluggards of the Combined Fleet, especially the Spanish ships, prevented d'Orvilliers from closing. By the following morning Hardy was off the Eddystone and the enemy had vanished, drawn away to the southward by a contact which turned out to be a fleet of Dutch Indiamen.

Hardy's despatch from the Eddystone was the first word of him which the Government had received since the appearance of the enemy. 'I shall do my utmost to draw them up Channel', he wrote; and the Ministers were now happy enough to see him come. They had had a fright, and were thankful to see their fleet inside the enemy and in reach of shelter and reinforcements. Everyone assumed that a battle was inevitable; but even the King now wrote of drawing the enemy towards the narrow waters of the Downs before engaging.[1] Every ship that could swim was pressed into service: the St Albans and Isis, just home from the West Indies and scarcely able to float; Arrogant, listed as unfit for service; Blenheim, reported by Shuldham to be irreparably bad and unfit to leave the harbour; and Amelia, which with the Blenheim had been refused by Keppel in the previous year. Arrogant, Blenheim, and St Albans were all listed as unfit to weather a storm. But everything that could fire a gun was needed. In the first three days of September six ships of the line joined the fleet, bringing its strength to forty-five.

August was out, and Hardy's ships were in immediate need of water. Darby's division which had been at sea since the middle of May was particularly low. Most of the fleet had begun to use their ground tier of water casks, which was only done in case of real necessity; and some ships had only a week's supply on board. The Admiralty's promise to supply beer and water at sea was impracticable, for the fleet's consumption was 150 tons a day. It was therefore absolutely necessary to come in to harbour. Sandwich would have preferred the fleet to remain at the seaward anchorage of St Helen's on the Isle of Wight instead of coming up to Spithead, partly for the sake of appearances and partly because Palliser and Mulgrave feared that it might be blockaded or attacked at anchor in Spithead. But Hardy came

[1] Sandwich, III, 62, 80, 86–7.

boldly up to the inner anchorage; and Middleton and Kempenfelt thought he was right. The fleet could replenish five times as fast at Spithead; and Kempenfelt saw no reason why it should not go out from there in line of battle if the enemy appeared.[1]

The politicians' chief reason for preferring St Helen's was their fear of public opinion. Hardy's retreat up the Channel, though fully justified, had created the image of a British fleet flying before the enemy; and the withdrawal to Spithead did nothing to improve appearances. Though North and the King did justice to Hardy's resolution in defying public clamour to speed the replenishment of his stores, all were anxious to see him away again. Mulgrave suggested from Spithead that Sandwich might come down in person again; and with the King's blessing he hustled off on the day after Hardy's arrival. His purpose was partly to discover the real state of the fleet and speed its provisioning; but also, as he said himself, to enforce the Ministry's views without committing it to any official correspondence at this critical moment. Thus for the third time in the campaign the First Lord sheltered behind an unofficial communication: if the fleet put to sea before it was ready, or gave battle and suffered defeat, no one should be able to say that Hardy had been forced to act against his better judgment. For all his ability Jemmy Twitcher in a fright cannot have been much loved by his admirals.[2]

Sandwich reached Portsmouth at 9.30 on the morning of 5 September. Mulgrave was waiting for him at the Commissioner's office, and they had a talk before Sandwich went out to see Hardy at Spithead. He found the Commander-in-Chief apparently eager to get to sea, and was convinced by Kempenfelt of the necessity of coming in to Spithead. The First Lord explained to Hardy 'many public and private reasons why he should not continue here', and returned to Portsmouth determined to stay till he saw the fleet depart. The next two days were devoted to the Victualling Office, whose operations Sandwich hoped he had quickened. He caught sight of several Opposition politicians poking about and fishing for information. Perhaps, like Keppel, they saw in his activity 'the affected appearance of despatch, with which the present First Lord of the Admiralty has so often covered his real neglect'.[3]

The spirit of the fleet seemed better than might have been expected from the feuds of the spring. Sandwich's informants were mainly his own friends; but Captain Walsingham, who was regarded as a Keppelite, wrote to him most warmly and declared that all party was laid aside. But, he added,

[1] G 2759, 2762, 2763; Sandwich, III, 59, 61.
[2] G 2759, 2764; Sandwich, III, 91, 96.
[3] G 2763; Keppel, II, 338.

'give us a man to command us that we have confidence in'. Here he put his finger on the trouble. There was little wrong with the fleet that a strict and trusted commander could not have cured. 'The fleet', said Kempenfelt, 'wants a sensible, active and strict officer at the head of it, to brace up relaxed discipline, to give alertness and activity to it, in which consists the great part of its force. There is none of that ardour remains now that upon extraordinary occasions urged everyone to try to have his ship first ready; but there is a supine languour and indifference reigns now: it is the epidemic disorder of the nation. . . .' Perhaps the Channel fleet was always too near to home comforts and Westminster politics to achieve the high polish that the best commanders could put on squadrons abroad. Perhaps even Hawke had failed here, for when Anson took over the Channel fleet in 1758 he was disappointed in the standard of discipline and manoeuvring which that renowned though unpopular commander had achieved.[1]

All this activity at Portsmouth was misdirected. For on the day when Hardy anchored at Spithead, the Combined Fleet was ordered home and turned for Brest. Thus ended the invasion of 1779, a prey to careless preparation and disjointed planning. But the government continued to agitate for the Channel fleet to sail, in ignorance of the enemy's departure. The fleet's replenishment became so drawn out that Sandwich could not wait to see it completed, and returned to London with its commander's promise that it would begin to drop down to St Helen's as soon as a dozen ships were ready. Hardy, however, remained at anchor throughout September, and even the Admiralty's efforts to get him as far as St Helen's were frustrated. Early in October he met a firm order to move down from Spithead with a declaration signed by his flag officers that so large a fleet could not use the seaward anchorage so late in the year. Yet we shall see that the Channel fleet had not finished its cruising, and that it might have done better service in port preparing for future operations than in vain patrolling of the Channel when the enemy had vanished for the winter.

[1] Barham, I, 295, 297–8; Sandwich, III, 17, 46, 92; G 2763, 2767.

PART FOUR

THE EDGE OF THE KNIFE
1780

CHAPTER XVII

TOWARDS THE CARIBBEAN

1. *Lord North and the People*

'Never did a deeper political gloom overspread England, than in the autumn of 1779.' Looking back on the crisis, Wraxall questioned whether the Dutch in the Medway or the defeat off Beachy Head had caused such despondency and discontent. The enemy's command of the Channel, the loss of St Vincent and Grenada, and d'Estaing's threat to Jamaica were misfortunes which might have made a Chatham falter. And soon political agitation at home was to erupt into new channels with dangerous violence. A storm was brewing such as the Ministry had never yet encountered.

On 10 September Lord North wrote to ask Germain for his advice on future diplomacy and strategy. But in the same letter he asked an ominous question of another kind. How could the Ministry be strengthened to meet the coming session of Parliament? The Ministry's future lay very much in the hands of Germain. The deadlock over the vacant Secretaryship of State was still unresolved. Wedderburn and Eden were hoping to bring in a professional diplomatist, Sir Joseph Yorke or Lord Stormont, who they imagined might be more accessible to their influence than a politician; and to Stormont the King and North inclined. But the Bedfords' protégé Lord Carlisle was still unbeneficed. There were signs that the Bedford group might desert the Ministry; so it was more than ever vital to conciliate Gower over his son-in-law. If Germain would surrender the Board of Trade, Carlisle could be provided for. Some tiny grain of resolution had momentarily asserted itself in the Prime Minister, and this was the purpose of his approach to Germain.

Germain could have been bought out with a peerage, but the King would not hear of it. 'He has not been of use in his department, and nothing but the most meritorious service could have wiped off his former misfortunes.' This ungenerous allusion had nothing to do with Germain's handling of the war. The King assessed his servants primarily by their political usefulness; and Germain's rash handling of the Howes had temporarily annoyed him. But while he vetoed the easy solution, he did push North into stating his difficulty candidly to Germain. Germain grumbled that Carlisle's promotion following on his peace mission would raise the expectations of the Americans; but after a token resistance he gave way, and the Board of Trade was at

Carlisle's disposal. The Board's revival as a separate institution was successfully attacked in the great campaign against sinecures which was soon to come.[1]

The way was now clear, and the King was anxious to have the business settled. But North had lapsed into nerveless procrastination. He let Carlisle leave London without getting his acceptance of the Board of Trade; and though Sandwich implored Robinson not to leave the Prime Minister's side till he had acted, North himself slipped out of London without seeing Stormont or writing to Carlisle. In the meantime a fresh blow had fallen. On being told of the proposed arrangements, Lord Gower had stopped North short with his own resignation from the Lord Presidency of the Council.[2]

Gower's reason was the Ministry's intolerable weakness and evasion, particularly in its handling of a crisis which was rapidly developing in Ireland. Soon afterwards he told the House of Lords that he had presided for years at the Council table, and had seen such things pass of late that no man of honour or conscience could sit there. He had supported the American War on principle, confident that the country's resources were equal to the effort; 'but to profit by those resources, energy and effect must be restored to government'.[3] Lord Weymouth followed Gower into retirement; and there seemed to be a general conspiracy of the Bedfords to force the King to give up North. Inside the Ministry, too, a hostile front was forming against the Prime Minister. Rigby and Wedderburn ran him down in conversation; and when Stormont entered the Cabinet he united with Thurlow in such a display of hostility that it scarcely seemed possible for North to sit with them. Nevertheless Thurlow, the most formidable of the Bedford group, did not follow his leaders out of office. The youngest member of the Cabinet, he had succeeded Bathurst as Lord Chancellor in 1778. Tough, intractable and outspoken, he was respected by the King for his energy and straightforwardness. In turn he respected Germain, but disliked Sandwich and despised the Prime Minister. His loyalty to the Ministry in the autumn of 1779 was of great importance.

The key to the Ministry's disunion was their despair of North. All were sure that the Government was less unpopular than the Opposition, and could survive with a draught of fresh blood. But as early as August North's behaviour on the Irish question had convinced Robinson that the Administration would 'blow up' as soon as Parliament re-assembled. 'Nothing done,

---

[1] G 2626, 2631, 2657, 2770-1, 2788; Sackville, II, 138-9, 141, 145. By 1780 Germain had recovered the King's confidence (see e.g. Walpole, Last Journals, II, 405, 413).

[2] G 2777, 2780, 2791; Abergavenny, 26.

[3] Parl. Hist., XX, 1176.

or attempting to be done, no attention to the necessary arrangements at home, none to Ireland, nothing to India, and very little I fear to foreign affairs, a Cabinet totally disjointed, *hating* I may say, but I am sure not loving each other, never acting with union even when they meet, looking forward with anxiety to the moment of their parting, can never do, can never direct the great affairs of the Kingdom. . . . Indeed my dear Sir it must blow up.' North still had spirits enough for eating and amusements, but none for business; and when he was pressed to deal with Ireland and India he complained that all his time was taken up in the Treasury, and 'fell into one of his distressing fits'. His temper seemed so altered that Robinson had much to endure from him.[1]

The King knew that he might be forced to approach sections of the Opposition, and in the autumn he actually drew up instructions for Thurlow to open negotiations. But he was still convinced that North could survive if he wished to. He must cast off his indecision, answer letters, canvas measures thoroughly before he launched them, and then push them through with decision. The will to survive was the King's; and by holding the Ministry together he harnessed the fortunes of the monarchy to the broken spirit of North.

For a moment North grew more cheerful. He seemed willing to go on, and two of his friends were appointed to replace Gower and Weymouth: Lord Hillsborough to the Southern Department, and Lord Bathurst to the Lord Presidency. So, with Stormont at the Northern Department, the patching of the Ministry was complete. But it added little political strength or administrative talent. Bathurst had been the least able Chancellor of the century and was now old and frail. Hillsborough was a King's Friend with a long career of public service; but though George III liked his creed he thought less of his abilities. 'I do not know a man of less judgment', he wrote; and summing up his servants after the fall of the Ministry: 'Lord Hillsborough always put things off to the last minute, and though an amiable man [was] the least a man of business I ever knew.'[2] The ablest of the new men was Stormont, a good scholar who spoke with grasp and precision. But his manner was stiff and constrained, and he lacked the political experience to lead in the House of Lords or the personality to dominate a crisis.

This was the team with which North went forward into the most difficult parliamentary session of his career. As November drew on his spirits drooped again, and he began to talk of his inadequacy and the need to retire while

[1] Add. MSS. 38212, ff. 57-8, 61-2, 201-2.
[2] Abergavenny, 15; G 3588.

the going was good. The difficulty as always was to know if he meant it. The King was mystified, and even Jenkinson believed for a moment that he would resign. But more cheerful thoughts broke through. 'I look upon all this', Jenkinson told the King, 'as nothing permanent, but as a disease of the mind, which goes and comes; and which as long as it lasts, is very unpleasant to those who have anything to do with him.'[1] Robinson's accounts of the distracted Prime Minister were certainly alarming; but Jenkinson thought there was more duplicity in North than Robinson allowed. He suspected that the Prime Minister's aim was to be able to say that the King had prevented him from retiring, and thus to throw the blame for every calamity on the royal shoulders.

On 1 December North was brought to the point of declaring that he would retire so that the Ministry could be broadened. Thurlow was unleashed, and approached Shelburne: he was repelled with contempt. The Opposition had good reason to despise the offer; for at that moment the neglected Irish problem came home to roost. The Lord-Lieutenant had sent over a mass of statistics in the summer so that the troubles of the Irish economy could be examined in London. But the idea of opening markets to Irish goods aroused a storm of opposition from the English manufacturing towns; and North promptly turned his back on the difficulty. In August and September Robinson failed completely to make him tackle it, and it was not till Gower resigned and Thurlow bared his teeth that the papers from Dublin were examined. In October work was begun in earnest by Robinson and Jenkinson; yet still neither they nor North treated the question as seriously as it deserved. Still North ridiculed the vagueness of the Irish demand for free trade as though no data had reached him; and still Robinson complained of the Lord-Lieutenant frittering away his majority in the Irish Parliament. On 15 November rioting broke out in Dublin. For two days the Crown's supporters were not safe in the streets. There was talk of challenging the ban on Irish wool imports with a shipment; and the situation was rapidly drifting towards a Boston Tea Party.[2]

Behind the movement stood the Volunteers. The summer's threat of invasion had produced a spontaneous Volunteer movement throughout Ireland. With some diffidence the Government had supplied them with arms, and a force was created whose opinions carried more weight than subservient votes in Dublin. Squeezed between English Protectionists and Irish Volunteers, the Ministry yielded to force. On 5 December the Cabinet resolved to grant concessions so generous that even the Irish were surprised. Papers which should have been studied months before were digested in a

[1] G 2854.
[2] See Butterfield, *George III, Lord North and the People*, Chap. IV.

feverish rush, and on the 13th the bill was introduced. But commercial concessions were no longer enough. Already Grattan was leading the Irish on in the wake of America with a demand for legislative independence.

Nor did concessions to Ireland silence the English Opposition. North's apathy had allowed the Ministry to drift into their enemies' net. 'Damn him,' said Thurlow, 'nothing can goad him forward, he is the very clog that loads everything.'[1]

From the beginning of the session Rockingham and Shelburne had been assailing the system by which George III underpinned the toppling Ministry. In the efforts of Jenkinson and Robinson they professed to find a secret and unconstitutional influence at work to increase the power of the Crown. In the Commons Fox rose to a crescendo of intemperate denunciation which was to do lasting damage to his career. He compared the King with Henry VI for his failures, and with James II for his arbitrary ambitions, and he talked darkly of the subject's right of rebellion. Early in December the two Opposition parties announced that they had joined forces, melting into one mass to rally public opinion against the power of the Crown.

The public was suddenly a reality. In 1779 the price of wheat touched one of the lowest points of the century, and the farming interest embarked on one of its cyclical Poujadist agitations against high taxation. At a great meeting in York the gentry erupted into radicalism, carrying the smaller freeholders with them. Their targets were abuses in public expenditure, the increasing power of the Crown, and the unrepresentative character of Parliament. An Association with a permanent committee was formed; twenty-eight counties and many cities followed the Yorkshire example; and a project for a national assembly or anti-Parliament took shape.

Like the Irish movement, the English Associations had a dangerous American parallel in the Congress system; and the scheme had quasi-revolutionary foundations which challenged the whole structure of oligarchical politics. But this aspect of the movement foretold the future rather than moulded the present. For the Ministry, the immediate danger was the junction of public agitation and parliamentary opposition, of the general clamour for 'economical reform' with the Rockinghams' grudge against the royal influence which excluded them from power. Burke now brought forward a plan of reform which would, by a double stroke, check public extravagance by cutting away the archaic tangle of sinecures and pensions, and simultaneously destroy the chief sources of ministerial patronage. With Burke and Fox at its head, the parliamentary offensive stormed forward into 1780.[2]

[1] Christie, 5.
[2] See Butterfield, Chap. VI.

2. A Case for Boldness

For Ministers burdened with the conduct of a great war, the political crisis was a heavy additional load. Their health and energy were taxed by long nights of exhausting parliamentary debate, and in office hours their attention was distracted by domestic problems. When Colonel Stuart arrived from America at the end of November he found the American Secretary and his colleagues entirely occupied with Ireland, and had great difficulty in getting their attention for Clinton's views on America.[1] The war planning that autumn was done in a disruptive atmosphere of political confusion.

But we must turn to the origins of the autumn planning in September. The approaching equinox heralded the end of the crisis in home waters, and statesmen could lift their eyes from daily alarms and take a longer view. The operations of the home fleet would soon be over, and fresh dispositions could be planned for the winter: dispositions which would shape the war in distant theatres for a year to come. The need to plan was brought home at the beginning of September by the return from the Leeward Islands of Admiral Barrington, radiating gloom about the state of the fleet and broadcasting his view that every island which the enemy attacked would fall. A few days later North invited the views of Sandwich on future naval operations, and of Germain on foreign policy and strategy.

The Prime Minister thus appeared to take the initiative. But it is possible that he was prompted by the King, who was pressing him hard at the time to settle the question of the vacant offices. King George was deeply worried by the absence of leadership. 'The mode in which Cabinet meetings are now conducted distresses me very much', he told Sandwich, 'and is the cause of numberless delays and ill-humour.' At any rate he did not intend to leave the strategic enquiry to the exertions of North, and he stepped in to quicken the machinery. He wrote to Lord Sandwich asking him to produce a firm plan within the week, which they could hammer out with Amherst before it went to the Cabinet. He filled out the letter with a brief lecture on sharing responsibilities: Ministers should take a firm part and risk something to save the Empire. Sandwich protested that he would never hang back; but Cabinet questions should be brought to a decision, and then reduced to writing as they had been in the past. He told the King that he had written to North recommending firmness and decision, and begging him to take the lead in the Cabinet. Whatever North may have lacked, it was not advice.[2]

---

[1] Wortley, 146 (misdated).

[2] Sandwich, III, 97, 143, 164; Sackville, II, 138–9; Butterfield, 70. Sandwich's virtuous protestation, however, should be compared with the motive for the visit to Portsmouth from which he had just returned (see above p. 296).

The enquiry which followed was the first systematic review of strategy since the intervention of Spain three months earlier. At that time it had been decided to hold on in America and to harass the Spaniards sporadically with local forces in the Caribbean and the Gulf of Mexico. But these had been interim decisions taken under the shadow of invasion. That danger was receding, and there would be some force in hand for a stronger policy.

The past summer had seen a gradual deterioration in the strategic situation: a narrowing everywhere of the margin of safety. The effect of Spanish enmity had been most immediately apparent in the Channel. There disaster had been staved off; but everywhere the pressure was slowly mounting. In the Mediterranean, Gibraltar was blockaded and Minorca threatened. In the West Indies, St Vincent and Grenada had been lost, and the command of the sea in the Leeward Islands had passed, if only temporarily, to the French. The next twelve months would see a gradual stretching of British resources. In America the effort had reached its peak, and there could be no expansion; nor was any change of plan proposed. The design of piecemeal reabsorption which Clinton had been given in January 1779 was the final one. No longer was each succeeding New Year to bring a revision: the course was set, and the British army was marching on the road to Yorktown.

The Cabinet did not wholly share Barrington's alarm for the Leeward Islands, for d'Estaing had gone and was supposed (though wrongly) to be returning to Europe. Nevertheless the Cabinet began to give the West Indies the prior claim to reinforcements. On this there was general agreement. But on the scale of the effort two views emerged: the cautious and the bold.

The case for boldness was put in a powerful memorandum by Middleton.[1] He was convinced that the war could be won only in the West Indies; that the whole of the Lesser Antilles were in peril; and that if Jamaica were lost the entire war effort would be undermined. The defence of the islands had always rested on naval superiority. This had been lost in the course of the summer; and unless ships could be found to restore it, a very large force of troops would have to be sent to strengthen the garrisons. But Middleton preferred a bolder policy. The offensive had always paid in the islands: 'to this we owe all our success in the last war'. If a large reinforcement was needed for defence, a larger one could take the French base at Martinique and end the danger for good.

The proposal aligned Middleton with Germain and the King as an opponent of half-measures and over-insurance, and its wisdom was shown by the recent loss of St Vincent in the presence of a superior British fleet. The King had grasped the central truth of the British situation, that the

[1] Undated version in Sandwich, III, 172; and a copy in CL, Shelburne, wrongly endorsed 'June 1779'.

threat of invasion at home must be boldly outstared: 'We must risk something, otherwise we shall only vegetate in this war. I own I wish either to get through it with spirit, or with a crash be ruined.' Instead of keeping its battle fleets in the Channel, the country must be willing to fight on the beaches; only thus could the ships be found to save the West Indies and the initiative be restored to England. Germain shared his feelings: a tame defensive war would be fatal.[1]

The opposition came, as the cautious view so often does in war, from the heads of the armed services. Amherst and Sandwich still feared for the British Isles. Amherst favoured an offensive in the West Indies very strongly; yet his strategist's instinct for seizing the initiative abroad struggled with his desire as Commander-in-Chief to hoard troops in his own command. He would spare no troops from England: the offensive should be fed by Clinton, who might switch troops southwards from Halifax and Rhode Island for the winter. He added that if Americans could be persuaded to join in plundering and settling the Spanish islands, the foundations might be laid for a reconciliation with the rebel colonies: precisely the scheme which the French had professed to fear from the start of the rebellion.[2] The King, however, took the wider view. Troops should be spared from home; and if the enemy fleet in Brest dispersed, the operation of reinforcing the West Indies should be combined with the relief of Gibraltar and Minorca.

But Amherst's doubts were echoed by Sandwich. The First Lord's attention was still riveted on the English Channel; and when his views were called for he was actually at Portsmouth trying to hurry Hardy's fleet to sea. His answer was a long apologia for the navy's weakness. He admitted that the condition of the Leeward Islands fleet was deplorable, and Jamaica in deadly peril; but he would spare no ships till the Channel operations were over. Like Amherst he could only suggest detaching ships and troops from America; and as for Gibraltar, they would have to try their luck with a small convoy or single ships running the Spanish blockade. 'We ought in my opinion to husband our strength and employ it only on those services which are of the most importance, and have a probability of being attended with success.'[3]

'The most important services' were precisely the question of strategic priorities on which the advocates of the offensive based their case. But in this war the departments too often overbore the Cabinet. Sandwich returned to London bearing a promise from Hardy to sail as soon as possible; and though the Admiral put off the moment as long as he could, he was ordered out to the mouth of the Channel early in October on intelligence that the

[1] Sandwich, III, 143; G 2773; Sackville, II, 141–2.
[2] Add. MSS. 38212, f. 96; G 2780.
[3] G 2776.

enemy were lying in the inner roads at Brest.[1] Till the middle of November forty sail of the line were cruising to cover the inbound trade, a mission more fit for frigates and a few coppered two-deckers.

This autumn cruise was ordered in the teeth of the Comptroller's advice. When the winter's strategy was first debated, Middleton had implored Sandwich not to prolong the Channel operations, but to bring in the foulest ships at once and leave the seas to a fast coppered squadron. He reminded him how Keppel's autumn cruise in 1778 had retarded the preparations in the spring, and that unless the refits could be spread over the winter the Navy Board would be swamped and the same delays repeated.[2] And more than this: till the Channel fleet was recalled, Gibraltar and the West Indies could not be succoured. Whether Sandwich acted from fear of an increasingly unlikely invasion, or dread that the loss of a convoy might further weaken his political position, the decision to prolong the Channel operations was evidently his own. A strong Prime Minister or Secretary of State was needed to overrule the partial views of the Service Ministers. North by temperament and Germain from his political solitude were unable to give the lead.[3]

3. The Rodney Expedition

The views of the war ministers were laid before the Cabinet on 16 September, and a compromise plan was accepted. As Amherst and Sandwich had urged, the West Indies were to be strengthened in the first instance from North America by ordering Arbuthnot to detach three ships of the line. Four ships of the line which were preparing for service in England would be sent under Rodney to throw a convoy into Gibraltar and proceed to the Leeward Islands; and when the Channel fleet returned from its cruise (which Sandwich said could not be till two months from its sailing date) five or six more coppered ships would follow them. The total reinforcement of ships should thus be at least a dozen. For military reinforcements the Cabinet also turned in the first instance to America: Clinton should be ordered to send what he could spare. But at all events 5,000 men should be sent, and if Clinton could not find them, the Cabinet would have to consider later what troops might be sent from England with the Channel ships.[4]

This plan was agreed in an atmosphere of tempered optimism; for if d'Estaing really returned to Europe, the British fleet in the Leeward Islands would enjoy a powerful superiority in the winter. About the 25th, however,

---

[1] Adm. 2/1336, f. 62.   [2] Sandwich, III, 177.

[3] Anson had insisted on autumn cruising in 1759, but the object was blockade and battle, not the aimless cruising which was all that Hardy could attempt.

[4] G 2776, 2781. At this point the Cabinet was unaware of Clinton's intention to attack Charleston.

intelligence arrived from the Channel Islands that, far from coming home, d'Estaing's fleet had gone north from the Lesser Antilles to San Domingo and probably from there to America. A merchantman spoken off Beachy Head confirmed the news; and though North remained sceptical, Germain faced the reality: if d'Estaing was at San Domingo, Jamaica was in peril.[1] He was in no panic, for he doubted if the French troops at San Domingo could conquer Jamaica before relief arrived; and in the meantime Grant and Byron could profit by d'Estaing's removal from the Leeward Islands to take the offensive as they had been ordered.[2]

Nevertheless Germain anticipated an uproar at home. Urging Clinton to spare troops for the West Indies in the winter, he added: 'Such a mark of attention to the security of the sugar colonies would give great pleasure to all ranks in this country.' He was right. The London sugar interest was in arms against and clamouring for immediate and effectual protection. The merchants reasoned from the loss of St Vincent and Grenada that a naval force alone was not enough, and demanded a large reinforcement of troops for Jamaica. But the government's attempts to soothe their fears ran into an embarrassing obstacle. When ships had been engaged and provisioned for a large draft of recruits, Amherst disavowed the War Office's instructions, and stood the fire of the whole Cabinet by refusing to send more than 200 men.[3]

Worse was to follow. On 8 October a report arrived from France that 6,000 troops were embarking for the Caribbean. So alarmed was William Knox that he composed a memorandum for Germain which he headed momentously 'Peace or War'. He argued that unless ships and troops could be spared immediately from home defence to reinforce the West Indies England could not face another campaign against the combined power of the Bourbons. If help could not be sent at once, there was only one thing to do: England must buy a separate peace with Spain.[4]

Soon after he received this note, Germain made an overture to Madrid; and we shall see that Knox's paper signalled an important strategic development. In the meantime preparations to help the islands began. A battalion was ordered to embark in the next Jamaica convoy; and on the day after Knox had written his memorandum Germain ordered the Admiralty to prepare 10,000 tons of shipping within a month; evidence perhaps that the Leeward Islands were now thought too vulnerable to be left to Clinton's

---

[1] Sandwich, III, 145; G 2786; CL, Clinton, 28 Sept. from de Grey; Sackville, II, 145; Knox, 162.

[2] CL, Germain, 8 Oct. to Gov. Burt.

[3] CL, Germain, 27 Sept. to Clinton; 30 Sept., 15 and 18 Oct. from West India interests; CO 137/75, ff. 64, 100, 128–31; WO 34/232, p. 58; Knox, 163.

[4] CL, Knox, IX, 28 (memo of 14 Oct.).

care.[1] Nevertheless the assembly of the relief proceeded with painful slowness. The first intelligence that the Combined Fleet was dispersing arrived about 20 October by a ship bound from Oporto to Ireland; and a week later the Cabinet asked Sandwich to produce his plan to relieve Gibraltar, and ordered secret preparations to be pushed on with all speed under cover of the West India reinforcement.

The great convoy with which Rodney was to relieve Gibraltar and the West Indies consisted of three separate parts: storeships and a battalion of troops for Gibraltar; the outward bound Jamaica trade, in whose ships the merchants had found room for a battalion and recruits to strengthen the island; and a battalion for the Leeward Islands, the first échelon of a larger force whose commander, General Vaughan, sailed with the convoy. The plan proposed by Sandwich was that Rodney should detach the West India shipping with a frigate escort at a safe distance from Brest, and proceed himself with the Gibraltar transports to the Straits. After forcing the Spanish blockade, he should leave the convoy to unload, and proceed with his squadron to the West Indies.

The escort to Gibraltar was at first intended to consist of Rodney's four ships of the line, with a fifth which would be dropped at Gibraltar to meet the homeward trade. But Sandwich rightly feared on reflection that five ships would not be enough to break the blockade, and suggested that Rodney should be accompanied as far as the Straits by a detachment from the Channel fleet. This was approved with the rest of the plan at a Cabinet meeting on 4 November. But the decision had serious implications for the timetable. If the expedition was not to be held up, the Channel ships would have to be brought in at once to prepare; but unhappily a frigate had returned a few days earlier from reconnoitring Brest, and reported that the Combined Fleet still intended an invasion. In spite of the advancing winter and the probability that some of Cordoba's ships had already gone home to Cadiz, the Cabinet agreed not weaken the Channel fleet. More weeks were lost before intelligence arrived from Brussels on 20 November that the French invasion army was to disperse. At last the Admiralty acknowledged the improbability of invasion and recalled the Channel fleet. Seventeen sail of the line under Admiral Digby began their preparations to accompany Rodney to Gibraltar.[2]

It would be wrong to omit the Prime Minister's contribution to these

[1] CO 5/254, f. 151.
[2] CL, Germain, 20 Oct.; Sandwich, III, 185-8; G 2837; WO 34/120, f. 140; WO 34/232, ff. 59-60; Adm. 2/1336, f. 68. The Combined Fleet was reported to have disarmed ten sixty-fours, but only in order to complete the crews of their larger ships (WO 34/186, f. 75).

arrangements. Money was needed to pay the Gibraltar garrison; but the army's grants for the year were exhausted, and a large number of bills drawn by the troops in America were due for payment before the meeting of Parliament. After much fussing the Treasury resolved the difficulty by borrowing from the civil list. This shuffling of accounts is North's only recorded intervention in the planning which followed his initial call for ideas. He did suggest timidly that Paul Jones's raiders in the Texel should be watched by a superior force; but this was so ill received by Sandwich that he hastily disavowed the idea and attributed it to Robinson.[1]

Rodney's force was slowly gathering on the south coast. To prevent a leakage, the troops and stores for Gibraltar were embarked under orders from the American Department as though for the West Indies, whither the pay for the Gibraltar garrison was also consigned. No officers belonging to the regiments at Gibraltar were sent with the convoy; and even the coal for the garrison was not procured directly from the usual Gibraltar contractor. Rodney's open orders were for the Leeward Islands, and the whole Gibraltar convoy was to be diverted at sea by sealed orders from the Southern Department. These precautions were so carefully followed that Amherst feared that the regiment for Gibraltar would be carried off to the Caribbean. Yet he need not have feared: Rodney's destination was widely reported in Portsmouth.[2]

Rodney was suffering from gout, and his comments on the dockyard were biting. Early in December he went out to Spithead in his flagship *Sandwich*. She was a veteran of the Seven Years War, and her main battery had been reduced from 32- to 24-pounders. Her fitting-out had been negligent, and neither officers nor men could sleep dry; but Rodney hotly (though privately) refuted the Opposition's contention that she was unfit for service. He was anxious to be off. Spithead was all noise and hurry, he told his wife: there was not a fraction of the trouble and work at sea.

All this time unpleasant though contradictory rumours of the enemy were flying about. D'Estaing was said to have left the West Indies for America, which was the truth; but a Bristol privateer brought news that he had attacked Jamaica. Down at Bath Knox exhausted his lungs in combating the story; but in London there was no escaping the clamour. On 8 December a meeting of Jamaica planters and merchants petitioned for a strong Jamaica squadron, pointing out the island's inability to get a message to windward to the Lesser Antilles if the French attacked. Germain promised that every-

[1] G 2817, 2836; Sandwich, III, 108.
[2] G 2836; CO 318/6, 6 Dec.; Adm. 2/108, 8 Dec.; Adm. 2/1336, 9 Dec.; Sandwich III, 185 n.; Knox, Extra-Official State Papers, I, 15–16.

thing would be done, and the same day Rodney's sailing orders directed him to relieve Jamaica if it were necessary. 'For God's sake', the First Lord exhorted him privately, 'go to sea without delay. You cannot conceive of what importance it is to yourself, to me, and to the public, that you should not lose this fair wind.' He begged him not to wait till all the Channel ships were fully provisioned and every frigate ready. Two frigates which arrived from Quebec, with sails and rigging much worn, and leaky decks and upper works, were thrown into the force for Gibraltar without a refit. 'I must once more repeat to you', Sandwich wrote again, 'that any delay in your sailing will have the most disagreeable consequences.' [1]

But out at Spithead there was still much to do. Ten ships were still short of provisions, and moderate weather was needed to victual them, while the frigates from Quebec had to complete their provisions from ships not under sailing orders. On the 11th it was blowing hard from the south-west: 'Ministers and merchants are eager to have me gone,' wrote Rodney, 'but I cannot command the seasons.' Still delays continued. But at last, three days from the end of the year, the vast fleet put to sea. Twenty-two sail of the line and thirty-nine victuallers and storeships were dropping down the Channel with the trade. The New Year was to dawn on the first naval successes of the war, seeming to herald the approach of victory in America. [2]

4. Pressure on Spain

Rodney's expedition had been assembled in an atmosphere of haste and alarm; but before it put to sea the dangers were beginning to dissolve. The great French reinforcement for the West Indies had not materialised; and in the Western Atlantic the alarm caused by d'Estaing's descent on the American coast had been dissipated. His repulse at Savannah was now known, his fleet was believed to have been shattered in a storm on leaving the American coast, and he had himself returned to Brest. The situation beyond the Atlantic was therefore stabilised. In the Leeward Islands Hyde Parker, with sixteen sail of the line, enjoyed an overwhelming superiority as a result of d'Estaing's departure, and could well spare some help for Jamaica if it was needed; and Rodney's reinforcement was on its way in advance of anything which might be sent out from Brest. [3]

In this happier atmosphere the Cabinet's ideas expanded. The news from

---

[1] Mundy, I, 205–6; Adm. 2/1336, 8 Dec.; G 2876; WO 34/122, f. 26; CO 137/75, ff. 206, 217.

[2] G 2873; Mundy, I, 209; Adm. 2/108, pp. 101–3.

[3] CL, Germain, 12 Dec. to Admiralty, and 17 Dec., deposition of prisoner; Add. MSS. 38212, f. 297; G 2883, 2885, 2887.

Savannah arrived on 20 December; and on Christmas Eve a full Cabinet not only confirmed the existing arrangement to send 5,000 troops to the Leeward Islands, but resolved to launch a new undertaking: 3,000 additional men with landing craft should be sent to Jamaica to attack the Spanish Main.[1]

This decision is often treated as a senseless dispersion of effort at a moment when England was hard pressed throughout the world; and it is true that it made the reinforcement of Canada impossible and threw the burden of aiding Haldimand on to the tautly stretched army of Clinton.[2] Yet to understand the Jamaican project one must look beyond the needs of particular theatres to the total picture of England's predicament: a perspective suggested by Knox's October memorandum on the need for peace with Spain. Dominating England's strategic freedom was her friendlessness. 'England till this time', said Sandwich, 'was never engaged in a war with the House of Bourbon thoroughly united, their naval forces unbroken, and having no other war or object to draw off their attention and resources. We unfortunately have an additional war upon our hands which essentially drains our finances, and employs a very considerable part of our navy and army: we have no friend or ally to assist us. ... '[3] Even Holland, the once staunch ally, had evaded her treaty obligation to help and was carrying the enemy's supplies. A quarrel over her rights as a neutral was coming to a head.

Germain was very conscious of the situation. He had written during the summer of the need for a quick victory in America, to release the country's resources against its European enemies. To North's enquiry about diplomatic policy he had replied that we need not despair of alliances, but must go out and seek them: they would not fall into the country's lap.[4] On the following day, September 14th, Lord Weymouth had written to urge the minister in St Petersburg, James Harris, to spare no effort to draw Russia into an alliance. This letter crossed one from Harris suggesting that a formal proposal should be sent to the Tsarina in King George's own hand. This reached the Northern Department in October, about the time when Stormont succeeded Weymouth. Stormont began a vigorous search for friends, and was soon in negotiation with Russia, authorising Harris to pursue an alliance, or, if Catherine preferred it, an armed mediation in Britain's favour.[5] At the same time a substantial effort, both military and diplomatic, was turned against Spain, the weaker partner in the Bourbon alliance. For as long as the Spanish navy was hostile, England was unlikely to achieve the superiority at sea on which the defence of her colonies and the waging of an aggressive war must depend.

[1] G 2896.   [2] CL, Germain, 20 Jan. 1780 to Clinton.
[3] G 2776.   [4] Sackville, II, 136, 141.
                          [5] Madariaga, 121–4.

In November the first steps were taken to open a negotiation. Extreme caution was needed, both to conceal it from the French and for reasons of prestige and internal policy. The Spanish manner of entering the war made it impossible for the British government to make the first official overture; and the certainty that Spain would raise the subject of Gibraltar made it essential that the Ministry should not be embarrassed by a premature disclosure in England. The first feelers had to be secret, unofficial and easy to disown. In the course of November the Prime Minister and the Secretaries of State were seeking some safe channel through which to sound the Spanish government; and the matter was not put through the Cabinet.

One feeler was put out by the new Secretary for the Southern Department. The King of Naples was the son of Charles III of Spain; and Lord Hillsborough approached his Minister in London with an assurance that England would welcome overtures for peace provided that they made no reference to the rebellious colonies.[1] He covered himself by saying that he spoke as a private person and not as a Minister. About the same time Commodore Johnstone was steering for the Tagus with a small squadron to cruise on the coast of Portugal. He was a politician with little sea experience; but he had been used in a diplomatic role with the Carlisle Peace Commission in America. On reaching Lisbon he made contact with a Portuguese merchant named Cantofer who was acquainted with Floridablanca. He claimed that he had conferred with North before his departure; that both North and the King desired a separate peace with Spain; and that they were willing to pay for it with Gibraltar. For Spanish help against the American rebels they would throw in Florida and a share of Newfoundland fisheries. Johnstone went so far as to write out a letter of introduction to North, which Cantofer could use if Floridablanca sent him to London. He was disowned when the British government established another channel of communication; yet he had envoy's pay and permission to live on shore at Lisbon,[2] and his conversations with Cantofer resemble so closely the means actually established as to suggest that all these overtures were part of a deliberate search for an opening.[3]

---

[1] Bemis, *Hussey-Cumberland Mission*, 18. This is the fullest study of the negotiations. See also, however, Coxe, *The Kings of Spain of the House of Bourbon*, especially for a valuable note by Richard Cumberland which is not used elsewhere.

[2] Lord Herbert (ed.), *Henry, Elizabeth and George*, 183.

[3] For the Johnstone overture see Bemis, *op. cit.*, Chap. III; Rutherford (*Mariner's Mirror*, 1942, p. 196). Shortly before formal negotiations were opened in April, 1780, another feeler was put out by Sir John Dalrymple, who had been called to Lisbon in October by 'family distress'. It was not treated seriously by Floridablanca; nor is it clear what the British government could hope to gain by it. Only two things suggest that Dalrymple may have been put up to it: his unexplained passport to Madrid, and the fact that he was in touch with Germain about a privateering venture (for which see Chap. XXI).

The channel used in the end was opened by Germain a day or two before Hillsborough dropped his hint to the Neapolitan Minister. The agent was an Irish priest named Hussey, who had been chaplain to the Spanish embassy in London. Which party took the initiative is uncertain. Hussey told Floridablanca that the subject was opened by Germain when he visited the American Department on behalf of some interned priests; but the British reports of his conversation suggest that it was Hussey who had dropped the first hints. This is not impossible, for he was an energetic and politically-minded priest on his way to a mitre, and his statement to the contrary may have been no more than an attempt to conceal his presumption from his Spanish masters. Yet this is not the end of the question. For Hussey was a known intelligence agent of the Spanish government, and since the departure of the ambassador he had been fed with military intelligence by a counter-spy in communication with Germain. There is a possibility that even if Hussey was induced to make the first move, the British had intended him to do so.[1]

In December Hussey travelled to Madrid, equipped with an unofficial letter from Germain assuring him that a formal overture would be welcomed. Richard Cumberland, the Secretary of the Board of Trade and a personal friend of Germain, had handled the preliminary talks with Hussey in November, and had received a strong impression from him that Spain dreaded attacks on her colonies in the coming year; and Hussey was accordingly furnished with a strong hint that the Spanish colonies were indeed to be assailed.[2] On 17 December, soon after his departure, a despatch from Jamaica announced the first success against the Spanish Main, the capture of Omoa; and three days

[1] Bemis, *op. cit.*, 19, n. 11; Sackville, I, 323–6. The origins of the negotiation remain obscure. Cumberland's account to Shelburne in May 1782 (in the British Museum: kindly communicated to me by Father J. S. Benedict Cullen) is as follows. Floridablanca had had no confidence in the Spanish Ambassador, Almadovar, and had maintained confidential communications with Hussey. When war broke out Hussey returned to England (as Superintending Priest for the Spanish prisoners according to the Spanish archives, though he told Cumberland his sole object was to purchase astronomical instruments). He remained in communication with Madrid as their intelligence agent, of which Cumberland was kept informed by William Wardlaw, a British agent. Wardlaw reported that Hussey talked much of his desire to see peace re-established, and Germain agreed that he should be sounded about this. Hussey accepted the invitation and opened himself on the subject, making the condition that their conversations should be kept secret from the rest of the Cabinet.

Thus the first move would appear to have come from the British side. But there is a doubtful circumstance: Wardlaw was a double spy, employed and paid by the Spaniards and known to them as acquainted with Germain. So it remains possible that Hussey paved the way for the conversations: Cumberland (Sackville, I, 328) believed that he was acting for the Spanish Court.

[2] Sackville, I, 327, 331; memoranda by Hussey in the Spanish archives, communicated by Fr. Cullen.

later came the news of the French repulse at Savannah. It was suggested that d'Estaing's failure might drive a wedge of misunderstanding between the rebels and their French allies; and if Rodney should succeed in relieving Gibraltar, the Spaniards might lose heart. Omoa and Savannah together must have led directly to the decision on Christmas Eve to mount the Jamaica expedition. Germain had always wanted to make Jamaica 'a thorn in the side of Spain', and on learning that Omoa was to be attacked he had hurried off small arms and Indian presents on board Rodney's convoy, without delaying to ship them in an ordnance transport. Its capture was the opening for which he had hoped when he first ordered the Governor of Jamaica to harass the Spanish Main. Troops, landing craft and gunboats should pour like an expanding torrent into the breach.[1]

The only opposition came where it might have been expected. Amherst characteristically approved of the object, but maintained that the troops could not be spared from home defence. In cutting down the draft of recruits for Jamaica a few weeks earlier, he had said that if ten times as many recruits had been available they would still have been needed to fill the regiments at home; and if he grudged a few recruits, how much more did he grudge complete and serviceable regiments. The new levies at home were not complete, and three battalions which were most ready for the expedition were earmarked for home defence. Once again Amherst's dual position was pulling him in two directions. The Cabinet hesitated to override his professional advice; but they feared the exhaustion of a prolonged defensive war, and carried the dispute to the King. George III supported them; and a few days later at Germain's instigation he exercised his prerogative as Captain-General to overrule Amherst and release the troops for Jamaica. On 7 January Brigadier-General Garth and four regiments were warned to prepare for embarkation.[2]

Garth's battalions and the one already despatched added a total reinforcement of five battalions to the two and a half already in Jamaica.[3] a strong shield, or a formidable striking force. Germain wrote variously of making Jamaica safe, dividing the Spaniards' attention, and alarming them for their own possessions: after the stroke on the Spanish Main, an assault on New Orleans.[4] This succession of blows following on the relief of Gibraltar should strengthen the British hand at Madrid. Knox had contemplated bartering West Florida and the Mosquito shore for a separate peace: what if instead we

---

[1] G 2886, 2890; CO 137/75, ff. 116–7, 206, 226.
[2] Knox, 163; WO 34/122, ff. 82–3; G 2896, 2898; WO 34/232, pp. 97, 313–14.
[3] Already in Jamaica: one battalion 60th, 79th, Dalrymple's (Loyal Irish). Despatched Nov.: 88th. Despatched Jan.: 85th, 92nd, 93rd, 94th.
[4] CL, Germain, 4 Jan. to Vaughan; Sackville, II, 283; Knox, 164; Adm. 2/1337, f. 45.

overran New Orleans and the whole Nicaraguan isthmus? Spain, incapable of defending her own possessions, could scarcely pretend to Gibraltar.

Yet the question remains: of what value were the malarial swamps and forests of Nicaragua compared with Gibraltar? The answer was a base in the Pacific. The Spanish Main had lured the English since the days of Drake; but the prize was no longer the gold of El Dorado, but the trade of the Spanish colonies and the markets of the opening Pacific. For this England had tried ten years earlier to gain a base in the Falkland Islands on the Cape Horn route, and had been frustrated by Spain. The Central American isthmus is to the Falkland Islands what Suez is to the Cape of Good Hope: a short route to the Eastern Seas. On the Pacific coast near Lake Nicaragua there was a good anchorage at Realejo which could be supplied with stores from the West Indies; and it was reckoned that a force from Jamaica could reach it in thirty days to attack the Spanish possessions on the western coast of America. Anson had believed that with such a base a fleet could be maintained in the Pacific, and would be a match for nearly double its own number coming round the Horn.[1]

---

[1] For the numerous papers connected with the Central American project, see Sackville, II, 153–8, 282–3; WO 34/112, f. 50; WO 34/116, f. 77; CL, Germain, Vol. 17, Nos 11, 17, 18, 36; *ibid.*, III. Suppl.; *ibid.*, 10 Dec. 1779, Robert White to de Grey; CL, Shelburne, Vol. 86, No 176; Dalrymple, *Memoirs of Great Britain*, Appendix, p. 32; CO 137/77, ff. 20, 113. As late as 1837 a pamphlet by Henry Fairbairn argued the superiority of the Gulf of Mexico route over the proposed Suez route to the east.

CHAPTER XVIII

THE LOSS OF THE INITIATIVE

1. *Admiral Rodney*

One's view of Sir George Rodney depended on whether one was a politician or a seaman, a creditor or a friend. He was a sociable man. Women and play were his pastimes; and his elegant, slightly effeminate presence was well-known at the dinner table, voluble and indiscreet. Like Wolfe he fought his future battles over the mahogany, always returning to his favourite subject, which was Sir George Rodney. The politicians saw him in a different light. He had been in Parliament and might be again, so he had power to be useful; but he had many enemies, and was widely distrusted on account of his financial embarrassments and his freedom with public funds.

Rodney had run into unexpected troubles when he returned from the Jamaican command in 1774. Expensive habits and a parliamentary election had run up large debts; and his immunity from his creditors as a Member of Parliament suddenly ceased when Parliament was dissolved a year before it had run its course.[1] Scarcely had he set foot on shore when he had to fly the country. His refuge was Paris; and in due course his half-pay and his pay as Rear-Admiral of Great Britain should have enabled him to clear his debts. But he was hampered by his conduct in Jamaica. He had spent public money with a lavish contempt for rules, seeking no estimates before work was commissioned, and meeting bills by drawing irregularly on Navy Board officials.[2] It was a happy moment for the Board. They had always resented his off-hand manner, and his pay was withheld till he should account for his expenditure, clear the imprest against him, and satisfy the other claimants to his emoluments. He could not come home to dispute his rights in person; for if his English creditors would have let him, the fresh creditors who sprang up in Paris would not. His wife came over in 1776 to lobby North and Sandwich to employ him; and it was rumoured that she was also instructed to open a subscription at White's to pay his gaming debts. Neither attempt succeeded. 'If Sir George will consider the thing impartially', Lord Sandwich told her, 'he will see that, though his merit as a sea officer is undeniable, there are reasons that make it impossible for me to prevail on His Majesty to appoint him to the command of a foreign station ... as a man in office,

[1] This and much of what follows I have learnt from Mr David Spinney.
[2] Adm. 2/549, pp. 3, 61, 76.

your husband has deprived me of the power of being useful to him.' With his affairs in such confusion, he could not be employed in a position of trust. But Sandwich always intended to use him when it became possible. He was an old friend and protector of the Admiral, though Rodney's frustrated solicitations strained their relations severely; and at the end of 1777 he promised to join with other friends in obtaining an income for him from the government till his affairs were straight enough to let him serve.[1]

When England broke with France in March 1778 and recalled her ambassador, Rodney was still in pawn to his Paris creditors. But in May he bought his freedom with a loan from old Marshal Biron; and after a few days spent in taking leave of Paris society, he reached England before the first shots were fired. But no employment came. His private affairs were still in confusion, and another year passed before he was considered fit to serve. Why he was offered the Leeward Islands command is not certain. Rodney himself put it about that he owed it to the King. This was probably no more than an attempt to deprive the First Lord of the credit, for we find Sandwich going out of his way to assure the uneasy George III that Rodney would have no opportunity to relieve his indigence by mishandling stores. Rodney separately assured both Sandwich and Germain that he was in their debt alone. Sandwich indeed claimed the credit after Rodney's first successes; but it is possible that Germain is the true claimant. Rodney had cultivated his friendship when he became American Secretary; and Germain's support of the proposal to bombard le Havre is only one of many references to his high opinion of the Admiral.[2] Richard Cumberland claimed in his *Memoirs* that it was he who brought Rodney's claim to serve before Germain, and that Germain got him the command.[3]

Rodney's appointment raised a clamour from the West India merchants, who knew all too much of him, and there was a movement among them to apply for Palliser instead. Not everyone believed like Sandwich that Rodney would be unable to raid the public till. Gregson, the Navy Board clerk, was characteristically a sceptic. He told Lord Shelburne that Rodney's secretary was a notorious scoundrel. 'The appointment of these two vultures is a proof of the vile influence that still reigns, and I doubt not but a certain Lord is to have a share in the plunder.'[4]

Rodney's first care was for his family. He immediately entered his four-

---

[1] Sandwich, I, 135; Williams Transcripts, 1 Oct. 1776, Sandwich to Lady Rodney, and 1 Dec. 1777, Rodney to Sandwich; information from Mr Spinney.
[2] See above, p. 287; and Knox, 167-8.
[3] Sackville, II, 19, 172-3; Sandwich, III, 205-6, 213, 222-3; Cumberland, *Memoirs*, 292-3; G 2782; Knox, 162; information from Mr Spinney.
[4] Sandwich, III, 155; CL, Shelburne, Vol. 146, No. 151.

teen-year-old son on board his flagship. In 1780 he appointed him commander of one ship, and on the same day promoted him captain in another. He had a *quid pro quo* to offer Sandwich. The First Lord was being tormented to promote a 'young man of fashion' for whom he could do nothing at home. This was Lord Robert Manners, a youth of the Rutland clan, whose pretensions illustrate the pressure to which Sandwich sometimes capitulated. In 1775 Sandwich had refused to make him a lieutenant in defiance of regulations. Manners had now achieved his lieutenancy; and as Rodney's fleet assembled he wrote bitterly complaining of Sandwich's neglect to promote him captain. 'It is trifling too much with one of the first families in the Kingdom. I hope to God some time or other to have it in my power to show my displeasure.' Sandwich begged Rodney to 'do something' for the youth, and Rodney was game. Eighteen months later he offered to promote any officer whom Amherst cared to name, asking at the same time for a company in the Guards for one of his sons; and on the present occasion he had no difficulty in obliging Sandwich. Though the ship in which Manners was serving played no part in Rodney's first victory, he promptly gave him the command of a seventy-four. Manners begged the Duke of Rutland to get it confirmed: 'you must use your whole influence to effect it; write to Keppel, to Sir John L[owther?] or Lord Mansfield immediately'. It is easy to fall in with Middleton's indictment of Sandwich's appointments, and to forget the ruthlessness with which the eighteenth-century nobility pursued its private interests. The real grievance of Sandwich's enemies was not his favouritism, but his adherence to rule. Lord Robert never lived to show his displeasure. He was mortally wounded at the battle of the Saints.[1]

The First Lord and Rodney took each other's measure but knew that they could use each other. Sandwich skilfully balanced conciliation of Rodney with economy of favours; and Rodney walked a similar tightrope, flattering Sandwich and Germain at each other's expense and indulging in a little abuse of the Ministry when he thought it safe. His relations with his fellow-officers were based on two simple rules. If he fell out with his equals, as he often did, he reported them as delinquents to the Admiralty; and his subordinates he kept in line with threats of punishment. Among his captains he had few friends or none. 'My eye on my captains frightened them more than the enemy', he boasted.

Yet Rodney ranks among the great admirals. His first asset was luck. He was never wounded throughout his long and active career, and in the American War he timed his entries perfectly. Not for him to contend with

---

[1] Mundy, I, 206–7; Rutland, III, 3, 22, 24–5; WO 34/134, f. 252 (29 June 1781, Rodney to Amherst). Manners seems to have been a conscientious officer. Mackenzie excepts him from his strictures on the naval captains before Yorktown.

great odds, like Howe and Hood. His first actions were fought against inferior Spanish squadrons which blundered into him; and he twice arrived in the West Indies with a reinforcement to re-establish equilibrium when Hood had faced a superior enemy through the winter. His health was now very bad, and he was often too ill to do his duty. Yet with his luck he still combined an intermittent driving force, and flashes of originality; boldness, resolution, and the suppleness which avoided quarrels with the Ministry.

2. The Relief of Gibraltar

On 4 January Rodney's great fleet had cleared the danger area. Four hundred miles west of Rochefort he slipped the West India convoy, and proceeded with the battle fleet and the supply ships for the Mediterranean garrisons. His luck was with him. West of Finisterre at daybreak on the 8th an enemy fleet was sighted: he had run into the track of a supply convoy for the enemy fleet in Cadiz. The *Bienfaisant* came up with a Spanish fifty-four, which struck to her; and six frigates and sixteen laden transports were overhauled and taken. The victuallers were added to the Gibraltar convoy, the rest of the prizes detached with an escort to England; and the captured fifty-four was renamed *Prince William* in compliment to Digby's midshipman.

Rodney proceeded down the coast of Portugal, speaking occasional vessels which reported a Spanish fleet off Cape St Vincent. The convoy passed the Cape on the 16th in good order and ready for battle; and shortly before noon the enemy was sighted. Rodney was ill in bed; but he crowded on sail, formed his fleet into line abreast, and as he drew near hoisted the signal for a general chase. With a fresh wind and the weather gauge his coppered ships swept down on the enemy, which were eleven of the line commanded by Don Juan de Langara.

The Spanish navy was unready to prevent the relief of Gibraltar. Numerous ships of the line were repairing in Cadiz, and twenty-five on their way from Brest had put in to Ferrol with damage. Langara's detachment alone was cruising to intercept Rodney, unaware that he had Digby's powerful squadron from the Channel. Langara had no frigates scouting; and, outnumbered two to one by faster ships which took the lee gauge as they came up to prevent his retreat, his defeat was certain. Towards five o'clock, soon after the action was joined, a Spanish seventy-gun ship blew up. Darkness was rushing on, but Rodney pursued the enemy into the blustering night, through bright intervals of moonlight chased by the racing clouds. At two in the morning when six ships of the line had been taken, he ordered the fleet to bring to. The situation was much like Collingwood's on the same coast after Trafalgar. A half gale and a heavy sea were driving the fleets towards the shoals, while prize-crews struggled to take possession of the captured ships. Two of the prizes were cast ashore; but four were brought out and returned to England.

Frigates were despatched to Tangier to urge the Consul to hasten fresh provisions to Gibraltar. 'Great Britain was again Mistress of the Straits', was Rodney's message. The Spanish blockading squadron was driven off, and the relieving fleet came through the storms to anchor off the Rock. Troops, stores, and provisions poured ashore to make the fortress safe. The reinforcement intended for Minorca was detained by General Eliott; but the stores were forwarded to Murray at Port Mahon.

The run of success was not yet ended. As Digby's squadron made its way home to the Channel, it met a Mauritius convoy outward bound from France, scattered it, and took several transports and a coppered sixty-four stored for four years with £60,000 on board. This encounter brought the prizes of the Gibraltar operation to six ships of the line besides three destroyed or wrecked; about thirty-six merchantmen; and £70,000 sterling. There was triumph in London, and for Rodney the freedom of the City and the thanks of both Houses. 'You have taken', wrote Sandwich, 'more line-of-battle ships than had been captured in any one action of either of the last preceding wars.'

Rodney, in the meantime, was pursuing his lonely course towards the West Indies with four ships of the line. He lamented that none of Digby's coppered ships had been allowed to accompany him. Yet he had himself kept one of Digby's ships at Gibraltar to bring home the transports when they were unladen; a course which was contrary to his orders and ominously disregarded the value of each single ship of the line to his hard-pressed country. In 1781 the same disregard was to keep ships from the vital battle off Yorktown.

3. The Loss of the Initiative

The month of Rodney's first victories saw the rapid assembly of the second Leeward Islands convoy. The transports gathered, four regiments received their marching orders and embarked; and the force sailed on 30 January under convoy of the *Intrepid*. Only the officer commanding the whole brigade knew their destination: the battalion commanders were left in the dark, and the naval escort was under sealed orders. The four additional regiments for Jamaica were to follow shortly. Thus in the course of the winter ten battalions embarked for the West Indies with a total strength of 7,000 rank and file besides recruits. This was a larger reinforcement than had been spared for North America in any year since 1776, and measures better than the words of statesmen the trend of British strategy. Since the beginning of the war twenty-two battalions had been sent to the West Indies from

England and America: a total of some 13,000 rank and file in addition to recruits.[1]

Three days after the *Intrepid*'s convoy sailed, some British sailors broke out of prison in Brest, seized a brig, and made sail for England. They reached Whitehaven on 6 February, bringing the news that a very powerful force under Admiral Guichen had been due to sail for the West Indies on the 3rd. The French crew of the brig confirmed that the force was fifteen sail of the line or more, with numerous frigates and fifteen or sixteen thousand troops; and its departure was reported by a Danish brig which left Brest on the 4th.[2] The plans of the enemy were beginning to take hold.

In the previous November the French Admiralty's planning staff had examined a number of plans in the light of the summer's failure in the Channel. The courses from which France had most to gain were the conquest of the British West Indies or decisive operations in the Indian Ocean; but the head of the department considered that with no preparations in hand it was now too late in the winter to reinforce these theatres. Operations in North America he considered too uncertain in cost, duration and results, and a war against English trade was unlikely to be decisive. He therefore concluded that France and Spain should adhere to the plan of invading the British Isles.

His government, however, decided otherwise. Vergennes had been discouraged in the course of 1779 by dissensions among the American rebels and the energy with which England had mobilised her resources. In the autumn the Spaniards withdrew the whole of their fleet from Brest to cover the siege of Gibraltar, and they were accompanied by four French ships of the line. The allies agreed to abandon the invasion for the present, and to make their main effort an offensive in the Antilles. Admiral Guichen would take a squadron to Martinique, where the French fleet would be maintained at a strength of at least twenty-five sail of the line, and the Spaniards promised twelve of the line and 10,000 troops for Havana. Elsewhere the British would merely be held. Two ships of the line were destined to reinforce the Indian Ocean and contain them in Asia; and a force under Admiral Ternay to prevent a collapse of the rebellion in America.

In England it had been known for some time that the French were preparing a reinforcement for Martinique; and on learning the great scale of Guichen's expedition Germain shrewdly penetrated the enemy's design. He guessed that as a result of the Spanish withdrawal to their home ports, the

---

[1] Yet another battalion (Rainsford's 99th) was sent to Jamaica in the summer of 1780, the eleventh to go from England within little more than six months. Seven companies were intercepted by the Spaniards.

[2] CL, Germain, 8 and 10 Feb. to Vaughan.

enemy had abandoned the invasion of England, and that the West Indies would now be the main theatre of war. The British government had been starving the defence of England for the sake of a West Indian offensive. Now it appeared that the French were moving in the same direction, and were likely to retain the initiative in the islands. But as yet Germain felt no alarm, and assured General Vaughan that the government would not allow a naval inferiority in the Leeward Islands. Of that there was no apparent fear, for twelve sail of the line were under orders for the West Indies: five of them well on their way with Rodney and the second Leeward Islands convoy, three more from North America, and four under Commodore Walsingham preparing to convoy the trade and Garth's battalions to Jamaica.[1]

At this juncture there occurred a characteristic naval miscarriage. An express arrived from Cork with the news that seven transports and a victualler for the Leeward Islands had separated from the *Intrepid's* convoy. Since they had not received their orders or been given a rendezvous they had been able to do nothing but turn back to port. Germain was in touch with the Admiralty at once, and a ship of the line intended for the next convoy was sent to Cork to take the stragglers out to General Vaughan without delay. Delay there was, however, for they remained wind-bound till the end of March. Germain, though vexed, remained unperturbed, confident that the French ships in the West Indies were in bad condition and short of stores, and would not be fit for operations before the arrival of Rodney.[2]

The news which began to change this prospect was the destination of Ternay's squadron. Its existence in Brest had been known for some time, but its strength had been reported as four or six ships of the line and its destination as the Indian Ocean. The Admiralty had merely ordered Hughes to retain the three ships of the line which had been recalled from India.[3] But by early March Ternay was thought to be bound for North America, and to be taking as many as a dozen ships of the line and 12,000 troops. With Arbuthnot's force at New York supposedly depleted by the detachment ordered to the West Indies in the past autumn, a considerable force would have to be sent to his help. It was not easy to spare a further detachment from the ships at home; but happily on 5 March Sandwich learnt of Digby's return from Gibraltar with the six prizes of the operation: the French sixty-four coppered, fully stored and ready for immediate service, and the Spaniards also said by Rodney to be in good shape. With this accession of strength, Sandwich suggested to the King that five ships of the line should be spared from home service and detached under Admiral Thomas Graves

[1] CL, Germain, 8 and 10 Feb. to Vaughan.
[2] *ibid.*, 12 Feb. to Knox and Col. St Leger; CO 5/99, f. 21.
[3] Adm. 2/1337, f. 21. For the earlier recall of Hughes's ships, see above, pp. 261–2.

to the American coast. The King agreed strongly, and only urged that the Navy Board should not follow the 'old scrupulous method' of reporting Rodney's prizes fit before they were purchased, but hasten on their equipment if a superficial survey suggested that they were sound. He had grasped how the battle for the initiative was running: 'The country that will hazard most will get the advantage in this war. By keeping our enemies employed, we shall perplex them more than by a more cautious, and consequently less active, line of policy.[1]

The King's wish for haste was being met. Already the Comptroller had agreed to purchase the prizes summarily, without removing their naval stores or bringing them into dock, and Amherst had given a similar undertaking for their guns and ordnance stores. Sandwich obtained North's support for the despatch of Graves's squadron, and on the evening of 7 March they put it to a Cabinet meeting. The Cabinet was persuaded. On Sandwich undertaking to have thirty other ships of the line ready for home service by 1 May, they agreed to spare six of the line for America.[2]

Where should the squadron go? Sandwich feared that Ternay's ultimate destination might be the West Indies or perhaps the southern colonies, and he wished the relief to go to Charleston, whence it would move north or south as might be necessary. 'Depend upon it', he assured Rodney when the decision to send the reinforcement was taken, 'you shall be nobly supported; and though the enemy, I am persuaded, means to make the West Indies the great scene of action, I hope we shall be able to give you a great superiority of force, or at least an equality, which with your conduct will be the same thing.' But Germain guessed otherwise about the enemy's intention. He was convinced that Ternay had a northerly destination, and suspected that it might be Canada rather than New York. It was true that New York had been weakened by the departure of Clinton's expedition to Charleston, and might tempt the enemy; but he was confident that the reduced state of Washington's army would prevent success. On the other hand Lafayette had just returned from France to Boston, and he was connected in Germain's mind with Canada. We know now that the French did not intend to conquer Canada for the Americans; but the rebels' hopes and dispositions, the promises held out to the Canadians, and reports of the French troops' equipment and commanders, all suggested that Quebec, Newfoundland or Halifax might be their objective. And Quebec and Halifax were very weak. It had been impossible to spare reinforcements from England for Canada; and Clinton, having failed to get troops through to the St Lawrence in the autumn, had switched everything he could spare into his southern offensive at Charleston.[3]

[1] G 2956; Sandwich, III, 204, 243.   [2] G 2961-2.
[3] Sandwich, III, 203, 206; CL, Germain, 15 March to Clinton and Robertson.

This reasoning convinced the Cabinet that the right destination for Graves was Halifax. Sandwich still disagreed, but he had gone out of London for the week-end and recorded his dissent by letter. The Cabinet also wished to add two ships to Graves's squadron, so that he could pursue and fight Ternay with his own force even if Arbuthnot did not join him. But in the First Lord's absence they would take no decision on either issue, and Germain wrote on 11 March begging him to come. 'Your Lordship's absence distressed us much; and we preferred delaying any decision upon this business rather than determining upon it without having your reasons at large.' On the 14th the whole Cabinet was assembled, and it was settled that Graves should be strengthened to eight sail of the line and should go to New York.[1]

From these shifting arrangements it is apparent that the initiative was passing to the enemy. There was little room to doubt that they had switched their main effort away from the Channel, and in Germain's words were bent on 'pushing the war with their whole strength in America'. At what point on the long front from Trinidad to Quebec the attacks would come had yet to be revealed; but in the long run the ebb and flow of the seasons would carry the forces to and fro, and the station commanders again received warnings to keep in constant touch and support each other. Amherst wished to suspend the allocation and despatch of recruits till the enemy's intention was clearer; but though Germain agreed that they should not leave the British Isles till there was no further possibility of invasion, he insisted that if the troops were to be available abroad in the present campaigning season transports must be ordered and all preparations made for their departure.[2]

In the course of March the danger that Ternay would go to the West Indies ebbed further. His preparations were less advanced than had been thought, and his force was smaller. He was now most unlikely to go to the Caribbean so near the approach of the hurricane season. It was therefore safe to presume that he was bound for North America, and Graves received orders on 25 March to sail as soon as his ships were ready.[3]

Nevertheless Germain, who had gone to the country for the Easter recess, remained uneasy about the Leeward Islands. He felt that the squadron which Walsingham was about to take out would be wasted at Jamaica, for Guichen was unlikely to attack to leeward till he had disposed of Rodney; and he regretted that Sandwich had not empowered Rodney to order Walsingham to rejoin him. He was still more unhappy when he learnt of the bad condition

---

[1] Sandwich, III, 244; Knox, 165–6; G 2968; CL, Germain, 8 April to Haldimand; Adm. 2/1337, f. 68.

[2] CL, Germain, 15 March to Robertson, Vaughan, Dalling and Admiralty; 17 March to Haldimand; CO 138/6, f. 53; Sandwich, III, 237–8; Knox, 167.

[3] Knox, 167; Adm. 2/108, p. 427.

of Rodney's fleet, of which Sandwich had hitherto said nothing: it turned out to be ill-found and undermanned. Knox took up the cudgels in Germain's absence and persuaded Sandwich that three of Walsingham's ships should remain with Rodney instead of proceeding to leeward. But still the First Lord remained confident of the issue: Germain was not. For though Walsingham had received his sailing orders on 7 March, he was still held up on the 25th and could not reach Rodney in time to assist him against the first impact of Guichen. Germain's only comfort was that Arbuthnot might have obeyed his orders and detached a force from New York.[1]

Germain would have sent another six ships to the western Atlantic, convinced that there was little to be feared at home; but he found that Sandwich would not risk the British Isles on any account. The need to strengthen Walsingham was intensified by intelligence from Cadiz of the Spanish expedition which was preparing to sail for Havana. Since Ternay's force for America was now thought to be only eight sail of the line, two of Graves's eight ships were taken from him and ordered straight out to the West Indies.[2]

A further suggestion from Knox was at first brushed aside by Sandwich. This was that Walsingham and his convoy should be escorted clear of Brest by Graves. But early in April when a sortie from Brest was more probable, Walsingham was still wind-bound at home, and the Admiralty adopted the suggestion. Graves was ordered to escort the West India convoy two hundred leagues south-west from the Lizard if he was ready when Walsingham sailed. Graves himself was having difficulty in preparing his squadron. Most of his ships were just back from Gibraltar, short of men and in need of repairs; and their depleted provisions and stores had to be brought up to the foreign service scale. He had to compete for resources with the Channel fleet which was fitting out at the same time, and it was not till the middle of April that he was ready. Then five of his ships, with crews unpaid, refused to unmoor. One ship gave in only under threat of force; but this mutiny produced no capital sentences, for the wages were due 'in strictness of the Act.' At last Graves's squadron dropped down the Channel, only to be wind-bound in Plymouth.[3]

Ternay sailed from Brest on 2 May with seven sail of the line. The news was on Germain's table on the following day, and with the wind easterly at last he hoped that Graves and Walsingham had both cleared the land. But he was wrong. Walsingham's convoy was still wind-bound in Torbay. For a further fortnight Graves waited to escort him; but at last, on Lord Mulgrave's suggestion, he was allowed to proceed separately to America,

---

[1] CL, Germain, 24 March, de Grey to Hughes; Sandwich, III, 206; Knox, 166-7.
[2] Ternay's real strength was seven. His eighth ship was fitted as a hospital ship.
[3] Adm. 2/108, p. 438; Knox, 166; G 3002; Sandwich, III, 151, 238-9.

and sailed on the 17th from Plymouth in the wake of Ternay. That day it was known that Solano had sailed from Cadiz for the West Indies. Still Walsingham remained in Torbay. 'Was ever anything so provoking as the detention of Walsingham, who has been wind-bound these three months?" Sandwich asked Rodney. But before either Graves or Walsingham could sail, news had arrived that in the West Indies the battle was already joined.[1]

4. Rodney in the Leeward Islands

The approach of the hurricane season in August 1779 had closed down the Leeward Islands theatre for its annual siesta. The departure of Barrington and Byron for England had left Rear-Admiral Hyde Parker in command with a very inferior force; but d'Estaing's removal to Savannah and then to Europe transformed the British inferiority into a decisive superiority of sixteen ships of the line against seven.

So large a margin of superiority had seemed the best guarantee that the British lead could be maintained in a reinforcement race. Germain expected the British strength to show results in the winter. Both Byron and General Grant had had authority to take the offensive; and in the latter part of the year the American Secretary had been urging their successors to attack the French islands. But his hopes were disappointed. Grant, like Byron, had gone home leaving temporary successors. He divided the command between his two senior brigadiers; and instead of handing over his instructions, he ordered them to confine themselves to the defence of their own islands. Shortage of transports was also said to have contributed to the army's immobility.[2]

The convoy which Rodney had detached on his way to Gibraltar arrived in February 1780, bringing General Vaughan and his leading battalion.[3] Major-General the Hon. John Vaughan, Lord Lisburne's brother, was the officer who had stormed Fort Montgomery in the Hudson Highlands in 1777, and he had returned from America with a high recommendation from Clinton. Major Wemyss's view of him is characteristically harsh: 'Without abilities, he was ill-tempered and capricious, ever censuring the conduct of others; particularly his senior officers.' Hyde Parker, however, took to him as soon as they met, and called him 'this active general'; and he had the rare merit of agreeing with Rodney.[4]

Vaughan intended to lose no time in waiting for the remainder of his

---

[1] Sandwich, III, 214, 282; Adm. 2/1338, f. 18; CL, Germain, 3 May to Vaughan.
[2] CL, Germain, 3 and 7 Dec. to Admiralty, 4 Dec. to Brig.-Gen. Prescott; CO 318/7, f. 100; Sandwich, III, 156; Adm. 2/1337, f. 3.
[3] A second battalion was forwarded to Jamaica.
[4] Fortescue, III, 340; Sparks MSS., Vol. 22, p. 215; Eg. 2135, f. 151.

troops from England. There were 3,700 men fit for duty in the Leeward Islands, besides 1,350 serving in the fleet, and as soon as he reached Barbados he began to re-concentrate the scattered battalions. He summoned troops from Brigadier Prescott at St Kitts, gathered up more from Antigua, and reached St Lucia on 20 March with the intention of recovering St Vincent. He learnt that Guichen's force from France was on its way, but trusted that it would not arrive till his own blow had been struck. With some hesitation Hyde Parker decided to support the military operation rather than try to intercept Guichen. But the General postponed the attack. A letter from Rodney, and news of approaching reinforcements of troops (part of the scattered second contingent) caused him to save his strength for a more important objective than St. Vincent. It was as well that he paused; for on the 22nd Guichen reached Martinique, unimpeded by the British fleet.[1]

The command of the sea thus passed to the enemy. Guichen had twenty-three sail of the line against Hyde Parker's seventeen; and all but one of the British ships had spent the last hurricane season in the islands. The day after his arrival, Guichen appeared off St Lucia with an amphibious force. But he had not yet collected the whole of his fleet; and deterred by the strength of the defences and news that Rodney had reached Barbados, he returned to Fort Royal. At the first opportunity Vaughan redistributed his troops to Antigua and St Kitts, realising that he must stand on the defensive till the balance at sea had been redressed.[2] Germain was far from alone in believing that a reasonable distribution of troops would help to secure the islands when the navy was weak. It was true that dispersal in garrisons would hamper the mounting of an offensive; and it was equally true that if the fleet was over-whelmed and the command of the sea totally lost, most of the British islands would be indefensible and their garrisons a gift to the enemy. But this was far from being the case when Rodney reached the islands. Though inferior to the French, he was strong enough to dispute the command with them; and if the islands had not been garrisoned, the fleet would have been chained to their defence and unable to seek the enemy.

Rodney's four ships of the line reached St Lucia on 27 March. The British now had enough ships to offer battle; and early in April the whole fleet of twenty-one sail of the line put out to cruise off Martinique. But the enemy did not stir from under the guns of Fort Royal; and leaving his coppered ships on watch, Rodney returned to Gros Islet Bay. Guichen's orders were of the equivocal kind which so often restricted French commanders. With the exception of St Lucia he was to evacuate any British possessions which he might take, after destroying the munitions, stores and fortifications; and

---

[1] Fortescue, III, 342–3; Sandwich, III, 157; CO 318/7, ff. 81, 86.
[2] CO 318/7, f. 88.

was 'to keep the seas as much as the English forces maintained in the Windward Islands might allow him, without too much compromising his own forces'.[1] In this spirit his next enterprise was launched. Instead of fighting for the command of the waters, he intended to seize Barbados by stealth. On the 13th he sailed with 3,000 troops. Rodney followed him, and by the evening of the 16th he was close enough to count the enemy. They had twenty-two ships of the line; he had twenty, and a ship of fifty guns. The forces were nicely balanced.[2] Throughout the night shadowing frigates kept touch with the French; and on the morning of 17 April the two fleets engaged in the second great general action of the war.

The course of the battle of Martinique was much like that of Keppel's action off Ushant, and indeed of most naval battles of the century. Only a great superiority of force could have overcome the drag of misunderstandings, inadequate signalling systems, and adherence to rule. Indecisive results brought violent recriminations. Rodney's plan was to concentrate on the enemy's rear. But if he explained it to his captains (as his physician wrote many years later that he had asserted) he failed to instil it. An ambiguous signal brought into play the captains' indoctrination in the Fighting Instructions, and they engaged along the whole length of the enemy's line. For the soldiers serving in the fleet it was hard to understand how so fair an opportunity had passed without a single enemy ship sunk or taken.

Rodney raged at the result, and hinted at a conspiracy to disgrace the British flag. One captain who had risen from the lower deck was court-martialled and broken, having no great connections to protect him. The rest escaped unpunished; but in private letters Rodney condemned most of his captains and all his flag officers. Sandwich saw the dissensions with horror. He assured Admiral Rowley repeatedly that he had heard nothing against him, and restrained 'Vinegar' Hyde Parker when he came home in a fury and threatened to publish. 'God forbid', he wrote,[3] 'that the West India fleet should produce another scene like Mathews and Lestock, or Keppel and Palliser.'

The French strategy of evasion gave some degree of moral superiority to the British, but the command of West Indian waters remained in dispute. The considerable British army which was now assembled in the islands could do nothing while the issue at sea remained in doubt. After the battle Rodney took up a position between the French fleet and its base, but Guichen declined to fight his way back and sheltered under the batteries of Guadeloupe.

---

[1] Chevalier, 185.
[2] Rodney: 20 ships of the line and a fifty – about 1,494 guns. Guichen: 22 ships of the line – about 1,546 guns. A French seventy-gun ship joined after the battle.
[3] Sandwich, III, 233.

Here he replenished his stores from neutral St Eustatius; and early in May he issued forth on a mission, as misguided as the last one, to seize St Lucia without a battle. Rodney sighted him on the 10th, and for eleven days the fleets manoeuvred in variable winds while Rodney tried to force a battle. Twice the fleets clashed indecisively before Guichen gave up his object and withdrew to Martinique. He had a strong and well-handled fleet; but the fatal French doctrine of seeking strategic results without tactical risks frustrated his intentions.

Rodney had reached the theatre in time with the vital reinforcement which held the balance. But he maintained that five more ships of the line would have given him a decisive victory.[1] And if all had gone as the Ministry had planned, he would have had them. We have seen how Walsingham's ships from England were held up for three months by the wind: if he had sailed in late February or early March he should have been in time for the fighting. But what had become of the three ships which Arbuthnot had been ordered to send from America? The orders had been signed nine months earlier, on 24 September, and entrusted to the *Bonetta* sloop. She sailed from Spithead on 4 October, but was dismasted in mid-Atlantic by a storm. For weeks she battled vainly under jury masts to fetch New York. By the New Year her water was running out, forty-three of her crew were sick, several dead, and the rest almost naked, for there had been no slops in store at Portsmouth when she sailed. On 10 January her captain gave up and bore away for the Bahamas. Five weeks later he reached New Providence, and sent fifty-four sick on shore. Then he tried to forward his despatches, but no vessel could be hired on any terms. He tried to refit his own, found all the artificers working on privateers, and appealed to the Governor for priority. But the Governor was technically a prisoner of war as a result of an American raid, and neither the civil nor the military authorities would accept his orders. The *Bonetta* lay helpless in the Bahamas till 1 May. Before then Arbuthnot had inferred the Admiralty's intentions from allusions in later despatches. In April he ordered three ships of the line to Rodney, and the first of these joined him too late on 17 June.[2]

On such a chain of circumstances – on storms, private interests, and quarrelling officials – the Cabinet's plans might founder. But there remains a charge against the Ministry to dispose of. It was pointed out by Keppel that by early May three enemy forces had sailed unmolested from Brest and Cadiz to cross the Atlantic.[3] He argued that Brest should have been blockaded, and

[1] Adm. 1/486, f. 431.
[2] Adm. 2/1336, f. 58; Adm. 2/108, 24 Sept., Admiralty to *Bonetta*; Adm. 1/486, ff. 524–5.
[3] Keppel, II, 340.

twelve of the line sent to intercept Solano off Cadiz. But Keppel's analysis suffered from his lack of official information. The fact seems to be that the Channel fleet was not ready for service; and while it may be possible to blame this in part on the prolonged cruising of the previous autumn, the real cause was the winter voyage to relieve Gibraltar. The stubborn defence which was to preserve the fortress exacted a continual though subtle drain on the nation's resources: nor was the Spanish effort wholly in vain. Not for the last time the relief of Gibraltar left the Channel fleet exhausted and unready when the season of expeditions came round.

5. The Jamaican Sphere

Rodney had scarcely dropped anchor after his second encounter with Guichen when two cruisers raced in from the coast of Portugal with startling intelligence. A Spanish fleet was on the way: Don Josef Solano had left Cadiz at the beginning of May with twelve sail of the line and a large force of troops. Rodney came out to intercept him. But Solano, sighting a British frigate low on the horizon, passed to the north; and while Rodney lay to windward of Martinique vainly waiting for the Spaniards, the French fleet slipped out of Fort Royal and joined them at Guadeloupe. The troopships were forwarded to Havana, and the combined fleets dropped down to Fort Royal. The enemy were now twenty-seven ships of the line, and Rodney had only eighteen still fit to stand in the line of battle.[1]

The command of West Indian waters had been lost. All convoys were stopped, and Rodney prepared to meet an attack on St Lucia. But the season was running out, and the danger was short-lived. Nor did Solano mean to assist in attacking British islands. His squadron was in no condition for operations: 'assez exacte image d'un gouvernement délabré', a French historian has remarked. The crews were overwhelmed by disease; and it is alleged that the captains had filled their storage space with merchandise for their own profit, and by now had consumed most of the provisions. Far from combining with the French, Solano demanded their protection on the next leg of his voyage to Cuba. Guichen, with orders to leave the Leeward Islands before the hurricane season, escorted Solano to the westward, and then made for Haiti. Here he found appeals from Gérard and Lafayette to come to the help of the Americans. But his orders were clear; and in the middle of August he sailed for Europe, leaving ten ships of the line at Haiti. At sea he opened his

---

[1] The Admiralty knew on 25 April that Solano was about to sail, and were correctly informed of his force and destination. This warning reached Rodney a few days after the cruisers from Portugal. A preliminary warning dated 30 March had been sent to Parker at Jamaica, but I have not found evidence that Rodney was sent one.

sealed orders, and found that his destination was Cadiz. His landfall was in due course to have its repercussions in London.

Thus ended the year's operations in the Leeward Islands. Rodney was soon joined by Walsingham's reinforcement, but he was in the dark about the enemy. His frigates had failed to track them, and he had captured misleading letters which indicated that the main force of the French would go to America. He had agreed with Vaughan to spend the hot weather in attacking Trinidad, which lay outside the hurricane latitudes; but instead he conformed to the supposed movements of the enemy. The Leeward Islands fleet was broken up, and only Commodore Hotham remained there with six sail of the line. Rowley and Walsingham with ten of the line took the outward trade and the troopships to Jamaica to hold the Spaniards in check, while Rodney himself escorted the homeward trade to St Kitts, and sent off his most damaged ships with the August and October convoys to England. At St Kitts his fears for America were confirmed by news that a French fleet and convoy had anchored off Rhode Island in July: it was Ternay's expedition from Brest. He gathered up ten sail of the line, and 'without a moment's hesitation flew with all despatch' to New York. There we shall meet him soon.

The Leeward Islands settled down to their summer sleep, and the troops to their torrid martyrdom. By the end of May nearly two men in every five were sick, and in June two regiments had to be drafted and their cadres sent home. In St Lucia, the most sickly of the islands, the three months from June till August saw 584 men dead; and the August return showed less than half the survivors fit for duty. In the whole of the islands from St Lucia to St Kitts were 120 companies of infantry, with only 3,554 men fit for duty, an average company strength of less than thirty.[1]

Before we follow Rodney to New York, we must go down with Walsingham's convoy to leeward, where Jamaica was threatened by the approach of Solano's expedition. Hitherto it had not been an active theatre. Governor Dalling had entered heart and soul into Germain's schemes to harass the Spanish Empire; but till the reinforcements from England arrived he had only two and a half battalions in the island, so wasted by sickness that he could only count on 1,200–1,300 men for duty. The Assembly had been frightened by d'Estaing's expected attack in 1779, and violently opposed the despatch of troops from the island. Nor was General Dalling the man to persuade them. He felt unequal to his political duties, and his relations with the planters were deplorable. There were constant quarrels with the Assembly; and a clash with the Attorney-General which led him to dismiss four assistant-judges had a

[1] CO 318/6, ff. 144, 253; CL, Germain, II, Suppl. A battalion serving in the fleet was much healthier.

humiliating conclusion when he was forced by the British government to restore them. The efficiency of the militia deteriorated with the spirit of the planters. Nor, as military commander, did he promote a better understanding with the navy. He was on bad terms with the Admiral, Sir Peter Parker, and conducted a dispute over the disposal of prisoners in a manner so unbefitting his rank as to earn a sharp rebuke from the American Secretary.

Dalling's ambition was to lead an expedition to the Spanish Main, in which he may have seen an escape from his civil duties.[1] His plan was to thrust across Nicaragua by the San Juan River and Lake Nicaragua to Realejo on the Pacific coast; and he ordered Captain Dalrymple to destroy the fort at Omoa and free his force for the more southerly thrust in Nicaragua. But Dalrymple was a very young man, and intoxicated by his success. He came to a private arrangement with the navy for the distribution of the plunder, depriving the Bay men who had helped him of their share. He then gave himself leave to go home, and departed leaving the Bay men to petition Dalling for their rights. Instead of destroying the fort, he left a weak garrison, and sent home with despatches the only officer capable of commanding it. The plan which Dalrymple preferred to Dalling's was to advance from Omoa across Guatemala, and attack the South Sea from Sansonate. But by November 1779 disease had reduced the garrison of Omoa to seventy-four men, mostly negroes, and the fort fell to a 'party-coloured rabble' scraped together by the President of Guatemala.[2]

Dalrymple's plan was laid before Germain by his brother Sir John. But the Secretary of State preferred Dalling's Nicaraguan design. Twenty-five years later Sir John Dalrymple told Lord Grenville that Germain had often afterwards regretted the decision; but whether the Dalrymples' Honduran scheme would have made better use of the available resources must remain in doubt.[3] In February 1780, before Germain's instructions and reinforcements reached him, Dalling opened his own offensive. Five hundred regulars and volunteers sailed from Jamaica, followed in March by a further 450. With the second wave was Dalrymple, who had been intercepted at Jamaica on his way to Europe, forgiven by Dalling and promoted major. Indians and settlers made the force about 1,500, of whom 500 were regular troops. Colonel Kemble commanded the expedition. His first wave met with many delays: the Indians had not arrived, and the settlers had not assembled the promised boats. The operation had started late in the season, and owing to these delays the rains would come on before it could be completed. At last the advance began. In

---

[1] CO 137/75, f. 196; CO 137/78, f. 222.

[2] CO 137/76, ff. 56, 82, 86, 113.

[3] CO 137/77, f. 20; Sackville, II, 282; Huntington Library, Stowe Papers, Admiralty Box 9 (20 Oct. 1806, Sir John Dalrymple to Lord Grenville).

stifling heat the force worked its way against the strong current of the San Juan, losing men all the time from sickness. In April it reached the fort which guarded the outlet of the river from Lake Nicaragua, and after a weary week of cannonading in which almost every gun was laid by Horatio Nelson or the Chief Engineer, the garrison capitulated.

'Thus', wrote Dalling, 'the communicating door to the South Sea being burst open, what hinders His Majesty . . . to carry the force of his northern army to the destruction of the Spanish power, operating with a southern squadron?'[1] But already the expedition had spent its effort. Reinforcements arriving from Jamaica were engulfed by sickness. Though the climate on the Lake was said to be healthier, Kemble abandoned the advance; and leaving a garrison in the fort he withdrew the rest of the survivors to the coast, where disease continued its ravages with increasing violence.

This was the unpromising situation when Brigadier Garth's regiments from England reached the Caribbean. The Cabinet had intended them to strike the main blow in Nicaragua, and had equipped them with the boats for want of which Dalling's force was held up. Dalling had by now committed his own regulars prematurely and without authority, and had spent his force. When Garth's reinforcements reached Barbados on 10 July they had been on board ship for twenty weeks, and fever and scurvy were rapidly carrying them off. In the West Indies the sickness grew worse, and when the convoy reached Jamaica a month later it had only 1,350 men fit for duty. By now the arrival of the French and Spanish squadrons at Haiti endangered Jamaica, and there could be little question of forwarding any of Garth's troops to the Main as Dalling had intended. At the end of August Dalrymple arrived from the Main to report that Kemble had determined to withdraw his force, leaving only a beachhead garrison. Dalling still hoped to maintain a foothold on Lake Nicaragua and resume the advance after the rains; but in November he yielded to necessity and withdrew the survivors.[2]

By then sickness was raging uncontrolled in Jamaica itself. The planters, who were so anxious to have troops for their protection,[3] would not pay for building barracks, and since no houses could be rented Garth's wretched force was encamped through the rains. Dalling predicted a very heavy mortality before the season for operations returned, and he was right. Between Garth's arrival and the end of the year, seven and a half battalions lost 1,100 dead, and half of the 3,000 survivors were sick. Two regiments

---

[1] I.e., troops based on Jamaica and a squadron rounding the Horn (CO 137/77, f. 149).

[2] CO 137/78, ff. 218, 224, 226.

[3] In July their agent in London petitioned Germain against sending more troops or inhabitants out of the island and thus disturbing the sugar work.

were drafted and sent home – Dalrymple's Loyal Irish reduced almost to a man, and the newly arrived Ninety-third scarcely able to muster a company.[1] So withered the attempt on the Spanish Main, 'ill concerted and worse executed' as Germain described it. 'It failed in the execution', Knox was to tell William Pitt a decade later, 'through the avarice and presumption of the then Governor of Jamaica in making the attack that he might share in the plunder, when he was only ordered to make the preparations.' Dismal though the operations became, and futile as they may appear if viewed solely in the context of the struggle for the Thirteen Colonies, they had their place in the wider battle. For their failure Germain bears no blame. He had relied from the beginning on Indians and adventurers to test the ground and create an opening into which regular troops might be thrown at the right moment to overturn the Spanish colonial government. His belief in the opportunity had better support than Dalling's, for it was shared by Archibald Campbell, the brave and sensible officer who had conquered Savannah and was now Lieutenant-Governor of Jamaica. Even after the expedition came to its faltering close, Germain hoped that the men and equipment could be switched against New Orleans; and that by desultory pressure Nicaragua might eventually be penetrated and settled by Americans as a friendly state, and 'a severe wound given to the Spanish monarchy'. In the course of 1781 the American recruits whom he and Amherst intended for the core of the enterprise began to come in. Odell's Loyal American Rangers and Lord Charles Montagu's South Carolina Rangers reached Jamaica: seasoned men from the rebel army and very fit for the enterprise. But by then the war was running in different channels, and soon every effort was to be concentrated on saving Jamaica.[2]

[1] CO 137/78, f. 218; CO 137/80, ff. 170, 220.
[2] Knox, 209; CO 137/78, ff. 165, 342; CO 137/80, ff. 41, 174, 259, 289, 307; CO 137/ 81, f. 5.

CHAPTER XIX

GAIN AND LOSS IN AMERICA

1. Clinton and the King's Peace

The danger to the Caribbean islands would have made inevitable the heavy shift of effort towards the West Indies in the winter of 1779–80, even if no offensive had been intended there. But it plainly challenged Germain's hope of a rapid settlement in America. The only troops which were spared to Clinton in the spring of 1780 were British and German recruits. No reinforcement whatever could be spared for Quebec; and Germain, fearing an attack on Canada when Clinton moved southwards to the Carolinas, ordered him to strengthen Haldimand as soon as the ice opened in the St Lawrence.[1] Already England was doing too much with too few resources: barely checking the enemy in the Leeward Islands, the northern American colonies and Gibraltar, while simultaneously attempting to mount offensives against the southern colonies and the Spanish Empire. Victory over the rebellion was desperately needed; yet as Knox had argued, the European enemies had to be checked or broken before Britain's own powers of resistance crumbled.

Yet Germain did not despair. The feeble resistance which Prevost had encountered in Georgia and South Carolina suggested that the population was indifferent to the rebel cause. In the depths of the winter Washington's impotence in the north was shown when both Manhattan and Staten Island were joined to the New Jersey shore by ice thick enough to bear the heaviest cannon, while floating ice in the Narrows prevented mutual support against attack. As Lord Rawdon wrote from Staten Island, the failure to fall on the separated British forces did not suggest a healthy cause. Germain noted the jealousies in Congress, and the growing reluctance to serve in the rebel army. He continued to hope that the revolution would crumble from within, and suggested to Clinton that next to the destruction of Washington's army the speediest means to end the rebellion would be to gain over some of his leading officers. That this hope was not unfounded a great treason was to show within the year.[2]

Clinton however was not the man to make the best of slender resources. In November, depressed by the surprise of Paulus Hook and Stony Point, he

[1] CL, Germain, 19 Jan. to Clinton.
[2] Add. MSS. 38213, ff. 146–9; Sackville, II, 143–5, with additions in CL, Germain. See also Verulam, 128.

gave way to his resentment at the low priority accorded to his command, and sent in his resignation again. Only recently one of Germain's parliamentary acquaintance had urged him to take a firmer line with commanders abroad: '. . . certainly if it has ever been the practice to give way to the caprices of officers, and to solicit them either to accept or to continue in command, that is not the way either to inspire respect or to secure cheerful execution of orders.' Germain's reply to Clinton was stiffer than the tone he had adopted a year earlier. He pointed out that the reinforcement was as large as the country could afford in present circumstances; and that the recent expeditions to Penobscot, Virginia, Georgia and the New England coast had demonstrated what his diminished force could still achieve with a little energy. His call to duty was in accents which might have fallen from the Duke of Wellington: 'In times like these every officer, every subject, is called upon to stand forth in the defence of his sovereign, and of his country; and if a general declines the service because the force he commands is not adequate to his wishes, or may not enable him to extend his offensive operations with that rapidity he might expect, by whom is this country to be served in dangerous and critical situations?' He begged him to see that there was at least as much honour in using slender forces with credit as in controlling overwhelming superiority. But this is an appeal to which only great-hearted commanders will respond.[1]

Clinton had 32,000 effectives of all ranks distributed from Nova Scotia to the Bahamas, or perhaps 27,000 fit for duty. With this force he could still hope to retain the initiative against the rebels, provided that the navy could keep open his lateral communications. There were only forty warships on the coast in the spring; enough to protect the army's movements so long as no French force intervened, but not to stop the enemy's privateers and strangle his trade. The British supply-line was also being throttled, and from Halifax to the West Indies there had been complaints in the course of 1779 that provisions were short and victualling ships overdue. But the source of this trouble was not the cruiser shortage in America: it was the delays to convoys in home ports from contrary winds and enemy fleets in the Channel. Germain regarded single armed ships as the solution. It had been the system employed before France entered the war and the Navy Board took over the victualling of the army from the Treasury. He had opposed without success the Navy Board's discharge of the armed transports, and would have liked to return the army victuallers to the Treasury, who did not insist on convoy.[2]

[1] CL, Germain, 10 Oct. from William Pulteney; CO 5/98, f. 250.
[2] Usher, 293–6; Royal Institution MSS., I, 419, 466, 471; II, 8; CL, Clinton, 7 July 1781 from Germain.

The expedition to South Carolina sailed from New York on 26 December 1779. The voyage was stormy, and it was not till the end of January that the force began to assemble on the coast of Georgia, having lost most of its

THE SOUTHERN COLONIES

siege train and horses.[1] Howitzers, mortars and ordnance stores were summoned from St Kitts to make good the loss, and forty-five guns were lent and manned by the fleet, so that on 1 April Clinton was able to break ground in front of Charleston. Here General Lincoln had concentrated the

[1] One dismasted transport drifted for eleven weeks with provisions for four, and fetched up at St Ives in Cornwall.

rebel forces. In bold irregular operations Tarleton and Ferguson broke the rebel cavalry guarding Lincoln's communications with the north and cut his last line of escape, while the siege parallels in front of the city were pushed steadily forward. Lincoln surrendered Charleston on 12 May; and at the cost of 250 casualties Clinton took more than 6,000 Americans in arms with 400 guns and three rebel frigates. The prisoners included ten weak Continental regiments, and by holding the city Lincoln had ensured the destruction of the army defending the Carolinas. These losses changed the Americans' tone on the exchange of prisoners; and before the end of the year the survivors of the Saratoga Convention had secured their release.

All was now set fair for the pacification of South Carolina. James Simpson, the former official whose favourable report had influenced Clinton's decision to attack the province, now found that loyalists with a clean record were fewer than he had expected, but he was still confident that the King's government could be re-established.[1] The time had come to test Germain's plan for a political settlement. But Clinton was reluctant to use his powers. A few days after the fall of Charleston he learnt that he was no longer to be sole Peace Commissioner, but was to share his powers with Admiral Arbuthnot. Clinton detested the Admiral. Arbuthnot was a rough old diamond who would not have been appointed to the command in ordinary circumstances. He was in his late sixties, not in good health, and wrote in a style so muddled as to make his despatches obscure and ambiguous. Like Samuel Hood he had been a dockyard commissioner, and was called forward to fill the gap caused by the Keppelite defections. Naturally he was grateful to Sandwich. 'I owe your Lordship too much not to devote my life to you', he was to write. His attachment has made him the target of the First Lord's critics. Sir Charles Laughton has held him up as 'a sample of the extremity to which the maladministration of Lord Sandwich had reduced the navy': 'a late survival . . . ignorant of the discipline of his profession . . . destitute of even a rudimentary knowledge of naval tactics . . . a coarse, blustering, foul-mouthed bully'. This is violent language, and not easy to support. Colonel Stuart credited him on first acquaintance with 'an openness and candour that does honour to human nature . . . he will be above a little paper war with Ministers'.[2]

It was Arbuthnot himself who had demanded his inclusion in the Peace Commission, and Germain had yielded under pressure from Sandwich. But Clinton characteristically felt the alteration as a personal slight; for the same mail brought a criticism of his conduct in the autumn and a hint of impatience with his failure to use his powers as Commissioner to restore any province to

[1] CO 5/99, f. 265.
[2] Sandwich, III, 258; IV, 170; DNB (Laughton's article on Arbuthnot); Wortley, 162.

the King's peace. He replied by asking permission to resign, unless the Commission were altered to give him a veto on the restoration of civil government. The truth was that he not only disliked Arbuthnot, but held views on pacification which were directly opposed to the Admiral's. Arbuthnot was eager to use the Commission; but 'at present', he wrote, 'we seem to be so wedded to our military power that it will not be parted with until it cannot be avoided'. He insisted on the immediate necessity at least of publishing the terms of the future political settlement, and ending the rule of military law; and he begged Germain for a peremptory order as the only means of overcoming Clinton's resistance. Coming events were to show the wisdom of hurrying slowly; yet on the need to declare their future intentions Arbuthnot was right. All that the two commanders could agree, however, was to promise clemency for rebels who would submit.[1]

With this Clinton turned the command in the Carolinas over to Cornwallis with 4,000 men, and embarked the remainder of the army for New York. He now knew that a French force was on its way to America, and his future operations would depend on its strength and intentions. But he had in mind an expedition to the Chesapeake and the seizure of a base at Norfolk, to curb the rebel trade and favour the operations of Cornwallis.[2]

2. Cornwallis in the Carolinas

Cornwallis had already begun the task of clearing South Carolina. Four garrisons secured a long base-line on the coast from Savannah to Georgetown, and three columns advanced into the interior. It was the best country for mounted troops which the British had encountered in America. The roads were of fine sand without stones or gravel, and the woods were clear of underbrush. Cornwallis commanded the main thrust on Camden; and learning that a Continental regiment was retreating before him, he detached Tarleton with his mounted infantry in pursuit. Dashing through Camden towards the North Carolina border, Tarleton covered more than 100 miles in fifty-four hours, overtook the enemy, and destroyed the last body of Continental troops in South Carolina. The whole province was now in British hands. Cornwallis cantoned his troops in the hot weather to cover the formation of loyalist militias, and returned to Charleston to settle the civil administration and prepare for the invasion of North Carolina.

In Charleston Cornwallis busied himself with the problems of political consolidation: the raising of a militia, and the purging of field officers of the

[1] CO 5/99, ff. 19, 24, 288; Sandwich, III, 138-9, 142; Sackville, II, 162, 166-7. On the galling inconveniences of life in New York under military rule, see Nelson, 144.
[2] CO 5/99, f. 255.

old rebel militia and members of the rebel Council. The rest of the disaffected were disarmed, and required to furnish provisions and transport instead of personal service. The export of rice to England was resumed, to restore the colony's prosperity. James Simpson was confident that in a month or two South Carolina would return to peace and loyalty, and looked forward impatiently to the restoration of the legislature.[1]

But while Cornwallis worked to consolidate, his gains were beginning to crumble. Thomas Sumter entered the field as a guerrilla leader and rapidly seduced many of the militia, while a regular force of Continentals was pushing south towards the border under Gates, the reputed victor of Saratoga. Cornwallis hurried up from Charleston to join the army, determined to take the offensive and save his hospitals and magazines. He had only 2,000 men,[2] but 1,500 of them were British regulars; and on 16 August he scattered Gates's force near Camden in a masterly attack. Kalb was killed, Gates fled 200 miles on the fastest horse in the American army, and of 4,000 Americans only 700 assembled again in North Carolina. Two days later Tarleton with 160 men surprised Sumter's band and killed or took 450 of them. For the second time a crushing victory had laid South Carolina at Cornwallis's feet.

Yet the triumph was delusive, and Cornwallis was far from clear how to use his victory. His troops had gained in reputation; but even measured against the enormous losses of the enemy he could ill afford his own: his 300 casualties in the battle were irreplaceable. Still more serious was the disappointing progress of pacification. A month earlier the country seemed to have submitted completely, and the people to be sincerely happy at their release from rebel tyranny. It had been possible to look forward to the complete extinction of the rebel cause by this time. But the approach of Gates had released a store of disaffection which had been wholly unsuspected.[3] Sumter's emergence was the signal for a general rising between the Peedee and the Santee. Oaths of allegiance were discarded, militia units deserted to the enemy, and fierce attacks were launched on British outposts. Nor did Gates's crushing defeat extinguish the flames.

Against this resurgent violence Cornwallis was helpless. He could execute militiamen who had deserted to the enemy after taking the oath of allegiance, and after the battle of Camden two or three of these deserters were picked out of a bunch of thirty and hanged. But in an auction of terror the rebels could always outbid him. His aim was to conciliate and pacify: theirs was

---

[1] Sackville, II, 169; Royal Institution MSS., II, 158.

[2] 1,944 rank and file, 2,239 of all ranks.

[3] Royal Institution MSS., II, 169–70, 173; Sackville, II, 185–6; Cornwallis-Wykeham-Martin, 325.

to stoke the flames of hatred. After the defeat at King's Mountain an elderly militia colonel who had always been a fair and open enemy to the rebels was hanged with eight other prisoners as a reprisal. Cornwallis was up against western frontiersmen, trained in savagery by their encroachments on the Indians; and his own policy was hampered by the high proportion of provincial troops in his army. Many an expedition contained no British troops; and the loyalist units gave the campaign the murderous character of a civil war. The rebels persecuted even neutrality, and little quarter was given. The loyalist regiments burned and ravaged in their turn. Tarleton's Legion became a by-word, and 'Tarleton's quarter' was the cry which blessed the rebels' massacre of surrendering militiamen at King's Mountain. In the face of rebel ruthlessness the long-oppressed loyalists were easily disheartened, and Cornwallis despaired of them: 'when I see a whole settlement running away from 20 or 30 robbers, I think they deserve to be robbed'.[1] The militia could not be trusted. The great mass of citizens who were neither dedicated rebels nor loyalists had returned to their allegiance from weariness of war and military service; and when they found themselves forced into a new militia to serve against their friends, they deserted in droves.[2]

The choice after Camden was not an easy one. According to Germain's plan the army should now act as a covering force while the liberated province was pacified by the loyalist militia. But after Gates's incursion Cornwallis was certain that he could not protect the province effectively except by taking the offensive and smashing the rebel strongholds in North Carolina. Two doubts suggest themselves. How was order to be maintained in his rear by a militia in which he had no confidence amidst a population envenomed by civil war? And where could his own advance be halted? When Savannah had been recovered the Governor had urged the invasion of South Carolina for the protection of Georgia: now South Carolina had been won, and it was necessary to attack North Carolina. Before Cornwallis's small force stretched the endless leagues of North Carolina and Virginia; and every mile it advanced would incur fresh obligations to loyalists. If Cornwallis was right, Germain's concept of a methodical and static consolidation was breaking down in face of the dynamic of rebel warfare.

Cornwallis was a commander who preferred the bolder course. Boldness

[1] Ross, *Cornwallis Correspondence*, I, 56–75. On the savagery which characterised the Southern war, see Nelson, 149. Alden (*The South* . . . 235) cites the hanging of five loyalists taken while marching to join Prevost at the beginning of 1779 as an early stimulus to the atrocious character of the struggle.

[2] Thus A. Turnbull explained the collapse of British control in South Carolina in a letter to Shelburne. (CL, Shelburne, Vol. 66, p. 641, letter of 1 Aug. 1781). The rebel South Carolina militia's failure to rise to the crisis of the British invasion in 1780 lends it probability. (see Alden, *The South* . . ., 239, 241).

had succeeded at Camden, and he chose it now. He appealed to Clinton to support him with a diversion in the Chesapeake: 'It may be doubted by some whether the invasion of North Carolina may be a prudent measure; but I am convinced it is a necessary one, and that if we do not attack that province, we must give up both South Carolina and Georgia, and retire within the walls of Charleston.' On 7 September the army moved northwards towards the border.

The first objective was Hillsborough, deep in North Carolina. But lack of forage slowed the army's progress, and on 22 September it had only reached Charlottetown. Here Cornwallis was in a known area of rebellion where his foraging parties were constantly harassed. Governor Martin, who had reported favourably on the inhabitants, issued proclamations urging the loyalists to embody; but few came in, probably because they could not get through the hovering rebel parties. Oppressed and intimidated, they dared not stir, though they promised to help when the army reached them. Then came news of a misfortune which turned the course of the campaign.

Major Ferguson had been advancing from Ninety-Six across the back parts of South Carolina towards Charlottetown to protect the army's rear against guerrillas. He was the most expert rifleman and partisan in the British Army, and he felt a confidence in his militia which few still shared. In pursuit of a rebel party which had attacked Augusta, he found himself suddenly in the presence of 1,400 mounted riflemen from beyond the mountains. Ferguson turned at bay on King's Mountain. He had 1,000 militiamen and was the only British man in his entire force; but he had a position of great natural strength and 100 picked Provincial troops, and was confident he could hold the mountain. But the slopes of the hill were forested. A storm of bullets rained on the militiamen as the backwoodsmen closed in from three sides. Ferguson was everywhere, animating his troops and cutting down white flags until he was killed. The survivors attempted to surrender, but two men with white flags were shot down, and the slaughter continued. At length a rebel officer was able to stop the firing. By then more than 300 of Ferguson's men were dead or too badly wounded to be moved; 700 became prisoners, some of them marked for the gallows.

The effect on Cornwallis was decisive. With a rebel force menacing his rear, further advance was impossible. The North Carolina loyalists had done nothing to justify the risk of invading their province, and the army's departure from South Carolina had put the British gains in peril. He broke off his offensive and fell back to a central position at Winnsborough from which he could support both Camden and Ninety-six. Here the army remained till the end of the year.

3. The French Established

In New York the fall of Charleston had produced a euphoria which even the approach of a French expedition could not damp. In the middle of July Lord Robert Manners heard predictions that North Carolina and Virginia would be overrun before the winter, Pennsylvania cowed by the British approach, and the Jerseys enabled to throw off the rebel yoke. Then would come a small expedition to re-occupy Rhode Island, and in the spring an attack on Boston.[1]

Everything, however, awaited the appearance of the French. If they did not come, Clinton hoped to mount his operation in the Chesapeake. But he felt cramped by the shortage of troops. The recruits from Europe had not yet reached him; for it will be remembered that the despatch of the 2,000 British recruits had been opposed by Amherst while there remained any possibility that England would be invaded.[2] When Ternay's destination became apparent in April, the Cabinet ordered them to sail. But when the German recruits reached England in June, there was only enough shipping for 1,400 of the British recruits. Germain ordered the Admiralty to appoint an escort and despatch the convoy to New York, and repeated the order on July 1. But we shall see that the naval situation at home interposed to prevent their despatch till the end of the summer, and they did not reach New York till the end of October.[3]

The army's dispositions in July were as follows[4]:

Rank and file:	Fit for duty	Total Effectives
Nova Scotia	1,862	3,145
New York and Long Island	14,285	20,048
South Carolina	4,870	6,733
Georgia	1,259	1,706
East Florida	351	457
West Florida	727	1,308
Bermuda	281	304
Providence	51	118
Totals	23,686	33,819

It will be seen from these figures that Clinton's only uncommitted reserve was at New York, where he could put about 5,000 fit men in the field after finding garrisons. He asked Cornwallis to spare 2,500 men; but

---

[1] Rutland, III, 31–2.   [2] Above, p. 327.
[3] G3002; CO 5/255, pp. 15, 21; below, p. 357.   [4] CO 5/100, f. 53.

Cornwallis could not afford to lose a man. To Germain Clinton complained of the shortage, so mortifying when another 10,000 men might end the war 'as far as the Hudson River'.[1]

But before any decision could be taken about future operations, Clinton had to reckon with the approach of Ternay.[2] He had now to pay the penalty for evacuating Rhode Island in the previous autumn – a penalty to which he had not been blind when he gave the order. A French force established there would be a permanent menace to all the British posts from Canada southwards. If Graves's squadron came in time there was one sure remedy: to attack and destroy the French expedition at the moment of its arrival. But Ternay must be given no time to strengthen the Newport peninsula or summon American reinforcements.

Clinton laid his plans accordingly. He considered two possible operations: a landing in the Sakonnet passage to the east of Rhode Island; or to take the expedition through the Conanicut Passage as d'Estaing had done in 1778 and land on the Rhode Island coast above Newport. An amphibious attack needs careful preparation, but Clinton had the time. By 22 June he had 6,000 troops ready, and had warned Arbuthnot to assemble transports. The Admiral had everything prepared so that Graves could be refitted on his arrival without crossing the bar at Sandy Hook. Thus each commander was alert and ready. But there was no bridge of understanding between them.

The two services had co-operated well during the siege of Charleston. But scarcely had the city surrendered when Arbuthnot's appointment to the Peace Commission re-opened the quarrel with Clinton. He now rejected both of Clinton's proposed attacks; but he pleaded ignorance of Rhode Island and refused to suggest an alternative plan.

Ternay, in the meantime, was approaching. Like Graves he had had his troubles. The Ministry of Marine had summoned the transports too late from Toulon, delaying the embarkation of the troops. Contrary winds then prevented his departure, and when he finally sailed on 2 May he was detained for several days in the Bay of Biscay by a westerly gale. He chose the southern passage, and south-west of Bermuda on 20 July he had a brush with an inferior British force under Commodore Cornwallis which had been escorting a homeward-bound convoy from the West Indies. But he pressed on to complete his own mission. Early in August he was sighted off Virginia; but on the 13th Graves arrived off New York after an eight weeks' passage by the southern route. He was refitted in six days, and his 700 sick were replaced with volunteers from New York. But on the 18th news arrived

---

[1] CO 5/100, ff. 49–52; Royal Institution MSS., II, 156.
[2] The following account relies largely on Willcox's analysis based on the Clinton Papers (*JMH*, 1945).

that Ternay had been at Rhode Island for a week. It has never been explained why Arbuthnot had no cruisers out to watch for the enemy, but the fact remains that for seven days the French had been fortifying their base unmolested. Graves was blamed in England for wasting time with a prize on his voyage; but though he arrived just a day after Ternay, an earlier arrival would have made little difference unless Rhode Island had been watched.

Arbuthnot now had ten sail of the line against Ternay's six; and as soon as he learnt that the French were at Newport he agreed with Clinton that the troops should be embarked and moved up Long Island Sound while the fleet reconnoitred the enemy. But on embarking his regiments Clinton discovered that Arbuthnot had used the transports' water to replenish the fleet, and the butts were empty. While they were being replenished the wind changed, and the East River became impassable. Not till the 27th did the transports reached Huntington Bay in the Sound.

Through sickness and the separation of a transport, the French had only 4,000 troops fit for duty, and no batteries had yet been constructed. But Clinton knew only that they had been in possession of Rhode Island for nearly three weeks, and the prospect of a *coup de main* was fading. Moreover, Washington's forces were gathering to threaten Staten Island, and he was nervous about his rear. Holding the force where it lay, he sent his A.D.C. to Arbuthnot, who sent back a message that the prospects were hopeless and he hoped the army would not come. The French, he said, had been reinforced with American militia and artillery, the fortifications were too strong to be assaulted, and the fleet could not provide a siege train as it had done at Charleston. Arbuthnot's report was decisive. Without seeing for himself, Clinton dropped back towards New York to await developments.

Early in August a flag of truce was sent to seek intelligence, and the officer reported that the harbour could be forced if troops could occupy one side of the passage. Arbuthnot proposed an immediate conference, and Clinton rode day and night through Long Island to join the Admiral. But when he reached Gardiner's Bay the anchorage was empty. Arbuthnot had put out on a report that the French were to sail, leaving not even a despatch boat in the bay. General Mathew and Brigadier Dalrymple were sent in pursuit, found the fleet on 19 August, and proposed the seizure of Conanicut Island if it would enable the fleet to force the passage. Arbuthnot replied that the attempt was hopeless without a full scale siege by 18-20,000 men.

So the opportunity passed untested, and the French obtained their lodgment in America, though even in September, when batteries had been armed in the entrance to the harbour, Ternay feared that the British would pass up the western passage between Conanicut Island and the mainland. The British commanders, angry and uneasy, settled down to fix the blame on each other.

Arbuthnot sent home long misleading reports and selections of correspondence to show that it was Clinton who had shrunk from the risk; and Clinton despatched Brigadier Dalrymple to demand the recall of Arbuthnot, the removal of the transports from naval control, and a reinforcement of at least 10,000 men. If these terms were not met, he asked leave to resign. Germain concluded that the failure was caused by a total want of confidence and communication between the two commanders: both were to blame.[1] Separated by 100 miles of Long Island Sound, and without previous agreement or present sympathy, it is no wonder that they missed the fleeting moment. Now a French squadron and a corps of troops were established in 'the best and noblest harbour in America': an anchorage too dangerous to blockade except in the summer, and with no shelter for the watching fleet nearer than the tip of Long Island, eighteen leagues to leeward.

4. Treason among the Rebels

The commander of the French troops was Lieutenant-General the Comte de Rochambeau. Distinguished service in the Seven Years War, and the command in 1779 of the picked assault force of Vaux's army of invasion, testified to his military abilities. His new assignment called for other qualities; and he had the temperance, loyalty and generosity which were needed for dealing with his strange allies. His orders were to land twelve battalions on Rhode Island and place himself under the command of Washington. To the American commander the plan of operations was left, with only the secret proviso that the French force should be kept together. Vergennes' hope was to strike a decisive blow on the rebel coast, exploiting the division of force and universal inferiority which he believed would be forced on the British in the summer of 1780. What he did not want was to further the American passion for expanding into Canada and Nova Scotia; but this was a political question for Luzerne in Philadelphia.

Though Vergennes' hopes were to be realised in due course, the moment was not ripe. Rochambeau arrived when American fortunes were running low. The French were shocked at the surrender of Charleston, and inclined to believe in southern indifference to the rebel cause. Luzerne, who had been in America long enough to judge, feared from the moderation of the British in South Carolina that they were contemplating a settlement with the northern states and the consolidation of their gains in the south. The new arrivals were horrified by what they found. Ternay, an orthodox officer and easily discouraged by the peculiar situation of the Americans, reported that the revolution was not so far advanced as Europe believed, and that a

[1] Sandwich, III, 258.

single highly placed traitor in the American ranks could decide the fate of a campaign; a fear soon shown to have substance. The state of the Continental forces was a shock for Rochambeau. 'Send us troops, ships, and money', he wrote home five days after his arrival; 'but do not count on these people nor on their resources, they have neither money nor credit, their forces only exist momentarily, and when they are about to be attacked in their own homes they assemble during the time of personal danger to defend themselves.' He had been told that France's commercial credits in America would support his force for a whole campaign: now he found that he could only supply his men till the end of the year. Money was needed. But still more he needed men, for Washington's aim was to attack New York, and he remembered d'Estaing's fiascos: '*il ne faut pas faire ici des affaires de Savannah*'. Not only the British believed that the rebellion had shallow roots.[1]

When Washington had learnt in the spring that the French were coming, he was deeply worried by the situation in the south. But though cramped by the poverty of his resources, he was naturally a bold and aggressive commander, and his instinct was to ease the pressure on Gates by a blow in the north. He suggested that if the whole British force remained at Charleston, the French should sail straight for Sandy Hook and burst into the port of New York. He foresaw that if they went first to Rhode Island, the events of 1778 would repeat themselves: the British would have time to obstruct the approaches to New York and receive help from England. This indeed was what happened. Clinton and Arbuthnot, like the Howes two years earlier, reached New York from the southward before the French appeared. But on this occasion the reinforcing squadron from England arrived almost simultaneously with the French; for Graves, sailing on the southern route, had better luck than Byron, and the British retained the naval superiority which Rochambeau needed to assault New York.

The allied offensive was therefore stillborn; and while Washington and Rochambeau were inactive, Clinton was planning a coup whose unmasking was to give the enemy one of their worst frights in the whole course of the war. Benedict Arnold, the hero of Quebec and Saratoga, had formed a treasonable correspondence with the British. Clinton had Germain's authority to use just such an opening, and Arnold's defection was the climax of an extensive correspondence with American traitors which fed the hope of a rebel collapse.[2] He commanded at West Point, the impenetrable key to the Highlands. It was a tremendous opening. Success would win all the forts in the Highlands, with their stores, siege guns, boats and men. If the blow did not break the war-weary Americans immediately, its effects should

[1] See correspondence in Sparks MSS., Vol. 78.
[2] See Carl van Doren, *The Secret History of the American Revolution*.

still be lasting and decisive; for Washington's lateral communications would be severed, and according to Arnold he 'would be obliged to fight or to disband his army for want of provisions'.[1]

At the last moment the plot miscarried. The negotiations were managed by Clinton's Adjutant-General, Major André. Returning from a conference with Arnold, he was cut off from his ship; and as he made his way back in disguise, protected as he hoped by Arnold's safe-conduct, he was searched by a rebel party which found incriminating papers in his boots. While Arnold fled to the British lines, André was sentenced to death.

Desperate efforts were made to save him. General Robertson went up the river to meet General Greene, who said that there was no treating about spies; to which Robertson replied that no military casuist in Europe would call André a spy. 'Greene now with a blush . . . told me that the army must be satisfied by seeing spies executed; but there was one thing would satisfy them – they expected, if André was set free, Arnold should be given up. This I answered with a look only, which threw Greene into confusion. I am persuaded André will not be hurt.'[2]

But Robertson was wrong. The Americans were angry and frightened; and after their shamefaced attempt to trade André's life for Arnold's they hanged him in the midst of their army, rejecting his petition to be shot. The first that Clinton knew of it was when André's servant came into the lines with his baggage. Four days after the hanging he received a peremptory demand from Washington for an explanation about the confinement of plotting prisoners of war in South Carolina; to which he managed to return a civil answer.

Arbuthnot in the meantime had been cruising off Rhode Island to intercept a second French reinforcement which was believed to be on its way. In the middle of September he returned to Gardiner's Bay resolved to wait there till the winter was well advanced. If the French evaded him, he intended to detach all but his own flagship to Rodney in the West Indies. But as we know, Rodney was even then approaching New York; and on the following day he appeared with ten sail of the line.[3]

Rodney's arrival brought a new element into the quarrels of New York. While Clinton and Arbuthnot continued their bickering, Arbuthnot set to with Rodney: 'You may guess how the service is carried on', wrote one of Rodney's captains.[4] Arbuthnot's grievance was said to be prize money:

[1] CO 5/100, f. 301. See above, pp. 143–4.
[2] CO 5/100, f. 189.
[3] CL, Germain, 13 Sept., from Arbuthnot.
[4] Rutland, III, 39.

'the loaves and fishes' had caused too much trouble already between the services and within the navy. But Rodney's own conduct does not bear close scrutiny, and he offered provocation which a wiser man than Arbuthnot might have found intolerable. He had come to America to fight Guichen; and since Guichen had gone to Europe he had no good reason for staying. Though he assumed the command of the station the moment he arrived, his flag never met Arbuthnot's; and while the battle fleet tossed in Gardiner's Bay, Rodney remained at New York to plunder Arbuthnot's resources and mar his dispositions. He stripped the storehouses, impressed 400 seamen, and carried off two frigates on his departure. Muddle and friction were the result. A convoy was about to fetch urgently needed supplies from Halifax. Rodney countermanded it, but did not inform Arbuthnot; and when three victuallers arrived from England on passage to Halifax Arbuthnot allowed them to proceed, imagining that supplies were already being shuttled from their destination.[1]

Rodney did not wholly ignore operations. He arrived full of the idea of attacking Rhode Island, but when Clinton showed him the correspondence with Arbuthnot he promptly dropped it. Clinton instead sent off the Chesapeake expedition which he had planned before the French arrival, and for which Rodney's presence allowed an ample naval superiority. On 16 October General Leslie sailed for Virginia with 2,500 men. A month later Rodney departed for the West Indies with his ten sail of the line, leaving eight with Arbuthnot, while two returned to England. He carried with him a powerful artillery of invective to use against the commanders in America. The war there, he wrote to Sandwich, was being conducted with 'a slackness inconceivable in every branch'; every useful post which was taken was unaccountably evacuated; and the abandoning of Rhode Island had been 'the most fatal measure that could possibly be adopted'. On the last point he spoke from ignorance of the circumstances. His criticisms of Clinton's inertia may have been just, but they were vitiated by a fact which Willcox has remarked: his own demands for action 'had been ineffective because they had never been made'.[2]

[1] Sackville, II, 190-1; Sandwich, III, 259; Adm. 1/486, ff. 414, 450, 464, 634 et seq.
[2] Mundy, I, 428-32; James, 239; JMH 1945, pp. 313-5.

CHAPTER XX

THE HOME FRONT

1. *The Command of the Channel Fleet*

As Graves and Walsingham sailed for the Western Atlantic, Hardy returned from his winter quarters at Greenwich to resume the command of the Channel fleet. The augeries were not favourable, for the slackness and indiscipline of which Rodney had complained are confirmed from other quarters. Middleton mentioned it in connection with the difficulty of introducing carronades. It had infected the lower deck, and when Graves's ships mutinied for their pay, Captain Samuel Hood, then Commissioner of Portsmouth Dockyard, wrote to his brother of the 'wonderful spirit of discontent in almost every ship which I am afraid is encouraged; this I am well assured of, proper exertions to prevent it is not used. Such a want of discipline and order throughout the fleet was never known before, or such a want of regard and attention to the good of the King's service. The negligence of officers in general is really astonishing, and God only knows to what extent the mischief will go.'[1] This was the general refrain. The seamen took their lead from the ships' officers; and the officers' slackness was tolerated by the admirals. The fleet did not need a better government or a better cause. It needed a better commander.

Sandwich believed that by wary management he was laying the hydra of faction asleep. His letters to Rodney showed the greatest care not to drive him the way of other commanders. He greeted the victory over Langara with the warmest praise, and claimed the credit for Rodney's receiving the thanks of Parliament and a pension. 'The worst of my enemies', he wrote, 'now allow I have pitched upon a man who knows his duty, and is a brave, honest, and able officer. I will not tire you with panegyric' – a pleasant fancy – 'but am not the less eager in dealing out all around me the praises due to your merit.'[2]

At the same time, however, Sandwich was anxious to do justice to his disgraced friend Palliser. There had been some support in the House of Commons for employing him; and encouraged by this Sandwich formed the plan of giving him Hardy's Governorship of Greenwich Hospital. He intended to compensate Hardy with the Lieutenant-Generalcy of Marines. Unfortunately North had already thought of the Marines for Rodney, and Barrington

---

[1] Sandwich, III, 275.   [2] Sandwich, III, 205-7.

had also applied for them. The King, who opposed Palliser's reinstatement because it would 'occasion noise' (as indeed it did), warned North of Sandwich's real motive for blocking Rodney's claim. Sandwich neatly outflanked them all by offering Rodney the Marines as an alternative to his pension, knowing well that he was anxious to provide for Lady Rodney, on whom half the pension would devolve. Rodney chose the pension.[1]

As matters turned out, Hardy did not have to be bought out of Greenwich. On 18 May, on the eve of receiving his orders for the Channel fleet, he dropped dead of a fit. A successor was needed at once, and the command was offered to Barrington. But Barrington since his return from the West Indies was a man with a grievance. He was dissatisfied with the recognition his capture of St Lucia had received, and when he had been asked to return to the Leeward Islands he had told Sandwich that he would never act as a Commander-in-Chief again. He now came to London, and in spite of Sandwich's persuasions refused the Channel command. He said that the strain and anxiety would kill him, and advised the First Lord to send for Keppel. Mulgrave interpreted this as a deep plot on Barrington's part to become First Lord himself; but his real motive seems to have been the one he gave to Sandwich, that he could not face the strain. He had no confidence in the Admiralty; and a couple of days later he opened his heart to Middleton. 'A man must see with my eyes, and have my feelings, before he can account for my refusing the command. If our superiors had those feelings, and only their King and country's interest at heart, we might in time be ourselves again. Had I been in command, what I have seen since I have been here would have made me run mad. A total relaxation of discipline, and the rule laid down by a great man that we are all alike, must in the end be productive of bad consequences.' A stouter heart and stronger nerves were wanted to reform the Channel fleet.[2]

Above all energy and drive were needed. 'If you wish success in your armies or fleets', Middleton advised Sandwich, 'look for persons of abilities of the middle age – I mean about forty – to conduct them.' But Barrington's refusal forced the Admiralty back on Francis Geary, who was aged about seventy. He was much liked as a man, and was not a politician. But more was needed. Since the previous autumn Kempenfelt had been preaching the doctrine that the fleet needed a driving personality. He did not subscribe to the notion that some magic in the British breed made them better seamen

[1] Knox, 165; G 2951, 2960; Sandwich, III, 208–9. Palliser's appointment does more credit to Sandwich's personal loyalty than to his political discretion. It brought on the most acrimonious and personal debate in the House of Commons which Wraxall could remember in fourteen years.

[2] G 3030; Sandwich, II, 363–4, III, 281; Barham, I, 366; Barrington Papers, II, 337–41.

than the French. In Keppel's campaign the enemy had managed their ships like seamen, and their frigates had shown an alertness not equalled by the British. 'The men who are best disciplined, of whatever country they are, will always fight the best.' But Geary was no more a leader than Hardy had been. He had been third in command to Hawke, but had never held an independent seagoing command, and had not been to sea at all for many years. 'The present person', wrote Kempenfelt, 'is brave, generous, and may perhaps have been a good officer; but he is wholly debilitated in his faculties, his memory and judgment lost, wavering and indeterminate in everything.' It was as well that the major operations of 1780 were not in the Channel.[1]

2. The Channel Operations

Sandwich's promise to have thirty sail of the line ready for home service by 1 May was not an easy undertaking to fulfill. The six prizes of the Gibraltar campaign had arrived at the beginning of March, and were promptly surveyed and taken into service. But in offering the Mediterranean command to Commodore Elliot, Sandwich had to warn him that he would not be allowed to fly his flag in a ship of the line. In present circumstances we could not weaken the home fleet except in the hope of obtaining a superiority elsewhere. England could not be superior in the Mediterranean, so recently a domain of the British navy, and a single ship of the line at Gibraltar would merely be thrown away from the defence of Britain.[2]

Though the enemy had also dispersed their forces abroad, and did not intend an invasion, they could still assemble nearly fifty sail of the line in European waters. But from the beginning there was no settled policy. The Spaniards were obsessed with the siege of Gibraltar; and the French, uneasy about the Cumberland negotiations in Madrid, were forced to defer to their wishes. '*Rien de nouveau pour le présent en Europe*', Vergennes reported to Ternay at the beginning of June. '*Il paroit que la campagne s'y passera en observation et que les grands coups s'il doit s'en porter se fraperont dans les Amériques.*'[3] Seven French sail of the line had accompanied the Spaniards home to Cadiz in the winter, and some vague idea was canvassed for a concentration there to command the mouth of the Channel in the late summer. All this was unknown to the British government. What was apparent, however, was that the enemy had already in part effected at Cadiz the concentration which had cost them so many vital weeks in 1779. Seven more ships of the line were believed to be fitting out at Toulon to join the main force; and there was every reason to expect that the whole armada would eventually work its way northward

---

[1] Barham, I, 297–8, 311, 329, 333; Sandwich, III, 275, 280.
[2] G 2962; Sandwich, III, 208.   [3] *Sic* (Doniol, IV, 287 n.).

to the Channel. All that lay in the power of the British fleet was to prevent such ships as remained in Brest from joining the enemy concentration.

Geary hoisted his flag on 24 May. His fleet was still six short of the thirty which Sandwich had promised, but another ten would be ready as soon as men came in. The ships immediately ready were powerful, thirteen of them of eighty guns and above, and none below seventy-four. They had moreover the inestimable advantage of copper. When Richard Cumberland embarked at Portsmouth in April for his mission to Spain, he walked Father Hussey round the dockyard so that he could see the tremendous display of stores which backed the fleet; and everything which they saw afloat floated on copper. The invention had proved its worth, and enthusiasm resounded on all sides. 'The *Courageux's* copper has answered beyond my hopes', Mulgrave had written in the last campaign, 'as her superiority in sailing is hardly credible.' Rodney declared that without copper-bottomed ships, he would not have brought Langara to action, and begged for all that Sandwich could send him. Middleton believed that if the navy could continue to stop Dutch shipments of copper to France and prevent the export of British rolled plates, the British lead in coppering could be maintained. 'This first of all naval improvements seems at this critical period the means which Providence has put into our power to extricate us from present danger.'[1]

On 27 May the Admiralty ordered Geary to go to sea as soon as twenty-four ships of the line were ready, and prevent the junction of the Cadiz and Brest fleets. He sailed on 8 June, hastened by a letter from old Lord Hawke urging him to get off Brest and 'watch those fellows as close as a cat watches a mouse', and till nearly the end of the month he cruised off Ushant watching for the French. But on the 28th he fell back to a station off the Lizard, pleading indeterminately his orders to protect the homeward-bound convoys and to prevent the enemy's concentration.

In the meantime a despatch had arrived from Commodore Johnstone on the coast of Portugal which faced the Cabinet with a difficult decision. Enemy squadrons were cruising off Finisterre and Cape St Vincent to intercept the British East and West India convoys. Should the Admiralty be ordered to detach from the Channel fleet to protect the convoys on the far side of the Bay? Or should the trade be risked to ensure the defence of home waters and the Soundings? On the 24th the Cabinet resolved that Geary should detach an admiral with ten sail of the line to cruise for not more than a month beyond the Bay.[2]

[1] CL, Germain, 21 April, Cumberland to Germain; Sandwich, III, 34, 175–6, 201; G 3510.
[2] G 3085; Barrington Papers, II, 343–5.

These orders were peremptory; but when he received them off the Lizard Geary hesitated. A Council of Flag Officers was called; and in view of the enemy's strength it was agreed not to divide the fleet. Instead the whole force sailed southwards for Finisterre. The recruits for America had even now not sailed, and Knox asked the Admiralty to hold them up till Geary returned to protect them. Germain derided the precaution: 'I trusted to the natural sloth of sea operations . . . and all I pray is that your precautions may not be better attended to than you desired.' His scepticism was justified. The troops grew sickly, the campaigning season waned, the Admiralty was sent peremptory orders that they should sail. Yet in the middle of August the recruits were still not away, and in spite of a favourable wind it looked as though the convoy would be held up for the convenience of the Treasury. 'I am sorry the money is likely to delay our transports from sailing', Germain wrote to Knox on the 13th, 'but the easterly wind seems so steady that I flatter myself they will go in spite of Admiralty, Treasury, etc.' His patience with naval arrangements wore thinner as the seasons passed.[1]

Geary returned off Ushant without sighting the enemy, and at the end of July the Jamaica convoy made its landfall safely: 'very heartening to the fat and greasy citizens', the odious Eden reported to Lord Carlisle, 'and not unacceptable to the public purse'.[2] He rubbed his hands too soon. A fine southerly wind carried an outward bound convoy to sea for the East and West Indies, escorted by Captain Moutray in the Ramillies, 64. Though the enemy were known to be cruising off Cadiz for the trade, he was ordered to rendezvous at Madeira, and his course took him straight through the danger area which Geary had just left. On 9 August, 250 miles west of Cape St Vincent, he ran into the enemy fleet. Against thirty-two sail of the line Moutray could do nothing to save his merchantmen, and he made off pursued by the fast squadron of the enemy. Of his convoy only three ships escaped. Sixty-one fell into the hands of the enemy: tall East Indiamen, and storeships, troops and merchandise much needed in the West Indies. The loss was valued at £1½ million, and 3,000 prisoners were taken. It was a fearful blow, not least to the Cumberland negotiations in Madrid.

When news of the disaster arrived, Geary and his fleet were at Spithead. In spite of orders to stay at sea as long as possible, he had been compelled to return for refreshment by the mounting scurvy, which had attacked one in seven of his men. Sandwich was as sorry to see him in port as he had been to see Hardy, and as anxious to get him away. The loss of another convoy, he told Geary, 'would occasion such distress to this country that no one can tell the consequences it might have'. Two regiments were shipped as marines

---

[1] Knox, 168; CL, Knox, 13 Aug. from Germain; CO 5/255, p. 27.
[2] Carlisle, 437.

to make up Geary's complements, and he was ordered to detach a squadron at once to protect the inward bound convoys if he could not take the whole fleet to sea. Geary replied by asking where he should cruise, as he could not simultaneously hinder the enemy's concentration and look for the homeward trade. The King acknowledged the dilemma, and applauded his wisdom in throwing the decision on the Admiralty. Before the end of August, however, the East and West India convoys were home, and North asked Sandwich to reconsider the purpose of detaching. The order was cancelled, and Geary was ordered to take the whole fleet to sea when it was ready.[1]

Geary's exchanges with the Admiralty made Barrington rejoice that he had refused the command. He suspected that the Board were preparing to lay all that went wrong on Geary's shoulders. To his brother the Bishop of Llandaff he denounced 'the duplicity and Jesuitical Correspondence of the Admiralty, who are at present frightened out of their senses . . . the wickedest herd that ever good men served under'. Holding these views, he was dismayed when Geary broke down. On 27 August the Commander-in-Chief applied for sick leave with the support of his doctors: 'The Admiral, thro' a constant fatigue and hurry of business added to an over anxiety of mind seems to have exhausted his strength.'[2]

At least one captain thought Geary would not be fit to serve again. Sandwich suggested however that he should have a short rest while Barrington took the fleet to sea. But Barrington refused to command, and sent a letter to the Admiralty offering to serve under any Admiral but one (presumably Palliser), or to strike his flag and make way for a junior officer.

Three or four days passed without an answer, and Barrington grumbled to his brother Lord Barrington that everyone was too immersed in electioneering to look to the good of the country. Here he did the Ministers an injustice. His letter had been greeted with utter consternation. Sandwich described it as criminal[3]; but Barrington was one of the most popular officers in the fleet, and his retirement would fan the flames which had been raised by Palliser's appointment to Greenwich. Mulgrave went down to Hinchingbrooke to talk it over with Sandwich, and they diagnosed a plot to bring back Keppel, with Geary a weak tool of Barrington. Sandwich concluded that they must resist intimidation. Barrington must go, and the fleet be sent to sea at once under Admiral Darby. North and the King were in complete agreement; they only feared that Sandwich's draft answer to

---

[1] Sandwich, III, 290–2; Adm. 2/1338, ff. 42, 46.

[2] James, 246; Barrington Papers, II, 347–9.

[3] ' . . . it is criminal in a military officer to make conditions with his Sovereign relative to his serving' (Williams, 208).

Barrington was too equivocal and would give him an opportunity to change his mind. The discussion was cut short by a second letter from Barrington. Geary had handed over his orders, and Barrington had refused them and handed the fleet over to the Port Admiral. This was so improper that the King could wait no longer. Since North had set out for Oxfordshire for the election, the King himself sent the order to the Admiralty for Barrington to strike his flag.[1]

To Pye went the Lieutenant-Generalcy of Marines which Barrington had sought. Nor was Barrington employed again by the North Ministry, though he returned after its fall as second-in-command in the Channel, and for a short time commanded off Ushant in the absence of Howe. Darby took over the Channel fleet and joined the Board of Admiralty, and Drake was transferred from the Downs to take a flag in the fleet for the remainder of the campaign. Darby had been promoted by Sandwich, apparently in order to preside at Palliser's court-martial, and had first hoisted his flag in the Channel fleet when Harland refused to serve in 1779. Now he succeeded to the chief command through the defection of another senior. He was hitherto undistinguished, but honest and personally respected, as even Keppel acknowledged. He had no enviable task. Barrington, by refusing to serve, had split the fleet again; and Middleton wrote speedily to Kempenfelt begging him, whatever his private feelings, not to widen the breach till the campaign was over. On 12 September Darby sailed to cruise and protect the trade.[2]

3. Repulse of the Opposition

The critical summer months had passed without a return of the alarms of 1779. Though Sandwich was shaken by the loss of the *Ramillies* convoy and the defection of Barrington, no enemy fleet had approached the Channel. In politics, too, the summer brought a respite; for the Opposition suffered a series of tactical reverses which brought their onslaught to a standstill.

The early months of the year had seen the Ministry riding out a great political storm, buffeted to and fro by protectionist interests, extra-parliamentary agitation, and onslaughts in the House of Commons. By the end of March it was at the point of collapse, and the Opposition seemed to be rushing the country gentlemen on towards the destruction of the King's government and the system on which it rested. In this parliamentary battle Lord North appeared at his best. His spinelessness in administration became flexibility in debate. Sober, reasonable and courteous, he slipped through

[1] Barrington Papers, II, 349-51; Rutland, III, 60; Barham, I, 367; Sandwich, III, 295-8, 300; G 3122, 3125-6.
[2] Keppel, II, 346; Barham, I, 369; Sandwich, III, 302.

his enemies' fingers, conceding the right of petitioners to be heard, and in the same breath making it clear that they were individuals and not the nation. At the Easter recess the exhausted combatants scattered to recruit their health. 'Economical reform' had been checked; but when the House re-assembled early in April the offensive was renewed from a different quarter: for Dunning opened the discussion of the forty Association petitions which lay on the table. The attack was now directed against the Crown; and in a full House Dunning carried his resolution that its powers should be diminished. Pressing their success, the Opposition carried a further motion that it was the duty of the House to redress the abuses. 'The blow seems to me decisive', wrote Horace Walpole; and North told the King that he must be allowed to retire at the end of the session.[1]

This was the climax of the assault; but the Opposition's triumph was deceptive. Radicalism was driving a wedge between the leaders of the Associations and the essentially conservative mass of the discontented gentry. The country gentlemen might agitate for lower taxes; but annual parliaments, reformed constituencies, and control of the King's household expenditure struck at their sense of property and their respect for the throne. The House rose for a week so that the young bloods of the Opposition could go down to the Newmarket races, and in their absence the Ministry organised its forces. The independents who had followed Dunning in the heat of the chase began to cool. On 13 April, while the Commons were still in recess, the Lords threw out the Contractors' Bill. On the 24th the House of Commons reassembled. The largest gathering in living memory heard Dunning propose that till grievances were redressed Parliament should not be prorogued or dissolved. It was an echo of the Long Parliament; and by fifty votes the government beat it down.

The Ministry had survived, and the end of the session brought time to breathe. Shelburne and Rockingham were moving apart, as the latter drew away from the radicals; and in the counties the majorities had already begun to rebel against the caucuses which dominated the Associations. Soon events at home and abroad were to consolidate the Ministry's success. Moderate opinion rallied against the fury of the Gordon riots; and the fall of Charleston ignited new hope that the long American struggle would be fought through to victory.

At the beginning of June, about the time when Geary put to sea, the Protestant Association's petition against the relief of Roman Catholics from certain minor disabilities was the signal for the worst rioting of the century. The poor of London were a force whose uncontrollable violence filled the

[1] See Butterfield, Chaps. VI and VII.

propertied classes with horror. Since Walpole had wisely shelved the Dissenters' claim for relief the mob had not come out for religion; but in the name of Protestantism June 1780 saw horrors unparallelled since the days of the Stuarts. The City was given over to arson and pillage; Lord Sandwich was attacked on his way to the House of Lords; Mansfield's house and splendid library in Bloomsbury were burnt; and even Stormont's distant villa at Ken Wood was threatened. As troops were drawn towards the capital, the Commanders-in-Chief in the Downs and Portsmouth were warned to watch the enemy coast in case the French should seize the opportunity to raid the English coastline.

The crisis called for political courage. The Aldermen of the City had countenanced the outbreak in order to undermine the Ministry, and the magistrates would not order the troops to open fire. Two Ministers kept cool heads. Throughout the riots and their judicial aftermath Stormont acted with alertness, persistence, and fair-mindedness; and Amherst showed himself ready if his colleagues would support him. At his request a Cabinet meeting was hastily called on 6 June, and the military forces to crush the riots were placed under his direct control. But the soldiers were still not empowered to shoot till the magistrates had read the Riot Act, and knowing that they were not allowed to protect themselves they were showing signs of sulkiness. But where was the courage to issue the order? The magistrates would not, and Amherst as a soldier could not. Lord Mansfield hedged about the law, and no lead could be expected from the Prime Minister. 'Nothing is done', wrote Robinson, 'no line fixed, the Cabinet to determine it – No Cabinet fixed – no previous meeting etc. etc.' The King presided at a meeting of the Privy Council, and asked the opinions of those who were present on the legality of opening fire without the reading of the Riot Act. There was much hesitation, for the suppression of the Wilkes riots had led to indictments for murder. The King then turned to the Attorney-General, who was present as an assessor. Wedderburn gave the clear and unequivocal answer he sought: if the mob was committing a felony and could not be prevented by other means, the troops should be ordered to fire, and the reading of the Riot Act was unnecessary.

It was enough. The rest of the Council plucked up their courage and unanimously concurred. King George, with the firmness whose want was to ruin the King of France within the decade, declared that as supreme magistrate he would see the decision carried into effect,[1] and signed an Order in Council himself. The rest lay with Amherst. The troops' morale was restored; and by the 8th fresh regiments were pouring into London and 'dealing death

[1] According to some accounts he said that at all events there was one magistrate in the Kingdom who would do his duty.

about pretty freely'. That night every street was patrolled by soldiers with orders to fire on any four persons who refused to disperse. Amherst estimated the dead and wounded as 458, others as more than 700. Order began to reappear through the smoke and ruins; and a Member of Parliament felt safe enough to lament 'the two most detestable extremes, a lawless mob, and a Military Government'.[1]

The Gordon Riots were to sear the memories of the ruling class for many years, and affected the course of politics more deeply and lastingly than the invasion panic of the previous year. And hard on the heels of the shooting a special issue of the *London Gazette* trumpeted the fall of Charleston. It was a great triumph, and came when the Opposition was cracking. Rockingham and his followers had rallied to the government against the riots, while the Catholic-hating Shelburne took an equivocal stand. This followed deeper division on Parliamentary Reform. Rockingham had wanted to shelve the issue for the sake of unity, while Shelburne favoured the reform of Parliament and encouraged the radical leaders of the county Associations. The moment seemed ripe for the Ministry to approach Rockingham for a coalition: if nothing came of it, it would smooth the way for another manoeuvre.

The Rockingham terms proved impossible: equivocal at the least on American Independence, exacting on economical reform, and to the King's ears outrageous about men: Secretaryships of State for Fox and Richmond, places for Portland, Manchester, Townshend and Burke. Fox, the King would swallow in any lucrative but not ministerial office – 'he never having had any principles can certainly act as his interest may guide him' – but Richmond's conduct towards the Court over a long period made him unacceptable in any capacity. Nor was the King willing to sacrifice Amherst and Sandwich. Amherst was not perfect, but he was better than any possible alternatives; and as for Sandwich, 'whatever his private failings may be, I know no man so fit for his department, he has now got out the finest fleet this country ever possessed'.[2]

The way was clear for the counter-stroke. On 1 July in Cabinet North threw out the idea of a sudden dissolution of Parliament and a general election. Eighteenth-century parliaments usually ran their full seven-year term; and the Opposition would be surprised and unbalanced by the

---

[1] G 3047, 3052; Wraxall, I, 347, 356–7; Campbell, *Lives of the Lord Chancellors*, VI, 128–30; Add. MSS. 38214, f. 51; WO 34/125, f. 115; Castro, *Gordon Riots*, VII, 231–4, 239–40; Wortley, 187; Lothian, 367. Wedderburn had his reward: Lord Chief Justice de Grey resigned to avoid trying the rioters, and Wedderburn at last obtained the Chief Justiceship of the Common Pleas.

[2] G 3099; Christie, 24–9. For what follows see Christie, 29–38 and 116–63.

announcement. Sandwich was enthusiastic, believing that the successes at home and abroad would swing the popular vote to the Ministry. The Treasury experts took a more sober view, for Robinson preferred the orthodox calculation of seats and members to the doubtful factor of public opinion. His first calculations were not reassuring; but an optimistic disposal of the doubtful seats transformed the outlook, and his final prediction was a majority of 128 for the government. On 1 September, in the middle of the Barrington crisis, the Opposition was stunned by the dissolution.

The election which followed was distinguished in that century by the clear principles which marked the parties, and there was an unusual number of contested elections. The Court and Ministry stood for the unity of the Empire and the maintenance of a protectionist control of the American economy; the Opposition, though divided on the terms of peace with the colonies, were united in their determination to end the war and to attack the executive's influence in Parliament. But alas for the calculations of psephologists! Far from gaining, the government lost about five seats. And Sandwich was proved as wrong as Robinson, for even the 'popular' constituencies failed the Ministry. When the new Parliament assembled, North would be conducting the great war on yet more precarious political foundations.

PART FIVE

CATASTROPHE
1781

CHAPTER XXI

THE SHADOWS GATHER

1. *The Strain on Resources*

By the autumn of 1780 England had been waging a great war for two and a half years with resources too slender to meet her commitments. To a remarkable degree, through the insistence of Germain and the King, she had been able to dispute the initiative with the enemy; and in introducing the army estimates towards the end of the year Jenkinson could without straining his case paint the past campaign in pleasing colours. The enemy armaments which were to exploit England's hour of distress had returned to Europe without attempting a single conquest, while England had recovered South Carolina and was pressing the colony's northern neighbour. Yet this was only part of the truth. For the despatch of the enemy's expeditions had shown how difficult it was for England to mould the course of strategy. And in this third September of the general war England's widening strategic commitments throughout the world were beginning to tell, and she was drifting into a situation which she was to face again between 1940 and 1942: so much to protect, such dispersion of force, so little prospect of a decisive concentration. The coming disaster in Virginia was the result of accumulating errors and misfortunes; but war is full of these, and they would not have proved decisive if Britain had been operating with a reasonable margin for flexibility. If England could keep afloat she might yet outstay her enemies. But she was on so tight a string that the misdirection of a single ship might mean disaster.

That the navy was at full stretch has been apparent in the operations of 1780. But the tautness throughout the system was now appearing in other branches of the war effort. The shipping situation, for one, was restricting the execution of plans. The old difficulty of supplying the army in America remained. None of the provisions for 1780 reached Clinton till October, and if the army had not been able to save its salt provisions by drawing on the resources of South Carolina during the siege of Charleston, there might have been a disastrous shortage long before supplies arrived from home.[1] These delays were blamed by Germain on the Navy Board's handling of the victuallers[2]; but the shortage went deeper than this, for not only had the year's recruits for Clinton been held up for transports, but in the autumn an offensive expedition was to yield priority for shipping to reinforcements for

[1] See Major Cockburn's memorandum of Dec. 1780 in CL, Germain, II, Suppl.
[2] See above, p. 339.

existing operations in America and the West Indies.[1] The allocation of shipping priorities was a new burden on Germain's department: a new and ominous restraint on strategy.

The army was also feeling the strain of prolonged war and expanding commitments. Clinton was calling for huge reinforcements, Canada was weak, and at the end of the year the emergence of Holland as an enemy was to call for additional garrisons from the Shetlands to India. The constant trickle of trained infantry across the Atlantic had outstripped recruiting. The wastage of British troops in the western Atlantic between 1777 and 1779 had been 15,664: only 4,786 recruits had been sent out to replace them. Though fresh regiments had been sent out 16,000 strong, the old regiments already in the theatres of war were wasting away.[2]

Not only had the casualties in the theatres of operations to be met, but new regiments raised and the ordinary wastage by desertion and disease at home and in overseas garrisons replaced. Yet the harvest of recruits was drying up. Two years earlier 24,000 men had been raised for the regular army in twelve months; in the next twelve months only 16,000; in the twelve months to September 1780 15,000. Though new regiments were being raised, the army's strength was actually shrinking. Three regiments had just been drafted in the West Indies for want of men; even the infantry in England had lost 100 or so in the past year; and the whole army, including the Irish establishment, was short of its authorised establishment by 27,000.[3]

In the first years of the American rebellion, recruits had been drummed up by tested expedients: short-term service, enlistment of Irish Catholics, and the pardoning of convicted criminals. But the great expansion after Saratoga outran these methods. Between 1778 and 1781, in addition to fencibles, volunteer corps, and the embodying of nearly 40,000 militia, there were raised thirty-one new regiments of foot and four of cavalry. To find the men the bounty was raised, and raised again. Physical requirements were lowered, and age limits widened. Volunteers were promised exemption from parish service after their discharge, and permission to set up in any trade wherever they wished. The idle and disorderly were made liable to impressment by the justices. Vain efforts were even made to obtain the Irish executive's assent to the raising of regiments officered by Irish Catholics.[4] Further

[1] Below, p. 376.

[2] Add. MSS. 38344, ff. 179–80; Add. MSS. 38375, ff. 74–5. These casualty figures do not include the Convention troops, of which the British component amounted to 2,880 rank and file.

[3] Add. MSS. 38344, ff. 162–3; WO 34/127, ff. 152–61.

[4] On this point see CL, Germain, 22 Dec. 1778 to Lord Buckinghamshire; in general Curtis, 51–71. For examples of forced enlistments, see J. of Army Hist. Research, Dec. 1956, p. 186.

compulsion, the Secretary at War argued, was wrong and useless: wrong because contrary to British principles of government, and useless because it would cause disturbances and desertion.[1]

The new regiments had had little difficulty in raising their men. More than half of the 15,000 recruits raised in the past twelve months had been for new levies, and the latest regiment to be raised had found its men quickly and relatively cheaply. It was the 'old' regiments which were failing. The Additional Companies which fed the battalions abroad were not getting a third of the numbers they had been recruiting when they were first established, and were failing to replenish the ranks of their regiments. One of their difficulties was the arbitrary drafting of the men they raised into other regiments, which made the Colonels and officers lose interest and send home bad N.C.O.s to recruit.[2]

Jenkinson, as Secretary at War, had protested to Amherst in the past at the raising of new regiments while the old ones were short of establishment[3]; and Amherst felt some sympathy, for new regiments were open to jobbery and led to rapid promotion of officers who had the luck to raise them. Nevertheless the high bounties which their officers gave to recruits for the sake of promotion tapped a source of men which was not open to the old regiments.

Drawing the logic from this, Jenkinson changed his ground. If the raising of new regiments was unavoidable, the establishments of the old should be reduced. His objection to uncompleted establishments was purely financial. As Secretary at War he was responsible for preparing the army estimates and defending them in the House of Commons. Depleted establishments were wasteful. Certain off-reckonings were swallowed up whatever the real numbers in the ranks, a loss which Jenkinson estimated at £30,000; and a further £100,000 remained unused in the hands of the Paymaster and the Regimental Agents to their own profit, while Parliament was asked to vote the same sums again for new regiments. Faced with the Estimates for 1781, Jenkinson wanted existing establishments to be cut back to a figure which the regiments could hope to complete.

But to Amherst the issue was not financial but military. The army had too few troops to meet essential commitments; and to reduce the paper establishments of regiments would not solve the difficulty. It would merely preclude the possibility of raising the old regiments to efficient strength: a battalion 700 strong was a much better fighting instrument than one of 560. Moreover he feared that to cut establishments would reveal to the enemy

[1] WO 34/127, 24 Oct. 1780, Jenkinson to Amherst.
[2] G 3208.
[3] Add. MSS. 38212, ff. 305–12.

how far the army was below its strength on paper. Jenkinson doubted if the enemy was really deceived, and pointed out that it had never been possible to keep establishments up towards the end of a war: indeed in 1760 on Amherst's own advice the establishments of regiments in the West Indies and America had been reduced to figures which they could maintain. He insisted that there were no serious military objections to the cuts, and real political and financial advantages.[1]

But Amherst stuck to his guns. It was his duty to present Jenkinson's proposals to the Cabinet, and he was able to press his case against them. He maintained that as no pay was issued except for effectives, the financial saving would be inconsiderable, though he admitted that under the present system some money lay dead for a time in the hands of individuals. As a result of his efforts he was able to tell Jenkinson that the Cabinet 'seemed' to think that the high establishments should be retained in the hope of filling them. But this was not the end of the matter. Jenkinson had had a Treasury training, and was still very close to North. The national debt had nearly doubled since the beginning of the war, and the next loan would have to be floated on extravagant terms. In Parliament, where the Opposition's campaign for economy had threatened even the King's Household, he expected trouble over the enormous extraordinaries of the troops in the West Indies and America. He demanded a more explicit instruction from the Commander-in-Chief on which to prepare the Estimates, and obtained the Prime Minister's support.[2]

Before the Cabinet would come to a decision about the reductions, they wanted to hear North and give Jenkinson an opportunity to appear before them in person. A date and time were agreed, and Jenkinson won his case. But if he could lean on the Prime Minister, Amherst could look to the King. When Amherst brought him the Cabinet's resolution, King George expressed his understanding that no reduction was intended in regiments which had a probability of completing their present establishments. Sixty-one battalions were cut instead of the seventy-six which Jenkinson had proposed: a paper reduction of 7,630 privates instead of 12,470. Amherst had saved what he could, but he considered that forty-nine of the reduced battalions were now tied to establishments well below the efficient strength for active service.[3]

[1] G 3266; WO 34/127, 31 Oct., North to Amherst, ff. 152–61, 184–6; WO 34/128, f. 15; Add. MSS. 38214, ff. 216–17; Add. MSS. 38383 (Jenkinson's draft speech).

[2] WO 34/127, ff. 184–6, 196; WO 34/128, f. 14; WO 34/235, p. 524; G 2343–4; WO 34/186, ff. 92–3.

[3] WO 34/127, f. 61; WO 34/235, pp. 245, 551–5; WO 4/112, pp. 12, 13, 27–8; Royal Institution MSS., II, 216. On 1 December Amherst wrote to Germain in connection with a proposal to raise a special corps: ' . . . it is the opinion of a very sensible and

The dispute over the reductions emphasised the handicap imposed on Jenkinson by his exclusion from the Cabinet. He was answerable for the army in the House of Commons, where he had to do solitary battle against several senior officers in opposition. He maintained that though it was for the Cabinet to decide the army's strength, he ought to have a voice in how to attain it. His constitutional position soon caused him further uneasiness. Early in the New Year the Cabinet resolved to raise forty independent companies in Ireland for the English establishment, in order to meet the expanding needs of home defence. But soon afterwards, on Amherst's representation that there were not enough troops for essential services, the Cabinet ordered six further regiments to be raised in the same manner. At this Jenkinson rebelled. He denounced the new regiments as jobs which he should have been given an opportunity to oppose in the Cabinet, and threatened to resign rather than have anything to do with them. This time he had the support of Amherst and Hillsborough, and the plan was dropped. It might have been killed at birth if Amherst had spoken up in Cabinet as Jenkinson had expected: he must indeed have wished for a seat beside the silent soldier at the Council table.[1]

2. The South Sea Enterprise

The outlook would have been very different if Spain could have been detached from the enemy alliance, and in the course of 1780 the attempt begun in the previous autumn had proceeded, at first hopefully. Though there is no evidence that Father Hussey was acting in collusion with the Spanish government when he approached Germain, his arrival in Madrid at the end of 1779 was, as he had predicted, not unwelcome. The Spanish situation was sufficiently embarrassing. They had counted on beating England in one campaign, taking their profit quickly, and then securing their own colonies from the contagion of rebellion by sacrificing the Americans. Now they faced prolonged war without the means to wage it. An immediate peace was alluring if they could get their price. They were not bound by treaty to the American rebels; and for Gibraltar Floridablanca was willing to forego the hope of other gains and desert the French alliance.

Hussey had made it clear from the beginning that Gibraltar was the vital condition for the Spaniards; and he confirmed it on his return to London at the end of January. The price was stiff, and even Knox had not suggested

intelligent officer, of high rank, now in America, that the compleating of the present corps in that country would be force sufficient to end the rebellion there'. (WO 34/235, p. 589).

[1] G 3236, 3266; Abergavenny, 41; Add. MSS. 38214, f. 216.

more than the sacrifice of West Florida and perhaps the lodgments on the Nicaraguan coast. But it is probable that when the first contacts were made the British Ministers concerned were willing to pay for peace with Gibraltar. Hussey reported to Madrid that Germain saw little difficulty, and if Commodore Johnstone was speaking the truth Lord North was also willing. Of Hillsborough's views there is no direct evidence at the time; but he was probably of the same mind, for in the following September both he and Stormont would have been happy to pay for peace with Gibraltar if public opinion would have allowed it. As Commodore Johnstone reminded Sandwich in a letter from the coast of Portugal, there had been cries of doom when Calais, Tangier and Louisburg were successively abandoned, yet England had survived and flourished without them.[1]

But when Hussey reappeared with the formal Spanish overture the Ministers could proceed no further without Cabinet approval. Four successive meetings were devoted to the subject, and a list of possible equivalents for Gibraltar was presented and discussed. In the end, however, the surrender of Gibraltar was rejected. Perhaps the decision was influenced by the news which arrived at that moment of Rodney's victory over Langara; but always in the background must have been the fear of public opinion, and we shall see that in the peace negotiations which ended the war it was the same force which wrecked the statesmen's hopes of exchanging Gibraltar. Hussey, indignant and disappointed at the decision, was soothed by Richard Cumberland, and sent a report to Floridablanca which, while warning him that Gibraltar could not form part of the basis of negotiation, held out the hope that it could subsequently be introduced. This letter was shown to Germain and Hillsborough, but was not officially communicated to the Cabinet.

In April Cumberland was despatched to Lisbon to further the negotiation. As a subordinate of limited experience he would not commit the government's prestige to his actions. He sailed without the power to discuss the one vital concession, and the decision to withhold Gibraltar meant that his mission could not succeed. He was, however, lured to Madrid by Floridablanca, who knew his instructions but hoped at the least to use his presence as a lever against the French. His appearance did indeed alarm Vergennes into making strategic concessions to the Spaniards; but it sowed confusion within the Bourbon ranks, disrupted their war planning, and opened the prospect of a mediated peace in 1781 if the British government had thought it necessary.[2]

[1] Doniol, IV, 502; Bemis, *Hussey-Cumberland Mission*, 95 n.; Sandwich, III, 190.

[2] For these negotiations see Bemis, *op. cit.*, supplemented for the British side by Coxe, *Kings of Spain* . . . Cumberland remained convinced that it was the Gordon Riots which disrupted the negotiation, and that between capture of Admiral Langara and the Riots a separate peace might have been attained without yielding Gibraltar.

In the meantime plans had been in hand for new and heavier blows against the Spanish Empire. When Brigadier Garth's expedition sailed for Jamaica to seize a base in the Pacific, two plans for privateering expeditions in the Pacific were in the air. One of them came from Sir John Dalrymple, Baron of the Scottish Exchequer and brother of the young officer whose capture of Omoa had triggered the Jamaica expedition. Acting with a consortium of Glasgow merchants, Dalrymple applied for government approval and subsidies for a squadron of privateers. Their notion was that the Spaniards would expect a twenty months' respite in the Pacific from the outbreak of war, since the declaration had come too late in the year to mount an expedition to round the Horn in the good months of December and January. But the voyages of Captain Cook had shown that there were two safe routes to the South Pacific at any season: from Britain by the Cape of Good Hope, and from India by the Philippines or New Holland. An expedition by these routes in the course of 1780 would catch the Spaniards unprepared. Dalrymple imagined a squadron of raiders from Britain sailing by the Cape of Good Hope and New Zealand to the south coast of Chile; running before the south wind to scour the coast as far as Panama; and thence to sell the prizes and refit in India or China. From there they could renew the cycle.[1]

This plan was taken seriously by Germain, and negotiations to mount it proceeded in the first half of 1780. But by the late summer the government took up the project on its own account, and the Glasgow 'tobacco lords' dropped out. The germ of the new plan was a proposal made in January 1780 by a somewhat different Scottish interest. William Fullarton and Thomas Mackenzie Humberston proposed to raise a pair of regiments and fit out warships to cruise in the Pacific and capture the Acapulco fleet. Humberston was a rich man who had helped his cousin Lord Seaforth to raise the Seventy-eighth Highlanders and bought the Seaforth estates; and Fullarton, with estates in Ayrshire and a seat in Parliament, was his closest friend. In February 1780 these lairds were given permission to raise their regiments without expense to government, and Germain ensured that this new threat was conveyed to the Spanish government.[2] In the next few months they raised the Ninety-eighth and Hundredth Foot, which, after splendid service in India, were disbanded at the peace. Humberston was at least a soldier; but Fullarton's commission was attacked as a piece of political favouritism to a civilian. Like Thomas Graham of Peninsular fame Fullarton came late to soldiering; and his brilliant services and original methods in India were to prove that the slow ladder of seniority was not the only way to make

---

[1] Harlow, 108; Dalrymple, *Memoirs of Great Britain*, Appendix, p. 32; Sackville, II, 153–8.

[2] Spanish memorandum by Hussey, communicated by Father Cullen.

good soldiers. He had been Secretary to Stormont in Paris, and Lord Shelburne described him in the House of Lords as 'commis and clerk'. At the instigation of Shelburne's pensioner Barré a duel resulted, and Shelburne was slightly wounded.[1]

But soon larger possibilities than mere buccaneering opened up in the Pacific. On 17 July 1780 came news of the reduction of Fort St Juan, which in Dalling's phrase promised to burst open the door to the South Sea. With the prospect of a Pacific base in Central America the government hoped for nothing less than to revolutionise the western coast of Spanish America from Chile to Mexico. The East India Company was interested; not because they believed in the American scheme – for they doubted if the areas could be held – but to serve their own purposes in the East Indies. The Company's genuine trading activities were by now mainly in China, with India as a source of goods for barter. But importing from China was a deficit trade; and to balance the account and stop the drain of silver the Company needed a market in the East Indian archipelago. Here were the gold and spices which were wanted in China. They had tried before to win a foothold. Manila had been captured in the Seven Years War, but too late to be retained at the peace; and between 1768 and 1775 a lodgment had been held in North Borneo, about the time of the attempt to secure the Falkland Islands base on the western route to the Pacific.

A plan for a joint Pacific expedition was approved by the Cabinet on 3 August. It was to consist of a ship of the line, the Ninety-eighth and Hundredth Regiments augmented to 1,000 men each, and 2,000 Company sepoys. The Company suggested as an initial step the seizure of the Dutch Spice Islands and of bases in the Spanish Philippines. Lord Hillsborough, who handled the negotiations as Secretary of State for the Southern Department, gave them a short answer on the Dutch islands, for bad as the country's relations with the United Provinces had become he still hoped to keep them out of the war; but by the end of September agreement was reached on the Spanish islands. Celebes would be taken by Company troops; Mindanao by the Crown regiments, to be handed over to the Company when the Pacific operations were completed. The augmentation of Fullarton's and Humberston's regiments began; troopships were ordered; and the sailing date was fixed for December 1780.[2]

In the course of September a privateer brought a Spanish frigate into Glasgow, with accounts of a rebellion in Spanish America and a treasure fleet in the River Plate which was to sail for Europe in December. Commodore Johnstone suggested a small expedition to capture the treasure, to

[1] Sackville, II, 282; WO 34/232, p. 386; Walpole, Last Journals, II, 385.
[2] G 3115; Harlow, 105-6, 136; WO 34/235, pp. 78, 85.

which the Cabinet agreed on 2 November; and it was decided three weeks later to unite the two forces for the initial operation in the River Plate. The South Sea expedition would then proceed on its way round the Cape of Good Hope.[1]

3. *The Gathering Storm*

The offensive for 1781 was planned to strike at the Spanish Empire, and with modest means. But it was never doubted that the main effort would be a defensive one against the French in the West Indies.[2] To this the main resources of England would have to be devoted, while in America Clinton hung on and exploited Cornwallis's successes with the resources he already had. Long before the final plan was settled for the South Sea expedition, the naval situation had begun to undergo profound changes, and offensive plans to give way before the pressure of events. The Cabinet was soon being shepherded into piecemeal improvisation, hampered at every turn by the shortage of men and ships.

The first alarm was the loss of the *Ramillies* convoy. The lost storeships for Rodney's fleet had to be replaced without waiting for the next general convoy at the end of October, and the remainder of a regiment of which seven companies had been taken had to be hurried out to Jamaica. So tight was the shipping shortage that Germain arranged with the Jamaica merchants to cram the troops into their ships in the next convoy.[3] Scarcely were these arrangements in hand when more alarming news arrived from the West Indies themselves. Rodney's fleet was in a deplorable condition, and Solano's squadron had joined the French. Though it was soon learnt that the French and Spaniards had separated, and that Walsingham had joined Rodney with his reinforcements, the enemy were in great strength and it was clear that the West Indies were still the main naval theatre.

It was the middle of September: the season which in other years had brought hopeful plans to wrest the initiative from the enemy. Now it had become a question of holding out against the swelling pressure. The urgent need was to replace Rodney's useless ships and get them home for major repairs and coppering. Sandwich came up to London, and with Middleton's advice and some pressure from the King it was resolved to bring in selected

---

[1] Harlow, 109–10; G 3170, 3190. If the whole Pacific scheme and its link with Jamaica is thought to be a wild aberration of a distracted government, it should be remembered that it was reconsidered in 1806, when Lord Grenville called in Sir John Dalrymple to expound the earlier plan. (Huntington Library, Stowe MSS., Admiralty Box 37).

[2] CO 318/6, f. 168 (4 July, Germain to Vaughan).

[3] Sandwich, III, 302; WO 34/127, f. 28; CO 318/6, f. 174.

ships from the Channel for docking, and from them to provide ten sail of the line for Rodney. In addition Arbuthnot should send him five from America in the winter even if Ternay wintered at Rhode Island. With these replacements Rodney could send home fourteen of his worst ships; and in the spring a force should be available at home to reinforce Arbuthnot.[1]

Troops were also needed. Thanks to the despatch of Garth's four battalions in the spring, Jamaica should be reasonably strong; but in the Leeward Islands Vaughan reported his force to be very weak and dispersed as a result of wastage and sickness. Germain promised him any help that could be spared from the unequal struggle in which the country was engaged.[2] But America too was clamouring. On 25 September Brigadier Dalrymple arrived with Clinton's report of the fiasco at Rhode Island and the flare-up in South Carolina. His tone was very gloomy, and he demanded 10,000 reinforcements.

This was out of the question. But with great difficulty three battalions were found in England, and to the alarm of the Dublin Castle executive three more were wrested from Ireland and replaced by the cadres of the drafted regiments from the Leeward Islands. Of these six battalions three were to go to Vaughan, with orders that they should be sent north to Clinton in the summer. It was too late in the year to send troops direct to New York; but the remaining three battalions were ordered by the southern route to Charleston. They were the first fresh regiments which Clinton had been sent for two years, and together with 1,000 recruits which were to sail with them and 2,800 Germain recruits who would sail in the spring they gave Clinton the promise of 6,000 reinforcements for the next campaign. At the very least this help should enable him to hold on and sustain Cornwallis. The Americans were certainly in great distress, and Rochambeau's men might not stand up well to the winter cold. No one could foretell what change of fortune might come with the spring. They could only wait and hope.[3]

The decision to send these troops swamped the resources of the Navy Board. The three regiments for the West Indies were found passages by the Jamaica merchants; but if troopships were allotted to the American reinforcement it would be impossible to lift the expedition which was being assembled for the River Plate and the South Sea. A choice was necessary. The Board was ordered to give priority to the reinforcements, and the sailing of the South Sea expedition was postponed.[4]

---

[1] Sandwich, III, 228, 233, 302; CL, Germain, 15 Sept. to Admiralty and 22 Sept. to Clinton; Adm. 2/1338, ff. 56, 66; G 3135; Adm. 1/311, passim.
[2] CO 318/6, f. 196.
[3] Lothian, 374; G 3155-6; CL, Germain, 6 Oct. to Admiralty; CO 318/6, f. 250.
[4] Adm. 2/1338, ff. 62, 70, 74, 78; WO 34/235, p. 546.

The forces for the westward got away gradually as shipping was scraped together.[1] Sir Samuel Hood, newly promoted from his Commissionership to flag rank, sailed with the troops and squadron for the Leeward Islands at the end of November, and the regiments for Charleston left in January. But throughout the autumn the sense of mounting pressure continued. There was intelligence from Paris of a squadron and military reinforcements preparing to sail for America, and Arbuthnot's orders to reinforce Rodney in the winter had to be made discretionary.[2] And more ominous than the movements of the enemy was the international scene.

The diplomatic offensive which had been opened in the autumn of 1779 had come to a halt. The Spanish negotiations had borne no direct fruit; and after a winter of hope the approach to Russia had collapsed. The policy of Catherine the Great seemed bewildering and irresolute; but by March 1780 she had equipped a fleet which was expected to come to the aid of the British. Then came the awakening. On 1 April 1780 the Russian Ambassador presented a declaration on neutral rights whose acceptance would have destroyed the British weapon of blockade. Far from finding help, England faced the hostility of a vast though shadowy combination of neutrals.[3]

In the summer of 1780 the Northern Powers began to band in a League of Armed Neutrality to open French and Spanish ports to the naval stores of the Baltic. Within a year of the Russian declaration, Russia, Sweden and Denmark would have 84 warships in commission to back their policy, and the League expanded swiftly. The Netherlands and the Empire adhered in 1781, Prussia and Portugal in 1782. For England the vital element in the Neutrality was Holland. Russian shipping was insignificant; Denmark would compromise; but if Holland obtained free access to enemy ports the blockade of naval stores would be torn to shreds. Friction with the Dutch had been mounting for some time. In the West Indies they were using St Eustatius as a contraband depot for the French islands and the rebel American colonies; and contrary to their own past practice as belligerents they adopted the doctrine that all trade in neutral bottoms was free from capture. The British government took its stand solely on the question of naval stores: it was willing to allow Dutch carrying in the French West Indies to continue uninterrupted, and to waive the Treaty of Alliance of 1678 if the Dutch would only stop this strategic traffic to French ports. When the Dutch refused to discuss the question in 1779 the British

---

[1] Adm. 2/1338, ff. 103–5.

[2] CL, Germain, 7 Oct. (intelligence) and 13 Oct. to Admiralty; Mundy, I, 402.

[3] The misunderstanding of Catherine's intentions was chiefly caused by Harris's reports from St Petersburg. The story is revealed in Madariaga, especially pp. 96, 171, 182, 197–8, 214–15.

government had announced that naval stores would not be allowed to pass through the Channel in Dutch bottoms.

The Dutch reply was to pass contraband down the Channel in their general convoys. Tension was increased in the autumn of 1779 by the aid and comfort they gave to the American raider Paul Jones; and on this provocation a British force stopped and searched the second of their Channel convoys. Shots were exchanged and a few ships seized. No satisfaction being given by Holland about either Paul Jones or naval stores, the British government in April 1780 suspended their commercial treaty privileges and subjected their shipping to the full rigour of the blockade. If the Dutch resisted the searching of their convoys, England would have to choose between abandoning this important strategic weapon and adding another naval power to their enemies. And war with Holland would be more dangerous if she adhered to the Armed Neutrality and invoked its aid. For a long time the Dutch hesitated to join the League, but in the second half of November 1780 the States-General voted to do so.

The British Ministers had read the signs and framed their policy.[1] They intended to fight the Dutch rather than let them carry for the enemy; and to prevent the quarrel from drawing in the Armed Neutrality, war had to be forced on Holland before her adhesion was ratified, and the real issue of neutral rights obscured. The Dutch had provided a pretext. Henry Laurens had recently been captured at sea on his way from America to Holland, carrying papers which revealed a negotiation between Congress and the Magistracy of Amsterdam. The opportunity was seized. Stormont demanded the disavowal and punishment of those concerned. No satisfactory reply was made, and an ultimatum followed. But on 15 December, before it expired, Stormont learnt from the British Minister at the Hague that Holland was hastening her accession to the Armed Neutrality. There was not a moment to lose. Stormont obtained the Cabinet's assent to the immediate withdrawal of the British Minister. The breach was final, and the method as planned. The ostensible issue was not neutral rights, and the League refused its help to the Dutch.

The breach was calculated: but was it wise? Not in the view of William Knox. France and Spain would have to pay more for their naval stores, but England would have to bear the far greater cost of a Dutch war, and had added twenty sail of the line to her enemies. An Austrian mediation was in the air, and Knox maintained that the Cabinet should have temporised till they knew what might come of it. Nor did he feel that the coercion of Holland had been properly discussed. He gives a description, which he must have had from Germain, of the Cabinet meeting which approved the ultimatum. North and Bathurst fell asleep at once, Hillsborough nodded and dropped

[1] G 3171, 3181.

his hat. Sandwich was overcome at first, but then rubbed his eyes and looked attentive. Stormont read the papers aloud and discussed them with Thurlow and Germain, while Amherst sat awake but as usual silent. The others then woke up and approved the proceedings.

This may indict the business methods of the North Ministry and the general habit of taking important decisions as an appendix to dinner. Yet the decision itself can be defended. 'It is allowed on all hands', an observer had recently remarked, 'that it will be impossible for France to fit out her fleets if she is prevented from carrying naval stores in Dutch bottoms from the Baltic.'[1] We have seen the stress which Middleton laid on stopping the Dutch supply of copper to the French dockyards; and Stormont shared the Admiralty's conviction that to stop the carriage of naval stores was vital. And although the Dutch navy was a serious embarrassment in the course of 1781 it is impossible, when one reflects on the favourable turn which the naval war was taking eighteen months later, to be sure that Stormont was wrong. Immediate steps were taken to reap the benefits of the breach. A total embargo was laid on the export of salt provisions to foreign ports in the West Indies, and Rodney was ordered to seize St Eustatius, the neutral warehouse of the French Leeward Islands. Two hours after the Cabinet resolution had been reported and approved by the King, the orders for the General and Admiral were on their way to Portsmouth, those for the Admiral being a transcript of the Secretary of State's letter to the Board of Admiralty. To the speed with which the Ministry had acted, Knox attributed the overhauling of a rich Dutch convoy which had left St Eustatius two days before the British forces arrived. Once more we find respect for the British effort on the far side of the Channel. Reflecting on the prompt and ubiquitous measures against the Dutch, the diplomatic historian Doniol wonders at 'the marvellous vigour which characterised that government throughout the struggle'.[2]

4. The End of the Initiative

The breach with Holland was the end of the South Sea expedition: and the decision to abandon it on 29 December 1780, marks the end of Britain's long struggle to retain a share of the strategic initiative against the odds which were massed against her. The reason for the decision was the East

[1] Dartmouth, III, 246.
[2] Knox, 271–2; Knox, Extra-official State Papers, I, 16; G 3222; Mundy, II, 6; Doniol, IV, 516. A lucid account of the intricate Anglo-Dutch negotiations is to be found in Bemis, *Diplomacy of the American Revolution*, showing how internal pressures and the skilful manipulation of trade regulations by France prevented the Dutch government from acceding to a compromise.

India Company's withdrawal of its contingent. The sepoys would be needed to secure India against attack from the Dutch bases in Ceylon and Sumatra. Instead of attacking the Spaniards in the Pacific, the British Cabinet resolved to turn what remained of the original force against the Dutch. For Holland held the keys to the east.

Hitherto the war had involved little fighting between the British and French in India. At the outset each side had only a single small ship of the line; and after one battle with Admiral Vernon the French squadron had withdrawn to its distant base at Mauritius, leaving the trading posts at Mahé and Pondicherry to be snapped up by the British. The balance of power in India depended utterly on the command of the sea: the British at Calcutta, Madras and Bombay were as dependent on the sea for supplies and mutual support as were Clinton's forces stretched between Nova Scotia and Florida. The reinforcement which Admiral Hughes brought out in 1779 was able to retain the British superiority at sea. But when the Dutch entered the war internal events in India were undermining the British position. By errors of policy which Hughes deplored, the Madras Presidency became engaged in simultaneous warfare with the Mahrattas and with Hyder Ali, the Sultan of Mysore. In June 1780 Hyder burst into the Carnatic with a vast and well-drilled army.

The war with Holland gave a new significance to Hyder's attack. For it gave France what she had lacked: an all-weather base in the Dutch island of Ceylon, which commanded both the coasts of India. The Dutch also held the Cape of Good Hope, a watering and provisioning station for fleets on passage, and the source of provisions for the French base at Mauritius. 'Whichever of these powers [England and France] shall possess the Cape, the same may govern India': the East India Company's contention was decisive. From this time a new principle appears in British strategy: to ensure that France did not become the successor in the Indian Ocean to the decaying power of Holland. Twice in the next twenty-five years Ceylon was occupied; three times expeditions were sent to seize the Cape of Good Hope. And the first of these Cape expeditions was launched at once. The 3,000 troops who had been gathered for the River Plate and the South Sea were switched to this new objective: a mission tactically offensive but strategically defensive. If the attack should fail, the 2,000 men of Humberston's and Fullarton's regiments originally intended for the Pacific should proceed to the defence of India.[1]

Scarcely had the British government committed the country to war with Holland when dreadful news arrived from St Lucia. A hurricane of

[1] Harlow, 108, 110; Richmond, *Navy in India*, 124–6; G 3223.

appalling violence had swept the Caribbean. A tidal wave had inundated part of Jamaica with great loss of human life and stock; and the Lesser Antilles were hit still harder. Every battery was destroyed on Barbados, which was outside the usual hurricane zone, and 4,000 lives were said to have been lost. On St Lucia every building was unroofed. General Vaughan's secretary and seven others were killed when his house collapsed, and he escaped in his nighshirt to exist for several days in negro clothing. The sick were lying in pools of water, and most of the ammunition was ruined. Every transport was driven ashore. Rodney, with his usual luck, was away at New York: but of the ships which remained in the islands, two of the line and ten cruisers were cast away or foundered, eight of the line and a fifty-gun ship were severely damaged, and one of the line bore away dismasted for England. The stores were destroyed, and the damage could not be repaired.

The Ministers could only hope that the enemy had suffered too, though since most of their force had left the Leeward Islands it could not be in the same degree. To reinforce the devastated islands was out of the question. The Dutch war and the Cape expedition absorbed too many ships, and as the year expired Gibraltar called again for assistance. On New Year's Day the Cabinet resolved that the home fleet should relieve the fortress for the second time, and pass a frigate convoy through the Straits to victual Minorca.

Here, again, the Ministry was responding to the pressure of events. The Spanish fixation on Gibraltar and Minorca may have drawn their forces away from operations which offered a more decisive effect on the war; yet now, as in the previous winter it diverted the Royal Navy to a defensive winter operation with serious consequences for its strength in the spring. The Opposition asserted, as Keppel had done when Gibraltar had last been relieved, that it was an unnecessary operation which ruled out a blockade of Brest. Amongst those who retrospectively clamoured for blockading Brest was Lord Howe, who not long before had rejected the station off Ushant as totally impracticable: so much for the motives of the Opposition's naval experts. Sandwich answered that Gibraltar would have fallen if it had not been relieved, and that the operation in itself gave a good chance of bringing a Spanish fleet to battle. 'What would have been said if Admiral Darby had been employed in watching the motions of the French fleet in the harbour of Brest, and Gibraltar had been taken?'[1]

Whether Gibraltar at that time was worth the effort is an open question. Some argued that it was not. Sea power in the Mediterranean did not yet involve the security of India, as it was to do from the time of Napoleon's Egyptian expedition; and the argument could be heard that Gibraltar's

[1] Sandwich, IV, 318, 353, 357.

function of keeping open England's moderate volume of Mediterranean trade was of marginal importance.[1] Throughout the eighty odd years since its capture, Ministers and Ambassadors had shown a remarkable willingness to bargain it away; and as recently as September Stormont and Hillsborough had thought it a cheap price to pay for peace with Spain.[2] The obstacle to the bargain was the prejudice and passion of the people, and Stormont shrank from advising the government to consider the step. So in the late winter the whole Channel fleet of England was drawn into operations for the relief of the fortress. The consequences were to be felt throughout the world.

5. The Two Sides of the Hill

India, the Mediterranean, the West Indies: everywhere the country's resources were being drawn in to hold the tide. A new naval theatre had been opened in the North Sea by the Dutch fleet lying athwart the Baltic trade route. In America Arbuthnot's fleet had nearly been called away to the help of Rodney; and if it had gone, the British troops in the Chesapeake would have fallen to the French at Rhode Island, who sallied out in the late winter to attack them. Time's hurrying footsteps echoed at the backs of the Ministers. 'The vast extent and enormous expense of the war will not admit of dilatory or languid movements', Germain warned Governor Dalling of Jamaica. No reinforcements could be spared from England to feed his offensive against the Spanish colonies; yet the national finances could not afford to leave any resources inactive, and if sickness and rain had caused Nicaragua to be abandoned, Dalling was to attack New Orleans with what he had.[3]

In this precarious situation they feared above all that Russia would enter the war in support of Holland. Towards the end of November the Cabinet had learnt that Catherine intended to offer her mediation to the belligerents; a prospect which had strengthened the case for hurrying on the breach with Holland before she joined Russia in the Armed Neutrality. The mediation could not be rejected, but it might be converted into a joint mediation with Austria to end the war on favourable terms. Meanwhile Russia had to be dissuaded from supporting the Dutch; and after witholding Gibraltar from the Spaniards, it was agreed to bribe Catherine with Minorca.

Feelers had been put out some time earlier through the Minister in Peters-

---

[1] See, for example, Mahon, Life of . . . Murray, 390; CL, Shelburne, Vol. 83, Nos. 14, 16, 17 etc. On the value of Gibraltar at the time, see Stetson Conn, Gibraltar in British Diplomacy in the Eighteenth Century, pp. 256–7, 259, 266–7.

[2] Above, p. 372.

[3] CO 137/78, ff. 266, 270.

burg. On 28 October 1780, in a final bid for Russian help, Lord Stormont had instructed Sir James Harris to discover whether the cession of some British colony might tempt Catherine to join us against France and Spain. This letter crossed with one from Harris, who had independently tested the ground and been told by Prince Potemkin that nothing but the cession of Minorca would induce Catherine to join us. There were powerful arguments in favour of paying the price; for Russia had long wanted a Mediterranean base, and as Knox pointed out in a study which he made of the situation, Russian occupation of the island would give lasting jealousy to France and Spain, and bind Russia and her northern allies to England. On 3 January the Cabinet decided to make the offer. It was a difficult choice. But as Stormont explained to the King, everything must be done 'to dispel if possible the northern storm', and a friendly Russian mediation leading to a favourable peace would be cheap at the price. In George III, however, the Cabinet encountered an apparently immovable obstacle; for he declared that he would never cede a possession which had not been conquered by the enemy.

So matters rested for several days; and on the 16th a bulky packet arrived from Harris reporting his further talks with Potemkin. The Prince had replied to his overture that distant colonies were of no use to Russia; but that for Minorca he believed Catherine .would go to any lengths. The deciphering of the key letter was not completed till the afternoon of the 17th, when it was forwarded to the King with Stormont's recommendation. Evidently there was still some delay; for if rumour was correct, it was a memorial delivered two days later by the Russian Minister on the war with Holland which finally drove home the seriousness of the outlook. The King cancelled his levée and for the second time since the beginning of the war summoned the Cabinet to his presence. This time his purpose was not to drive them on, but to hear their views. Seating the Ministers round a table, he invited their opinions. Someone asked who should speak first; and the King replying that he would not point to anyone, Sandwich said that it was usual for the youngest to begin. He thus ensured that Thurlow, who was hostile to the cession, should not have the first word. For three and a half hours they discussed the question, and it was Sandwich who converted the King. The First Lord knew too well the delicacy of the naval balance. Russia, he argued, intended in any event to profit from the belligerents' difficulties. If she declared for the enemy England would lose not merely Minorca, but Gibraltar, Canada, the American colonies and the West Indies. Even if Catherine remained neutral, he asked what hope there was of ending the war without some equally valuable concession. He turned the King's favourite argument to his purpose: with Russia against us, 'we shall never again figure as a leading power in Europe, but think ourselves happy if we can drag on for some years a contemptible existence as a commercial state'. Minorca seemed a small price for an alliance which might save the country.[1]

Catherine refused the bait, for her real preoccupation was with the Ottoman Empire, and she could not afford serious distractions in the west. Nor could the Austrians be tempted by an offer to re-open the Scheldt.[2] The mediation, however, proceeded, and the terms which were produced in May had much to attract England. France at that moment was willing if necessary to sacrifice the Americans for the sake of peace: to accept a basis of *uti possidetis* which would leave England in possession of South Carolina and Georgia, much of North Carolina, a foothold in Virginia, the neighbourhood of New York, and a base in the Penobscot River which would enable her to lay effective claim to most of Maine. But the very reasons which made Vergennes willing induced the British Cabinet to reject the opportunity. The French finances were near the breaking point, their joint campaign with the Spaniards had misfired in the West Indies, the Americans seemed to be near the end of their physical and moral resources. The southern colonies were collapsing one by one before the British advance, and the French commanders and Minister in America were in despair with the rebels. In February Franklin had passed on a solemn warning from Washington that the situation demanded the most vigorous efforts or a peace. For many months Vergennes had feared a separate peace between Spain and England: if the operations of 1781 did not bring the success which had eluded the allies for four successive years, a settlement would be inevitable.[3]

Most of this was known to the British government. 'This war like the last will prove one of credit', the King had recently said; and there was evidence, some of it in the captured papers of Henry Laurens, that the short purse of France was nearly empty. Almost at the moment of the mediation, intelligence from France reported the dismissal of Neckar for opposing further war expenditure, and the consequent fall on the French Exchange. 'The best men', said the report, 'consider M. Neckar's retreat as a fatal stab to the credit of France, and to the independence of America'. The hope of a French financial collapse was widely held. 'One lucky blow in the West Indies will give us peace', General Murray wrote from Minorca, 'for I judge the enemy finds the expense of the war as intolerable as we do.'[4]

---

[1] Sandwich, IV, 23–6; Walpole, *Last Journals*, II, 442; G 3202–3, 3230, 3237, 3245–6; Knox, 272, 291; Bemis, *Diplomacy of the American Revolution*, 180–1; Malmesbury Corr., I, 299, 315–21, 323–6. See also Madariaga, 239–42, 284–5.

[2] Madariaga, 287.

[3] Bemis, *Diplomacy of the American Revolution*, 181–7, and *Hussey-Cumberland Mission*, 113–24.

[4] Bemis, *Hussey-Cumberland Mission*, 111; G 3155, 3166, 3249, 3315, 3342, 3344, 3347, 3355, 3357; Knox, 176; Mahon, *Murray*, 392; Knox, *Extra-Official State Papers*, I. 27.

In their financial embarrassment the French were known to be deeply worried by the condition of the Americans. Since the spring of 1780 a steady trickle of reports had told of the rebel's weakness and disunity. Much of this was opinion, but there were facts to support it: the collapse in South Carolina, the separatism of Ethan Allen in Vermont, the treason of Arnold. In Paris Silas Deane was hatching further treachery. In the New Year there were two serious mutinies in Washington's army, and Clinton soared from sullen gloom to the peaks of optimism. With proper reinforcements and superiority at sea the coming campaign could break the rebellion: 'I have all to hope, and Washington all to fear.'[1]

As this picture unfolded in London, it seemed likely that if England could keep afloat, American resistance would at last collapse. Germain's hopes rested on Cornwallis and his army in the south. When the news of the victory at Camden arrived in December 1780 he was confident that Cornwallis would sweep forward into Virginia and join hands with the force in the Chesapeake. Then perhaps the authority of Congress would at last be undermined and public opinion in the colonies would turn in our favour. The news of rebel difficulties which accumulated in the New Year confirmed his hopes.

Indeed [he wrote to Clinton at the end of the winter], so very contemptible is the rebel force now in all parts, and so vast is our superiority, that no resistance on their part is to be apprehended than can materially obstruct the progress of the King's arms in the speedy suppression of the rebellion, and it is a pleasing though at the same time mortifying reflection when the duration of the rebellion is considered . . . that the American levies in the King's service are more in number than the whole of the enlisted troops in the service of the Congress.[2]

These were the hopes for which the British fought on. They fought for complete victory, or at the least for a peace which would not acknowledge the right of other powers to mediate between England and her colonies. 'I am fully convinced', North told the House of Commons in the New Year, 'that the means possessed by this country, when vigorously exerted, constitute the only mode of obtaining a just and an honourable peace.' If the country could go doggedly on, avoiding defeat and preventing losses,

[1] Sackville, II, 160, 168, 206; CL, Germain, June 1780 (intelligence), 27 Aug. 1780, 24 and 27 Feb. 1781; G 3262; Wortley, 171; Lothian, 382; CO 5/101, f. 10 et seq. When Wilmington, North Carolina, was occupied by the British, one of the signatories to the Declaration of Independence wrote a lament which compares with anything written by the English opponents of North: 'A country on the verge of ruin – a corrupt or what is worse an ideot Assembly – an indolent executive – Treasurers without money – a military without exertion – punctilios superseding duty . . . ' etc. (Duke University MSS., 13 Feb. 1781, Wm. Hooper to James Iredell).

[2] CL, Clinton, 5 Dec. 1780, 7 Feb. and 7 March 1781, from Germain.

the enemy might relinquish the field. It would be a narrow thing, and the hurricane in the Leeward Islands had unseated the naval calculations. But in the New Year there were still two reasonable grounds to hope that the naval balance could be restored. The Spaniards would probably give battle to Darby when he relieved Gibraltar, and suffer a second defeat; and Rodney had enough ships in the Leeward Islands to intercept and beat the French reinforcements before they reached Martinique.

On the French side of the Channel Neckar might be silenced, but Vergennes did not deceive himself. Like George III he knew that credit and time were vital: 'This war has gone too slowly; it is a war of hard cash, and if we drag it out the last shilling may not be ours.' The coming campaign must be decisive, said a memorandum to the Spaniards: 'everything urges us to end the war; the means for waging it daily decrease, and the European situation may change at any moment.'[1]

The Spaniards, however, were an obstacle to the search for a decision. They had frustrated the renewal of the invasion plan in 1780, and after drawing the French into a Caribbean campaign had given no effective co-operation. In the early winter Vergennes tried to interest them in another attempt to invade the British Isles in 1781; but now they saw Gibraltar and Minorca within their grasp, and did not mean to conquer them in the Channel. Their own plan was to concentrate the fleets in the Straits, overwhelm Britain's Mediterranean garrisons, and follow up the victory by attacking Jamaica. They obtained a promise of six French ships of the line to join them at Cadiz. With the lever of the Cumberland negotiations, the weaker and less efficient ally was forcing the stronger into her wake: to the Mediterranean instead of the Channel, to Jamaica and Florida instead of the Lesser Antilles and the rebel colonies.

An alternative to the invasion of England was to reinforce Rochambeau for a decisive effort in America. Rochambeau's son reached Versailles late in 1780 with his demands for reinforcements and supplies. Money was sent at once; but Vergennes hesitated to grant him troops. They might yet be needed for invading England; and the death of the Empress Maria-Theresa and the impending mediation had plunged European affairs into uncertainty. Nor was it clear what additional French troops could achieve in America: their arrival might merely encourage the rebels to let their own army filter away.

These questions remained unresolved through the early months of 1781. Nevertheless a striking force was collected in Brest, to sail in March when its destination was decided. A containing force was also prepared for the Indian Ocean. By January the British preparations to attack the Cape had

[1] Doniol, IV, 516, 544.

been discovered and their purpose identified. The French had already been discussing a plan to reinforce the Cape and Mauritius, and the decision was now taken. Eleven hundred troops and five sail of the line commanded by Suffren were to leave Brest with the main striking force in March.

As these preparations went forward, the main plan at last took shape. It was decided not to reinforce America directly from France: Rochambeau's force would remain an auxiliary corps under Washington, and the Americans would be sent the means to keep twelve or fifteen thousand troops of their own on foot. The main fleet under de Grasse would go to the West Indies. There it would co-operate with the Spaniards if they had a plan; and in the hot weather it would sail north in great strength to join Ternay's squadron on the American coast. What de Grasse should do there was left to circumstances. If the worst happened and the American army disintegrated, he had orders to evacuate Rochambeau's corps to the West Indies: so much had the winter mutinies at Morristown shaken the trust of the French.[1]

When these orders were given, the preparations were already near completion. Castries, the new Minister of Marine, went down to Brest to superintend the fleet's departure; and on 22 March de Grasse sailed with twenty ships of the line for Martinique. The hopes of France went with him.

[1] Doniol, IV, 544–50.

CHAPTER XXII

THE DEFENCE OF THE EAST ATLANTIC

1. *Gibraltar and the Cape*

The resolution on New Year's Day to send the Channel Fleet to Gibraltar had implications far graver than the similar decision of the previous winter. Rodney's relieving force had been clear of the Channel before the end of the year: Darby had still to receive his orders and assemble his ships and convoy. Nor was the fleet ready. Many of his ships had been withdrawn in the early autumn to make up Hood's reinforcement for the West Indies; but the twenty-two sail of the line which remained with him stayed at sea longer even than Hardy's fleet in 1779, for at the end of October it put out to intercept Guichen's return from the West Indies. But the enemy did not intend to risk Guichen and his convoy off Ushant. Their main fleet was with the Spaniards at Cadiz; and there Guichen was brought. Early in November the whole French fleet of thirty-eight sail of the line sailed for its home port. As it came northwards Sir Samuel Hood left Spithead for the West Indies, little suspecting the danger towards which his convoy was steering. Happily for the British Empire the enemy was sighted off Finisterre by the *Crescent* frigate, which turned northwards to search for the Channel fleet. Approaching the Channel she met Hood with his convoy, and with this warning he held a northerly course to keep out of the enemy's track. The French entered Brest without incident on 3 January. In the meantime Darby had returned on 21 December for his winter refit after a vain cruise of two months in the Bay of Biscay.

Once again winter cruising had exercised a disastrous influence on future strategy. Though the relief of Gibraltar was decided on 1 January, it was not till 13 March that Darby could sail; and such was the shortage of men that if Amherst had had his way and withdrawn the two regiments on loan to the fleet, four or five capital ships would have been immobilised and the expedition could never have sailed.[1] Instead of a winter relief, the Channel fleet was going to Gibraltar at the very moment when it was needed for the spring operations in home waters. Even now his convoy was not complete. His storeships were with him; but the loading of provisions in the depot at Cork had been held up waiting for victualling transports to return from

[1] WO 34/236, pp. 403, 763; WO 34/122, ff. 82–3.

abroad. They were now loaded; but to send them up the Channel at the last moment to Spithead would have been a gamble on an alternation of westerly and easterly winds. Instead, Darby seized an east wind to take him down the Channel, and sailed for Cork to pick up the victuallers. But by ill fortune a change of wind held the victuallers in harbour, and ten more days were lost in sight of the bleak hills of County Cork before they could join him at sea.[1] Had Darby been able to press straight on, he might have met de Grasse's West India reinforcements as they sailed from Brest and changed the course of history. But he was still far off on the Irish coast. The shipping shortage had combined with the winds to impose a fatal delay.

Darby took the whole fleet of twenty-eight sail of the line, for thirty-two Spaniards were lying in his course to intercept him. His ships were now well manned and fitted, and if he had to fight the odds would not be too heavy. Against the lengthening chances at sea a victory would have counted heavily. But the delay in sailing cheated the Ministry of this hope; for when Darby at last approached Gibraltar the Spaniards had gone into Cadiz for provisions. Darby's convoy unloaded under fire in Gibraltar bay, and when the fleet obtained a wind to take it home, thirty or forty empty transports were ready to accompany it.[2]

The movement of the Channel fleet was used to cover the Cape expedition, which sailed with it. The naval force was commanded by Commodore Johnstone; and very ungrateful he was, for he complained loudly that the cancelling of his River Plate enterprise would cost him a hundred thousand in prize money. Johnstone was a hot-tempered politician with modest naval experience but a lot of influence. He had never commanded a post-ship till 1779, when he was given a small squadron on the coast of Portugal; but he was a nephew of Lord Elibank and General Murray, and an East India House politician. His military colleague was General Medows, a veteran of the Seven Years War and commander of the brigade which had repulsed d'Estaing at St Lucia: a thorough professional soldier, an excellent tactician and manager of troops; sweet-tempered and popular but of firm character. He had three battalions of infantry, though most of them were still raw recruits[3]; and Johnstone's task force was two ships of the line and three of fifty guns.

Nine days after the British fleet's departure, there sailed from Brest de Grasse's great fleet and convoy for the West Indies; and with it went Suffren's five sail of the line and 1,100 troops for the Cape and Mauritius.

[1] Keppel, II, 349 ff.; Sandwich, IV, 330, 348.
[2] G 3229, 3262; Eg. 2135, f. 156; Sandwich, IV, 4–6, 34.
[3] Actually three battalions, (2/42nd., 98th, 100th), two of them very strong, and four Additional Companies: about 2,600 rank and file.

The Bailli de Suffren, an obese untidy little man of energy and courage, had served under d'Estaing in the western Atlantic, and there he had confirmed his belief that the current French naval doctrine was false. He was convinced that the first object of a fleet must be to destroy the enemy's. On 16 April he was approaching Porto Praya in the Cape Verde Islands for water and minor repairs when he sighted Johnstone's expedition lying in the anchorage. It was in disorder and inferior strength, and Suffren bore down in headlong attack. He was completely unexpected, and confusion reigned in the British fleet: Colonel Fullarton had to swim from the shore to rejoin his ship. Somehow, through mismanagement by the French captains, Johnstone was able to beat off the enemy and pursue them; but at nightfall he broke off the chase and rejoined his transports, leaving Suffren to make his way unhindered to the Cape.

Johnstone lingered at Porto Praya for another fortnight, and when he reached the Cape the enemy were ready. Suffren's troops were ashore, and the Dutch Governor, already warned by a French frigate of the British declaration of war, had landed the guns of five Dutch East Indiamen. The British expedition had been outpaced and thwarted. The naval officers thought at once of prize money, and wanted to switch the whole force back to the River Plate enterprise.[1] Fullarton supported them; but Medows's orders were clear. He had not been sent on a 'buccaneering party', and if the Cape could not be taken, the two battalions originally intended for the east should proceed to India. Johnstone then formally proposed that Medows should land and attack the Cape, while warning him that he could not guarantee to maintain communications with the shore: a characteristic device which would have thrown the responsibility on the military commander. Medows declined the invitation, and insisted on being forwarded to India. So Johnstone detached the convoy with two ships of the line and one fifty-gun ship; and though he knew the strength of Suffren's force at the Cape, he adhered to the letter of his instructions and turned back with two fifties to take some prizes to St Helena. Very different was the conduct of Medows. From a warship at sea he had learnt of Hyder Ali's successes. In spite of peremptory orders to detach one battalion to the West Indies, he framed his conduct to the new circumstances and took all his regiments to India. Very different might have been the coming struggle in the east if Johnstone had acted like him.[2]

[1] When some Dutch East Indiamen were attacked in Saldanha Bay, Captain Pasley much resented the participation of the army and its consequent claim to a share of the spoils.

[2] WO 34/135, f. 225. For further information on the above operations see Willcox in *American Neptune*, 1945; Rutherford in *Mariner's Mirror*, 1942; Castex, *Manoeuvre de la Praya*; Richmond; Harlow.

2. The Price of Gibraltar

Darby's absence left not a single ship in full operational order at home, except a few which were preparing for foreign service. Nothing was left to molest de Grasse and Suffren, who sailed to upset the balance in the West Indies and Indian Ocean; nothing to cover the convoys in British waters; nothing to hold the Dutch in check except one or two bad ships which might just do for North Sea service.

When Darby sailed for Gibraltar, the forces in enemy ports were accurately known, but their destination could not be penetrated. The French-inspired reports that they would send a force to America were treated with suspicion, and on 7 March Germain guessed that they had still to make up their minds. Even when it was almost certain that de Grasse had sailed, it was still not known whether his force was bound for America, the West Indies, or both; or whether it might instead join the Spaniards at Cadiz and dispute Darby's passage to Gibraltar. The French delay in forming their plans had made it virtually impossible to discover them in advance; but it is difficult to explain why no cruiser observed the fleet as it left Brest or tracked its course: a sloop was sent to look into the port the day after the enemy had sailed. In defence of the Admiralty Sandwich later maintained that the intelligence service on land was more regular and accurate than unsupported cruisers reconnoitring Brest. This may have been true, though if rumour is correct Stormont did not believe it: yet it did not remove the need to watch enemy fleet movements at sea, and the fact remains that de Grasse was not shadowed. For twelve days after his departure the British Cabinet was uncertain that he had gone.[1]

About 30 March it was learnt that part of the enemy fleet was bound for the Indian Ocean. Its access to the harbour of Ceylon and the known connection of the French with Hyder Ali gave the news a serious twist. If the enemy won control of Indian waters and landed an army, they would find an ally already lodged in the Madras Presidency, and could overwhelm the handful of British troops and sepoys who held the sky suspended. The East India Company appealed for help and was swiftly answered. The *Monarca*, 68, a prize of Rodney's Moonlight Battle, was ordered to India, and a regiment which the Company 'thankfully' accepted was to follow in company transports. A few days brought news still blacker. Hyder's invasion of the Carnatic had caught the British dispersed and unprepared; and in September 1780 he had destroyed a force of nearly 4,000 men under Colonel Baillie.

[1] CO 318/8, f. 23; Mundy, II, 59–61; Adm. 2/1339, f. 47; Add. MSS. 38344, f. 243; Walpole, *Last Journals*, II, 482.

Amherst had already opposed the despatch of troops, with a warning that the forces at home were 16,000 below the numbers needed for home defence. He had posed the question whether to risk a further decrease, or to send only recruits from England and to raise Swiss or other foreign troops for the Company. When Baillie's defeat was considered, the Cabinet attended to the warning: it resolved that only recruits should be added to the reinforcement, and that the Company must negotiate for Swiss or Germans. But at all hazards ships had to be found, and the Cabinet agreed to send out two additional ships of the line at once, and two more in October.[1]

By now it was probable that none of de Grasse's fleet was to go directly to America. The general guess was that he would reach the West Indies without a decided superiority and too late in the season; and that after provisioning the French islands he would go north to 'revive the dying cause of rebellion'. Yet till the Channel fleet returned from Gibraltar, not a ship could be spared to follow him. The first charge on the country's reserves was India; for there, as Sandwich told Rodney, everything was at stake.[2]

The convoy for India could not sail till Darby's return, for there was nothing to protect it against a raiding squadron from Brest. From the first the safety of the convoys in the absence of the Channel fleet had worried Sandwich. Cruisers went out to the westward to stop the inbound convoys and divert them north about; and the German reinforcements collected in the Weser were sent round the north of Scotland to America instead of being brought down the Channel to join a convoy at Spithead. To cover this northern traffic and the Baltic trade a cruiser force commanded by Captain Stewart in a seventy-four was sent to patrol the seas between Norway and Scotland, and a working base with a small garrison was established in the Shetlands.[3] These arrangements were largely successful. The German troops slipped away before the Dutch came out from the Texel, and the homeward bound Jamaica convoy was met and diverted round the north of Scotland. But the cruisers missed a convoy laden with the plunder of St Eustatius, and on 2 May it ran into a raiding squadron under la Motte-

---

[1] Add. MSS. 38315, f. 42; WO 34/132, ff. 44, 58; WO 34/236, p. 501; G 3270, 3274, 3297, 3300, 3311–2, 3334–9. General Faucit who had negotiated the 'Hessian' treaties, re-opened negotiations in Germany; and a Mr Erskine, who had been seeking permission to raise a regiment in Switzerland, was authorised to raise one for the Company. But French influence in Switzerland was at a peak, and the cantons took stringent measures to prevent Erskine from recruiting (see Giddey in *Schweiz. Zeitschr. für Gesch.*, 1954). Eventually two Hanoverian battalions reached India.

[2] CO 318/8, f. 54; CO 5/101, f. 170; Mundy, II, 106–7.

[3] Half a battalion of Scottish Fencibles was convoyed to Lerwick in March, leading to representations by Stormont on the undefended state of the Scottish coast.

Picquet. Commodore Hotham made the signal to scatter, but two-thirds of his convoy was captured by the enemy.[1]

This misfortune was accompanied by intelligence that the Dutch fleet had sailed from the Texel. They had not been expected to be ready before the end of May, and Hyde Parker was hurried off to Portsmouth to scrape a force together. The *Princess Amelia*, 80, and *Buffalo*, 60, both unfit for foreign service, were made ready, and Sandwich considered appropriating the two ships of the line which were waiting to sail to India. But Darby fortunately arrived from Gibraltar on 20 May. The Channel was now safe, and on the 28th the *Sultan*, 74, and *Magnanime*, 64, received their sailing orders for the convoy to India. Two of Darby's returning ships were ordered to the North Sea to face the Dutch; and three more were at last spared for America, and one for the West Indies. But after their voyage to Gibraltar they had to complete their stores to foreign service scale, and it would be some time before they could sail. America's real protection against de Grasse was a swift pursuit from the West Indies; and knowing that Rodney intended to come home, Sandwich begged him to remain at his post and take the critical decisions.[2]

The delay in despatching these reinforcements was directly caused by the decision to relieve Gibraltar. They did not reach America till the crisis was past, and their absence added to the accumulation of misfortunes which composed the disaster at Yorktown. Wise after the event, the Opposition led by Keppel maintained that if Darby had forwarded part of his fleet straight to the West Indies from Gibraltar, as had been done when Rodney relieved the fortress, the whole course of the war beyond the Atlantic would have been changed. A tidy argument can be marshalled to support the contention. Four of Darby's ships were actually ordered to America and the West Indies as soon as they returned from Gibraltar. If they had been equipped for foreign service before Darby sailed, and had gone straight out to Rodney from Gibraltar, they would have reached the West Indies sooner than de Grasse with his cumbrous convoy, and enabled Rodney to master the French.

But in strategy tidy arguments are usually achieved by ignoring the complex of facts and guesses which form decisions. To send out ships intact and in good condition to Rodney it might have been necessary to

[1] Mundy, II, 59–61; CL, Germain, 20 March, to Admiralty; G 3270; Sandwich, IV, 7, 18; Adm. 2/1339, ff. 40–2.

[2] G 3316, 3327, 3348; James, 448; Sandwich, IV, 48; Adm. 2/1339, f. 83. For the state of the naval forces at home between March and the end of May, compare lists in Sandwich, IV, 40–2, 332–3.

forego the hope of a battle with the Spaniards off Cadiz. It might just have been possible to equip the ships for foreign service in time, and the danger of Darby's reduced force being intercepted by the Spaniards on its return might have been accepted. But there were other considerations. When the decision to relieve Gibraltar was taken in January and the preparation of the fleet began, de Grasse's force had not been assembled; and even when Darby sailed in March the enemy's destination was not known. There would have been a risk of sending the reinforcements to the wrong destination. It may be argued that it would have made no difference whether the ships went to the West Indies or to America, since sooner or later they would have joined the vital concentration. Yet the enemy's unsuspected reinforcement of India proves the danger of strategic surprise. Would it have been right to reduce the exiguous home fleet still further before it was known whether the whole of de Grasse's force was to leave Europe? Risks had to be accepted in home waters; but the summer was to see a bitter struggle in the North Sea for the Baltic trade, while to the westward Darby never had more than twenty-six ships of the line to face nearly fifty French and Spaniards. Facing an option of difficulties, it was reasonable for the Cabinet to trust that Rodney would rise to the occasion. In full possession of what followed, one must regret that Rodney was not reinforced from Gibraltar if it could have been done: in the circumstances of Darby's departure it is impossible to say that it should have been.[1]

3. The Defence of Trade

On 5 June Hyde Parker sailed for the North Sea to face the Dutch. He had four ships of the line, and two heavy frigates which could stand in the line of battle against the Dutch. Two of the ships of the line were rated as unfit for foreign service; but the other two had come from Darby's Channel fleet on its return from Gibraltar, and with the detachments ordered to the West Indies and America reduced the force immediately available in the Channel to twenty-one of the line. It is reasonable to ask whether the command of the North Sea was a proper object for the overburdened navy, important though the Greenland and Baltic trades might be. But more than this was at stake. With the British weakness in the Western Approaches, the North Sea had become a back door for the inward bound Atlantic shipping and the despatch of reinforcements to America. And through the North Sea came the Baltic naval stores which furnished the fleets of the belligerents: it was to stop the Dutch traffic in naval stores that England had accepted the risks of fighting Holland, and there was intelligence to show

[1] The question is briefly touched on in Sandwich, IV, 315–16.

how much the French and Spanish navies feared the stoppage. Even at the crisis of the campaign, when Darby faced odds of more than two to one in the Channel, the North Sea squadron was maintained in full force to check the Dutch.[1]

Hyde Parker saw the Baltic convoy safe to Elsinore, where he was joined under Admiralty arrangements by Commodore Stewart with his seventy-four from the Shetlands, and at the end of July he sailed for home with 120 merchantmen. On 5 August he crossed the track of the Dutch fleet with a convoy off the Dogger Bank. Both Admirals shed their merchantmen and turned to fight.

England and Holland had not fought for 100 years; but though their navy had diminished, the Dutch were still the tough obstinate seamen who had stood the hammering battles of the reign of Charles II. Admiral Zoutman had eight ships in his line of battle against Parker's seven, with 460 guns against 446. For four hours the little squadrons fought line to line, till both became unmanageable and drew apart. In this fiercest naval battle of the war, the Dutch suffered 545 casualties, the British 100 fewer. A good Dutch ship foundered in the night after the battle; and while the British merchantmen went on to their destination, the Dutch convoy turned back, not to sail again that year. The advantage therefore lay with the British. Parker, however, returned to the Nore in a rage at the state of his squadron. Rodney had described him as a dangerous man with a violent temper, and hostile in the highest degree to the Ministry. Considering the pressure on the navy and the Admiralty's assessment of the Dutch fleet, his force had been adequate. But he refused a knighthood, resigned his command, and would serve no more. He was succeeded by Stewart, under whose protection two more Baltic convoys came home in the autumn.[2]

The same pressure of commerce protection which drew Parker's ships into the North Sea deflected Darby's Channel fleet from what, in a strictly naval view, was its primary task. When the fleet returned from Gibraltar, the French home fleet under Guichen was nearly ready in Brest; and on the principle that the first object of a fleet was to fight and beat the enemy, the British Channel fleet could have performed no more important task than to intercept Guichen. A victory off Ushant would have come too late to alter the course of events beyond the Atlantic; but it might have

[1] G 3401; Sandwich, IV, 96.

[2] Add. MSS. 38344, ff. 237, 246; Sandwich, IV, 18, 59 n., 88; G 3316; Keppel, II, 355–6, 363 n.; Adm. 2/1340, f. 31; James, 310–11. It was alleged that another ship of the line could have been sent out to Parker in time for the battle, but that she was negligently sent to the rendezvous at the Gunfleet instead. The précis in Sandwich, IV, 88–9, seems to dispose of this. On the other side it is argued that Hyde Parker should have used his single-decked frigates in his line of battle.

restored the country's sense of proportion when the blow fell at Yorktown, and even made it possible to save Minorca, which was soon to be attacked. But the loss of the St Eustatius convoy had shaken the Cabinet. Public opinion and public credit were more sensitive to convoy losses than to neglected strategic opportunities, whose effects took longer to appear and were less measurable. England's power in the eighteenth century resembled Holland's in the seventeenth: it depended not on land or population but on a credit structure based on trade. There was common belief that England's credit was an inflated balloon which would collapse if it were punctured: a financial panic or a revolt of the City might deprive the government of the means to wage a war. Now that la Motte-Picquet had tasted blood, it looked as though the Channel would have to be scoured continually to protect the shipping. By precautions against further convoy losses the Cabinet resigned the chance of intercepting Guichen.

To have the fleet off Brest before Guichen sailed, it would have been necessary to bring the ships from Gibraltar straight in to revictual. Instead, Darby was ordered to leave ten sail of the line in the Soundings to look for la Motte. This detachment came in on 4 June, and it would still have been possible to prepare twenty-one ships of the line in time to meet Guichen's twenty. This was the Cabinet's intention. But at that moment it was learnt that a Jamaica convoy was due in the Soundings. The idea of collecting a strong force off Brest was thrown aside, and Darby was ordered to sail at once and cover the convoy with whatever ships were ready. He set out at once for Portsmouth; cannibalised the complements of other ships to complete those which were ready; and sailed on 9 June with nine sail of the line, made up to twelve by subsequent reinforcements. On the 18th the Admiralty learnt that the precaution had been unnecessary. The *Juno* frigate had found the Jamaica convoy and diverted it north about; and in any case la Motte's squadron was no longer cruising. Darby was now told that he would be reinforced to go off Brest in strength. But the chance had been lost: on the 23rd Guichen sailed for Cadiz with eighteen sail of the line to join the Spaniards.[1]

Though de Grasse had already departed unobserved, there still seems to have been no continuous watch on Brest. At the beginning of July the Admiralty had no more than 'reason to think' that Guichen had gone, and no news whatever of the course he had steered.[2] The Channel fleet was blown up the Channel to Torbay early in July, to learn that the French had sailed.

[1] Two others had collided and returned to Brest. Sandwich, IV, 10, 44–5; G 3348, 3353; Adm. 2/1339, ff. 93, 98, 112, 116.
[2] A sloop had been detailed to watch Brest, but she used to come into Plymouth at intervals (Adm. 2/1339, ff. 71, 89; G 3367; Keppel, II, 356).

Darby's beer and sauerkraut were nearly finished, scurvy had broken out, and he sailed for Spithead for provisions and reinforcements. If he had failed to stop Guichen, the trade at least was safe. The Jamaica convoy had been diverted, convoys from Charleston and the Leeward Islands had come safely home and the outward bound East Indiamen had been seen clear of the danger area. In the Soundings as in the North Sea the country's seaborne commerce continued to flow, though at a price. The nation's overtaxed resources had forced a hard choice on the government.

4. Return of the Combined Fleet

The reinforcement for America was commanded by Admiral Digby, Arbuthnot's successor as Commander-in-Chief and Peace Commissioner. His three ships, like Graves's in the previous year, had been delayed by a pay-mutiny and contrary winds.[1] Now the uncertainty about Guichen's movements imposed a further delay of several days so that the Channel fleet could escort him to sea. Darby, having landed his sick and replenished his provisions, was ready to sail on 19 July, and duly saw Digby's ships into the Atlantic before turning south to cruise off Finisterre for the enemy.

The French and Spaniards had made a prompter use of their concentration than in the past. By early July Guichen was with Cordoba at Cadiz, and on the 23rd they sailed to cover the passage of an expedition to Minorca. The army landed on 18 August, and General Murray's garrison of 2,700 men was invested in St Philip's Castle by 14,000 French and Spanish soldiers, while a Spanish squadron cruised off Port Mahon to stop reinforcements and supplies.

Having seen the Minorca expedition on its way, the Combined Fleet turned northwards with forty-nine sail of the line to command the approaches to the Channel. Off Finisterre Darby learnt from a Portuguese merchantman that this overwhelming force was between him and his base, and he hastened back to defend the Channel. On 25 August the British fleet anchored in Torbay. Leaving a frigate off the Start to watch for the enemy, Darby stretched his battle fleet in a crescent of two lines to defend the anchorage. But the Admiralty was incredulous of the news. Much false intelligence had come from merchantmen, and it was known from continental sources that Minorca had been attacked. They concluded that Darby's Portuguese had seen a convoy outward bound from Cork, and assured the Lord Mayor of Bristol that the news of the Combined Fleet was false. They had every reason to avert unnecessary panic: when la Motte-Picquet had been cruising in May, there had been signs of it at Plymouth again; and men had been

[1] The *Canada* had mutinied for pay in arrears through the negligence of her last captain, Sir George Collier (Sandwich, IV, 343 n).

taken from repair work in the dockyard to make a boom, as though la Motte with his six ships would storm the Sound. 'It is ships and not booms we are in want of at present', Middleton had written. This time the Admiralty did not intend a false alarm to lock up their resources. On 27 August Darby was ordered to sea to cover the approach of a second Jamaica convoy which was reported to be the most valuable ever sent. Two days later the Admiralty had news of a large French convoy from the Ile de Rhé which they concluded was what the Portuguese had seen. But on the 30th came news of a large fleet off the Scillies, and on the following day the *Agamemnon* on her way to the East Indies sighted between forty-four and forty-seven sail of the line thirty leagues east of the Lizard.[1]

It seemed too late in the year for an invasion, and there was no intelligence of transports on the French coast. But the rich Jamaica convoy and another from the Leeward Islands were approaching the danger area. Darby sent out a pair of frigates to meet them; and the Admiralty, taking no chances after the loss of the St Eustatius convoy, ordered out every cruiser on which they could lay their hands. Frigates went out from the Clyde, Dublin and the Bristol Channel; and at Robinson's suggestion revenue cutters on the west coast of Ireland were borrowed and sent out with naval officers to seek the convoys.[2] In the meantime reinforcements were hastily fitted out for the fleet. There was a certain nervousness in the air. The King suggested sending Navy Board Commissioners down to the three great dockyards, for the sake of appearances even if it did no good. Sandwich and Middleton resisted the waste of the Navy Board's time: by then the ships at Portsmouth and Plymouth were out of the shipwrights' hands, and their equipment depended entirely on the captains and the Port Admirals. But a Commissioner was sent down to Sheerness to see what he could do.[3]

At the moment of the Combined Fleet's appearance, the Dutch convoy which Parker had turned back to the Texel in August was ready to sail again for the Baltic. Stewart, whose ship had been at home for repairs, was on the point of taking out a reinforcement to join the watching screen and intercept them; a mission so important that in spite of the need for ships in the Channel the Cabinet agreed he should proceed. Even if he joined Darby instead, the Channel fleet would not be strong enough to fight, and as Robinson wrote to Sandwich, the stopping of the Dutch convoy would deliver 'the most effectual blow that perhaps could be given to the French and Spanish navies'.[4]

[1] Add. MSS. 38216, f. 349; Sandwich, IV, 37, 39, 334; G 3393; Adm. 2/1340, ff. 66, 70, 79, 81, 101.
[2] Sandwich, IV, 53–4, 59–60.
[3] Sandwich, IV, 53; G 3402, 3404.   [4] G 3400–1; Sandwich, IV, 96.

Without Stewart's ships or the three which were going abroad, the Channel fleet would have only twenty-nine sail of the line. It was not easy to know how to use them; and Sandwich was bombarded with conundrums by Palliser, Mulgrave and Darby. Was it right to leave the fleet in a defensive anchorage while convoys were threatened? In Torbay it was probably safe except in a strong east wind; but it had no refuge to retire to if an enemy attack succeeded, and would be as well placed at Spithead to exploit the enemy's difficulties if they were driven up Channel and damaged by a gale. And if the British fleet stayed in Torbay and the enemy passed up Channel to Spithead, would it not have to follow them and risk the difficult passage through the Needles? Should the smaller two-deckers be sent into the North Sea to join Stewart, in case the French and Spaniards meant to detach a force to cover their naval stores from the Baltic? Should the fleet be ordered to the westward to watch the enemy closely?[1]

The central question was whether to send the fleet to the westward against the French and Spaniards. The King, ever hopeful, had fastened on a report from Flanders that the enemy were to detach a squadron against the victualling depot at Cork; and if this happened he wanted Darby to go out and attack the remainder of the Combined Fleet. He launched his usual appeal for boldness. 'This country, with such numerous enemies, must be ruined unless what we want of strength is made up in activity and resolution. Caution has certainly made this war less brilliant than the former; and if that alone is to direct our operations, with the load of debt we labour under, without much foresight it is easy to tell we must be great losers.'[2]

When this appeal reached Sandwich, the latest intelligence put the enemy at forty-four to forty-seven sail of the line, and it was clear that they had not detached. The First Lord scented danger; and already a letter was on its way from Darby demanding 'an order fully signed' for his protection. For the past two years Sandwich had been wary of risking his name on an order without Cabinet authority. Darby's instructions were 'a matter of too much magnitude to be decided by any single person', and he asked the King to procure a Cabinet meeting. Several of the Ministers were out of London for the summer. Dartmouth was absent as usual; so was Bathurst; and Thurlow, convalescing on Gower's good cooking at Trentham, thought naval operations could be managed without a lawyer. North, however, had returned from Oxfordshire as soon as he heard of the enemy's appearance; and on 6 September Sandwich managed to collect the half dozen Ministers who were concerned with the war.[3] He had before him a draft order for Darby

[1] Sandwich, IV, 50–2, 55–8, 60–1.
[2] Sandwich, IV, 53, 55.
[3] G 3404; Carlisle, 520; Gore-Browne, *Thurlow*, 163; Sandwich, IV, 53.

composed by Middleton. The Comptroller's view was that nothing could be gained by giving battle: there was no great object at stake to justify the risk, and an indecisive action would still leave the enemy in command of the Channel with his superior numbers. But he believed it was still possible to protect the trade: his solution was copper. Instead of fighting, Darby's coppered fleet should exploit its speed. 'I still think it practicable to save our colonies by a proper use of this first of naval improvements.'[1]

The Cabinet approved. Darby was ordered to put to sea without waiting for further reinforcements, seek the enemy, and hover with his coppered ships to watch for an opening. Thus he should be able to protect both the homeward convoys and the Irish coast. This was a tough assignment, as Darby complained. With half the enemy's numbers he was expected to cover two great convoys and prevent a descent on Ireland, and with his small force he doubted if he could do any one of these things. The enemy probably had some coppered ships which could bring him to action and hold him till their slower vessels came up. In these doubts there was no timidity. 'Our situation will certainly be critical', Mulgrave wrote from Torbay, 'but there is a manliness and plain firm sense about Admiral Darby that will make him do everything for the best . . . You must not suffer him to be run down by clamour; he is a plain but valuable man; his arrangements are judicious.'[2]

Darby waited a few days for Kempenfelt to rejoin the fleet from sick leave and command a division; and on 15 September he sailed with twenty-seven ships of the line. It was almost exactly two years since Hardy had begun to move his fleet out for the final cruise of the invasion year; and again the enemy had gone. On the insistence of Cordoba the French and Spaniards had separated on 5 September, the day before Darby's orders were agreed by the Cabinet. On the 14th the military commander at Plymouth reported a general belief that the French were in Brest and the Spaniards on their way home; but not till the 22nd did intelligence arrive from Brussels and Paris which was thought sufficiently reliable to act on. By then Darby had vanished to the westwards, and his absence was to exert an unhappy influence on future strategy.[3]

---

[1] Sandwich, IV, 61-2; CL, Shelburne, Vol. 151, No. 2.
[2] Sandwich, IV, 13, 63, 65-6.
[3] WO 34/137, ff. 173, 187; Adm. 2/1340, f. 105; Sandwich, IV, 13-14.

CHAPTER XXIII

'CORNWALLIS LED A COUNTRY DANCE'

1. *Germain and Clinton*

By a slender margin the year's operations in home waters passed without serious misfortune. Gibraltar had been relieved, the trade and reinforcements had sailed, and even the intervention of the Dutch had not been allowed to close the North Sea and the Baltic. The only shadows had been the loss of the St Eustatius convoy and the attack on Minorca. In the presence of superior enemy forces England had been able to keep open her maritime communications.

These containing operations were based on a deliberate resolution to take risks at home, calculating on the ineffectiveness of the combined allies. By forfeiting the initiative in Europe Britain had allowed the enemy to attack Minorca, casting a shadow over the Mediterranean theatre. All this was for the sake of the East and West Indies, and to enable Cornwallis to maintain his offensive towards Virginia. By the end of the summer the fairest hopes in America were already blighted; but in early October Germain still expected enough of Virginia to be recovered to justify the Commissioners in restoring civil government to the colony, and the royal Governor was ordered to return to America like the Governors of Georgia and the Carolinas. At that very moment French siege-guns were pounding Germain's hopes to pieces.

Considering the universal pressure on the country's resources, Clinton had received generous reinforcements. The Cabinet had been unable to meet his demand for 10,000 men, but it will be remembered that they were able to promise him 6,000, with three more regiments to come from the West Indies at the end of the summer. In the event the promise was not completely fulfilled, for we shall find that of the three promised West India battalions only one reached America. Clinton's other demands received an unequivocal rebuff. Against his demand for the recall of the Admiral and his removal from the Peace Commission, Sandwich supported Arbuthnot; and Germain, who was sick of Clinton's jealousies, asked his emissary Dalrymple to put the demand in writing and laid it before the Cabinet. Arbuthnot's eventual removal was agreed: in due course he should be sent to Jamaica to succeed Sir Peter Parker whose relief was due. But for the sake of harmony between the services, Arbuthnot's successor would be on the Peace Commission. If

Clinton did not like this compromise, he should resign his command to Cornwallis.[1]

If Clinton resigned, Germain and Sandwich agreed that Arbuthnot should remain, to avoid the difficulty of replacing him. Sandwich was confident that Clinton would go; but Germain doubted it, for the General acted 'more from caprice than common sense', He talked to Colonel Bruce, who was to take the Cabinet's answers to Clinton, and impressed on him that no good could come of Clinton's distrust. He must either remain in his command in a good humour and rely on being supported as strongly as the situation allowed, or resign and come home. Not that Germain had any confidence in Clinton: he remembered Burgoyne too well. 'When we act with such a man', he wrote, '. . . we must be cautious not to give him any opportunity of doing a rash action under the sanction of what he may call a positive order.' But he could not dismiss him; and though Clinton guessed his resignation was expected, he would not go.[2]

The drive on Virginia was constantly pressed on Clinton in the coming months: 'The recovery of the southern provinces, and the prosecution of the war by pushing our conquests from south to north, is to be considered as the chief and principal object for the employment of all the forces under your command.' The obstacle which Germain feared was Clinton himself, with his four houses in New York, his officers busy with their theatricals, his train of commissaries and quartermasters making their fortunes. All this had been described to him by Rodney. 'In this war', the Admiral wrote after his visit to New York, 'I am convinced the sword should cut deep.' He was not alone in thinking that the entire American War had been run by *fainéant* Generals.[3]

Through the first half of 1781 Germain waited to hear that the advance to Virginia was completed. At the end of 1780 he had learnt with bitter disappointment that Leslie's force at Portsmouth had been withdrawn from the Chesapeake to reinforce Cornwallis, for he had regarded the post there as a vital part of the southern plan. Leslie's was the second withdrawal from the Chesapeake; and Germain remonstrated in terms so strong that he thought the letter might precipitate Clinton's resignation. The rebel supply depots in Virginia on which their southern army depended had not

[1] Willcox, *JMH*, 1945, p. 316; Knox, 171; CL, Germain, 4 and 13 Oct. to Clinton; G 3160. Willcox's study is based on the papers in the William Clements Library and supersedes previous studies of the Yorktown campaign.

[2] Sandwich, III, 256–9; Sackville, II, 185; CO 5/102, f. 38; Knox, 174; CO 5/103, f. 124.

[3] CL, Clinton, 7 Feb. from Germain; CO 5/101, ff. 169, 311; Sackville, II, 192 ff.; Knox, 172.

been attacked, their supply line had not been cut. Once more the loyalists had been deserted. A valuable naval station had been thrown away, and the Chesapeake reopened to rebel imports and French reinforcements. The waste of effort was intolerable. With the Dutch in the war, England could not afford to lock up her resources indefinitely in America. 'Every advantage must therefore be seized, every occasion profited of, and the public service be made the great motive and object of all our actions.'[1]

The exhortation to waste no resources was a common one at this stage of the war; but the criticism was not wholly fair. Leslie had moved on his own initiative in response to an appeal from Cornwallis. Clinton's only failure was that he had given Leslie no strong orders to the contrary, and he replaced Leslie's force by one from New York commanded by the renegade Arnold, with stronger instructions to hold on to Portsmouth. As for Germain's contention that Leslie should have marched across Virginia, it rested on a total misreading of the situation, and is a rare instance of what Germain's critics have always alleged to have been a general habit of ignorant interference. The worst of the letter is that Germain should have felt compelled to write in these terms at all to a Commander-in-Chief. His feelings about Clinton may be gauged from an exhortation he sent him in May: 'that the war should be conducted upon a permanent and settled plan of conquest, always securing and preserving what has been recovered, and not by desultory enterprises, taking possession of places at one time, and abandoning them at another, which never can bring the war to a conclusion, or encourage the people to avow their loyalty and exert their endeavours to relieve themselves from the tyranny of the rebel rulers . . .'. He urged 'decision in council, and activity, vigour and perseverance in execution'.[2] Germain had tried giving Clinton his head within broad lines of policy, and nothing had been achieved; he had tried to lever him out, and had failed. Such want of confidence as he now showed was likely to rock Clinton's unsteady judgment in the coming campaign.

Germain's hopes now rested on the energy, ambition and proved leadership of Cornwallis; and Cornwallis may have suspected it, for his aide-de-camp returned from England about the time when Colonel Bruce was charged with Germain's admonition to Clinton, and probably in the same ship.[3] Be that as it may, the rift between Clinton and Cornwallis dates from this time. Hitherto they had worked together amicably; and Cornwallis's dormant commission as Commander-in-Chief, which has been wrongly blamed for their misunderstandings, had been no more than

[1] CO 5/101, ff. 1–4.
[2] CO 5/101, f. 311.
[3] Bruce took the southerly winter route by Charleston.

a normal precaution that the command should not devolve on a German general.[1]

2. The Bankruptcy of the Southern Offensive

Cornwallis had left America at the end of 1778 because of the illness of his wife. He returned in 1779 because her death had made England unendurable to him. He did not expect any brilliant developments in the theatre, but wished to rejoin his friends on active service: 'I love that army, and flatter myself that I am not quite indifferent to them.' His courage and integrity won him the devotion of officers and men. 'A good officer', wrote the uncharitable Wemyss, who served under him in the south, 'devoted to the service of his country . . . beloved by the army.' 'Deservedly the favourite of every person of every rank under his command', Germain's nephew George Damer reported. To General William Amherst in England there was a refreshing momentum about his campaign of 1780 which provided, he said, a rare exception to the system established in America of showing vigour in money-making alone.[2]

In Cornwallis Germain had a General who believed wholeheartedly in the advance on Virginia. He had long been convinced that the only way to protect South Carolina was to push northwards. As long as the enemy had a nucleus of regular troops the occupied areas could never be properly garrisoned or pacified. Around the Continentals gathered the hordes of militiamen, to be defeated and dispersed at great cost in British lives, only to assemble again as soon as the Continentals rallied. Haldimand was to expound the problem a year later, when he explained the impossibility of penetrating New England with the force in Canada.

It is not the number of troops Mr Washington can spare from his army that is to be apprehended, it is the multitude of militia and men in arms ready to turn out at an hour's notice at the shew of a single regiment of Continental Troops that will oppose this attempt.[3]

The British situation in the Carolinas was not unlike that of the Napoleonic armies in Spain when Wellington hovered on the Portuguese frontier. As long as they were able to disperse, they could check the guerrillas and secure their supplies, and eventually would bring the population to acquiesce in their rule. But whenever they had to concentrate against a regular force

[1] A dormant commission for Vaughan had actually been signed when Cornwallis offered to return to America in April 1779.

[2] Cornwallis Wykeham-Martin, 319; Harvard, Sparks MSS., Vol. 22, p. 215; Sackville, II, 211; Add. MSS. 38215, f. 42 (17 Dec. 1780, Gen. William Amherst to Jenkinson).

[3] CO 5/106, p. 356.

they released their hold on the countryside, and the flames of civil war burst forth. If Cornwallis could have destroyed Greene's Continentals and overrun their base in Virginia, the pacification of the south might have proceeded with system and success.

The advance to the north would expose South Carolina to a bold and swift-moving enemy. Cornwallis and Germain were both aware of the risk, but they believed that if Clinton would threaten Virginia and Maryland from the north, the enemy would be forced to pull back their southern army.[1] Cornwallis only waited for the arrival of Leslie's reinforcement from the Chesapeake to resume his offensive. It reached Charleston in the middle of December; and while it was marching up country to join him, Cornwallis made his final arrangements. A small force was sent by sea to occupy Wilmington on the North Carolina coast, where it would hold a new supply base on the flank of the coming advance; and contrary to Clinton's instructions orders were given to destroy the fortifications of Charleston. On 7 January Cornwallis marched with only 4,000 men. Of this intention he had sent no word to Clinton.

Nathanael Greene, who had replaced Gates in command of the American southern army after its defeat at Camden, was too weak to stand and fight. But he was a bold and resourceful commander in adversity, and believed that with the help of the militia and guerrillas he could absorb the blow and ruin Cornwallis's army. Without hesitation he seized the initiative and struck at the British communications. Dividing his force, he joined hands with the guerrillas and took the offensive against Cornwallis's strategic flanks. He could not be disregarded. To save the posts at Ninety-six and Augusta, Cornwallis split his own force, and sent Tarleton in pursuit of Greene's western detachment. Tarleton quickly gained contact with the enemy and attacked them impetuously at Cowpens. But the American commander, Morgan, handled his Continentals and militia with skill, and Tarleton was routed with the loss of most of his infantry. It was one of the few tactical defeats suffered by British regulars in the course of the war; and the 800 casualties were a disastrous loss to Cornwallis.

Cornwallis rushed forward to cut off the Americans, destroying his baggage to speed his pursuit. But Greene had taken control of Morgan's force and slipped away behind the flooded Catawba. Leaving rearguards of militia to dispute the passage of the river, he fell back with his regulars on Guilford to draw Cornwallis deep into the heart of the rebel country. Thus started the great retreat to the River Dan. Greene hoped to make a second Saratoga by drawing the weakened British force onto his own

---

[1] Cornwallis Corr., I, 111; CL, Germain, 4 Oct. 1780 to Clinton.

reserves. He failed, but he made something like a second Trenton instead. Over winter roads, swollen creeks and unbridged rivers Cornwallis followed him, marching sometimes thirty miles in a day, losing men through sickness, skirmishes and desertions, but with Greene always slipping across the next river just ahead of him. The rearmost American troops marched forty miles in sixteen hours to cross the Dan in time. Cornwallis had gained 200 miles of ground and reached the Virginia border, only to place himself in a position of the utmost difficulty. His force was depleted, provisions were short, the country unsecured, the enemy intact. There was no question of crossing the river.

It was a classic instance of the arrested offensive. The British fell back to a position between Hillsborough and Salisbury where Cornwallis hoped to collect the loyalists and command the road system. Greene let him go, for his own reinforcements had not reached him; but his light troops crossed the Dan to hang on Cornwallis's flanks. Few loyalists could make their way through to the British army; and one party which tried it was caught and massacred on the road by Harry Lee.

Early in March Greene was ready to advance. Cornwallis still had 1,900 men; but though Greene had only 1,490 Continental infantry, of whom less than half had been in action, militia and volunteers swelled his army to 4,400. They were of varying merit; but all could inflict casualties, and they could be replaced if they fell. From Morgan's success at Cowpens Greene had learnt to use his militia as a screen of marksmen rather than in the regular order of battle. With this force, unsure in quality but overwhelming in numbers, Greene awaited the British at Guilford Court House. There Cornwallis fought one of the most remarkable actions of the war. Sharing their hardships, he led his 1,900 tired and hungry men against 4,400 Americans, with no information to guide him except that he was overwhelmingly outnumbered; and after a desperate struggle with the best of the Continentals he dislodged the enemy and took their guns. Yet this brilliant feat of arms was no real victory. It cost more than 500 casualties. These losses, with the exhaustion of the troops and the lack of provisions, prevented a pursuit. In vain he had expended more than a quarter of his force. He no longer had the men to pursue his conquests.

In search of provisions the British fell back towards the Cape Fear River to gain touch with Wilmington. But the enemy commanded the steep banks of the river, and no supplies came through. Greene himself now turned from Cornwallis and struck deep in his rear towards South Carolina. But Cornwallis hesitated to follow. Supplies would be difficult, and he feared the prospect of opposed river crossings on the march: another Guilford would destroy him. Sending a warning of Greene's approach to Lord

Rawdon in South Carolina, he led his own force down to the coast at Wilmington, which he reached with 1,435 rank and file. His officer casualties had been particularly severe, and the two battalions of the Guards Brigade had only a captain and five subalterns fit for duty.[1]

Thus was proclaimed the bankruptcy of the policy of reconquest from the south, and the situation foretold so long ago by General Murray and General Harvey had come to pass. Again and again the Americans came forward to accept defeat. The Continental army's power of recuperation was astounding, and in defeat it had nothing vital to yield. 'Greene', said Mackenzie, 'is . . . entitled to great praise for his wonderful exertions; the more he is beaten, the further he advances in the end. He has been indefatigable in collecting troops, and leading them to be defeated.'

As long as Greene's army survived, a seemingly inexhaustible supply of militia rallied to it on the battlefield, while irregulars roamed the British foraging areas and terrorised the loyalists. Decisive victory could have broken the cycle. So might the weariness and exhaustion of the rebel militia, if the British army remained in being. But from indecisive victories the British regiments could never recover. Nearly six years earlier Murray had prophesied the danger: 'if the business is to be decided by numbers, the enemy's plan should be to lose a battle with you every week, until you are reduced to nothing'. And General Harvey's words echoed down the years: 'our army will be destroyed by damned driblets'.[2]

3. The March to Yorktown

The great adventure was over. No longer could Cornwallis's depleted force expect to sweep the rebellion from North Carolina and Virginia. But though the campaign had been lost the war was not. If the British could hold on to what they held and avoid defeats, the enemy might yet disintegrate under their difficulties. Cornwallis might have returned to save South Carolina from Greene, and played out the game to the end. What that end might have been no one can be sure.

To enable Cornwallis to return, the commandant at Charleston had prepared a flotilla to carry his force from Wilmington along the Waccamaw River and so to Charleston. But Cornwallis would not accept the delay of waiting for transports, the loss of his cavalry horses, and the humiliation of a retreat. He still clung to the grander vision. At Wilmington he learnt that

[1] Duke University MSS., XVIII-F (20 April, O'Hara to Duke of Gloucester).
[2] Mackenzie, 673; CL, Germain, encl. in Murray's of 27 Aug. 1776; above, p. 85. A recent vindication of the southern militia is Robert C. Pugh's 'The Revolutionary Militia's Role in the Southern Campaign, 1780–1.' (William and Mary Quarterly, 1957).

General Phillips had joined Arnold in Virginia with a reinforcement, and on 10 April he wrote to him about future plans.

Now, my dear friend, what is our plan? Without one we cannot succeed, and I assure you that I am quite tired of marching about the country in quest of adventures. If we mean an offensive war in America, we must abandon New York, and bring our whole force into Virginia. . . . If our plan is defensive, mixed with desultory expeditions, let us quit the Carolinas (which cannot be held defensively while Virginia can be so easily armed against us) and stick to our salt pork at New York, sending now and then a detachment to steal tobacco.[1]

This letter at least contained a general plan for subduing the rebellion, which was more than any commander had produced since the collapse of the Hudson Valley strategy at Saratoga. Through it filter gleams of impatience with Clinton's direction of the war. But there is also a hint of a gambler's desperation. He still clung to the belief that Virginia was the key, and to get it he would risk South Carolina and abandon New York, giving up all that had been gained for the sake of a new start. He showed no recognition of New York's importance: of the security it gave to Canada, its position in relation to the separatist movement in Vermont, its role as a naval base. He did not believe that Greene would follow him; but at least Greene had uncovered Virginia by his advance on Camden, and on 25 April Cornwallis and his little army marched for the Chesapeake.

His departure sealed the fate of South Carolina and Georgia. For though the British forces in the deep South still outnumbered Greene, they were scattered in ten garrisons to control the countryside. Greene advanced against Camden. Lord Rawdon marched out with 800 men against 1,200 and at the age of twenty-six won the first victory of his distinguished career. But Hobkirk's Hill was no more than a costly breathing space to secure his withdrawal. Now the outlying posts fell rapidly. Augusta surrendered, and Ninety-Six was evacuated with difficulty. The British were pressed rapidly back till nothing remained of their southern conquests beyond the neighbourhoods of Charleston and Savannah. These they held till the peace.

Though Clinton had not been told of Cornwallis's intention to advance into North Carolina, it would be wrong to suppose that he had disapproved of it. On the contrary, from the swiftness of the advance and his knowledge of Greene's weakness he expected that Cornwallis would soon consolidate his hold on North Carolina. He should then be able to spare troops to enable the New York army to take the offensive. Arnold had tried to persuade him

[1] Cornwallis Corr., II, 87.

that an attack up the Hudson would capture the forts of the Highlands by a few days' siege; but Clinton was unconvinced, and intended to operate in the northern end of Chesapeake Bay towards Philadelphia, and clear the Delaware peninsula. He was convinced that the necessary loyalist support to establish royal government did not exist in Virginia, and that if the British cause had numerous friends anywhere outside the Carolinas and Georgia, they would probably be found at the head of the Chesapeake, in Pennsylvania.[1]

The only obstacle he saw was his shortage of troops, and he characteristically wrote that with the 10,000 reinforcements he had asked for he would have no doubt of success. The first shock came in the second half of April when he learnt how much Cornwallis's force had been whittled away. It was clear that he could expect no reinforcements from there; but it was another month before Cornwallis's announcement that he intended to cast loose from South Carolina and march for Virginia gave him real cause for uneasiness about the south. He guessed that Greene would not be drawn after Cornwallis, and that the loss of South Carolina would follow.[2] If Germain was deluded about the situation in the southern colonies, the generals in the theatre had shared his errors.

The widening gulf of misunderstanding between Clinton and Cornwallis was due in part to the difficulties of communication; but it was due much more to Clinton's failure to exercise control. Throughout the three years of his command he had never laid down broad lines of policy or imposed a master-plan: instead he had criticised the government's suggestions and grumbled at the size of his force. His failure to dominate the theatre is measured in a letter he wrote to Cornwallis at the beginning of August. He said that from his high opinion of Cornwallis's talents he had left him full liberty to act as he judged best, while Clinton confined himself to supplying his wants from New York, restricted to the defensive by the reinforcements which he had sent to the south.[3] Thus by his own confession he had resigned not only the most active field command but much of the strategic initiative in the theatre to his subordinate, contenting himself with the comfortable passivity of New York. It is scarcely surprising that his efforts to take up the reins again would be neither confident nor effective.

Cornwallis's march to Virginia was not opposed, and on 20 May he joined hands with Arnold near Richmond, to learn that General Phillips had died a week earlier. The only enemy regular troops in the area were a small force

---

[1] CO 5/102, ff. 13, 20, 171.
[2] Ibid., ff. 42, 130.
[3] CO 5/103, f. 77.

under Lafayette, and having failed to bring these to battle Cornwallis made eastwards for Williamsburg in the Virginian Tidewater to await word from Clinton. The Commander-in-Chief had already suggested an incursion by water towards Philadelphia to destroy magazines and stores. This Cornwallis opposed, still insisting that if the war was to be waged offensively Virginia was the only province worth the effort. When, however, Clinton's instructions arrived on the 26th they revealed how diametrically opposed the views of the two Generals had become. He would have no truck with an offensive in Virginia; and unless Cornwallis was prepared to try the area at the head of the Chesapeake, he was ordered to choose a safe defensive post at Williamsburg or Yorktown, retain enough troops for Clinton's favourite desultory water movements, and send back the balance of his force to New York.

Clinton's lack of intellectual honesty appears in this despatch. To prove that Cornwallis had troops to spare he calculated his numbers in effectives, instead of in men present and fit for duty, the method of reckoning which he demanded that Germain should use. Though he rejected Virginia as too tough a nut to crack, he described the militia opposing Cornwallis as ill-armed, inexperienced, and 'full as spiritless as the militia of the southern provinces': yet two days earlier, describing the dangers of his own position at New York to the Secretary of State, he had referred to the surrounding militia as 'warlike, inveterate and numerous'.[1]

Clinton's wish for the return of troops to New York was no longer dictated by a desire to take the offensive. For a new and menacing picture was taking shape. From intercepted despatches he had learnt that Washington and Rochambeau intended a great effort against the city, and that they would probably be supported by a fleet and troops from the West Indies.[2] His force in New York and Long Island had been reduced to fewer than 10,000 rank and file present and fit (the method of reckoning which suited him in this instance), a force well below the accepted margin of safety if the enemy should control the surrounding water. Though no effort by the Americans alone could dislodge the British from the colonies, the intervention of a French fleet and army might enable them to inflict such irreparable loss as would destroy the country's will to fight on.

It is odd that when he realised the precariousness of the naval situation, he thought first of New York with its large garrison and powerful entrenchments. For Cornwallis, perched precariously on the threshold of Virginia with no fortress of refuge, offered an easier target. Of this Clinton had already had warning. In March the French squadron at Rhode Island had

[1] CO 5/102, ff. 154, 171.
[2] CO 318/7, f. 135.

attempted to land troops in the Chesapeake to attack Arnold's detachment. Arbuthnot had brought the enemy to action at sea, and frustrated them; but if they obtained a naval force strong enough to seal the Chesapeake, the position of the army in Virginia would be precarious indeed.

When Cornwallis received the order to fortify Williamsburg or Yorktown, he replied that neither place could be held by the reduced force which would remain with him when he had sent troops to New York. In any case he questioned the wisdom of holding Yorktown (which he called sickly and Clinton healthy). It would always be exposed to a French attack, and experience had shown that it could make no diversion in favour of the Carolinas. While this letter was on its way, he acted on the views it expressed. He abandoned the Williamsburg peninsula on which Yorktown stood, and crossed the James River to Arnold's former post at Portsmouth, which a small force could hold. Here he prepared to send back a detachment to New York.[1]

Thus the army sheered away from the Yorktown trap. But when Clinton received Cornwallis's letter he had second thoughts. Cornwallis's post in Virginia was intended not only to form a springboard for a future offensive in the Chesapeake, but to protect a fleet anchorage in the York River or Hampton Roads. For this the possession of the Williamsburg peninsula was vital, and Clinton was prepared to forego the reinforcement of New York to hold it. Accordingly he ordered Cornwallis to retain the whole of his force if he needed it; to fortify Old Point Comfort at the tip of the Williamsburg peninsula, which commanded Hampton Roads from the north; and to hold Yorktown too if he thought it necessary to the security of Old Point Comfort.[2]

This was the first that Cornwallis had heard of a harbour for ships of the line. He cancelled the reinforcements for New York, and ordered his Engineer to reconnoitre Old Point Comfort with some naval officers. But their report was adverse. The Point would be very difficult to fortify, it would not close the channel to the enemy, and because of the conformation of the shore line and the deep water close in, it would not protect British ships from attack. Cornwallis thereon took a decision for which he afterwards pleaded a positive order from Clinton: instead of Old Point Comfort he would

[1] Cornwallis Corr., I, 103, 105, 108.
[2] CO 5/102, ff. 248, 272. Fortescue (III, 396) states that Clinton was induced to rescind his first orders by the receipt of Germain's letter of 2 May, with 'positive commands . . . that not a man was to be withdrawn from the Chesapeake'. Germain's letter, quoted on p. 403 above, does not support this interpretation. Its intention was to urge Clinton to pursue a settled and permanent plan of conquest, and gave him full liberty to act as changing circumstances might require. As Clinton knew, it had been written without the knowledge of French intentions which Clinton now possessed.

fortify Yorktown, with a post at Gloucester on the opposite shore of the York River, to protect the only anchorage where ships of the line could lie in safety.

A French ship of the line had wintered at Yorktown in 1779-80, and works had been raised to protect her against attack from the sea. But against a landward attack the position was very weak. Cornwallis warned Clinton that it commanded no country and he would need a superiority in the field to enable him to obtain forage and supplies. What he failed to make clear was that Yorktown was bad defensive ground in itself: he had indeed said so, but with reference to his earlier situation when he had expected to be deprived of more than half his force for New York.

Cornwallis reckoned that he would need six weeks to fortify the ground without ruining his troops' health in the heat; and he was very short of entrenching tools, though more than 3,000 had been sent to the Chesapeake from New York. Through the hot August days his men toiled at the field works, which, their commander wrote to Clinton on 27 August, 'will be a work of great time and labour, and after all, I fear, [will] not be very strong'. Four days later a French ship of the line and two frigates appeared in the mouth of the river. A naval lieutenant rode down to the end of the peninsula with an escort of dragoons; and from Old Point Comfort he counted thirty or forty enemy ships within the Capes. The trap had sprung.[1]

[1] Cornwallis Corr., I, 107-12, 116-7; CO 5/103, ff. 69, 130.

CHAPTER XXIV

THE ANATOMY OF DISASTER

1. *Washington and Clinton*

It was on 8 May that the Comte de Rochambeau learnt that his son and
Admiral Barras had landed at Boston with the instructions for the year
from France. Barras had come to assume the command of the squadron at
Rhode Island, for Ternay had died in the winter. The two commanders
could now look forward to the arrival of a superior fleet from the West
Indies to wrest the initiative from the British. It was not before time. For
the past two years the war in the north had been sunk in torpor. Washington
had few men and no funds; and indifference and war-weariness were
spreading. A victory was wanted; but as Washington had said, 'no land
force can act decisively unless accompanied by a maritime superiority'.

On 21 May Rochambeau conferred with Washington at Wethersfield in
Connecticut. They had before them intercepted despatches which revealed
the British government's intention to consolidate from the south and drive
Washington behind the Hudson. Rochambeau favoured a campaign in the
south; but Washington held to his view that New York was still the place
to strike, and obtained agreement. The French troops would march for the
Hudson to serve under his command. Washington hesitated to leave the
fleet at Newport without the troops' protection, and wanted it to retire to
the safety of Boston; but with some difficulty Barras persuaded him that it
should remain at the strategic point at Rhode Island from which it could
swoop on the English lodgments.

Rochambeau's corps set out on its march through the hills of western
Connecticut, and joined Washington near New York early in July. But it
was soon plain that the British position was too strong to be carried. On the
21st Washington threw forward a strong screen of troops and made a
thorough reconnaissance with the French generals. What they saw was
discouraging. The defences looked strong, and Clinton had as many men in
them as the combined forces of Washington and Rochambeau. Without
command of the sea they could do nothing: the course of the campaign
must depend on de Grasse's fleet. To him Rochambeau appealed after
the Wethersfield Conference. The Americans, he wrote, were at the end
of their resources, and de Grasse must bring four or five thousand troops
from the West Indies to operate in the Chesapeake or force a passage

into New York harbour. On 14 August de Grasse's reply arrived. It was precise and encouraging. He would bring his whole fleet and 3,000 troops; would sail on 13 August from San Domingo for the Chesapeake; and would stay till 13 October, when he must return to the Caribbean to support the Spaniards. Within that period Washington must complete his operations.

About the time when this letter arrived, news was received which decisively ruled out an attack on New York. The 2,400 German reinforcements which had slipped round the north of Scotland in May had joined Clinton. Washington had long been alarmed for Virginia, where Lafayette and his little force were in constant danger of being trapped by Cornwallis and annihilated; and he now resolved to turn his back on Clinton and strike at Cornwallis. It was a brave decision. He would leave half his American force to guard the Highlands, but they were only 2,500 men. Admiral Barras, who wanted to take his squadron on a separate expedition to Newfoundland, had to be persuaded to come to the Chesapeake and bring the French siege-train, which was too heavy to be moved by land. Under pressure from Rochambeau he agreed, with a justifiable warning that he might be intercepted by the British at sea. Thus every resource was gathered for a decisive concentration; and two days after the receipt of de Grasse's letter 7,000 French and American regulars marched for the Chesapeake.

The northern regiments showed visible discontent at being removed so far from their homes, but were pacified as they passed through Philadelphia by an overdue issue of hard cash borrowed from the French. The army moved rapidly. In fifteen days the Americans covered 200 miles. It was a period of great anxiety for Washington. He had no word of de Grasse, and was racked by fear that the British fleet would ruin his hopes by occupying the Chesapeake. But as he rode south from Philadelphia on 5 September an express came up the road with despatches which set his mind at rest: de Grasse and his fleet were inside the Chesapeake. 'I have never seen a man moved by greater or more sincere joy', said the Duc de Lauzun. The French troops had already disembarked; and their commander, General St Clair, had placed himself under the orders of the young Lafayette till Rochambeau should arrive. It was an act of significant generosity. For it was by such good feeling and willingness to take the wider view that the French had achieved the coup which Germain had always expected of the British forces. In the short season when operations in the West Indies were dormant, they had switched their land and sea forces northwards to achieve a decisive concentration. Its success would depend on the British commanders' response; and to understand what followed we must turn back to the spring operations in the Caribbean.

2. *Rodney and de Grasse*

Rodney had returned from his foray to America in December 1780 to the devastation of the great hurricane. He appealed in strong terms to Germain for reinforcements, for he was certain that in the coming year his own theatre would be the decisive one. 'Here and here only the French expect a much superior fleet than they had last year, and by intercepted letters they will certainly have one' – 'Jamaica, my Lord, can be in no danger while I command to leeward' – 'Depend upon it, my Lord, here will be the war.' He suggested a single Commander-in-Chief for the West Indies and America; and his own choice for the appointment is not hard to guess.[1]

Reinforcements, of course, were on their way. In January Hood's squadron arrived from England to make good the wastage, and with them the three battalions which were intended to go on to Clinton in the summer. Sir Samuel Hood had been obtained from the Captains' List by a special promotion when Darby and William Drake had refused the offer to be second-in-command to Rodney. He had been Commissioner at Portsmouth since the beginning of the French war, an appointment due both to his ability and to his connections.[2] Though this appointment did not usually lead to further service at sea, he had been dissatisfied for some time that his juniors were flying commodores' pennants, and had been asking to have his flag and go to sea. As soon as it was decided to reinforce the Leeward Islands, Sandwich obtained Cabinet authority to send him. There followed the special promotion of captains, with the usual stretching to oblige other connections; and thus the future Lord Hood obtained his flag.[3]

Though Hood's arrival gave Rodney the temporary command of the sea, the enemy islands were believed to be strongly garrisoned, and General Vaughan saw no hope of capturing them. Rodney had asked Clinton to lend him troops for the winter when he was at New York; but with Cornwallis's winter offensive building up in the Carolinas Clinton had felt unable to spare any. 'What could we not have done', Rodney asked rhetorically in March, 'had Clinton sent an army with me?'[4] It was a kind of cry heard all too often in every quarter, not least from Clinton himself.

Rodney's confidence in the security of the Jamaica command was not well conceived. The island itself might be secure against a sudden blow, but Sir Peter Parker had other responsibilities for which he was ill provided. His

[1] Sackville, II, 194–5.
[2] Hood was married to the daughter of Edward Linzee, mayor of Portsmouth, who wrote to Sandwich that his appointment gratified 'all our political friends' (Williams Transcripts).
[3] Sandwich, III, 232; G 3137, 3152.   [4] Mundy, II, 58.

force, after the first convoy of the year went home, was little more than equal to the four French ships of the line at San Domingo, to say nothing of the eight sound Spaniards at Havana.[1] The government at home relied on him to protect West Florida; but when the French and Spanish squadrons sailed from Havana in April to support an attack on Pensacola he was powerless to stop them. The navy, it is true had used less than its most honest endeavours to reinforce the garrison. When the Spanish Governor of Louisiana opened the attack, Governor Dalling had sent a regiment recruited from American rebel prisoners to General Campbell's assistance, but the two warships in which they sailed returned without landing them. One had spoken a sloop which reported that Pensacola had fallen, and instead of checking the intelligence she captured a French frigate and returned to Jamaica with her prize. The second ship took some prizes, commandeered twenty-three of the soldiers to work them, and after standing by to see them clear of danger, she bore away on 29 March for Jamaica without attempting to reconnoitre Pensacola, and chased and took two more prizes as she returned. After a leisurely concentration, the Spaniards broke ground at the end of April, and a few days later their batteries opened. After a week's firing they had nearly exhausted their efforts when one of their shells rolled in at the open door of a bomb-proof magazine. The explosion caused a hundred casualties and demolished a redoubt, and the Spaniards stormed in and after one repulse gained a footing within the works. Under their close fire Campbell's men could not work their guns, and on 9 May he surrendered. West Florida was gone.[2]

Rodney opened his own campaign with an easier task, for at the end of January he received the Cabinet's order to attack St Eustatius. Vaughan and Rodney moved at once, The defenceless island capitulated without resistance, and a convoy of thirty merchantmen with a Dutch sixty-gun ship which had just cleared the harbour was pursued and captured. The booty in the island was immense. For years it had been supplying the enemy islands and the Americans. Ships had cleared openly for St Eustatius from British ports, or detached themselves from convoys bound for St Kitts. Naval officers had long complained of the breach in the blockade, which they were powerless to prevent; and Rodney found ample evidence in the Dutch warehouses that British subjects had been systematically supplying the enemy. He retaliated with wholesale confiscations, to the benefit of his pocket.

[1] The Spaniards were reported to be able to send seven ships of the line and one of fifty guns to sea. But both Monteil and Solano were reported to be old and cautious (CO 137/80, f. 83).
[2] CO 137/80, ff. 223 et seq.; Add. MSS. 38216, f. 332; Royal Institution MSS., II, 286; Sandwich, IV, 127.

Horace Walpole condemned the giving of the captured property to the captors as a 'savage and dangerous precedent'. Though the naval blockade was useless as long as British merchants supplied the enemy with impunity, the merchants knew their Locke, and based their case on a higher law than mere necessity of war. The confiscation ordinances tended 'to injure civil contracts, which are founded on the Law of Nature, and which form the most sacred bond of society'. Rodney and Vaughan were to pay dearly for their sacrilege. The Duke of Wellington expressed the matter with his usual dry relevance: 'at St Eustatius . . . was found a vast quantity of British property, which was certainly contraband, and, moreover, was intended for the supply of the public enemies of the state. The captors claimed this property as prize; there was a long law-suit upon the subject, which was decided against them.'[1]

The plunder so vainly appropriated held Rodney like a magnet. He virtually handed over the operational command to Hood, cancelled attacks on the Dutch colonies of Surinam and Curaçao, and remained for three months at St Eustatius with Vaughan collecting and despatching the treasure, much of which was to fall into the hands of la Motte-Picquet. The Admiral and General appointed agents for the plunder without any authority, which lay in the hands of the officers and ships' companies of the fleet in conjunction with the army. When Germain heard of his stay at St Eustatius he feared that de Grasse would not be intercepted before he reached Martinique; and he was right. Though warning of a French reinforcement reached Rodney in February, he detached Hood with only eighteen sail of the line to intercept it, keeping another ship cruising and three with his flag at St Eustatius. At first Hood was stationed out at sea to the eastward of Martinique to meet de Grasse as he approached; but when the enemy did not appear, Rodney ordered him to close in and blockade the four French ships of the line in Martinique to cover the sailing of his convoy from St Eustatius. Hood remonstrated, but in vain; and instead of meeting de Grasse to windward in the open sea the British fleet was in the close waters off Fort Royal. The French were able to manoeuvre their transports into safety along the shore of the island, and the four ships in Fort Royal joined de Grasse's twenty, giving him a superiority of six. Short of seamen, and with four ships damaged and leaking, Hood finally despaired of a close action and withdrew to St Lucia.

Thus was disappointed the Cabinet's hope of intercepting de Grasse.

[1] G 2776; Sackville, II, 278–9, 291–2, 202–5; CL, Germain, Thoughts on the Caribbean Station; Petition of West India Planters and Merchants (printed copy in CL, Shelburne, Vol. 79, p. 173); CO 318/7, ff. 110–11, 117–18; Walpole, *Last Journals*, II, 455; Gurwood, *Selections from Despatches of Wellington*, 115.

Germain still thought that the advanced season would prevent him from attacking the British islands, and the danger now appeared to lie in America; for there intelligence indicated that de Grasse would sail with most of his force, including Monteil's ships at San Domingo. On 4 July he was still confident that Rodney's pursuit and the arrival of Digby's three ships from England would produce a superiority in American waters, and that the longed-for naval victory would pave the way for a West Indian offensive in the winter. But it will be remembered that Digby's reinforcement was held up at home till the 19th awaiting the protection of the Channel fleet; and before then Germain received from Clinton the intercepted despatches on the Wethersfield conference, confirming the enemy's expectations of ships and troops from the West Indies, and revealing the extent of their hopes. Germain was unwell, and the despatches made him feel worse. Extracts from the letters were sent to Rodney, with a firm order to watch and follow de Grasse, leaving 'a sufficient force for the protection of the islands'. But it was now too late to influence the campaign from London, and the order did not reach the Leeward Islands till the crisis had come. The Ministry could only trust that Rodney would obey his standing orders to support the American station, of which he had recently been reminded. It remains to be seen how far he fulfilled the Cabinet's hopes.[1]

Germain had underestimated de Grasse's enterprise. He had assumed that he would not have the time or the force to attack the British islands. But de Grasse had counted Hood's fleet, and he lost not a moment. Within three days of anchoring at Fort Royal he was off with 1,200 troops to attack St Lucia, while a second force assailed Tobago. Brigadier St Leger's defences on St Lucia proved strong and resolutely manned, and the whole French force was switched to support the Tobago landing, where the insignificant garrison capitulated two days before Rodney made his leisurely appearance on 4 June. On the following day he met the French fleet. He had the weather gauge and twenty ships against twenty-four, and Hood thought he might have fought with advantage. But with night coming on Rodney feared that the French would entangle his fleet among the Grenadines or decoy it into the westerly current between Grenada and the mainland. Yet Grenada was still far to leeward, the Grenadines were more than twenty miles away on the following morning, and he had the moonlight he had used against Langara. Thus he missed his second chance to bring de Grasse to battle. Rodney was

[1] CO 318/8, f. 114; CO 5/102, ff. 154, 197; Knox, 178; Sandwich, IV, 138; Adm. 2/1340, 14 July to Rodney and Digby. On July 29th the Cabinet resolved to send at least five more ships of the line to the West Indies, a decision which merged into the autumn planning which followed (G 3379).

tired and ill after eighteen months abroad. If the fresher and younger Hood had commanded, the French fleet might have been dealt a blow to spoil its American operations.

De Grasse's primary task was to support the Spaniards if they had a plan; but he found that Don Solano was preparing a winter attack on Florida and had no immediate intention of taking the offensive. The French fleet was therefore free for several months to pursue its secondary object, and intervene on the American coast. On 5 July it sailed from Martinique for San Domingo, where it joined Monteil's squadron on the 16th. Here de Grasse found appeals from Rochambeau and Luzerne which told him of the critical situation in Virginia. He responded generously. At San Domingo were French troops brought out by Guichen in 1780, at the Spaniards' disposal for their winter campaign, and he borrowed 3,000 under promise to return them by the end of October. From the Spaniards at Cuba he obtained a loan of money. And taking his courage in his hands, he gathered his whole fleet for the enterprise. Ten of his ships of the line had served a long time in the West Indies, and his government had ordered them home for repair; but he swept them up. Nothing was left to convoy the trade to France, and it stayed at San Domingo for the rest of the year. There may be truth in Captain White's remark [1]: 'If the British government had sanctioned or a British admiral had adopted such a measure, however necessary to carry an important political operation, the one would have been turned out and the other would have been hung. No wonder they succeeded and we failed.' In America eight French ships of the line faced seven British; and on 5 August twenty-seven French ships of the line and a fifty-gun ship were standing northward from San Domingo to join them. The fate of the British forces scattered along the American seaboard would depend on Rodney.

Rodney had long expected de Grasse to go north to America, and as early as the beginning of May he had warned the Admiral at New York to expect them. But when a frigate reported in the second week of July that the enemy had sailed from Martinique, his latest intelligence from home was that only fourteen French ships of the line would go to America, while de Grasse himself would return to Europe with the trade. It did not occur to either Rodney or Hood that the French Admiral might hold up his convoys, and Rodney prepared to disperse his own Leeward Islands trade to its destinations in Britain and Jamaica. The fleet sailed to Antigua for stores, and proceeded north to St Eustatius to despatch the convoys. On 31 July the Jamaica convoy sailed under escort of the *Sandwich*, which was

[1] Quoted in Sandwich, IV, 134.

destined for the Port Royal yard as she was too crazy for the voyage to England. With her went the *Torbay* and *Prince William*, under strict orders to leave the convoy off the end of Jamaica and proceed to America. On the following day the homeward-bound convoy sailed with two ships of the line, one an old-fashioned sixty and the other due for repairs.

Rodney himself sailed with the homeward convoy in the *Gibraltar*. She too required a refit, and Rodney thought that the composition bolts and fastenings which she needed could be fitted quicker in England than at Jamaica or Halifax. Moreover, he argued that her great draught of twenty seven feet made her unsuitable for the American station as she could not cross the bar at Sandy Hook. Yet she would have gone there if Rodney had not taken her to ferry him home. He felt very ill and exhausted; but if his health had improved at sea he had intended to steer for America. In the latitude of Bermuda he left the convoy and stood to the northward, hoping that he would recover in the cooler weather; but he felt no better and turned for England. On reaching Plymouth he judged the *Gibraltar* sound enough to go out and join the out-numbered Channel fleet. About the crisis beyond the Atlantic he confessed no fears. 'I have not a doubt', he wrote to Germain, 'but his Majesty's fleet will be superior on the coast and prevent the enemy's designs, provided the officers who command will do their duty.'[1]

The departure of Rodney and the convoys left Hood with fourteen ships of the line. But another ten days passed before he sailed for America, for he was held back by intelligence that la Motte-Picquet had reached Martinique from Europe and then that the enemy had left some ships of force in the islands. These reports proved false, and at dawn on 10 August he sailed from Antigua. The fleet on which the safety of Clinton's army depended had only fourteen of the twenty ships of the line which had been in the Leeward Islands at the end of July; and only one regiment of the three which General Vaughan had been ordered to send to Clinton. Vaughan, somewhat like his predecessor Grant, had gone home leaving no instructions to send troops to America; but his temporary successor, Brigadier Christie, grasped the importance of the crisis and embarked the Fortieth Regiment in the fleet. The pattern of the British movement was not unlike the French: it was the proportion and timing which were different.[2]

3. *The Fight for the Chesapeake*

In American waters Arbuthnot had at last handed over his command and departed. Throughout the first half of the year all concert between the

[1] G 3318; Sandwich, IV, 134; Mundy, II, 144, 153; CL, Germain, 15 Sept. from Rodney.

[2] CO 318/7, f. 128. *cf.* above, p. 329.

army and navy in America had been disrupted by his quarrels with Clinton, who continued to tell his friends that one or other of them must go, but showed no willingness that it should be himself. But the old Admiral had for some time past been asking for relief. Digby was on his way to replace him, and the Admiralty intended that he should relieve Sir Peter Parker at Jamaica. But Arbuthnot no longer had the health for active service. He had been having fits which resulted in prolonged unconsciousness, loss of sight in one eye, and impaired memory. After fifty-five years in the service, he felt that he could be of no more use; and on 4 July he handed over his command to Thomas Graves, and sailed for England without waiting for his relief.[1]

Graves was the officer whom Ternay had outpaced to America in 1780. Though he had made an unusually fast passage, his alleged delay with a prize was under enquiry; and though he was backed by his friend Lord North, the Admiralty did not intend him to succeed Arbuthnot as Commander-in-Chief. Of this he was unaware, and the First Lord's correspondence suggests double-dealing. He had assured Graves that the purpose of the enquiry was to clear him, and that he would personally silence criticism; so that Graves's confidence in his word was shattered in September when he learnt that he was to be superseded by a junior officer and friend of Sandwich, and was to serve as third in command at Jamaica. North had protested feebly. 'It will not be enough for me to say that this disgrace must have been the lot of somebody', he wrote to Sandwich. 'I shall lose all political honour and consequence if, when a disgrace is to be suffered, my friend is chosen as the proper object of it.' The reader may decide which politician the transaction reveals in the more curious light.[2]

As yet in ignorance of his fall, Graves applied himself to the difficult task of obtaining Clinton's co-operation. When Rochambeau's troops marched to join Washington, there seemed to be a chance of remounting the attack on Rhode Island which had broken down in 1780.[3] The French squadron lay at Newport with only 450 troops and some militia to protect it, and their siege train at Providence; and Mackenzie, who knew Rhode Island intimately, had no doubt that the new plan would succeed. Arbuthnot had feared that de Grasse would fall on him if he lingered off Rhode Island, and wanted to shelter the whole squadron in New York. But Graves took the threat from the Caribbean more lightly, and agreed to make the attempt. The attack, however, was postponed by Cornwallis's retention of his whole force in Virginia; and in the meantime Graves received instructions

[1] Sandwich, III, 250, 265-7; Sackville, II, 191.
[2] Sandwich, III, 270; IV, 207-8; Adm. 1/489, Graves's of 24 Sept. 1781.
[3] What follows relies on Willcox's study in J.M.H., 1945.

by the *Hornet* sloop to watch for a rebel convoy on its way from France to Boston. 'There is every reason', Lord Stormont had informed Sandwich, 'to believe that it is one of the most important supplies the French have ever sent the rebels', and that it was 'considered by the rebels themselves as furnishing them with the only possible means of carrying on the war'.[1]

To go off Boston when de Grasse was expected from the West Indies was a serious risk; yet when the fortunes of the rebellion were so desperate an important stroke against their supplies might be decisive. Graves took the chance, and on 21 July his whole fleet rounded Cape Cod and stood in towards Boston. By this decision still more ships were whittled away from the force which would face de Grasse.

Thick fog blanketed Boston Bay. The ships groped cautiously in fear of collision, and the fog guns boomed out their warnings to friend and foe. To search for shipping in these conditions was useless, and on 16 August Graves returned to Sandy Hook to resume the discussion of the attack on Newport. There was probably a week in hand before de Grasse's arrival, and the arrival of the German reinforcements enabled Clinton to play his part. But the fleet had suffered in Boston Bay and was not fit for immediate action. Two of Graves's six ships of the line had already been damaged during the French sortie in the spring, and their refitting had been delayed and their defects aggravated by the cruise off Boston. They could only now begin their long delayed repairs; and though another ship returned from the Halifax yard Graves had only five ready for service.

In Graves's absence a sloop from Rodney had reached New York with the news of de Grasse's departure from the Leeward Islands; but her captain, instead of seeking Graves out, had chased and captured a privateer, only to be taken in turn by three others.[2] Graves now learnt the news from a duplicate despatch; and on the following day Clinton, who was preparing to cross the Harlem River and interrupt Washington's foraging, learnt that the enemy had left White Plains. As August crept on he watched their progress across the Hudson and through New Jersey. His only hope of stopping them was a swift pursuit to fasten on Washington before he crossed the Delaware; but still he clung to New York, imagining that Washington had turned his attack from Manhattan to Staten Island, and continuing with his own plans against Newport. On the 20th he reported to Germain that Cornwallis was making progress with his entrenchments at Yorktown, and could be expected to send reinforcements to New York.[3] There was intelligence from Philadelphia that de Grasse was bringing his whole fleet and a large military force,

---

[1] Sandwich, IV, 141; Adm. 2/1338, f. 77.   [2] James, 284.

[3] CO 5/103, ff. 97, 124. Mackenzie, pp. 606, 639, outlines a ruthless advance into the Jerseys for which he thought 9,000 men could be spared.

and from Newport that Barras's squadron was preparing for sea. But Clinton and Graves believed that this was mostly talk. On 28 August Sir Samuel Hood arrived off Sandy Hook with his fourteen ships of the line from Antigua; but still there was no news of de Grasse, and Graves was convinced that the mountain would bring forth a mouse.

Hood suspected no more than Graves the full magnitude of the crisis. But he knew that time was vital. He refused to bring his fleet in over the bar. Going in by boat he found Graves and Clinton discussing the attack on Rhode Island, and persuaded the Admiral to bring his ships out of the harbour. On the 31st the fleet of nineteen sail of the line and one of fifty guns united off Sandy Hook. They should have been more. Graves's two absent ships of the line were still refitting, and two fifties were cruising or conducting convoys. The two ships which Rodney had sent by way of Jamaica had gone into harbour contrary to his orders, and had been ordered by Sir Peter Parker to strengthen the homeward-bound convoy as far as their ways lay together.[1] Parker had been begged by Rodney to detach every ship of his own which he could spare to America; but Rodney's own example must excuse him for sending home with the convoy three ships, all of which had been out of English yards for three years or more. This left him a single ship to face the Spaniards at Cuba, and he kept her.

As the fleet gathered off Sandy Hook Graves learnt that Barras had sailed from Newport. To attack Rhode Island now would be useless, and he weighed at once for the Chesapeake, confident that Barras was bound for the south and hoping to fall on him with his overwhelming superiority. On 5 September he sighted the Capes of Virginia. Out of Lynnhaven Bay a great French fleet was beating: it was not Barras's ships from Rhode Island, but de Grasse's from the West Indies. Three of his ships of the line and a fifty were supporting the army in the mouth of the James River; but even without them he had twenty-four ships against nineteen, and ranged 1,800 guns against 1,400. He did not need victory, but only the control of the Chesapeake. An indecisive battle would serve his purpose: it was a situation well adapted to French doctrine.

The battle for the Chesapeake followed the typical eighteenth century pattern. When the British had superior numbers they often beat the French: when they did not, they drew. Graves's fight against superior numbers was a tactical draw and a strategic defeat with every usual feature: a missed opportunity at the outset, signalling confusion, poor support from the subordinate Admirals, the British ships shattered aloft at the end of the action.

[1] The two ships were off the east end of Jamaica on 8 August, and might well have joined Graves in time. They regained this position on the 28th, and did not leave the convoy till 22 September, off San Salvador in the Bahamas (Adm. 51/740).

Graves's second in command, perhaps uneasy about his own part in the battle, criticised his Commander-in-Chief after the event, as Palliser had criticised Keppel; though unlike Palliser he won the ear of historians. Rodney sneered, and Hood said that Rodney's presence would have produced a decisive victory; yet exactly three months earlier Rodney himself had refused to engage de Grasse at all with better odds than Graves enjoyed. In the subsequent paper engagements it is Graves who appears to best advantage. He claimed that if he had been properly seconded, four or five of the French van would have been cut to pieces; but he did not impute cowardice or treason. 'The signal was not understood. I do not mean to blame anyone, my Lord. I hope we all did our best.' This was a generosity to which few contemporary admirals could have risen.

At sunset de Grasse drew away; and on calling for reports from his ships and learning how much his own fleet had been shattered, Graves decided it would be imprudent to re-engage. Throughout the 6th the two fleets lay refitting in sight of each other. On the 7th and 8th the enemy had the wind, and Graves' damaged ships could not have engaged them if he had wished to do so. At a Council of War on the day after the battle, Hood had pressed Graves to make for the Chesapeake; and had this been done it is possible that Cornwallis's fate would have been different. Barras would have been unable to bring the siege train up the river when he reached it on the 10th from Rhode Island, and the army at Yorktown might have been able to protract its defence beyond the time limit which de Grasse had set for the operation. Alternatively, Cornwallis might have been enabled to cross the James River and march for the Carolinas, or the York and race for New York, while the British fleet impeded pursuit. Both these courses were feared by Rochambeau, and difficult though they would have been, they might have succeeded. Yet other questions must be asked. What would have happened to the British fleet? Blockaded in the river, short of provisions, without hope of reinforcements or supplies, its anchorage perhaps made untenable by batteries on the shore, it would have released Cornwallis only to take his place in the trap. The French would have commanded the sea and been at liberty to shift their troops at will against Charleston or even New York. Perhaps the stakes were high enough to justify the risks. But important though the loss of Cornwallis's army was to prove, the loss of the fleet would have been a worse disaster. The surrender at Yorktown was to break the British will to continue the fight for the colonies; but the destruction of Graves's ships would have put it out of the country's power to limit the defeat. The Leeward Islands and Jamaica would have fallen. New York would have been assaulted or starved. India could not have been defended. And if the French had permitted it, Nova Scotia and Canada would have passed to American rule.

4. The World Turned Upside Down

The opportunity to enter the Chesapeake passed on the 9th. The French vanished under a press of sail, and when Graves reconnoitred the estuary on the 13th the combined fleets of de Grasse and Barras lay inside the Capes in overwhelming strength. There was nothing to be done but return to New York for repairs, supplies and reinforcements. One ship of the line which was too leaky to be salvaged was set on fire and abandoned, and on 19 September the remainder reached Sandy Hook.

In the meantime Clinton had embarked a relieving force of troops at New York, and only waited for the Admiral's word to sail to Cornwallis's rescue. This was now impossible, and having missed the chance to grapple Washington on the near side of the Delaware, he lacked the numbers to pursue him overland to Virginia, even if he could have forced the great rivers in his path. Nor did he think Washington would be turned from his purpose by a diversion at New York.

The first reports from Cornwallis were not unduly alarming. When de Grasse had first appeared and landed his troops at Jamestown, Cornwallis had taken up a position outside Yorktown, as his works were not ready to be defended. On 16 September he feared little before the end of October; but on the following day he learnt that the Rhode Island squadron had joined the enemy, and his tone changed. On the 23rd Clinton received a solemn warning that if he could not relieve him soon, he must prepare to hear the worst; and on the 24th a Council of War resolved to take every risk to relieve Cornwallis as soon as the fleet was ready. There was one slender hope: that the French might lie where the violence of the tide would enable the British to slip past them into the York River. The military force would be stripped to the bone. The regiments would embark in battleships, without camp equipment, horses or women; and the battalion guns would have only men's harness to drag them.

On the day of this decision Digby arrived with his three ships from England, and agreed to serve for the time being under Graves, as Graves's flagship could not be spared for Jamaica. Two more ships came forward from repairs, and on 10 October the *Prince William* and *Torbay* from their detention at Jamaica. But even now the fleet was not ready. The repairs and refitting had gone forward slowly, hampered by empty storehouses and victualling yards and the shortage of artificers. These were administrative excuses on which the navy seized to throw the blame for the delay on the Admiralty; but not all onlookers were convinced. One who was not was Major Mackenzie. He was a dispassionate staff officer, and by no means uncritical of the army's own discipline: he had reflected on the bad example set by the British generals who, unlike the Germans, had remained on shore when the troops embarked in their transports. He records on 1 October that naval officers from captains downwards talked of the superiority of the French fleet and the impossibility of destroying it with fireships. Several of the captains were on shore more often than on board their ships, and behaved as though they were commanding guardships at Portsmouth rather than battle-damaged vessels preparing for a desperate enterprise. 'They . . . appear more ready to censure the conduct of others than to refit their own ships.' The failure off the Chesapeake had reopened the healing sores of the fleet. 'The spirit of party prevails in the greatest degree', Mackenzie was to write later, 'and our officers seem more anxious to ruin their private enemies, than those of their country.' 'A most destructive spirit of party prevails . . . some espousing the part and opinions of one Admiral, some of another, and others abusing them all.'[1]

Even with the new arrivals the fleet would have only twenty-five sail of the line and two of fifty guns to fight thirty-six of the enemy who might be holding a defended anchorage. Five fireships were prepared, and Graves used his reprieve in the command to fill them with officers who were his own friends. At last on 16 October some of the ships began to move down to Staten Island.

If the navy are not a little more active [Mackenzie confided to his diary] they will not get a sight of the Capes of Virginia before the end of this month, and then it will be too late. They do not seem to be hearty in the business, or to think that the saving that army is an object of such material consequence. One of the Captains has exposed himself so much as to say, that the loss of two line of battle ships in effecting the relief of that army, is of much more consequence than the loss of it. Sir Samuel Hood appears to be the only man of that Corps who is urgent about the matter . . . . The others think too much of the superiority of the French fleet, and say ours is by no means equal to the undertaking.[2]

It was not till the 19th that the expedition sailed, and old General Robertson declared that with more exertion it might have been out five days sooner.[3] But Cornwallis had been given time by the enemy to put his works in order, and he wrote cheerfully and had provisions to last till the middle of November. The relief was a desperate undertaking; but the army was eager to rescue the universal favourite Cornwallis, and Clinton did not

[1] Mackenzie, 653, 687, 690.
[2] Mackenzie, 664. Willcox (*Amer. Hist. Rev.*, LII.) is convinced that the navy's heart was not in the attempt, and that the delay in refitting reflected their fears. If this was so, the Admirals should have stated their doubts firmly to Clinton; but anyone who recalls Lord Keith's conduct off Cadiz in 1800 will realise that an Admiral required less moral courage to sabotage a military operation than to oppose it.
[3] *Ibid.*, 675.

despair. ''Tis not a move of choice but of necessity. If Lord Cornwallis's army falls, I should have little hope of seeing British Dominion re-established in America, as our country cannot replace that Army. If we do not try to save it, we cannot succeed; if we do, we may.'[1] But off Virginia the fleet picked up a small boat with a white man and two negroes from the Chesapeake. They had escaped from Yorktown with the news that the rescue came too late.

On the night of 29 September Cornwallis had retired from his outer position, and concentrated his force in the narrow belt of his main defences above the York River. He had just over 6,000 rank and file against 16,000,[2] but was confident that he could hold out for a considerable time in the expectation of relief. The enemy broke ground in front of his lines, and on the evening of 9 October their batteries began to pound his earthworks. Forty heavy guns and sixteen mortars appeared to be firing. Men fell fast and the fresh earth began to crumble. On the night of 11th the enemy opened their second parallel within 300 yards; and two nights later they stormed the two advanced redoubts protecting the British left, which were swiftly incorporated in their second parallel. The bombardment had already been so effective that by now Cornwallis dared not show a gun to their old batteries. On the 16th, the last day of de Grasse's promised period of co-operation, two sorties forced the redoubts covering two new batteries, and spiked eleven guns; but the work was done hurriedly, and they were soon in action again. One desperate resort was left: to ship the whole force across the York River to Gloucester and try to slip away to the north. It was tried that night, but when part of the force was across the weather grew rough and the attempt was abandoned. There was no more to be done. In the morning Cornwallis judged that his works would be ripe for assault in many places by midday. His artillery ammunition was exhausted, and only 3,273 rank and file remained fit for duty in the Yorktown position. To stand an assault would be madness, and he took the decision to surrender. On the afternoon of the 18th the army moved out in good order to lay down its arms to the French and Americans; and tradition says that it marched to the melancholy tune of *The World Turned Upside Down*.[3]

> If ponies rode men, and if grass ate the cows,
> And cats should be chased into holes by the mouse . . .
> If summer were spring, and the other way 'round,
> Then all the world would be upside down.

[1] Lothian, 398.
[2] Enemy rank and file: French 7,800, Continentals 5,800, Virginian militia, 3,000.
[3] See Freeman, V, 388.

5. Conclusion

In six weeks Clinton's situation had been transformed from stalemate to catastrophe. Nothing known to him at the end of August had suggested any unusual danger to Cornwallis. Though he knew from intercepted letters that the enemy intended to attack New York or the Chesapeake with the help of de Grasse, the conclusion he drew from the intelligence was very different from what followed. He assumed that the British superiority at sea would be maintained; that the enemy's operations would therefore fail; and that at the end of the summer the French would withdraw all their troops to the West Indies and cease to help the rebels. Time was therefore on his side. He had only to avoid risks: 'because it was now manifest that, if we could only persevere in escaping affront, time alone would soon bring about every success we could wish'.[1]

Often in the past British detachments had held lodgments on the Chesapeake and other parts of the enemy coastline. At Rhode Island and Savannah they had been attacked by superior French fleets, but a firm resistance had soon deterred the French admiral and raised difficulties between the French and Americans. And without a superior fleet there was little Washington could do to dislodge the British, for even if he could scrape together enough troops and artillery to attack them, sea power gave them better lateral communications and they could reasonably hope to relieve their threatened detachment. Washington needed two months to move from White Plains and reduce Cornwallis: it took Graves five days to move from Sandy Hook to the Chesapeake.

That Cornwallis's safety depended on superiority at sea Clinton well knew. He said so repeatedly in retrospect; and he had said it long before, and had been assured by his government that at least an equality would be maintained in American waters. On this assumption he proceeded: de Grasse overturned it. The troops from the West Indies gave Washington a sufficient force to pen Cornwallis inside the Yorktown defences; the naval battle enabled the French to move a siege train into the Chesapeake, with only six laborious miles to haul the guns from Jamestown; and the presence of a superior fleet prevented rescue or relief. Cornwallis's fate was then virtually sealed. A stronger position could only have prolonged the defence by a few days, and even if Graves had managed to refit his fleet faster, it could scarcely have forced its way through the enemy. If Cornwallis had escaped across the York River to Gloucester, it is conceivable that by forced marches without baggage he might have reached New York; but 300 miles of country

[1] Willcox, *J.M.H.*, 1945, pp. 322–3 (quotation from Clinton's later Narrative).

intersected by great rivers and guarded by a hostile militia were not easily traversed with the speed to elude a determined pursuit.

If Clinton can be blamed for allowing the situation to develop, it is because his passivity at New York resigned the initiative to Washington. He made no attempt to interfere with the numerically inferior enemy camped about him at the end of August. Yet it must be remembered that till the last moment Washington had no intention of marching to Virginia; that Clinton was deluded about his intentions when he eventually crossed the Hudson; and that he acted on the assumption that his control of the sea would enable him to reinforce Cornwallis. Not till 6 September, when he learnt that an enemy fleet was in the Chesapeake, did he have cause for real alarm; nor did he know the result of Graves's battle for another week. With justice he could say that the disaster was caused by the want of the promised naval superiority.

The margin between success and disaster at sea was so narrow that as one reviews the previous twelve months one laments at every turn some twist of events which might have turned the scales if it had happened otherwise: if only Gibraltar had not called for relief; if only Hyder's success in the Carnatic had not coincided with Suffren's reinforcement for the Indian Ocean; if only Digby's ships could have sailed sooner to join Graves; if only Rodney had intercepted de Grasse before he reached Martinique, or fought him to a standstill at Tobago; if only Sir Peter Parker had not held back the *Prince William* and *Torbay* at Jamaica; if only Graves had kept his squadron together. Yet war is not a matter of exact calculation, for the fog of uncertainty which shrouds it makes errors inevitable. Minor errors are balanced by those of the enemy, and can be retrieved if one is operating with an adequate margin of force. England in 1781 was not. In all the western theatres her fleets were operating with inferior numbers; and this could be redressed only by an accurate assessment of risks and a determination to stake everything at the crucial point.

This was not done. In Jamaica two ships of the line were delayed for convoy work, and a third was uselessly retained. Nor did Graves collect his whole force at the beginning of September, though he knew a French fleet was likely to appear. But in the last analysis the campaign was lost in the Leeward Islands. There Rodney was in touch with de Grasse; from there alone could a sense of the magnitude of the danger have been conveyed to Graves and Parker; from there relief was expected. Yet while de Grasse brought twenty-eight two-decked ships to America, Hood brought fourteen. 'To this inferiority', Clinton told Germain,[1] '. . . and to this alone, is our present misfortune to be imputed.'

[1] CO 5/103, f. 254.

When de Grasse sailed for America in July there were still twenty-four operational British ships of the line in the West Indies; and these combined with Graves's squadron could have beaten de Grasse off the Chesapeake before Barras joined him. Most or all of the British force could have gone to America. Instead six went home, and another began a long refit at Jamaica. All these seven were in need of repair; but unsoundness is relative, and de Grasse took ten ships to America which had been ordered home for refits. It is clear that Rodney's own ship could have gone to America if he had thought it necessary, and the same must have been true of most of the others. Sir Peter Parker kept another sound ship convoying on the Jamaica station. There remained sixteen: two of these Rodney delayed by sending them with the trade to Jamaica, where Parker matched his sense of urgency and delayed them again. The dissipation of these ten ships had one single cause. Rodney acted on old intelligence from Europe, and assumed that de Grasse would send only a detachment to America. Rarely has strategic surprise played so decisive a role in war; and it was due to the vision and daring of de Grasse. It is strange that the man whose courage decided the war was soon to be a prisoner in the flagship of his outwitted opponent.[1]

[1] The above figures are based on Sandwich, IV, 125–7.

PART SIX

AN EMPIRE SALVAGED

CHAPTER XXV

SAVING THE SHIP

1. The News of Yorktown

On 12 October, when the loose earth was flying from the Yorktown ramparts and the British guns were falling silent under the pounding of the siege-batteries, Germain was looking forward to a campaign by Cornwallis in Maryland when the weather cooled. This hope was not as wild as it seems in the after-knowledge of de Grasse's strength and Washington's march to Virginia. The rebels' affairs were shown to be desperate that summer in the intercepted correspondence of Washington and Lafayette; and news from other sources indicated increasing animosities within the rebel organs of government, which only French men and money or a British disaster could prevent from developing into open schism. That the French shared this view was apparent from the deciphered letters of Rochambeau, which referred to the possible disintegration of the rebel army and the withdrawal of the whole of the French force to the Caribbean. In these circumstances Washington's intention to attack New York seemed mere folly. The existing garrison was enough to stop him; and there were large British and German reinforcements on the way, whose arrival 'when the rebellion is in so declining a stage' was expected to exert a strong pull on the doubters among the rebels, and enable Clinton to maintain the momentum of his Chesapeake offensive. Even in the New York area the American Department hoped that Clinton could take the offensive against the stores which Rochambeau was leaving unprotected at Rhode Island.[1]

Germain was alert to the threat from de Grasse. But he relied on a rapid pursuit by Rodney, on Digby's three ships on passage from England, and on the arrival of the military reinforcements before the French troops from the West Indies could intervene. The first shadow of doubt was cast by Rodney's cocksure arrival at Plymouth in September. The information he brought of Hood's delay in leaving the West Indies made it probable that he would reach America too late if de Grasse risked the trade for the sake of speed. But the time had long passed when intervention from Britain could change the course of events.[2]

[1] CL, Clinton, 7 July and 4 Oct. from Germain; CL, Germain, 23 June from Geo. Rome, 26 and 31 July to Haldimand; CO 5/103, f. 115.

[2] CL, Germain, 26 and 31 July to Haldimand; Knox, 179.

The news of Graves's indecisive battle off the Chesapeake reached England in the middle of October. No one could guess its ultimate effect on Cornwallis; but even at the best it dashed the hope of a naval victory which would restore the initiative to England and bring an honourable peace within her grasp. 'I nearly think this Empire ruined', wrote the King; and a Treasury official lamented the wear and tear of indecisive war. 'Nevertheless I am inclined to hope we shall get through the plunge half drowned, and a proper object for the care of the Humane Society . . . Shall we ever have another victory on that element which we used to command?' Germain by now had long since despaired of the navy. 'It is no use our fleet sailing from Torbay', he had written sarcastically a few days earlier of Darby's command, 'as we cannot be alarmed for the Channel and we never cruise in stations to alarm the enemy.'[1]

By early November Cornwallis's critical situation was apparent. An officer home from America thought he would break out towards the Carolinas; but Germain did not allow so vain a hope to delude him, and the whole world hung on the news from New York. If the relieving force failed to get through, wrote Sandwich, 'there is, I fear, an end of all our expectations of a favourable conclusion of the American war, and consequently all hopes of a peace in which the power and riches of this country are not to be annihilated . . .' Even Lord Carlisle's frivolous circle recognised how much depended on the event: even George Selwyn was stirred, though more heated by Lord North's unfeeling way of granting a favour. Carlisle himself, now in Dublin as Lord-Lieutenant, waited with deep anxiety for the news which was expected from America about 27 November. 'The fate of England seems to me to be set upon one cast' – 'what a tremendous and awful moment'.[2]

The news was in Paris first. Vergennes told Franklin on 20 November of Cornwallis's capitulation. Clinton's despatch which reached Germain's office at midnight on Sunday 25th had been written off the Chesapeake and left little room to hope that Cornwallis could be saved; but the truth had already arrived from Paris at midday, by the packet boat which had taken the Comte de Jarmac to Calais. Germain, if Wraxall's story is true, set off at once from Pall Mall in a hackney carriage, picked up Stormont in Portland Place, and went on to Thurlow in Bloomsbury. There they determined to tell North. Between one and two o'clock Germain arrived in Downing Street. North, he told Wraxall, took the news 'as he would have taken a ball in the breast'. Germain knew what the

---

[1] G 3426; Sandwich, IV, 181 n. (cf. 162); Knox, 180; CL, Knox, 1 Oct. from Germain.

[2] G 3439; Knox, 180; Sandwich, IV, 201; Carlisle, 531–5.

image meant, for a musket ball in the breast had struck him down at Fontenoy.[1]

North flung open his arms, and paced up and down the room exclaiming 'Oh God! it is all over.' This was the universal feeling. Parliament was to assemble on the Tuesday; and at the Cockpit meeting of government supporters on the previous evening there were many long faces. 'What we are to do after Lord Cornwallis's catastrophe, God knows', Antony Storer wrote to Carlisle; 'or how anybody can think there is the least glimmering of hope for this nation surpasses my comprehension'. Lord Gower told the same story of universal dismay when he arrived in London a few days later: the town in mourning, every face clouded with sorrow, 'and the wisest and most intelligent asking each other what was next to be done, to which the wisest and most intelligent could give no answer'.[2]

On the face of it this despair does not explain itself: 7,000 troops had been lost, and with them the foothold in the Chesapeake, but there were still 30,000 effectives in America. Halifax, New York, Charleston, Savannah, and St Augustine remained in British hands; de Grasse and his reinforcements could not linger with Washington; and the rebel finances and military power were no less straitened than they had been before the capitulation. For a moment the rebels would be heartened by the victory, and the loyalists staggered, and it would be impossible to resume offensive operations for a long time. But perseverence in adversity and continuing steady pressure might even now break the spirit of the rebellion.

But it was the timing of the blow which mattered. Eight months earlier, if Arbuthnot's fleet had been absent in the West Indies and Ternay had brought off his coup in the Chesapeake against Arnold, it would have had no comparable effect: indeed it would have averted the later disaster by making it impossible for Cornwallis to march on Virginia. But the summer's events had changed the picture: defeats in India, the loss of West Florida and Tobago, heavy losses of merchant shipping, Minorca invaded, the French and Spanish fleets riding once more in the mouth of the Channel. Now the load of taxes and the 'frightful unfunded debt'[3] were felt in earnest. The country gentlemen of England had borne the burden for more than six years. They had seen their money poured into the enormous expenses of the American command; and well might they now rebel at further efforts to

---

[1] Wraxall, II, 433–6; Marlow, 87; Walpole, *Last Journals*, II, 474. Ross (Cornwallis Corr., I, 129 n.) points out the discrepancy in Wraxall's story, that the despatch from Clinton did not reach London till midnight, and did not make Cornwallis's capitulation a certainty. But the much more positive news from France was in London during the day, and Wraxall's story may well be accurate.

[2] Carlisle, 535, 542.

[3] Barrington, *Life*, 189.

fill the bottomless well of Clinton's consumption. Yet the real issue was not financial: the country had lost its nerve. Yorktown was a victory of French sea power; and the same power could strike again in the Caribbean and India. Already enemy preparations in Brest were drawing Britain's wasting resources away from the relief of the beleaguered garrison of Minorca. Some voices could still argue that the independence of America would mean the loss of all Britain's colonies; of the West Indies, India, and Newfoundland, and with them her fisheries, commerce and naval power.[1] Yet by continuing the struggle they seemed to be risked more certainly and quickly. Peace might be the country's only salvation.

2. The Loss of Minorca

Yet the struggle was not over; and though London mourned, Vergennes was not deceived. He did not believe that final victory had been won at Yorktown. 'History', he said, 'offers few examples of a success so complete; but one would be wrong to believe that it means an immediate peace; it is not in the English character to give up so easily.'[2] And he was right. For the war still had more than a year to run. Nor did Yorktown mean the immediate annihilation even of the Ministry: Lord North's administration still had four months of life. To understand its final efforts one must turn back to the planning which had been going on while the news from Yorktown was awaited.

The news that Minorca was to be attacked reached England in the second half of August; but the appearance of the enemy fleets in the Channel soon afterwards precluded any immediate relief. An officer set out overland through Belgium and southern Germany to see if help could be sent from Tuscany, and found that through the error of the enemy cruisers a ship had escaped from Mahon in the hope of bringing in a thousand Corsicans. The hope of getting in was a strong north-west wind, common enough in the Gulf of Lions, to blow the enemy cruisers to leeward. The captain of the ship reported that the garrison had been surprised by the enemy landing, and on retiring into the fort had abandoned essential provisions and stores. Meanwhile in England Amherst had been investigating the possibility of throwing in supplies in cutters. Army officers were confident that cutters from England or Leghorn could get in without difficulty; but though Sandwich came up from Blackheath to find some sea officers who were familiar with the harbour, he knew it well himself and could not imagine the Spaniards would allow anything to enter.[3]

[1] Lothian, 406.   [2] Doniol, IV, 688.
[3] WO 34/136, f. 293; WO 34/137, f. 206; WO 34/138, ff. 109, 126, 191; WO 34/237, p. 606.

On 22 September, however, intelligence arrived from Brussels that the French and Spanish Atlantic fleets had dispersed to their home ports in a sickly and damaged condition; and Lord Stormont instantly proposed the recall of half a dozen of Darby's Channel ships for a prompt and secret effort to save the island. Middleton was consulted, and his advice was to revictual Darby's fastest ships at sea, embark the regiments which were serving in the fleet as marines, and send them straight away to the Mediterranean with a strong cruiser force. Sandwich demurred. He thought it impracticable to store and revictual the ships at sea, or to use the marine regiments as reinforcements. Middleton gave way, but begged for the sake of secrecy that no captains known to be reserved for home service should be sent, nor troops embarked till the last possible moment. About 27 September it was learnt that the expected Leeward Islands convoy was safe in Cork, and that the Jamaica convoy was not yet due; and on that day the Cabinet resolved to send seven sail of the line with 700 troops to relieve Minorca. Five cruisers were sent out to recall the Channel fleet; but Darby by then was cruising uselessly far to the west and southward, and it was not till he was making for home on 1 November that he received his orders of recall. On 1 November, nearly six weeks after the Cabinet recalled him, he brought the fleet in to Spithead with rigging worn and water exhausted; and by then the situation had changed utterly. For news was filtering in of the enemy's preparations, and once again the initiative was passing to the French.[1]

The French government intended five ships of the line for the West Indies to replace the returning ships of de Grasse and support the major Spanish effort against Jamaica. But in spite of their recent successes in the western hemisphere, a decision in the West Indies still seemed far off. They could not afford to prolong the war, and were persuaded that the quickest way to end it was a decisive blow in India. The author of this plan was Dupleix's old collaborator, the Marquis de Bussy: he proposed the seizure of Bombay or Surat, an attack on the British on the Upper Ganges in conjunction with the Moguls, and assistance to Hyder Ali for the capture of Madras. Suffren was to be given a decisive naval superiority by a reinforcement of ten sail of the line with 4,200 troops to procure a decision on land. For secrecy the force was to sail in small detachments. The first two ships of the line left Brest in November, picked up de Bussy under an assumed name at Cadiz, and made for Teneriffe to await the next échelon of the reinforcement. A second detachment, of three ships of the line, was due to sail in December with the West India reinforcement, much as Suffren had sailed with de Grasse.

[1] Adm. 2/1340, f. 105; G 3421-2; CL, Shelburne, Vol. 151, Nos. 3-4; Sandwich, IV, 67-8, 329-30.

They would be escorted as far as Madeira by a dozen ships of the line under Guichen, who would then join the Spaniards at Cadiz to prevent a third winter relief of Gibraltar.[1]

If the French sailed uninterrupted, they would certainly reach both India and the West Indies decisively in advance of any British reinforcement; and both theatres were in the greatest danger. As the news of these preparations began to reach Whitehall, and the Ministry gathered its resources to meet the challenge, a despatch arrived from Murray at Minorca which suggested that the relief of the island could wait. Murray wrote that the proper time to relieve him was January or February, when the enemy fleets could not keep the seas in the Gulf of Lions and a small naval escort would be enough. He was confident that he could hold out till the spring; and pressed by the enemy preparations in Brest and the delayed return of the Channel Fleet, the Cabinet on 1 November thankfully postponed the relief of Minorca and ordered the systematic preparation of troops and stores to sail early in the New Year.[2]

So intimately is the story of Minorca linked with the decisions of the autumn that it will be as well to take it to its conclusion. Early in December General Rainsford set out overland from London with the news that a regiment and a supply convoy were coming with an escort of two frigates. The regiment embarked on 19 December, but contrary winds detained it. At length at the end of January Captain Man of the *Cerberus* frigate took the convoy to sea; but he was blown back to Falmouth early in February, and before he could sail again Minorca had fallen.[3] General Murray's hopes of holding out had been defeated by disease. About the turn of the year scurvy had appeared in the garrison; and on 5 February only 600 decrepit infantry and 200 seamen remained fit for any kind of duty. Murray, on whose defences the enemy had as yet made little impression, was forced to surrender to 14,000 besieging troops; and the emaciated survivors boasted that the victors could take little credit for capturing a hospital. A single cargo of lemons might have changed the story.[4]

---

[1] Richmond, *Navy in India*, 318 *et seq.*, and Appendix II.

[2] G 3438.

[3] Add. MSS. 23658; WO 34/142, f. 172; Adm. 2/1341, ff. 32 *et seq.*, 59, 61.

[4] Murray's garrison consisted of two British and two Hanoverian battalions. A fifth battalion had been intercepted and detained at Gibraltar by Eliott in January 1780. Whether the relief convoy could have landed its troops and stores if it had passed the Spanish blockade is open to question. Colonel Pringle's ship had passed the enemy's shore batteries in November under cover of a bombardment from the fortress, but the harbour was made unsafe by enemy shelling and she had to leave immediately. The Lieutenant-Governor wrote that a relieving fleet would have to send men in at night in small boats (WO 34/139, ff. 82-3, 239).

3. The Work of Salvage

The first wind of the preparations in Brest reached Lord Stormont by 20 October. It reported only the West India component of the expedition, which was said to consist of seven to ten ships of the line and five regiments of infantry; and the fact that its commander was Vaudreuil, who had been Governor of San Domingo, strengthened the impression that it was intended to attack Jamaica. When the news arrived, the British reinforcements for both the East and West Indies had already been allocated: India was to have six sail of the line, and Rodney was to take eight out to the Leeward Islands.[1] A brief explanation of the Indian reinforcement is necessary. It will be remembered that on the news of Suffren's sailing and Hyder Ali's victory over Baillie, three ships of the line had been sent to India in April and May of 1781, and two more had been intended to take out the October convoy.[2] At the same time it had been decided that no more British troops could be spared; but by August there was intelligence that Dutch ships and French troops were to be sent to the Indian Ocean; and while the two ships of the line promised for the autumn sailed at once, it was resolved that 2,000 British troops, including 300 dismounted dragoons, should sail with the October convoy.[3] Two new regiments of foot and one of light dragoons were hastily formed from existing units[4]; and two Hanoverian battalions were later obtained and added to the force. But the two ships of the line which sailed in August had met the French and Spanish fleets in the mouth of the Channel; and instead of proceeding to India they had been added to Darby's fleet at Torbay, with which they remained till the end of the Channel operations. It was to replace and strengthen this diverted reinforcement that six other ships were earmarked for India; and we shall see that both ships and troops eventually sailed in the New Year.

Rodney's force for the West Indies was raised from eight to ten in consequence of the news from Brest.[5] But all his ships were either fitting in the dockyards, or were out with the Channel fleet and would require extensive fitting and storing before they could go abroad. Vaudreuil's force would be ready to sail before them, and if it joined de Grasse in the West Indies there would be nothing to shield Jamaica. The garrison, in spite of the reinforcement in 1780 and the subsequent arrival of troops recruited from

[1] Sandwich, IV, 69 (distribution of navy at 11 Oct.).

[2] See above, pp. 391–2

[3] Adm. 2/1340, f. 52; G 3379.

[4] Burgoyne's Light Dragoons by drafts from other regiments of light dragoons, Sandford's and Rowley's Foot from Independent Companies.

[5] By 7 Nov. (Sandwich, IV, 73–4), but I have found no record of the date of the Cabinet decision.

rebel prisoners in America, had by now been reduced to about 2,000 fit men distributed between ten different units.[1] Unless Vaudreuil's departure could be prevented or delayed, the island was lost. Could the navy at home find the strength both to reinforce the distant stations and to stop the enemy's squadrons from leaving Brest? This was the dilemma which confronted the Cabinet.

October 20th was a Saturday, but Stormont managed to collect four Ministers at his office. North, Hillsborough, and Amherst were present, and Germain was close enough at hand to leave his opinion with Stormont; but Sandwich, through some oversight at the Admiralty, had not received his summons. The meeting agreed that it was vital to intercept or at least retard Vaudreuil; but without the First Lord nothing could be decided about the means. When Sandwich appeared on the Monday it was found that there was no choice: Darby's water was nearly exhausted, and he must be found and brought in to replenish it before a detachment could go off Brest.[2]

It was agreed that warnings should be sent off to all the commanders in the West Indies by a fast ship, with reminders to those in the Leeward Islands of their responsibility for Jamaica. After the meeting Germain approved drafts to the military commanders, and departed to his Northamptonshire house to marry his daughter, leaving Knox to fair-copy the despatches. They were sent to the Admiralty for forwarding on the following Saturday, 27 October, and Knox imagined that an express had been sent off with them to the frigate which was standing by. Another week-end passed, and on the Tuesday he saw the Secretary to the Admiralty and discovered that the despatches were still in London. Stephens explained that he had no instructions to write to the naval commanders, and could do nothing till Sandwich returned to London that day. Knox protested that Germain had produced a draft of the necessary orders but that Sandwich had uncharacteristically said that he required no authority from a Secretary of State on this occasion. But when the First Lord reappeared at the Admiralty on Wednesday 31st he sent for Knox, and said that Germain must have misunderstood him: he could not write the despatches without the King's commands, and must have an instruction from the Secretary of State immediately. Knox gave him Germain's draft from which to prepare the despatches, and promised him a formal letter to follow.[3]

Sandwich was in bad health that autumn, whether from the Chancellor's

---

[1] Rank and file fit for duty (return of 1 Dec.: CO 137/82, f. 59).
[2] G 3427-9.
[3] CL, Germain, 31 Oct. from Knox. Though Germain was not listed as present at the Cabinets of the 20th and 24th, it is clear that he saw both Stormont and Sandwich.

attacks on him in the summer or (as the ennobled Wedderburn was pleased to hazard)[1] from certain private exploits above the rate of his vigour. He certainly looked ill and exhausted. But in Knox's eyes his conduct was not excused by sickness: it followed an established Admiralty pattern. 'It does not become me to say it except to your Lordship', he told Germain, 'but to the insufficiency of their instructions when no directions are given them, much of our delays and disappointments are owing, and if your Lordship does not determine to give the orders yourself instead of leaving it to Lord Sandwich to make them out from a minute of Cabinet things will never be better.'

The writing of the despatches was not the only direction in which Sandwich was raising obstacles. The plan to intercept Vaudreuil was also in trouble. By now reports had swelled the Brest expedition to eighteen ships of the line including a component for India. The British Channel fleet had been reduced by ships sent home for docking to twenty-three. Of these ten were earmarked for India and the West Indies, and Sandwich declared that if they sailed as planned, the thirteen remaining ships would be too few: Vaudreuil could not be intercepted. In any case they would be too late, he added, since they must return to revictual before they went off Brest. Knox was much shaken by the conversation. If Vaudreuil was allowed to sail, he would be in the West Indies long before the British reinforcements could be fitted for foreign service and added to the fleet at Antigua. In the absence of his chief he turned for help to another Secretary of State, and appealed to Lord Stormont. Stormont was visibly startled to learn that Sandwich had abandoned hope of stopping the French; but he soon regained his ministerial poise with the dictum that 'we always talked as if we had that power to do what we thought fit, but we ought only to consider what was best to be done with our means'.

This aphorism contained a grain of truth; but it reveals the attitude of the professional adviser rather than the imaginative leader, and Stormont had fallen in too readily with Sandwich's departmental pessimism. It was Knox who rose to the occasion. The case, he told Stormont, stood thus. At this moment Hood had enough ships beyond the Atlantic to face de Grasse, who would have to send home the ten ships he had detained for the Yorktown operation. The key to the situation was Vaudreuil's force in Brest, which must be prevented from sailing till our own West India reinforcement was ready; and Knox believed it could be done. The French never sailed with a convoy while a British squadron was at sea; and in any case their transports had first to be gathered from Lorient, Rochefort, and Bordeaux, which could not be done in the presence of a British fleet. Inferior numbers did

[1] Carlisle, 529.

not matter, for even with inferior numbers a coppered squadron would prevent the French from sailing: fifteen ships to the south of Belle-Isle would be enough. While Vaudreuil was held fast, the British ships for the West Indies could be despatched one by one as they completed, and would thus reach Antigua before him. With such a British force assembled to windward, no French or Spanish admiral would risk his ships on the hostile lee shore of Jamaica.[1]

All this Knox retailed to Germain on 31 October, begging him to send his views to Stormont in time for the next day's Cabinet meeting. Germain's reply measures the practised obstructiveness of the Admiralty. It was vain, he wrote, to argue about plans and operations when one could not discover the state of the navy. If Sandwich approved of a plan, we seldom lacked the means to execute it; but if he disliked it, official difficulties occurred, and the state of the fleet was such that no new measures could be pursued. At this moment the West Indies could not be saved unless eight ships were sent immediately; and if England could not at the same time have a dozen ships cruising in the Bay of Biscay we must fairly declare that we could not continue the war. He promised to send a few lines to Stormont, though his own opinions or Stormont's would mean little unless the Admiralty seriously adopted them.[2]

To find the necessary force the Cabinet considered breaking into the reinforcement which was earmarked for India. But while the interception of Vaudreuil hung in the balance, anxiety for India had been growing. On 14 October, together with the news of Graves's indecisive and fatal engagement off the Chesapeake, came the belated news of Commodore Johnstone's failure to capture the Cape. The East India Company at once asked the government to make a second attempt with the troops then under orders for India; and they renewed their demand on 31 October when de Bussy's force was discovered. The scheme was rejected, to their disappointment; yet they were luckier than they knew, for only on 8 November did the Cabinet dismiss the possibility of withdrawing some of the reinforcement for India to stop Vaudreuil.[3]

Nevertheless the American Department's battle to intercept Vaudreuil was won. Darby's fleet arrived at Spithead on 5 November, and fourteen ships of the line and a fifty were ordered to prepare for the interception. Sandwich's insistence on bringing them home was justified; for most of

[1] CL, Germain, Knox's of 31 Oct.
[2] Knox, 180.
[3] G 3426, 3440. For the Company's negotiations with Hillsborough, see Harlow, 121–125, whose strictures on the government for rejecting the proposal do not however take account of the naval situation.

them had to shift their standing and running rigging, and their ground tiers of water casks had to be broken up since the fresh water had been used and they had been filled with sea water. All this was slow work in the short November days, with tempestuous weather interrupting the traffic from the shore. The time for action was slipping past, and the enemy might sail at any moment.[1]

Darby was suffering from scurvy, and on his recommendation Kempenfelt received orders to command the intercepting force. Ten days later, on November 24th the Admiralty ordered him to sail as soon as his force was ready, or with such ships as he thought necessary for his task. Since this task was defined as the interception of a convoy guarded by fourteen sail of the line and four more *armées en flûte*, he was left in some bewilderment. Was he meant to sail with fewer than the fourteen originally appointed? The answer was revealed the same evening in a private letter from the First Lord, warning him not to count on two or three of his ships: 'but if you stay for them, the object you have in view will [be] at an end'. This characteristic proceeding was not to Kempenfelt's taste. If the Admiralty wanted him to sail with less than his whole force, he asked Middleton, why should they not give him an order and shoulder the responsibility? Middleton agreed, and told Lord Sandwich so. Though at least one sound ship lay with the North Sea squadron in the Downs the Board insisted on retaining her there to watch the Dutch, and she was released to Kempenfelt only on 7 December, too late for the operation. The intercepting squadron never reached more than twelve of the line and a fifty. They were not ready to sail till November was out; and by then the worst was known from America.[2]

4. The Reinforcement Race

Cornwallis's surrender in no way deflected the Cabinet's attention from Jamaica. Whether or not the American War was to continue, the Cabinet agreed that in the present circumstances it would be wrong to send fresh units to replace Cornwallis's lost regiments. Jamaica was another matter. The campaigning season was over in America, de Grasse was certain to return to the Caribbean. The danger there was imminent, and immediately after the news of Yorktown the Merchants and Planters petitioned (for the

[1] Sandwich, IV, 75–6.
[2] Sandwich, IV, 74–5, 326; Adm. 2/1340, f. 118; Barham, I, 351, 354; Adm. 1/95, 7 Dec. to Capt. Edwards; Adm. 2/111, p. 401. Sandwich stated that the North Sea ship (*Bellona*, 74) was detained by a defective mainmast. Her orders to join Kempenfelt were issued on 7 December. Another ship in the Downs, the *Fortitude*, 74, was stated to have been on shore and to want docking, but possibly might have gone out on a short cruise (Sandwich, IV, 324, 326).

second time that autumn) for naval and military help. A couple of days later a despatch from the island revealed that in the Pensacola capitulation the Spaniards had stipulated that the garrison might go anywhere except to Jamaica: a further confirmation of their intention to attack it. News of de Grasse varied; but one report said that he had taken the whole of his great fleet from America to the West Indies.[1]

To save Jamaica was the great task of the moment, and the last great operation launched by Germain. The first need was good commanders. General Mathew, the commander of the Chesapeake expedition of 1779, was going out to the Leeward Islands to replace Vaughan, who had come home. But a change was urgently needed in Jamaica, where Governor Dalling had reduced the government to quarrelsome atrophy and the militia to sullen worthlessness. He had long since sought permission to hand over to the Lieutenant-Governor and come home to draw his salary *in absentia*, and had been first granted permission and then peremptorily ordered to return. But still he lingered; and on 5 December a meeting of the Privy Council ordered him to leave the island in terms which admitted no delay. Fortunately the former order had at last taken effect, and he had sailed for home on 24 November, still plotting to draw his salary as an absentee. The Lieutenant-Governor remained in command. This was Brigadier-General Archibald Campbell, who had conquered Georgia, and there was an immediate change of spirit. The executive's harmony with the assembly was restored, and money which had been refused for defence in November was now forthcoming. The spirit and discipline of the militia improved; and Campbell set to work to strengthen the island's defences, repairing unserviceable cannon, and linking Port Royal to the north and east sides of the island with a signalling system to give early warning of the enemy's approach. He was determined to spin out a stubborn defence till help could reach him.[2]

What help he could expect depended on the creation of a superior fleet to windward by reinforcing faster than the enemy. The Cabinet assumed that Hood had returned to the Leeward Islands from New York, and hoped that Digby had spared him some ships from the American station. On 1 December Digby was sent orders to send every ship which he could afford; and the same Cabinet meeting agreed that all the ships at home which were now ready for the West Indies should sail at once without waiting for the trade. Their commander, Rodney, had been taking surgical advice and convalescing at Bath since his return in September; and while the effects of his great miscalculation were unfolding in America he had

---

[1] G 3462; CO 137/80, ff. 31, 181; CO 137/81, f. 45; CO 5/103, ff. 263–4.
[2] CO 137/81, ff. 171, 183, 185; CO 137/82, ff. 57, 105–7, 149–50, 219; Knox, 185.

been rewarded with the Vice-Admiralty of Great Britain in succession to Hawke. Down he went to Portsmouth carrying Admiralty orders to sail at once with whatever was ready. Of the ten ships under his command he found four ready at Portsmouth, and two more were waiting at Plymouth to join him.[1]

[1] G 3452; Adm. 2/1340, f. 128; Mundy, II, 169.

CHAPTER XXVI

THE SHIP AFLOAT

1. *Rodney Away*

From Portsmouth Rodney sent Germain his usual tirade against the dockyard: 'the backwardness of everything, the slowness of their motions astonishes me'. He lamented that Kempenfelt's squadron had not been ordered to accompany him to the West Indies and return to Europe in time for the next summer's operations.[1] Here his egoism had twisted his judgment. Kempenfelt's ships were not stored and victualled for foreign service; and had they been kept in port and prepared to accompany Rodney, they would not only have missed Vaudreuil in the Bay of Biscay, but could not have been home and re-equipped till very late in the next year's European campaign. But Rodney's suggestion was scarcely made when Kempenfelt, far out on the wintry seas fifty leagues from Ushant, sighted the enemy convoy.

The French put to sea on 10 December. There were only five ships of the line for the West Indies and two for the Indian Ocean; but they were escorted by the twelve with which Guichen was to join the Spaniards off Gibraltar. Together these made nineteen fully armed ships of the line instead of the expected fourteen; and Kempenfelt had only twelve of the line and a fifty. He sighted the enemy on the 12th, forming a line of battle on his lee bow. But by negligence for which Guichen afterwards tendered his resignation, the French battle fleet was stationed to leeward of the convoy. Kempenfelt grasped the enemy's mistake and swooped under full sail on the defenceless transports. Fourteen prizes were taken out of the 100 enemy sail, and five more coming out from Bordeaux to joint the convoy were added later by the *Agamemnon*. The next day a frigate reconnoitred the whole French line from just out of gunshot, and her report of its strength convinced Kempenfelt that no more could be done. Detaching a fireship to the Leeward Islands with a warning for Hood, he returned to harbour.

The Ministry was much criticised for sending out so small a force. In private Middleton, and in Parliament Howe and Keppel, declared that if Rodney's ships and perhaps the squadron preparing for India had gone out with Kempenfelt, he could have decided the fortunes of the war in the Bay of Biscay. But it is far from clear that this could have been done. One or at most two ships might possibly have been spared from the Downs, though

[1] Sackville, II, 215 (a favourite theme with Rodney: see, *ibid.*, 205–6).

till the end of November the Dutch were expected to leave the Texel; but all the India ships and most of Rodney's were unready when Kempenfelt sailed on 2 December, and they were unready because ill fortune had delayed the return of the Channel fleet in October. Perhaps a few of Rodney's might have been sent away with Kempenfelt, to proceed on to the West Indies; but the real reason for not sending them was the underestimation of the enemy's strength. Kempenfelt's coppered ships would have been enough to stand up to the expected fourteen of the enemy encumbered with a convoy, for even against nineteen he managed to inflict a serious loss of stores and to capture a thousand troops; and the taking of the Bordeaux ships lends credit to Knox's argument that an earlier watch by a small squadron could have prevented the convoy's assembly. The real charge to which the Ministers must answer is their ignorance of the true strength of the enemy. Faulty intelligence is an inevitable part of war; yet it must be admitted that Sandwich had too often allowed the enemy ports to lie unwatched, and had relied too much on the intelligence service operating through Brussels and Amsterdam. He maintained that intelligence by land was more regular and accurate than what unsupported cruisers could obtain. Two years earlier, however, Stormont had been struck on taking office by the inadequacy of the intelligence network: '. . . there is at present a want of regular and immediate secret intelligence that is highly prejudicial to your Majesty's service'. Now with Kempenfelt on the point of sailing he was still dissatisfied. He had said in conversation (Lord Hertford retailed to Walpole) that we had no intelligence; and that though he had repeatedly tried to arrange for cutters to lie off the French seaports and collect information, he could not prevail on Sandwich to provide them.[1]

The reaction of the Ministry to Kempenfelt's partial success was not gratitude but disappointment and alarm. Not everyone can have shared the King's feeling that he might have hit harder and persisted longer[2]; but it was apparent that the enemy's warships and most of their transports had got clean away and must be powerfully pursued. Kempenfelt's report, which arrived on 18 December, indicated that nine of the enemy ships were bound for the West Indies. Happily this was false; but it was believed. Five ships of the line were added to Rodney, bringing his force to fifteen, while a further five were ordered to prepare for foreign service in case they were wanted. The decision was taken and the order given before the inevitable appeal from the merchants.[3]

[1] G 2877; Sandwich, IV, 329; Walpole, Last Journals, II, 482.
[2] Sandwich, IV, 78.
[3] Adm. 1/95, Kempenfelt's of 14 Dec.; Adm. 2/1340, f. 146; Sandwich, IV, 227-8; CO 137/81, f. 193.

It was now known that Digby had lent Hood four of his North American ships, and intended to send him all but one of the others before the end of the year. Hood would therefore have about twenty-two sail of the line, which Rodney's fifteen would bring up to a maximum of about thirty-seven. Assuming that de Grasse would take all or most of the two French fleets from the Chesapeake to the West Indies, but would have to send home the ships in need of refits, and that Vaudreuil's reinforcement was indeed nine as Kempenfelt reported, the British force should be just enough for safety if it arrived in time.

Middleton, however, who was consulted by the Board, considered that even twenty reinforcements from home would not be enough, in view of Vaudreuil's advantage in the race; for by the time of Rodney's arrival the French would probably have made their junction with the Spaniards. It was now vital to obtain a superiority of four or five ships of the line by sending out singly every three-decker which could be got ready within a fortnight, with a sufficient number of two-deckers. Jamaica could then probably be saved and its assailants destroyed.

This argument was developed in a memorandum which he sent to the First Lord on Christmas Day (and, with an eye to the future, to Lord Shelburne on Christmas Eve). Its interest is academic, for later developments made its adoption unnecessary; but it gives much food for thought about the principles on which the naval war had been conducted. For Middleton adopted the view which Germain and the King had advocated since the Spanish intervention in 1779. Without an overall superiority at sea, the colonies could be defended only by seeking a decisive local superiority at the expense of home waters, and inflicting a defeat on the enemy in distant seas. 'If the absurd system of starving every other service to make up an insufficient western squadron is still to prevail we shall not only lose island after island in sight of fleets that are still too weak to protect them, but see every possession belonging to Great Britain with the troops left for their defence in the hands of the enemy.'

Yet the trade and military convoys must continue to sail from home ports, and invasion be prevented. To achieve this in the absence of most of the major units of the fleet Middleton suggested a daring plan. The outward-bound convoys from the Channel should sail in the early spring before the enemy took station to the westward, escorted by forty-four gun frigates to free the fifties for the line of battle. The homeward convoys must be brought in north-about, and the vital area in home waters would then be the North Sea. To obtain a decisive superiority he proposed to send there every three-decker left at home (for the western station would be too dangerous for them if the enemy's main fleet proved to be coppered as was reported). Every other ship not employed in the western squadron should accompany them. By these dispositions the western squadron would be relieved of responsibility for the trade. Its only mission would be to prevent invasion, and under an able flag officer fifteen or twenty of the fastest two-deckers would be enough. Victualled for five months, coming in to Torbay only when the enemy went into port, and hanging constantly on the skirts of the French fleet, they could prevent it from passing invasion convoys across the Channel.[1]

These plans Sandwich submitted to Kempenfelt, who had no doubt discussed them with Middleton and endorsed them whole-heartedly.[2] It would be open to the enemy to detach to the North Sea from their own fleet to support the Dutch; but he thought they were unlikely to penetrate the British scheme in time to disrupt it in the coming summer. They would believe with good reason that we could not ward off simultaneously their blows in the West Indies and in home waters. To save the West Indies we must accept inferiority at home, and rely on the army to defeat invasion.

Four days after Middleton's memorandum reached Sandwich, the Cabinet agreed that the five provisional additions to Rodney's force of fifteen should proceed, sailing singly as Middleton had suggested without waiting till all were ready. Middleton's pressure may well have prompted the decision, for Sandwich appears to have remained hesitant. A few days later he reported the 'good news' that de Grasse's fleet had been seen at Martinique, with only twenty-eight sail including frigates, and with many topmasts down and signs of damage after its passage from America. He concluded, too readily, that de Grasse had not brought the whole French fleet from America, and that Hood would not be much inferior; and evidently he reopened the question of the five additional reinforcements, for three days later North replied through Robinson that 'he thought it determined and fixed, and that there could not be a doubt about it in his opinion'.[3]

Rodney, in the meantime, had been struggling to get away. From the ill-liked dockyard at Portsmouth he dropped down to Plymouth, which he liked no better, and he was soon laying about him and stirring up the port authorities. 'I hate this place', he told his wife on Christmas day. 'I have taught them briskness and activity, which all the ports much want.' Soon he was boasting of the quickened tempo: 'Such is the effect of fear. They knew there was no trifling with me.' From Admiral Milbank he extorted the crews of ships in need of repair, leaving in exchange his own sick in the hospital. Milbank complained to the Admiralty that Rodney had assumed

[1] CL, Shelburne, Vol. 151, Nos. 7, 9; Barham, II, 37–40.

[2] Sandwich, IV, 80–2.

[3] G 3487; Add. MSS. 38217, f. 231; Sandwich, IV, 229. For the composition of Rodney's reinforcement, see note on p. 453 below.

the direction of all the ships preparing to join him. 'I certainly have', said Rodney, 'and have obliged their commanders, and the officers of his Majesty's dock-yard here, to use every despatch possible in fitting them for service.'[1]

By the end of the year nothing except the wind blowing up the Sound detained the Admiral in whose hands Sandwich wrote that the fate of the empire depended. On 7 January the wind veered to the west; and by the 8th it had come round far enough to the northward for Rodney to sail with twelve ships of the line and a promise of three more to follow. Out in the Channel a violent contrary wind was blowing, and he put back to shelter in Torbay. But on the 14th he cleared the land. The wind was a fierce westerly gale and the sea, mountains high, was rolling in towards the Breton coast. To weather Ushant with a fleet in these conditions was no certainty, but Rodney knew how much the public service urged the risk, and carrying a press of sail he cleared it by a mere two leagues.[2]

2. The Race is Won

Rodney was fairly away; and as he departed, news came into London which lightened the prospect to the westward. On Christmas day a gale had completed the business begun by Kempenfelt. Guichen's fleet was scattered, and he had returned to Brest with most of the French West India reinforcement. Only Vaudreuil himself with two ships of the line and a few transports proceeded to his destination, where he joined de Grasse on 2 February; and when the remainder sailed again in February Rodney was far ahead.

The squadron for India was commanded by Admiral Bickerton, and it sailed on 6 February. He was to keep well to the westward to avoid the large enemy forces in Spanish ports, and refresh his ships at Rio de Janeiro if it was necessary. East India Company messengers set out overland for India to arrange for frigates to meet him with the latest intelligence as he approached Madras.[3]

Thus India and the West Indies were provided for, on a very large scale; and the future pattern of events in those theatres was now virtually settled, so far as it was determined in Europe. There remained only details to be tidied up: the disposal of the force at Jamaica, and the possibility of intercepting Guichen when he sailed again. As soon as the news that he had turned back was known Stormont had sought royal assistance to hasten the Admiralty's measures. The King responded with a letter which urged the First Lord to

[1] Mundy, I, 214; II, 174, 176.
[2] *Ibid.*, 176, 182–3, 185, 195; Adm. 2/1341, f. 14. On investigation Williams (471) says that Rodney's criticism of the dockyards 'seems generally without substance'.
[3] Adm. 2/1341, ff. 10, 26.

strain every nerve to intercept the French; and falling into Sandwich's own idiom, he reminded him how much it would strengthen his hand when he faced the coming naval enquiry in Parliament.[1]

Sandwich consulted Middleton, whose answer provides a comment on the view that in every circumstance the proper policy was a close blockade of Brest. If the necessary force could indeed be prepared in time, by using the ships which were preparing to follow Rodney, it would need up to a dozen frigates and four or five cutters to scout for the enemy in the thick wintry seas. If the battle fleet cruised till March it would not be fit for further service till May, and the frigates needed for early Atlantic convoys would be worn out. In spite of this effort Guichen might nevertheless escape, and the West India ships would have to follow with all speed to join Rodney. But Middleton believed that the proper place to intercept Guichen was at his destination. Hood's squadron should be collected at Barbados in constant readiness to join Rodney, with its frigates thrown out in a long 150-mile chain to the eastward, trusting to its windward position to deter de Grasse from attacking other islands in the meantime. As soon as Guichen's convoy was sighted, Rodney should put out to destroy it.[2]

In spite of his advice, the Cabinet resolved on the following day to attempt the interception in Europe, and ordered that the sailing of Rodney's five 'reserved' ships should be postponed. But evidently it proved impossible to collect an adequate force, for Sandwich told Robinson a month later that the large detachments to the West Indies and India put the interception of Guichen out of the question.[3] Guichen sailed again on 11 February without interruption, accompanied by three or four ships of the line for India, and two with a convoy for the West Indies. Two of Rodney's 'reserved' ships had already been released to him, and sailed with a convoy of troops and stores, under the protection as far as Madeira of Bickerton's East India squadron. His total reinforcement was thus seventeen sail of the line.[4]

It was these West Indian arrangements which produced Germain's last dispute with Sandwich, By now their disagreements were so notorious that Fox had said he would regard him as a principal witness when Sandwich was impeached. Germain spent much of January at his Northamptonshire house for political reasons which will appear; and shortly before his return

[1] G 3494; Sandwich, IV, 82–3. 'You will do great service to this Kingdom and add considerably to your popularity', Sandwich had told Hood in November.
[2] CL, Shelburne, Vol. 151, No. 8 (16 Jan., Middleton to Sandwich): printed in Sandwich, IV, 78–80 with variations, and the suggested date December 1781, which from internal evidence cannot be correct.
[3] G 3499; Abergavenny, 50.
[4] See note below, p. 453.

the Cabinet resolved that the Admiral at Jamaica should send his capital ships to the Leeward Islands to strengthen Rodney. Sandwich asked Knox to obtain a letter of authority for the order from the Secretary of State. At that moment it was still thought that Guichen had got clear away with his reinforcement for the West Indies, and Knox pointed out that by the time the order reached Jamaica, the whole French fleet would probably have gone down to San Domingo, and that the Jamaica ships might then be intercepted as they beat up through the Windward Passage. The draft instruction which he sent Germain for his signature made the arrangement depend on the enemy not being before Jamaica. Germain strongly approved of the amendment, and in that form the order was sent.

Knox had told Sandwich that still more objectionable in Germain's eyes was a direction in the draft order that Graves should remain with Rowley at Jamaica. Germain, he said, thought that Graves should be recalled for his conduct off the Chesapeake; and if the Jamaica merchants learnt that he was to remain at Jamaica they would demand Germain's removal. Sandwich replied that Graves's brother-in-law Lord North would not allow him to be disgraced, and that instead of recalling him he would ask him privately to apply for leave to come home. To this characteristic device Knox replied that it would mean a delay of six or eight months during which Graves might succeed to the command of the whole fleet of England.[1]

The extent to which the indecisive battle off the Chesapeake had determined the fate of Cornwallis had yet to make its full impact on the public, and judging by past precedents Graves's failure would certainly lead to a clamour against him. At the end of January Germain demanded that he should be brought to trial. But Sandwich had had enough of courts-martial, and properly replied that the Chesapeake despatch showed no criminality: 'for want of success I can never allow to come under that description'. He refused to order a court-martial, unless sufficient grounds were supplied by the American Department and the King's pleasure signified by an order from a Secretary of State. Germain instructed Knox to prepare the material for the Admiralty; but the time had passed when an individual would take the responsibility for the trial on his shoulders, and he refused to give the order till the papers had been considered by the Cabinet. It was a curious encounter: Germain, whose life had been blighted by a court-martial, seeking a scapegoat for Yorktown; and Sandwich, whose protection of Graves had hitherto been at the best half-hearted, determined to save him from trial. But Sandwich had burnt his fingers already by court-martialling an admiral who had failed to win a victory; while Germain, who had struggled to obtain his

[1] G 3491; Sackville, II, 295; Adm. 2/1341, f. 2; Knox, *Extra-Official State Papers*, I, Appendix p. 7.

own trial, held that an innocent man should not fear to face his judges. 'I would never', he had once declared in a parliamentary attack on Lord Mansfield, 'oppose the minutest scrutiny into my behaviour. However much condemned by the envy or malice of enemies, I would at least shew that I stood acquitted in my own mind. *Qui fugit judicium, ipso teste, reus est.*' Sandwich's apology for Graves's supersession in America stands contrasted in its tone and depths: 'In times such as these', he told him in the last days of the Ministry, 'it is not enough to have drawn or executed instructions properly: blame must be laid somewhere, and it is a mere accident where the fault will be laid.'[1]

Amid such manoeuvring and mutual mistrust the last days of the Ministry dragged out. Germain believed that the dispersal of Guichen's fleet and Rodney's superior reinforcements ended the threat to Jamaica for the present year. Intelligence, however, indicated that the enemy still intended the attack.[2] Of Guichen's second departure there was a stream of conflicting reports: he was to sail about 8 February with three ships of the line for the West Indies and three, with two more *en flûte*, for India; or with five for the West Indies; with 3,500 troops, or with 5-6,000. At last, on 23 February, a report arrived from the *Arethusa*, which had been watching Brest since Kempenfelt's return, that on the 12th she had seen a large fleet coming out.[3]

[1] Knox, 181; Marlow, 290; Sandwich, IV, 209. Graves was not court-martialled.
[2] CO 137/82, f. 77; Adm. 2/1341, ff. 44, 45, 70.
[3] Adm. 2/1340, f. 147; Adm. 2/1341, f. 75.

NOTE

Rodney's seventeen ships from England were made up as follows:

8 Nov. 8 in the original list; 1 Dec, to sail with him at once.
    2 in the original list ; 1 Dec, to follow with convoy.

18 Dec. The two latter not to wait for convoy but to sail at once.
    5 Channel ships added (*Namur, Duke, Agamemnon, Hercules, Valiant*)

    2 newly commissioned ships provisionally added (*Warrior*, new; *Magnificent*, from refit)

    —
17
    —

Also provisionally added but not eventually sent:
    2 North Sea ships
    1 just commissioned
    —
20
    —

It was a gloomy scene as February drew into March. The French had recovered St Eustatius in a manner disgraceful to the garrison; Minorca had unexpectedly surrendered; in the Leeward Islands Hood had been contending with a force which outnumbered him by nearly two to one, and the fall of St Kitts was hourly expected. Yet the prospect was not all darkness. Quebec and Nova Scotia were intact. The lodgments on the American coast at New York, Charleston and Savannah could not be disturbed by the rebels without a French fleet. And though India and Jamaica were threatened, reinforcements were on their way which would turn the scales and alter the course of the war.

3. Victory

To the Americans Yorktown had opened a splendid vista. With the French commanding the sea, they could treat the British positions along their coast as marooned detachments, to be punched out one by one with the help of Rochambeau's troops; and Washington was eager to strike at once against Charleston or at least the little post at Wilmington. But the vision faded. De Grasse had his obligations to the Spaniards, whose ambitions lay in the Caribbean; and once again the Spanish alliance was drawing the French away from their own obligations. His allotted time in America was spent; and the victors parted, looking forward to renewed co-operation in 1782 for the capture of Charleston or New York. De Grasse removed all his ships of the line from American waters,[1] and without them Washington could not move his siege guns south against Charleston.

The British had never doubted that the French would return to take the offensive in the West Indies after the hurricane months. The disaster in the Chesapeake did not shake this view; and on his return to New York Hood announced that he would return to the Caribbean, reinforced with every ship which the American command could spare. Against his strong objections Graves sailed for Jamaica in the London as he had been ordered, taking a seventy-four to a station where she would be useless; but Digby responded with four ships of the line, followed by two more in December when the enemy's intentions were clarified. Few, perhaps, of his predecessors would have done as much, and this disinterested conduct, which left him with only a single ship of over fifty guns on the American station, brought much relief when it was known in London on 16 December. 'Admiral Digby cannot be sufficiently recommended', Germain told the King.[2]

---

[1] He left only the two-decked frigate Romulus of 44 guns, which had been used in the line by the Rhode Island squadron and is sometimes mistaken for a ship of the line.

[2] Sandwich, IV, 197–215; Adm. 1/490, passim; G 3471.

The garrisons of the British Leeward Islands were now sadly depleted. The May return at the end of the healthy winter season was to show only 2,159 men present and fit for duty; and on the vital island of St Lucia four and a half battalions had only 654 healthy men. Their protection was thus thrown entirely on the British Admiral, crippling his freedom of movement. 'The very defenceless state of all our islands through the want of troops will always oblige him to act on the defensive', Lord Robert Manners wrote a little later, 'as no island is safe but the one we are immediately protecting ...'.

Hood had twenty-two sail of the line fit for service at the beginning of 1782, when the North American ships had all joined him. Against these de Grasse could range thirty. He had brought thirty-three ships of the line from America, and was joined by another in the West Indies. Of the ten ships of the line which should have gone home in the previous summer, three were sent down to San Domingo together with one of the Rhode Island ships to convoy the much-delayed trade to Europe; but the rest, at some risk, he retained.[1]

De Grasse's main objective was Jamaica; but he could not store and victual his fleet till the expected convoy arrived from France, and he used the waiting period to attack the British Leeward Islands. St Eustatius had been surprised by the Marquis de Bouillé before Hood's return from America, and de Grasse's first choice was Barbados, where the inferior British squadron lay; but after two unsuccessful attempts to work to windward, he turned against St Kitts on 11 January and besieged the garrison on Brimstone Hill. Hood, short of provisions and stores after his voyage from New York, made for Antigua to replenish them; and embarking General Prescott with five hundred troops he sailed to the relief of St Kitts. His hope was to surprise the French at anchor; but on the voyage one of his ships of the line ran on board a frigate, and precious time was lost in repairing her – the parallel with Graves's caution off the Chesapeake has been well made – and thus the French had time to learn of the British approach and put to sea.[2] By a fine feat of seamanship Hood slipped into the position they had left; and anchoring on the edge of a bank so that the enemy could not anchor outside his line, he repulsed de Grasse in two attacks on 26 January.

In this position Hood could hope to foil the enemy. The French siege guns had been lost in a wrecked transport, he had taken a frigate laden with munitions, and he had the garrison commander's word that Brimstone

---

[1] Three of the ships he had brought to America in 1781 foundered at sea on their way to England as prizes after the battle of the Saints, and one of Barras's squadron was condemned at Halifax.

[2] Possibly to protect their supplies from Martinique; but de Grasse had previously put out from the Chesapeake rather than be attacked at anchor. See Sandwich, IV, 217.

Hill could hold out. But he forgot the character of the inhabitants. At the foot of the hill lay guns and ammunition which they had refused to remove; and with these and some ships' cannon the enemy battered down the defences and forced the garrison's surrender. There was no longer duty or safety in the anchorage; and in the night of 14 February the British squadron stole away. 'A very unofficerlike action', said Rodney, 'and tending to discourage the fleet in general, by a British fleet of twenty-two sail cutting their cables, putting out their lights, and running away from an enemy's fleet of only twenty-seven sail of the line.' This comment once again reveals more of Rodney than of Hood, and reminds us that Graves is in good company among the admirals who have refused to fight to a decision against such odds.

De Grasse followed up his success by taking the little islands of Nevis and Montserrat. The events on Nevis will show the dilemma which faced the smaller islands under enemy attack. When the French fleet stood in, the only defence was three hundred militiamen indifferently armed and trained, and a few bad cannon without a single artilleryman to direct their fire. The Council considered the propriety of a token resistance. But they had neither trained their militia nor prepared redoubts, and judged it wiser not to irritate the enemy. Two of them went down to St Kitts to negotiate a capitulation. The terms were satisfactory: the inhabitants were allowed to behave as neutrals and export their produce anywhere in neutral vessels. Only the negroes and poorer whites imperilled the happy arrangement by their communications with the British.[1]

Demerara and Essequibo rapidly followed Nevis into the French maw.[2] But help was at hand. On 25 February Rodney joined Hood at sea with his twelve sail of the line and repaired to St Lucia, where five more arrived in ones and twos from England. Superiority had passed to the British; and had Rodney intercepted the reinforcements and convoy which he learnt were on their way from France, the enemy fleet would have been reduced to helplessness and the French islands to starvation. But Rodney assumed that the convoy would come in to Martinique as usual from the south. Hood disagreed, and suggested as Middleton had done that the watch should stretch northwards as far as the latitude of Guadeloupe.[3] They were right; and on 20 March the French convoy anchored safely in Fort Royal Bay. De Grasse thus received his reinforcements and provisions, and was ready for the next move: the junction with Don Solano's fleet at San Domingo, and the invasion of Jamaica.

Rodney lay watching him from St Lucia. On 5 April he learnt that troops

[1] Pares, *West India Fortune*, 97–9.
[2] They had been captured from the Dutch by British privateers.
[3] See above, p. 451, and Sandwich, IV, 217, 243–6.

had embarked; and on the evening of the 7th came the expected word from his cruisers. The enemy were on the move. The battle fleet with which de Grasse intended to conquer Jamaica numbered thirty-three ships of the line, and two ships of fifty guns shepherded the convoy. His numbers were made up as follows:

West India ships returned from America	23	
Barras's squadron from Rhode Island	5	
Ship which had remained in West Indies?. . . .	1	(*Magnifique*)
Total in Western Atlantic, Jan. 1782	29	
Reinforcements from Europe, 1782	4	
Total, 7 April	33	

Not present

Escorting trade to Europe	4	(3 de Grasse, 1 Barras)
Unready at Martinique	1	(de Grasse)
Dropped out since St Kitts	1	(de Grasse)
	6	

Rodney had thirty-six ships of the line. Thus the hopeless inferiority of the previous September had been converted in the course of the winter into a significant superiority by heavy reinforcement from home. These were the elements which composed his fleet:

Hood's squadron from America	12[1]	
Lent by Digby	5	
From refit at Antigua	1	(*Russell*)
From England at end of 1781	1	(*St Albans*)
Total Jan. 1782.	19	
Reinforcement of 1782	17	
Total 7 April	36	

Not present

Local convoy	1	(*Prudent*, 64, from Digby)
To Jamaica with convoys for refits .	3	(all from Hood)
	4	

To the disgust of at least one captain, Rodney waited for daylight to sail, though the fleet lay in an open bay.[2] Nevertheless the French, with their cumbrous convoy, could not keep their lead. Early on the 9th Hood with the advanced squadron overtook the enemy, and it became clear that de

[1] Including the two ships which joined him from Jamaica after the battle of the Chesapeake. One of his original 14 had been abandoned and burnt after the battle, and three others were worn out or crippled and refitting (see list of ships not present).

[2] The following account is based on James, Chevalier and Sandwich, IV.

Grasse's hope of achieving his object by evasion was doomed. Instead he had a chance to crush the British van, which had felt the wind as it emerged from the lee of Dominica and had become widely separated from the main body. Its mutilation would have enabled the French to proceed to Jamaica with little fear of interruption; but de Grasse refused the opportunity. Instead of falling on Hood, he modified his plan of evasion. He would send his convoy to the safety of Guadeloupe, draw Rodney away, throw off the pursuit, and return to pick up the convoy for the next lap of the voyage. He sent only a detachment against Hood, not to crush him but to win time for the convoy's retreat. In calms and shifting breezes sporadic actions took place between the northern end of Dominica and the Iles des Saintes, the French keeping their distance for fear of the British carronades.

Now began the erosion of de Grasse's strength. The pursuit continued throughout the 10th, and that night the *Jason* ran on board the *Zélé* and retired with damage to Guadeloupe, where she was followed by the *Caton*, whose masts had suffered in the action of the 9th. More time was lost when two ships dropped to leeward and had to be supported. The next night the *Zélé* collided again with the flagship, lost her bowsprit and foremast, and had to be taken in tow by a frigate to Guadeloupe. At daybreak she was sighted from the British fleet, six miles to leeward with the French fleet twelve to fifteen mile off on the port bow. In the hope of drawing de Grasse back to her rescue, Rodney detached four ships in chase, and the manoeuvre succeeded. The French turned back; and though the chasing ships were recalled and the *Zélé* was soon in safety, de Grasse persisted on his course and drew into action.

For the first time in the war a British Admiral engaged a main fleet of the enemy with the one vital requisite for victory: a heavy superiority in ships and guns. He had thirty-six ships of the line, and de Grasse had been reduced to thirty. Whether Rodney made the best use of his advantage – whether he broke the French line by long considered design, and whether the design was his own; whether the French would have suffered more if he had kept them closely engaged from to leeward; whether the pursuit was lax: these points are still debated, but they do not matter to our theme. By the end of the day de Grasse was a prisoner and five French ships of the line were in Rodney's hands; two more struck to Hood a week later. The survivors rallied under Vaudreuil at San Domingo, and with a fresh arrival from Martinique they numbered twenty-six French ships and with a dozen Spaniards. But Rodney was on their heels, and the great attack on Jamaica, to which all the enemy's movements since Yorktown had been directed, was abandoned. The battle of the Saints had yielded a limited harvest, and the enemy were not broken; and yet there was some truth in Rodney's boast to Sandwich:

'You may now despise all your enemies.' But the architects of the victory were no longer in power.

4. The Anatomy of Victory

In the *Parliamentary History* the naval strategy of the American War is reduced to a simple matter of discovering the enemy's strength and over-matching it: to a rational calculation which could only be upset by the laziness, cowardice or stupidity of Ministers. The manner in which Rodney's superiority at the battle of the Saints was achieved proves the poverty of the view.

In the first place Rodney's great reinforcement was despatched on false intelligence of the French expedition from Brest, and before anything could be known of de Grasse's strength in the Caribbean. If de Grasse had sent ten ships home instead of four, the British reinforcement would have been excessive; if he had kept all ten, and had not lost two in collisions immediately before the battle, it would have been inadequate.

Many other accidents might have intervened to alter the balance. If Darby had come home from his Channel cruise as soon as he was recalled, a decisive force might have been ready to intercept the French reinforcements off Brest. What would have been the consequence? De Grasse would have been deprived of the four ships which Vaudreuil was taking out to him; but Rodney would probably not have been given the seven ships which were added to his squadron on Kempenfelt's failure. If an interception had been achieved by using Bickerton's force which was preparing for India, there might have been the added misfortune of Bickerton's absence from the Battle of Cuddalore, and India as well as the West Indies would have suffered by Guichen's interception. If scurvy had been expected at Minorca, a relief by a battle fleet might have been attempted at all costs in December: it would then have been difficult or impossible to give Rodney the additional seven ships, most of which were taken from the Channel fleet. If Guichen's force had not been scattered by the Christmas storm, the French reinforcements and supplies would have reached Martinique in time for de Grasse to depart for Jamaica before Rodney arrived to challenge him.

The superiority which gave Rodney the victory was the outcome not of precise calculation and circumstances foreseen, but of intelligent guesswork and a determination to concentrate on the most vital of many competing claims; and in the last resort of the incalculable but not impartial factor which generally favours the side with most in hand: the factor of luck.

CHAPTER XXVII

THE END OF THE MINISTRY

1. *The Departure of Germain*

Parliament had assembled two days after the news of Yorktown, on 27 November. Both Germain and Sandwich were said to seem shaken by the blow – the latter 'near to death with fatigue and mortification'. But Lord North's parliamentary equanimity was unshaken, and the debate on the Address was carried by 89 votes. The leaders of the Opposition were quite unprepared to exploit the disaster, and the interval since the news had been too short for them to gather their forces or form a plan. Their wild talk of vermin, scaffolds and the day of reckoning made little impact on a House deeply moved by the national crisis. 'It is strange they should never have learnt that to show exultation in a public calamity makes them odious.'[1]

The Opposition had been in a state of demoralisation for the past eighteen months. Since the Gordon Riots and the initial successes in South Carolina they had made no headway against the Ministry. A large majority of the House of Commons had accepted the Dutch War as just and necessary; and even Cornwallis's failure in the Carolinas had not persuaded them that the reconquest of America was hopeless. Nevertheless the opening success of the Ministry in the new session concealed only momentarily the gravity of the political crisis. In the course of the brief sitting which ended on 20 December there were five debates on the future of the American War, and this became the crucial question for the government's survival. There were signs that some of the Ministry's supporters would no longer give North their vote for pursuing the struggle. Like former wars the present one had nearly doubled the national debt; and the country gentlemen would not continue indefinitely to pour a high land tax into the American War without return. When the Christmas recess arrived, most of the English county members were opposed to the continuation of the American struggle.

Lord North had warned his colleagues in the previous winter that he could not finance the war for more than another year; and in the course of the present session he moved, like most of his colleagues, towards the belief that America must be abandoned. The King of course would never freely accept this conclusion; and within the Cabinet Germain resisted it to the end. His attitude was clear, firm, and rational: 'that we can never

[1] Carlisle, 539, 541. This chapter owes much to I. R. Christie's *The End of North's Ministry*.

continue to exist as a great or powerful nation after we have lost or renounced the sovereignty of America'. He foretold a continuing connection between America and France; the loss of Britain's American trade followed soon by that of Nova Scotia, Newfoundland and Canada; enemy cruiser bases in Bermuda and the Bahamas to strangle the homeward bound West India trade in time of war; and the West Indies themselves, bereft of all supplies except from England, soon to fall to the French and Americans.[1]

Germain did not pretend that the hope of recovering America was bright. The betrayal of the loyalists in the Yorktown capitulation might prevent them from trusting to British protection again. But he believed that the future of Britain depended on keeping what was still held, and fighting through to a settlement on a basis of *uti possidetis*. In possession of New York, Charleston and Savannah we would safeguard the extensive trade which he believed was going through them, and retain summer stations and staging posts from which winter operations could be mounted in the West Indies. Thus, he contended, the huge death-rate in the Caribbean could be reduced, by seasoning troops from Europe and providing cool cantonments in the hot weather. If one considers how in the next war with France the British army was wrecked by West Indian diseases, one cannot lightly dismiss this part of his argument.[2]

How the struggle could be continued he suggested at the King's request in a memorandum circulated to the Cabinet. With superiority at sea Nova Scotia, Penobscot, New York, Charleston, Savannah and East Florida could all be defended by the forces already there; and any surplus could take up the plan so often recommended but never seriously adopted, of attacking the rebel coasts in conjuction with inroads from Canada, and supporting any loyalists bold enough to trust us after Yorktown. On the treatment of the loyalists in the Yorktown capitulation he felt great bitterness[3]; and he touched

---

[1] Wraxall Memoirs, II, 465; CL, Germain, preamble to the memorandum printed in Sackville, II, 216. This, though dated 1782 by the Clements Library in the Germain and Shelburne papers, seems to me to belong to the period between 28 Nov. (cf. G 3449) and 8 Dec. (cf. reference to possibility that no more fresh corps may be sent to America, and Cabinet Minute in G 3462).

[2] Preamble, *loc. cit.* Ideally, he said, troops should sail from England for the West Indies on 1 September, to arrive at the opening of the healthy campaigning season in the Caribbean; but at that time enemy fleets were in the Channel, inward bound convoys were expected, and no escort could be spared. Reinforcements therefore tended to sail later, and arrive about the beginning of the hot weather: if they could be sent to a summer station in America their losses could be avoided. The contention is supported in Mackenzie, 554; and cf. table of losses in Appendix I, below.

[3] He ordered the Admiralty to court-martial the captain of the Yorktown cartel ship (the ill-famed *Bonetta*) for refusing to take off more than a dozen loyalists and neglecting those he did take. (CO 5/255, p. 124).

too on the indiscipline and indiscriminate plundering of rebels and loyalists by the army, and the failure to establish civil government. There must be, he said, one person with full power to treat and pardon, to direct the great outlines of operations, to end the jealousies and misunderstandings of commanders. Even if limited offensives proved beyond the present means, Britain should remain in a situation to receive and protect the Americans if their dislike of their war government and of the French should turn them towards us. At all costs, we must hold what we had.[1]

In all this there was no new talisman of victory: only the wearied repetition of a formula which he still believed to be right. On 8 December the Cabinet took its decision to send only recruits to America, precluding any more ambitious plan. On the 14th Germain could still declare in the House of Commons that the Ministry was unanimous against abandoning America. How unanimous, North demonstrated by quitting the Treasury bench and withdrawing to a seat behind it, while Germain faced his attackers alone. The disunity within the Ministry was shown at a Cabinet meeting the same day, when a total silence was preserved on the pressing subjects of the Commons debate and plans for America.[2]

Germain was certain that changes were being discussed. If the Ministry was to survive, scapegoats were needed. As Sandwich told Admiral Graves, the choice of victims was a matter of chance rather than justice; and Sandwich and Germain, the director of the navy and the chief protagonist of coercing the rebels, were the natural sacrifices. Dundas and Rigby, who had despaired of recovering America, were determined that the two ministers must go and independence be recognised: their defection would mean the loss of a dozen votes, and with desertions among the country gentlemen it would kill the government's majority. Germain was inflexible in his opinions, but he did not intend to cling to office: a wealthy man living within his means, he was not, like Sandwich and Carlisle, impelled to seek office by financial necessity, and his only private ambition was a peerage to erase the stain of Minden. When the King suggested Carleton as a proper successor to Clinton, he replied that though he could not serve with Carleton after the letters they had exchanged, the King was unlikely to leave the seals in his hands for long. He warned the King that among the real friends of government dislike of the American War was general, and that men of high office and great political connections desired an accommodation. Before Christmas he urged the King to release him, and perhaps offer the American Department and the Admiralty to the Opposition; but in vain.

The cause of the delay was a deadlock between the Prime Minister and

[1] G 3449; Knox, 272; Sackville, II, 216.
[2] G 3462, 3470.

the King. The King insisted that if Germain retired his successor must equally oppose independence for America. Under this condition North would have liked to bring in Jenkinson; but if Jenkinson refused, he would have preferred to retain Germain's capable support in the House of Commons.[1]

Thus the American Department was thrown into confusion, as the Northern Department had been in 1779. Though Germain still held the seals no decision could be taken about Clinton's successor, nor any instructions issued for the next campaign. On 23 December the Cabinet agreed at an amicable meeting to relieve Clinton; but while Germain stayed in office Carleton could not be named as his successor. On the same day North had a meeting at the King's suggestion with Stormont and Hillsborough, the two Secretaries of State on whom peace negotiations would fall. Their conversation was the exact counterpart of many which North had had with the King. He was despondent about the war, talked of the country's reserves as nearly exhausted, but was against saying so in public. He thought that such sovereignty as could now be maintained over the rebellious colonies was not worth fighting for, adding that the King did not agree with him. But he showed no intention of adopting Independence, spoke in a general way against discussing terms of peace in public, and was disposed to wait on events and see what might come of negotiations with Holland. About Carleton and Germain he would not commit himself.[2]

The King had no objection to Germain having his peerage and retiring, provided it was understood that the cause of his retirement was Carleton's appointment and not the abandonment of the struggle; but he would not move a step in the matter till a successor was found for the American Department. North was in perplexity. Though he had hedged to the Secretaries of State about America, he revealed his true feelings to Robinson: 'You see there is no great objection to changing men, but a very great one to changing measures, and that it will be expected from me to take upon myself *alone* to carry on that plan which appears to me in our present circumstances ruinous and impracticable.'[3]

The King, then, was willing to dispense with Germain but not with his policy; while the Prime Minister, though he disliked the policy, would have been willing to retain the man. Germain was not admitted behind the scenes, but from the King's hedging about Carleton he guessed that his own removal was in the wind if the King could penetrate North's views on America. He therefore thought it 'more proper and decent to keep out of the way' till his future was decided; and with the King's permission he went down

[1] G 3468, 3470, 3478; Knox, 273; Sackville, I, 140–1.
[2] G 3475, 3477, 3483, 3485. [3] G 3485; Abergavenny, 46.

to Drayton, leaving Knox in charge of the office and freeing the ministerial coteries from the embarrassment of his presence.

January drew on without a decision. 'We go on here with our usual amusements', Germain wrote from Drayton on the 10th, 'as if all were peace and quiet. Lord North perhaps is doing the same at Bushey; but if he intends to make any change among us, it is almost time to let us into the secret.' Knox in the meantime had been unreliably informed of the proposed changes, and went to see North with a message from Germain which he read aloud. North interrupted him to say it was measures, not men which should be changed; and at the end he launched into a protestation that his own department occupied his full attention. Where, he demanded, was he to find taxes to produce £800,000? Last year he had said he could do it for one year only: he had fulfilled his engagement and now wished he were out: the enemy would not make peace with us. At this point Knox reminded him of Guichen's misfortune and Rodney's consequent superiority in the West Indies, and suggested his old project of trying to detach France's allies. North's reply was to walk about the room and call for his post chaise. Knox took this as a civil way of telling him to get out of the room, and he went.[1]

It was high time for Germain to return to the game. Back in London on the 15th, he had an audience with the King two days later, and asked him point blank whether he was still to regard himself as Secretary of State. The King replied, by his own account, that no decision had yet been taken; and Germain described North's rebuff of Knox, and pressed for an answer. He declared that he would never retract what he had said about American Independence, and would rather leave office now than be forced to it later, as must certainly happen if vigorous measures were not pursued. He left the closet with a promise that North would send for him.[2]

The next morning a summons for Germain arrived from Downing Street. Knox scribbled Robinson a hasty line to warn the Prime Minister not to be inattentive, and to tell him that he had disposed Germain to treat with the Americans on the basis of *uti possidetis* and a truce. Robinson hurried to Downing Street; but when North came down he went, not into his room, but into a Cabinet meeting on Admiralty business. To this, and not to a private conference, Germain found that he had been summoned. He sat the meeting out; but finding that North had no intention of speaking to him he came away 'in a monstrous passion', and wrote a letter of resignation to the King. Knox slipped away to Downing Street to fetch Robinson, who persuaded Germain to hold the letter back till after the week-end.[3]

[1] Knox, 18, 274; Sackville, II, 295.   [2] Knox, 274-5; G 3497.
[3] Knox, 275.

The King had written to North as he had promised; but he enclosed the letter in a despatch box with some signed warrants, and North had thrown the whole contents to a clerk without looking at them. The truth emerged on the Monday morning, the 21st, when he received a sharp rebuke from the King for his neglect of Germain. He had now kept the American Secretary's fate in suspense for six weeks, to his own discredit and the detriment of military preparations. The King added that on one point he would ever agree with his American Secretary: a separation from America would be the end of Britain as a Great Power, and would make his own situation intolerable. North's reply made his dilemma clear. Though many of the Ministry's supporters would turn unreliable if Germain stayed in office, they objected to his views rather than his person: peace with America was necessary, even at the cost of England's sovereignty. Since the King agreed with Germain, was it right that he rather than North should be forced to go?[1]

But did North mean it? His friends had heard these tones too often to be sure. Robinson reported him as determined to go on, but in very low spirits, which he attributed not to his differences with the King on policy, but to the annual tribulation of the approaching budget. At any rate North sent Germain a civil note, and saw him on the following day. He told him flatly that it was impossible to continue the war: America was lost, and it was vain to think of recovering it. Germain offered to treat on the basis of *uti possidetis*, but North was sure that only independence would now be accepted. Then, said Germain, he must look out for another Secretary of State. The Prime Minister described the difficulty of finding a competent successor in the House of Commons, since Jenkinson would not take the office. He promised to give Germain his decision before he went to the House on the following day. But, he ended sadly, Germain's removal would solve nothing, since the King stood immovable on independence.[2]

Such was Germain's account of the interview. But North carried off the impression that if nothing was done and no one rendered ill offices, everything might go on as before: Germain's views on America had not after all differed from his own as much as might have been expected, and the

[1] G 3501, 3503. That there was substance in the charge that North's delays were disrupting military preparations is suggested by the arrangements to ship the 2,700 recruits to New York. Not till 20 February did Germain's successor instruct the Admiralty to provide transports. A month later he ordered that shipping should if necessary be hired at a high price owing to the importance of the reinforcement; but on 21 March he learnt that the Navy Board could procure no shipping, and ordered it to apply to the Ordnance, which had 5,000 tons available. When another month had gone by the new Ministry was asking for a progress report (CO 5/255, pp. 132, 137, 139, 194).

[2] G 3502; Knox, 275–6; Sackville, I, 76.

only subject not open to compromise was the appointment of Carleton. So Germain heard no more; and North continued on his blinkered way, half paralysed by George III's declaration that if Germain was to be removed for opposing independence, the King must be removed as well. Parliament re-assembled; and Rigby and Dundas let it be known that they would not attend the House while Germain was in office. On this Germain wrote to North again on the 30th, when more than a week had passed since their interview, demanding the answer he had been promised as an absolute necessity so that his Department could function: the mails were about to be made up for America and the West Indies, and proper instructions were needed for the Commanders-in-Chief as well as an answer to Clinton's application to resign. No answer was returned; but as North came out from the Closet on the following day, he said that Germain's wish was reasonable, but the worst of it was that Jenkinson refused to take his office.[1]

This was enough. From that moment, says Knox, Germain considered himself as out. Meeting Hillborough, he learnt that Welbore Ellis was to be sounded as his successor, and if that failed the American Department would be merged in the Southern Department. To the King's surprise Ellis accepted the office on 5 February, and Germain's days in the American Department drew to their close. One of his last despatches authorised Clinton to hand over to General Robertson and leave America; and he begged him for the last time not to sacrifice the loyalists outside Charleston and Savannah by over-insuring at New York. On 9 February he paid his farewell to his office, and recommended Knox's application for a pension to the Prime Minister. And so he departed, having borne for more than six years the main burden of a great war.[2]

2. The Fall of the Ministry

Perhaps the Opposition had spent the recess consulting their constituents as they had promised: one contemplates with pleasure the Christmas activity of Thomas Pitt, who elected himself for Old Sarum, or of the incorruptible Barré, returned by Lord Shelburne for Calne. They came back refreshed to Westminister with a determination to keep the members together, and by numerous call of the House they succeeded in keeping attendance at an unusually high level. Lord North added nothing positive to his own strength when he replaced Germain with Welbore Ellis, a correct and ageing politician whose services had always been at the government's disposal.

[1] G 3507; Knox, 276; Sackville, I, 77.
[2] CO 5/104, f. 181; Knox, 276; Lothian, 408; Abergavenny, 48.

In the December debates Thomas Pitt had denounced the Ministers as a set of puppets dancing to the orders of a deadly secret influence. It was a stale story; but never perhaps had George III come nearer to the Opposition's conception of him than in the months after Yorktown, when his determination not to give up America blocked every effort to abandon a policy which had lost the support of the public. Germain had defied the Opposition to remove the Ministers by parliamentary means and impeach them; to which Mr. Byng had replied that the Ministers were protected by a phalanx of hired supporters. 'Give us only an honest Parliament, and we should then see if security and impunity would result from impeachment.'

Byng was wide of the mark. The Ministry, like every stable Ministry of the century, rested ultimately on the confidence and support of a proportion of the independent country gentlemen; and as long as North was free to change its composition and policies, the country gentlemen were likely to remember their duty to the throne and the social order, and to prefer the King's government to the ranting factions of the Opposition. But time was to show that no important section of the Opposition could now be bought in; and the King's refusal to end the American War alienated the country gentlemen and threw him on the mercy of the men he feared and hated.

The first assault was launched against the Admiralty. Sandwich, unlike Germain, intended to fight for his position. He could not afford to lose it: 'unless I retire with a pension', he was to write, 'my finances will be in the utmost disorder'.[1] He had courted the naval enquiry, and in as public a form as possible; and he had carefully canvassed and primed his colleagues. He worked hard to collect the materials for his defence, and succeeded in assembling impressive evidence of his administrative achievements. He faced his attackers prepared and confident.[2]

But Fox did not intend to bore the squires with administration. He confined himself to recent operations; and for this Sandwich was less prepared, and the charges were less easy to answer. The outcome of operations, as he said, did not decide the question whether the orders given had been right[3]; but though his defence was spirited, Fox's catalogue of the past year's reverses shook the House. On 7 February the government's majority was only 22 – which 'makes Lord North horrid sick'.[4] On a second motion on the 20th the majority remained steady, but an ominous number of deserters were absent or voted with the Opposition. Most significant of all, only ten county members voted with the Ministry.

---

[1] Abergavenny, 52.
[2] Ibid., 46–8; Add. MSS. 38217, ff. 216, 228; Sandwich, IV, 281–301, 308–14, 355 ff.
[3] Above, pp. xvi–xvii.
[4] Christie, 312: for the enquiry in general, see ibid., 305–19.

Dundas was later to say that if Sandwich had been jettisoned in time the Ministry would have survived.[1] The defence of the Admiralty eroded the majority; and on 22 February the Opposition switched its attack and opened a new offensive against the American War. An address against its further prosecution was barely defeated, and Dundas declared that the government was converted and that the retirement of Germain meant the repudiation of the policy of coercion. But this was less than the truth; for unless the King yielded, the Ministers' hands were tied, and they could not adopt a new or a firm policy. When the motion was re-introduced on the 27th Welbore Ellis could only declare that he and North did not differ from the Opposition on the principle of the question, but solely on the expediency. This was not enough. Fox had called North a mere puppet of the King and his friends – 'of that infernal spirit which really governs' – and it had become evident to many independents who had no wish to displace the Ministry that only a check imposed by the House of Commons could turn the King from the policy which the nation had rejected. Sir Gilbert Elliot, who detested the Foxites and their joy at the national disasters, now repudiated the American War: he 'now plainly saw that the nation, the House of Commons and the ministers had been for a long time in the wrong'. In the division more than forty of the Ministry's friends deserted, and about half of them voted with the Opposition. 'I perfectly agree', said one of them, ' . . . in detesting the views of some of the faction leaders in opposition, and in wishing to support the King's government.' But by 19 votes the House abandoned the coercion of America.[2]

This defeat was not the end of the Ministry or the policy. A few days later North opened his budget as usual, and it was apparent that the condemnation of the war was not synonymous with the fall of the men who had waged it. But North warned the King that the Ministry must be reconstructed with help from the ranks of the Opposition. Thurlow was authorised to approach the Bedfords, but in vain, for on the American question the King would yield no ground. The royal reply to the address was evasive, and close by the King's chair stood Benedict Arnold. Only the return of twenty-eight deserters saved the government from immediate defeat; but on 4 March a resolution passed the House which declared all who should advise or try to prosecute offensive war in America for the purpose of reducing the colonies to obedience by force to be enemies of their country. This was the end of the policy. Two days later Germain's successor notified the Commanders-in-Chief of the Commons' decision.

Yet still the Ministry remained, unshaken by the loss of Minorca and the

[1] Abergavenny, 51.
[2] Christie, 319–40.

imminent fall of St Kitts. North declared that he would stay until the House thought fit to remove him, and the Opposition was forced to advance from its defeat of the policy to the censure of the men themselves. On the 8th the government survived by only ten votes. Dundas, whose Scotch phalanx held the balance, declared that the government could not be carried on with this majority – a majority, as North told the King, where defeat would have meant the immediate removal of the Ministers.[1] Nothing except fresh blood could now save the Ministry. The Bedfords and Grafton had refused their services; Shelburne would not join a broad-bottom administration; and the King, having by the obstinacy of his prolonged defence expended every reserve which could cover his retreat, was now face to face with Shelburne and Rockingham. The Closet was about to be stormed.

The last hopeless resort was tried: Thurlow sounded Lord Rockingham. The reply was crushing. The Marquess claimed to speak for all the components of the Opposition, and his terms meant unconditional surrender: full power to grant independence to America; the full programme of economical reform; full power for Rockingham to name the Ministers and exclude all who were 'obnoxious'.[2] Still the King struggled in the net; and Robinson's lists showed further defections in the House of Commons. Rather than yield, the King hinted at abdication. On 15 March Sir John Rous, a Suffolk independent, was put up to propose a motion of no further confidence in the Ministry. The majority shrank to nine; and three days later another independent member, Thomas Grosvenor, informed the Prime Minister that he spoke for a group of country gentlemen who had resolved no longer to oppose the clear sense of the House of Commons. To North this was decisive. For years he had talked intermittently of resigning: now, almost too late, he spoke out firmly. 'The torrent is too strong to be resisted: Your Majesty is well apprised that, in this country, the Prince on the throne, cannot, with prudence, oppose the deliberate resolution of the House of Commons.' 'Your Majesty has graciously and steadily supported the servants you approve as long as they could be supported . . . Your Majesty. . . can lose no honour if you yield at length.'[3]

There was nothing to be done but abandon the present Ministers entirely and approach Rockingham and Shelburne. This was North's advice; but the King had already said that he would not treat personally with the leaders of the Opposition: if North resigned before he had decided on his course, 'you will certainly for ever forfeit my regard'.[4] But North was desperate. A motion for the removal of the Ministers was down for the 20th, and he believed

---

[1] Abergavenny, 51; G 3546.
[2] G 3551, 3555–6, 3565.
[3] Christie, 365.
[4] G 3567.

it might be carried: he would quit office under the unparallelled stigma of a vote in the Journals for his removal. From this disgrace he implored the King to save him; and by the afternoon of the 20th he had prevailed. When Lord Surrey rose to propose the removal of the Ministers, North rose simultaneously. After an hour or more of debate Surrey gave way; and Lord North announced the Ministry's resignation. The House adjourned at once. 'Good night, gentlemen', said North to the stranded throng at the door, 'you see what it is to be in the secret.' And stepping into his waiting carriage he rolled away into the gathering dusk.[1]

[1] Wraxall, II, 607. For the final struggles of the Ministry, see Christie, 340–69.

CHAPTER XXVIII

THE NEW BROOMS

1. *The Sack of the Fortress*

The Rockingham Ministry took office on 27 March 1782. Never had there been such a massacre. The new rulers were numerous and vengeful, and every place that could be cleared was needed. The fallen administration was 'shot by platoons and in corps'. Every Minister went except Thurlow; virtually the whole Court except the King's Bedchamber. In Dublin Lord Carlisle learnt of his dismissal as Lord-Lieutenant of the East Riding by reading it in the *Gazette*, a breach of the 'decent forms to be observed between gentlemen', and resigned the Lord-Lieutenancy of Ireland. The Lords of Trade were spared from the slaughter only to fall victims to judicious principle: Burke's bill to abolish the Board was revived, and Edward Gibbon was 'stripped of a convenient salary' which had promoted his comfort for the past three years.

The Secretaryships of State were re-organised, and the American Department abolished; but the Cabinet, instead of shrinking, was swelled from nine to eleven members through the inclusion of the Master-General of the Ordnance, the Chancellor of the Exchequer (separated from the head of the Treasury because Rockingham was a peer), and the Chancellor of the Duchy of Lancaster. Rockingham was Prime Minister and First Lord of the Treasury, with his guiding spirit Fox as Foreign Secretary; Shelburne took the other Secretaryship, in charge of domestic, Irish and colonial affairs; Richmond the Ordnance. Amherst lost his post as Commander-in-Chief to Conway, and his Lieutenant-Generalcy of the Ordnance to Sir William Howe. Middleton's wish for professional knowledge at the Admiralty was gratified by the elevation of Keppel to the head of the Board.

In the army, there were not many changes apart from the fall of Amherst. General Irwin was removed from the command in Ireland to make way for Burgoyne, who had filled his long divorce from military activity by composing a comic opera, and was now rewarded for his opposition to North with a Privy Councillorship and the command of a regiment. Carleton had already been ordered to relieve Clinton, and the appointment stood. Mathew was retained in the Leeward Islands and Campbell confirmed in Jamaica: neither appointment was a conspicuous political plum, or offered much except danger and disease. But for the dissident Admirals the day had dawned and the looting began. For Keppel, now the political head of his profession, there was promotion and a peerage; for Harland, who had refused to serve in 1779, promotion and a seat at the Board. Darby was ejected from the Channel fleet to make way for Lord Howe, who obtained an English peerage; and Barrington accepted the command of one of his divisions. Hyde Parker's resignation after his North Sea battle was rewarded with the command in India. Rodney was superseded by Sandwich's East India House opponent, Hugh Pigot, who like Harland became Admiral of the Blue and a member of the Board. Dismissals alone could not make vacancies for all the asking faces, and Keppel hoped to revive the sinecure of Major-General of Marines, which, as the King remarked,[1] 'will not increase his popularity though it may his dependents'. But Palliser, surprisingly, was spared. After an interval Fox demanded his removal from Greenwich. Keppel wanted to do it, but shuffled; and Shelburne saved him on the grounds that the right moment had passed.

In his own office Shelburne made a somewhat curious impression on Germain's old subordinates. He was one of the most intelligent Ministers of the century; yet Knox heard Sir Stanier Porten of the Southern Department say, 'God be thanked I am not to be under you again.' Knox had long ago been told by a predecessor[2] that Shelburne was the most difficult of all Ministers to please, and he found it was true. Drafts were endlessly revised, but despatches remained unanswered, and Knox could obtain no instructions for preparing drafts. Finally he was summoned to the 'Jesuit's' house in Berkeley Square on a Sunday night between ten and eleven o'clock with all the unanswered despatches, and refused to go. On taking office Shelburne had told Knox he would continue to employ him, and asked him to keep another member of the department away from him, as he could not bear to see anyone he meant to part with: 'a fair confession, I thought', says Knox, 'of weakness of nerves, notwithstanding all his bustle and high tone.' In the end Knox was turned out without notice two days after Shelburne had said he hoped he would continue.[3]

Rodney's recall was decided by the Cabinet at an after-dinner meeting eight days after the battle of the Saints. Keppel, who had long ago stood silent while Byng was condemned, is said to have opposed it, but to have let his own interest moderate his counsel, and to have insisted only that the recall should be put through a Secretary of State. This evasion of an unpleasant task was not unoticed by George III, for about the same time Keppel was

[1] G 3783.
[2] Sir Richard Sutton, who retired from an under-secretaryship of state with a baronetcy in 1772.
[3] Knox, 283–6. See also his *Extra-Official State Papers*, I, 21–4, 30–1, 38.

sounding Shelburne about removing Palliser, while refusing to be mixed up in it himself; conduct in both cases which the King despised.[1]

On 1 May the Secretary to the Admiralty penned the administration's first communication to Rodney. 'Lord Viscount Keppel', he began, 'having signified his Majesty's pleasure that Hugh Pigot, Esq, Admiral of the Blue, be appointed to relieve you in the command of his Majesty's ships in Barbadoes and the Leeward Islands, I am commanded by my Lords Commissioners of the Admiralty to acquaint you therewith . . .'[2]

Pigot, newly raised to the Board of Admiralty and the rank of full Admiral, had been a Rear-Admiral at the beginning of the war. He had benefited by the rapid wartime promotion without ever hoisting his flag, and to small experience as a captain he had added none as an admiral. Hitherto his main war work had been the organisation of a pressure group in favour of his brother Lord Pigot, illegally deposed from the Governorship of Madras, whose case the Opposition had taken up in 1777. This was the officer chosen to replace England's most successful Admiral.

Pigot hoisted his flag in the *Jupiter* to sail for the West Indies. But on 18 May arrived the news that Rodney had won the most complete victory of the war. Frantically the Ministers tried to undo their work. A King's messenger sped out of London that morning, and at two in the afternoon of the 19th he dismounted at the Port Admiral's office in Plymouth, having covered the road in twenty-eight hours.[3] He was too late: Pigot had gone. A cutter put out to chase him; but the *Jupiter* had vanished into the Atlantic, pursuing her inexorable course to Barbados.

Within four days the news of Hood's capture of two more ships of the line completed the tale of Rodney's success. 'You will find Rodney has taken some more ships', Sheridan wrote to Thomas Grenville in Paris. 'The unluckiness of his recall, I think, appears to increase with its ill effect; and people don't seem to fancy Pigott.'[4] Rodney's toll in the course of the war was now seventeen ships of the line destroyed or taken, with a Dutch, a French, and two Spanish Admirals. The Ministry could do nothing but put the best face on it. Before the hero returned he was created a peer of Great Britain, with a pension of £2,000, which on his death was settled for ever on the title. There was a peerage for Hood, and baronetcies for Drake and Affleck.

2. The Order of Withdrawal

The Rockingham government had policies as well as places: it was dedicated to the liquidation of the American War and the making of peace. The

[1] James, 357; G. 3676–7, 3699–3700.
[2] Mundy, II, 326.   [3] *Ibid.*, II, 307 n.
[4] Buckingham, *Memoirs of the Court and Cabinets of George III*, I, 32.

negotiations with America lay with Shelburne's department, and his envoy Oswald was rapidly translated to Paris to sound Franklin, while Fox's accredited envoy Thomas Grenville opened talks with the European belligerents. The way was long and difficult, and in July the death of Rockingham and the withdrawal of Fox from the Ministry left Shelburne as Prime Minister with the whole negotiation in his hands. While the Cabinet searched the thickets for a way out of the country's difficulties, it had still to bear the inherited burden of the war; and the course of the last campaign would powerfully influence the terms of the peace.

About their great line of strategy they came to office in complete agreement. The army was to be withdrawn from America, and part of it redeployed to strengthen the West Indies. The executive orders to Carleton were resolved on three days after the Ministry was established. He was to leave for America without delay to take over a unified command which would include Canada and Newfoundland; to evacuate New York, Charleston and Savannah; and St Augustine too if circumstances justified it. With the evacuated regiments he was to reinforce the West Indies as he thought necessary, and to ship the remainder of the troops to Halifax. If evacuation proved difficult or was prevented by an enemy attack, an early capitulation on terms which would secure the main object was preferable to an obstinate defence without a rational purpose. Carleton was authorised to inform the Americans of his intention to withdraw, and was promised a new peace commission so that he could negotiate on liberal terms if it proved expedient.[1]

Dining with a large party at Lord Hillsborough's Knox was surprised by Lord Denby calling in a loud voice, 'Knox, what are you going to do with all the troops you are taking away from Charleston and New York?' Knox replied he knew nothing about removing troops. 'No', said Denby, and swore he knew it, for one of the Cabinet had told him so. Knox retailed the conversation to Shelburne, and says that he continued: 'Your Cabinet, my Lord, is too numerous for secrecy, and especially as there are some in it who were never in the habit of keeping secrets, and they cannot resist the pleasure of the display of their importance.' His dismissal soon afterwards is not wholly surprising.[2]

For the West Indies no immediate measures seemed necessary: Rodney was already away with sufficient reinforcements, and for the future the Cabinet looked to Carleton's regiments from America. On learning that St Kitts and other islands had fallen before Rodney's arrival, Shelburne wrote to the Generals in the Caribbean urging them to keep Carleton

[1] G 3618; CO 5/106, pp. 1-13.
[2] Knox, 285.

informed of their situation. His letter to General Mathew is an odd mixture of incitement to enterprise and cautious reservations. But to Rodney, who had asked where to send the fleet in the hurricane season, no communication was made.[1]

The coming redeployment and evacuation of America was an operation so vast and secret that Shelburne ordered Admiral Digby to correspond with and receive his orders directly from a Secretary of State.[2] But more than a special chain of command, serious preparations were needed. None were made: no transports were prepared, nor any steps taken to redeploy the existing shipping for the great withdrawal. It was unfortunate, as Middleton admitted, that the Ministry had not taken office till the spring, with so little time to plan their measures; yet the fact remains that they had ordered the evacuation of the vast army in America with no thought to the means. It was not for want of advice. A few days after Keppel had taken over at the Admiralty, Middleton saw a newspaper report of the intended evacuation, and called on him to discuss it. He explained that the simultaneous evacuation of New York and Charleston with their cannon, provisions and stores would call for 85,000 tons of shipping or three times as much as was in hand. He suggested that the Charleston garrison should be left till the withdrawal from New York was completed: 40–50,000 tons of shipping would then be enough and could be obtained. In any event, he said, the American station would have to be warned to retain all their transports and convert their victuallers to troopships; water casks must be prepared; and provisions ready to sail from the British Isles for New York and Charleston must be diverted. But nothing was done. Transports and victuallers lay idle at Spithead for months, and were then allowed to sail fully laden for Canada and the West Indies with no orders to take part in the withdrawal. Stores and provisions were shipped to garrisons that were to be moved, tying up the transports and adding to the material which would have to be shifted or abandoned. By Middleton's calculation fifteen months' supply of stores were allowed to sail for New York and Charleston after the decision to evacuate them. These omissions, he said, lost a whole year in completing the withdrawal; and had the war continued through 1783 they would have prevented an offensive in the West Indies.[3]

The strategic implications of the withdrawal were also under fire. In Jamaica General Archibald Campbell expected the abandonment of the southern colonies to expose his homeward-bound convoys to heavy losses as they came up the American coast to feel for the trade wind: the effect, he told Knox, would be harmful 'to a degree beyond what the

[1] CO 318/19, f. 133; CO 137/82, f. 173; Mundy, II, 328.
[2] CO 5/255, p. 141.
[3] Barham, II, 47–50, 76–9.

speculative politicians have calculated'. The same thought had already struck Middleton, who pointed out that the dangers were augmented by the Spanish capture of New Providence in the Bahamas. He urged the immediate recovery of Providence, and the establishment of cruiser bases there and in Bermuda to protect the trade. After the evacuation of America there would be no port for cruisers on the coastline from Halifax to Jamaica, and he suggested the strange possibility of reoccupying Rhode Island. Nor was Middleton convinced that the abandonment of New York was of advantage to a West Indian offensive. Germain had suggested in his last memorandum on the American War that without America troops in the Caribbean would have no healthy summer station; and Middleton advanced the same idea. Only a limited force could act together in any place in the West Indies; but the climate and fighting would call for frequent reinforcements, which were best assembled and acclimatised in the healthy station at New York, with only a two-months' round trip for the transports to St Lucia.[1]

The news of Rodney's victory suggested immediately that troops evacuated from America might take the offensive in the Caribbean and recover the lost islands. But though the proposal was made on 21 May and expressed to Carleton as a hope on 5 June, no practical steps were taken to evacuate the rebel colonies. By the end of July it was clear to Middleton that the evacuation of New York could not be completed that autumn, and an alternative must be considered: the troops intended for the West Indies might be detached, leaving the remainder to winter in New York, while the surplus transports began the removal of stores to Halifax. He suggested bringing Pigot's fleet from the Leeward Islands to assist in the movement of troops, providing the equivalent of 6,000 tons of transports. The question was raised in the Cabinet on 2 August by Lord Ashburton; and it was agreed that Pigot should be ordered to bring his fleet to America in the hurricane season. The Cabinet still hoped that the whole force at New York could be removed before the winter with the help of transports from the St Lawrence, though it was improbable that Carleton could embark the families and effects of all the loyalists who wished to leave. Not that the Ministry felt any strong sense of obligation to the loyalists – Carleton's orders had made no provision for bargaining in their favour – but the new Secretary, Thomas Townshend, threw out the idea that Carleton might be able to hold on to some port and make the embarkation in stages. This vague hope characterises the whole plan, a plan based on orders for the Leeward Islands fleet which should have been given many weeks earlier. On 14 August Carleton was informed that an active war was now to be opened

[1] Knox, 188; CL, Shelburne, Vol. 151, Nos. 14, 17.

in the West Indies. He was ordered to embark all the troops which could serve there, assume the command in the West Indies himself, and take the offensive. Townshend gave him full liberty to make any alterations which he thought necessary in the execution of the plans: 'All that can be done on this side of the water is, to chuse an officer fit for the command, to point out the objects to him, and to give him full and ample credit and confidence in his measures for the attainment of them.' These were words which Germain might have used to Sir William Howe in the early days of the rebellion. But Germain would not have been content with this: he would have made strenuous efforts to provide the means.[1]

3. The Fleet in Home Waters

The Cabinet's usual summer preoccupation was home defence, and the new men had brought some ideas in their baggage. Richmond, on taking over the Ordnance, obtained engineers' reports on the defences of Portsmouth and Plymouth, and personally inspected those of Chatham. They were found unsafe against heavy cannon, and the Cabinet authorised the expenditure of £¼ million to make the three great dockyards as safe for the summer as time and circumstances allowed.[2] Shelburne revived an idea of the Elder Pitt: a fleet of transports maintained in constant readiness to carry troops wherever they were needed. He suggested hiring 20,000 tons of shipping to be stored, victualled and fitted for troops. The idea was good in itself, but the country's shipping resources were already under heavy strain, which the coming evacuation of America would increase. The Navy Board could obtain no bids for the hire of transports, and passed the requisition to the Board of Ordnance, who collected 5,000 tons of shipping by the end of July.[3]

The Ministers were allowed no breathing space before they were thrown into the problems of the naval campaigning season. While the Ministry was forming, news arrived of an expedition assembling in Brest; and it was also known that in Cadiz Guichen was about to bring home some Dutch East India ships and the San Domingo convoy, which had been delayed in the West Indies when de Grasse sailed for the Chesapeake. The Channel fleet was not ready for sea, but there was no major force to be feared in Brest, and at the beginning of April a dozen ships of the line which

---

[1] CL, Shelburne, Vol. 151, Nos. 15, 18; G 3771, 3862, 3864; CL, Sydney, IV, Ashburton's memo. to Townshend of 2 Aug.; Adm. 2/1341, f. 152; CO 5/106, pp. 57, 291–308, 314.
[2] CL, Shelburne, Vol. 136.
[3] Ibid., Vol. 151, Nos. 19–20.

were ready were sent out under Barrington to watch Brest and look for the expedition and the convoy. They were to cruise between Belle-Isle and Ushant till the 25th; and on the 20th a frigate sighted a French convoy escorted by two sixty-fours with a third en flûte. Barrington gave chase, and during the night Jervis in the Foudroyant, 80, overhauled and took one of the enemy sixty-fours. The ship en flûte, with 500 troops and naval stores, surrendered to the Queen, and twelve out of the eighteen transports were captured. The convoy was bound for India, and the losses, added to Kempenfelt's captures in December, were a heavy blow to the hopes of de Bussy.[1]

Before the main fleet could take up the watch it was learnt, first that la Motte-Picquet had slipped out of Brest to join Guichen, and then that Guichen's immensely valuable convoy had left the shelter of Ferrol and Corunna and fetched Bordeaux in safety.[2] This last news arrived on 7 May; and the same day Howe's orders to go off Brest were countermanded. In April the Admiralty had learnt that fourteen Dutch two-deckers were lying ready in the Texel to force their way down the Channel and join the French. The Flying Fish now came in from the Dutch coast, having seen the enemy anchored outside the Texel. Tromp in the Medway was evidently remembered; and while militia were hastily thrown into the Landguard fort off Harwich, Howe was ordered to the Downs to attack the Dutch fleet. He was off the South Foreland on 11 May; but on entering the North Sea his crews were struck down by the crippling epidemic of influenza which was sweeping across Europe, and finding that the Dutch had re-entered the Texel he returned to the Channel under Cabinet orders. A force under Sir John Ross was left to guard the North Sea, but it too was driven back to the Downs by sickness in the middle of June, and a weakly defended Baltic convoy was lucky to get home in safety.[3]

Another convoy was not so fortunate. The Franco-Spanish fleet sailed from Cadiz on 4 June under the command of Cordoba. As it worked its way northwards towards the end of the month it met a British convoy outward-bound for Newfoundland, and captured eighteen merchantmen. Early in July the Brest squadron of eight sail of the line joined the flag, giving Cordoba a fleet of forty sail of the line to command the mouth of the Channel.

Howe had sailed for the westward at the end of June to cover a Jamaica convoy which was due in the Soundings. Almost at once he learnt from

[1] G 3615; Adm. 2/1341, ff. 80, 85; Chevalier, 330–4; James, 366.
[2] G 3695; Adm. 2/1341, ff. 103–5.
[3] CL, Shelburne, Vol. 168, 17 Apr. from Keppel; G 3720–1, 3731, 3774, 3810–11; James, 367; Chevalier, 335.

neutrals that the Combined Fleet was in the chops of the Channel, and on 12 July he sighted it to windward south-south-east of the Scillies. He had only twenty-five sail of the line; and resolving to gain the windward position he boldly took his fleet by night between the Scillies and Land's End. La Motte-Picquet had given chase with the eight ships of the fast squadron, but finding himself out of supporting distance of the main fleet he was forced to draw back. '*Quelle journée, Monseigneur, nous avons manquée par la pesanteur des vaisseaux espagnols!*' he lamented in his report. It was not the only debt which Howe would owe to Sandwich's legacy of copper.[1]

Howe did not sight the Jamaica convoy; but a heavy gale drove the enemy off their station in the chops of the Channel as it approached, and Sir Peter Parker brought it safely home. This was a stroke of luck; yet the new Ministry had thrown one convoy straight into the arms of the enemy, while the Baltic fleet had been saved only by the passiveness of the Dutch. The new government was pursuing the same policy as their predecessors. Once again an inferior fleet had disputed the command of the Channel, while the superiority in the North Sea for which Middleton had pleaded had been sacrificed to the Western Squadron; for on the approach of the Combined Fleet five ships of Ross's North Sea squadron had been ordered to the Channel. The King mentioned 'the propriety of getting the fleet for the North Sea out as soon as possible for the defence of our northern trade'; and Middleton was in despair. The Dutch fleet was reported at sea again, with the apparent intention of going north about to join the French and Spaniards; and instead of the Atlantic convoys being brought round Scotland through a commanded North Sea, the whole strength of the home fleet was again being thrown to the west to form a force which could never hope to match the enemy. Two West India convoys were approaching the Channel, a Baltic fleet would soon be ready to return from Elsinore, a convoy for India and more than 300 ships for America and the West Indies was waiting to sail. Everywhere there was danger or delay. The failure to give early protection to the North Sea might prevent the Baltic trade from making a second voyage that year, while the Dutch safely escorted their own East and West India convoys into the open sea.[2]

4. *The Third Relief of Gibraltar*

Cordoba's Combined Fleet quit the Channel at the end of July to cover the siege of Gibraltar. The British government had known for some time that the enemy's main effort in Europe would be against Gibraltar; and ammunition, provisions and reinforcements were needed for the garrison.

[1] James, 369; Chevalier, 335.
[2] G 3817, 3820, 3849; Adm. 2/1341, f. 130; Barham, II, 52–4.

There was now a real need to throw the Home Fleet's strength to the west-ward; but because the North Sea had been sacrificed to the Channel in the preceding weeks, the Baltic convoy was still imprisoned at Elsinore, and with the Leeward Islands convoy approaching the north of Scotland the return of a force to the North Sea could not be delayed. A straight prefer-ence for the North Sea rather than the Channel was no longer possible: neither Gibraltar nor the northern trade could wait.

Middleton was summoned to the First Lord on 22 July, to learn that Gibraltar would be relieved as soon as the enemy quit the Channel. This was the first Middleton had heard of it, and guessing that the loading of the transports was not in hand, he asked if the Treasury had been warned. Keppel referred him to young William Pitt, the twenty-three year old Chancellor of the Exchequer, and on the following day Middleton attended a conference at the Treasury.

Pitt was in the chair. He showed the Comptroller a list of the supplies to be sent to Gibraltar, and asked how it could be done. The intention was to send the relief in September. Middleton greatly preferred the immediate despatch of a small squadron, which Keppel had proposed; and he pointed out that though nothing had been done to prepare and load transports, the bulky item of provisions was lying ready at Spithead in a convoy for New York, where they were not needed. There was now a surplus of provisions in America, and he suggested that the whole of the New York supply should be diverted to Gibraltar, and a vessel quickly loaded in the Thames with the mixed articles not supplied by contract. Two days later he saw Keppel again, and learnt more about the government's general intentions, including the transfer of troops from New York to the Leeward Islands. 'No plan, however, is yet settled to carry these measures into execution,' he noted; 'and what might be done, at this moment, with a few ships, cannot be executed, in a few weeks, with our whole force.' For the failure to prepare the Gibraltar supplies he blamed the numerous Cabinet and its ineffective chairman. Shelburne, he wrote, had not the weight or ability to obtain decisions: he lacked method, application, and knowledge of his job, and for lack of weight could carry no plan into execution. For lack of proper directions the Comptroller's work could not begin: he could 'get no fixed plan from any of the ministers, and therefore can lay none on my part, for preparation'.[1]

The Comptroller's plan for an immediate relief had the King's support, for the grand attack on the fortress was imminent; but Shelburne, pleading the technical question of the entrance to the Bay, dared not decide, and predicted that the Cabinet would find the decision equally difficult.[2] The plan was not

[1] Barham, II, 54–6, 74.   [2] G 3862–3.

adopted, and the relief was hung up for weeks while the Treasury and Ordnance assembled their cargoes. Keppel was proclaiming the need to bring home the Baltic fleet with its naval stores before anything else was attempted, and the general futility of looking beyond the problems of the moment. Shelburne turned to the Comptroller for better advice. Middleton now thought that the chance to relieve Gibraltar with a small force had been lost, and that when the transports were ready the whole fleet would be needed. But he suggested that the interval while the transports were loading should be used to bring home the Baltic fleet.[1] Probably as a result of this advice the Cabinet on 14 August resolved that Howe should enter the North Sea with all the ships which were ready, and cruise as far as the Naze of Norway to cover the inbound convoys. But later in the day doubt set in. The Cabinet began to wonder whether Howe could return from the northward in time to sail for Gibraltar by the first week in September, and instructed the First Lord that the plan should depend on Howe's answer to the question.[2]

Keppel went down to Portsmouth on the 16th, as Sandwich had sometimes done, to supervise the preparations. The weather was bad and work at a standstill; but from the 18th the refitting went ahead with speed, and when the First Lord returned to London on the 21st there was little more to be done but pay the men. But the Gibraltar transports were not yet assembled. The victuallers and storeships in the Thames were expected in the Downs on the 28th or 29th if they had a westerly wind to take them out of the river; but they would then have to wait for an east wind to blow them through the Straits of Dover.[3]

Keppel returned to London to find that Shelburne had decided to suspend the North Sea operation in favour of Gibraltar. On the 23rd Howe's North Sea orders were cancelled, and he was ordered to sail for Gibraltar as soon as the victuallers and storeships joined him. But the next morning the Cabinet veered again. Howe was now to reinforce the North Sea squadron to a strength of fifteen; and with these Admiral Milbanke would proceed off the Texel, make sure that the Dutch fleet was not at sea, and summon the Baltic convoy from Elsinore. But instead of remaining to cover its passage, he was to rejoin Howe with the first easterly wind.[4]

Milbanke saw the Dutch lying in the Texel, summoned the convoy, and returned as he had been ordered. The transports from London river also

---

[1] G 3877-8; CL, Shelburne, Vol. 151, No. 37 (wrongly dated Nov. 1782). The Duke of Grafton in his Memoirs ascribes this plan to Keppel, who of course had the task of 'selling' it to the Cabinet.
[2] G 3880-1.
[3] G 3895.
[4] G 3887, 3899, 3900, 3903.

passed the Straits, and on the 6th were off the Isle of Wight with a fair easterly wind. Had the whole convoy sailed at once, Middleton reckoned that they might have been at Gibraltar by the 20th, and home for an early autumn refit. But instead of being joined by the fleet at sea, the transports were brought in to Spithead. The fleet did not sail till the 11th, lost its fair wind, and took another month to fetch the Straits, by which time the main crisis at Gibraltar had long been weathered. In the interval before it sailed, the detachment which had returned from the North Sea lay idle for five days while the Baltic convoy was making its unprotected passage from Elsinore. 'There is fault or want of judgment or both somewhere', wrote Middleton, 'and the City will be in an uproar if the fleet from the Sound does not appear soon.... There can be no good peace if the war is not better conducted.' Happily the Dutch did not come out, and on 21 September the Baltic convoy was reported on the Yorkshire coast.[1]

'This last business', Middleton noted, 'is the worst managed of any in the whole war.' In the midst of these rapid changes of plan Lord Mulgrave had written to Sandwich from the Channel fleet: 'The whole of this summer's proceedings in our line must I think show your administration to great advantage.' About the same time an important letter about the peace negotiations arrived from Oswald in Paris; and when one recalls the Opposition sneers at Ministerial 'haymaking' in the August of 1779, it seems curious that August 1782 saw Shelburne's Cabinet scattered so wide that it would have taken a week to call a meeting.[2]

Two days after the relief sailed from Spithead, the enemy launched his great attack on Gibraltar. The siege was now in the hands of the duc de Crillon, the victor of Minorca. He had found that the Spaniards, with the experience of 1705 and 1727, saw no hope of taking the fortress by a land assault; and an orthodox naval bombardment on the sea flank of the defences would be crushed by the rain of bombs and heated shot from the British batteries. But with peace in sight the fall of Gibraltar had to be hastened, and a solution emerged. For the grand attack which was now intended, a French engineer officer had designed a special weapon: floating batteries of timber so thick as to be impenetrable by shot or bombs, and protected against fire by a pump-driven circulation of water. Ten were built, mounting 152 heavy cannon. Their fire was to be co-ordinated with that of the Spanish gunboats and

---

[1] CL, Shelburne, Vol. 151, No. 26; Barham, II, 66–7, 73; G 3931, 3939.

[2] Sandwich, IV, 424; G 3891. Thurlow evidently considered diplomacy to be no more a lawyer's province than naval strategy: on 19 September an urgent alteration to Oswald's commission had to be sent to Derbyshire so that he could attach the Seal to it. (CL, Sydney, Vol. V, Nos. 6–9). Cf. above, p. 399.

the batteries in the siege lines, bringing 398 pieces of ordnance to bear to crush the 86 British guns in the sector which the floating batteries were to attack.

Crillon was in haste. Though the first trial of the pumps had flooded the interiors of the batteries, he would not allow time to correct the faults: instead the water channels were sealed off except on the exteriors. On the evening of September 12th he ordered Admiral Moreno to attack on the following day. The notice was short: too short to co-ordinate the elements of the plan. No co-operation had been arranged with the Combined Fleet, which had arrived that very day, or even with the sloops and gunboats based on Algeciras; and no arrangements had been made to tow the batteries out of action to repair damage or extinguish fires. Nevertheless under threat of removal Moreno accepted his orders.

The grand assault of September 13th was a total failure. The floating batteries were anchored in too extended a line: they were exposed to excessive British fire, and the furthest of them were beyond the supporting range of the siege-line batteries, which in any case ran out of ammunition in the afternoon. At nightfall slow fires were burning in two of the batteries. They could have been extinguished if arrangements had been made for towing out action, but instead the batteries had to be abandoned and destroyed. At two in the morning a dozen British gunboats emerged from Gibraltar, and finding the remaining batteries unprotected by Spanish sloops or gunboats they attacked the southern end of the line, moving up relentlessly through the carnage to destroy the entire line of batteries.

So ended Crillon's hope of carrying the fortress by attack, and the siege reverted to a blockade. Gibraltar might yet have been starved into surrender; and the Combined Fleet of forty-nine sail of the line lay at Algeciras to prevent a relief. But the thirty-five Spanish ships were in lamentable condition, and Cordoba could not use them with confidence in battle. In contrast, Howe was coming south with thirty-four sail of the line, all coppered and with no barnacled laggards among them. The fleet had a first-rate commander whom it trusted, it was well trained, and the admiral had confided in his captains.

On October 10th a storm from the south-west struck the enemy fleet. One ship of the line drove ashore on the Spanish coast, another under the guns of Gibraltar, where it was taken, and a third was blown through the Straits into the Mediterranean. The next evening, while the enemy lay becalmed in Algeciras, a northerly breeze brought Howe into the Straits; but though four transports got in to Gibraltar, the rest of the convoy was carried into the Mediterranean by the currents through the transport masters' neglect of their instructions, and the fleet was forced to follow. Cordoba might have sealed the Straits against their return, but he was more concerned to recover his missing ship than to give battle; and pushing into the Mediterranean in search of it he enabled Howe to slip between the Combined Fleet and the Straits. He declined a close action, and on the 16th an east wind enabled Howe to summon the convoy from the African coast and bring it to anchor under the batteries of Gibraltar.

Thus the final relief of the fortress was accomplished. On the 19th Howe was away into the Atlantic ahead of the enemy. On the following day the Combined Fleet had the weather gauge, and he prepared to fight. But once again the enemy refused a close action, and eventually drew off and vanished. Howe detached eight ships of the line to the West Indies, and set his course for Portsmouth.[1]

5. The Comptroller Compares

Sir Charles Middleton had long maintained a correspondence on naval affairs with Lord Shelburne; and Shelburne's advent to office released a storm of paper from the Comptroller. It is easy to be wise without responsibility, and Middleton's hastily scribbled memoranda were written from the shelter of an administrative office; yet if his criticism of Sandwich is to be allowed any weight, his criticisms of the Rockingham and Shelburne administrations must not be discounted. Before the summer was out Middleton regarded his new masters with less favour than the old.

His diagnosis of the trouble was simple, and familiar: it was ministerial ignorance and incapacity. The bridge between conception and execution had vanished, for no one in the new administration knew the procedure for executing a strategic decision. The Cabinet was too large; Shelburne as Prime Minister lacked the weight, ability and application to carry a plan into execution; and the Secretaries of State were ineffective. He lectured Shelburne as North, with very different motives, had lectured the King. 'War is a comprehensive business; the minister who conducts it must think of nothing else.' The Prime Minister must grasp the whole detail of the war, or appoint reliable Secretaries of State. 'The want of a minister to connect

---

[1] Chevalier's account of the operations attributed the Combined Fleet's failure to engage closely to Howe's superior speed. But the British accounts make it clear that Howe was ready to fight these odds if the enemy were willing. It is curious that this was the man who had said in Parliament of Kempenfelt's brush with Guichen that his whole force should have been taken. It is one more instance of the varying worth of parliamentary criticism.

In defending the Preliminaries of the peace, Howe later said that his ships were in bad shape; and Shelburne claimed that he had complained of the fleet's discipline (Barrow, *Life of . . . Howe*, 170–1). But these assertions are entangled with the issue of the peace-terms, and probably with the animosity between Shelburne and Keppel. In the face of the fleet's success against a superior enemy, they must be treated with reserve.

and control the several departments prevented . . . every useful measure from being carried into execution.'[1]

He had always pressed for professional knowledge at the Board of Admiralty, but now that he had a professional First Lord his attitude to the administration was curious. In the autumn of 1782 he wrote thus to Shelburne:

unless the naval force is conducted in the Cabinet by professional knowledge, judgment and method, it cannot prove equal to the many services that will be expected from it. The misapplication of a single ship will be felt in the present contest, and it has been [due] to this omission more than any other that we are under present difficulties.

. . . and it is proper to observe how necessary it is to settle an early plan in the Cabinet for the application of the fleet, and to have every possible information laid before them before it can be concluded.[2]

The truth is that the professional element which Middleton had wanted on the Board was himself. He urged Shelburne in a long letter to bring the Comptroller to the Board, for it would, he said, immediately remedy the evil caused by delay in correspondence and transmission of orders between departments. To this ambition Keppel was not an aid but a hindrance: 'as the alteration . . . will naturally give jealousy to the first Lord as a *seaman*, though greedily embraced by every landman [sic] who may preside there, I should advise a delay of this measure till such an event takes place'.

The advantages which a Comptroller from the nature of his office must have in point of naval knowledge is so well known, that every first Lord of the Admiralty whether Sea or Land finds it necessary to consult him on every subject of moment. Should this alteration therefore take place, it will become less material than it has been hitherto, whether the first Lord be of the sea or land, and probably better of the latter kind if a very able one of the former cannot be found.[3]

On the eve of the peace, in January 1783, Middleton wrote of the difficulty of obtaining the co-operation of a professional First Lord in reforming the Navy Board:

That experience in the civil part of the office, which an unremitting application to the duties of my place has given me, must be as little in his possession as in that of a landman (sic), and the innovation which I consider a necessary part of the plan,[4] he will consider an affront to his skill, and a cheque on his conduct . . . till the business of the Navy Department is far advanced, it will be necessary, if my experience

---

[1] Barham, II, 56, 78, 296.
[2] CL, Shelburne, Vol. 151, No. 37.
[3] *Ibid.*, No. 39.
[4] I.e., the promotion of the Comptroller to a seat at the Board.

is to be turned to public account, that a landsman (*sic*), in case of a vacancy at the Admiralty be placed at the head of it. He should be a man of rank, and the design of his being offered that station, be candidly laid before him ... when the plan of reformation is once completed, the Admiralty Board may then take that professional form that may be judged most proper.[1]

In retrospect Middleton found much to be said for Sandwich: perhaps he found the choleric Keppel less patient of remonstrance. 'The military part of the service', he wrote to Sandwich in 1789 on a rumour that he had been offered the Admiralty, 'has since that time been brought to a proper sense of distinction between your Lordship's conduct and those that followed you in office.' 'Who', he wrote of civil reforms in the Admiralty, 'has so great a right to the credit of all this as your Lordship?' This may have been no more than the judicious buttering of a possible chief; but on his favourite topic of patronage he endorsed two drafts of old letters with these words: 'He was called a jobber, but they are all equally so, and indeed more so than ever I found him to be, though more secret in their manner.' 'All his successors, notwithstanding their great pretensions to a regard for the public service, have proceeded in the same way.' It was the age, not the man, which was at fault.[2]

[1] CL, Shelburne, Vol. 151, No. 53.
[2] Barham, II, 10, 30, 315, 316.

CHAPTER XXIX

THE SKY SUSPENDED

1. *The Last Autumn*

'It has been some time determined', Shelburne informed General Mathew, 'that a very effective war shall be carried on in the West Indies.' But when he wrote it was already the middle of August, and the plan to draw on America for a Caribbean offensive gradually merged in the general autumn planning. Early in September a winter reinforcement of eight ships of the line was allocated to the West Indies from the fleet which was about to relieve Gibraltar, and it was agreed that the German princes should be asked to make their troops in America available for any part of the world. By now the Ministers were casting their net more widely in search of enterprises to justify the abandonment of America. 'I beseech you to remember, my dear Mr Townshend', Shelburne wrote to his successor in the Home and Colonial Department, 'that the evacuation of New York can never be justified but by active measures elsewhere . . .' Some of the objects proposed were as diffuse as any for which North's government had been attacked. Shelburne lingered on the idea of seizing the Canary Islands; and a plan to renew the abortive expeditions against South America was put in train by the Cabinet, with a squadron of warships and several thousand troops. Middleton got a hint of it from Keppel, and at once sent Shelburne a list of the necessary preparations with a request for Treasury action.[1]

On 15 September a despatch arrived from Carleton, reporting the evacuation of Savannah and declaring that with the present supply of shipping Charleston could not be evacuated that year nor New York even in 1783. At the beginning of October Shelburne, considerably out of his depth, sent the Comptroller a questionnaire on future operations. What was the probability that Carleton had evacuated New York? If he had not, what were the best means of having it '*instantly*' done; and what offensive measures could be counted on at that season with the troops withdrawn? Could a force be fitted out at home in time to round the Horn this season? What could be done to succour India with troops and ships? Middleton replied that there was not the slightest possibility that New York had been evacuated; for however positive Carleton's orders might have been, there was the inescapable fact that the victuallers sent abroad had not been ordered to assemble

[1] CO 318/9, f. 197; G 3909–10; CL, Sydney, V, 10 Sept.; CL, Shelburne, Vol. 151, No. 27.

at New York, and it was now too late to withdraw this season without abandoning the immense accumulation of stores, baggage and provisions. By November, however, there should be 35,000 tons of transports at New York, enough to remove the stores and provisions in the course of the winter as a preliminary to the general withdrawal. Any offensive by Carleton's troops must therefore depend on what detachment he might decide to spare. As for the Pacific expedition, ships from England could round the Horn if they sailed at the end of November: 1,800 troops could be embarked in warships and coppered transports by then, and he admitted that they could do great mischief to the Spaniards by supporting their rebellious colonies. Nevertheless he strongly opposed the project. The first need was defence. Any ships sent to the Pacific were lost for the remainder of the war; and to part even with 50-gun ships, which he had always insisted ought to be in the line of battle, might forfeit the remaining islands in the West Indies. If Shelburne was sure of his object and determined to execute it, the force should be kept down to the scale of the abandoned project of 1780, and consist of 40-gun ships and frigates with only 1,600 to 1,800 troops, which could be supported by a larger force in the following autumn when New York had been evacuated and India and the West Indies were safe. We must not embarrass ourselves with too many objects at once, he wrote: this had been the misfortune of 1782. Unless much dexterity was used this winter to remove the stores from New York, 65,000 tons of transport shipping would be tied up abroad without a hope of any being returned to England. He dreaded the consequences: 'Your Lordship is not so much conversant with this business as I am, nor can you foresee the difficulties that must arise from it, if our future plans are not founded on firmer ground than they have been hitherto.'[1]

Middleton's advice evidently had some influence, for the secret expedition was reduced to 1,000 troops, and the escort to frigates with a single fifty-gun ship.[2] But the orders to fit out the warships were not given till December, and by then the situation had changed. Autumn after autumn the North Ministry had seen its initiative gradually extinguished as the enemy's superior resources took command of the situation, and this last year was no different. The enemy intended to renew the attack on Jamaica in 1783 by reinforcing Vaudreuil with thirty French and Spanish ships of the line from Cadiz. The preparation of this force was known in London by December. Eight more British ships of the line were ordered to be fitted out and sent to the West Indies, carrying two regiments for the Jamaica garrison; and the troops for the secret expedition were ordered to rendezvous at Barbados, in case they

[1] CO 5/106, p. 329; CL, Shelburne, Vol. 151, Nos. 29–31.
[2] G 4022; CO 318/9, f. 322.

were urgently needed for the defence of Jamaica or other islands. Middleton protested, as he had done a year earlier[1] when Rodney's reinforcements were being assembled, that Jamaica would be in great danger unless the naval reinforcement was decisively superior; and two more ships of the line were added before the end of the year.[2]

Once more, therefore, the New Year opened on the prospect of a great battle for the Caribbean. But with Gibraltar saved, diplomacy was at last on the move. On 30 November preliminary articles of peace had been signed between England and America, and on 21 January private information reached England that the preliminaries with France and Spain had been signed. An immediate armistice went into effect, the main reinforcements were cancelled, and the Ministers braced themselves for the political battle to defend the terms of the peace.

2. Final Operations in the Western Atlantic

Little remains but to relate how the American War ebbed away and Jamaica remained secure against the last efforts of the Bourbons; and how, in eastern waters far beyond the knowledge of the Ministers, Admiral Hughes and Sir Eyre Coote with the North government's reinforcements fought out the contest with Suffren to save the British dominion in India.

When de Grasse left the American coast after Yorktown, Washington had proposed an overland attack on Canada in conjuction with the French land forces which remained with him. But Rochambeau had verbal instructions to evade any such proposal, for it was no part of French policy that the Americans should establish themselves without a rival on the Atlantic seaboard. Without French troops the Continental army could not mount a serious offensive anywhere, and the northern states settled down to their usual

---

[1] Above, p. 448.
[2] G 4023; CO 318/9, f. 322; CL, Shelburne, Vol. 151, No. 51; Adm. 2/1341, f. 167. The reinforcements intended for the West Indies at the end of the year were as follows:

Ships of the line:

Detached by Howe, October	8
Sailed 7 December	1
Under orders at end of year	10
	—
	19
	—

Troops:

To sail early January with two of the above ships of the line: 1,500 men for Jamaica (68th and 81st Regiments).
To sail with the trade after 10 January, escorted by two other of above ships: 1,000 (for Barbados, provisionally for a secret service).

winter slumbers. The south remained equally passive. Rawdon had departed to recover his health after withdrawing the outlying garrisons; and in September his successor, Colonel Stuart, fought a desperate and indecisive little action with Greene at Eutaw Springs. The two forces then drew apart, and the British retired into Charleston. Greene's difficulties were as great as those of the British, and there was no more serious fighting on the southern front.

At New York Clinton was left throughout the winter of 1781-2 with almost no naval force to protect him. All his posts to the southward depended on his ability to reinforce them by sea: there were reports that a Spanish attack was intended against St Augustine and Savannah, and in the spring of 1782 their capture of New Providence in the Bahamas brought them uncomfortably close to Florida and to the homeward track of the Jamaica convoys. But New York could not be attacked without a fleet; and de Grasse was unlikely for the moment to disengage himself from the Caribbean operations against Jamaica. With the advice of a Board of General Officers Clinton resolved to spare 2,000 men from the southern colonies for Jamaica.

But much of Clinton's time in the expiring weeks of his command was taken up with loyalist problems. The failure to protect the loyalists in the Yorktown capitulation gave rise to fears that the serving loyalists, abandoned to vengeful enemies, might lose heart once for all. General Robertson suggested a proclamation threatening retaliation for injuries done to them by the rebels; and in spite of his prolonged opposition to the revival of civil government in New York, Clinton was even prepared to re-open the courts for the purpose.[1] The bitterness between rebels and loyalists, however, was such that there was little fear of committed loyalists going over to the enemy or being received by them. The more serious risk was that in default of British protection they would protect themselves. The war in America trembled constantly on the knife-edge between civilised conventions and atrocious barbarity: how precariously the decencies were preserved was soon made harshly clear.

To co-ordinate the operations of loyalist irregulars at New York, they had been placed under the control of a Board of Loyalists, under whose direction they raided and plundered the rebel coast in an atrocious spirit of reprisal. Early in April a rebel militia captain named Huddy, who was believed to have murdered a loyalist, was removed from a prison ship in New York under pretence of exchanging him, and hanged on the rebel shore of New Jersey with a notice pinned on his breast threatening one-for-one reprisals. Whether or not Huddy was guilty, the loyalists could produce a fearful list of atrocities against their friends. The Board of Loyalists had evidently authorised Captain Lippencote to commit the murder, though it

[1] CO 5/104, f. 198.

disowned him. Clinton was greatly distressed: he believed that the Board
had deliberately put Huddy through the ordinary prison, in order to involve
the army and navy and excite the war of indiscriminate retaliation for which
they thirsted. Their action had every prospect of success. Washington and
his council of war resolved to retaliate; and having received no positive
requital from Clinton he ordered the British captains who were unconditional prisoners in his hands to draw lots for a victim. The American officer
responsible for the choice allowed the lot to fall on an officer who was
protected by the Yorktown capitulation, and Captain Asgill of the First
Guards found himself under close arrest in readiness for the gallows if Lippencote were not handed over or brought to justice. But for Clinton to convict
Lippencote was not easy. The Board of Loyalists maintained that he was
not amenable to a court-martial, he refused to plead, and the court adjourned
while the Crown lawyers considered the case.

This hideous problem confronted Carleton when he reached New York at
the end of April. 'Upright, zealous, and attentive in the discharge of every
duty'.[1] he came in high hopes of conciliating the rebels. With determined
civility he reminded Washington that the rebels had been trying loyalists
for going over to the British since the passing of their Treasons Act; and he
pointed out the implications. In a civil war, he said, there could be no treason,
or each side would be able to frame its own laws to massacre the other.
His overture received the usual blank obstruction. Washington referred
him to the civil power; and the Governor of New Jersey referred him back
to Washington. In arresting Captain Asgill Washington had overstepped
the laws of civilisation and of war. He had seized a hostage without waiting
for justice to be denied; and through his agent's negligence he had violated
the Yorktown capitulation. The field officers of the Yorktown army
appealed from the Americans to the French, and both de Grasse and Vergennes interposed. Congress was already embarrassed by the case, and the
trial and acquittal of Lippencote enabled Washington to withdraw from an
awkward predicament. Carleton promised to pursue enquiries. But he
pointed out that the case arose from a series of reciprocal horrors perpetrated
by the New Jersey rebels and the refugees: men of liberal minds and high
office should rise above such vulgar malignity.[2]

Carleton had come to America convinced that if the great mass of
Americans could recognise their own interests, they would choose a reunion
with England on terms like those which had recently been granted to Ireland.
To negotiate this reconciliation was the great mission which had induced

[1] Major Wemyss in Sparks MSS., Vol. 22, p. 221.
[2] The British and loyalist documents on the case, with rebel depositions, are in
CO 5/105, esp. pp. 147, 291, 315.

him to cross the Atlantic again. But at the beginning of August his hopes were shattered by news that a general negotiation had opened in Paris, with the concession of independence a probability. This blow brought the Shelburne Ministry its first taste of an angry General, an experience its members had often rejoiced to see falling on Lord North. Carleton wrote at once to Shelburne for leave to resign his command, as he could see no prospect of being of further use. His recriminations to General Conway carried familiar notes: he had been hurried out of England to be a mere Inspector of Embarkations; he had been got out of the way of more favoured soldiers; he would serve no more out of Europe. By the end of the year his repeated request to resign led the Cabinet to order General Grey out to relieve him; but the war ended and the exchange was never made.[1]

As soon as he reached New York Carleton had realised that complete evacuation that year was impossible for lack of transports. He chose, therefore, to begin his withdrawal from the rebel colonies in the south, where two of his three posts were at the mercy of the first serious attacker. The evacuation of Savannah was completed by the middle of July, but it required the whole of Carleton's 10,000 tons of shipping. Even so it was only made possible by the use of canoes and boats on inland waterways, which carried off the Indians, negroes and refugees to St Augustine, whose evacuation had therefore to be suspended. The evacuation of Charleston would have required three times the tonnage used at Savannah, and could not be undertaken. In the meantime New York stood on the defensive. No further offensive operations on land were intended; but on the sea Admiral Digby was in some embarrassment about his cruising policy, for while, as Peace Commissioner, he had received a strong resolution of the House of Commons against the continuation of the American War, he had no orders as Admiral to desist from capturing rebel shipping. With Carleton's support he decided to continue.[2]

Carleton condemned New York as a bad defensive post, and in spite of six years of British occupation 'but very, very little obliged to art'. In the absence of a fleet he drew in his posts to tighten his perimeter; but he thought that half a dozen French ships of the line could drive him from the town and his main magazines in a few hours, and divide his force into separate parts. At the end of July thirteen French ships of the line were sighted off the Capes of Virginia; and though Digby had only a single

[1] CO 5/106, pp. 325, 365; CL, Shelburne, Vol. 68, p. 253. The candidate favoured by Richmond and Conway seems to have been General Dalling: a fitting counterpart to Admiral Pigot (G 3960).
[2] CO 5/106, p. 49, 211, 329.

sixty-four and two fifty-gun ships, he determined to defend the bar at Sandy Hook with a miscellaneous force.[1]

The French squadron had come with Vaudreuil from the West Indies. When both sides had dressed the wounds of the battle of the Saints and despatched their convoys, Vaudreuil had been able to slip away from the hurricane latitudes and make for Boston, where his squadron underwent a prolonged refit. A detachment of the British fleet followed at its leisure, unsure of the enemy's destination and towing prizes which retarded its progress. Pigot's situation was much to be pitied, wrote Hood, for he had 'no one about him capable of affording wholesome advice which, without the smallest imputation to him as he has been so long on land and never hoisted his flag or commanded a squadron before, I should think could not be unwelcome'. George III could now savour one of the pleasures of Opposition, the criticising of commanders: the delay in following the French, he wrote to Keppel, 'does not do great credit to the activity or decision of those that have and do command that fleet'.[2]

Pigot remained in harbour at New York till the middle of October, when he returned to the Leeward Islands, leaving Hood with twelve ships of the line to watch Vaudreuil. Early in November news reached Hood that the French and Spanish fleets intended to unite at San Domingo to renew the attack on Jamaica; and knowing that Vaudreuil would not be ready to leave Boston till the middle of December, he followed Pigot to the Caribbean to prevent the enemy concentration. There he stood guard over Jamaica till March 1783, grumbling that Pigot would not come down from the Leeward Islands to support him. But Pigot's position was difficult. Enemy forces were known to be coming from Europe, and though Hood was certain that they would come straight to San Domingo or Cuba, the garrisons in the Leeward Islands had shrunk so low that it was impossible to leave them to their own protection. At the end of the year five regiments in St Lucia, Antigua and Barbados could muster only 1,570 fit men between them.[3]

In Jamaica Archibald Campbell had never doubted that the attempt which had been stopped by Rodney's victory would be renewed when the hurricane season ended in November; but he did not allow the prospect to paralyse him, and kept up incursions on the Spanish Main to recover and protect the British settlements. These expeditions were conducted with the economy of force which Germain had always advocated: shoremen and Indians cemented with a few Provincials were enough for the purpose. Nevertheless, though a regiment from England had reached him in April 1782,[4] and 700

---

[1] CO 5/106, pp. 49, 267, 329; Adm. 1/490, f. 121.
[2] James, 359; G 3940.   [3] CO 318/10, p. 79.
[4] Fourteenth Regiment, in the convoy which sailed with Bickerton.

recruits in June, he asked to be made up to 4,000 effectives by the end of the hurricane season. This could not be done. To the very end the military situation in the Caribbean remained in the balance, because Carleton lacked the shipping in America to withdraw from New York and Charleston. Though Hood was in the offing and hoped for a naval battle, it must have been with relief that Campbell published the armistice on the last day of April 1783.

3. Hyder and Suffren

The last news from India which we recorded had arrived in April 1781, and told of Colonel Baillie's disaster in the previous September at the hands of Hyder Ali. Throughout 1781 and 1782 a ferocious struggle was fought for the empire of India; but news of its progress reached England slowly, and only now has the moment come to bring the story to its conclusion. Yet it will be remembered how the situation in the east deflected British resources from other tasks: how a squadron was drawn eastwards in the critical invasion year 1779; how in the latter part of 1780 the war with Holland abruptly ended the proposed Pacific expedition in favour of an attack on the Cape of Good Hope and the eventual reinforcement of India; how further reinforcements were drawn from England in the critical year of Yorktown to counter Hyder and Suffren; how a squadron under Admiral Bickerton was spared early in 1782 while the force to save Jamaica was being assembled. The British position in India was singularly vulnerable. The Company's forces were small and dispersed, and a relatively weak French intervention could turn the balance in favour of the country powers. France, a great military power, did not need her navy to defend her coasts as England did, and unless Brest was blockaded could act offensively where she pleased. Labourdonnais had pointed this out before the Seven Years War; and the East India Company had been so conscious of it as to believe that only neutralisation could save India.[1]

In America a handful of French regiments intervened with decisive effect. In India, much further from Europe and with no considerable European population, the leverage which such a force could exert was vastly greater. Few troops of the British army had ever served in India: operations on land were mainly the affair of the Company's European troops and sepoys, and the first regular troops sent by the North government were Lord Macleod's Regiment which sailed at the end of 1778. In January 1781, after Baillie's defeat, Sir Eyre Coote had only 1,600 Europeans in Madras, including two Company regiments. But as the war drew towards its close, the Ministry built up in response to enemy movements the largest force of British regulars

[1] See Richmond, introduction to *The Navy in India*.

which had ever served there. General Medows went on with four battalions from the abortive Cape expedition in 1781; and the reinforcements despatched with Admiral Bickerton in the last weeks of the Ministry contained a regiment of cavalry (the first European Horse to serve in India), two battalions of British infantry, and two of Hanoverians. The whole European force in India thus came to compare in size with the garrison of Jamaica. Ten thousand miles from home, these troops were the force which saved the Carnatic.

INDIA

Like the army in America, the force in southern India was dependent on the sea for its reinforcements, supplies and lateral movements. After the initial clash of 1778 the French fleet withdrew from the coast of India for two and a half years, and Hyder launched his attack without its help. But in January 1781, as Sir Eyre Coote marched to relieve the Carnatic garrisons beset by Hyder, Admiral d'Orves descended with six two-deckers and joined Hyder at Pondicherry. De Grasse and Washington in their different degrees were to present no more formidable combination when they united in the Chesapeake a few months later. Coote was at Cuddalore, utterly dependent on seaborne supplies; Admiral Hughes was at Bombay, assured that the French had brought no troops and oblivious of Coote's real danger. Had the enemy persisted, they could have starved the only British force in southern India into surrender. But, knowing that reinforcements were on the way from Europe, the Governor of Mauritius had ordered d'Orves to return by April with his force intact. Like d'Estaing in America, he quit the coast with his mission uncompleted, and two rice vessels reached Coote from Madras when he had been reduced to two days' supplies. The external threat removed, Coote launched the astounding campaign in which 8,500 Europeans and sepoys crushed ten times their numbers at Porto Novo.[1]

When the approaching monsoon ended the campaign in August, news of the war with Holland had reached Madras, seven months after its outbreak. Suffren was known to have reached Mauritius; and to forestall his attack it was necessary to deny him the use of Dutch bases, for Trincomalee in Ceylon was the only all-weather harbour in the Bay of Bengal. The British had no natural harbour on the Coromandel coast of India; and in the violent northeast monsoon from October to January no fleet could remain on the coast. Ships retiring to Bombay to escape the monsoon or refit after battle would leave the Madras coast at the enemy's mercy for several months. It had happened in 1759; and Hughes and Coote urged the Governor that the Dutch ports must be seized, and Hyder driven back from the coast and deprived of French support. Their advice was adopted. The Dutch mainland port of Negapatam was taken in November 1781, and in January a small force stormed the main fort at Trincomalee. But success was short-lived. Suffren was at hand, and a desperate struggle of eighteen months was to decide the fate of India.

If the British government's arrangements had been properly executed, Hughes would have confronted Suffren's eleven French ships of the line with twelve or fourteen; and the Rockingham Ministry might have inherited a victory in India to match Rodney's in the Caribbean. Commodore Johnstone had brought two ships of the line and three fifty guns as far as the Cape; the *Monarca* and a fifty-gun ship had followed him closely; and the *Sultan* and *Magnanime* sailed in June 1781. But greed, neglect and shortsightedness were to frustrate the concentration.

Though Johnstone knew Suffren's strength, it will be remembered that he adhered to the letter of his instructions and turned back from the Cape

[1] The following account of operations in India relies chiefly on James, *The British Navy in Adversity*; Richmond, *The Navy in India*; Fortescue, *History of the British Army*; and Harlow, *Founding of the Second British Empire*.

with two of his fifty-gun ships to escort some prizes to St Helena.[1] On his way he fell in with the 'fifty' which had followed him from home; and in the full knowledge that Suffren would give the French a superiority in the Indian Ocean, he ordered her to cruise off the Cape and Mauritius instead of hastening on to join Hughes. Her captain obeyed, perhaps not unwillingly, and taking two prizes he brought them back to St Helena, from which he sailed for the second time eight weeks after his first arrival. On his second passage he was taken by the French; and the odds east of the Cape lengthened from ten British two-deckers against eleven French to nine against twelve.

Captain Gell's *Monarca* had joined Hughes with a healthy complement after the shortest possible passage; the three ships forwarded from the Cape by Johnstone, which had left England before her, arrived three months later after a long and circuitous voyage, barely in time for the first clash with Suffren and with their crews ravaged by disease. But the *Sultan* and *Magnanime* were still absent. They had sailed a few weeks behind the *Monarca*, but had wasted time at St Helena and in towing a prize to Madras, and arrived on the last day of March 1782, 'more like hospital ships than men of war'. Such was the execution of ministerial designs on which the fate of India might depend.

The odds might indeed have been worse, for as soon as Suffren joined him d'Orves had sailed from Mauritius to attack Hughes before Johnstone's reinforcement reached him. Had he gone straight to Trincomalee he would have succeeded, but winds and currents carried him to the north of Madras. Hughes was able to return from Trincomalee, and the French found him lying under the Madras batteries with nine sail of the line.[2]

D'Orves had handed over his command to Suffren, who declined to attack the British under the batteries. But the clash was not long delayed, for Hughes followed him to sea, and fought the first of their five fierce battles. Suffren had about 800 guns against 600, and intended his rear to double on the British rear and crush it; but his second in command failed him, and after an indecisive struggle the fleets parted in a squall at dusk.

Thus Suffren's first bid for the command of the sea was foiled. Nevertheless he landed 3,000 French troops at Porto Novo without hindrance; and Hyder, who was so discouraged that he had begun to withdraw from the Carnatic, took fresh heart and resumed the offensive. With his help the French troops captured Cuddalore, obtaining a base on the coast and a supply port for Hyder. The conditions for a sustained French intervention had been achieved.

[1] See above, p. 390.
[2] Including fifty-gun ships. The convention deplored by Middleton whereby fifties were not used in the line of battle was not observed by the small forces in Indian waters.

Suffren had orders to return to Mauritius and refit, but he was of tougher metal than d'Orves; and recognising that withdrawal would be fatal to the alliance with Hyder, he remained in Indian waters. Hughes did not intend to renew the fight: his first need was to reinforce the weak garrison of Trincomalee, and though the two laggard ships from England had joined him, he did not intend to risk a battle which might force him to relinquish his object. But battle was forced on him. Suffren regarded no other operations as profitable till he had won a decision at sea; and on 12 April, while Rodney and de Grasse were fighting for Jamaica at the Saints, Hughes and Suffren fought off Ceylon for India. Again the results were indecisive, and Trincomalee received its reinforcement.

4. The Last Battles

Both sides were aware that the crisis had yet to come. For de Bussy's plan was in train to bring the Indian struggle to a climax, and the North Ministry's counter-move was unrolling.[1] One of the government's last acts had been the despatch of Admiral Bickerton with six sail of the line and a convoy of troops. Sailing in February 1782 he got safely away: the French reinforcement was not so fortunate. The second French detachment to sail was mauled by Kempenfelt and then driven back by a storm, and only two storeships proceeded to the rendezvous. When this force sailed again in April it fell in with Barrington, who took two ships of the line and drove the third back to Brest with its convoy.[2] Thus only about half of the ten ships intended for Suffren reached Mauritius, where the raging plague caused a seventy-four to be burnt as too pestiferous for service. The military force was also whittled down by Kempenfelt and Barrington, and still further reduced by a detachment left to protect the Cape from Bickerton; and at Mauritius hundreds more were swept off by the plague.

Both Hughes and Suffren knew that Bickerton was on the way, and Suffren determined to stake a throw on a third battle while the odds remained in his favour. Hughes was lying at Negapatam to protect that place and Trincomalee; and here on 6 July 1782 the fleets re-engaged. The fight was fierce, the casualties were heavy, the tactical results once again indecisive. Much now depended on speedy repairs. But instead of going straight to Madras, Hughes lingered at Negapatam expecting Bickerton; and when he eventually went to Madras and completed his repairs, Suffren was ready to strike again. Appearing off Trincomalee, he offered the garrison the honours of war for a speedy capitulation, and they surrendered virtually without resistance only two days before Hughes returned to their relief.

[1] Above, p. 437.   [2] See above, p. 478.

For the British the loss seemed disastrous. While the French now had a safe refitting base off southern India, Hughes had none nearer than Bombay; nor could he round Ceylon with a damaged fleet in the monsoon. Another punishing battle might therefore prove fatal; and defying the Madras Council he retired to Bombay, where Bickerton joined him.

To all appearances southern India lay at the enemy's mercy. But the calculations of oceanic strategy were as deceptive to the French as they so often were to the British. Expecting de Bussy, Suffren planned a decisive stroke against Madras for the spring of 1783, and to ensure a safe rendezvous with the reinforcement he withdrew from the scene of action to Sumatra. But the grander design miscarried. For at Sumatra Suffren learnt that de Bussy, who was due in September with ten sail of the line, had been delayed by the Mauritius plague. He could not be expected till February, and then with only four ships. The French government had hoped for a decisive contribution from the Dutch, who had eight two-deckers ready at home and seven in the East Indies. But though a force sailed from the Texel, it never passed the Cape but stayed to protect the colony. Nor did the squadron at Batavia stir. Perhaps it was deterred by Commodore Johnstone's false instructions to attack Java and Sumatra, of which the French obtained a copy; perhaps by the East India Company's attack in 1781, when China ships based on Bencoolen in Sumatra had swept up all the Dutch settlements on the west coast of the island. Here again a minor and apparently irrelevant offensive may have served to retain the initiative and exercise unforeseen pressure on the plans of the enemy.[1]

Thus Suffren was disappointed of Dutch help; nor could he wait at Sumatra for de Bussy's retarded junction, for by February Hughes and Bickerton might return with disastrous effect to southern India. He therefore took the risk of returning on his own to Ceylon, where de Bussy followed and joined him in early March. They did not know that peace was already spreading across the world. They knew only that with fifteen ships against eighteen they had no hope of a decisive naval victory. In its dying moments the North government had achieved a superiority in both the East and West India commands.

Yet the command of the water could still be held in dispute while de Bussy's troops delivered the decisive blow on land. Suffren had the greatness to see that the French army at Cuddalore, not the fleet at Trincomalee, now held the key to decision. Though the British fleet might appear at any minute, he rushed de Bussy's troopships to Cuddalore escorted by his coppered warships, and escaping interception by a hair's breadth returned to Trincomalee.

[1] For the Sumatra operations see Harlow, 136–40; for the false instructions, *Mariner's Mirror*, 1942, pp. 202–3,

The army at Cuddalore now consisted of 3,000 Europeans, 3,000 French sepoys, and 5,000 Mysore infantry and cavalry. Against these the British marched from Madras in April with 1,700 Europeans, 8,000 sepoys and 1,000 native cavalry. These might have been enough in the hands of Coote, but he died at the end of April, leaving General James Stuart in command. Stuart marched slowly forward and reached Cuddalore at the beginning of June. Five days were then spent in landing stores from the fleet, while the French rapidly entrenched a formidable covering position. This was attacked on the 13th, and though the losses were heavy Stuart dislodged the enemy and drove them into the town.

At this critical moment Suffren appeared. He had only fifteen ships against Hughes's eighteen, and 1,000 guns against 1,200; but unlike most French admirals of the day he was willing to expose his fleet for a great object. Hughes's fleet was short of water, and his best hope was to obtain the weather gauge and win a decisive victory which would release him to go in search of water and provisions. But scurvy had so ravaged his crews that though he had more ships and guns than the enemy he had fewer seamen. In a line-to-line engagement on 20 June the French inflicted heavier casualties than the British. Hughes then bore away for Madras in search of water, abandoning the command of the coast to the enemy; and Suffren landed 2,000 men to strengthen de Bussy.

The British army's situation was serious. Though it was obtaining cattle in plenty, the troops were tired and the enemy with their reinforcements much more numerous. A French sortie from Cuddalore was repulsed with loss, but everything depended on reinforcements. Stuart had summoned the force in the south of the Presidency, and in spite of the Governor Lord Macartney's counter-order Colonel Fullarton was marching up to his help. Whether Stuart would have been forced to retreat with the loss of his siege-train, or could have liquidated the French bridge-head in India with the help of Fullarton, was not to be decided. For on 28 June, with Fullarton within three days march, news arrived that five months earlier the Preliminaries of peace had been signed. The struggle had opened in a grey dawn at Lexington; its last shot was fired eight years later on the other side of the world outside a dusty town in southern India.

NOTE
European Troops in India

(1) At outset of fighting in 1780:
  1/73rd Highlanders (Macleod's) (now 71st)
  Madras European Infantry (later 102nd Foot)
  Company regiment from Bengal (later 101st Foot)

(2) Reinforcements which arrived late in 1781:

2/42nd Highlanders (now 73rd)
Fullarton's Regiment (98th – later disbanded)
Humberston's Regiment (100th – later disbanded)
78th Highlanders (now 72nd) – sent in May 1781

} Medows's Cape Expedition

(3) Reinforcements of 1782 (arrived winter 1782/3):

23rd Light Dragoons (Burgoyne's)
Sandford's Regiment (101st – later disbanded)
Rowley's Regiment (102nd – later disbanded)
Two Hanoverian battalions

CONCLUSION

CONCLUSION

1. The Peace

In the months between Yorktown and the battle of the Saints it must have seemed to many that peace could be achieved only on disastrous and humiliating terms. An army had been destroyed in America; all the British Caribee islands except Antigua and Barbados had gone, West Florida was lost and Jamaica seemed doomed. In India Hyder Ali remained in the centre of the Carnatic, French troops had landed at Porto Novo, and the reinforcements on their way with de Bussy might turn the scales decisively against the British power. Not only the loss of the American colonies but the total overthrow of the Peace of 1763 might be feared.

Yet that winter was only a trough in the changing fortunes of the war. Yorktown, which had caused the country to despair, was less a proof of British impotence than an uncovenanted mercy to the enemy. For the alliance was staggering under the burden of the war. Vergennes had made his preparations to sell American independence if necessary at a mediated negotiation, and the rebels themselves were at the end of their resources. The collapse of the enemy alliance, for which King George and Germain had waited as they continued the struggle, was no chimera: it was averted by Yorktown, but the internal stresses existed and in the skilful hands of Shelburne were turned to account.[1]

For the lonely Shelburne, unfitted to conduct a war, to manage his Cabinet or to explain his intentions, was better suited to the secret paths of diplomacy. With his vision of a future Atlantic trading community, he grasped that America was the partner in the enemy alliance to whom concessions should be made: to whom the wide plains beyond the Alleghenies should be opened, even at the expense of Canada's claim to the fur-trapping lands south of the Great Lakes; whose independence should be conceded without conditions if the speed of the negotiation required it. These surrenders made, England could contend for the restoration in the rest of the world of

[1] The negotiations are analysed from a British angle in Harlow: for the discussions on Gibraltar see esp. pp. 342–61, on which the following account greatly relies. See also Bemis, *Diplomacy of the American Revolution*, which perhaps underestimates the strength of the British hand in the negotiations; and Stetson Conn, *Gibraltar in British Diplomacy in the Eighteenth Century*, which attributes the Spanish failure to obtain Gibraltar to the designs of Vergennes (p. 236), but does not make sufficient allowance for the strength of English public opinion and the division in the Cabinet. For an admirable summary of the negotiations, see J. Steven Watson, *The Reign of George III*, 252–7.

the situation of 1763. In the American negotiators he was matched by shrewd, hard men for whom *raison d'état* was as decisive a consideration as it was for the more experienced French. Suspicious of Vergennes and alarmed by Spanish claims on the Mississippi, they pushed the negotiation on, relinquishing their claims to Canada and financial indemnity. The Preliminaries of 30 November 1782 were signed before Vergennes was informed; and though the signing did not in law remove America from the struggle, it was clear that they might quit the war in fact if France and Spain unduly prolonged their own negotiations.

The Bourbon Powers had indeed been protracting their negotiation through the summer, hoping that Gibraltar would fall to their September attack. Its failure and the arrival of Howe's relieving convoy a month later destroyed this expectation; and France opened negotiations in earnest. Though bound by treaty to support the Spanish claim to Gibraltar, she had no interest in Spain's recovery of the fortress; for Vergennes knew that the jealousy of England which it kept alive in Madrid was the foundation of the Family Compact. Nor was he happy to see the war prolonged. He feared that the situation was tilting against the Bourbons. Rodney's campaign in the West Indies had put an end to their factitious supremacy in the western Atlantic, their navies' morale was low, and a total silence from the commanders in India suggested that de Bussy's stroke had gone astray. Even if the war situation had looked more promising it might have been unwise to prolong the struggle; for the French finances were collapsing, and the ambitions of Austria and Russia required the Bourbons' attention in Europe. The Spanish Court, however, saw things in a different light. They desperately desired to gain Gibraltar and to expel the interloping British from the Gulf of Mexico, the 'waterfront' of their decaying American Empire[1]; and they professed an optimism about the next expedition against Jamaica which Vergennes could not share. France now stood pinched between Spanish intransigence and the rising confidence of England.

For in the British Cabinet itself divisions were appearing as the crisis of the negotiation approached. Shelburne, with the support of Pitt, Thomas Townshend, Grantham and Thurlow, favoured the rapid conclusion of peace even at the cost of Gibraltar. The King agreed: he regarded the loss of the American colonies as a betrayal by his people, who had thrown over the great object of the struggle when the House of Commons had voted against the war in America. He counted on the East and West Indies to restore the country's prosperity and was opposed to sacrifices in those areas for the sake of Gibraltar. Shelburne for his part may even have regarded the fortress as a liability which permanently damaged British relations with

[1] Harlow, 342.

Spain; for he had been impressed by Richard Cumberland with the idea that 'no accommodation can be sincere as long as the fortress is withheld'.[1] But Keppel and Richmond would have none of it. Rather than lose Gibraltar they would fight on; and as the negotiation proceeded they drew Grafton, Conway and Camden into their camp.

Caught between Spain and England, Vergennes soon found himself obliged to consider buying Gibraltar for his ally with a French possession. When the suggestion was first made by Spain, he greeted it with indignation; but the same idea was soon to be put forward by Shelburne in London. Vergennes was anxious to break the deadlock in the negotiations before the meeting of Parliament on 27 November, and on the afternoon of the 20th his emissary Rayneval re-appeared without warning in London. Shelburne saw him at nine that evening, and they talked into the small hours of the morning. On his own responsibility and with the King's approval he told Rayneval that England would consider the cession of Gibraltar in return for restitution by Spain of all her captures (Minorca, West Florida and the Bahamas), with the addition of either Porto Rico or one of two groups of French islands: Martinique and St Lucia, or Dominica and Guadeloupe. France might be compensated with the Spanish part of San Domingo.

On the following afternoon Shelburne faced the Cabinet with these proposals. The meeting was stormy, with violent opposition from Keppel and Richmond. They had swallowed the American terms a few days earlier, and were in no mood to give way to the Bourbons. But Shelburne carried the waverers. Vergennes for his part could not be expected to receive the new proposals with enthusiasm; but Rayneval had been persuaded by Shelburne, and succeeded in persuading Vergennes, that the survival of the present British Ministry was of vital interest to France, and depended on a tolerable peace. Vergennes set to work on the Spanish Ambassador in Paris; but a seven hours' conference was needed to bring the tormented man to reason. At last Aranda put down on paper a compromise proposal: if France would yield Dominica and Guadeloupe for Gibraltar, Spain would give up Minorca; but he insisted that she must keep West Florida, and that Britain must abandon her settlements on the Main. With these proposals Rayneval returned to London, where he arrived in the early hours of 3 December.

But in Rayneval's absence English opinion had hardened. For the secret of the new proposals had leaked out. The City was clamouring against the proposal that France should acquire Spanish San Domingo, and the whole

---

[1] G 3919, 3962, 3984, 3987, 4004, 4021. That Cumberland's advice was given weight in Ministerial circles is suggested by the presence of a copy of his memorandum among the papers of Lord Walsingham, who was Under-Secretary in the American Department and in 1786 was offered the Madrid Embassy.

country was violently opposed, as Hillsborough and Stormont had maintained it was,[1] to yielding Gibraltar on any terms. Now even the King began to veer. He was against another year's war and would have closed with the new offer if it could not be bettered, yet he greatly preferred St Lucia and Martinique to Guadeloupe with Dominica, which was a captured British island. The Cabinet was brought to agree to the offer, but insisted that if Spain retained West Florida she must pay for it with Trinidad. Even this agreement was reached only after a bitter eight-hour wrangle. The Cabinet was now split into two almost equal halves; and in a heated statement to the King Richmond declared that he had agreed to the American terms only in order to stand the firmer against France and Spain: Guadeloupe was negligible, and nothing could compensate for the loss of Gibraltar, 'the brightest jewel of the Crown'.[2]

Vergennes was stunned by the new developments. But as Shelburne had guessed, he could not afford to imperil the conclusion of peace without a further effort, and he now put forward two new propositions. First, France might add St Lucia to Dominica and Guadeloupe; and since this would make Martinique insecure, she would exchange that island with Britain for an equivalent in India or the West Indies. Alternatively, if the British government would confidentially inform the French what they would offer Spain to drop her claim to Gibraltar, France would undertake the negotiation with Spain on the British behalf. King George would have preferred the first proposition if he could have found an equivalent to yield for Martinique, for he believed that peace would be incomplete unless we got rid of 'this proud fortress' of Gibraltar, the source of constant lurking enmity with Spain.[3] But no equivalent could be offered by which England would not be the loser; and the Cabinet, taking up the second proposition, agreed to make the roundest possible offer to Spain. If she would forget Gibraltar, she should have Minorca and both the Floridas.

Vergennes placed this offer before Aranda; and to his astonishment and relief the Spanish Ambassador accepted on the spot. So the peace was concluded. With Holland a final settlement was not reached till 1784, but it followed the pattern determined by the Great Powers. France recovered St Lucia, but of her conquests in the Lesser Antilles she retained only Tobago. In Newfoundland she recovered the islands of St Pierre and Miquelon, with an extension of her fishing rights along the west coast; in India her trading posts were restored, but she did not recover a military or political footing as she had once hoped. Spain gained the most in terms of territory: not Gibraltar, but Minorca and West Florida which she had captured, and

[1] Above, p. 372.
[2] G 4005, 4007, 4009.
[3] G 4020–1, 4034.

East Florida which she had not. In return she restored the Bahamas to Britain, and acknowledged the British right to cut Honduras logwood within defined boundaries. Holland who had contributed least to the allied war-effort, gained nothing. Indeed she was lucky to retain Trincomalee, which Britain would have retained if France had appropriated the Cape. England retained Negapatam on the mainland of India, obtained the right to navigate and trade freely in the Spice Islands, and refused to discuss the question of Neutral Rights which had brought Holland into the war.

The peace was made, and Shelburne had now to defend it in Parliament. He had worked in secret. His colleagues resented their exclusion, and he had not explained his far-reaching hopes that a new mercantile understanding would emerge from the settlement with America. Keppel, soon to resign, made a last vain protest against the Bourbon peace. He argued that the 109 ships of the line in service could fight on against the 123 French and Spaniards, many of which were in a deplorable condition; could win a decisive battle in the West Indies, pull down the naval power of our enemies, and obtain a better peace. Shelburne called on Sir John Jervis to combat the argument; and the future victor of St Vincent produced perhaps the most unrestrained indictment of the navy's condition which emerged in the whole course of the war. He argued 'the crazy state of our ships', the neglect of the officers and indiscipline of the men, the wretched state of the dockyards, the supineness and corruption in the departments; and, on a strategic plane, the improbability of forcing the enemy to decisive battle. Is this a credible picture? It bears no resemblance to the fleet with which Hood had manoeuvred at St Kitts and Rodney at the Saints, or to the Channel fleet with which Howe had relieved Gibraltar. Inevitably ships deteriorated towards the end of a long war, but the enemy were in worse case than the British. Almost at the same moment off San Domingo Sir Samuel Hood was writing that, formidable though the enemy were, 'we should never again be in so good a condition for recovering the nation's honour, as at this present moment nothing is wanting, I am very confident, to effect it, but unanimity at home and a regard to whom the King's fleets and armies are trusted'.[1]

Keppel quit the Ministry as soon as the preliminaries were signed. Richmond remained at the Ordnance, which he professed to regard as a purely military post, but withdrew from the Cabinet. 'I know', he wrote to a friend,

that this country wants peace and that after the waste of men and money we have had, that further exertions must be difficult to make; but as by the Treaty with America

[1] Keppel, II, 403–4; CL, Shelburne, Vol. 72, p. 523; G 406, 40642.

we had in fact agreed with her there was little doubt but we should soon have detached her from France or at least have had in her a very cool enemy. I am persuaded that this circumstance must have operated on France, and that her fleet and that of Spain were in a very bad condition, whilst ours was more numerous and in better order than it had been at any period. Under these circumstances I think that if we had stuck to our first and better terms we should have had them, or that if our enemies had been obstinate we had the fairest prospect in the course of next summer of striking some essential blow against their fleet, besides attacking the weak possessions of Spain already much distressed by the rebellion in her provinces.[1]

This reasoning follows to a remarkable degree the view once held by George III and Germain, though the King had since abandoned it in his bitterness at the surrender to America.

Richmond's disgust was focused on the yielding of Trincomalee and Tobago; but the peace terms were not the only reason to mistrust the government. Shelburne had excited the fears of conservatives with a radical programme of internal reform which made even Fox look like a comparatively safe man. He had no feeling for the sense of the House of Commons, and in spite of warnings he believed that his majority was secure. Fox was waiting to exploit the miscalculation. On 17 February the debates on the peace treaties began, and a week later Shelburne resigned after defeats in both Houses. Once more the King faced an alliance of the main Opposition parties, determined to force their way into office. For six weeks he refused to accept the inevitable, and the country was virtually without an executive; but early in April 1783 he sent for the coalition's leaders. On the 26th of that month a new Secretary of State wrote his first despatches to the commanders in the Leeward Islands, belatedly announcing the cancellation of the South Sea expedition. For their different reasons both Mathew and Pigot must have read them with curious feelings. For the signature at the foot of the page was North's.

2. Reflections on a Lost War

In the first days of the Rockingham Ministry a friend of Charles Fox had met one of Rochambeau's aides de camp in Ratisbon. They discussed the American War. 'No opinion was clearer', the Frenchman said, 'than that though the people of America might be conquered by well disciplined European troops, the country of America was unconquerable.'[2]

[1] Duke University MSS., XVIII F (27 Jan. 1783, Richmond to the Bishop of Exeter: printed, from the Richmond papers, in Olson, The Radical Duke, 193–4). Cf. General Haldimand: 'My soul is completely bowed down with grief at seeing that we (with no absolute necessity), have humbled ourselves so much as to accept such humiliating boundaries'. (Riedesel Memoirs, II, 169).

[2] CL, Shelburne, Vol. 34, No. 2 (16 April 1782, John Trevor to Fox).

This was true, and if England had been opposed by a united population, her effort to recover the rebellious colonies would have been vain from the beginning. She might indeed have destroyed the Continental Army, occupied all the centres of population, and dispersed the rebel assemblies. But what would have followed? The causes of the rebellion might have remained, and the bitterness of the civil war would certainly have survived. Guerrilla fighting might have been kept up indefinitely till Britain tired of the contest and withdrew from a country she could not govern, leaving a very different America to emerge from the anarchy.[1]

Yet though it may be that Britain never evolved a constructive political plan, her military effort was based on a better reasoned concept than mere reconquest and policing by her handful of regular troops. She relied, as General Robertson had said, on helping the good Americans to overcome the bad: the British army would break the power of the rebels, and organise and support the loyalists who would police the country.

The reader may feel that the loyalists have not been sufficiently examined. Yet we are faced by a society in turmoil and confusion. Were there errors in the political handling of the Americans? We enter the nightmare world of loyalist literature: a looking-glass world in which rebels are fiends incarnate, and the British generals avoid victory in order to line their pockets with bribes and plunder or to favour the political Opposition at home: a world in which Shelburne conducts his peace negotiations to promote his stock-jobbing, and even the loyalist ranks are infiltrated by highly placed fellow-travellers of the rebels. If Thomas Jones can claim on one page that a Drogheda massacre at Fort Washington would have ended the war, and on another that a general emulation of Carleton's leniency to prisoners would have been decisive, how shall posterity judge? How could run-of the-mill soldiers cope with the situation? It seemed impossible to satisfy the loyalists, persecuted, robbed and bitter, and at the same time to conciliate the rebels. General Howe attempted to hold the balance, and disappointed every group.[2] The loyalists complained that he was too lenient to the rebels; the troops that he was too kind to the civil population as a whole; the population that he was lax in protecting them from the troops. The problem needed a strong and imaginative administrator. The revolution was an unprecedented event, and no guidance could be sought from history. Only a Viceroy of genius, with his hands freed from the direct control of military operations in the field, might have risen above the tide of spiritual disorder which engulfed New York.

---

[1] There is an interesting discussion of this in R. R. Palmer, *Age of the Democratic Revolution.*

[2] Howe's problem is discussed in Anderson, 232–3.

It is certain that the loyalists were not a majority, nor were they evenly distributed. But the British government relied on war-weariness (of which there were ample signs) to make the bulk of the population subside with relief into acquiescence. And had they destroyed the organised armies of the rebellion they might well have succeeded.

Yet was it ever possible to destroy the rebel armies? It has been argued that Washington had only to lie back in the mountains and avoid battle; and that the British, dependent on navigable rivers for their communications, could not penetrate the country far and fast enough to force him to fight. 'In such a country as America', the Duke of Wellington was to write, 'very extensive, thinly peopled, and producing but little food in proportion to their extent, military operations by large bodies are impracticable, unless the party carrying them on has the uninterrupted use of a navigable river, or very extensive means of land transport, which such a country can rarely supply.'[1] But Wellington was thinking specifically of operations based on Canada; and before Saratoga Washington gave Howe several opportunities to destroy the main body of the rebel army.

It is generally assumed that even if Britain had an opportunity to reconquer America in the first two years of the war, it ended at Saratoga: that thereafter the rebels, with victory behind them and the promise of supplies from their European ally, were able to hold their own; while the British, over-extended and deprived of their command of the seas, allowed the strength of their American offensive to ebb as they struggled to defend their other possessions. But this is an over-simplification. When the King and Germain persisted in the struggle against mounting difficulties, they believed that victory was still possible, and that the effort was proportioned to the stakes. And there were good grounds for their hopes.

If England could have won the command of the oceans, the game would have been in her hands. France would have been unable to deploy her military power beyond the seas; and England, after sweeping up as many of the French and Spanish islands in the Caribbean as she thought necessary to her prosperity and security, would have been free to concentrate her military resources in America. With another 10,000 men and the assured command of American waters, even Clinton should have been able to destroy or paralyse Washington's army. The seizure of the Hudson Highlands, or a strong offensive in Virginia, could have made it impossible for Washington to detach against Cornwallis in the Carolinas; and freed from the necessity of holding his own force together or plunging forward in pursuit of Greene, Cornwallis might well have consolidated his hold on South Carolina and expanded methodically northwards. What he needed was security from outside

[1] Gurwood, *Selections from the Wellington Despatches*, No. 879.

intervention to enable him to disperse his regular battalions, support and supervise his militia, and hunt down guerrilla bands with his mobile columns. Whether the victory would have proved worth winning in the long run is a speculation which the historian of the war is not obliged to face: it is enough that it could have been won.

But all this depended on maritime superiority, which proved elusive. Decisive naval victory was rare in the days of sail; and in the past two wars it had taken several years of sustained pressure to wear down the enemy's resources and establish a clear control of ocean communications. In the American War attrition was a slower process, for the French government's resources were not depleted by a land war in Europe. Moreover the two Bourbon powers, whose fleets had been worn down in succession in the past contests, entered the American War almost together. Against these odds it was out of the question to maintain the close and sustained blockade of Brest which in the Seven Years War had been both a substitute for battle and a means of forcing it. Still less was it possible to challenge the combined fleets of France and Spain at their main point of effort in European waters.

Yet even without the unqualified and general command of the sea, it might have been possible to retain a high degree of strategic initiative. Though the Royal Navy's efficiency had been eroded by peace, over-confidence, and political feuding, its past victories gave it the moral advantage over the enemy, who never shook off their consciousness of it; and in spite of French efforts in the years of peace, the administrative and planning machinery of the British navy remained inherently better. Germain and George III strove to win the initiative by boldness and surprise, and to gain a local superiority in a vital theatre which would lead to victory.

There were difficulties in the way: difficulties of space, time and weather. The spring expeditions were held up by slow preparations and contrary winds until the enemy fleet was ready to threaten their passage, so that further delay was imposed to await the protection of the Channel fleet. Thus Clinton's reinforcements for 1779 arrived so late as to give him reasons for a barren campaign; Garth's fresh regiments for Jamaica in 1780 arrived too late to feed the offensive on the Spanish Main; and their escorting squadron with which Rodney might have snatched a victory in the Leeward Islands arrived when the opportunity had passed. Uncertainty and miscalculations about the enemy hampered planning: ignorance of d'Estaing's destination in 1778 yielded the initiative to the enemy; miscalculations of French plans in 1779 led to a naval inferiority in the West Indies and prevented the switching of troops to Clinton; uncertainty in 1780 enabled the French to wrest a superiority in the western theatres while Sandwich refused to reduce the home fleet. The uncertain communications across the Atlantic frustrated the Admiralty's intention to reinforce the Leeward Islands from America in 1780. All these difficulties weighed heavily because England had no margin of force to redress an error; for as Sandwich once told an officer, the misplacing of a single ship became a grave misfortune.

Only one thing could have relieved the pressure. The navy's strategic reserve was the home fleet. If the risk of invasion could have been defied and more ships detached abroad, the local superiority which England needed could have been achieved. But the fear of invasion haunted Sandwich, the Admiralty and the country. It was this which prevented the early despatch of Byron in 1778 to counter d'Estaing in America; which delayed the despatch of Rodney in the autumn of 1779; which prevented the strengthening of Graves and Walsingham when they sailed in 1780. A second danger in European waters also drew the navy's strength irresistibly into the defensive: the threat to the Mediterranean garrisons. The first winter relief of Gibraltar and Minorca delayed the refitting of the Channel fleet, and thus the departure of Graves to America in pursuit of Ternay; and the second relief under Darby delayed the despatch of reinforcements to Graves on the eve of Yorktown. The final relief which sailed in September 1782 would have been impossible if the Home Fleet had been further reduced for the sake of overseas theatres. Germain and the King resisted the constant pressure to over-insure in the English Channel, and it is probable that without their intervention losses in the West Indies would have been still heavier; but not till 1782 was the superiority for which they had been striving achieved in the Lesser Antilles.

A sustained strategic boldness requires mutual trust between the leaders and a solid foundation of popular support. Perhaps Lord North was excessively nervous of his parliamentary majority; yet the internal tensions of his Cabinet and the public suspicion which surrounded Germain and Sandwich made it impossible to be sure that the country would accept an occasional reverse as the price of boldness.

The cautious and disjointed strategy which resulted was echoed by the timidity of the commanders in America. The decision to use a large army against the rebels had been based on the need for a quick victory, and its only justification would have been a succession of rapid and decisive blows to destroy the military and political organs of the rebellion: for a slow and remorseless grinding in which military victory in the field played no part, the great army would have been an expensive and vulnerable tool. But to achieve victory a spirit of enterprise was needed. 'Happy the army in which an untimely boldness frequently appears', wrote Clausewitz; and among the younger officers in America there were seeds of bold and aggressive leadership. But among the Generals only Cornwallis showed himself to be a bold commander in the field; for Burgoyne was a mere gambler with 'more sail than ballast'. And at the very top there was petrification. While the American commanders were products of a revolutionary situation in which timid men did not rise, learning the trade of war as they practised it, with everything to lose by defeat and everything to gain by victory, Howe and Clinton were members of a stable political community who had arrived and could not be shaken from their perch. They had only to play the game safely to draw their emoluments and retain their position. Their fertility of invention was spent in devising reasons for inaction.

In the Cabinet the leading opponent of boldness was Sandwich. Jealous of his department's autonomy, he also shared his naval colleagues' obsession with the idea of invasion; and to this fear was added a personal fear of blame as misfortunes accumulated. This was not the stuff of which great war ministers are made; and Sandwich became the chief advocate of a policy which yielded the initiative to the enemy and could only have led to disaster if it had not been resisted. Nor was he an easy colleague in a co-operative enterprise. Yet his merits were considerable. The political contentions which marred his twelve years at the Admiralty, and the bitterness born of defeat, were to deny him recognition of his department's great administrative achievements. For the successful navy of 1782 was his creation.[1] 'Our natural rivals', runs a memorial of 1783 among the Shelburne papers on the peacetime navy, '. . . bending their whole force to the creation of a fleet that has for its bases extensive, invaluable sugar colonies, compared with which our West Indian islands are but mole hills, have advanced with hasty strides towards an equality with us, which equality they doubtless would more nearly have gained, but for an exertion on our part, that must astonish every person that considers it, and that would indeed have been impossible in any circumstances, but those of a war that threatened our existence as a nation.'[2]

In Germain Sandwich faced a hostile critic of his department and the chief opponent of his strategy of conservation. The American Secretary's sanguine temperament drew him always towards an aggressive strategy. It might be argued that in this war optimism was not the most necessary attribute in high places: that it was more necessary to withdraw from the war by an act of political discretion than to wage it in a spirit of military optimism. But the initiative in diplomacy did not lie with Germain: his task was to wage the war, and he was convinced of its necessity. More than anyone he ensured that the war was not reduced to a crippling defensive, leading

---

[1] See his memorandum on the navy of 1782 in Sandwich, IV, 361–4.
[2] CL, Shelburne, Vol. 72, p. 237.

to the loss of every colony and to defeat in detail throughout the world. He was not a great war minister, yet both as an administrator and planner he had much to commend him. In a more popular cause, and against odds less heavy, he would have won a place in history at least as respectable as that which is held by the Pitts, Dundases and Castlereaghs of the wars against Revolutionary France and Napoleon.

3. *The Aftermath*

In March 1783 the Lieutenant-Governor of Gibraltar invested General Eliott with the Order of the Bath. The artillerymen who had served the guns of the fortress through nearly four years of siege prepared an emblematic firework for the night: it celebrated the defeat of Spain's chief ambition, but it might equally have celebrated the peace as a whole. America, for whose recovery England had endured so much, was gone for ever, and a valuable Mediterranean base and trading port had been lost at Minorca; yet the losses in the West Indies were light, and in the Indian Ocean England had emerged with greater advantages than she had won in 1763. 'The more I reflect', wrote the King, '. . . the more I thank Providence for having through so many difficulties, among which the want of union and zeal at home is not to be omitted, enabled so good a peace . . . to be concluded.'[1]
. . Yet though the peace as a whole was infinitely less damaging than might once have been expected, the loss of America was a fearful defeat. The King tried to console himself with the thought that separation might after all be for the best: 'knavery seems to be so much the striking feature of its inhabitants that it may not in the end be an evil that they become Aliens to this Kingdom'.[2] But it would not work. Though he announced the American treaty to Parliament with dignity, all who heard him were struck by the choke in his voice as he spoke the word 'independence'.
    The impact of the defeat was profound. 'If it shall please God to prolong my life to another war some years hence', wrote Lord Hood, 'I shall look to the event of it with fear and trembling, unless by the all powerful inter-ference of the Divine Providence, we become an united and rational people.'[3] It was not the memory of the political feuding which dismayed the country, but a general disgust with the established politicians. 'Unhappy England', a nobleman had written after Yorktown, 'bankrupt in genius as well as other resources does not offer one man . . . capable of preserving the Empire. An exuberancy of declamatory eloquence is to be found in either House of

[1] G 4081.   [2] G 3978.   [3] G 4062.

Parliament. But an individual where experience, judgment, integrity, sound discretion unite is not the produce of this season.'[1] This feeling was general, and it attainted the leaders of the Opposition as well as Lord North and his colleagues. And for the first time the official classes had begun to question the fabric of the Whig oligarchy. The losing struggle had tested the system and exposed its weakness. Was it right that the administration of the army should be at the mercy of a haphazard and occasional organisation implemented at the King's pleasure? That the public purse should support a huge system of sinecures and patronage? That public indignation could be ignored in the House of Commons? That knowledge of finance in a public servant should be a matter for derision?[2]

From the outbreak of the next struggle the war machine began to undergo important changes. From 1793 there was always a Commander-in-Chief to supervise the army's discipline and training at home, and the Secretary at War was relegated to a financial and administrative role with powers more clearly limited and defined. Permanent military districts brought regiments constantly under the eye of a general officer. In the same year a Secretary of State for War was created, to direct the army's operations and speak for it in Cabinet and Parliament.

In the years of peace William Pitt began the huge task of administrative reform. Perhaps the pre-eminence accorded to him in war and peace owed something to the feeling that under Lord North the country had been 'ruined by distinct Departmental Ministers'.[3] His reforms had their roots in two Commissions instituted by North in the course of the American War. When Burke introduced his bill for economical reform in 1780, North had promised his assistance to investigate the public accounts. A parliamentary Commission was formed; but North also created a statutory Commission which, though attacked by the Opposition because it was composed of officials, was a more effective instrument. It was empowered to examine witnesses on oath, and its chief objects were first, to examine current accounts and secondly, to recommend speedier accounting procedures, so that reasonably accurate statements should be available if required by Parliament, and that balances in hand at the end of the year should be immediately available for spending.[4] In the next seven years the Commission wrote fifteen long reports, which Pitt published as parliamentary papers and made the basis of his efforts for administrative reform.

The operational experience of the war was also remembered. The tactical

[1] Lothian, 412.
[2] On the last point, see Binney, 255–6.
[3] Lothian, 412.
[4] Binney, 9.

lessons were observed not only in England but on the Continent.[1] Though handicapped by the rigid training of the rank and file, British and Hessians had proved adept students as the fighting went on. Always superior in the open, they soon learnt to fight on equal terms in close country. Provincial units such as Simcoe's and Tarleton's marched as fast and struck as suddenly as the best of the rebels; but the ordinary regiments of the line also incorporated the rifle and polished their open order drills till they were capable of beating the Americans at their own game. British officers returned home convinced that fire-power was everything and the shock of the bayonet obsolete, and a struggle ensued between these proponents of a more open flexible tactical order and those who stood by the Frederickean close order. In Germany, too, returning officers were influential, among them Captain Ewald of the Hessian Jägers, with many tactical successes against the Americans to his credit, who rose to be a lieutenant-general, wrote works on light infantry, and served with distinction in the French Revolutionary Wars. Some of the best soldiers who emerged in Prussia's struggle with Napoleon had served in America; and men like Gneisenau brought back the seeds of heresy from which a regenerated army was to grow after the defeat of the old order at Jena.

The war was remembered with horror by the statesmen who had shared in its direction. Ex-opponents of North eagerly supported internal enemies of the French Revolution in Europe: Burke and William Windham the French emigrés, and the Grenvilles the Dutch royalists. But no one who, like George III and Dundas, had held responsibility in the American War, would touch them. When Lord Grenville promised great results in 1799 from the help of the Dutch population, Dundas shook his head: 'I cannot forget the American War, where we were so miserably disappointed in the promised and expected co-operation.'[2] A year later the King recalled the immensity of the supply problem when he opposed the expedition to Egypt: 'if means were not taken to supply the troops as completely as the army in America had been by Lord North's Treasury, he should consider them as devoted to famine and destruction'.[3]

One lesson, however, was misapplied. The American War had been largely fought and decided in the West Indies. And when the struggle with France was renewed the Cabinet turned without hesitation to that theatre. The flower of the army was drawn irresistibly away from the periphery of Europe to perish among the fevers of the Antilles.

[1] See Fuller, *British Light Infantry in the Eighteenth Century*; Curtis, *Organisation of the British Army* . . .; Fortescue, IV.

[2] *Dropmore Papers*, V, 215.

[3] Matheson, *Life of Lord Melville*, 290.

4. The Fates of Men

The end of the war did not bring the total eclipse of the men who had waged it. Neither Germain nor Sandwich returned to Cabinet office; but North, though perhaps tired of the responsibilities of power, came back with Fox in 1783 for the sake of his followers. The clean sweep of the tarnished men was not completed till 1784, when Pitt assembled his Cabinet; and then Fox and Shelburne were annihilated equally with North. Yet many of North's old colleagues escaped political extinction. Stormont, who served in the Fox-North Coalition, was Lord President of the Council in Pitt's Cabinet in 1794. Lord Gower, purged of guilt by his resignation in 1779, served with Pitt for many years as Lord President and Lord Privy Seal, and became a Marquess. Thurlow and Wedderburn monopolised the Lord Chancellorship for eighteen years. Amherst reappeared as Commander-in-Chief when the struggle with France was resumed in 1793. Most of North's able under-ministers went on: Jenkinson and Dundas to high political office and earldoms, Eden to a distinguished diplomatic career and a barony. Middleton, as Baron Barham, succeeded to Sandwich's old position at the head of the Admiralty in the year of Trafalgar.

In the navy total eclipse was difficult. Hyde Parker achieved it when his ship foundered on the voyage to take up his command in India. But for those who survived there was no retirement. Sir Peter Parker, of Charleston and Jamaica, worked his way up by mere longevity to the head of the list, and died in 1811 after eleven years as Admiral of the Fleet. But others lived on more splendidly. From the Admirals and Captains who had served in the dark years of the American War emerged the great school of seamen who held Revolutionary France in check. The most remarkable survivor was Lord Howe. After four years as First Lord of the Admiralty in Pitt's Ministry, he returned on the outbreak of the next war to the command in the Channel, and in 1794 beat the Brest fleet on the Glorious First of June. He retained the confidence of his seamen to the end, and when the fleet mutinied at Spithead in 1797 he was sent down to reassure the crews and bring them back to their duty.

Two Admirals who shared the honours of the First of June received Irish peerages: Thomas Graves, whose failure off the Chesapeake had ruined Cornwallis, and Alexander Hood, whose altered log-book at the trial of Keppel had made him unjustly notorious. Graves was badly wounded and retired with a pension; but Hood, as Lord Bridport, succeeded Howe in the Channel command, and instituted the close blockade of Brest which became the foundation of subsequent success. He was followed in the Channel by two distinguished captains of the American War, Jervis as

Earl of St Vincent and William Cornwallis, the General's brother. The Mediterranean, which became the twin pillar of British supremacy, was commanded in turn by Lord Hood, Hotham and Jervis. When the war was renewed in 1803 their burden was taken up by two men who had been young captains under Sir Peter Parker on the Jamaica station: Nelson till his death in battle at Trafalgar, and Collingwood till he died at sea from unremitting toil five years later.

Of the Generals only one went on to greatness, though field officers like Charles Stuart and John Moore rose to fill their place. Burgoyne withdrew largely from political life after the fall of the Fox-North Coalition, wrote a comedy, and begot four children by a popular singer. Clinton refused an Irish barony in 1783 on the ground that Keppel, Howe and Germain had been advanced two steps in the peerage[1]: he died as Governor of Gibraltar in 1795. Sir William Howe served as a district commander in England in the next war. But Cornwallis within a few years became Governor-General and Commander-in-Chief in India, where great political and territorial changes were under way, with Archibald Campbell as Governor of Madras and Medows giving his cheerful and self-sacrificing service. When Cornwallis came home Pitt's war ministry leant on him heavily, and he became in turn Master-General of the Ordnance, Viceroy of Ireland, and plenipotentiary for negotiating the Peace of Amiens. In 1805 at the age of sixty-five he reluctantly accepted a second appointment as Governor-General of India, and died the same year at Ghazipur.

Of the three statesmen most closely connected with the war, Lord North was the only one to be recalled to high office, and his dismissal in 1783 (accompanied inevitably by a ludicrous anecdote) was the end of his official career. For the rest of his life he acted with the Opposition against Pitt, his followers in the House dwindling till by 1788 they numbered only seventeen. By then his eyes were failing, and his last years were passed with never-failing patience and good humour in total blindness. In 1790 his aged father's death brought him at last the Guilford title and the wealth from which his father had always refused him an adequate allowance. But he did not enjoy them long. Two years and a day later he died of dropsy at the age of sixty.

It was a sad end for a man who in his own way had been a distinguished politician. He belongs to that strange procession who reigned under the classical constitution at the Treasury: Walpole, Newcastle, the Younger Pitt and Liverpool. All but Pitt were once ridiculed as venal avoiders of trouble or mere figureheads. Yet of none of them was this just. In that conservative oligarchy a stable executive was achieved by careful conciliation of interests

[1] CL, Clinton, to C. J. Fox, after 10 July 1783.

and balancing of rewards. North formed his Ministry after a decade of unstable politics; and he held it together for twelve years with the support of the King and the House of Commons. His tragedy was that the second half of his administration was burdened with a contentious and unsuccessful war for which his very qualities unfitted him; and he left a legend of ineptitude which is only half the story.

Of the two men on whom his failings threw the main burden of the war, Sandwich largely retired from public life on the fall of the Ministry. He lived mainly at Hinchingbrooke, and died in London a few months before Lord North at the age of seventy-three. Throughout his long career as diplomatist and statesman he had remained on the army list, and died the senior general in the army. In the days of his eclipse he was regarded with affection by men who had served him. Middleton was not alone in remembering him. The rehabilitated Palliser, in undisturbed possession of Greenwich, wrote a few days after the armistice asking permission to have his old chief's portrait painted. He intended to leave it to the Hospital as a testimony 'of my remembering to the last days of my life your Lordship's friendship and kindness to me, as well in my days of adversity as prosperity'. The portrait by Gainsborough still hangs at Greenwich; and the Royal Marines possess an Opie painted three years later by subscription of the officers, 'your own children, brought into the service or promoted by your Lordship'.[1]

Germain retired with a peerage; but malice was not silenced by his fall, and there lay before him 'one of the last and most painful trials of his life'.[2] Lord Carmarthen[3] moved in the House of Lords that his presence while under the sentence of a court-martial would be derogatory to the honour of the House; and the motion was repeated on the day when the new Viscount Sackville took his seat. Carmarthen was privately applauded by his friend Lord Pembroke for resisting the countenancing of Sackville's cowardice and sodomy; and there is little doubt that the old enmities of Minden were still at work, for the two men were friends of the Ligoniers and Pembroke had once been aide-de-camp to Granby. But their actions were the less excusable since both had been content to serve at Court till 1780 with the North administration. It was too much for the Lords to stomach. Personal attacks on a Minister in office were one thing, insults to a private person another. This was 'a motion cruel and ill-mannered, not becoming one man of quality to another; at the same time an unpardonable insult to the Crown'; 'in every light odious, and tended to destroy the

[1] Sandwich, IV, 425.
[2] Cumberland, *Character*, 20.
[3] Afterwards 5th Duke of Leeds.

best prerogative of the Crown, that of pardon'. Germain thought of challenging Carmarthen after his first speech; but as Walpole wrote, 'it is not a *cas combattable*. It is more offensive than if it was'.[1] On taking his seat and enduring Shelburne's crocodile tears and the vulgar abuse of Richmond and Abingdon, he replied with temperance and generosity.

Lord Sackville lived three more years, and continued to speak regularly in Parliament, dividing his time between Stoneland, Drayton and Pall Mall. In the country he lived the life of an old-fashioned squire, reproving the choir's singing on Sunday, helping the unfortunate, and entertaining his friends with lavish hospitality. He struggled to forget the resentments which his misfortunes had accumulated, and he did not find it easy. When Lord Carmarthen was given office by Pitt at the end of 1783 he refused his support to the new administration, in spite of the pleas of Pitt, Thurlow, and his nephew the Duke of Dorset.[2] On his deathbed he struggled to extinguish one last grudge before he took the Sacrament. We must leave him at the last to his friends; and though resentment had betrayed him to moments of passion, yet a friend could assert that it had not spoilt his nature. 'The same Providence that gave him strength to endure', wrote Richard Cumberland, 'laid afflictions upon him to put that strength to the trial: I am warranted in saying they neither hardened his heart, depressed his spirit, nor soured his temper. . . .'

Cumberland was with him two days before he died, and gives an account of Lord Sackville's last words to him when he took the Sacrament. 'You see me now', said Sackville, 'in those moments when no disguise will serve, and when the spirit of a man must be proved; I have a mind perfectly resigned and at peace within itself . . . Tell me not of all that passes in health and pride of heart, these are the moments in which a man must be searched; and remember that I die, as you see me, happy and content.'[3]

It may well have been true.

---

[1] Carlisle, 572, 576; Walpole, *Last Journals*, II, 496; Herbert, *Pembroke Papers*, 195. Carmarthen's account is in the Leeds Political Memoranda, 53–8. Other peers who joined in this attack were Chatham (son of the war leader at the time of Minden), Southampton (Fitzroy, who had brought one of Ferdinand's orders to Sackville), the Duke of Rutland (Granby's son), and Derby (Burgoyne's nephew).

[2] Sackville, I, 80–4.   See also Valentine, 485.

[3] Cumberland, *Character*, 15, 23. His last years are also described by Wraxall.

APPENDIX

THE ARMY

Dispositions of Cavalry and Infantry [1]

Effectives of all ranks: including Provincials and Germans unless otherwise indicated

	April 75	Sept. 75	Mar. 76	Dec. 76	Aug. 77	Feb. 78	Oct. 78	July 79	Mar. 80	Sept. 80	Mar. 81	Sept. 81	Mar. 82
Cavalry (South Britain)	3,322	3,330	3,253	3,192	3,085	3,143	4,388	5,378	5,866	5,860	5,835	5,844	5,803
Infantry (South Britain)	7,290	9,145	10,319	9,673	10,783	11,328	16,864	17,649	19,249	20,783	19,091	21,914	21,865
Militia (South Britain)	—	—	—	—	—	—	32,213	33,573	36,287	36,973	30,500	36,440	36,606
TOTAL (South Britain)	10,612	12,475	13,572	12,865	13,868	14,471	53,465	56,600	61,402	63,616	55,426	64,198	64,274
Additional Companies raising for the infantry	—	—	—	2,763	2,031	3,408	3,020	3,282	4,588	3,438	2,583	3,023	3,247
North Britain (i.e. Scotland)	1,745	1,831	2,300	2,043	2,116	2,132	4,354	4,954	5,651	7,102	5,856	5,850	5,892
Embarked for service	—	—	—	‖358	—	—	—	—	6,194	3,637	6,203	4,868	5,872
Jersey	174	332	303	280	269	264	840	1,359	1,332	2,182	2,132	2,776	2,761
Guernsey	169	175	172	172	162	162	743	1,226	1,342	2,099	1,922	2,214	1,795
Africa	157	109	84	64	64	116	116	437	333	208	343	270	270
Gibraltar	3,064	3,085	3,188	3,142	3,141	3,110	5,031	4,930	5,874	5,786	5,666	5,560	5,336
Minorca	2,168	2,193	2,243	2,223	2,210	2,199	2,183	2,151	2,134	2,132	2,077	2,035	2,035
East India (excluding East India Company troops)	—	—	—	—	—	—	1,099*	1,009*	1,009*	1,245*	1,210	1,099	1,062

Medows expedition	—	—	—	—	—	—	—	—	—	—	—	2,784
West Indies and on passage	1,983	1,976	1,937	3,145	3,315	1,860	1,751	8,119	9,290	11,153	9,745	10,087	8,756
North America	6,991§	10,502§	14,374§	20,741‡	23,694‡	50,156§	39,637	35,942	33,466	32,149	30,531	35,641	34,463
Under orders for North America	—	—	6,957	—	—	—	—	—	—	—	—	—	—
Convention Army†	—	—	—	—	—	6,277	4,175	3,617	3,617	3,617	2,794	2,684	1,535
Canada	—	—	6,835	7,767	—	6,647	7,507	7,471	7,471	7,471	8,976	8,976	10,225
GENERAL TOTAL including militia	27,063	32,678	45,130	54,631	57,637	77,878	112,239	131,691	142,386	147,152	135,464	149,282	150,310
Wanting to complete	3,521	2,842	14,663	10,311	7,305	?	?	?	?	?	?	?	?

* On passage.
† The troops under the Convention of Saratoga were not considered to be prisoners of war and continued to be included in returns.
‡ British troops only
§ Including Canada.
‖ Under orders for Great Britain.

[1] From Lord North's return-books in the William Clements Library: the figures are the latest known in England at the date given. The Irish Establishment is omitted, as I have not found any continuous series of Irish returns.

Men raised for the British Establishment, 1774–80

These figures were compiled by Jenkinson before introducing the army estimates in December 1780. They exclude militia and fencibles.

Sept. 1774 to Sept. 1775 3,575 of which none were for new levies
Sept. 1775 to Sept. 1776 11,063 of which 2,124 were for new levies
Sept. 1776 to Sept. 1777 6,882 of which none were for new levies
Sept. 1777 to Sept. 1778 23,978 of which 12,984 were for new levies
Sept. 1778 to Sept. 1779 16,154 of which 5,576 were for new levies
Sept. 1779 to Sept. 1780 15,233 of which 8,392 were for new levies

76,885   29,076

Provincial Rank and File in America

Dec. 1777	3,738	Dec. 1779	6,757
June 1778	4,628	Dec. 1780	8,201
Dec. 1778	6,326	May 1781	8,151
June 1779	6,504		

(WO 34/139, f. 133.)

West Indies Reinforcements

Regiments sent from the British Isles, October 1776 to February 1780, with their wastage on passage. Recruits for regiments already in the West Indies are not included.

Destination	Embarked	Regiment	Rank and file embarked	Died on passage Number	Died on passage Percentage
Jamaica	1776 Oct.	Dalrymple's	491	9	1¾
Jamaica	1779 March	79th	1,007	83	8⅛
Jamaica	1779 Nov.	88th	758	25	3¼
Leeward Is.	1779 Dec.	89th	683	40	5¾
Leeward Is.	1780 Jan.	90th	701	94	13¼
Leeward Is.	1780 Jan.	91st	710	160	22½
Jamaica	1780 Jan.	85th	643	40	6¼
Leeward Is.	1780 Jan.	86th	683	60	8¾
Leeward Is.	1780 Jan.	87th	674	37	5½
Jamaica	1780 Feb.	93rd	667	111	16½
Jamaica	1780 Feb.	94th	710	179	25⅛
Jamaica	1780 March	92nd	710	94	13⅛

Totals for the above twelve regiments: 8,437 embarked
7,506 landed
932 died on passage
11 % average loss

The lowest losses are among troops sent fairly early in the winter; the highest, among troops who sailed after December and were delayed on passage.

Five more regiments were sent to the West Indies before the end of the war.

(Add. MSS. 38345, ff. 16–17.)

A Consignment of Camp Equipment

The equipment listed below was shipped in two transports in April 1780, and is reproduced as a typical shipment to the Western Atlantic.

	For General Vaughan (Leeward Islands)	For General Clinton
Private tents with poles, pins etc.	4,826	4,875
Bell tents with poles, pins etc.	132	392
Drum cases	220	520
Powder bags	110	266
Hatchets	1,826	4,922
Kettles and bags	1,826	4,892
Canteens	8,412	22,858
Haversacks	8,412	22,420
Camp colours	132	312
Axes		6
Scythes		240
Lots Forage Cords	For Seventeenth	240
Picket ropes	Light Dragoons	30
Water buckets		48
Great mallets		12
Picket posts		180

(WO 34/124, ff. 236–8.)

BIBLIOGRAPHY OF CITATIONS

I. Manuscript Materials

PUBLIC RECORD OFFICE

Admiralty

Adm. 1/484–90, 505. (Admirals' Despatches, North America).
Adm. 2/99–108 (Orders and Instructions).
Adm. 2/1333–41 (Secret Orders and Letters).
Adm. 51/740 (Captain's log of *Prince William*).

Colonial Office

CO 5/93–106 (Secretary of State – America – military despatches).
CO 5/167 (Secretary of State to Secretary at War).
CO 5/174 (Commander-in-Chief to Germain).
CO 5/253 (précis on military operations against the colonies).
CO 5/254–5 (Secretary of State to Admiralty).
CO 42/36–7 (Canada).
CO·137/75–83 (Jamaica).
CO 318/5–10 (West Indies).

State Papers

SP 78/305–6 (France).

War Office

WO 4/112 (establishments).
WO 17/1154–5 (monthly returns).
WO 26/31 (reductions).
WO 34/110–42, 186–91, 226–237 (Amherst Papers).

BRITISH MUSEUM

Add. MSS. 21680 (Haldimand).
Add. MSS. 23658 (Rainsford).
Add. MSS. 29914 (Jervis).
Add. MSS. 34187 (Lisburne).
Add. MSS. 34413–5 (Auckland).
Add. MSS. 37833–5 (Robinson).
Add. MSS. 38208–17; 38343–5; 38375; 38383; 38433–42 (Liverpool).
Add. MSS. 38650A (miscellaneous).
Eg. 2135 (Lisburne).

WILLIAM CLEMENTS LIBRARY, ANN ARBOR, MICHIGAN

Clinton Papers (Letters from Secretary of State).
Germain Papers.

Knox Papers.
Lacaita-Shelburne Papers.
Shelburne Papers (Vols. 34, 66–9, 72, 78–9, 83–8, 136, 142, 146, 151).
Sydney Papers (Vols. 1–5).
Wedderburn Papers.

HOUGHTON LIBRARY, HARVARD
Sparks MSS. (Vols. 22, 75, 77, 78).

MERTON HALL, NORFOLK:
A few papers of the 2nd Lord Walsingham.

PRINCETON UNIVERSITY LIBRARY
Berthier Papers (topographical information).

DUKE UNIVERSITY LIBRARY (a few letters)
Iredell MSS.
MSS. Series XVIII (British).

HUNTINGTON LIBRARY, SAN MARINO, CALIFORNIA
Stowe Papers (some miscellaneous letters).

LONGLEAT, WARMINISTER, WILTSHIRE (Marquess of Bath)
Papers of Lord Weymouth:
Thynne Papers, Vols. XXXVIII-XXXIX.
American Affairs 1777–9 (unbound bundle).

SCONE PALACE, PERTHSHIRE
Papers of Lord Stormont. Not sorted or available for inspection, but copies of a few
papers were furnished through the kindness of Lord Mansfield.

WILLIAMS TRANSCRIPTS FROM THE SANDWICH PAPERS
Copies of Lord Sandwich's patronage letters lent by Mr M. J. Williams. These are
taken from the transcripts in the National Maritime Museum, Greenwich.

II. Original Printed Materials

ABERGAVENNY: MSS of the Marquess of Abergavenny (Hist. MSS. Comm., 1887).
ALMON, JOHN: *Biographical, Literary and Political Anecdotes* (1797).
Annual Register.

BARHAM, CHARLES MIDDLETON, LORD: *Letters and Papers* (Navy Records Society,
1907).
BARRINGTON, ADM. THE HON. SAMUEL: *The Barrington Papers* (Navy Records
Society, 1941).

BARRINGTON, ADM. THE HON. SAMUEL: Some letters of (*Mariner's Mirror*, 1934).
BATHURST: MSS. of Earl Bathurst (Hist. MSS. Comm., 1923).
BUCKINGHAM AND CHANDOS, 2ND DUKE OF: *Memoirs of the Court and Cabinets of George III* (1853), Vol. I.
BUTLER, CHARLES: *Reminiscences* (1822).

CARLISLE: MSS. of the Earl of Carlisle (Hist. MSS. Comm., 1897).
CHARLEMONT: MSS. of James, 1st Earl of Charlemont (Hist. MSS. Comm. 1891).
CLINTON'S NARRATIVE: see Willcox.
CORNWALLIS: *Correspondence of Charles, 1st Marquess Cornwallis* (ed. Charles Ross, 1859).
CORNWALLIS WYKEHAM-MARTIN, see Wykeham-Martin.
COSTIN, W.C., and J. S. WATSON: *The Law and Working of the Constitution: Documents, 1660–1914* (1952).
CUMBERLAND, RICHARD: *Memoirs* (1807).
CUMBERLAND, RICHARD: *Character of the late Lord Sackville* (1785).

DALRYMPLE, SIR JOHN: *Memoirs of Great Britain and Ireland* (1788).
DARTMOUTH: MSS of the Earl of Dartmouth (Hist. MSS. Comm., 1895).
Dropmore Papers: see Fortescue.
DUCANE: MSS. of Lady Ducane (Hist. MSS., 1905).

English Historical Documents:
    Vol. X, ed. D. B. Horn and Mary Ransome (1957).
    Vol. XI, ed. A. Aspinall and E. Anthony Smith (1959).

FORTESCUE, J. W.: see George III.
FORTESCUE, J. B., MSS. of, preserved at Dropmore (Hist. MSS. Comm., 1906), Vol. V
FOX: *Memorials and Correspondence of Charles James Fox* (ed. Lord John Russell) (1853).

GAGE, GENERAL THOMAS: *Correspondence* (ed. C. E. Carter) (1931).
GEORGE III: *Correspondence 1760–83* (ed. J. W. Fortescue) (1927–8).
GIBBON, EDWARD: *Autobiography* (ed. John Murray) (1897).
GRAFTON, 3RD DUKE OF: *Autobiography and Correspondence* (ed. W. R. Anson) (1898).
GURWOOD: see Wellington.

HASTINGS: MSS. of the late R. Hastings (Hist. MSS. Comm., 1934).
HATCH, M. M. (ed.): 'Letters of Captain Sir John Jervis to Sir Henry Clinton, 1774-82' (*American Neptune*, 1947).
HERBERT, LORD (ed.): *Henry, Elizabeth and George, 1734–80* (1934).
HERBERT, LORD (ed.): *The Pembroke Papers 1780–94* (1950).
HOWE, LIEUT.-GENERAL SIR WILLIAM: *Orderly Book* (ed. B. F. Stevens) (1890).
HOWE, LIEUT.-GENERAL SIR WILLIAM: *Narrative ... in a Committee of the House of Commons* (1780).
HUTCHINSON, P. E. (ed.): *Diary and Letters of Thomas Hutchinson* (1886).

JAMES, REAR ADM. BARTHOLOMEW: *Journal 1752-1828* (Navy Records Society, 1896).
JONES, THOMAS: *History of New York during the Revolutionary War* (1879).
KNOX: MSS of Captain H. V. Knox (Hist. MSS. Comm., Various VI, 1909).

[KNOX, WILLIAM]: *Extra-Official State Papers addressed to . . . Lord Rawdon . . . by a late Under Secretary of State* (1789).

LEEDS: *Political Memoranda of Francis, 5th Duke of Leeds* (ed. O Browning) (1884).
LLOYD, MAJOR-GEN: 'Major-General Lloyd's Plan to conquer America' (*Political Magazine*, June 1781).
LOTHIAN: MSS. of the Marquess of Lothian (Hist. MSS. Comm., 1905).

MACKENZIE: *The Diary of Frederick Mackenzie* (1930).
MALMESBURY, LORD (ed.): *Diaries and Correspondence of James Harris, 1st Earl of Malmesbury* (1845). Vol. I.
MALMESBURY, LORD: *Letters of 1st Earl of Malmesbury, his family and friends* (1870).

Parliamentary History of England, ed. William Cobbett (1806 ff.).
PASLEY, ADM. SIR THOMAS: *Private Sea Journals 1778-82* (1931).
PEMBROKE: see Herbert.

RIEDESEL, MME. DE: *Letters and Memoirs . . . by Mme. Riedesel* (1827).
ROUND: MSS of James Round (Hist. MSS. Comm., 14 Rep., App. IX, 1895).
Royal Institution: *American MSS. in the Royal Institution of Great Britain* (Hist. MSS. Comm., 1904-9).
RUTLAND: MSS. of the Duke of Rutland (Hist. MSS. Comm., 1905), Vol. III.

SACKVILLE: see Stopford-Sackville.
SANDWICH: *Private Papers of John, Earl of Sandwich* (Navy Records Society, 1933).
STEVENS, B. F.: see Howe.
STOCKDALE: *Memoirs of the life and writings of the Rev. Percival Stockdale* (1809).
STOPFORD-SACKVILLE: MSS. of Mrs Stopford-Sackville (Hist. MSS. Comm., 1904, 1910).
STUART WORTLEY, MRS E. (ed.): *A Prime Minister and his Son* (1925).

TORRINGTON: *The Torrington Diaries*, ed. C. B. Andrews (abridged by Fanny Andrews, 1954).
TURGOT, A. R. J: *Œuvres* (1923), Vol. V.

VERULAM: MSS of the Earl of Verulam (Hist. MSS. Comm., 1906).

WALPOLE, HORACE: *The Last Journals of Horace Walpole, 1771-83* (ed. Doran) (1859).
WALPOLE, HORACE: *Correspondence*, the Yale Edition (ed. W. S. Lewis) (1937-).
WELLINGTON, 1ST DUKE OF: *Selections from the Despatches and General Orders of the Duke of Wellington* (ed. Lieut.-Colonel Gurwood, 1851 edn.).
WILLCOX, W. B. (ed.): *The American Rebellion: Sir Henry Clinton's Narrative* (1954).
WORTLEY: see Stuart Wortley.

WRAXALL, SIR NATHANIEL: *Historical Memoirs of his own Time* (1836).
WRAXALL, SIR NATHANIEL: *Posthumous Memoirs of his own Time* (1836).
WYKEHAM-MARTIN: MSS. of Cornwallis Wykeham-Martin (Hist. MSS. Comm., Various VI, 1909).

III. General Works

This list is a guide to citations and not a catalogue of the literature in the field. Works marked with an asterisk contain useful source material.

ALBION, R. G, *Forests and Sea Power* (1926).
ALDEN, J. R.,*The South in the Revolution, 1763-89* (1957).
ALDEN, J. R., *The American Revolution* (1954).
*ALMON, JOHN, *Biographical, Literary and Political Anecdotes* (1797), Vol. III.
ANDERSON, T. S., *The Command of the Howe Brothers* (1936).

*BARRINGTON, SHUTE, *Political Life of Viscount Barrington* (1814).
BARROW, SIR JOHN, *Life of Richard, Earl Howe* (1835).
BASYE, A. H., *The Lords Commissioners of Trade and Plantations, 1748-82* (1925).
BASYE, A. H., 'The Secretary of State for the Colonies, 1768-82' (*Amer. Hist. Rev.*, XXVIII).
BEATSON, ROBERT, *Naval and Military Memoirs of Great Britain from 1727 to 1' '3* (1804).
BEMIS, S. F., *Diplomatic History of the United States* (1937).
BEMIS, S. F., *Diplomacy of the American Revolution* (1935).
BEMIS, S. F., *The Hussey-Cumberland Mission and American Independence* (1931).
BEMIS, S. F., 'British Secret Service and the Franco-American Alliance' (*Amer. Hist. Rev.*, XXIX).
BINNEY, J. E. D., *British Public Finance and Administration, 1774-92* (1958).
BOYD, J. P.,'Silas Deane: Death by a kindly teacher of treason?' (*William and Mary Quarterly*, 1959).
BRADLEY, A. G., *Lord Dorchester* (1929).
BROOMFIELD, J. H., 'The Keppel-Palliser Affair, 1778-9' (*Mariner's Mirror*, 1961).
BURT, A. L., *Guy Carleton, Lord Dorchester 1724-1808* (Can. Hist. Assn, revised 1955).
BURT, A. L., 'The Tragedy of Chief Justice Livius' (*Can. Hist. Rev.*, 1924).
BURT, A. L., 'The Quarrel between Germain and Carleton, an inverted story' (*Can. Hist. Rev., 1930*).
BUTTERFIELD, HERBERT, *George III, Lord North and the People, 1779-80* (1949).
BUTTERFIELD, HERBERT, 'Lord North and Mr Robinson' (*Camb. Hist. J.*, 1937).

CAMPBELL, JOHN LORD, *Lives of the Lord Chancellors* (3rd Engl. Edn. Vol. VI).
CASTEX, R., *Manœuvre de la Praya, 1781* (1912).
CASTRO, J. P. DE, *The Gordon Riots* (1926).
CHEVALIER, E., *Histoire de la marine française, 1774-83* (1877).
CHRISTIE, I. R., *The End of North's Ministry, 1780-2* (1958).

CLARK, JANE, 'The Command of the Canadian Army in 1777' (Can. Hist. Rev., 1929).

CLODE, C. M., The Military Forces of the Crown – their Administration and Government (1869).

CONN, STETSON, Gibraltar in British Diplomacy in the Eighteenth Century (1942).

COULTER, see Lloyd.

*COVENTRY, GEORGE, A Critical Enquiry regarding the real author of Junius (1825).

COXE, WILLIAM, Memoirs of the Kings of Spain of the House of Bourbon . . . 1700–88 (1815).

CURTIS, E. E., Organisation of the British Army in the American Revolution (1926).

*DONIOL, H., Histoire de la participation de la France à l'établissement des États-Unis (1886–92).

VAN DOREN, CARL, Secret History of the American Revolution (1941).

VON EELKING, MAX, The German Allied Troops in the North American War of Independence (transl. J. G. Rosengarten, 1893).

*VON EELKING, MAX, Memoirs, and Letters and Journals, of Major-General Riedesel (transl. W. L. Stone, 1868).

ELLIOT, see Minto.

ELLIS, KENNETH, The Post Office in the Eighteenth Century (1958).

FEILING, KEITH, The Second Tory Party (1938).

*FITZMAURICE, LORD EDMOND, Life of William, Earl of Shelburne (1912).

*FONBLANQUE, E. B. DE, Political and Military Episodes . . . derived from the life and correspondence of the Rt. Hon. John Burgoyne (1876).

FORTESCUE, J. W., A History of the British Army (Vol. III, 1911).

FOY, GEN. M. S., History of the War in the Peninsula (1829).

FREEMAN, D. S., George Washington (Vols. IV and V, 1951–2).

FULLER, J. F. C., British Light Infantry in the Eighteenth Century (1925)

GIDDEY, ERNEST, James Francis Erskine et son régiment suisse 1779–86 (Schweizerische Zeitschr. für Geschichte, 1954).

GIPSON, L. H., The British Empire before the American Revolution (1939–49). Esp. Vol. VII.

GORE-BROWNE, ROBERT, Chancellor Thurlow (1953).

GRAHAM, G. S., 'Considerations on the War of American Independence' (Bull. Inst. Hist. Research, 1949).

HARLOW, V. T., Founding of the Second British Empire, 1763–93 (1952).

HUNT, R. M., Life of Sir Hugh Palliser (1844).

JAMES, W. M., The British Navy in Adversity (1926).

*KEPPEL, THOMAS, Life of Augustus, Viscount Keppel (1842).

LACOUR-GAYET, G., La marine militaire de France sous le règne de Louis XVI (1905).

LEWIS, MICHAEL, The Navy of Britain (1948).

LLOYD, C. and COULTER, J. S. L., *Medicine and the Navy:* III – 1714–1815 (1961).
LONG, J. C., *Lord Jeffrey Amherst* (1933).
LOWELL, E. J., *The Hessians* (1884).

MADARIAGA, ISABEL DE: *Britain, Russia, and the Armed Neutrality of 1780* (1962).
MAHAN. A. T., *Major Operations of the Navies in the American War of Independence* (1913).
MAHON, R. H., *Life of General the Hon. James Murray* (1921).
MARLOW, LOUIS, *Sackville of Drayton* (1948).
MATHIAS, PETER, *The Brewing Industry in England, 1700–1830* (1959).
*MINTO, COUNTESS OF (ed.), *Life and Letters of Gilbert Minto* (1874).
*MINTO, COUNTESS OF (ed.), *Notes from the Minto MSS.* (1862).
*MUNDY, MAJ.-GEN. G. B., *Life and Correspondence of Lord Rodney* (1830).

NAMIER, L. B., *Structure of Politics at the Accession of George III* (1929).
NAMIER, L. B., *England in the Age of the American Revolution* (1930).
NELSON, W. H., *The American Tory* (1961).
NICKERSON, HOFFMAN, *The Turning Point of the Revolution* (1928).

OLSON, A. G., *The Radical Duke: Career and Correspondence of Charles Lennox, third Duke of Richmond* (1961).

PACK, S. W. C., *Admiral Lord Anson* (1960).
PALMER, R. R., *Age of the Democratic Revolution* (1959).
PARES, RICHARD, *George III and the Politicians* (1953).
PARES, RICHARD, *War and Trade in the West Indies, 1739–63* (1936).
PARES, RICHARD, *A West India Fortune* (1950).
PATTERSON, A. TEMPLE, *The Other Armada* (1960).
PHILLIPS, C. J., *History of the Sackville Family* (1929).
PORRITT, EDWARD, *The Unreformed House of Commons* (1903).
PUGH, ROBERT C., 'The Revolutionary Militia in the Southern Campaign, 1780–1' (*William and Mary Quarterly*, 1957).

REILLY, ROBIN, *The Rest to Fortune: The Life of Major-General James Wolfe* (1960).
RICHMOND, SIR HERBERT, *The Navy in India, 1763–83* (1931).
RICHMOND, SIR HERBERT, *The Navy in the War of 1739–48* (1920).
RIEDESEL, see Eelking.
RITCHESON, C. R., *British Politics and the American Revolution* (1954).
RODDIS, L. H., *James Lind* (1951).
RODNEY, see Mundy.
RUTHERFORD, G., 'Sidelights on Commodore Johnstone's Expedition to the Cape' (*Mariner's Mirror*, 1942).

SHY, JOHN W., 'A New Look at Colonial Militia' (*William and Mary Quarterly*, 1963).
STEPHENSON, O. W., 'The Supply of Gunpowder in 1776' (*Amer. Hist. Rev.*, XXX).
SUTHERLAND, L. S., *The East India Company in Eighteenth-Century Politics* (1952).

THAYER, THEODORE, *Pennsyslvania Politics and the Growth of Democracy* (1953).

THOMSON, M. A., *The Secretaries of State, 1681–1782* (1932).

USHER, R. G., 'Civil Administration of the British Navy during the American Revolution' (unpubl. thesis, Univ. of Michigan, 1942).

VALENTINE, ALAN, *Lord George Germain* (1961).

WARD, CHRISTOPHER, *War of the Revolution* (ed. J. R. Alden) (1952).

WATSON, J. STEVEN, *The Reign of George III* (1760–1815).

WILLCOX, W. B., 'Rhode Island in British Strategy, 1780–1' (*Amer. Hist. Rev.*, 1945).

WILLCOX, W. B., 'The British Road to Yorktown: a Study in Divided Command' (*Amer. Hist. Rev.*, 1946).

WILLCOX, W. B., 'British Strategy in America, 1778' (*J. Mod. Hist.*, 1948).

WILLCOX, W. B., 'Battle of Porto Praya, 1781' (*Amer. Neptune*, 1945).

WILLCOX, W. B., see also Wyatt.

WILLIAMS, M. J., 'The Naval Administration of the Fourth Earl of Sandwich, 1771–82' (Oxford, unpublished thesis, 1962).

WYATT, FREDERICK AND WILLCOX, W. B., 'Sir Henry Clinton: a Psychological Exploration in History' (*William and Mary Quarterly*, 1959).